CRITIQUE OF PURE REASON

IMMANUEL KANT (1724–1804) was born in Königsberg, the son of a strap maker. "The history of the life of Immanuel Kant," wrote the poet Heine in a brief biographical sketch, "is hard to write, inasmuch as he had neither life nor history, for he lived a mechanically ordered and abstract old bachelor life in a quiet retired street in Königsberg, an old town on the northeast border of Germany. I do not believe that the great clock of the cathedral there did its daily work more dispassionately and regularly than its compatriot Immanuel Kant. Rising, coffee drinking, writing, reading college lectures, eating, walking, all had their fixed time, and the neighbors knew that it was exactly half past three when Immanuel Kant in his grey coat, with his bamboo cane in his hand, left his house door and went to the Lime tree avenue, which is still called, in memory of him, the Philosopher's Walk." From 1740–46 Kant studied at the University of Königsberg. For the next nine years he supported himself as a private tutor, and then returned to the University in 1755 as a *Privatdozent*. In 1770 he was made a full professor and he continued to lecture for another twenty-seven years. Unlike many philosophers, Kant was highly respected and revered through most of his life and mourned at his death. His principal works are: CRITIQUE OF PURE REASON (1781), *Prolegomena to Any Future Metaphysics* (1783), *Metaphysic of Ethics* (1785), *Critique of Practical Reason* (1788), and *Religion within the Bounds of Pure Reason* (1793).

FRIEDRICH MAXIMILIAN MÜLLER was born in Dessau, Germany, December 6th, 1832, son of the poet Wilhelm Müller. As orientalist and comparative philologist, he is best known for his 51-volume set of *The Sacred Books of the East*. Müller's translation of CRITIQUE OF PURE REASON first appeared in 1881. He died in Oxford, England on October 28, 1900.

A NOTE ON THIS EDITION

The Anchor edition of *Critique of Pure Reason* is taken from the translation by F. Max Müller. Except for the deletion of two lengthy translator's prefaces, the text, including final additions and corrections, is complete here. The text is a translation of the first edition of the *Critique* (1781), with material new to the second edition supplied in italics. This second edition material includes footnotes, outright additions to the text, and revisions or replacements of certain passages that appeared in the first edition and were subsequently deleted by Kant. These passages from the first edition have been retained, enclosed in brackets, and are followed by their replacements in italics.

The original paginations of the first and second editions are shown (*e.g.,* [A:3–4; B:4–6]–the "A" and "B" referring to the first and second editions respectively) at the top of each right-hand page and refer to the text on that and the facing page. The page references within the body of the text refer to pages in the Anchor edition.

Kant's textual notes are indicated by symbols; the translator's notes are numbered.

CRITIQUE
OF PURE REASON

·

IMMANUEL KANT

TRANSLATED INTO ENGLISH BY

F. MAX MÜLLER

ANCHOR BOOKS

Doubleday & Company, Inc.
Garden City, New York

The Anchor Books edition of
Critique of Pure Reason is
published by arrangement with the
Macmillan Company, New York

Anchor Books edition: 1966

Printed in the United States of America

TABLE OF CONTENTS

TO HIS EXCELLENCY
THE ROYAL MINISTER OF STATE
BARON VON ZEDLITZ

Dedication

SIR,

To further, so far as in us lies, the growth of the sciences is to work in your Excellency's own interest, your own interest being intimately connected with them, not only through the exalted position of a patron of science, but through the far more intimate relation of a lover and enlightened judge. For that reason I avail myself of the only means within my power of proving my gratitude for the gracious confidence with which your Excellency honours me, as if I too could help toward your noble work.

[Whoever delights in a speculative life finds with moderate wishes the approval of an enlightened and kind judge a powerful incentive to studies the results of which are great, but remote, and therefore entirely ignored by vulgar eyes.]

To you, as such a judge, and to your kind attention I now submit this book, placing all other concerns of my literary future under your special protection, and remaining with profound respect[1]

Your Excellency's
Most obedient Servant,
IMMANUEL KANT.

KÖNIGSBERG, *March* 29, 1781.

[1] The second paragraph is left out and the last sentence slightly altered in the Second Edition.

Motto to Second Edition

baco de verulamio

Instauratio magna: Praefatio

De nobis ipsis silemus: de re autem, quae agitur, petimus, ut homines eam non opinionem, sed opus esse cogitent; ac pro certo habeant, non sectae nos alicujus aut placiti, sed utilitatis et amplitudinis humanae fundamenta moliri. Deinde ut suis commodis aequi . . . in commune consulant, . . . et ipsi in partem veniant. Praeterea, ut bene sperent, neque Instaurationem nostram ut quiddam infinitum et ultra mortale fingant, et animo concipiant; quum revera sit infiniti erroris finis et terminus legitimus.

TABLE OF CONTENTS
TO THE FIRST EDITION

Instead of this simple Table of Contents, later editions have
a much fuller one, which, as Rosenkranz observes, obscures
rather than illustrates the articulation of the book:

TABLE OF CONTENTS

PREFACE[1]

Our reason (Vernunft) has this peculiar fate that, with reference to one class of its knowledge, it is always troubled with questions which cannot be ignored, because they spring from the very nature of reason, and which cannot be answered, because they transcend the powers of human reason.

Nor is human reason to be blamed for this. It begins with principles which, in the course of experience, it *must* follow, and which are sufficiently confirmed by experience. With these again, according to the necessities of its nature, it rises higher and higher to more remote conditions. But when it perceives that in this way its work remains for ever incomplete, because the questions never cease, it finds itself constrained to take refuge in principles which exceed every possible experimental application, and nevertheless seem so unobjectionable that even ordinary common sense agrees with them. Thus, however, reason becomes involved in darkness and contradictions, from which, no doubt, it may conclude that errors must be lurking somewhere, but without being able to discover them, because the principles which it follows transcend all the limits of experience and therefore withdraw themselves from all experimental tests. It is the battle-field of these endless controversies which is called *Metaphysic*.

There was a time when Metaphysic held a royal place among all the sciences, and, if the will were taken for the deed, the exceeding importance of her subject might well have secured to her that place of honour. At present it is the fashion to despise Metaphysic, and the poor matron, forlorn and forsaken, complains like Hecuba, *Modo maxima rerum, tot generis natisque potens—nunc trahor exul, inops* (Ovid, Metam. xiii. 508).

[1] This preface is left out in later editions, and replaced by a new preface; see p. xxviii below.

At first the rule of Metaphysic, under the dominion of the dogmatists, was despotic. But as the laws still bore the traces of an old barbarism, intestine wars and complete anarchy broke out, and the sceptics, a kind of nomads, despising all settled culture of the land, broke up from time to time all civil society. Fortunately their number was small, and they could not prevent the old settlers from returning to cultivate the ground afresh, though without any fixed plan or agreement. Not long ago one might have thought, indeed, that all these quarrels were to have been settled and the legitimacy of her claims decided once for all through a certain physiology of the human understanding, the work of the celebrated *Locke*. But, though the descent of that royal pretender, traced back as it had been to the lowest mob of common experience, ought to have rendered her claims very suspicious, yet, as that geneal-ogy turned out to be in reality a false invention, the old queen (Metaphysic) continued to maintain her claims, everything fell back into the old rotten dogmatism, and the contempt from which metaphysical science was to have been rescued, re-mained the same as ever. At present, after everything has been tried, so they say, and tried in vain, there reign in philosophy weariness and complete indifferentism, the mother of chaos and night in all sciences but, at the same time, the spring or, at least, the prelude of their near reform and of a new light, after an ill-applied study has rendered them dark, confused, and useless.

It is in vain to assume a kind of artificial indifferentism in respect to enquiries the object of which cannot be indifferent to human nature. Nay, those pretended indifferentists (how-ever they may try to disguise themselves by changing scholastic terminology into popular language), if they think at all, fall back inevitably into those very metaphysical dogmas which they profess to despise. Nevertheless this indifferentism, showing itself in the very midst of the most flourishing state of all sciences, and affecting those very sciences the teachings of which, if they could be had, would be the last to be sur-rendered, is a phenomenon well worthy of our attention and consideration. It is clearly the result, not of the carelessness, but of the matured judgment* of our age, which will no longer

---

* We often hear complaints against the shallowness of thought in our own time, and the decay of sound knowledge. But I do not see that sciences which rest on a solid foundation, such as mathematics, physics, etc., deserve this reproach in the least. On the contrary, they maintained their old reputation of solidity, and with regard to

rest satisfied with the mere appearance of knowledge. It is, at the same time, a powerful appeal to reason to undertake anew the most difficult of its duties, namely, self-knowledge, and to institute a court of appeal which should protect the just rights of reason, but dismiss all groundless claims, and should do this not by means of irresponsible decrees, but according to the eternal and unalterable laws of reason. This court of appeal is no other than the *Critique of Pure Reason*.

I do not mean by this a criticism of books and systems, but of the faculty of reason in general, touching that whole class of knowledge which it may strive after, unassisted by experience. This must decide the question of the possibility or impossibility of metaphysic in general, and the determination of its sources, its extent, and its limits—and all this according to fixed principles.

This, the only way that was left, I have followed, and I flatter myself that I have thus removed all those errors which have hitherto brought reason, whenever it was unassisted by experience, into conflict with itself. I have not evaded its questions by pleading the insufficiency of human reason, but I have classified them according to principles, and, after showing the point where reason begins to misunderstand itself, solved them satisfactorily. It is true that the answer of those questions is not such as a dogma-enamoured curiosity might wish for, for such curiosity could not have been satisfied except by juggling tricks in which I am no adept. But this was not the intention of the natural destiny of our reason, and it became the duty of philosophy to remove the deception which arose from a false interpretation, even though many a vaunted and cherished dream should vanish at the same time. In this work I have chiefly aimed at completeness, and I venture to maintain that there ought not to be one single metaphysical problem that has not been solved here, or to the solution of which the key at least has not been supplied. In fact Pure

physics, even surpass it. The same spirit would manifest itself in other branches of knowledge, if only their principles had first been properly determined. Till that is done, indifferentism and doubt, and ultimately severe criticism, are rather signs of honest thought. Our age is, in every sense of the word, the age of criticism, and everything must submit to it. Religion, on the strength of its sanctity, and law, on the strength of its majesty, try to withdraw themselves from it; but by so doing they arouse just suspicions, and cannot claim that sincere respect which reason pays to those only who have been able to stand its free and open examination.

Reason is so perfect a unity that, if its principle should prove insufficient to answer any one of the many questions started by its very nature, one might throw it away altogether, as insufficient to answer the other questions with perfect certainty.

While I am saying this I fancy I observe in the face of my readers an expression of indignation, mixed with contempt, at pretensions apparently so self-glorious and extravagant; and yet they are in reality far more moderate than those made by the writer of the commonest essay professing to prove the simple nature of the soul or the necessity of a first beginning of the world. For, while he pretends to extend human knowledge beyond the limits of all possible experience, I confess most humbly that this is entirely beyond my power. I mean only to treat of reason and its pure thinking, a knowledge of which is not very far to seek, considering that it is to be found within myself. Common logic gives an instance how all the simple acts of reason can be enumerated completely and systematically. Only between the common logic and my work there is this difference, that my question is,—what can we hope to achieve with reason, when all the material and assistance of experience is taken away?

So much with regard to the completeness in our laying hold of every single object, and the thoroughness in our laying hold of all objects, as the material of our critical enquiries—a completeness and thoroughness determined, not by a casual idea, but by the nature of our knowledge itself.

Besides this, certainty and clearness with regard to form are two essential demands that may very properly be addressed to an author who ventures on so slippery an undertaking.

First, with regard to certainty, I have pronounced judgment against myself by saying that in this kind of enquiry it is in no way permissible to propound mere opinions, and that everything looking like a hypothesis is counterband, that must not be offered for sale at however low a price, but must, as soon as it has been discovered, be confiscated. For every kind of knowledge which professes to be certain *a priori,* proclaims itself that it means to be taken for absolutely necessary. And this applies, therefore, still more to a definition of all pure knowledge *a priori,* which is to be the measure, and therefore also an example, of all apodictic philosophical certainty. Whether I have fulfilled what I have here undertaken to do, must be left to the judgment of the reader; for it only behoves the author to propound his arguments, and not to determine beforehand the effect which they ought to produce on his judges. But, in order to prevent any unnecessary weakening of those arguments, he may be allowed to point out himself certain passages which, though they refer to collateral objects only, might occasion some mistrust, and thus to counteract in time the influence which the least hesitation of the reader in respect to these minor points might exercise with regard to the principal object.

I know of no enquiries which are more important for determining that faculty which we call understanding (Verstand), and for fixing its rules and its limits, than those in the Second Chapter of my Transcendental Analytic, under the title of 'Deduction of the Pure Concepts of the Understanding.' They have given me the greatest but, I hope, not altogether useless trouble. This enquiry, which rests on a deep foundation, has two sides. The one refers to the objects of the pure understanding, and is intended to show and explain the objective value of its concepts *a priori*. It is, therefore, of essential importance for my purposes. The other is intended to enquire into the pure understanding itself, its possibility, and the powers of knowledge on which it rests, therefore its subjective character; a subject which, though important for my principal object, yet forms no essential part of it, because my principal problem is and remains, What and how much may understanding (Verstand) and reason (Vernunft) know without all experience? and not, How is the faculty of thought possible? The latter would be an enquiry into a cause of a given effect; it would, therefore, be of the nature of an hypothesis (though, as I shall show elsewhere, this is not quite so); and it might seem as if I had here allowed myself to propound a mere opinion, leaving the reader free to hold another opinion also. I therefore warn the reader, in case my subjective deduction should not produce that complete conviction which I expect, that the objective deduction, in which I am here chiefly concerned, must still retain its full strength. For this, what has been said may possibly by itself be sufficient.

Secondly, as to clearness, the reader has a right to demand not only what may be called logical or discursive clearness, which is based on concepts, but also what may be called æsthetic or intuitive clearness produced by intuitions, i.e. by examples and concrete illustrations. With regard to the former I have made ample provision. That arose from the very nature of my purpose, but it became at the same time the reason why I could not fully satisfy the latter, if not absolute, yet very just claim. Nearly through the whole of my work I have felt doubtful what to do. Examples and illustrations seemed always to be necessary, and therefore found their way into the first sketch of my work. But I soon perceived the magnitude of my task and the number of objects I should have to treat; and, when I saw that even in their driest scholastic form they would considerably swell my book, I did not consider it expedient to extend it still further through examples and illustrations required for popular purposes only. This work can never satisfy the popular taste, and the few who know, do not require that help which, though it is always welcome, yet might here have defeated its very purpose. The Abbé Terrasson[2] writes indeed that, if we measured the greatness of a book, not by the number of its pages, but by the time we require for mastering it, many a book might be said to be much shorter, if it were not so short. But, on the other hand, if we ask how a complicated, yet in principle coherent whole of speculative thought can best be rendered intelligible, we might be equally justified in saying that many a book would have been more intelligible, if it had not tried to be so very intelligible. For the helps to clearness, though they may be missed[3] with regard to details, often distract with regard to the whole. The reader does not arrive quickly enough at a survey of the whole, because the bright colours of illustrations hide and distort the articulation and concatenation of the whole system, which, after all, if we want to judge of its unity and sufficiency, are more important than anything else.

Surely it should be an attraction to the reader if he is asked to join his own efforts with those of the author in order to carry out a great and important work, according to the plan here proposed, in a complete and lasting manner. Metaphysic, according to the definitions here given, is the only one of all sciences which, through a small but united effort, may count on such completeness in a short time, so that nothing will remain for posterity but to arrange everything according to its own views for didactic purposes, without being able to add anything to the subject itself. For it is in reality nothing but an inventory of all our possessions acquired through Pure Reason, systematically arranged. Nothing can escape us, because whatever reason produces entirely out of itself, cannot

---

[2] Terrasson, Philosophie nach ihrem allgemeinen Einflusse auf alle Gegenstände des Geistes und der Sitten, Berlin, 1762, p. 117.
[3] Rosenkranz and others change *fehlen* into *helfen,* without necessity, I think.

hide itself, but is brought to light by reason itself, so soon as the common principle has been discovered. This absolute completeness is rendered not only possible, but necessary, through the perfect unity of this kind of knowledge, all derived from pure concepts, without any influence from experience, or from special intuitions leading to a definite kind of experience, that might serve to enlarge and increase it. *Tecum habita et noris quam sit tibi curta supellex* (Persius, Sat. iv. 52).

Such a system of pure (speculative) reason I hope myself to produce under the title of 'Metaphysic of Nature.' It will not be half so large, yet infinitely richer than this Critique of Pure Reason, which has, first of all, to discover its source, nay, the conditions of its possibility, in fact, to clear and level a soil quite overgrown with weeds. Here I expect from my readers the patience and impartiality of a judge, there the goodwill and aid of a fellow-worker. For however completely all the principles of the system have been propounded in my Critique, the completeness of the whole system requires also that no derivative concepts should be omitted, such as cannot be found out by an estimate *a priori,* but have to be discovered step by step. There the synthesis of concepts has been exhausted, here it will be requisite to do the same for their analysis, a task which is easy and an amusement rather than a labour.

I have only a few words to add with respect to the printing of my book. As the beginning had been delayed, I was not able to see the clean sheets of more than about half of it. I now find some misprints. The antinomy of pure reason from p. 306 to p. 330 has been arranged in a tabular form, so that all that belongs to the thesis stands on the left, what belongs to the antithesis on the right side. I did this in order that thesis and antithesis might be more easily compared.

PREFACE TO THE SECOND EDITION. 1787.

Whether the treatment of that class of knowledge with which reason is occupied follows the secure method of a science or not, can easily be determined by the result. If, after repeated preparations, it comes to a standstill, as soon as its real goal is approached, or is obliged, in order to reach it, to retrace its steps again and again, and strike into fresh paths; again, if it is impossible to produce unanimity among those who are engaged in the same work, as to the manner in which their common object should be obtained, we may be convinced that such a study is far from having attained to the secure method of a science, but is groping only in the dark. In that case we are conferring a great benefit on reason, if we only find out the right method, though many things should have to be surrendered as useless, which were comprehended in the original aim that had been chosen without sufficient reflection.

That *Logic,* from the earliest times, has followed that secure method, may be seen from the fact that since *Aristotle* it has not had to retrace a single step, unless we choose to consider as improvements the removal of some unnecessary subtleties, or the clearer definition of its matter, both of which refer to the elegance rather than to the solidity of the science. It is remarkable also, that to the present day, it has not been able to make one step in advance, so that, to all appearance, it may be considered as completed and perfect. If some modern philosophers thought to enlarge it, by introducing *psychological* chapters on the different faculties of knowledge (faculty of imagination, wit, etc.), or *metaphysical* chapters on the origin of knowledge, or the different degrees of certainty according to the difference of objects (idealism, scepticism, etc.), or lastly, *anthropological* chapters on prejudices, their causes and remedies, this could only arise from their ignorance of the peculiar nature of logical science. We do not enlarge, but we only disfigure the sciences, if we allow their respective limits to be confounded: and the limits of logic are definitely fixed by the fact, that it is a science which has nothing to do but fully to exhibit and strictly to prove all formal rules of thought (whether it be *a priori* or empirical, whatever be its origin or its object, and whatever be the impediments, accidental or natural, which it has to encounter in the human mind).

That logic should in this respect have been so successful, is due entirely to its limitation, whereby it has not only the right, but the duty, to make abstraction of all the objects of knowledge and their differences, so that the understanding has to deal with nothing beyond itself and its own forms. It was, of course, far more difficult for reason to enter on the secure method of science, when it has to deal not with itself only, but also with objects. Logic, therefore, as a kind of preparation (*propaedeutic*) forms, as it were, the vestibule of the sciences only, and where real knowledge is concerned, is presupposed for critical purposes only, while the acquisition of knowledge must be sought for in the sciences themselves, properly and objectively so called.

If there is to be in those sciences an element of reason, something in them must be known *a priori,* and knowledge may stand in a twofold relation to its object, by either simply *determining* it and its concept (which must be supplied from elsewhere), or by making it *real* also. The former is *theoretical,* the latter *practical knowledge* of reason. In both the *pure* part, namely, that in which reason determines its object entirely *a priori* (whether it contain much or little), must be treated first, without mixing up with it what comes from other sources; for it is bad economy to spend blindly whatever comes in, and not to be able to determine, when there is a stoppage, which part of the income can bear the expenditure, and where reductions must be made.

Mathematics and *physics* are the two theoretical sciences of reason, which have to determine their *objects a priori:* the former quite purely, the latter partially so, and partially from other sources of knowledge besides reason.

Mathematics, from the earliest times to which the history of human reason can reach, has followed, among that wonderful people of the Greeks, the safe way of a science. But it must not be supposed that it was as easy for mathematics as for logic, in which reason is concerned with itself alone, to find, or rather to make for itself that royal road. I believe, on the contrary, that there was a long period of tentative work (chiefly still among the Egyptians), and that the change is to be ascribed to a *revolution,* produced by the happy thought of a single man, whose experiment pointed unmistakably to the path that had to be followed, and opened and traced out for the most distant times the safe way of a science. The history of that intellectual revolution, which was far more important than the discovery of the passage round the celebrated Cape of Good Hope, and the name of its fortunate author, have not been preserved to us. But the story preserved by Diogenes Laertius, who names the reputed author of the smallest elements of ordinary geometrical demonstration, even of such as, according to general opinion, do not require to be proved, shows, at all events, that the memory of the revolution, produced by the very first traces of the discovery of a new method, appeared extremely important to the mathematicians, and thus remained unforgotten. A new light flashed on the first man who demonstrated the properties of the isos-

celes triangle[4] (whether his name was *Thales* or any other
name), for he found that he had not to investigate what he
saw in the figure, or the mere concept of that figure, and
thus to learn its properties; but that he had to produce (by
construction) what he had himself, according to concepts *a
priori,* placed into that figure and represented in it, so that, in
order to know anything with certainty *a priori,* he must not
attribute to that figure anything beyond what necessarily follows from what he has himself placed into it, in accordance
with the concept.

It took a much longer time before physics entered on the
high way of science: for no more than a century and a half has
elapsed, since Bacon's ingenious proposal partly initiated that
discovery, partly, as others were already on the right track,
gave a new impetus to it,—a discovery which, like the former,
can only be explained by a rapid intellectual revolution. In
what I have to say, I shall confine myself to natural science,
so far as it is founded on *empirical* principles.

When Galilei let balls of a particular weight, which he had
determined himself, roll down an inclined plain, or Torricelli
made the air carry a weight, which he had previously determined to be equal to that of a definite volume of water; or
when, in later times, Stahl* changed metal into lime, and lime
again into metals, by withdrawing and restoring something, a
new light flashed on all students of nature. They comprehended
that reason has insight into that only, which she herself produces on her own plan, and that she must move forward with
the principles of her judgments, according to fixed law, and
compel nature to answer her questions, but not let herself be
led by nature, as it were in leading strings, because otherwise
accidental observations, made on no previously fixed plan, will
never converge towards a necessary law, which is the only
thing that reason seeks and requires. Reason, holding in one
hand its principles, according to which concordant phenomena
alone can be admitted as laws of nature, and in the other hand
the experiment, which it has devised according to those principles, must approach nature, in order to be taught by it: but

[4] Kant himself in a letter to Schütz (Darstellung seines Lebens
von seinem Sohn, Halle, 1835, Band. II. S. 208) pointed out the
mistake which appears in the preface to the 2nd edition, namely,
gleichseitig (equilateral), instead of gleichschenkelig (isosceles).
* I am not closely following here the course of the history of the
experimental method, nor are the first beginnings of it very well
known.

not in the character of a pupil, who agrees to everything the master likes, but as an appointed judge, who compels the witnesses to answer the questions which he himself proposes. Therefore even the science of physics entirely owes the beneficial revolution in its character to the happy thought, that we ought to seek in nature (and not import into it by means of fiction) whatever reason must learn from nature, and could not know by itself, and that we must do this in accordance with what reason itself has originally placed into nature. Thus only has the study of nature entered on the secure method of a science, after having for many centuries done nothing but grope in the dark.

Metaphysic, a completely isolated and speculative science of reason, which declines all teaching of experience, and rests on concepts only (not on their application to intuition, as mathematics), in which reason therefore is meant to be her own pupil, has hitherto not been so fortunate as to enter on the secure path of a science, although it is older than all other sciences, and would remain, even if all the rest were swallowed up in the abyss of an all-destroying barbarism. In metaphysic, reason, even if it tries only to understand *a priori* (as it pretends to do) those laws which are confirmed by the commonest experience, is constantly brought to a standstill, and we are obliged again and again to retrace our steps, because they do not lead us where we want to go; while as to any unanimity among those who are engaged in the same work, there is so little of it in metaphysic, that it has rather become an arena, specially destined, it would seem, for those who wish to exercise themselves in mock fights, and where no combatant has, as yet, succeeded in gaining an inch of ground that he could call permanently his own. It cannot be denied, therefore, that the method of metaphysic has hitherto consisted in groping only, and, what is the worst, in groping among mere concepts.

What then can be the cause that hitherto no secure method of science has been discovered? Shall we say that it is impossible? Then why should nature have visited our reason with restless aspiration to look for it, as if it were its most important concern? Nay more, how little should we be justified in trusting our reason if, with regard to one of the most important objects we wish to know, it not only abandons us, but lures us on by vain hopes, and in the end betrays us! Or, if hitherto we have only failed to meet with the right path, what indications are there to make us hope that, if we renew our researches, we shall be more successful than others before us?

The examples of mathematics and natural science, which by one revolution have become what they now are, seem to me sufficiently remarkable to induce us to consider, what may have been the essential element in that intellectual revolution which has proved so beneficial to them, and to make the experiment, at least, so far as the analogy between them, as sciences of reason, which metaphysic allows it, of imitating them. Hitherto it has been supposed that all our knowledge must conform to the objects: but, under that supposition, all attempts to establish anything about them *a priori,* by means of concepts, and thus to enlarge our knowledge, have come to nothing. The experiment therefore ought to be made, whether we should not succeed better with the problems of metaphysic, by assuming that the objects must conform to our mode of cognition, for this would better agree with the demanded possibility of an *a priori* knowledge of them, which is to settle something about objects, before they are given us. We have here the same case as with the first thought of Copernicus, who, not being able to get on in the explanation of the movements of the heavenly bodies, as long as he assumed that all the stars turned round the spectator, tried, whether he could not succeed better, by assuming the spectator to be turning round, and the stars to be at rest. A similar experiment may be tried in metaphysic, so far as the *intuition* of objects is concerned. If the intuition had to conform to the constitution of objects, I do not see how we could know anything of it *a priori;* but if the object (as an object of the senses) conforms to the constitution of our faculty of intuition, I can very well conceive such a possibility. As, however, I cannot rest in these intuitions, if they are to become knowledge, but have to refer them, as representations, to something as their object, and must determine that object by them, I have the choice of admitting, either that the *concepts,* by which I carry out that determination, conform to the object, being then again in the same perplexity on account of the manner how I can know anything about it *a priori;* or that the objects, or what is the same, the experience in which alone they are known (as given objects), must conform to those concepts. In the latter case, the solution becomes more easy, because experience, as a kind of knowledge, requires understanding, and I must therefore, even before objects are given to me, presuppose the rules of the understanding as existing within me *a priori,* these rules being expressed in concepts *a priori,* to which all objects of experience must necessarily conform, and with which they must agree. With regard to objects, so far as they are conceived by reason only, and conceived as necessary, and which can never be given in experience, at least in that form in which they are conceived by reason, we shall find that the attempts at conceiving them (for they must admit of being conceived) will furnish afterwards an excellent test of our new method of thought, according to which we do not know of things anything *a priori* except what we ourselves put into them.*

This experiment succeeds as well as we could desire, and promises to metaphysic, in its first part, which deals with concepts *a priori,* of which the corresponding objects may be given in experience, the secure method of a science. For by thus changing our point of view, the possibility of knowledge *a priori* can well be explained, and, what is still more, the laws which *a priori* lie at the foundation of nature, as the sum total of the objects of experience, may be supplied with satisfactory proofs, neither of which was possible with the procedure hitherto adopted. But there arises from this deduction of our faculty of knowing *a priori,* as given in the first part of metaphysic, a somewhat startling result, apparently most detrimental to the objects of metaphysic that have to be treated in the second part, namely, the impossibility of going with it beyond the frontier of possible experience, which is precisely the most essential purpose of metaphysical science. But here we have exactly the experiment which, by disproving the opposite, establishes the truth of our first estimate of the knowl-

---

* This method, borrowed from the student of nature, consists in our looking for the elements of pure reason in that *which can be confirmed or refuted by experiment.* Now it is impossible, in order to test the propositions of pure reason, particularly if they venture beyond all the limits of possible experience, to make any experiment with their *objects* (as in natural science); we can therefore only try with *concepts* and *propositions* which we admit *a priori,* by so contriving that the same objects may be considered on one side as objects of the senses and of the understanding in experience, and, on the *other,* as objects which are only thought, intended, it may be, for the isolated reason which strives to go beyond all the limits of experience. This gives us two different sides to be looked at; and if we find that, by looking on things from that twofold point of view, there is an agreement with the principle of pure reason, while admitting one point of view only, there arises an inevitable conflict with reason, then the experiment decides in favour of the correctness of that distinction.

edge of reason *a priori,* namely, that it can refer to phenomena
only, but must leave the thing by itself as unknown to us,
though as existing by itself. For that which impels us by necessity to go beyond the limits of experience and of all phenomena, is the *unconditioned,* which reason postulates in all
things by themselves, by necessity and by right, for everything
conditioned, so that the series of conditions should thus become complete. If then we find that, under the supposition of
our experience conforming to the objects as things by themselves, it is *impossible to conceive* the unconditioned *without
contradiction,* while, under the supposition of our representation of things, as they are given to us, not conforming to them
as things by themselves, but, on the contrary, of the objects
conforming to our mode of representation, that *contradiction
vanishes,* and that therefore the unconditioned must not be
looked for in things, so far as we know them (so far as they
are given to us), but only so far as we do not know them (as
things by themselves), we clearly perceive that, what we at
first assumed tentatively only, is fully confirmed.* But, after
all progress in the field of the supersensuous has thus been
denied to speculative reason, it is still open to us to see, whether
in the practical knowledge of reason *data* may not be found
which enable us to determine that transcendent concept of the
unconditioned which is demanded by reason, in order thus,
according to the wish of metaphysic, to get beyond the limits
of all possible experience, by means of our knowledge *a priori,*
which is possible to us for practical purposes only. In this
case, speculative reason has at least gained for us room for
such an extension of knowledge, though it had to leave it
empty, so that we are not only at liberty, but are really called
upon to fill it up, if we are able, by *practical data* of reason.†

---

* This experiment of pure reason has a great similarity with that
of the *chemists,* which they sometimes call the experiment of *reduction,* or the *synthetical process* in general. The *analysis* of the
metaphysician divided pure knowledge *a priori* into two very heterogeneous elements, namely, the knowledge of things as phenomena
and of things by themselves. *Dialectic* combines these two again,
to bring them into *harmony* with the necessary idea of the *unconditioned,* demanded by reason, and then finds that this harmony
can never be obtained, except through the above distinction, which
therefore must be supposed to be true.
† In the same manner the laws of gravity, determining the movements of the heavenly bodies, imparted the character of established
certainty to what Copernicus had assumed at first as an hypothesis
only, and proved at the same time the invisible force (the New-

The very object of the critique of pure speculative reason consists in this attempt at changing the old procedure of metaphysic, and imparting to it the secure method of a science, after having completely revolutionised it, following the example of geometry and physical science. That critique is a treatise on the method (*Traité de la méthode*), not a system of the science itself; but it marks out nevertheless the whole plan of that science, both with regard to its limits, and to its internal organisation. For pure speculative reason has this peculiar advantage that it is able, nay, bound to measure its own powers, according to the different ways in which it chooses its own objects, and to completely enumerate the different ways of choosing problems; thus tracing a complete outline of a system of metaphysic. This is due to the fact that, with regard to the first point, nothing can be attributed to objects in knowledge *a priori,* except what the thinking subject takes from within itself; while, with regard to the second point, reason, so far as its principles of cognition are concerned, forms a separate and independent unity, in which, as in an organic body, every member exists for the sake of all others, and all others exist for the sake of the one, so that no principle can be safely applied in *one* relation, unless it has been carefully examined in *all* its relations, to the whole employment of pure reason. Hence, too, metaphysic has this singular advantage, an advantage which cannot be shared by any other science, in which reason has to deal with objects (for *Logic* deals only with the form of thought in general) that, if it has once attained, by means of this critique, to the secure method of a science, it can completely comprehend the whole field of knowledge pertaining to it, and thus finish its work and leave it to posterity, as a capital that can never be added to, because it has only to deal with principles and the limits of their employment, which are fixed by those principles

tonian attraction) which holds the universe together, which would have remained for ever undiscovered, if Copernicus had not dared, by an hypothesis, which, though contradicting the senses, was yet true, to seek the observed movements, not in the heavenly bodies, but in the spectator. I also propose in this preface my own view of metaphysics, which has so many analogies with the Copernican hypothesis, as an hypothesis only, though, in the Critique itself, it is proved by means of our representations of space and time, and the elementary concepts of the understanding, not hypothetically, but apodictically; for I wish that people should observe the first attempts at such a change, which must always be hypothetical.

themselves. And this completeness becomes indeed an obligation, if it is to be a fundamental science, of which we must be able to say, *'nil actum reputans, si quid superesset agendum.'*

But it will be asked, what kind of treasure is it which we mean to bequeath to posterity in this metaphysic of ours, after it has been purified by criticism, and thereby brought to a permanent condition? After a superficial view of this work, it may seem that its advantage is *negative* only, warning us against venturing with speculative reason beyond the limits of experience. Such is no doubt its primary use: but it becomes *positive,* when we perceive that the principles with which speculative reason ventures beyond its limits, lead inevitably, not to an *extension,* but, if carefully considered, to a *narrowing* of the employment of reason, because, by indefinitely extending the limits of sensibility, to which they properly belong, they threaten entirely to supplant the pure (practical) employment of reason. Hence our *critique,* by limiting sensibility to its proper sphere, is no doubt *negative;* but by thus removing an impediment, which threatened to narrow, or even entirely to destroy its practical employment, it is in reality of *positive,* and of very important use, if only we are convinced that there is an absolutely necessary practical use of pure reason (the moral use), in which reason must inevitably go beyond the limits of sensibility, and though not requiring for this purpose the assistance of speculative reason, must at all events be assured against its opposition, lest it be brought in conflict with itself. To deny that this service, which is rendered by criticism, is a *positive* advantage, would be the same as to deny that the police confers upon us any positive advantage, its principal occupation being to prevent violence, which citizens have to apprehend from citizens, so that each may pursue his vocation in peace and security. We had established in the analytical part of our critique the following points:—First, that space and time are only forms of sensuous intuition, therefore conditions of the existence of things, as phenomena only; Secondly, that we have no concepts of the understanding, and therefore nothing whereby we can arrive at the knowledge of things, except in so far as an intuition corresponding to these concepts can be given, and consequently that we cannot have knowledge of any object, as a thing by itself, but only in so far as it is an object of sensuous intuition, that is, a phenomenon. This proves no doubt that all speculative knowledge of reason is limited to objects of *experience;* but it should be carefully borne in mind, that this leaves it perfectly open to us, to *think* the same objects as things by themselves, though we cannot *know* them.* For otherwise we should arrive at the absurd conclusion, that there is phenomenal appearance without something that appears. Let us suppose that the necessary distinction, established in our critique, between things as objects of experience and the same things by themselves, had not been made. In that case, the principle of causality, and with it the mechanism of nature, as determined by it, would apply to all things in general, as efficient causes. I should then not be able to say of one and the same being, for instance the human soul, that its will is free, and, at the same time, subject to the necessity of nature, that is, not free, without involving myself in a palpable contradiction: and this because I had taken the soul, in both propositions, in *one and the same sense,* namely, as a thing in general (as something by itself), as, without previous criticism, I could not but take it. If, however, our criticism was true, in teaching us to take an object in two senses, namely, either as a phenomenon, or as a thing by itself, and if the deduction of our concepts of the understanding was correct, and the principle of causality applies to things only, if taken in the first sense, namely, so far as they are objects of experience, but not to things, if taken in their second sense, we can, without any contradiction, think the same will when phenomenal (in visible actions) as necessarily conforming to the law of nature, and so far, *not free,* and yet, on the other hand, when belonging to a thing by itself, as not subject to that law of nature, and therefore *free.* Now it is quite true that I may not *know* my soul, as a thing by itself, by means of speculative reason (still less through empirical observation), and consequently may not know freedom either, as the quality of a being to which I attribute effects in the world of sense, because, in order to do this, I should have to know such a being as determined in its existence, and yet

* In order to *know* an object, I must be able to prove its possibility, either from its reality, as attested by experience, or *a priori* by means of reason. But I can *think* whatever I please, provided only I do not contradict myself, that is, provided my conception is a possible thought, though I may be unable to answer for the existence of a corresponding object in the sum total of all possibilities. Before I can attribute to such a concept objective reality (real possibility, as distinguished from the former, which is purely logical), something more is required. This something more, however, need not be sought for in the sources of theoretical knowledge, for it may be found in those of practical knowledge also.

as not determined in time (which, as I cannot provide my concept with any intuition, is impossible). This, however, does not prevent me from *thinking* freedom; that is, my representation of it contains at least no contradiction within itself, if only our critical distinction of the two modes of representation (the sensible and the intelligible), and the consequent limitation of the concepts of the pure understanding, and of the principles based on them, has been properly carried out. If, then, morality necessarily presupposed freedom (in the strictest sense) as a property of our will, producing, as *a priori data* of it, practical principles, belonging originally to our reason, which, without freedom, would be absolutely impossible, while speculative reason had proved that such a freedom cannot even be thought, the former supposition, namely, the moral one, would necessarily have to yield to another, the opposite of which involves a palpable contradiction, so that *freedom,* and with it morality (for its opposite contains no contradiction, unless freedom is presupposed), would have to make room for the *mechanism* of nature. Now, however, as morality requires nothing but that freedom should only not contradict itself, and that, though unable to understand, we should at least be able to think it, there being no reason why freedom should interfere with the natural mechanism of the same act (if only taken in a different sense), the doctrine of morality may well hold its place, and the doctrine of nature may hold its place too, which would have been impossible, if our critique had not previously taught us our inevitable ignorance with regard to things by themselves, and limited everything, which we are able to *know* theoretically, to mere phenomena. The same discussion as to the positive advantage to be derived from the critical principles of pure reason might be repeated with regard to the concept of *God,* and of the *simple nature* of our *soul;* but, for the sake of brevity, I shall pass this by. I am not allowed therefore even to *assume,* for the sake of the necessary practical employment of my reason, *God, freedom,* and *immortality,* if I cannot *deprive* speculative reason of its pretensions to transcendent insights, because reason, in order to arrive at these, must use principles which are intended originally for objects of possible experience only, and which, if in spite of this, they are applied to what cannot be an object of experience, really changes this into a phenomenon, thus rendering all *practical extension* of pure reason impossible. I had therefore to remove *knowledge,* in order to make room for *belief.* For the dogmatism of meta-

physic, that is, the presumption that it is possible to achieve
anything in metaphysic without a previous criticism of pure
reason, is the source of all that unbelief, which is always very
dogmatical, and wars against all morality.

If, then, it may not be too difficult to leave a bequest to posterity, in the shape of a systematical metaphysic, carried out
according to the critique of pure reason, such a bequest is not
to be considered therefore as of little value, whether we regard
the improvement which reason receives through the secure
method of a science, in place of its groundless groping and
uncritical vagaries, or whether we look to the better employment of the time of our enquiring youth, who, if brought up
in the ordinary dogmatism, are early encouraged to indulge
in easy speculations on things of which they know nothing,
and of which they, as little as anybody else, will ever understand anything; neglecting the acquirement of sound knowledge, while bent on the discovery of new metaphysical
thoughts and opinions. The greatest benefit however will be,
that such a work will enable us to put an end for ever to all
objections to morality and religion, according to the Socratic
method, namely, by the clearest proof of the ignorance of our
opponents. Some kind of metaphysic has always existed, and
will always exist, and with it a dialectic of pure reason, as being natural to it. It is therefore the first and most important
task of philosophy to deprive metaphysic, once for all, of its
pernicious influence, by closing up the sources of its errors.

In spite of these important changes in the whole field of science, and of the *losses* which speculative reason must suffer
in its fancied possessions, all general human interests, and all
the advantages which the world hitherto derived from the
teachings of pure reason, remain just the same as before. The
loss, if any, affects only the *monopoly of the schools,* and by
no means the *interests* of *humanity.* I appeal to the staunchest
dogmatist, whether the proof of the continued existence of our
soul after death, derived from the simplicity of the substance,
or that of the freedom of the will, as opposed to the general
mechanism of nature, derived from the subtle, but inefficient,
distinction between subjective and objective practical necessity,
or that of the existence of God, derived from the concept of
an *Ens realissimum* (the contingency of the changeable, and
the necessity of a prime mover), have ever, after they had
been started by the schools, penetrated the public mind, or
exercised the slightest influence on its convictions? If this has
not been, and in fact could not be so, on account of the unfit-

ness of the ordinary understanding for such subtle speculations; and if, on the contrary, with regard to the first point,
the hope of a *future life* has chiefly rested on that peculiar
character of human nature, never to be satisfied by what is
merely temporal (and insufficient, therefore, for the character
of its whole destination); if with regard to the second, the
clear consciousness of *freedom* was produced only by the clear
exhibition of duties in opposition to all the claims of sensuous
desires; and if, lastly, with regard to the third, the belief in a
great and wise *Author of the world* has been supported entirely
by the wonderful beauty, order, and providence, everywhere
displayed in nature, then this possession remains not only undisturbed, but acquires even greater authority, because the
schools have now been taught, not to claim for themselves any
higher or fuller insight on a point which concerns general human interests, than what is equally within the reach of the
great mass of men, and to confine themselves to the elaboration of these universally comprehensible, and, for moral purposes, quite sufficient proofs. The change therefore affects the
arrogant pretensions of the schools only, which would fain be
considered as the only judges and depositaries of such truth
(as they are, no doubt, with regard to many other subjects),
allowing to the public its use only, and trying to keep the key
to themselves, *quod mecum nescit, solus vult scire videri.* At
the same time full satisfaction is given to the more moderate
claims of speculative philosophers. They still remain the exclusive depositors of a science which benefits the masses without their knowing it, namely, the critique of reason. That
critique can never become popular, nor does it need to be so,
because, if on the one side the public has no understanding
for the fine-drawn arguments in support of useful truths, it is
not troubled on the other by the equally subtle objections. It is
different with the schools which, in the same way as every man
who has once risen to the height of speculation, must know
both the pro's and the con's and are bound, by means of a
careful investigation of the rights of speculative reason, to
prevent, once for all, the scandal which, sooner or later, is
sure to be caused even to the masses, by the quarrels in which
metaphysicians (and as such, theologians also) become involved, if ignorant of our critique, and by which their doctrine
becomes in the end entirely perverted. Thus, and thus alone,
can the very root be cut off of *materialism, fatalism, atheism,
free-thinking, unbelief, fanaticism,* and *superstition,* which may
become universally injurious, and finally of *idealism* and *scep-*

ticism also, which are dangerous rather to the schools, and can scarcely ever penetrate into the public. If governments think proper ever to interfere with the affairs of the learned, it would be far more consistent with their wise regard for science as well as for *society,* to favour the freedom of such a criticism by which alone the labours of reason can be established on a firm footing, than to support the ridiculous despotism of the schools, which raise a loud clamour of public danger, whenever the cobwebs are swept away of which the public has never taken the slightest notice, and the loss of which it can therefore never perceive.

Our critique is not opposed to the *dogmatical procedure* of reason, as a science of pure knowledge (for this must always be dogmatical, that is, derive its proof from sure principles *a priori*), but to *dogmatism* only, that is, to the presumption that it is possible to make any progress with pure (philosophical) knowledge, consisting of concepts, and guided by principles, such as reason has long been in the habit of employing, without first enquiring in what way, and by what right, it has come possessed of them. Dogmatism is therefore the dogmatical procedure of pure reason, *without a previous criticism of its own powers;* and our opposition to this is not intended to defend either that loquacious shallowness which arrogates to itself the good name of popularity, much less that scepticism which makes short work with the whole of metaphysic. On the contrary, our critique is meant to form a necessary preparation in support of a thoroughly scientific system of metaphysic, which must necessarily be carried out dogmatically and strictly systematically, so as to satisfy all the demands, not so much of the public at large, as of the schools, this being an indispensable condition, as it has undertaken to carry out its work entirely *a priori,* and thus to the complete satisfaction of speculative reason. In the execution of this plan, as traced out by the critique, that is, in a future system of metaphysic, we shall have to follow in the strict method of the celebrated Wolf, the greatest of all dogmatic philosophers, who first showed (and by his example called forth, in Germany, that spirit of thoroughness, which is not yet extinct) how the secure method of a science could be attained only by a legitimate establishment of principles, a clear definition of concepts, an attempt at strictness of proof, and an avoidance of all bold combinations in concluding. He was therefore most eminently qualified to raise metaphysics to the dignity of a science, if it had only occurred to him, by criticism of the organum, namely, of pure reason itself, first to prepare his field,—an omission to be ascribed, not so much to himself as to the dogmatical spirit of his age, and with regard to which the philosophers of his own, as well as of all previous times, have no right to reproach each other. Those who reject, at the same time, the method of Wolf, and the procedure of the critique of pure reason, can have no other aim but to shake off the fetters of *science* altogether, and thus to change work into play, conviction into opinion, and philosophy into philodoxy.

With regard to this second edition, I have tried, as was but fair, to do all I could in order to remove, as far as possible, the difficulties and obscurities which, not perhaps without my fault, have misled even acute thinkers in judging of my book. In the propositions themselves, and their proofs, likewise in the form and completeness of the whole plan, I have found nothing to alter, which is due partly to the long-continued examination to which I had subjected them, before submitting them to the public, and partly to the nature of the subject itself. For pure speculative reason is so constituted that it forms a true organism, in which everything is *organic,* the whole being there for the sake of every part, and every part for the sake of the whole, so that the smallest imperfection, whether a fault or a deficiency, must inevitably betray itself in use. I venture to hope that this system will maintain itself unchanged for the future also. It is not self-conceit which justifies me in this confidence, but the experimental evidence produced by the identity of the result, whether we proceed progressively from the smallest elements to the whole of pure reason, or retrogressively from the whole (for this also is given by the practical objects of reason) to every single part; the fact being, that an attempt at altering even the smallest item produces at once contradictions, not only in the system, but in human reason in general. With regard to the *style,* however, much remains to be done; and for that purpose, I have endeavoured to introduce several improvements into this second edition, which are intended to remove, first, misapprehensions in the Æsthetic, especially with regard to the concept of time: secondly, obscurities in the deduction of the concepts of the understanding: thirdly, a supposed want of sufficient evidence, in proving the propositions of the pure understanding: fourthly, the false interpretation put on the paralogisms with which we charged rational psychology. To this point (only to the end of the first chapter of transcendental Dialectic) do the changes of style and representation* extend, and no further. Time was too short for doing more, nor did I, with regard to the rest, meet with any misapprehensions on the part of competent and impartial judges. These, even though I must not name them

* The only thing which might be called an addition, though in the method of proof only, is the new refutation of *psychological idealism*, and the strict (and as I believe the only possible) proof of the objective reality of external phenomena on p. 176. That idealism may be considered entirely innocent with respect to the essential aims of metaphysic (though it is not so in reality), yet it remains a scandal to philosophy, and to human reason in general, that we should have to accept the existence of things without us (from which we derive the whole material of knowledge for our own internal sense) on faith only, unable to meet with any satisfactory proof an opponent, who is pleased to doubt it. (See p. 337.) It will probably be urged against this proof that, after all, I am immediately conscious of that only which is within me, that is, of my *representation* of external things, and that consequently it must still remain uncertain whether there be outside me anything corresponding to it or not. But by internal *experience* I am conscious of *my existence in time* (consequently also, of its determinability in time); and this is more than to be conscious of my representation only, and yet identical with the *empirical consciousness of my existence,* which can be itself determined only by something connected with my existence, yet outside me. This consciousness of my existence in time is therefore connected as identical with the consciousness of relation to something *outside* me; so that it is experience, and not fiction, sense, and not imagination, which indissolubly connects the external with my internal sense. The external sense is by itself a relation of intuition to something real outside me; and its real, in contradistinction to a purely imaginary character, rests entirely on its being indissolubly connected with internal experience, as being the condition of its possibility. This is what happens here. If with the *intellectual consciousness* of my existence in the representation, *I am,* which accompanies all my judgments and all acts of my understanding, I could at the same time connect a determination of that existence of mine by means of *intellectual intuition,* then that determination would not require the consciousness of relation to something outside me. But although that intellectual consciousness comes first, the inner intuition, in which alone any existence can be determined, is sensuous and dependent on the condition of time; and that determination again, and therefore internal experience itself, depends on something permanent which is not within me, consequently on something outside me only, to which I must consider myself as standing in a certain relation. Hence the reality of the external sense is necessarily connected, in order to make experience possible at all, with the reality of the internal sense; that is, I am conscious, with the same cer-

with that praise which is due to them, will easily perceive in the proper place, that I have paid careful attention to their remarks.

These improvements, however, entail a small loss to the reader. It was inevitable, without making the book too voluminous, to leave out or abridge several passages which, though not essential to the completeness of the whole, may yet, as useful for other purposes, be missed by some readers. Thus only could I gain room for my new and more intelligible representation of the subject which, though it changes absolutely nothing with regard to propositions, and even to proofs, yet deviates so considerably from the former, in the method of the treatment here and there, that mere additions and interpolations would not have been sufficient. This small loss, which every reader may easily supply by reference to the first edition, will I hope be more than compensated for by the greater clearness of the present.

I have observed with pleasure and thankfulness in various publications (containing either reviews or separate essays) that the spirit of thoroughness is not yet dead in Germany, but has only been silenced for a short time by the clamour of a fashionable and pretentious licence of thought, and that the difficulties which beset the thorny path of my critique, which is to lead to a truly scientific and, as such, permanent, and therefore most necessary, science of pure reason, have not

---

tainty, that there are things outside me which have a reference to my sense, as that I exist myself in time. In order to ascertain to what given intuitions objects outside me really correspond (these intuitions belonging to the *external sense,* and not to the faculty of imagination), we must in each single case apply the rules according to which experience in general (even internal) is distinguished from imaginations, the proposition that there really is an external experience being always taken for granted. It may be well to add here the remark that the *representation of something permanent* in existence is not the same as a *permanent representation;* for this (the representation of something permanent in existence) can change and alternate, as all our representations, even those of matter, and may yet refer to something permanent, which must therefore be something external, and different from all my representations, the *existence* of which is necessarily involved in the *determination* of my own existence, and constitutes with it but one experience, which could never take place internally, unless (in part) it were external also. The *how* admits here of as little explanation as the permanent in time in general, the co-existence of which with the variable produces the concept of change.

discouraged bold and clear heads from mastering my book. To these excellent men, who so happily blend thorough knowledge with a talent for lucid exposition (to which I can lay no claim), I leave the task of bringing my, in that respect far from perfect, work to greater perfection. There is no danger of its being refuted, though there is of its being misunderstood. For my own part, I cannot henceforth enter on controversies, though I shall carefully attend to all hints, whether from friends or opponents, in order to utilise them in a future elaboration of the whole system, according to the plan traced out in this *propaedeutic*. As during these labours I have advanced pretty far in years (this very month, into my sixty-fourth year), I must be careful in spending my time, if I am to carry out my plan, of furnishing a metaphysic of nature, and a metaphysic of morals, in confirmation of the truth of my critique both of speculative and of practical reason, and must leave the elucidation of such obscurities as could at first be hardly avoided in such a work, and likewise the defence of the whole, to those excellent men who have made it their own. At single points every philosophical treatise may be pricked (for it cannot be armed at all points, like a mathematical one), while yet the organic structure of the system, considered as a whole, has not therefore to apprehend the slightest danger. Few only have that pliability of intellect to take in the whole of a system, if it is new; still fewer have an inclination for it, because they dislike every innovation. If we take single passages out of their connection, and contrast them with each other, it is easy to pick out apparent contradictions, particularly in a work written with all the freedom of a running speech. In the eyes of those who rely on the judgment of others, such contradictions may throw an unfavourable light on any work; but they are easily removed, if we ourselves have once grasped the idea of the whole. And, if a theory possesses stability in itself, then this action and reaction of praise and blame, which at first seemed so dangerous, serve only in time to rub off its superficial inequalities: nay, secure to it, in a short time, the requisite elegance also, if only men of insight, impartiality, and true popularity will devote themselves to its study.

KÖNIGSBERG, April, 1787.

INTRODUCTION

I

THE IDEA OF TRANSCENDENTAL PHILOSOPHY

[Experience is no doubt the first product of our under-standing, while employed in fashioning the raw material of our sensations. It is therefore our first instruction, and in its progress so rich in new lessons that the chain of all future generations will never be in want of new information that may be gathered on that field. Nevertheless, experience is by no means the only field to which our understanding can be confined. Experience tells us what is, but not that it must be necessarily as it is, and not otherwise. It therefore never gives us any really general truths, and our reason, which is particu-larly anxious for that class of knowledge, is roused by it rather than satisfied. General truths, which at the same time bear the character of an inward necessity, must be independent of ex-perience,—clear and certain by themselves. They are therefore called knowledge *a priori,* while what is simply taken from ex-perience is said to be, in ordinary parlance, known *a posteriori* or empirically only.

Now it appears, and this is extremely curious, that even with our experiences different kinds of knowledge are mixed up, which must have their origin *a priori,* and which perhaps serve only to produce a certain connection between our sensu-ous representations. For even if we remove from experience everything that belongs to the senses, there remain neverthe-less certain original concepts, and certain judgments derived from them, which must have had their origin entirely *a priori,* and independent of all experience, because it is owing to them that we are able, or imagine we are able, to predicate more of the objects of our senses than can be learnt from mere experience, and that our propositions contain real generality and strict necessity, such as mere empirical knowledge can never supply.]

I

Of the Difference between Pure and Empirical Knowledge

That all our knowledge begins with experience there can be no doubt. For how should the faculty of knowledge be called into activity, if not by objects which affect our senses, and which either produce representations by themselves, or rouse the activity of our understanding to compare, to connect, or to separate them; and thus to convert the raw material of our sensuous impressions into a knowledge of objects, which we call experience? In respect of time, therefore, no knowledge within us is antecedent to experience, but all knowledge begins with it.

But although all our knowledge begins with experience, it does not follow that it arises from experience. For it is quite possible that even our empirical experience is a compound of that which we receive through impressions, and of that which our own faculty of knowledge (incited only by sensuous impressions), supplies from itself, a supplement which we do not distinguish from that raw material, until long practice has roused our attention and rendered us capable of separating one from the other.

It is therefore a question which deserves at least closer investigation, and cannot be disposed of at first sight, whether there exists a knowledge independent of experience, and even of all impressions of the senses? Such knowledge *is called a* priori, *and distinguished from* empirical *knowledge, which has its sources a* posteriori, *that is, in experience.*

This term a priori, however, is not yet definite enough to indicate the full meaning of our question. For people are wont to say, even with regard to knowledge derived from experience, that we have it, or might have it, a priori, because we derive it from experience, not immediately, *but from a general rule, which, however, has itself been derived from experience. Thus one would say of a person who undermines the foundations of his house, that he might have known a priori that it would tumble down, that is, that he need not wait for the experience of its really tumbling down. But still he could not know this entirely* a priori, *because he had first to learn from experience that bodies are heavy, and will fall when their supports are taken away.*

We shall therefore, in what follows, understand by knowledge a priori *knowledge which is absolutely independent of all experience, and not of this or that experience only. Opposed to this is empirical knowledge, or such as is possible* a posteriori *only, that is, by experience. Knowledge* a priori, *if mixed up with nothing empirical, is called pure. Thus the proposition, for example, that every change has its cause, is a proposition* a priori, *but not pure: because change is a concept which can only be derived from experience.*

II

We are in Possession of Certain Cognitions *a priori*, and even the Ordinary Understanding is never without them

All depends here on a criterion, by which we may safely distinguish between pure and empirical knowledge. Now experience teaches us, no doubt, that something is so or so, but not that it cannot be different. First, then, if we have a proposition, which is thought, together with its necessity, we have a judgment a priori; *and if, besides, it is not derived from any proposition, except such as is itself again considered as necessary, we have an absolutely* a priori *judgment. Secondly, experience never imparts to its judgments true or strict, but only assumed or relative universality (by means of induction), so that we ought always to say, so far as we have observed hitherto, there is no exception to this or that rule. If, therefore, a judgment is thought with strict universality, so that no exception is admitted as possible, it is not derived from experience, but valid absolutely* a priori. *Empirical universality, therefore, is only an arbitrary extension of a validity which applies to most cases, to one that applies to all: as, for instance, in the proposition, all bodies are heavy. If, on the contrary, strict universality is essential to a judgment, this always points to a special source of knowledge, namely, a faculty of knowledge* a priori. *Necessity, therefore, and strict universality are safe criteria of knowledge* a priori, *and are inseparable one from the other. As, however, in the use of these criteria, it is sometimes easier to show the contingency than the empirical limita-*

tion[1] of judgments, and as it is sometimes more convincing to prove the unlimited universality which we attribute to a judgment than its necessity, it is advisable to use both criteria separately, each being by itself infallible.

That there really exist in our knowledge such necessary, and in the strictest sense universal, and therefore pure judgments a priori, is easy to show. If we want a scientific example, we have only to look to any of the propositions of mathematics; if we want one from the sphere of the ordinary understanding, such a proposition as that each change must have a cause, will answer the purpose; nay, in the latter case, even the concept of cause contains so clearly the concept of the necessity of its connection with an effect, and of the strict universality of the rule, that it would be destroyed altogether if we attempted to derive it, as Hume does, from the frequent concomitancy of that which happens with that which precedes, and from a habit arising thence (therefore from a purely subjective necessity), of connecting representations. It is possible even, without having recourse to such examples in proof of the reality of pure propositions a priori within our knowledge, to prove their indispensability for the possibility of experience itself, thus proving it a priori. For whence should experience take its certainty, if all the rules which it follows were always again and again empirical, and therefore contingent and hardly fit to serve as first principles? For the present, however, we may be satisfied for having shown the pure employment of the faculty of our knowledge as a matter of fact, with the criteria of it.

Not only in judgments, however, but even in certain concepts, can we show their origin a priori. Take away, for example, from the concept of a body, as supplied by experience, everything that is empirical, one by one; such as colour, hardness or softness, weight, and even impenetrability, and there still remains the space which the body (now entirely vanished) occupied: that you cannot take away. And in the same manner, if you remove from your empirical concept of any object, corporeal or incorporeal, all properties which experience has taught you, you cannot take away from it that property by which you conceive it as a substance, or inherent in a substance (although such a concept contains more determinations than that of an object in general). Convinced, therefore, by

[1] According to an emendation adopted both by Vaihinger and Adickes.

*the necessity with which that concept forces itself upon you,
you will have to admit that it has its seat in your faculty of
knowledge* a priori.

But[2] what is still more extraordinary is this, that certain
kinds of knowledge leave the field of all possible experience,
and seem to enlarge the sphere of our judgments beyond the
limits of experience by means of concepts to which experience
can never supply any corresponding objects.

And it is in this very kind of knowledge which transcends
the world of the senses, and where experience can neither
guide nor correct us, that reason prosecutes its investigations,
which by their importance we consider far more excellent and
by their tendency far more elevated than anything the understanding can find in the sphere of phenomena. Nay, we risk
rather anything, even at the peril of error, than that we
should surrender such investigations, either on the ground of
their uncertainty, or from any feeling of indifference or contempt. *These inevitable problems of pure reason itself are,*
God, Freedom, *and* Immortality. *The science which with all
its apparatus is really intended for the solution of these problems, is called* Metaphysic. *Its procedure is at first* dogmatic,
*i.e. unchecked by a previous examination of what reason can
and cannot do, before it engages confidently in so arduous an
undertaking.*

Now it might seem natural that, after we have left the solid
ground of experience, we should not at once proceed to erect
an edifice with knowledge which we possess without knowing
whence it came, and trust to principles the origin of which is
unknown, without having made sure of the safety of the foundations by means of careful examination. It would seem natural, I say, that philosophers should first of all have asked the
question how the mere understanding could arrive at all this
knowledge *a priori,* and what extent, what truth, and what
value it could possess. If we take natural to mean what is just
and reasonable, then indeed nothing could be more natural.
But if we understand by natural what takes place ordinarily,
then, on the contrary, nothing is more natural and more intelligible than that this examination should have been neglected
for so long a time. For one part of this knowledge, namely,
the mathematical, has always been in possession of perfect

[2] The Second Edition gives here a new heading:—III, Philosophy
requires a science to determine the possibility, the principles, and
the extent of all cognitions *a priori.*

trustworthiness; and thus produces a favourable presumption with regard to other parts also, although these may be of a totally different nature. Besides, once beyond the precincts of experience, and we are certain that experience can never contradict us, while the charm of enlarging our knowledge is so great that nothing will stop our progress until we encounter a clear contradiction. This can be avoided if only we are cautious in our imaginations, which nevertheless remain what they are, imaginations only. How far we can advance independent of all experience in *a priori* knowledge is shown by the brilliant example of mathematics. It is true they deal with objects and knowledge so far only as they can be represented in intuition. But this is easily overlooked, because that intuition itself may be given *a priori,* and be difficult to distinguish from a pure concept. Thus inspirited by a splendid proof of the power of reason, the desire of enlarging our knowledge sees no limits. The light dove, piercing in her easy flight the air and perceiving its resistance, imagines that flight would be easier still in empty space. It was thus that Plato left the world of sense, as opposing so many hindrances to our understanding, and ventured beyond on the wings of his ideas into the empty space of pure understanding. He did not perceive that he was making no progress by these endeavours, because he had no resistance as a fulcrum on which to rest or to apply his powers, in order to cause the understanding to advance. It is indeed a very common fate of human reason first of all to finish its speculative edifice as soon as possible, and then only to enquire whether the foundation be sure. Then all sorts of excuses are made in order to assure us as to its solidity, or to decline altogether such a late and dangerous enquiry. The reason why during the time of building we feel free from all anxiety and suspicion and believe in the apparent solidity of our foundation, is this:—A great, perhaps the greatest portion of what our reason finds to do consists in the analysis of our concepts of objects. This gives us a great deal of knowledge which, though it consists in no more than in simplifications and explanations of what is comprehended in our concepts (though in a confused manner), is yet considered as equal, at least in form, to new knowledge. It only separates and arranges our concepts, it does not enlarge them in matter or contents. As by this process we gain a kind of real knowledge *a priori,* which progresses safely and usefully, it happens that our reason, without being aware of it, appropriates under that pretence propositions of a totally different character, adding to given concepts new and strange ones *a priori*, without knowing whence they come, nay without even thinking of such a question. I shall therefore at the very outset treat of the distinction between these two kinds of knowledge.

IV

Of the Distinction between Analytical and Synthetical Judgments

In all judgments in which there is a relation between subject and predicate (I speak of affirmative judgments only, the application to negative ones being easy), that relation can be of two kinds. Either the predicate B belongs to the subject A as something contained (though covertly) in the concept A; or B lies outside the sphere of the concept A, though somehow connected with it. In the former case I call the judgment analytical, in the latter synthetical. Analytical judgments (affirmative) are therefore those in which the connection of the predicate with the subject is conceived through identity, while others in which that connection is conceived without identity, may be called synthetical. The former might be called illustrating, the latter expanding judgments, because in the former nothing is added by the predicate to the concept of the subject, but the concept is only divided into its constituent concepts which were always conceived as existing within it, though confusedly; while the latter add to the concept of the subject a predicate not conceived as existing within it, and not to be extracted from it by any process of mere analysis. If I say, for instance, All bodies are extended, this is an analytical judgment. I need not go beyond the concept connected with the name of body, in order to find that extension is connected with it. I have only to analyse that concept and become conscious of the manifold elements always contained in it, in order to find that predicate. This is therefore an analytical judgment. But if I say, All bodies are heavy, the predicate is something quite different from what I think as the mere concept of body. The addition of such a predicate gives us a synthetical judgment.

[It becomes clear from this,

1. That our knowledge is in no way extended by analytical judgments, but that all they effect is to put the concepts which we possess into better order and render them more intelligible.

2. That in synthetical judgments I must have besides the

concept of the subject something else (*x*) on which the understanding relies in order to know that a predicate, not contained in the concept, nevertheless belongs to it.

In empirical judgments this causes no difficulty, because this *x* is here simply the complete experience of an object which I conceive by the concept A, that concept forming one part only of my experience. For though I do not include the predicate of gravity in the general concept of body, that concept nevertheless indicates the complete experience through one of its parts, so that I may add other parts also of the same experience, all belonging to that concept. I may first, by an analytical process, realise the concept of body through the predicates of extension, impermeability, form, etc., all of which are contained in it. Afterwards I expand my knowledge, and looking back to the experience from which my concept of body was abstracted, I find gravity always connected with the before-mentioned predicates. Experience therefore is the *x* which lies beyond the concept A, and on which rests the possibility of a synthesis of the predicate of gravity B with the concept A.]

Empirical judgments, as such, are all synthetical; for it would be absurd to found an analytical judgment on experience, because, in order to form such a judgment, I need not at all step out of my concept, or appeal to the testimony of experience. That a body is extended, is a proposition perfectly certain a priori, and not an empirical judgment. For, before I call in experience, I am already in possession of all the conditions of my judgment in the concept of body itself. I have only to draw out from it, according to the principle of contradiction, the required predicate, and I thus become conscious, at the same time, of the necessity of the judgment, which experience could never teach me. But, though I do not include the predicate of gravity in the general concept of body, that concept, nevertheless, indicates an object of experience through one of its parts: so that I may add other parts also of the same experience, besides those which belonged to the former concept. I may, first, by an analytical process, realise the concept of body, through the predicates of extension, impermeability, form, etc., all of which are contained in it. Afterwards I expand my knowledge, and looking back to the experience from which my concept of body was abstracted, I find gravity always connected with the before-mentioned predicates, and therefore I add it synthetically to that concept as a

*predicate. It is, therefore, experience on which the possibility
of the synthesis of the predicate of gravity with the concept
of body is founded: because both concepts, though neither of
them is contained in the other, belong to each other, though
accidentally only, as parts of a whole, namely, of experience,
which is itself a synthetical connection of intuitions.*

In synthetical judgments *a priori,* however, that help is entirely wanting. If I want to go beyond the concept A in order
to find another concept B connected with it, where is there
anything on which I may rest and through which a synthesis
might become possible, considering that I cannot have the advantage of looking about in the field of experience? Take the
proposition that all which happens has its cause. In the concept
of something that happens I no doubt conceive of something
existing preceded by time, and from this certain analytical
judgments may be deduced. But the concept of cause is entirely outside that concept, and indicates something different
from that which happens, and is by no means contained in
that representation. How can I venture then to predicate of
that which happens something totally different from it, and to
represent the concept of cause, though not contained in it, as
belonging to it, and belonging to it by necessity? What is here
the unknown *x,* on which the understanding may rest in order
to find beyond the concept A a foreign predicate B, which
nevertheless is believed to be connected with it? It cannot be
experience, because the proposition that all which happens has
its cause represents this second predicate as added to the subject not only with greater generality than experience can ever
supply, but also with a character of necessity, and therefore
purely *a priori,* and based on concepts. All our speculative
knowledge *a priori* aims at and rests on such synthetical, i.e.
expanding propositions, for the analytical are no doubt very
important and necessary, yet only in order to arrive at that
clearness of concepts which is requisite for a safe and wide
synthesis, serving as a really new addition to what we possess
already.

[We have here a certain mystery* before us, which must
be cleared up before any advance into the unlimited field of a

---

* If any of the ancients had ever thought of asking this question,
this alone would have formed a powerful barrier against all systems of pure reason to the present day, and would have saved many
vain attempts undertaken blindly and without a true knowledge of
the subject in hand.

pure knowledge of the understanding can become safe and trustworthy. We must discover on the largest scale the ground of the possibility of synthetical judgments *a priori;* we must understand the conditions which render every class of them possible, and endeavour not only to indicate in a sketchy outline, but to define in its fulness and practical completeness, the whole of that knowledge, which forms a class by itself, systematically arranged according to its original sources, its divisions, its extent and its limits. So much for the present with regard to the peculiar character of synthetical judgments.]

V

In all Theoretical Sciences of Reason Synthetical Judgments *a priori* are contained as Principles

1. All mathematical judgments are synthetical. This proposition, though incontestably certain, and very important to us for the future, seems to have hitherto escaped the observation of those who are engaged in the anatomy of human reason: nay, to be directly opposed to all their conjectures. For as it was found that all mathematical conclusions proceed according to the principle of contradiction (which is required by the nature of all apodictic certainty), it was supposed that the fundamental principles of mathematics also rested on the authority of the same principle of contradiction. This, however, was a mistake: for though a synthetical proposition may be understood according to the principle of contradiction, this can only be if another synthetical proposition is presupposed, from which the latter is deduced, but never by itself. First of all, we ought to observe, that mathematical propositions, properly so called, are always judgments a priori, *and not empirical, because they carry along with them necessity, which can never be deduced from experience. If people should object to this, I am quite willing to confine my statement to pure mathematics, the very concept of which implies that it does not contain empirical, but only pure knowledge* a priori.

At first sight one might suppose indeed that the proposition $7+5=12$ *is merely analytical, following, according to the principle of contradiction, from the concept of a sum of 7 and 5. But, if we look more closely, we shall find that the concept of the sum of 7 and 5 contains nothing beyond the union of both sums into one, whereby nothing is told us as to what* *this single number may be which combines both. We by no means arrive at a concept of Twelve, by thinking that union of Seven and Five; and we may analyse our concept of such a possible sum as long as we will, still we shall never discover in it the concept of Twelve. We must go beyond these concepts, and call in the assistance of the intuition corresponding to one of the two, for instance, our five fingers, or, as Segner does in his arithmetic, five points, and so by degrees add the units of the Five, given in intuition, to the concept of the Seven. For I first take the number 7, and taking the intuition of the fingers of my hand, in order to form with it the concept of the 5, I gradually add the units, which I before took together, to make up the number 5, by means of the image of my hand, to the number 7, and I thus see the number 12 arising before me. That 5 should be added to 7 was no doubt implied in my concept of a sum $7 + 5$, but not that that sum should be equal to 12. An arithmetical proposition is, therefore, always synthetical, which is seen more easily still by taking larger numbers, where we clearly perceive that, turn and twist our conceptions as we may, we could never, by means of the mere analysis of our concepts and without the help of intuition, arrive at the sum that is wanted.*

Nor is any proposition of pure geometry analytical. That the straight line between two points is the shortest, is a synthetical proposition. For my concept of straight *contains nothing of magnitude (quantity), but a quality only. The concept of the* shortest *is, therefore, purely adventitious, and cannot be deduced from the concept of the straight line by any analysis whatsoever. The aid of intuition, therefore, must be called in, by which alone the synthesis is possible.*

[It is true that some few propositions, presupposed by the geometrician, are really analytical, and depend on the principle of contradiction: but then they serve only, like identical propositions, to form the chain of the method, and not as principles. Such are the propositions, a=a, *the whole is equal to itself, or* $(a+b)>a$, *that the whole is greater than its part. And even these, though they are valid according to mere concepts, are only admitted in mathematics, because they can be represented in intuition.]*[3] *What often makes us believe that the predicate of such apodictic judgments is contained in our concept, and the judgment therefore analytical, is merely the*

---

[3] This paragraph from *It is true* to *intuition* seems to have been a marginal note, as shown by Dr. Vaihinger.

ambiguous character of the expression. We are told that we ought *to join in thought a certain predicate to a given concept, and this necessity is inherent in the concepts themselves. But* the *question is not what we* ought *to join to the given concept, but what we* really think *in it, though confusedly only, and then it becomes clear that the predicate is no doubt inherent in those concepts by necessity, not, however, as thought in the concept itself, but by means of an intuition, which must be added to the concept.*

2. Natural science (physica) contains synthetical judgments *a priori* as principles. *I shall adduce, as examples, a few propositions only, such as, that in all changes of the material world the quantity of matter always remains unchanged: or that in all communication of motion, action and reaction must always equal each other. It is clear not only that both convey necessity, and that, therefore, their origin is* a priori, *but also that they are synthetical propositions. For in the concept of matter I do not conceive its permanency, but only its presence in the space which it fills. I therefore go beyond the concept of matter in order to join something to it* a priori, *which I did not before conceive in it. The proposition is, therefore, not analytical, but synthetical, and yet* a priori, *and the same applies to the other propositions of the pure part of natural science.*

3. Metaphysic, *even if we look upon it as hitherto a tentative science only, which, however, is indispensable to us, owing to the very nature of human reason, is meant to* contain synthetical knowledge a priori. *Its object is not at all merely to analyse such concepts as we make to ourselves of things* a priori, *and thus to explain them analytically, but to expand our knowledge* a priori. *This we can only do by means of concepts which add something to a given concept that was not contained in it; nay, we even attempt, by means of synthetical judgments* a priori, *to go so far beyond a given concept that experience itself cannot follow us: as, for instance, in the proposition that the world must have a first beginning. Thus, according at least to its intentions, metaphysic consists merely of synthetical propositions* a priori.

VI

The General Problem of Pure Reason

Much is gained if we are able to bring a number of investigations under the formula of one single problem. For we thus not only facilitate our own work by defining it accurately, but enable also everybody else who likes to examine it to form a judgment, whether we have really done justice to our purpose or not. Now the real problem of pure reason is contained in the question, How are synthetical judgments *a priori* possible?

That metaphysic has hitherto remained in so vacillating a state of ignorance and contradiction is entirely due to people not having thought sooner of this problem, or perhaps even of a distinction between analytical *and* synthetical *judgments. The solution of this problem, or a sufficient proof that a possibility which is to be explained does in reality not exist at all, is the question of life or death to metaphysic. David Hume, who among all philosophers approached nearest to that problem, though he was far from conceiving it with sufficient definiteness and universality, confining his attention only to the synthetical proposition of the connection of an effect with its causes* (principium causalitatis), *arrived at the conclusion that such a proposition* a priori *is entirely impossible. According to his conclusions, everything which we call metaphysic would turn out to be a mere delusion of reason, fancying that it knows by itself what in reality is only borrowed from experience, and has assumed by mere habit the appearance of necessity. If he had grasped our problem in all its universality, he would never have thought of an assertion which destroys all pure philosophy, because he would have perceived that, according to his argument, no pure mathematical science was possible either, on account of its certainly containing synthetical propositions* a priori; *and from such an assertion his good sense would probably have saved him.*

On the solution of our problem depends, at the same time, the possibility of the pure employment of reason, in establishing and carrying out all sciences which contain a theoretical knowledge a priori *of objects, i.e. the answer to the questions*

How is pure mathematical science possible?

How is pure natural science possible?

As these sciences really exist, it is quite proper to ask, How *they are possible? for that they must be possible, is proved by their reality.**

But as to metaphysic, *the bad progress which it has hitherto made, and the impossibility of asserting of any of the metaphysical systems yet brought forward that it really exists, so far as its essential aim is concerned, must fill every one with doubts as to its possibility.*

Yet, in a certain sense, this kind of knowledge *also must be looked upon as given, and though not as a science, yet as a natural disposition* (metaphysica naturalis) *metaphysic is real. For human reason, without being moved merely by the conceit of omniscience, advances irresistibly, and urged on by its own need, to questions such as cannot be answered by any empirical employment of reason, or by principles thence derived, so that we may really say, that all men, as soon as their reason became ripe for speculation, have at all times possessed some kind of metaphysic, and will always continue to possess it. And now it will also have to answer the question*

How is metaphysic possible, as a natural disposition? *that is, how does the nature of universal human reason give rise to questions which pure reason proposes to itself, and which it is urged on by its own need to answer as well as it can?*

As, however, all attempts which have hitherto been made at answering these natural questions (for instance, whether the world has a beginning, or exists from all eternity) have always led to inevitable contradictions, we cannot rest satisfied with the mere natural disposition to metaphysic, that is, with the pure faculty of reason itself, from which some kind of metaphysic (whatever it may be) always arises; but it must be possible to arrive with it at some certainty as to our either knowing or not knowing its objects; that is, we must either decide that we can judge of the objects of these questions, or of the power or want of power of reason, in deciding anything upon them,—therefore that we can either enlarge our pure reason with certainty, or that we have to impose on it fixed and firm

---

* *One might doubt this with regard to pure natural science; but one has only to consider the different propositions which stand at the beginning of real (empirical) physical science, those, for example, relating to the permanence of the same quantity of matter to the* vis inertiae, *the equality of action and reaction, etc., in order to become convinced that they constitute a* physica pura, *or* rationalis, *which well deserves to stand by itself as an independent science, in its whole extent, whether narrow or wide.*

limits. This last question, which arises out of the former more general problem, would properly assume this form,

How is metaphysic possible, as a science?

The critique of reason leads, therefore, necessarily, to true science, while its dogmatical use, without criticism, lands us in groundless assertions, to which others, equally specious, can always be opposed, that is, in scepticism.

Nor need this science be very formidable by its great prolixity, for it has not to deal with the objects of reason, the variety of which is infinite, but with reason only, and with problems, suggested by reason and placed before it, not by the nature of things, which are different from it, but by its own nature; so that, if reason has only first completely understood its own power, with reference to objects given to it in experience, it will have no difficulty in determining completely and safely the extent and limits of its attempted application beyond the limits of all experience.

We may and must therefore regard all attempts which have hitherto been made at building up a metaphysic dogmatically, as non-avenu. *For the mere analysis of the concepts that dwell in our reason* a priori, *which has been attempted in one or other of those metaphysical systems, is by no means the aim, but only a preparation for true metaphysic, namely, the answer to the question, how we can enlarge our knowledge* a priori *synthetically; nay, it is utterly useless for that purpose, because it only shows what is contained in those concepts, but not by what process* a priori *we arrive at them, in order thus to determine the validity of their employment with reference to all objects of knowledge in general. Nor does it require much self-denial to give up these pretensions, considering that the undeniable and, in the dogmatic procedure, inevitable contradictions of reason with itself, have long deprived every system of metaphysic of all authority. More firmness will be required in order not to be deterred by difficulties from within and resistance from without, from trying to advance a science, indispensable to human reason (a science of which we may lop off every branch, but will never be able to destroy the root), by a treatment entirely opposed to all former treatments, which promises, at last, to ensure the successful and fruitful growth of metaphysical science.*

It will now be seen how there can be a special science serving as a critique of pure reason. [Every kind of knowledge is called pure, if not mixed with anything heterogeneous. But more particularly is that knowledge called absolutely pure, which is not mixed up with any experience or sensation, and is therefore possible entirely *a priori*.] Reason is the faculty which supplies the principles of knowledge *a priori*. Pure reason therefore is that faculty which supplies the principles of knowing anything entirely *a priori*. An Organum of pure reason ought to comprehend all the principles by which pure knowledge *a priori* can be acquired and fully established. A complete application of such an Organum would give us a System of Pure Reason. But as that would be a difficult task, and as at present it is still doubtful whether and when such an expansion of our knowledge is here possible, we may look on a mere criticism of pure reason, its sources and limits, as a kind of preparation for a complete system of pure reason. It should be called a critique, not a doctrine, of pure reason. Its usefulness would be negative only, serving for a purging rather than for an expansion of our reason, and, what after all is a considerable gain, guarding reason against errors.

I call all knowledge *transcendental* which is occupied not so much with objects, [as with our *a priori* concepts of objects.] *as with our manner of knowing objects, so far as this is meant to be possible* a priori. A system of such concepts might be called Transcendental Philosophy. But for the present this is again too great an undertaking. We should have to treat therein completely both of analytical knowledge, and of synthetical knowledge *a priori*, which is more than we intend to do, being satisfied to carry on the analysis so far only as is indispensably necessary in order to recognise in their whole extent the principles of synthesis *a priori*, which alone concern us. This investigation which should be called a transcendental critique, but not a systematic doctrine, is all we are occupied with at present. It is not meant to extend our knowledge, but only to rectify it, and to become the test of the value of all *a priori* knowledge. Such a critique therefore is a preparation for a New Organum, or, if that should not be possible, for a Canon at least, according to which hereafter a complete system of a philosophy of pure reason, whether it serve for an expansion or merely for a limitation of it, may be carried out, both analytically and synthetically. That such a system is possible, nay that it need not be so comprehensive as to prevent the hope of its completion, may be gathered from the fact that it would have to deal, not with the nature of things, which is endless, but with the understanding which judges of the nature of things, and this again so far only as its knowledge *a priori* is concerned. Whatever the understanding possesses *a priori,* as it has not to be looked for without, can hardly escape our notice, nor is there any reason to suppose that it will prove too extensive for a complete inventory, and for such a valuation as shall assign to it its true merits or demerits.

Still less ought we to except here a criticism on the books and systems treating of pure reason, but only on the faculty of pure reason itself. It is only if we are in possession of this, that we possess a safe criterion for estimating the philosophical value of old and new works on this subject. Otherwise, an unqualified historian and judge does nothing but criticise the groundless assertions of others by means of his own, which are equally groundless.

II

DIVISION OF TRANSCENDENTAL PHILOSOPHY

Transcendental Philosophy is with us an idea (of a science) only, for which the critique of pure reason should trace, according to fixed principles, an architectonic plan, guaranteeing the completeness and certainty of all parts of which the building consist. *It is a system of all principles of pure reason.* The reason why we do not call such a critique a transcendental philosophy in itself is simply this, that in order to be a complete system, it ought to contain likewise a complete analysis of the whole of human knowledge *a priori.* It is true that our critique must produce a complete list of all the fundamental concepts which constitute pure knowledge. But it need not give a detailed analysis of these concepts, nor a complete list of all derivative concepts. Such an analysis would be out of place, because it is not beset with the doubts and difficulties which are inherent in synthesis, and which alone necessitate a critique of pure reason. Nor would it answer our purpose to take the responsibility of the completeness of such an analysis and derivation. This completeness of analysis, however, and of derivation from such *a priori* concepts as we shall have to deal with presently, may easily be supplied, if only they have first been laid down as perfect principles of synthesis, and nothing is wanting to them in that respect.

All that constitutes transcendental philosophy belongs to the critique of pure reason, nay it is the complete idea of transcendental philosophy, but not yet the whole of that philosophy itself, because it carries the analysis so far only as is requisite for a complete examination of synthetical knowledge *a priori.*

The most important consideration in the arrangement of such a science is that no concepts should be admitted which contain anything empirical, and that the *a priori* knowledge shall be perfectly pure. Therefore, although the highest principles of morality and their fundamental concepts are *a priori* knowledge, they do not belong to transcendental philosophy, because the concepts of pleasure and pain, desire, inclination, free-will, etc., which are all of empirical origin, must here be presupposed. Transcendental philosophy is the wisdom of pure speculative reason. Everything practical, so far as it contains motives, has reference to sentiments, and these belong to empirical sources of knowledge.

If we wish to carry out a proper division of our science systematically, it must contain first *a doctrine of the elements,* secondly, *a doctrine of the method* of pure reason. Each of these principal divisions will have its subdivisions, the grounds of which cannot however be explained here. So much only seems necessary for previous information, that there are two stems of human knowledge, which perhaps may spring from a common root, unknown to us, viz. *sensibility* and the *understanding,* objects being given by the former and thought by the latter. If our sensibility should contain *a priori* representations, constituting conditions under which alone objects can be given, it would belong to transcendental philosophy, and the doctrine of this transcendental sense-perception would necessarily form the first part of the doctrine of elements, because the conditions under which alone objects of human knowledge can be given must precede those under which they are thought.

CRITIQUE OF PURE REASON

I

THE ELEMENTS OF TRANSCENDENTALISM

THE ELEMENTS OF TRANSCENDENTALISM

FIRST PART

TRANSCENDENTAL ÆSTHETIC

§ 1[1]

Whatever the process and the means may be by which knowledge reaches its objects, there is one that reaches them directly, and forms the ultimate material of all thought, viz. intuition (Anschauung). This is possible only when the object is given, and the object can be given only (to human beings at least) through a certain affection of the mind (Gemüth).

This faculty (receptivity) of receiving representations (Vorstellungen), according to the manner in which we are affected by objects, is called sensibility (Sinnlichkeit).

Objects therefore are given to us through our sensibility. Sensibility alone supplies us with intuitions (Anschauungen). These intuitions become thought through the understanding (Verstand), and hence arise conceptions (Begriffe). All thought therefore must, directly or indirectly, go back to intuitions (Anschauungen), i.e. to our sensibility, because in no other way can objects be given to us.

The effect produced by an object upon the faculty of representation (Vorstellungsfähigkeit), so far as we are affected by it, is called sensation (Empfindung). An intuition (Anschauung) of an object, by means of sensation, is called empirical. The undefined object of such an empirical intuition is called phenomenon (Erscheinung).

In a phenomenon I call that which corresponds to the sensation its *matter;* but that which causes the manifold matter of the phenomenon to be perceived as arranged in a certain order, I call its *form.*

Now it is clear that it cannot be sensation again through which sensations are arranged and placed in certain forms. The matter only of all phenomena is given us *a posteriori;* but their form must be ready for them in the mind (Gemüth)

---

[1] These section numbers do not appear in the first edition.

a priori, and must therefore be capable of being considered as separate from all sensations.

I call all representations in which there is nothing that belongs to sensation, *pure* (in a transcendental sense). The pure form therefore of all sensuous intuitions, that form in which the manifold elements of the phenomena are seen in a certain order, must be found in the mind *a priori.* And this pure form of sensibility may be called the pure intuition (Anschauung).

Thus, if we deduct from the representation (Vorstellung) of a body what belongs to the thinking of the understanding, viz. substance, force, divisibility, etc., and likewise what belongs to sensation, viz. impermeability, hardness, colour, etc., there still remains something of that empirical intuition (Anschauung), viz. extension and form. These belong to pure intuition, which *a priori,* and even without a real object of the senses or of sensation, exists in the mind as a mere form of sensibility.

The science of all the principles of sensibility *a priori* I call *Transcendental Æsthetic.** There must be such a science, forming the first part of the Elements of Transcendentalism, as opposed to that which treats of the principles of pure thought, and which should be called *Transcendental Logic.*

In Transcendental Æsthetic therefore we shall first isolate sensibility, by separating everything which the understanding adds by means of its concepts, so that nothing remains but empirical intuition (Anschauung).

Secondly, we shall separate from this all that belongs to sensation (Empfindung), so that nothing remains but pure

---

* The Germans are the only people who at present (1781) use the word *æsthetic* for what others call criticism of taste. There is implied in that name a false hope, first conceived by the excellent analytical philosopher, Baumgarten, of bringing the critical judgment of the beautiful under rational principles, and to raise its rules to the rank of a science. But such endeavours are vain. For such rules or criteria are, according to their principal sources, empirical only, and can never serve as definite *a priori* rules for our judgment in matters of taste; on the contrary, our judgment is the real test of the truth of such rules. It would be advisable therefore to drop the name in that sense, and to apply it to a doctrine which is a real science, thus approaching more nearly to the language and meaning of the ancients with whom the division into αἰσθητὰ καὶ νοητά was very famous (or to share that name in common with speculative philosophy, and thus to use æsthetic sometimes in a transcendental, sometimes in a psychological sense).

intuition (reine Anschauung) or the mere form of the phenomena, which is the only thing which sensibility *a priori* can supply. In the course of this investigation it will appear that there are, as principles of *a priori* knowledge, two pure forms of sensuous intuition (Anschauung), namely, *Space* and *Time*. We now proceed to consider these more in detail.

FIRST SECTION OF THE TRANSCENDENTAL ÆSTHETIC

§ 2

Of Space

By means of our external sense, a property of our mind (Gemüth), we represent to ourselves objects as external or outside ourselves, and all of these in space. It is within space that their form, size, and relative position are fixed or can be fixed. The internal sense by means of which the mind perceives itself or its internal state, does not give an intuition (Anschauung) of the soul (Seele) itself, as an object, but it is nevertheless a fixed form under which alone an intuition of its internal state is possible, so that whatever belongs to its internal determinations (Bestimmungen) must be represented in relations of time. Time cannot be perceived (angeschaut) externally, as little as space can be perceived as something within us.

What then are space and time? Are they real beings? Or, if not that, are they determinations or relations of things, but such as would belong to them even if they were not perceived? Or lastly, are they determinations and relations which are inherent in the form of intuition only, and therefore in the subjective nature of our mind, without which such predicates as space and time would never be ascribed to anything?

In order to understand this more clearly, let us first consider space.

1. Space is not an empirical concept which has been derived from external experience. For in order that certain sensations should be referred to something outside myself, i.e. to something in a different part of space from that where I am; again, in order that I may be able to represent them (vorstellen) as side by side, that is, not only as different, but as in different places, the representation (Vorstellung) of space must already be there. Therefore the representation of space

cannot be borrowed through experience from relations of external phenomena, but, on the contrary, this external experience becomes possible only by means of the representation of space.

2. Space is a necessary representation *a priori*, forming the very foundation of all external intuitions. It is impossible to imagine that there should be no space, though one might very well imagine that there should be space without objects to fill it. Space is therefore regarded as a condition of the possibility of phenomena, not as a determination produced by them; it is a representation *a priori* which necessarily precedes all external phenomena.

[3. On this necessity of an *a priori* representation of space rests the apodictic certainty of all geometrical principles, and the possibility of their construction *a priori*. For if the intuition of space were a concept gained *a posteriori*, borrowed from general external experience, the first principles of mathematical definition would be nothing but perceptions. They would be exposed to all the accidents of perception, and there being but one straight line between two points would not be a necessity, but only something taught in each case by experience. Whatever is derived from experience possesses a relative generality only, based on induction. We should therefore not be able to say more than that, so far as hitherto observed, no space has yet been found having more than three dimensions.]

4. (*3*) Space is not a discursive or so-called general concept of the relations of things in general, but a pure intuition. For, first of all, we can imagine one space only and if we speak of many spaces, we mean parts only of one and the same space. Nor can these parts be considered as antecedent to the one and all-embracing space and, as it were, its component parts out of which an aggregate is formed, but they can be thought of as existing within it only. Space is essentially one; its multiplicity, and therefore the general concept of spaces in general, arises entirely from limitations. Hence it follows that, with respect to space, an intuition *a priori*, which is not empirical, must form the foundation of all conceptions of space. In the same manner all geometrical principles, e.g. 'that in every triangle two sides together are greater than the third,' are never to be derived from the general concepts of side and triangle, but from an intuition, and that *a priori*, with apodictic certainty.

[5. Space is represented as an infinite quantity. Now a general concept of space, which is found in a foot as well as in an ell, could tell us nothing in respect to the quantity of the space. If there were not infinity in the progression of intuition, no concept of relations of space could ever contain a principle of infinity.]

4. *Space is represented as an infinite given quantity. Now it is quite true that every concept is to be thought as a representation, which is contained in an infinite number of different possible representations (as their common characteristic), and therefore comprehends them: but no concept, as such, can be thought as if it contained in itself an infinite number of representations. Nevertheless, space is so thought (for all parts of infinite space exist simultaneously). Consequently, the original representation of space is an* intuition a priori, *and not a concept.*

§ 3

Transcendental Exposition of the Concept of Space

I understand by transcendental exposition (Erörterung), *the explanation of a concept, as of a principle by which the possibility of other synthetical cognitions* a priori *can be understood. For this purpose it is necessary, 1. That such cognitions really do flow from the given concept. 2. That they are possible only under the presupposition of a given mode of explanation of such concept.*

Geometry is a science which determines the properties of space synthetically, and yet a priori. *What then must be the representation of space, to render such a knowledge of it possible? It must be originally intuitive; for it is impossible from a mere concept to deduce propositions which go beyond that concept, as we do in geometry (Introduction, p. 10). That intuition, however, must be* a priori, *that is, it must exist within us before any perception of the object, and must therefore be pure, not empirical intuition. For all geometrical propositions are apodictic, that is, connected with the consciousness of their necessity, as for instance the proposition, that space has only three dimensions; and such propositions cannot be empirical judgments, nor conclusions from them (Introduction, p. 3).*

How then can an external intuition dwell in the mind anterior to the objects themselves, and in which the concept of objects can be determined a priori? *Evidently not otherwise*

*than so far as it has its seat in the subject only, as the formal
condition under which the subject is affected by the objects
and thereby is receiving an* immediate representation, *that is,*
intuition *of them; therefore as a form of the external* sense *in
general.*

It is therefore by our explanation only that the possibility
of geometry *as a synthetical science* a priori *becomes intelligible. Every other explanation, which fails to account for this
possibility, can best be distinguished from our own by that
criterion, although it may seem to have some similarity with
it.*

Conclusions from the Foregoing Concepts

a. Space does not represent any quality of objects by themselves, or objects in their relation to one another; i.e. space
does not represent any determination which is inherent in the
objects themselves, and would remain, even if all subjective
conditions of intuition were removed. For no determinations
of objects, whether belonging to them absolutely or in relation
to others, can enter into our intuition before the actual existence of the objects themselves, that is to say, they can never
be intuitions *a priori.*

b. Space is nothing but the form of all phenomena of the
external senses; it is the subjective condition of our sensibility,
without which no external intuition is possible for us. If then
we consider that the receptivity of the subject, its capacity of
being affected by objects, must necessarily precede all intuition
of objects, we shall understand how the form of all phenomena
may be given before all real perceptions, may be, in fact, *a
priori* in the soul, and may, as a pure intuition, by which all
objects must be determined, contain, prior to all experience,
principles regulating their relations.

It is therefore from the human standpoint only that we can
speak of space, extended objects, etc. If we drop the subjective condition under which alone we can gain external intuition, that is, so far as we ourselves may be affected by
objects, the representation of space means nothing. For this
predicate is applied to objects only in so far as they appear
to us, and are objects of our senses. The constant form of this
receptivity, which we call sensibility, is a necessary condition
of all relations in which objects, as without us, can be perceived; and, when abstraction is made of these objects, what
remains is that pure intuition which we call space. As the

peculiar conditions of our sensibility cannot be looked upon as conditions of the possibility of the objects themselves, but only of their appearance as phenomena to us, we may say indeed that space comprehends all things which may appear to us externally, but not all things by themselves, whether perceived by us or not, or by any subject whatsoever. We cannot judge whether the intuitions of other thinking beings are subject to the same conditions which determine our intuition, and which for us are generally binding. If we add the limitation of a judgment to a subjective concept, the judgment gains absolute validity. The proposition 'all things are beside each other in space,' is valid only under the limitation that things are taken as objects of our sensuous intuition (Anschauung). If I add that limitation to the concept and say 'all things, as external phenomena, are beside each other in space,' the rule obtains universal and unlimited validity. Our discussions teach therefore the reality, i.e. the objective validity, of space with regard to all that can come to us externally as an object, but likewise the *ideality* of space with regard to things, when they are considered in themselves by our reason, and independent of the nature of our senses. We maintain the empirical reality of space, so far as every possible external experience is concerned, but at the same time its transcendental ideality; that is to say, we maintain that space is nothing, if we leave out of consideration the condition of a possible experience, and accept it as something on which things by themselves are in any way dependent.

With the exception of space there is no other subjective representation (Vorstellung) referring to something external, that would be called *a priori* objective. [This subjective condition of all external phenomena cannot therefore be compared to any other. The taste of wine does not belong to the objective determinations of wine, considered as an object, even as a phenomenal object, but to the peculiar nature of the sense belonging to the subject that tastes the wine. Colours are not qualities of a body, though inherent in its intuition, but they are likewise modifications only of the sense of sight, as it is affected in different ways by light. Space, on the contrary, as the very condition of external objects, is essential to their appearance or intuition. Taste and colour are by no means necessary conditions under which alone things can become to us objects of sensuous perception. They are connected with their appearance, as accidentally added effects only of our peculiar organisation. They are not therefore representations *a priori,* but are dependent on sensation (Empfindung), nay taste even on an affection (Gefühl) of pleasure and pain, which is the result of a sensation. No one can have *a priori,* an idea (Vorstellung) either of colour or of taste, but space refers to the pure form of intuition only, and involves no kind of sensation, nothing empirical; nay all kinds and determinations of space can and must be represented *a priori,* if concepts of forms and their relations are to arise. Through it alone is it possible that things should become external objects to us.]

With the exception of space there is no other subjective representation, referring to something external, that could be called a priori *objective. For from none of them can we derive synthetical propositions* a priori, *as we can from the intuition in space § 3. Strictly speaking, therefore, they can claim no ideality at all, though they agree with the representation of space in this, that they belong only to the subjective nature of sensibility, for instance, of sight, of hearing, and feeling, through the sensations of colours, sounds, and heat. All these, however, being sensations only, and not intuitions, do not help us by themselves to know any object, least of all* a priori.

My object in what I have said just now is only to prevent people from imagining that they can elucidate the ideality of space by illustrations which are altogether insufficient, such as colour, taste, etc., which should never be considered as qualities of things, but as modifications of the subject, and which therefore may be different with different people. For in this case that which originally is itself a phenomenon only, as for instance, a rose, is taken by the empirical understanding for a thing by itself, which nevertheless, with regard to colour, may appear different to every eye. The transcendental conception, on the contrary, of all phenomena in space, is a critical warning that nothing which is seen in space is a thing by itself, nor space a form of things supposed to belong to them by themselves, but that objects by themselves are not known to us at all, and that what we call external objects are nothing but representations of our senses, the form of which is space, and the true correlative of which, that is the thing by itself, is not known, nor can be known by these representations, nor do we care to know anything about it in our daily experience.

SECOND SECTION OF THE TRANSCENDENTAL ÆSTHETIC

§ 4

Of Time[2]

I. Time is not an empirical concept deduced from any experience, for neither coexistence nor succession would enter into our perception, if the representation of time were not given *a priori*. Only when this representation *a priori* is given, can we imagine that certain things happen at the same time (simultaneously) or at different times (successively).

II. Time is a necessary representation on which all intuitions depend. We cannot take away time from phenomena in general, though we can well take away phenomena out of time. Time therefore is given *a priori*. In time alone is reality of phenomena possible. All phenomena may vanish, but time itself (as the general condition of their possibility) cannot be done away with.

III. On this *a priori* necessity depends also the possibility of apodictic principles of the relations of time, or of axioms of time in general. Time has one dimension only; different times are not simultaneous, but successive, while different spaces are never successive, but simultaneous. Such principles cannot be derived from experience, because experience could not impart to them absolute universality nor apodictic certainty. We should only be able to say that common experience teaches us that it is so, but not that it must be so. These principles are valid as rules under which alone experience is possible; they teach us before experience, not by means of experience.[3]

IV. Time is not a discursive, or what is called a general concept, but a pure form of sensuous intuition. Different times are parts only of one and the same time. Representation,

[2] In the Second Edition the title is, Metaphysical exposition of the concept of time, with reference to par. 5, Transcendental exposition of the concept of time.

[3] I retain the reading of the First Edition, *vor derselben, nicht durch dieselbe. Von denselben*, the reading of later editions, is wrong; the emendation of Rosenkranz, *vor denselben, nicht durch dieselben*, unnecessary. The Second Edition has likewise *vor derselben*.

which can be produced by a single object only, is called an intuition. The proposition that different times cannot exist at the same time cannot be deduced from any general concept. Such a proposition is synthetical, and cannot be deduced from concepts only. It is contained immediately in the intuition and representation of time.

V. To say that time is infinite means no more than that every definite quantity of time is possible only by limitations of one time which forms the foundation of all times. The original representation of time must therefore be given as unlimited. But when the parts themselves and every quantity of an object can be represented as determined by limitation only, the whole representation cannot be given by concepts (for in that case the partial representations come first), but it must be founded on immediate intuition.

§ 5

Transcendental Exposition of the Concept of Time

I can here refer to [see footnote p. 5] where, for the sake of brevity, I have placed what is properly transcendental under the head of metaphysical exposition. Here I only add that the concept of change, and with it the concept of motion (as change of place), is possible only through and in the representation of time; and that, if this representation were not intuitive (internal) a priori, no concept, whatever it be, could make us understand the possibility of a change, that is, of a connection of contradictorily opposed predicates (for instance, the being and not-being of one and the same thing in one and the same place) in one and the same object. It is only in time that both contradictorily opposed determinations can be met with in the same object, that is, one after the other. Our concept of time, therefore, exhibits the possibility of as many synthetical cognitions a priori as are found in the general doctrine of motion, which is very rich in them.

Conclusions from the foregoing concepts

a. Time is not something existing by itself, or inherent in things as an objective determination of them, something therefore that might remain when abstraction is made of all subjective conditions of intuition. For in the former case it would be something real, without being a real object. In the latter it could not, as a determination or order inherent in things themselves, be antecedent to things as their condition, and be known and perceived by means of synthetical propositions *a priori*. All this is perfectly possible if time is nothing but a subjective condition under which alone[4] intuitions take place within us. For in that case this form of internal intuition can be represented prior to the objects themselves, that is, *a priori*.

b. Time is nothing but the form of the internal sense, that is, of our intuition of ourselves, and of our internal state. Time cannot be a determination peculiar to external phenomena. It refers neither to their shape, nor their position, etc., it only determines the relation of representations in our internal state. And exactly because this internal intuition supplies no shape, we try to make good this deficiency by means of analogies, and represent to ourselves the succession of time by a line progressing to infinity, in which the manifold constitutes a series of one dimension only; and we conclude from the properties of this line as to all the properties of time, with one exception, i.e. that the parts of the former are simultaneous, those of the latter successive. From this it becomes clear also, that the representation of time is itself an intuition, because all its relations can be expressed by means of an external intuition.

c. Time is the formal condition, *a priori*, of all phenomena whatsoever. Space, as the pure form of all external intuition, is a condition, *a priori*, of external phenomena only. But, as all representations, whether they have for their objects external things or not, belong by themselves, as determinations of the mind, to our inner state, and as this inner state falls under the formal conditions of internal intuition, and therefore of time, time is a condition, *a priori*, of all phenomena whatsoever, and is so directly as a condition of internal phenomena (of our mind) and thereby indirectly of external phenomena also. If I am able to say, *a priori*, that all external phenomena are in space, and are determined, *a priori*, according to the relations of space, I can, according to the principle of the internal sense, make the general assertion that all phenomena, that is, all objects of the senses, are in time, and stand necessarily in relations of time.

If we drop our manner of looking at ourselves internally, and of comprehending by means of that intuition all external intuitions also within our power of representation, and thus take objects as they may be by themselves, then time is nothing. Time has objective validity with reference to phenomena

---

[4] Read *allein* instead of *alle*.

only, because these are themselves things which we accept as objects of our senses; but time is no longer objective, if we remove the sensuous character of our intuitions, that is to say, that mode of representation which is peculiar to ourselves, and speak of things in general. Time is therefore simply a subjective condition of our (human) intuition (which is always sensuous, that is so far as we are affected by objects), but by itself, apart from the subject, nothing. Nevertheless, with respect to all phenomena, that is, all things which can come within our experience, time is necessarily objective. We cannot say that all things are in time, because, if we speak of things in general, nothing is said about the manner of intuition, which is the real condition under which time enters into our representation of things. If therefore this condition is added to the concept, and if we say that all things as phenomena (as objects of sensuous intuition) are in time, then such a proposition has its full objective validity and *a priori* universality.

What we insist on therefore is the empirical reality of time, that is, its objective validity, with reference to all objects which can ever come before our senses. And as our intuition must at all times be sensuous, no object can ever fall under our experience that does not come under the conditions of time. What we deny is, that time has any claim on absolute reality, so that, without taking into account the form of our sensuous condition, it should by itself be a condition or quality inherent in things; for such qualities which belong to things by themselves can never be given to us through the senses. This is what constitutes the transcendental ideality of time, so that, if we take no account of the subjective conditions of our sensuous intuitions, time is nothing, and cannot be added to the objects by themselves (without their relation to our intuition) whether as subsisting or inherent. This ideality of time, however, as well as that of space, should not be confounded with the deceptions of our sensations, because in their case we always suppose that the phenomenon to which such predicates belong has objective reality, which is not at all the case here, except so far as this objective reality is purely empirical, that is, so far as the object itself is looked upon as a mere phenomenon. On this subject see a previous note, in section 2, on Space.

Explanation

Against this theory which claims empirical, but denies absolute and transcendental reality to time, even intelligent men have protested so unanimously, that I suppose that every reader who is unaccustomed to these considerations may naturally be of the same opinion. What they object to is this: Changes, they say, are real (this is proved by the change of our own representations, even if all external phenomena and their changes be denied). Changes, however, are possible in time only, and therefore time must be something real. The answer is easy enough. I grant the whole argument. Time certainly is something real, namely, the real form of our internal intuition. Time therefore has subjective reality with regard to internal experience: that is, I really have the representation of time and of my determinations in it. Time therefore is to be considered as real, not so far as it is an object, but so far as it is the representation of myself as an object. If either I myself or any other being could see me without this condition of sensibility, then these self-same determinations which we now represent to ourselves as changes, would give us a kind of knowledge in which the representation of time, and therefore of change also, would have no place. There remains therefore the empirical reality of time only, as the condition of all our experience, while absolute reality cannot, according to what has just been shown, be conceded to it. Time is nothing but the form of our own internal intuition.* Take away the peculiar condition of our sensibility, and the idea of time vanishes, because it is not inherent in the objects, but in the subject only that perceives them.

The reason why this objection is raised so unanimously, and even by those who have nothing very tangible to say against the doctrine of the ideality of space, is this. They could never hope to prove apodictically the absolute reality of space, because they are confronted by idealism, which has shown that the reality of external objects does not admit of strict proof, while the reality of the object of our internal perceptions (the perception of my own self and of my own status)

---

* I can say indeed that my representations follow one another, but this means no more than that we are conscious of them as in a temporal succession, that is, according to the form of our own internal sense. Time, therefore, is nothing by itself, nor is it a determination inherent objectively in things.

is clear immediately through our consciousness. The former might be merely phenomenal, but the latter, according to their opinion, is undeniably something real. They did not see that both, without denying to them their reality as representations, belong nevertheless to the phenomenon only, which must always have two sides, the one when the object is considered by itself (without regard to the manner in which it is perceived, its quality therefore remaining always problematical), the other, when the form of the perception of the object is taken into consideration; this form belonging not to the object in itself, but to the subject which perceives it, though nevertheless belonging really and necessarily to the object as a phenomenon.

Time and space are therefore two sources of knowledge from which various *a priori* synthetical cognitions can be derived. Of this pure mathematics give a splendid example in the case of our cognitions of space and its various relations. As they are both pure forms of sensuous intuition, they render synthetical propositions *a priori* possible. But these sources of knowledge *a priori* (being conditions of our sensibility only) fix their own limits, in that they can refer to objects only in so far as they are considered as phenomena, but cannot represent things as they are by themselves. That is the only field in which they are valid; beyond it they admit of no objective application. This ideality of space and time, however, leaves the truthfulness of our experience quite untouched, because we are equally sure of it, whether these forms are inherent in things by themselves, or by necessity in our intuition of them only. Those, on the contrary, who maintain the absolute reality of space and time, whether as subsisting or only as inherent, must come into conflict with the principles of experience itself. For if they admit space and time as subsisting (which is generally the view of mathematical students of nature) they have to admit two eternal infinite and self-subsisting nonentities (space and time), which exist without their being anything real, only in order to comprehend all that is real. If they take the second view (held by some metaphysical students of nature), and look upon space and time as relations of phenomena, simultaneous or successive, abstracted from experience, though represented confusedly in their abstracted form, they are obliged to deny to mathematical propositions *a priori* their validity with regard to real things (for instance in space), or at all events their apodictic certainty, which cannot take place *a posteriori*, while the *a priori* conceptions of space and time are, according to their opinion, creations of our imagination only. Their source, they hold, must really be looked for in experience, imagination framing out of the relations abstracted from experience something which contains the general character of these relations, but which cannot exist without the restrictions which nature has imposed on them. The former gain so much that they keep at least the sphere of phenomena free for mathematical propositions; but, as soon as the understanding endeavours to transcend that sphere, they become bewildered by these very conditions. The latter have this advantage that they are not bewildered by the representations of space and time when they wish to form judgments of objects, not as phenomena, but only as considered by the understanding; but they can neither account for the possibility of mathematical knowledge *a priori* (there being, according to them, no true and objectively valid intuition *a priori*), nor can they bring the laws of experience into true harmony with the *a priori* doctrines of mathematics. According to our theory of the true character of these original forms of sensibility, both difficulties vanish.

Lastly, that transcendental æsthetic cannot contain more than these two elements, namely, space and time, becomes clear from the fact that all other concepts belonging to the senses, even that of motion, which combines both, presuppose something empirical. Motion presupposes the perception of something moving. In space, however, considered by itself, there is nothing that moves. Hence that which moves must be something which, as in space, can be given by experience only, therefore an empirical datum. On the same ground, transcendental æsthetic cannot count the concept of change among its *a priori* data, because time itself does not change, but only something which is in time. For this, the perception of something existing and of the succession of its determinations, in other words, experience, is required.

§ 8

GENERAL OBSERVATIONS ON TRANSCENDENTAL ÆSTHETIC

In order to avoid all misapprehensions it will be necessary, first of all, to declare, as clearly as possible, what is our view with regard to the fundamental nature of sensuous knowledge. What we meant to say was this, that all our intuition is nothing but the representation of phenomena; that things which we see are not by themselves what we see, nor their relations by themselves such as they appear to us, so that, if we drop our subject or the subjective form of our senses, all qualities, all relations of objects in space and time, nay space and time themselves, would vanish. They cannot, as phenomena, exist by themselves, but in us only. It remains completely unknown to us what objects may be by themselves and apart from the receptivity of our senses. We know nothing but our manner of perceiving them, that manner being peculiar to us, and not necessarily shared in by every being, though, no doubt, by every human being. This is what alone concerns us. Space and time are pure forms of our intuition, while sensation forms its matter. What we can know *a priori*—before all real intuition, are the forms of space and time, which are therefore called pure intuition, while sensation is that which causes our knowledge to be called *a posteriori* knowledge, i.e. empirical intuition. Whatever our sensation may be, these forms are necessarily inherent in it, while sensations themselves may be of the most different character. Even if we could impart the highest degree of clearness to our intuition, we should not come one step nearer to the nature of objects by themselves. We should know our mode of intuition, i.e. our sensibility, more completely, but always under the indefeasible conditions of space and time. What the objects are by themselves would never become known to us, even through the clearest knowledge of that which alone is given us, the phenomenon.

It would vitiate the concept of sensibility and phenomena, and render our whole doctrine useless and empty, if we were to accept the view (of Leibniz and Wolf), that our whole sensibility is really but a confused representation of things, simply containing what belongs to them by themselves, though smothered under an accumulation of signs (Merkmal) and partial concepts, which we do not consciously disentangle. The distinction between confused and well-ordered representation is logical only, and does not touch the contents of our knowledge. Thus the concept of Right, as employed by people of common sense, contains neither more nor less than the subtlest speculation can draw out of it, only that in the ordinary practical use of the word we are not always conscious of the manifold ideas contained in that thought. But no one would say therefore that the ordinary concept of Right was sensuous, containing a mere phenomenon; for Right can never become a phenomenon, being a concept of the understanding, and representing a moral quality belonging to actions by themselves. The representation of a Body, on the contrary, contains nothing in intuition that could belong to an object by itself, but is merely the phenomenal appearance of something, and the manner in which we are affected by it. This receptivity of our knowledge is called sensibility. Even if we could see to the very bottom of a phenomenon, it would remain for ever altogether different from the knowledge of the thing by itself.

This shows that the philosophy of Leibniz and Wolf has given a totally wrong direction to all investigations into the nature and origin of our knowledge, by representing the difference between the sensible and the intelligible as logical only. That difference is in truth transcendental. It affects not the form only, as being more or less confused, but the origin and contents of our knowledge; so that by our sensibility we know the nature of things by themselves not confusedly only, but not at all. If we drop our subjective condition, the object, as represented with its qualities bestowed on it by sensuous intuition, is nowhere to be found, and cannot possibly be found; because its form, as phenomenal appearance, is determined by those very subjective conditions.

It has been the custom to distinguish in phenomena that which is essentially inherent in their intuition and is recognised by every human being, from that which belongs to their intuition accidentally only, being valid not for sensibility in general, but only for a particular position and organisation of this or that sense. In that case the former kind of knowledge is said to represent the object by itself, the latter its appearance only. But that distinction is merely empirical. If, as generally happens, people are satisfied with that distinction, without again, as they ought, treating the first empirical intuition as purely phenomenal also, in which nothing can be found belonging to the thing by itself, our transcendental distinction is lost, and we believe that we know things by themselves, though in the world of sense, however far we may carry our investigation, we can never have anything before us but mere phenomena. To give an illustration. People might call the rainbow a mere phenomenal appearance during a sunny shower, but the rain itself the thing by itself. This would be quite right, physically speaking, and taking rain as something which, in our ordinary experience and under all possible relations to our senses, can be determined thus and thus only in our intuition. But if we take the empirical in general, and ask, without caring whether it is the same with every particular observer, whether it represents a thing by itself (not the drops of rain, for these are already, as phenomena, empirical objects), then the question as to the relation between the representation and the object becomes transcendental, and not only the drops are mere phenomena, but even their round shape, nay even the space in which they fall, are nothing by themselves, but only modifications or fundamental dispositions of our sensuous intuition, the transcendental object remaining unknown to us.

The second important point in our transcendental æsthetic is, that it should not only gain favour as a plausible hypothesis, but assume as certain and undoubted a character as can be demanded of any theory which is to serve as an organum. In order to make this certainty self-evident we shall select a case which will make its validity palpable.

Let us suppose that space and time are in themselves objective, and conditions of the possibility of things by themselves. Now there is with regard to both a large number of *a priori* apodictic and synthetical propositions, and particularly with regard to space, which for this reason we shall chiefly investigate here as an illustration. As the propositions of geometry are known synthetically *a priori*, and with apodictic certainty, I ask, whence do you take such propositions? and what does the understanding rely on in order to arrive at such absolutely necessary and universally valid truths? There is no other way but by concepts and intuitions, and both as given either *a priori* or *a posteriori*. The latter, namely empirical concepts, as well as the empirical intuition on which they are founded, cannot yield any synthetical propositions except such as are themselves also empirical only, that is, empirical propositions, which can never possess that necessity and absolute universality which are characteristic of all geometrical propositions. As to the other and only means of arriving at such knowledge through mere concepts or intuitions *a priori,* it must be clear that only analytical, but no synthetical knowledge can ever be derived from mere concepts. Take the proposition that two straight lines cannot enclose a space and cannot therefore form a figure, and try to deduce it from the concept of straight lines and the number two; or take the proposition that with three straight lines it is possible to form a figure, and try to deduce that from those concepts. All your labour will be lost, and in the end you will be obliged to have recourse to intuition, as is always done in geometry. You then give yourselves an object in intuition. But of what kind is it? Is it a pure intuition *a priori* or an empirical one? In the latter case, you

would never arrive at a universally valid, still less at an apodictic proposition, because experience can never yield such.
You must therefore take the object as given *a priori* in intuition, and found your synthetical proposition on that. If you
did not possess in yourselves the power of *a priori* intuition,
if that subjective condition were not at the same time, as to
the form, the general condition *a priori* under which alone the
object of that (external) intuition becomes possible, if, in fact,
the object (the triangle) were something by itself without any
reference to you as the subject, how could you say that what
exists necessarily in your subjective conditions of constructing
a triangle, belongs of necessity to the triangle itself? For you
could not add something entirely new (the figure) to your concepts of three lines, something which should of necessity belong to the object, as that object is given before your knowledge of it, and not by it. If therefore space, and time also,
were not pure forms of your intuition, which contains the *a
priori* conditions under which alone things can become external objects to you, while, without that subjective condition,
they are nothing, you could not predicate anything of external
objects *a priori* and synthetically. It is therefore beyond the
reach of doubt, and not possible only or probable, that space
and time, as the necessary conditions of all experience, external and internal, are purely subjective conditions of our
intuition, and that, with reference to them, all things are phenomena only, and not things thus existing by themselves in
such or such wise. Hence, so far as their form is concerned,
much may be predicated of them *a priori,* but nothing whatever of the things by themselves on which these phenomena
may be grounded.

*II. As a confirmation of this theory of the ideality both of
the external and of the internal sense, and therefore of all objects of the senses as mere phenomena, we may particularly
remark, that everything in our knowledge which belongs to intuition (excluding therefore the feelings of pain and pleasure,
and the will, which are no knowledge at all) contains nothing
but mere relations, namely, of the places in an intuition (extension), change of places (motion), and laws, according to
which that change is determined (moving forces). Nothing is
told us thereby as to what is present in the place, or what, besides the change of place, is active in the things. A thing by
itself, however, cannot be known by mere relations, and we
may, therefore, fairly conclude that, as the external sense
gives us nothing but representations of relations, that sense*

can contain in its representation only the relation of an object to the subject, and not what is inside the object by itself. The same applies to internal intuition. Not only do the representations of the external senses constitute its proper material with which we fill our mind, but time, in which these representations are placed, and which precedes even our consciousness of them in experience, nay, forms the formal condition of the manner in which we place them in the mind, contains itself relations of succession, coexistence, and that which must be coexistent with succession, namely, the permanent. Now that which, as a representation, can precede every act of thinking something, is the intuition: and, if it contains nothing but relations, then the form of intuition. As this represents nothing except what is being placed in the mind, it can itself be the manner only in which the mind, through its own activity, that is, by this placing of its representation, is affected by itself, in other words, an internal sense with respect to its form. Whatever is represented by a sense is so far always phenomenal, and we should therefore have either to admit no internal sense at all, or the subject, which is its object, could be represented by it as phenomenal only, and not, as it might judge of itself, if its intuition were spontaneous only, that is, if it were intellectual. The difficulty here lies wholly in this, how a subject can have an internal intuition of itself: but this difficulty is common to every theory. The consciousness of self (apperception) is the simple representation of the ego, and if by it alone all the manifold (representations) in the subject were given spontaneously, the inner intuition would be intellectual. In man this consciousness requires internal perception of the manifold, which is previously given in the subject, and the manner in which this is given in the mind without spontaneity, must, on account of this difference, be called sensibility. If the faculty of self-consciousness is to seek for, that is, to apprehend, what lies in the mind, it must affect the mind, and can thus only produce an intuition of itself. The form of this, which lay antecedently in the mind, determines the manner in which the manifold exists together in the mind, namely, in the representation of time. The intuition of self, therefore, is not, as if it could represent itself immediately and as spontaneously and independently active, but according to the manner in which it is internally affected, consequently as it appears to itself, not as it is.

III. If I say that the intuition of external objects and the self-intuition of the mind, represent both (viz. the objects and the *mind*) *in space and time, as they affect our senses, that is, as they appear, I do not mean, that these objects are mere* illusion. *For the objects, as phenomena, nay, even the properties which we ascribe to them, are always looked upon as something really given: and all we do is, that, as their quality depends only on the manner of intuition on the part of the subject in relation to a given object, we distinguish the object, as* phenomenon, *from itself, as an object by itself. Thus, if I assert that the quality of space and time, according to which, as a condition of their existence, I accept both external objects and my own soul, lies in my manner of intuition and not in these objects by themselves, I do not mean to say that bodies* seem *only to exist outside me, or that my soul* seems *only to be given in my self-consciousness. It would be my own fault, if I changed that, which I ought to count as phenomenal, into mere illusion.**

This cannot happen, however, according to our principle of the ideality of all sensuous intuitions; on the contrary, it is only when we attribute objective reality *to those forms of intuition that everything is changed inevitably into mere* illusion. *For if we take space and time as properties that ought to exist as possible in things by themselves, and then survey the absurdities in which we should be involved in having to admit that two infinite things, which are not substances, nor something inherent in substances, but nevertheless must be something existing, nay, the necessary condition of the existence of all things, would remain, even if all existing things were removed, we really cannot blame the good Bishop Berkeley for degrading bodies to mere illusion. Nay, it would follow that even our own existence, which would thus be made dependent on*

---

* *Phenomenal predicates can be attributed to the object in its relation to our sense: as for instance to the rose its red colour, and its scent. But what is merely illusion can never be attributed to an object as a predicate, for the simple reason that the illusion attributes to the object by itself something which belongs to it only in its relation to the senses, or to a subject in general: as for instance the two handles, which were formerly attributed to Saturn. That which is never to be found in the object itself, but always in its relation to a subject, and is inseparable from its representation by a subject, is phenomenal, and the predicates of space and time are therefore rightly attributed to objects of the senses, as such. In this there is no illusion. If, on the contrary, I were to attribute to the rose* by itself *redness, handles to Saturn, and extension to all external objects, without restricting my judgment to the relation of these objects to a subject, we should have illusion.*

the independent reality of such a non-entity as time, must become a mere illusion, an absurdity which hitherto no one has been guilty of.

IV. In natural theology, where we think of an object which not only can never be an object of intuition to us, but which even to itself can never be an object of sensuous intuition, great care is taken to remove all conditions of space and time from its intuition (for all its knowledge must be intuitive, and not thought, which always involves limitation). But how are we justified in doing this, when we have first made space and time forms of things by themselves, such as would remain as conditions of the existence of things a priori, even if the things themselves had been removed? If conditions of all existence, they would also be conditions of the existence of God. If we do not wish to change space and time into objective forms of all things, nothing remains but to accept them as subjective forms of our external as well as internal intuition, which is called sensuous, for the very reason that it is not originally spontaneous, that is such, that it could itself give us the existence of the objects of intuition (such an intuition, so far as we can understand, can belong to the First Being only), but dependent on the existence of objects, and therefore possible only, if the faculty of representation in the subject is affected by them.

It is not necessary, moreover, that we should limit this intuition in space and time to the sensibility of man; it is quite possible that all finite thinking beings must necessarily agree with us on this point (though we cannot decide this). On account of this universal character, however, it does not cease to be sensibility, for it always is, and remains derivative (intuitus derivativus), not original (intuitus originarius), and therefore not intellectual intuition. For the reason mentioned before, the latter intuition seems only to belong to the First Being, and never to one which is dependent, both in its existence and its intuition (which intuition determines its existence with reference to given objects). This latter remark, however, must only be taken as an illustration of our æsthetic theory, and not as a proof.

Conclusion of the Transcendental Æsthetic

Here, then, we have one of the requisites for the solution of the general problem of transcendental philosophy, How are synthetical propositions a priori possible? namely, pure intuitions a priori, space and time. In them we find, if in a judg-

ment a priori *we want to go beyond a given concept, that which can be discovered* a priori, *not in the concept, but in the intuition corresponding to it, and can be connected with it synthetically. For this very reason, however, such judgments can never go beyond the objects of the senses, but are valid only for objects of possible experience.*

THE ELEMENTS OF TRANSCENDENTALISM

SECOND PART

TRANSCENDENTAL LOGIC

INTRODUCTION

THE IDEA OF A TRANSCENDENTAL LOGIC

I

Of Logic in General

Our knowledge springs from two fundamental sources of our soul; the first receives representations (receptivity of impressions), the second is the power of knowing an object by these representations (spontaneity of concepts). By the first an object is *given* us, by the second the object is *thought,* in relation to that representation which is a mere determination of the soul. Intuition therefore and concepts constitute the elements of all our knowledge, so that neither concepts without an intuition corresponding to them, nor intuition without concepts can yield any real knowledge.

Both are either pure or empirical. They are empirical when sensation, presupposing the actual presence of the object, is contained in it. They are pure when no sensation is mixed up with the representation. The latter may be called the material of sensuous knowledge. Pure intuition therefore contains the form only by which something is seen, and pure conception the form only by which an object is thought. Pure intuitions and pure concepts only are possible *a priori,* empirical intuitions and empirical concepts *a posteriori.*

We call *sensibility* the *receptivity* of our soul, or its power of receiving representations whenever it is in any wise affected, while the *understanding,* on the contrary, is with us the power of producing representations, or the *spontaneity* of knowledge. We are so constituted that our intuition must always be sensuous, and consist of the mode in which we are affected by objects. What enables us to think the objects of our sensuous intuition is the understanding. Neither of these qualities or faculties is preferable to the other. Without sensibility objects would not be given to us, without understanding they would not be thought by us. *Thoughts without contents are empty, intuitions without concepts are blind.* Therefore it is equally necessary to make our concepts sensuous, i.e. to add to them their object in intuition, as to make our intuitions intelligible, i.e. to bring them under concepts. These two powers or faculties cannot exchange their functions. The understanding cannot see, the senses cannot think. By their union only can knowledge be produced. But this is no reason for confounding the share which belongs to each in the production of knowledge. On the contrary, they should always be carefully separated and distinguished, and we have therefore divided the science of the rules of sensibility in general, i.e. æsthetic, from the science of the rules of the understanding in general, i.e. logic.

Logic again can be taken in hand for two objects, either as logic of the general or of a particular use of the understanding. The former contains all necessary rules of thought without which the understanding cannot be used at all. It treats of the understanding without any regard to the different objects to which it may be directed. Logic of the particular use of the understanding contains rules how to think correctly on certain classes of objects. The former may be called *Elementary Logic*, the latter the *Organum* of this or that science. The latter is generally taught in the schools as a preparation for certain sciences, though, according to the real progress of the human understanding, it is the latest achievement, which does not become possible till the science itself is really made, and requires only a few touches for its correction and completion. For it is clear that the objects themselves must be very well known before it is possible to give rules according to which a science of them may be established.

General logic is either pure or applied. In the former no account is taken of any empirical conditions under which our understanding acts, i.e. of the influence of the senses, the play of imagination, the laws of memory, the force of habit, the inclinations, and therefore the sources of prejudice also, nor of anything which supplies or seems to supply particular kinds of knowledge; for all this applies to the understanding under certain circumstances of its application only, and requires experience as a condition of knowledge. General but pure logic has to deal with principles *a priori* only, and is a *canon of the understanding and of reason,* though with reference to its formal application only, irrespective of any contents, whether empirical or transcendental. General logic is called applied, if it refers to the rules of the use of our understanding under the subjective empirical conditions laid down in psychology. It therefore contains empirical principles, yet it is general, because referring to the use of the understanding, whatever its objects may be. It is neither a canon of the understanding in general nor an organum of any particular science, but simply a catharticon of the ordinary understanding.

In general logic, therefore, that part which is to constitute the science of pure reason must be entirely separated from that which forms applied, but for all that still general logic. The former alone is a real science, though short and dry, as a practical exposition of an elementary science of the understanding ought to be. In this logicians should never lose sight of two rules:—

1. As general logic it takes no account of the contents of the knowledge of the understanding nor of the difference of its objects. It treats of nothing but the mere form of thought.

2. As pure logic it has nothing to do with empirical principles, and borrows nothing from psychology (as some have imagined); psychology, therefore, has no influence whatever on the canon of the understanding. It proceeds by way of demonstration, and everything in it must be completely *a priori.*

What I call applied logic (contrary to common usage according to which it contains certain exercises on the rules of pure logic) is a representation of the understanding and of the rules according to which it is necessarily applied *in concreto,* i.e. under the accidental conditions of the subject, which may hinder or help its application, and are all given empirically only. It treats of attention, its impediments and their consequences, the sources of error, the states of doubt, hesitation, and conviction, etc., and general and pure logic stands to it in the same relation as pure ethics, which treat only of the necessary moral laws of a free will, to applied ethics, which consider these laws as under the influence of sentiments, inclinations, and passions to which all human beings are more or less subject. This can never constitute a true and demonstrated science, because, like applied logic, it depends on empirical and psychological principles.

II

Of Transcendental Logic

General logic, as we saw, takes no account of the contents of knowledge, i.e. of any relation between it and its objects, and considers the logical form only in the relation of cognitions to each other, that is, it treats of the form of thought in general. But as we found, when treating of Transcendental Æsthetic, that there are pure as well as empirical intuitions, it is possible that a similar distinction might appear between pure and empirical thinking. In this case we should have a logic in which the contents of knowledge are not entirely ignored, for such a logic which should contain the rules of pure thought only, would exclude only all knowledge of a merely empirical character. It would also treat of the origin of our knowledge of objects, so far as that origin cannot be attributed to the objects, while general logic is not at all concerned with the origin of our knowledge, but only considers representations (whether existing originally *a priori* in ourselves or empirically given to us), according to the laws followed by the understanding, when thinking and treating them in their relation to each other. It is confined therefore to the form imparted by the understanding to the representations, whatever may be their origin.

And here I make a remark which should never be lost sight of, as it extends its influence on all that follows. Not every kind of knowledge *a priori* should be called transcendental (i.e. occupied with the possibility or the use of knowledge *a priori*), but that only by which we know that and how certain representations (intuitional or conceptual) can be used or are possible *a priori* only. Neither space nor any *a priori* geometrical determination of it is a transcendental representation; but that knowledge only is rightly called transcendental which teaches us that these representations cannot be of empirical origin, and how they can yet refer *a priori* to objects of experience. The application of space to objects in general would likewise be transcendental, but, if restricted to objects of sense, it is empirical. The distinction between transcendental and empirical belongs therefore to the critique of knowledge, and does not affect the relation of that knowledge to its objects.

On the supposition therefore that there may be concepts, having an *a priori* reference to objects, not as pure or sensuous intuitions, but as acts of pure thought, being concepts in fact, but neither of empirical nor æsthetic origin, we form by anticipation an idea of a science of that knowledge which belongs to the pure understanding and reason, and by which we may think objects entirely *a priori*. Such a science, which has to determine the origin, the extent, and the objective validity of such knowledge, might be called *Transcendental Logic,* having to deal with the laws of the understanding and reason in so far only as they refer *a priori* to objects, and not, as general logic, in so far as they refer promiscuously to the empirical as well as to the pure knowledge of reason.

III

Of the Division of General Logic into Analytic and Dialectic

What is truth? is an old and famous question by which people thought they could drive logicians into a corner, and either make them take refuge in a mere circle,[1] or make them confess their ignorance and consequently the vanity of their whole art. The nominal definition of truth, that it is the agreement of the cognition with its object, is granted. What is wanted is to know a general and safe criterion of the truth of any and every kind of knowledge.

It is a great and necessary proof of wisdom and sagacity to know what questions may be reasonably asked. For if a question is absurd in itself and calls for an answer where there is no answer, it does not only throw disgrace on the questioner, but often tempts an uncautious listener into absurd answers, thus presenting, as the ancients said, the spectacle of one person milking a he-goat, and of another holding the sieve.

If truth consists in the agreement of knowledge with its object, that object must thereby be distinguished from other objects; for knowledge is untrue if it does not agree with its object, though it contains something which may be affirmed of other objects. A general criterium of truth ought really to be valid with regard to every kind of knowledge, whatever the objects may be. But it is clear, as no account is thus taken of the contents of knowledge (relation to its object), while truth concerns these very contents, that it is impossible and absurd to ask for a sign of the truth of the contents of that knowledge,

[1] The First Edition has *Diallele,* the Second, *Dialexe.*

and that therefore a sufficient and at the same time general mark of truth cannot possibly be found. As we have before called the contents of knowledge its material, it will be right to say that of the truth of the knowledge, so far as its material is concerned, no general mark can be demanded, because it would be self-contradictory.

But, when we speak of knowledge with reference to its form only, without taking account of its contents, it is equally clear that logic, as it propounds the general and necessary rules of the understanding, must furnish in these rules criteria of truth. For whatever contradicts those rules is false, because the understanding would thus contradict the general rules of thought, that is, itself. These criteria, however, refer only to the form of truth or of thought in general. They are quite correct so far, but they are not sufficient. For although our knowledge may be in accordance with logical rule, that is, may not contradict itself, it is quite possible that it may be in contradiction with its object. Therefore the purely logical criterium of truth, namely, the agreement of knowledge with the general and formal laws of the understanding and reason, is no doubt a *conditio sine qua non*, or a negative condition of all truth. But logic can go no further, and it has no test for discovering error with regard to the contents, and not the form, of a proposition.

General logic resolves the whole formal action of the understanding and reason into its elements, and exhibits them as principles for all logical criticism of our knowledge. This part of logic may therefore be called *Analytic*, and is at least a negative test of truth, because all knowledge must first be examined and estimated, so far as its form is concerned, according to these rules, before it is itself tested according to its contents, in order to see whether it contains positive truth with regard to its object. But as the mere form of knowledge, however much it may be in agreement with logical laws, is far from being sufficient to establish the material or objective truth of our knowledge, no one can venture with logic alone to judge of objects, or to make any assertion, without having first collected, apart from logic, trustworthy information, in order afterwards to attempt its application and connection in a coherent whole according to logical laws, or, still better, merely to test it by them. However, there is something so tempting in this specious art of giving to all our knowledge the form of the understanding, though being utterly ignorant as to the contents thereof, that general logic, which is meant to be a mere canon of criticism, has been employed as if it were an organum, for the real production of at least the semblance of objective assertions, or, more truly, has been misemployed for that purpose. This general logic, which assumes the semblance of an organum, is called *Dialectic*.

Different as are the significations in which the ancients used this name of a science or art, it is easy to gather from its actual employment that with them it was nothing but a logic of semblance. It was a sophistic art of giving to one's ignorance, nay, to one's intentional casuistry, the outward appearance of truth, by imitating the accurate method which logic always requires, and by using its topic as a cloak for every empty assertion. Now it may be taken as a sure and very useful warning that general logic, if treated as an organum, is always an illusive logic, that is, dialectical. For as logic teaches nothing with regard to the contents of knowledge, but lays down the formal conditions only of an agreement with the understanding, which, so far as the objects are concerned, are totally indifferent, any attempt at using it as an organum in order to extend and enlarge our knowledge, at least in appearance, can end in nothing but mere talk, by asserting with a certain plausibility anything one likes, or, if one likes, denying it.

Such instruction is quite beneath the dignity of philosophy. Therefore the title of Dialectic has rather been added to logic, as a critique of dialectical semblance; and it is in that sense that we also use it.

IV

Of the Division of Transcendental Logic into Transcendental Analytic and Dialectic

In transcendental logic we isolate the understanding, as before in transcendental æsthetic the sensibility, and fix our attention on that part of thought only which has its origin entirely in the understanding. The application of this pure knowledge has for its condition that objects are given in intuition, to which it can be applied, for without intuition all our knowledge would be without objects, and it would therefore remain entirely empty. That part of transcendental logic therefore which teaches the elements of the pure knowledge of the understanding, and the principles without which no object can be thought, is transcendental Analytic, and at the same time a logic of truth. No knowledge can contradict it without losing at the same time all contents, that is, all relation to any object, and therefore all truth. But as it is very tempting to use this pure knowledge of the understanding and its principles by themselves, and even beyond the limits of all experience, which alone can supply the material or the objects to which those pure concepts of the understanding can be applied, the understanding runs the risk of making, through mere sophisms, a material use of the purely formal principles of the pure understanding, and thus of judging indiscriminately of objects which are not given to us, nay, perhaps can never be given. As it is properly meant to be a mere canon for criticising the empirical use of the understanding, it is a real abuse if it is allowed as an organum of its general and unlimited application, by our venturing, with the pure understanding alone, to judge synthetically of objects in general, or to affirm and decide anything about them. In this case the employment of the pure understanding would become dialectical.

The second part of transcendental logic must therefore form a critique of that dialectical semblance, and is called transcendental Dialectic, not as an art of producing dogmatically such semblance (an art but too popular with many metaphysical jugglers), but as a critique of the understanding and reason with regard to their hyperphysical employment, in order thus to lay bare the false semblance of its groundless pretensions, and to reduce its claims to discovery and expansion, which was to be achieved by means of transcendental principles only, to a mere critique, serving as a protection of the pure understanding against all sophistical illusions.

TRANSCENDENTAL LOGIC

Transcendental Analytic

Transcendental Analytic consists in the dissection of all our knowledge *a priori* into the elements which constitute the knowledge of the pure understanding. Four points are here essential: first, that the concepts should be pure and not empirical; secondly, that they should not belong to intuition and sensibility, but to thought and understanding; thirdly, that the concepts should be elementary and carefully distinguished from derivative or composite concepts; fourthly, that our tables should be complete and that they should cover the whole field of the pure understanding.

This completeness of a science cannot be confidently accepted on the strength of a mere estimate, or by means of repeated experiments only; what is required for it is an idea of the totality of the *a priori* knowledge of the understanding, and a classification of the concepts based upon it; in fact, a systematic treatment. Pure understanding must be distinguished, not merely from all that is empirical, but even from all sensibility. It constitutes therefore a unity independent in itself, self-sufficient, and not to be increased by any additions from without. The sum of its knowledge must constitute a system, comprehended and determined by one idea, and its completeness and articulation must form the test of the correctness and genuineness of its component parts.

This part of transcendental logic consists of two books, the one containing the *concepts,* the other the *principles* of pure understanding.

TRANSCENDENTAL ANALYTIC

Book I

ANALYTIC OF CONCEPTS

By Analytic of concepts I do not understand their analysis, or the ordinary process in philosophical disquisitions of dissecting any given concepts according to their contents, and thus rendering them more distinct; but a hitherto seldom attempted dissection of the faculty of the understanding itself, with the sole object of discovering the possibility of concepts *a priori,* by looking for them nowhere but in the understanding itself as their birthplace, and analysing the pure use of the understanding. This is the proper task of a transcendental philosophy, all the rest is mere logical treatment of concepts. We shall therefore follow up the pure concepts to their first germs and beginnings in the human understanding, in which they lie prepared, till at last, on the occasion of experience, they become developed, and are represented by the same understanding in their full purity, freed from all inherent empirical conditions.

ANALYTIC OF CONCEPTS

Chapter I

METHOD OF DISCOVERING ALL PURE CONCEPTS OF THE UNDERSTANDING

When we watch any faculty of knowledge, different concepts, characteristic of that faculty, manifest themselves according to different circumstances, which, as the observation has been carried on for a longer or shorter time, or with more or less accuracy, may be gathered up into a more or less complete collection. Where this collection will be complete, it is impossible to say beforehand, when we follow this almost mechanical process. Concepts thus discovered fortuitously only, possess neither order nor systematic unity, but are paired in the end according to similarities, and, according to their contents, arranged as more or less complex in various series, which are nothing less than systematical, though to a certain extent put together methodically.

Transcendental philosophy has the advantage, but also the duty of discovering its concepts according to a fixed principle. As they spring pure and unmixed from the understanding as an absolute unity, they must be connected with each other, according to *one* concept or idea. This connection supplies us at the same time with a rule, according to which the place of each pure concept of the understanding and the systematical completeness of all of them can be determined *a priori,* instead of being dependent on arbitrary choice or chance.

TRANSCENDENTAL METHOD OF THE DISCOVERY OF ALL
PURE CONCEPTS OF THE UNDERSTANDING

SECTION I

Of the Logical Use of the Understanding in General

We have before defined the understanding negatively only, as a non-sensuous faculty of knowledge. As without sensibility we cannot have any intuition, it is clear that the understanding is not a faculty of intuition. Besides intuition, however, there is no other kind of knowledge except by means of concepts. The knowledge therefore of every understanding, or at least of the human understanding, must be by means of concepts, not intuitive, but discursive. All intuitions, being sensuous, depend on affections, concepts on functions. By this function I mean the unity of the act of arranging different representations under one common representation. Concepts are based therefore on the spontaneity of thought, sensuous intuitions on the receptivity of impressions. The only use which the understanding can make of these concepts is to form judgments by them. As no representation, except the intuitional, refers immediately to an object, no concept is ever referred to an object immediately, but to some other representation of it, whether it be an intuition, or itself a concept. A judgment is therefore a mediate knowledge of an object, or a representation of a representation of it. In every judgment we find a concept applying to many, and comprehending among the many one single representation, which is referred immediately to the object. Thus in the judgment that all bodies are divisible,[1] the concept of divisible applies to various other concepts, but is here applied in particular to the concept of body, and this concept of body to certain phenomena of our experience. These objects therefore are represented mediately by the concept of divisibility. All judgments therefore are functions of unity among our representations, the knowledge of an object being brought about, not by an immediate representation, but by a higher one, comprehending this and several others, so that many possible cognitions are collected into one. As all acts of the understanding can be reduced to judgments, the understanding may be defined as *the faculty of judging*. For we saw before that the understanding is the faculty of thinking, and thinking is knowledge by means of concepts, while concepts, as predicates of possible judgments, refer to some representation of an object yet undetermined. Thus the concept of body means something, for instance, metal, which can be known by that concept. It is only a concept, because it comprehends other representations, by means of which it can be referred to objects. It is therefore the predicate of a possible judgment, such as, that every metal is a body. Thus the functions of the understanding can be discovered in their completeness, if it is possible to represent the functions of unity in *judgments*. That this is possible will be seen in the following section.

METHOD OF THE DISCOVERY OF ALL PURE CONCEPTS OF
THE UNDERSTANDING

SECTION II

§ 9

Of the Logical Function of the Understanding in Judgments

If we leave out of consideration the contents of any judgment and fix our attention on the mere form of the under-

---

[1] *Veränderlich* in the First Edition is rightly corrected into *theilbar* in later editions, though in the Second it is still *veränderlich*.

standing, we find that the function of thought in a judgment can be brought under four heads, each of them with three subdivisions. They may be represented in the following table:—

I
Quantity of Judgments
Universal.
Particular.
Singular.

II
Quality
Affirmative.
Negative.
Infinite.

III
Relation
Categorical.
Hypothetical.
Disjunctive.

IV
Modality
Problematical.
Assertory.
Apodictic.

As this classification may seem to differ in some, though not very essential points, from the usual technicalities of logicians, the following reservations against any possible misunderstanding will not be out of place.

1. Logicians are quite right in saying that in using judgments in syllogisms, singular judgments may be treated like universal ones. For as they have no extent at all, the predicate cannot refer to part only of that which is contained in the concept of the subject, and be excluded from the rest. The predicate is valid therefore of that concept, without any exception, as if it were a general concept, having an extent to the whole of which the predicate applies. But if we compare a singular with a general judgment, looking only at the quantity of knowledge conveyed by it, the singular judgment stands to the universal judgment as unity to infinity, and is therefore essentially different from it. It is therefore, when we consider a singular judgment (*judicium singulare*), not only according to its own validity, but according to the quantity of knowledge which it conveys, as compared with other kinds of knowledge, that we see how different it is from general judgments (*judicia communia*), and how well it deserves a separate place in a complete table of the varieties of thought in general, though not

in a logic limited to the use of judgments in reference to each other.

2. In like manner infinite judgments must, in transcendental logic, be distinguished from affirmative ones, though in general logic they are properly classed together, and do not constitute a separate part in the classification. General logic takes no account of the contents of the predicate (though it be negative), it only asks whether the predicate be affirmed or denied. Transcendental logic, on the contrary, considers a judgment according to the value also or the contents of a logical affirmation by means of a purely negative predicate, and asks how much is gained by that affirmation, with reference to the sum total of knowledge. If I had said of the soul, that it is not mortal, I should, by means of a negative judgment, have at least warded off an error. Now it is true that, so far as the logical form is concerned, I have really affirmed by saying that the soul is non-mortal, because I thus place the soul in the unlimited sphere of non-mortal beings. As the mortal forms one part of the whole sphere of possible beings, the non-mortal the other, I have said no more by my proposition than that the soul is one of the infinite number of things which remain, when I take away all that is mortal. But by this the infinite sphere of all that is possible becomes limited only in so far that all that is mortal is excluded from it, and that afterwards the soul is placed in the remaining part of its original extent. This part, however, even after its limitation, still remains infinite, and several more parts of it may be taken away without extending thereby in the least the concept of the soul, or affirmatively determining it. These judgments, therefore, though infinite in respect to their logical extent, are, with respect to their contents, limitative only, and cannot therefore be passed over in a transcendental table of all varieties of thought in judgments, it being quite possible that the function of the understanding exercised in them may become of great importance in the field of its pure *a priori* knowledge.

3. The following are all the relations of thought in judgments:—

a. Relation of the predicate to the subject.

b. Relation of the cause to its effect.

c. Relation of subdivided knowledge, and of the collected members of the subdivision to each other.

In the first class of judgments we consider two concepts, in the second two judgments, in the third several judgments in their relation to each other. The hypothetical proposition, if perfect justice exists, the obstinately wicked is punished, contains really the relation of two propositions, namely, there is a perfect justice, and the obstinately wicked is punished. Whether both these propositions are true remains unsettled. It is only the consequence which is laid down by this judgment.

The disjunctive judgment contains the relation of two or more propositions to each other, but not as a consequence, but in the form of a logical opposition, the sphere of the one excluding the sphere of the other, and at the same time in the form of community, all the propositions together filling the whole sphere of the intended knowledge. The disjunctive judgment contains therefore a relation of the parts of the whole sphere of a given knowledge, in which the sphere of each part forms the complement of the sphere of the other, all being contained within the whole sphere of the subdivided knowledge. We may say, for instance, the world exists either by blind chance, or by internal necessity, or by an external cause. Each of these sentences occupies a part of the sphere of all possible knowledge with regard to the existence of the world, while all together occupy the whole sphere. To take away the knowledge from one of these spheres is the same as to place it into one of the other spheres, and to place it in one sphere is the same as to take it away from the others. There exists therefore in disjunctive judgments a certain community of the different divisions of knowledge, so that they mutually exclude each other, and yet thereby determine in their totality the true knowledge, because, if taken together, they constitute the whole contents of one given knowledge. This is all I have to observe here for the sake of what is to follow hereafter.

4. The modality of judgments is a very peculiar function, for it contributes nothing to the contents of a judgment (because, besides quantity, quality, and relation, there is nothing else that could constitute the contents of a judgment), but refers only to the nature of the copula in relation to thought in general. Problematical judgments are those in which affirmation or negation are taken as possible (optional) only, while in assertory judgments affirmation or negation is taken as real (true), in apodictic as necessary.* Thus the two judg-

---

* As if in the first, thought were a function of the understanding, in the second, of the faculty of judgment, in the third, of reason; a remark which will receive its elucidation in the sequel.

ments, the relation of which constitutes the hypothetical judgment (*antecedens et consequens*) and likewise the judgments the reciprocal relation of which forms the disjunctive judgment (members of subdivision), are always problematical only. In the example given above, the proposition, there exists a perfect justice, is not made as an assertory, but only as an optional judgment, which may be accepted or not, the consequence only being assertory. It is clear therefore that some of these judgments may be wrong, and may yet, if taken problematically, contain the conditions of the knowledge of truth. Thus, in our disjunctive judgment, one of its component judgments, namely, the world exists by blind chance, has a problematical meaning only, on the supposition that some one might for one moment take such a view, but serves, at the same time, like the indication of a false road among all the roads that might be taken, to find out the true one. The problematical proposition is therefore that which expresses logical (not objective) possibility only, that is, a free choice of admitting such a proposition, and a purely optional admission of it into the understanding. The assertory proposition implies logical reality or truth. Thus, for instance, in a hypothetical syllogism the *antecedens* in the major is problematical, in the minor assertory, showing that the proposition conforms to the understanding according to its laws. The apodictic proposition represents the assertory as determined by these very laws of the understanding, and therefore as asserting *a priori*, and thus expresses logical necessity. As in this way everything is arranged step by step in the understanding, inasmuch as we begin with judging problematically, then proceed to an assertory acceptation, and finally maintain our proposition as inseparably united with the understanding, that is as necessary and apodictic, we may be allowed to call these three functions of modality so many varieties or momenta of thought.

METHOD OF THE DISCOVERY OF ALL PURE
CONCEPTS OF THE UNDERSTANDING

SECTION III

§ 10

*Of the Pure Concepts of the Understanding, or of the
Categories*

General logic, as we have often said, takes no account of
the contents of our knowledge, but expects that representations will come from elsewhere in order to be turned into
concepts by an analytical process. Transcendental logic, on
the contrary, has before it the manifold contents of sensibility
a priori, supplied by transcendental æsthetic as the material
for the concepts of the pure understanding, without which
those concepts would be without any contents, therefore entirely empty. It is true that space and time contain what is
manifold in the pure intuition *a priori*, but they belong also
to the conditions of the receptivity of our mind under which
alone it can receive representations of objects, and which
therefore must affect the concepts of them also. The spontaneity of our thought requires that what is manifold in the
pure intuition should first be in a certain way examined, received, and connected, in order to produce a knowledge of it.
This act I call *synthesis*.

In its most general sense, I understand by synthesis the act
of arranging different representations together, and of comprehending what is manifold in them under one form of
knowledge. Such a synthesis is pure, if the manifold is not
given empirically, but *a priori* (as in time and space). Before
we can proceed to an analysis of our representations, these
must first be given, and, as far as their contents are concerned,
no concepts can arise analytically. Knowledge is first produced by the synthesis of what is manifold (whether given
empirically or *a priori*). That knowledge may at first be crude
and confused and in need of analysis, but it is synthesis
which really collects the elements of knowledge, and unites
them to a certain extent. It is therefore the first thing which

we have to consider, if we want to form an opinion on the first origin of our knowledge.

We shall see hereafter that synthesis in general is the mere result of what I call the faculty of imagination, a blind but indispensable function of the soul, without which we should have no knowledge whatsoever, but of the existence of which we are scarcely conscious. But to reduce this synthesis to concepts is a function that belongs to the understanding, and by which the understanding supplies us for the first time with knowledge properly so called.

Pure synthesis in its most general meaning gives us the pure concept of the understanding. By this pure synthesis I mean that which rests on the foundation of what I call synthetical unity *a priori*. Thus our counting (as we best perceive when dealing with higher numbers) is a synthesis according to concepts, because resting on a common ground of unity, as for instance, the decade. The unity of the synthesis of the manifold becomes necessary under this concept.

By means of analysis different representations are brought under one concept, a task treated of in general logic; but how to bring, not the representations, but the pure synthesis of representations, under concepts, that is what transcendental logic means to teach. The first that must be given us *a priori* for the sake of knowledge of all objects, is the manifold in pure intuition. The second is, the synthesis of the manifold by means of imagination. But this does not yet produce true knowledge. The concepts which impart unity to this pure synthesis and consist entirely in the representation of this necessary synthetical unity, add the third contribution towards the knowledge of an object, and rest on the understanding.

The same function which imparts unity to various representations in one judgment imparts unity likewise to the mere synthesis of various representations in one intuition, which in a general way may be called the pure concept of the understanding. The same understanding, and by the same operations by which in concepts it achieves through analytical unity the logical form of a judgment, introduces also, through the synthetical unity of the manifold in intuition, a transcendental element into its representations. They are therefore called pure concepts of the understanding, and they refer *a priori* to objects, which would be quite impossible in general logic.

In this manner there arise exactly so many pure concepts of the understanding which refer *a priori* to objects of intuition in general, as there were in our table logical functions in all possible judgments, because those functions completely exhaust the understanding, and comprehend every one of its faculties. Borrowing a term of Aristotle, we shall call these concepts *categories,* our intention being originally the same as his, though widely diverging from it in its practical application.

TABLE OF CATEGORIES

I

Of Quantity

Unity.
Plurality.
Totality.

II

Of Quality

Reality.
Negation.
Limitation.

III

Of Relation

Of Inherence and Subsistence (*substantia et accidens*).
Of Causality and Dependence (cause and effect).
Of Community (reciprocity between the active and the passive).

IV

Of Modality

Possibility.   Impossibility.
Existence.   Non-existence.
Necessity.   Contingency.

This then is a list of all original pure concepts of synthesis, which belong to the understanding *a priori,* and for which alone it is called pure understanding; for it is by them alone that it can understand something in the manifold of intuition, that is, think an object in it. The classification is systematical, and founded on a common principle, namely, the faculty of judging (which is the same as the faculty of thinking). It is not the result of a search after pure concepts undertaken at haphazard, the completeness of which, as based on induction only, could never be guaranteed. Nor could we otherwise understand why these concepts only, and no others, abide in the pure understanding. It was an enterprise worthy of an acute thinker like Aristotle to try to discover these fundamental concepts; but as he had no guiding principle he merely picked them up as they occurred to him, and at first gathered up ten of them, which he called *categories* or *predicaments*. Afterwards he thought he had discovered five more of them, which he added under the name of *post-predicaments*. But his table remained imperfect for all that, not to mention that we find in it some modes of pure sensibility (*quando, ubi, situs,* also *prius, simul*), also an empirical concept (*motus*), none of which can belong to this genealogical register of the understanding. Besides, there are some derivative concepts, counted among the fundamental concepts (*actio, passio*), while some of the latter are entirely wanting.

With regard to these, it should be remarked that the categories, as the true fundamental concepts of the pure understanding, have also their pure derivative concepts. These could not be passed over in a complete system of transcendental philosophy, but in a merely critical essay the mention of the fact may suffice.

I should like to be allowed to call these pure but derivative concepts of the understanding the *predicabilia,* in opposition to the *predicamenta* of the pure understanding. If we are once in possession of the fundamental and primitive concepts, it is easy to add the derivative and secondary, and thus to give a complete image of the genealogical tree of the pure understanding. As at present I am concerned not with the completeness, but only with the principles of a system, I leave this supplementary work for a future occasion. In order to carry it out, one need only consult any of the ontological manuals, and place, for instance, under the category of causality the *predicabilia* of force, of action, and of passion; under the category of community the *predicabilia* of presence and resistance; under the predicaments of modality the *predicabilia* of origin, extinction, change, etc. If we associate the categories among themselves or with the modes of pure sensibility, they yield us a large number of derivative concepts *a priori,* which it would be useful and interesting to mark and, if possible, to bring to a certain completeness, though this is not essential for our present purpose.

I intentionally omit here the definitions of these categories, though I may be in possession of them.[2] In the sequel I shall dissect these concepts so far as is sufficient for the purpose of the method which I am preparing. In a complete system of pure reason they might be justly demanded, but at present they would only make us lose sight of the principal object of

[2] See, however, Karl's remarks on p. 241 of First Edition.

our investigation, by rousing doubts and objections which, without injury to our essential object, may well be relegated to another time. The little I have said ought to be sufficient to show clearly that a complete dictionary of these concepts with all requisite explanations is not only possible, but easy. The compartments exist; they have only to be filled, and with a systematic topic like the present the proper place to which each concept belongs cannot easily be missed, nor compartments be passed over which are still empty.

§ 11

This table of categories suggests some interesting considerations, which possibly may have important consequences with regard to the scientific form of all knowledge of reason. For it is clear that such a table will be extremely useful, nay, indispensable, in the theoretical part of philosophy, in order to trace the complete plan of a whole science, *so far as it rests on concepts* a priori, *and to divide it systematically* according to fixed principles, *because that table contains all elementary concepts of the understanding in their completeness, nay, even the form of a system of them in the human understanding, and indicates therefore all the* momenta *of a projected speculative science, nay, even their* order. *Of this I have given an example elsewhere.* Here follow some of the considerations.*

The first is, *that this table, which contains four classes of the concepts of the understanding, may, in the first instance, be divided into two sections, the former of which refers to objects of intuition* (pure, as well as empirical), *the latter to the existence of those objects* (either in their relation to each other, or to the understanding).

The first section I shall call that of the mathematical, *the second, that of the* dynamical *categories. The first section has no correlates, which are met with in the second section only. Must not this difference have some ground in the nature of the understanding?*

Our second remark is, *that in every class there is the same member of categories, namely three, which again makes us ponder, because generally all division* a priori *by means of concepts must be dichotomy. It should be remarked also,*

* *Metaphysical Elements of Natural Science.*

*that the third category always arises from the combination of
the second with the first. Thus* totality *is nothing but plurality
considered as unity;* limitation *nothing but reality connected
with negation;* community *is the causality of a substance as
determining another reciprocally; lastly,* necessity, *the existence which is given by possibility itself. It must not be supposed, however, that therefore the third category is only a
derivative, and not a primary concept of the pure understanding. For the joining of the first and second concepts, in order
to produce the third, requires an independent act of the understanding, which is not identical with the act that produces
the first and second concepts. Thus the concept of a number
(which belongs to the category of totality) is not always possible when we have the concepts of plurality and unity (for
instance, in the concept of the infinite); nor can we understand
by simply combining the concept of a* cause *and that of a*
substance, *the* influence, *that is, how a substance can become
the cause of something in another substance. This shows that
a separate act of the understanding is here required, and the
same applies to all the rest.*

Third observation. *With regard to one category, namely,
that of* community, *which is found in the third class, its accordance with the form of a disjunctive judgment, which corresponds to it in the table of logical functions, is not so evident as elsewhere.*

*In order to become quite certain of that accordance, we
must remark that in all disjunctive judgments their sphere
(that is, all that is contained in them) is represented as a
whole, divided into parts (the subordinate concepts), and that,
as one of them cannot be contained under the other, they are
conceived as co-ordinate, not as subordinate, determining each
other, not in one direction only, as in a series, but reciprocally,
as in an aggregate (if one member of the division is given, all
the rest are excluded, and* vice versa).

A similar connection is conceived in a whole of things, *in
which one, as effect, is not subordinated to another as the
cause of its existence, but is co-ordinated with it, simultaneously and reciprocally, as cause of the determination of the
other (as, for instance, in a body of which the parts reciprocally attract and repel each other). This is a kind of connection totally different from that which exists in a mere relation
of cause to effect (of ground to consequence), for here the
consequence does not reciprocally determine the ground
again, nor (as in the case of the Creator and the creation)*

*constitute with it a whole. The process of the understanding,
in representing to itself the sphere of a divided concept, is the
same as that by which it thinks a thing as divisible: and in
the same manner in which, in the former, the members of a
division exclude each other, and are yet connected in one
sphere, the understanding represents to itself the parts of the
latter as existing (as substances), each independent of the
rest, and yet united in a whole.*

§ 12

In the transcendental philosophy of the ancients there is
another chapter containing concepts of the understanding
which, though they are not counted among the categories,
are yet considered by them as concepts a priori of objects. If
so, they would increase the number of the categories, which
cannot be. They are set forth in the famous proposition of
the Schoolmen, 'quodlibet ens est unum, verum, bonum.' Now,
although the inferences to be drawn from this principle
(yielding nothing but tautological propositions) were very
meagre, so that modern metaphysicians mention it almost by
courtesy only, a thought which has maintained itself so long,
however empty it may seem, deserves an investigation with
regard to its origin, nay, leads us to suspect that it may have
its foundation in some rule of the understanding which, as
often happens, has only been wrongly interpreted. What are
supposed to be transcendental predicates of things are nothing
but logical requirements and criteria of all knowledge of things
in general, whereby that knowledge is founded on the categories of quantity, namely, unity, plurality, and totality. Only,
instead of taking them as materially belonging to the possibility of things by themselves, they (the predicates, or rather
those who employed them) used them, in fact, in their formal
meaning only, as forming a logical requisite for every kind
of knowledge, and yet incautiously made these criteria of
thought to be properties of the things by themselves. In every
cognition of an object there is unity of concept, which may
be called qualitative unity, so far as we think by it only the
unity in the comprehension of the manifold material of our
knowledge: as, for instance, the unity of the subject in a
play, or a speech, or a fable. Secondly, there is truth, in respect to the deductions from it. The more true deductions
can be made from a given concept, the more criteria are there

of its objective reality. This might be called the qualitative
plurality *of criteria, which belong to a concept as their common ground (but are not conceived in it, as quantity).
Thirdly, there is* completeness, *which consists in this, that the
plurality together leads back to the unity of the concept, according completely with this and with no other concept,
which may be called the* qualitative completeness (*totality*).
*This shows that these logical criteria of the possibility of
knowledge in general do nothing but change the three categories of quantity, in which the unity in the production of the
quantum must throughout be taken as* homogeneous, *for the
purpose of connecting* heterogeneous *elements of knowledge
also in one consciousness, by means of the quality of the cognition as the principle of the connection. Thus the criterion
of the possibility of a concept (but not of its object) is the
definition of it, in which the* unity *of the concept, the* truth *of
all that may be immediately deduced from it, and lastly, the*
completeness *of what has been deduced from it, supply all
that is necessary for the constitution of the whole concept.
In the same manner the* criterion *of an hypothesis consists,
first, in the intelligibility of the* ground *which has been admitted* for the sake of explanation, *or of its* unity (*without
any auxiliary hypothesis*); *secondly, in the* truth *of the consequences to be deduced from it (their accordance with themselves and with experience)*; *and lastly, in the* completeness
*of the ground admitted for the explanation of these conse-
quences, which point back to neither more nor less than what
was admitted in the hypothesis, and agree in giving us again,
analytically* a posteriori, *what had been thought synthetically*
a priori. *The concepts of unity, truth, and perfection, therefore, do not supplement the transcendental table of the categories, as if it were imperfect, but they serve only, after the
relation of these concepts to objects has been entirely set aside,
to bring their employment under general logical rules, for the
agreement of knowledge with itself.*

TRANSCENDENTAL ANALYTIC

Chapter II

OF THE DEDUCTION OF THE PURE CONCEPTS OF THE UNDERSTANDING

Section I

§ 13

Of the Principles of a Transcendental Deduction in General

Jurists, when speaking of rights and claims, distinguish in every lawsuit the question of right (*quid juris*) from the question of fact (*quid facti*), and in demanding proof of both they call the former, which is to show the right or, it may be, the claim, the *deduction*. We, not being jurists, make use of a number of empirical concepts, without opposition from anybody, and consider ourselves justified, without any deduction, in attaching to them a sense or imaginary meaning, because we can always appeal to experience to prove their objective reality. There exist however illegitimate concepts also, such as, for instance, chance, or fate, which through an almost general indulgence are allowed to be current, but are yet from time to time challenged by the question *quid juris*. In that case we are greatly embarrassed in looking for their deduction, there being no clear legal title, whether from experience or from reason, on which their claim to employment could be clearly established.

Among the many concepts, however, which enter into the complicated code of human knowledge, there are some which are destined for pure use *a priori,* independent of all experience, and such a claim requires at all times a deduction,[3] because proofs from experience would not be sufficient to establish the legitimacy of such a use, though it is necessary to know how much concepts can refer to objects which they

[3] That is a transcendental deduction.

do not find in experience. I call the explanation of the manner how such concepts can *a priori* refer to objects their transcendental deduction, and distinguish it from the empirical deduction which shows the manner how a concept may be gained by experience and by reflection on experience; this does not touch the legitimacy, but only the fact whence the possession of the concept arose.

We have already become acquainted with two totally distinct classes of concepts, which nevertheless agree in this, that they both refer *a priori* to objects, namely, the concepts of space and time as forms of sensibility, and the categories as concepts of the understanding. It would be labour lost to attempt an empirical deduction of them, because their distinguishing characteristic is that they refer to objects without having borrowed anything from experience for their representation. If therefore a deduction of them is necessary, it can only be transcendental.

It is possible, however, with regard to these concepts, as with regard to all knowledge, to try to discover in experience, if not the principle of their possibility, yet the contingent causes of their production. And here we see that the impressions of the senses give the first impulse to the whole faculty of knowledge with respect to them, and thus produce experience which consists of two very heterogeneous elements, namely, matter for knowledge, derived from the senses, and a certain form according to which it is arranged, derived from the internal source of pure intuition and pure thought, first brought into action by the former, and then producing concepts. Such an investigation of the first efforts of our faculty of knowledge, beginning with single perceptions and rising to general concepts, is no doubt very useful, and we have to thank the famous Locke for having been the first to open the way to it. A deduction of the pure concepts *a priori*, however, is quite impossible in that way. It lies in a different direction, because, with reference to their future use, which is to be entirely independent of experience, a very different certificate of birth will be required from that of mere descent from experience. We may call this attempted physiological derivation (which cannot properly be called deduction, because it refers to a *quaestio facti*), the explanation of the possession of pure knowledge. It is clear therefore that of these pure concepts *a priori* a transcendental deduction only is possible, and that to attempt an empirical deduction of them is mere waste of time, which no one would think of except those who have never understood the very peculiar nature of that kind of knowledge.

But though it may be admitted that the only possible deduction of pure knowledge *a priori* must be transcendental, it has not yet been proved that such a deduction is absolutely necessary. We have before, by means of a transcendental deduction, followed up the concepts of space and time to their very sources, and explained and defined their objective validity *a priori*. Geometry, however, moves along with a steady step, through every kind of knowledge *a priori,* without having to ask for a certificate from philosophy as to the pure legitimate descent of its fundamental concept of space. But it should be remarked that in geometry this concept is used with reference to the outer world of sense only, of which space is the pure form of intuition, and where geometrical knowledge, being based on *a priori* intuition, possesses immediate evidence, the objects being given, so far as their form is concerned, through their very knowledge *a priori* in intuition. When we come, however, to the pure concepts of the understanding, it becomes absolutely necessary to look for a transcendental deduction, not only for them, but for space also, because they, not being founded on experience, apply to objects generally, without any of the conditions of sensibility; and, speaking of objects, not through predicates of intuition and sensibility, but of pure thought *a priori,* are not able to produce in intuition *a priori* any object on which, previous to all experience, their synthesis was founded. These concepts of pure understanding, therefore, not only excite suspicion with regard to the objective validity and the limits of their own application, but render even the concept of space equivocal, because of an inclination to apply it beyond the conditions of sensuous intuition, which was the very reason that made a transcendental deduction of it, such as we gave before, necessary. Before the reader has made a single step in the field of pure reason, he must be convinced of the inevitable necessity of such a transcendental deduction, otherwise he would walk on blindly and, after having strayed in every direction, he would only return to the same ignorance from which he started. He must at the same time perceive the inevitable difficulty of such a deduction, so that he may not complain about obscurity where the object itself is obscure, or weary too soon with our removal of obstacles, the fact being that we have either to surrender altogether all claims to the knowledge of pure reason—the most favourite field of all philosophers, because extending beyond the limits of all possible experience —or to bring this critical investigation to perfection.

It was easy to show before, when treating of the concepts of space and time, how these, though being knowledge *a priori*, refer necessarily to objects, and how they make a synthetical knowledge of them possible, which is independent of all experience. For, as no object can appear to us, that is, become an object of empirical intuition, except through such pure forms of sensibility, space and time are pure intuitions which contain *a priori* the conditions of the possibility of objects as phenomena, and the synthesis in these intuitions possesses objective validity.

The categories of the understanding, on the contrary, are not conditions under which objects can be given in intuition, and it is quite possible therefore that objects should appear to us without any necessary reference to the functions of the understanding, thus showing that the understanding contains by no means any of their conditions *a priori*. There arises therefore here a difficulty, which we did not meet with in the field of sensibility, namely, how subjective conditions of thought can have objective validity, that is, become conditions of the possibility of the knowledge of objects. It cannot be denied that phenomena may be given in intuition without the functions of the understanding. For if we take, for instance, the concept of cause, which implies a peculiar kind of synthesis, consisting in placing according to a rule after something called A something totally different from it, B, we cannot say that it is *a priori* clear why phenomena should contain something of this kind. We cannot appeal for it to experience, because what has to be proved is the objective validity of this concept *a priori*. It would remain therefore *a priori* doubtful whether such a concept be not altogether empty, and without any corresponding object among phenomena. It is different with objects of sensuous intuition. They must conform to the formal conditions of sensibility existing *a priori* in the mind, because otherwise they could in no way be objects to us. But why besides this they should conform to the conditions which the understanding requires for the synthetical unity of thought, does not seem to follow quite so easily. For we could quite well imagine that phenomena might possibly be such that the understanding should not find them conforming to the conditions of its synthetical unity, and all might be in such confusion that nothing should appear in the succession of phenomena which could supply a rule of synthesis, and correspond, for instance, to the concept of cause and effect, so that this concept would thus be quite empty, null, and meaningless. With all this phenomena would offer objects to our intuition, because intuition by itself does not require the functions of thought.

It might be imagined that we could escape from the trouble of these investigations by saying that experience offers continually examples of such regularity of phenomena as to induce us to abstract from it the concept of cause, and it might be attempted to prove thereby the objective validity of such a concept. But it ought to be seen that in this way the concept of cause cannot possibly arise, and that such a concept ought either to be founded *a priori* in the understanding or be surrendered altogether as a mere hallucination. For this concept requires strictly that something, A, should be of such a nature that something else, B, follows from it necessarily and according to an absolutely universal rule. Phenomena no doubt supply us with cases from which a rule becomes possible according to which something happens usually, but never so that the result should be necessary. There is a dignity in the synthesis of cause and effect which cannot be expressed empirically, for it implies that the effect is not only an accessory to the cause, but given by it and springing from it. Nor is the absolute universality of the rule a quality inherent in empirical rules, which by means of induction cannot receive any but a relative universality, that is, a more or less extended applicability. If we were to treat the pure concepts of the understanding as merely empirical products, we should completely change their character and their use.

§ 14

Transition to a Transcendental Deduction of the Categories

Two ways only are possible in which synthetical representations and their objects can agree, can refer to each other with necessity, and so to say meet each other. Either it is the object alone that makes the representation possible, or it is the representation alone that makes the object possible. In the former case their relation is empirical only, and the representation therefore never possible *a priori*. This applies to phenomena with reference to whatever in them belongs to sensation. In the latter case, though representation by itself (for we do not speak here of its[4] causality by means of the will) cannot produce its object so far as its existence is concerned, nevertheless the representation determines the object *a priori*, if through it alone it is possible to know anything as an object. To know a thing as an object is possible only under two conditions. First, there must be intuition by which the object is given us, though as a phenomenon only, secondly, there must be a concept by which an object is thought as corresponding to that intuition. From what we have said before it is clear that the first condition, namely, that under which alone objects can be seen, exists, so far as the form of intuition is concerned, in the soul *a priori*. All phenomena therefore must conform to that formal condition of sensibility, because it is through it alone that they appear, that is, that they are given and empirically seen.

Now the question arises whether there are not also antecedent concepts *a priori*, forming conditions under which alone something can be, if not seen, yet thought as an object in general; for in that case all empirical knowledge of objects would necessarily conform to such concepts, it being impossible that anything should become an object of experience without them. All experience contains, besides the intuition of the senses by which something is given, a concept also of the object, which is given in intuition as a phenomenon. Such concepts of objects in general therefore must form conditions *a priori* of all knowledge produced by experience, and the objective validity of the categories, as being such concepts *a priori*, rests on this very fact that by them alone, so far as the form of thought is concerned, experience becomes possible. If by them only it is possible to think any object of experience, it follows that they refer by necessity and *a priori* to all objects of experience.

There is therefore a principle for the transcendental deduction of all concepts *a priori* which must guide the whole of our investigation, namely, that all must be recognised as conditions *a priori* of the possibility of experience, whether of intuition, which is found in it, or of thought. Concepts which supply the objective ground of the possibility of experience are for that very reason necessary. An analysis of the experience in which they are found would not be a deduction, but a mere illustration, because they would there have an accidental character only. Nay, without their original rela-

---

[4] Read *deren* instead of *dessen*.

tion to all possible experience in which objects of knowledge occur, their relation to any single object would be quite incomprehensible.

[There are three original sources, or call them faculties or powers of the soul, which contain the conditions of the possibility of all experience, and which themselves cannot be derived from any other faculty, namely, sense, imagination, and apperception. On them is founded—

1. The synopsis of the manifold *a priori* through the senses.

2. The synthesis of this manifold through the imagination.

3. The unity of that synthesis by means of original apperception.

Besides their empirical use all these faculties have a transcendental use also, referring to the form only and possible *a priori*. With regard to the senses we have discussed that transcendental use in the first part, and we shall now proceed to an investigation of the remaining two, according to their true nature.]

Locke, for want of this reflection, and because he met with pure concepts of the understanding in experience, derived them also from experience, and yet acted so inconsistently *that he attempted to use them for knowledge which far exceeds all limits of experience. David Hume saw that, in order to be able to do this, these concepts ought to have their origin* a priori; *but as he could not explain how it was possible that the understanding should be constrained to think concepts, which by themselves are not united in the understanding, as necessarily united in the object, and never thought that possibly the understanding might itself, through these concepts, be the author of that experience in which its objects are found, he was driven by necessity to derive them from experience (namely, from a subjective necessity, produced by frequent association in experience, which at last is wrongly supposed to be* objective, *that is, from habit). He acted, however, very consistently, by declaring it to be impossible to go with these concepts, and with the principles arising from them, beyond the limits of experience. This empirical deduction, which was adopted by both philosophers, cannot be reconciled with the reality of our scientific knowledge* a priori, *namely, pure* mathematics *and general natural science, and is therefore refuted by facts. The former of these two celebrated men opened a wide door to* fantastic extravagance, *because reason, if it has once established such pretensions, can no longer be checked by vague praises of moderation; the other, thinking that he had once discovered so general an illusion of our faculty of knowledge, which had formerly been accepted as reason, gave himself over entirely to scepticism. We now intend to make the experiment whether it is not possible to conduct reason safely between these two rocks, to assign to her definite limits, and yet to keep open for her the proper field for all her activities?*

I shall merely premise an explanation *of what I mean by the* categories. *They are concepts of an object in general by which its intuition is regarded as determined with reference to one of the* logical functions *in judgments. Thus the function of the* categorical *judgment was that of the relation of the subject to the predicate; for instance, all bodies are divisible. Here, however, with reference to the pure logical employment of the understanding, it remained undetermined to which of the two concepts the function of the subject, or the predicate, was to be assigned. For we could also say, some divisible is body. But by bringing the concept of body under the category of substance, it is determined that its empirical intuition in experience must always be considered as subject and never as predicate only. The same applies to all other categories.*

OF THE DEDUCTION OF THE PURE CONCEPTS OF THE UNDERSTANDING

SECOND SECTION

Transcendental Deduction of the Pure Concepts of the Understanding

§ 15

Of the Possibility of Connecting (*conjunctio*) in General

The manifold of representations may be given in an intuition which is purely sensuous, that is, nothing but receptivity, and the form of that intuition may lie a priori *in our faculty of representation, without being anything but the manner in which a subject is affected. But the connection (conjunctio) of anything manifold can never enter into us through the senses, and cannot be contained, therefore, already in the pure form of sensuous intuition, for it is a spontaneous act of the power of representation; and as, in order to distinguish this from sensibility, we must call it understanding, we see that all connecting, whether we are conscious of it or not, and whether we connect the manifold of intuition or several concepts together, and again, whether that intuition be sensuous or not sensuous, is an act of the understanding. This act we shall call by the general name of* synthesis, *in order to show that we cannot represent to ourselves anything as connected in the object, without having previously connected it ourselves, and that of all representations* connection *is the only one which cannot be given through the objects, but must be carried out by the subject itself, because it is an act of its spontaneity. It can be easily perceived that this act must be originally one and the same for every kind of connection, and that its dissolution, that is, the* analysis, *which seems to be its opposite, does always presuppose it. For where the understanding has not previously connected, there is nothing for it to disconnect, because, as connected, it could only be given by the understanding to the faculty of representation.*

But the concept of connection includes, besides the concept of the manifold and the synthesis of it, the concept of the *unity* of the manifold also. *Connection is representation of the synthetical unity of the manifold.* *

The representation of that unity cannot therefore be the result of the connection; on the contrary, the concept of the connection becomes first possible by the representation of unity being added to the representation of the manifold. And this unity, which precedes a priori all concepts of connection, must not be mistaken for that category of unity of which we spoke on p. 66; for all categories depend on logical functions in judgments, and in these we have already connection, and therefore unity of given concepts. The category, therefore, presupposes connection, and we must consequently look still higher for this unity as qualitative (see p. 66, § 12), in that, namely, which itself contains the ground for the unity of different concepts in judgments, that is, the ground for the very possibility of the understanding, even in its logical employment.

§ 16

The Original Synthetical Unity of Apperception

It must be possible *that the I think should accompany all my representations: for otherwise something would be represented within me that could not be thought, in other words, the representation would either be impossible or nothing, at least so far as I am concerned. That representation which can be given before all thought, is called* intuition, *and all the manifold of intuition has therefore a necessary relation to the* I think *in the same subject in which that manifold of intuition is found. That representation, however (that* I think), *is an act of spontaneity, that is, it cannot be considered as belonging to* sensibility. *I call it* pure apperception, *in order to distinguish it from empirical apperception, or* original apperception *also, because it is that self-consciousness which by producing the representation,* I think (*which must accompany all*

Whether the representations themselves are identical, and whether therefore one can be thought analytically by the other, is a matter of no consequence here. The consciousness *of the one has always to be distinguished from the consciousness of the other, so far as the manifold is concerned; and everything here depends on the synthesis only of this (possible) consciousness.*

*others, and is one and the same in every act of conscious-
ness), cannot itself be accompanied by any other. I also call
the unity of it the transcendental unity of self-consciousness
in order to indicate that it contains the possibility of knowledge
a priori.*

*For the manifold representations given in any intuition
would not all be my representations, if they did not all belong
to one self-consciousness. What I mean is that, as my representations (even though I am not conscious of them as such)
they must be in accordance with that condition, under which
alone they can stand together in one common self-consciousness, because otherwise they would not all belong to me. From
this original connection the following important conclusion
can be deduced.*

*The unbroken identity of apperception of the manifold that
is given in intuition contains a synthesis of representations
and is possible only through the consciousness of that synthesis. The empirical consciousness, which accompanies various
representations, is itself various and disunited, and without
reference to the identity of the subject. Such a relation takes
place, not by my simply accompanying every relation with
consciousness, but by my adding one to the other and being
conscious of that act of adding, that is, of that synthesis. Only
because I am able to connect the manifold of given representations in one consciousness, is it possible for me to represent
to myself the identity of the consciousness in these representations, that is, only under the supposition of some synthetical
unity of apperception does the analytical unity of apperception become possible.**

** This analytical unity of consciousness belongs to all general con-
cepts, as such. If, for instance, I think red in general, I represent
to myself a property, which (as a characteristic mark) may be
found in something, or can be connected with other representations; that is to say, only under a presupposed possible synthetical
unity can I represent to myself the analytical. A representation
which is to be thought as common to different representations,
looked upon as belonging to such as possess, besides it, something
different. It must therefore have been thought in synthetical unity
with other (though only possible) representations, before I can
think in it that analytical unity of consciousness which makes it
conceptus communis. The synthetical unity of apperception is,
therefore, the highest point with which all employment of the understanding, and even the whole of logic, and afterwards the whole
of transcendental philosophy, must be connected; ay, that faculty
the understanding itself.*

The thought that the representations given in intuition belong all of them to me, is therefore the same as that I connect them in one self-consciousness, or am able at least to do so; and though this is not yet the consciousness *of the* synthesis *of representations, it nevertheless presupposes the possibility of this synthesis. In other words, it is only because I am able to comprehend the manifold of representations in one consciousness, that I call them altogether my representations, for otherwise, I should have as manifold and various a self as I have representations of which I am conscious. The synthetical unity of the manifold of intuitions as given* a priori *is therefore the ground also of the identity of that apperception itself which precedes* a priori *all definite thought. Connection, however, does never lie in the objects, and cannot be borrowed from them by perception, and thus be taken into the understanding, but it is always an act of the understanding, which itself is nothing but a faculty of connecting* a priori, *and of bringing the manifold of given representations under the unity of apperception, which is, in fact, the highest principle of all human knowledge.*

It is true, no doubt, that this principle of the necessary unity of apperception is itself identical, and therefore an analytical proposition; but it shows, nevertheless, the necessity of a synthesis of the manifold which is given in intuition, without which synthesis it would be impossible to think the unbroken identity of self-consciousness. For through the Ego, *as a simple representation, nothing manifold is given; in the intuition, which is different from that, it can be given only, and then, by* connection, *be thought in one consciousness. An understanding in which, by its self-consciousness, all the manifold would be given at the same time, would possess* intuition; *our understanding can do nothing but think, and must seek for its intuition in the senses. I am conscious, therefore, of the identical self with respect to the manifold of the representations, which are given to me in an intuition, because I call them, altogether, my representations, as constituting* one. *This means, that I am conscious of a necessary synthesis of them* a priori, *which is called the original synthetical unity of apperception under which all representations given to me must stand, but have to be brought there, first, by means of a synthesis.*

§ 17

The Principle of the Synthetical Unity of Apperception is the Highest Principle of all Employment of the Understanding

The highest principle of the possibility of all intuition, in relation to sensibility, was, according to the transcendental Æsthetic, that all the manifold in it should be subject to the formal conditions of space and time. The highest principle of the same possibility in relation to the understanding is, that all the manifold in intuition must be subject to the conditions of the original synthetical unity of apperception.*

All the manifold representations of intuition, so far as they are given us, are subject to the former, so far as they must admit of being connected in one consciousness, to the latter; and without that nothing can be thought or known by them, because the given representations would not share the act of apperception (I think) in common, and could not be comprehended in one self-consciousness.

The understanding *in its most general sense is the faculty of* cognitions. *These consist in a definite relation of given representations to an object; and an* object *is that in the concept of which the manifold of a given intuition is* connected. *All such connection of representations requires of course the unity of the consciousness in their synthesis: consequently, the unity of consciousness is that which alone constitutes the relation of representations to an object, that is, their objective validity, and consequently their becoming cognitions, so that the very possibility of the understanding depends on it.*

The first pure cognition of the understanding, therefore, on which all the rest of its employment is founded, and which at the same time is entirely independent of all conditions of sensu-

---

* *Space and time, and all portions thereof, are* intuitions, *and consequently single representations with the manifold of their content. (See the transcendental Æsthetic.) They are not, therefore, mere* concepts, *through which the same consciousness, as existing in many representations, but intuitions through which many representations are brought to us, as contained in one and in its consciousness; this latter, therefore, is compounded, and these intuitions represent the unity of consciousness as* synthetical, *but yet as* primitive. *This character of* singleness *in them is practically of great importance (see § 25).*

ous intuition, is this very principle of the original synthetical unity of apperception. Space, the mere form of external sensuous intuition, is not yet cognition: it only supplies the manifold of intuition a priori for a possible cognition. In order to know anything in space, for instance, a line, I must draw it, and produce synthetically a certain connection of the manifold that is given, so that the unity of that act is at the same time the unity of the consciousness (in the concept of a line), and (so that) an object (a determinate space) is then only known for the first time. The synthetical unity of consciousness is, therefore, an objective condition of all knowledge; a condition, not necessary for myself only, in order to know an object, but one to which each intuition must be subject, in order to become an object for me, because the manifold could not become connected in one consciousness in any other way, and without such a synthesis.

No doubt, that proposition, as I said before, is itself analytical, though it makes synthetical unity a condition of all thought, for it really says no more than that all my representations in any given intuition must be subject to the condition under which alone I can ascribe them, as my representations, to the identical self, and therefore comprehend them, as synthetically connected, in one apperception through the general expression, I think.

And yet this need not be a principle for every possible understanding, but only for that which gives nothing manifold through its pure apperception in the representation, I am. An understanding which through its self-consciousness could give the manifold of intuition, and by whose representation the objects of that representation should at the same time exist, would not require a special act of the synthesis of the manifold for the unity of its consciousness, while the human understanding, which possesses the power of thought only, but not of intuition, requires such an act. To the human understanding that first principle is so indispensable that it really cannot form the least concept of any other possible understanding, whether it be intuitive by itself, or possessed of a sensuous intuition, different from that in space and time.

§ 18

What is the Objective Unity of Self-consciousness?

The transcendental unity *of apperception connects all the manifold given in an intuition into a concept of an object. It is therefore called* objective, *and must be distinguished from the* subjective unity *of consciousness, which is a form of the* internal sense, *by which the manifold of intuition is empirically given, to be thus connected. Whether I can become* empirically *conscious of the manifold, as either simultaneous or successive, depends on circumstances, or empirical conditions. The empirical unity of consciousness, therefore, through the association of representations, is itself phenomenal and wholly contingent, while the pure form of intuition in time, merely as general intuition containing the manifold that is given, is subject to the original unity of the consciousness, through the necessary relation only of the manifold of intuition to the one,* I think,—*that is, through the pure synthesis of the understanding, which forms the a priori ground of the empirical synthesis. That unity alone is, therefore, valid objectively; the empirical unity of apperception, which we do not consider here, and which is only derived from the former, under given conditions* in concreto, *has subjective validity only. One man connects the representation of a word with one thing, another with another, and the unity of consciousness, with regard to what is empirical, is not necessary nor universally valid with reference to that which is given.*

§ 19

The Logical Form of all Judgments consists in the Objective Unity of Apperception of the Concepts contained therein

I could never feel satisfied with the definition of a judgment in general, given by our logicians, who say that it is the representation of a relation between two concepts. Without disputing with them in this place as to the defect of that explanation, that it may possibly apply to categorical, but not to hypothetical and disjunctive judgments (the latter containing, not a relation of concepts, but of judgments themselves),—

*though many tedious consequences have arisen from this mis-
take of logicians,—I must at least make this observation, that
we are not told in what that relation consists.**

But, if I examine more closely the relation of given cognitions in every judgment, and distinguish it, as belonging to the
understanding, from the relation according to the rules of reproductive imagination (which has subjective validity only),
I find that a judgment is nothing but the mode of bringing
given cognitions into the objective *unity of apperception. This
is what is intended by the copula* is, *which is meant to distinguish the objective unity of given representations from the
subjective. It* (the copula is) *indicates their relation to the original apperception, and their necessary* unity, *even though the
judgment itself be empirical, and therefore contingent; as, for
instance, bodies are heavy. By this I do not mean to say that
these representations belong* necessarily *to each other, in the
empirical intuition, but that they belong to each other by
means of the* necessary unity *of apperception in the synthesis
of intuitions, that is, according to the principles of the objective determination of all representations, so far as any cognition is to arise from them, these principles being all derived
from the principle of the transcendental unity of apperception.
Thus, and thus alone, does the relation become a judgment,
that is, a relation that is valid objectively, and can thus be kept
sufficiently distinct from the relation of the same representations, if it has subjective validity only, for instance, according
to the laws of association. In the latter case, I could only say,
that if I carry a body I feel the pressure of its weight, but not,
that it, the body, is heavy, which is meant to say that these two
representations are connected together in the object, whatever
the state of the subject may be, and not only associated or
conjoined in the perception, however often it may be repeated.*

* *The lengthy doctrine of the four syllogistic figures concerns
categorical syllogisms only, and though it is really nothing but a
trick for obtaining the appearance of more modes of concluding
than that of the first figure, by secretly introducing immediate conclusions* (consequentiae immediatae) *among the premisses of a
pure syllogism, this would hardly have secured its great success,
had not its authors succeeded, at the same time, in establishing
the exclusive authority of categorical judgments, as those to which
all others must be referred. This as we showed in § 9, p. 55 ff. is
wrong.*

§ 20

All Sensuous Intuitions are subject to the Categories as to Conditions under which alone their Manifold Contents can come together in one Consciousness

The manifold which is given us in a sensuous intuition is necessarily subject to the original synthetical unity of apperception, because by it alone the unity of intuition becomes possible (§ 7). That act of the understanding, further, by which the manifold of given representations (whether intuitions or concepts) is brought under one apperception in general, is the logical function of a judgment (§ 19). The manifold, therefore, so far as it is given in an empirical intuition, is determined with regard to one of the logical functions of judgment, by which, indeed, it is brought to consciousness in general. The categories, however, are nothing but these functions of judgment, so far as the manifold of a given intuition is determined with respect to them (§ 13, p. 68 ff.). Therefore the manifold in any given intuition is naturally subject to the categories.

§ 21

Note

The manifold, contained in an intuition which I call my own, is represented through the synthesis of the understanding, as belonging to the necessary unity of self-consciousness, and this takes place through the category.*

This category indicates, therefore, that the empirical consciousness of the manifold, given in any intuition, is subject to a pure self-consciousness a priori, in the same manner as the empirical intuition is subject to a pure sensuous intuition which likewise takes place a priori.

In the above proposition a beginning is made of a deduction *of the pure concepts of the understanding. In this deduction, as the categories arise in the understanding only,* independent

---

* *The proof of this rests on the represented unity of intuition, by which an object is given, and which always includes a synthesis of the manifold which is given for an intuition, and contains the relation of the latter to the unity of apperception.*

of all sensibility, *I ought not yet to take any account of the manner in which the manifold is given for an empirical intuition, but attend exclusively to the unity which, by means of the category, enters into the intuition through the understanding. In what follows (§ 26) we shall show, from the manner in which the empirical intuition is given in sensibility, that its unity is no other than that which is prescribed by the category (according to § 20) to the manifold of any given intuition. Thus only, that is, by showing their validity a priori with respect to all objects of our senses, the purpose of our deduction will be fully attained.*

There is one thing, however, of which, in the above demonstration, I could not make abstraction: namely, that the manifold for an intuition must be given antecedently to the synthesis of the understanding, and independently of it;—how, remains uncertain. For if I were to imagine an understanding, itself intuitive (for instance, a divine understanding, which should not represent to itself given objects, but produce them at once by his representation), the categories would have no meaning with respect to such cognition. They are merely rules for an understanding whose whole power consists in thinking, that is, in the act of bringing the synthesis of the manifold, which is given to it in intuition from elsewhere, to the unity of apperception; an understanding which therefore knows nothing by itself, but connects only and arranges the material for cognition, that is, the intuition which must be given to it by the object. This peculiarity of our understanding of producing unity of apperception a priori by means of the categories only, and again by such and so many, cannot be further explained, any more than why we have these and no other functions of judgment, and why time and space are the only forms of a possible intuition for us.

§ 22

The Category admits of no other Employment for the Cognition of Things, but its Application to Objects of Experience

We have seen that to think an object is not the same as to know an object. In order to know an object, we must have the concept by which any object is thought (the category), and likewise the intuition by which it is given. If no corresponding

intuition could be given to a concept, it would still be a thought, so far as its form is concerned: but it would be without an object, and no knowledge of anything would be possible by it, because, so far as I know, there would be nothing, and there could be nothing, to which my thought could be referred. Now the only possible intuition for us is sensuous (see Æsthetic); the thought of any object, therefore, by means of a pure concept of the understanding, can with us become knowledge only, if it is referred to objects of the senses. Sensuous intuition is either pure (space and time), or empirical, i.e. if it is an intuition of that which is represented in space and time, through sensation as immediately real. By means of pure intuition we can gain knowledge a priori of things as phenomena (in mathematics), but only so far as their form is concerned; but whether there are things which must be perceived, according to that form, remains unsettled. Mathematical concepts, by themselves, therefore, are not yet knowledge, except under the supposition that there are things which admit of being represented by us, according to the form of that pure sensuous intuition only. Consequently, as things in space *and* time *are only given as perceptions (as representations accompanied by sensations), that is, through empirical representations, the pure concepts of the understanding, even if applied to intuitions a priori, as in mathematics, give us knowledge in so far only as these pure intuitions, and therefore through them the concepts of the understanding also, can be applied to empirical intuitions. Consequently the categories, by means of intuition, do not give us any knowledge of things, except under the supposition of their possible application to empirical* intuition; *they serve, in short, for the possibility of empirical* knowledge *only, which is called* experience. *From this it follows that the categories admit of no other employment for the cognition of things, except so far only as these are taken as objects of possible experience.*

§ 23

The foregoing proposition is of the greatest importance, for it determines the limits of the employment of the pure concepts of the understanding with reference to objects, in the same manner as the transcendental Æsthetic determined the limits of the employment of the pure form of our sensuous intuition. Space and time are conditions of the possibility of how objects can be given to us, so far only as objects of the senses, therefore of experience, are concerned. Beyond these limits they represent nothing, for they belong only to the senses, and have no reality beyond them. Pure concepts of the understanding are free from this limitation, and extend to objects of intuition in general, whether that intuition be like our own or not, if only it is sensuous and not intellectual. This further extension, however, of concepts beyond our sensuous intuition, is of no avail to us; for they are in that case empty concepts of objects, and the concepts do not even enable us to say, whether such objects be possible or not. They are mere forms of thought, without objective reality: because we have no intuition at hand to which the synthetical unity of apperception, which is contained in the concepts alone, could be applied, so that they might determine an object. Nothing can give them sense and meaning, except our sensuous and empirical intuition.

If, therefore, we assume an object of a non-sensuous intuition as given, we may, no doubt, determine it through all the predicates, which follow from the supposition that nothing belonging to sensuous intuition belongs to it, that, therefore, it is not extended, or not in space, that its duration is not time, that no change (succession of determinations in time) is to be met in it, etc. *But we can hardly call this knowledge, if we only indicate how the intuition of an object* is not, *without being able to say what is contained in it, for, in that case, I have not represented the possibility of an object, corresponding to my pure concept of the understanding, because I could give no intuition corresponding to it, but could only say that our intuition did not apply to it. But what is the most important is this, that not even a single category could be applied to such a thing; as, for instance, the concept of substance, that is, of something that can exist as a subject only, but never as a mere predicate. For I do not know whether there can be anything corresponding to such a determination of thought, unless empirical intuition supplies the case for its application. Of this more hereafter.*

§ 24

Of the Application of the Categories to Objects of the Senses in General

The pure concepts of the understanding refer, through the mere understanding, to objects of intuition, whether it be our own, or any other, if only sensuous intuition, but they are, for that very reason, mere forms of thought, *by which no definite object can be known. The synthesis, or connection of the manifold in them, referred only to the unity of apperception, and became thus the ground of the possibility of knowledge* a priori, *so far as it rests on the understanding, and is therefore not only transcendental, but also purely intellectual. Now as there exists in us a certain form of sensuous intuition* a priori, *which rests on the receptivity of the faculty of representation (sensibility), the understanding, as spontaneity, is able to determine the internal sense through the manifold of given representations, according to the synthetical unity of apperception, and can thus think synthetical unity of the apperception of the manifold of* sensuous intuition a priori, *as the condition to which all objects of our (human) intuition must necessarily be subject. Thus the categories, though pure forms of thought, receive objective reality, that is, application to objects which can be given to us in intuition, but as phenomena only; for it is with reference to them alone that we are capable of intuition* a priori.

This synthesis *of the manifold of sensuous intuition, which is possible and necessary* a priori, *may be called* figurative (synthesis speciosa), *in order to distinguish it from that which is thought in the mere category, with reference to the manifold of an intuition in general, and is called intellectual synthesis* (synthesis intellectualis). *Both are transcendental, not only because they themselves are carried out* a priori, *but because they establish also the possibility of other knowledge* a priori.

But this figurative synthesis, if it refers to the original synthetical unity of apperception only, that is, to that transcendental unity which is thought in the categories, must be called the transcendental synthesis of the faculty of imagination, in order thus to distinguish it from the purely intellectual synthesis. Imagination is the faculty of representing an object even without its presence *in intuition. As all our intuition is sensuous, the faculty of imagination belongs, on account of the subjective condition under which alone it can give a corresponding intuition to the concepts of the understanding, to our sensibility. As, however, its synthesis is an act of spontaneity, determining, and not, like the senses, determinable only, and therefore able to determine a priori the senses, so far as their form is concerned, according to the unity of apperception, the faculty of imagination is, so far, a faculty of determining our sensibility a priori, so that the synthesis of the intuitions, according to the categories, must be the transcendental synthesis of the faculty of imagination. This is an effect, produced by the understanding on our sensibility, and the first application of it (and at the same time the ground of all others) to objects of the intuition which is only possible to us. As figurative, it is distinguished from the intellectual synthesis, which takes place by the understanding only, without the aid of the faculty of imagination. In so far as imagination is spontaneity, I call it occasionally productive imagination: distinguishing it from the reproductive, which in its synthesis is subject to empirical laws only, namely, those of association, and which is of no help for the explanation of the possibility of knowledge a priori, belonging, therefore, to psychology, and not to transcendental philosophy.*

*   *   *   *   *   *   *

This is the proper place for trying to account for the paradox, which must have struck everybody in our exposition of the form of the internal sense (§ 6, p. 42); namely, how that sense represents to the consciousness even ourselves, not as we are by ourselves, but as we appear to ourselves, because we perceive ourselves only as we are affected internally. This seems to be contradictory, because we should thus be in a passive relation to ourselves; and for this reason the founders of the systems of psychology have preferred to represent the internal sense as identical with the faculty of apperception, while we have carefully distinguished the two.

What determines the internal sense is the understanding, and its original power of connecting the manifold of intuition, that is, of bringing it under one apperception, this being the very ground of the possibility of the understanding. As in us men the understanding is not itself an intuitive faculty, and could not, even if intuitions were given in our sensibility, take them into itself, in order to connect, as it were, the manifold of its own intuition, the synthesis of the understanding, if con-

sidered by itself alone, is nothing but the unity of action, of which it is conscious without sensibility also, but through which the understanding is able to determine that sensibility internally, with respect to the manifold which may be given to it (the understanding) according to the form of its intuition. The understanding, therefore, exercises its activity, under the name of a transcendental synthesis *of the faculty of imagination, on the passive subject to which it* belongs *as a faculty, and we are right in saying that the internal sense is affected by that activity. The apperception with its synthetical unity is so far from being identical with the internal sense, that, as the source of all synthesis, it rather applies, under the name of the categories, to the manifold of* intuitions in general, *that is, to objects in general before all sensuous intuition; while the internal sense, on the contrary, contains the mere form of intuition, but without any connection of the manifold in it, and therefore, as yet, no* definite *intuition, which becomes possible only through the consciousness of the determination of the internal sense by the transcendental act of the faculty of imagination (the synthetical influence of the understanding on the internal sense) which I have called the figurative synthesis.*

This we can always perceive in ourselves. We cannot think a line without drawing it in thought; we cannot think a circle without describing it; we cannot represent, at all, the three dimensions of space, without placing, from the same point, three lines perpendicularly on each other; nay, we cannot even represent time, except by attending, during our drawing a straight line (which is meant to be the external figurative representation of time) to the act of the synthesis of the manifold only by which we successively determine the internal sense, and thereby to the succession of that determination in it. It is really motion, as the act of the subject (not as the determination of an object*), therefore the synthesis of the manifold in space (abstraction being made of space, and our attention fixed on the act only by which we determine the internal sense, *according to its form), which first produces the very concept of succession. The understanding does not, therefore, find in the in-*

---

* *Motion of an object in space does not belong to a pure science, consequently not to geometry, because the fact that a thing is moveable cannot be known* a priori, *but from experience only. Motion, however, considered as describing a space, is a pure act of successive synthesis of the manifold in external intuition in general by means of productive imagination, and belongs therefore, by right, not only to geometry, but even to transcendental philosophy.*

ternal sense such a connection of the manifold, but produces it by affecting the internal sense. It may seem difficult to understand how the thinking ego can be different from the ego which sees or perceives itself (other modes of intuition being at least conceivable), and yet identical with the latter as the same subject, and how, therefore, I can say: I, as intelligence and thinking subject, know myself as an object thought so far as being given to myself in intuition also, but like other phenomena, not as I am to the understanding, but only as I appear to myself. In reality, however, this is neither more nor less difficult than how I can be, to myself, an object, and, more especially, an object of intuition and of internal perceptions. But that this must really be so, can clearly be shown—if only we admit space to be merely a pure form of the phenomena of the external senses—by the fact that we cannot represent to ourselves time, which is no object of external intuition, in any other way than under the image of a line which we draw, a mode of representation without which we could not realise the unity of its dimension; or again by this other fact that we must always derive the determination of the length of time, or of points of time for all our internal perceptions, from that which is represented to us as changeable by external things, and have therefore to arrange the determinations of the internal sense as phenomena in time, in exactly the same way in which we arrange the determinations of the external senses in space. If, then, with regard to the latter, we admit that by them we know objects so far only as we are affected externally, we must also admit, with regard to the internal sense, that by it we only are, or perceive ourselves, as we are internally affected by ourselves, in other words, that with regard to internal intuition we know our own self as a phenomenon only, and not as it is by itself.*

* I do not see how so much difficulty should be found in admitting that the internal sense is affected by ourselves. Every act of attention gives us an instance of it. In such an act the understanding always determines the internal sense, according to the connection which it thinks, to such an internal intuition as corresponds to the manifold in the synthesis of the understanding. How much the mind is commonly affected thereby anybody will be able to perceive in himself.

§ 25

In the transcendental synthesis, however, of the manifold of representations in general, and therefore in the original synthetical unity of apperception, I am conscious of myself, neither as I appear to myself, nor as I am by myself, but only that I am. This representation *is an act of* thought, *not of* intuition. *Now, in order to* know *ourselves, we require, besides the act of thinking, which brings the manifold of every possible intuition to the unity of apperception, a definite kind of intuition also by which that manifold is given, and thus, though my own existence is not phenomenal (much less a mere illusion), yet the determination of my existence* * *can only take place according to the form of the internal sense, and in that special manner in which the manifold, which I connect, is given in the internal intuition. This shows that I have no* knowledge *of myself as I am, but only as I appear to myself. The consciousness of oneself is therefore very far from being a knowledge of oneself, in spite of all the categories which constitute the thinking of an* object in general, *by means of the connection of the manifold in an apperception. As for the knowledge of an object different from myself I require, besides the thinking of an object in general (in a category), an intuition also, to determine that general concept, I require for the knowledge of my own self, besides consciousness, or besides my thinking myself, an intuition also of the manifold in me, to determine that thought. I exist, therefore, as such an intelligence, which is simply conscious of its power of con-*

---

*The I think *expresses the act of determining my own existence. What is thus given is the existence, but what is not yet given, is the manner in which I am to determine it, that is, in which I am to place within me the manifold belonging to it. For that purpose self-intuition is required, which depends on an* a priori *form, that is, on time, which is sensuous, and belongs to our receptivity of what is given to us as determinable. If, then, I have not another self-intuition which, likewise* before *the act of* determination, *gives the* determining *within me, of the spontaneity of which I am conscious only, as* time *gives the determinable, I cannot determine my existence as that of a spontaneously acting being, but I only represent to myself the spontaneity of my thinking, that is, of the act of determination, my existence remaining sensuous only, that is, determinable, as the existence of a phenomenon. It is, however, on account of this spontaneity that I call myself an intelligence.*

nection, but with respect to the manifold that has to be connected, is subject to a limiting condition which is called the internal sense, according to which that connection can only become perceptible in relations of time, which lie entirely outside the concepts of the understanding. Such an intelligence, therefore, can only know itself as it appears to itself in an intuition (which cannot be intellectual and given by the understanding itself), and not as it would know itself, if its intuition were intellectual.

§ 26

Transcendental Deduction of the Universally Possible Employment of the Pure Concepts of the Understanding in Experience

In the metaphysical deduction of the categories their a priori origin was proved by their complete accordance with the general logical functions of thought, while in their transcendental deduction we established their possibility as knowledge a priori of objects of an intuition in general (§ 20, 21). Now we have to explain the possibility of our knowing a priori, by means of the categories, whatever objects may come before our senses, and this not according to the form of their intuition, but according to the laws of their connection, and of our thus, as it were, prescribing laws to nature, nay, making nature possible. Unless they were adequate to that purpose, we could not understand how everything that may come before our senses must be subject to laws which have their origin a priori in the understanding alone.

First of all, I observe that by the synthesis of apprehension I understand the connection of the manifold in an empirical intuition, by which perception, that is, empirical consciousness of it (as phenomenal), becomes possible.

We have forms of the external as well as the internal intuition a priori, in our representations of space and time: and to these the synthesis of the apprehension of the manifold in phenomena must always conform, because it can take place according to that form only. Time and space, however, are represented a priori, not only as forms of sensuous intuition, but as intuitions themselves (containing a manifold), and therefore with the determination of the unity of that manifold in them (*see transcendental Æsthetic**). *Therefore* unity of the synthesis *of the manifold without or within us, and consequently a* connection *to which everything that is to be represented as determined in space and time must conform, is given* a priori *as the condition of the synthesis of all* apprehension simultaneously with *the intuitions, not* in *them, and that synthetical unity can be no other but that of the connection of the manifold of any* intuition whatsoever *in an original consciousness, according to the categories, only applied to our* sensuous intuition. *Consequently, all synthesis, without which even perception would be impossible, is subject to the categories; and as experience consists of knowledge by means of connected perceptions, the categories are conditions of the possibility of experience, and valid therefore* a priori *also for all objects of experience.*

*   *   *   *   *   *   *   *

If, for instance, I raise the empirical intuition of a house, through the apprehension of the manifold contained therein, into a perception, the necessary unity *of space and of external sensuous intuition in general is presupposed, and I draw, as it were, the shape of the house according to that synthetical unity of the manifold in space. But this very synthetical unity, if I make abstraction of the form of space, has its seat in the understanding, and is in fact the category of the* synthesis of the homogeneous *in intuition in general: that is, the category of* quantity, *to which that synthesis of apprehension, that is, the perception, must always conform.*†

* *Space, represented as an object (as required in geometry), contains more than the mere form of intuition, namely, the* comprehension *of the manifold, which is given according to the form of sensibility, into a* perceptible *(intuitable) representation, so that the* form of intuition *gives the manifold only, while the* formal intuition *gives unity of representation. In the Æsthetic I had simply ascribed this unity to sensibility, in order to show that it precedes all concepts, though it presupposes a synthesis not belonging to the senses, and by which all concepts of space and time become first possible. For as by that synthesis (the understanding determining the sensibility) space and time are first given as intuitions, the unity of that intuition* a priori *belongs to space and time, and not to the concept of the understanding. (See § 24.)*

† *In this manner it is proved that the synthesis of apprehension, which is empirical, must necessarily conform to the synthesis of apperception, which is intellectual, and contained in the category entirely* a priori. *It is one and the same spontaneity, which there, under the name of imagination, and here, under the name of understanding, brings connection into the manifold of intuition.*

Or if, to take another example, I perceive the freezing of water, I apprehend two states (that of fluidity and that of solidity), and these as standing to each other in a relation of time. But in the time, which as internal intuition *I make the foundation of the phenomenon, I represent to myself necessarily synthetical* unity *of the manifold, without which that relation could not be given as* determined *in an intuition (with reference to the succession of time). That synthetical unity, however, as a condition* a priori, *under which I connect the manifold of* any intuition, *turns out to be, if I make abstraction of the permanent form of my intuition, namely, of time, the category of* cause, *through which, if I apply it to my sensibility, I determine everything that happens, according to its relation in time. Thus the apprehension in such an event, and that event itself considered as a possible perception, is subject to the concept of the relation of cause and effect. The same applies to all other cases.*

*   *   *   *   *   *   *   *

Categories are concepts which a priori *prescribe laws to all phenomena, and therefore to nature as the sum total of all phenomena* (natura materialiter spectata). *The question therefore arises, as these laws are not derived from nature, nor conform to it as their model (in which case they would be empirical only), how we can understand that nature should conform to them, that is, how they can determine* a priori *the connection of the manifold in nature, without taking that connection from nature. The solution of that riddle is this.*

It is no more surprising that the laws of phenomena in nature must agree with the understanding and its form a priori, *that is, with its power of* connecting *the manifold in general, than that the phenomena themselves must agree with the form of sensuous intuition* a priori. *For laws exist as little in phenomena themselves, but relatively only, with respect to the subject to which, so far as it has understanding, the phenomena belong, as phenomena exist by themselves, but relatively only, with respect to the same being so far as it has senses. Things by themselves would necessarily possess their conformity to the law, independent also of any understanding by which they are known. But phenomena are only representations of things, unknown as to what they may be by themselves. As mere representations they are subject to no law of connection, except that which is prescribed by the connecting faculty. Now that which connects the manifold of sensuous intuition is the faculty of imagination, which receives from the understanding the unity of its intellectual synthesis, and from sensibility the manifoldness of apprehension. Thus, as all possible perceptions depend on the synthesis of apprehension, and that synthesis itself, that empirical synthesis, depends on the transcendental, and, therefore, on the categories, it follows that all possible perceptions, everything in fact that can come to the empirical consciousness, that is, all phenomena of nature, must, so far as their connection is concerned, be subject to the categories. On these categories, therefore, nature (considered as nature in general) depends, as on the original ground of its necessary conformity to law (as* natura formaliter spectata). *Beyond the laws, on which* nature in general, *as a lawful order of phenomena in space and time depends, the pure faculty of the understanding is incapable of prescribing* a priori, *by means of mere categories, laws to phenomena. Special laws, therefore, as they refer to phenomena which are empirically determined, cannot be completely derived from the categories, although they are all subject to them. Experience must be superadded in order to know such special laws: while those other* a priori *laws inform us only with regard to experience in general, and what can be known as an object of it.*

§ 27

Results of this Deduction of the Concepts of the Understanding

We cannot think any object except by means of the categories; we cannot know any subject that has been thought, except by means of intuitions, corresponding to those concepts. Now all our intuitions are sensuous, and this knowledge, so far as its object is given, is empirical. But empirical knowledge is experience, and therefore no knowledge a priori is possible to us, except of objects of possible experience only.*

* *Lest anybody should be unnecessarily frightened by the dangerous consequences of this proposition, I shall only remark that the categories are not limited for the purpose of thought by the conditions of our sensuous intuition, but have really an unlimited field. It is only the knowledge of that which we think, the determining of an object, that requires intuition, and even in the absence of intuition, the thought of the object may still have its true and useful consequences, so far as the subjective use of reason is concerned. That use of reason, however, as it is not always*

This knowledge, however, though limited to objects of experience, is not, therefore, entirely derived from experience, for both the pure intuitions and the pure concepts of the understanding are elements of knowledge which exist in us a priori. Now there are only two ways in which a necessary harmony of experience with the concepts of its objects can be conceived; either experience makes these concepts possible, or these concepts make experience possible. The former will not hold good with respect to the categories (nor with pure sensuous intuition), for they are concepts a priori, and therefore independent of experience. To ascribe to them an empirical origin, would be to admit a kind of generatio aequivoca. *There remains, therefore, the second alternative only (a kind of system of the* epigenesis *of pure reason), namely, that the categories, on the part of the understanding, contain the grounds of the possibility of all experience in general. How they render experience possible, and what principles of the possibility of experience they supply in their employment on phenomena, will be shown more fully in the following chapter on the transcendental employment of the faculty of judgment.*

Some one might propose to adopt a middle way between the two, namely, that the categories are neither self-produced first principles a priori of our knowledge, nor derived from experience, but subjective dispositions of thought, implanted in us with our existence, and so arranged by our Creator that their employment should accurately agree with the laws of nature, which determine experience (a kind of system of preformation of pure reason). But, in that case, not only would there be no end of such an hypothesis, so that no one could know how far the supposition of predetermined dispositions to future judgments might be carried, but there is this decided objection against that middle course that, by adopting it, the categories would lose that necessity which is essential to them. Thus the concept of cause, which asserts, under a presupposed condition, the necessity of an effect, would become false, if it rested only on some subjective necessity implanted in us of connecting certain empirical representations according to the rule of causal relation. I should not be able to say that the effect is connected with the cause in the object (that is, by necessity), but only, I am so constituted that I cannot think these represen-

---

directed to the determination of the object, that is, to knowledge, but also to the determination of the subject, and its volition, cannot be treated of in this place.

*tations as connected in any other way. This is exactly what the
sceptic most desires, for in that case all our knowledge, resting
on the supposed objective validity of our judgments, is nothing but mere illusion, nor would there be wanting people to say
they know nothing of such subjective necessity (which can only
be felt); and at all events we could not quarrel with anybody
about what depends only on the manner in which his own
subject is organised.*

Comprehensive View of this Deduction

*The deduction of the pure concepts of the understanding
(and with them of all theoretical knowledge a priori) consists
in representing them as principles of the possibility of experience, and in representing experience as the determination of
phenomena in space and time,—and, lastly, in representing that
determination as depending on the principle of the original
synthetical unity of apperception, as the form of the understanding, applied to space and time, as the original forms of
sensibility.*[5]

DEDUCTION OF THE PURE CONCEPTS OF THE UNDERSTANDING

SECTION II

Of the a priori Grounds for the Possibility of Experience

[That a concept should be produced entirely *a priori* and
yet refer to an object, though itself neither belonging to the
sphere of possible experience, nor consisting of the elements
of such an experience, is self-contradictory and impossible. It
would have no contents, because no intuition corresponds to it,
and intuitions by which objects are given to us constitute the
whole field or the complete object of possible experience. An
a priori concept therefore not referring to experience would be
the logical form only of a concept, but not the concept itself by
which something is thought.

If therefore there exist any pure concepts *a priori*, though

[5] Kant does not carry the division into paragraphs in his second
edition further, because, as he says, he has to treat no more of
elementary concepts, and prefers, in representing their employment,
to adopt a continuous treatment, without paragraphs.

they cannot contain anything empirical, they must nevertheless all be conditions *a priori* of a possible experience, on which alone their objective reality depends.

If therefore we wish to know how pure concepts of the understanding are possible, we must try to find out what are the conditions *a priori* on which the possibility of experience depends, nay, on which it is founded, apart from all that is empirical in phenomena. A concept expressing this formal and objective condition of experience with sufficient generality might properly be called a pure concept of the understanding. If we once have these pure concepts of the understanding, we may also imagine objects which are either impossible, or, if not impossible in themselves, yet can never be given in any experience. We have only in the connection of those concepts to leave out something which necessarily belongs to the conditions of a possible experience (concept of a spirit), or to extend pure concepts of the understanding beyond what can be reached by experience (concept of God). But the elements of all knowledge *a priori,* even of gratuitous and preposterous fancies, though not borrowed from experience (for in that case they would not be knowledge *a priori*) must nevertheless contain the pure conditions *a priori* of a possible experience and its object, otherwise not only would nothing be thought by them, but they themselves, being without data, could never arise in our mind.

Such concepts, then, which comprehend the pure thinking *a priori* involved in every experience, are discovered in the categories, and it is really a sufficient deduction of them and a justification of their objective validity, if we succeed in proving that by them alone an object can be thought. But as in such a process of thinking more is at work than the faculty of thinking only, namely, the understanding, and as the understanding, as a faculty of knowledge which is meant to refer to objects, requires quite as much an explanation as to the possibility of such a reference, it is necessary for us to consider the subjective sources which form the foundation *a priori* for the possibility of experience, not according to their empirical, but according to their transcendental character.

If every single representation stood by itself, as if isolated and separated from the others, nothing like what we call knowledge could ever arise, because knowledge forms a whole of representations connected and compared with each other. If therefore I ascribe to the senses a synopsis, because in their intuition they contain something manifold, there corresponds to it always a synthesis, and receptivity can make knowledge possible only when joined with spontaneity. This spontaneity, now, appears as a threefold synthesis which must necessarily take place in every kind of knowledge, namely, first, that of the *apprehension* of representations as modifications of the soul in intuition, secondly, of the *reproduction* of them in the imagination, and, thirdly, that of their *recognition* in concepts. This leads us to three subjective sources of knowledge which render possible the understanding, and through it all experience as an empirical product of the understanding.

Preliminary Remark

The deduction of the categories is beset with so many difficulties and obliges us to enter so deeply into the first grounds of the possibility of our knowledge in general, that I thought it more expedient, in order to avoid the lengthiness of a complete theory, and yet to omit nothing in so essential an investigation, to add the following four paragraphs with a view of preparing rather than instructing the reader. After that only I shall in the third section proceed to a systematical discussion of these elements of the understanding. Till then the reader must not allow himself to be frightened by a certain amount of obscurity which at first is inevitable on a road never trodden before, but which, when we come to that section, will give way, I hope, to a complete comprehension.

I

Of the Synthesis of Apprehension in Intuition

Whatever the origin of our representations may be, whether they be due to the influence of external things or to internal causes, whether they have arisen *a priori* or empirically as phenomena, as modifications of the mind they must always belong to the internal sense, and all our knowledge must therefore finally be subject to the formal condition of that internal sense, namely, time, in which they are all arranged, joined, and brought into certain relations to each other. This is a general remark which must never be forgotten in all that follows.

Every representation contains something manifold, which could not be represented as such, unless the mind distinguished the time in the succession of one impression after another; for as contained in one moment, each representation can never be anything but absolute unity. In order to change this manifold into a unity of intuition (as, for instance, in the representation of space), it is necessary first to run through the manifold and then to hold it together. It is this act which I call the synthesis of apprehension, because it refers directly to intuition which no doubt offers something manifold, but which, without a synthesis, can never make it such, as it is contained in *one* representation.

This synthesis of apprehension must itself be carried out *a priori* also, that is, with reference to representations which are not empirical. For without it we should never be able to have the representations either of space or time *a priori,* because these cannot be produced except by a synthesis of the manifold which the senses offer in their original receptivity. It follows therefore that we have a pure synthesis of apprehension.

II

Of the Synthesis of Reproduction in Imagination

It is no doubt nothing but an empirical law according to which representations which have often followed or accompanied one another, become associated in the end and so closely united that, even without the presence of the object, one of these representations will, according to an invariable law, produce a transition of the mind to the other. This law of reproduction, however, presupposes that the phenomena themselves are really subject to such a rule, and that there is in the variety of these representations a sequence and concomitancy subject to certain rules; for without this the faculty of empirical imagination would never find anything to do that it is able to do, and remain therefore buried within our mind as a dead faculty, unknown to ourselves. If cinnabar were sometimes red and sometimes black, sometimes light and sometimes heavy, if a man could be changed now into this, now into another animal shape, if on the longest day the fields were sometimes covered with fruit, sometimes with ice and snow, the faculty of my empirical imagination would never be in a position, when representing red colour, to think of heavy cinnabar. Nor, if a certain name could be given sometimes to this, sometimes to that object, or if that the same object could sometimes be called by one, and sometimes by another name, without any rule to which representations are subject by themselves, would it be possible that any empirical synthesis of reproduction should ever take place.

There must therefore be something to make this reproduction of phenomena possible by being itself the foundation *a priori* of a necessary synthetical unity of them. This becomes clear if we only remember that all phenomena are not things by themselves, but only the play of our representations, all of which are in the end determinations only of the internal sense. If therefore we could prove that even our purest intuitions *a priori* give us no knowledge, unless they contain such a combination of the manifold as to render a constant synthesis of reproduction possible, it would follow that this synthesis of the imagination is, before all experience, founded on principles *a priori*, and that we must admit a pure transcendental synthesis of imagination which forms even the foundation of the possibility of all experience, such experience being impossible without the reproductibility of phenomena. Now, when I draw a line in thought, or if I think the time from one noon to another, or if I only represent to myself a certain number, it is clear that I must first necessarily apprehend one of these manifold representations after another. If I were to lose from my thoughts what precedes, whether the first parts of a line or the antecedent portions of time, or the numerical unities representing one after the other, and if, while I proceed to what follows, I were unable to reproduce what came before, there would never be a complete representation, and none of the before-mentioned thoughts, not even the first and purest representations of space and time, could ever arise within us.

The synthesis of apprehension is therefore inseparably connected with the synthesis of reproduction, and as the former constitutes the transcendental ground of the possibility of all knowledge in general (not only of empirical, but also of pure *a priori* knowledge), it follows that a reproductive synthesis of imagination belongs to the transcendental acts of the soul. We may therefore call this faculty the transcendental faculty of imagination.

III

Of the Synthesis of Recognition in Concepts

Without our being conscious that what we are thinking now is the same as what we thought a moment before, all reproduction in the series of representations would be vain. Each representation would, in its present state, be a new one, and in no wise belonging to the act by which it was to be produced by degrees, and the manifold in it would never form a whole, because deprived of that unity which consciousness alone can impart to it. If in counting I forget that the unities which now present themselves to my mind have been added gradually one to the other, I should not know the production of the quantity by the successive addition of one to one, nor should I know consequently the number, produced by the counting, this number being a concept consisting entirely in the consciousness of that unity of synthesis.

The very word of concept (Begriff) could have suggested this remark, for it is the *one* consciousness which unites the manifold that has been perceived successively, and afterwards reproduced into one representation. This consciousness may often be very faint, and we may connect it with the effect only, and not with the act itself, i.e. with the production of a representation. But in spite of this, that consciousness, though deficient in pointed clearness, must always be there, and without it, concepts, and with them, knowledge of objects are perfectly impossible.

And here we must needs arrive at a clear understanding of what we mean by an object of representations. We said before that phenomena are nothing but sensuous representations, which therefore by themselves must not be taken for objects outside our faculty of representation. What then do we mean if we speak of an object corresponding to, and therefore also different from our knowledge? It is easy to see that such an object can only be conceived as something in general $= x$: because, beside our knowledge, we have absolutely nothing which we could put down as corresponding to that knowledge.

Now we find that our conception of the relation of all knowledge to its object contains something of necessity, the object being looked upon as that which prevents our knowledge from being determined at haphazard, and causes it to be determined *a priori* in a certain way, because, as they are all to refer to an object, they must necessarily, with regard to that object, agree with each other, that is to say, possess that unity which constitutes the concept of an object.

It is clear also that, as we can only deal with the manifold in our representations, and as the x corresponding to them (the object), since it is to be something different from all our representations, is really nothing to us, it is clear, I say, that the unity, necessitated by the object, cannot be anything but the formal unity of our consciousness in the synthesis of the manifold in our representations. Then and then only do we say that we know an object, if we have produced synthetical unity in the manifold of intuition. Such unity is impossible, if the intuition could not be produced, according to a rule, by such a function of synthesis as makes the reproduction of the manifold *a priori* necessary, and a concept in which that manifold is united, possible. Thus we conceive a triangle as an object, if we are conscious of the combination of three straight lines, according to a rule, which renders such an intuition possible at all times. This *unity of rule* determines the manifold and limits it to conditions which render the unity of apperception possible, and the concept of that unity is really the representation of the object $= x$, which I think, by means of the predicates of a triangle.

No knowledge is possible without a concept, however obscure or imperfect it may be, and a concept is always, with regard to its form, something general, something that can serve as a rule. Thus the concept of body serves as a rule to our knowledge of external phenomena, according to the unity of the manifold which is thought by it. It can only be such a rule of intuitions because representing, in any given phenomena, the necessary reproduction of their manifold elements, or the synthetical unity in our consciousness of them. Thus the concept of body, whenever we perceive something outside us, necessitates the representation of extension, and, with it, those of impermeability, shape, etc.

Necessity is always founded on transcendental conditions. There must be therefore a transcendental ground of the unity of our consciousness in the synthesis of the manifold of all our intuitions, and therefore also a transcendental ground of all concepts of objects in general, and therefore again of all objects of experience, without which it would be impossible to add to our intuitions the thought of an object, for the object

is no more than that something of which the concept predicates
such a necessity of synthesis.

That original and transcendental condition is nothing else
but what I call *transcendental apperception*. The consciousness of oneself, according to the determinations of our state,
is, with all our internal perceptions, empirical only, and always
transient. There can be no fixed or permanent self in that
stream of internal phenomena. It is generally called the *internal sense,* or the empirical apperception. What is necessarily
to be represented as numerically identical with itself, cannot
be thought as such by means of empirical data only. It must
be a condition which precedes all experience, and in fact renders it possible, for thus only could such a transcendental supposition acquire validity.

No knowledge can take place in us, no conjunction or unity
of one kind of knowledge with another, without that unity of
consciousness which precedes all data of intuition, and without
reference to which no representation of objects is possible.
This pure, original, and unchangeable consciousness I shall call
transcendental apperception. That it deserves such a name
may be seen from the fact that even the purest objective unity,
namely, that of the concepts *a priori* (space and time), is possible only by a reference of all intuitions to it. The numerical
unity of that apperception therefore forms the *a priori* condition of all concepts, as does the manifoldness of space and
time of the intuitions of the senses.

The same transcendental unity of apperception constitutes,
in all possible phenomena which may come together in our
experience, a connection of all these representations according
to laws. For that unity of consciousness would be impossible,
if the mind, in the knowledge of the manifold, could not become conscious of the identity of function, by which it unites
the manifold synthetically in one knowledge. Therefore the
original and necessary consciousness of the identity of oneself
is at the same time a consciousness of an equally necessary
unity of the synthesis of all phenomena according to concepts,
that is, according to rules, which render them not only necessarily reproducible, but assign also to their intuition an object,
that is, a concept of something in which they are necessarily
united. The mind could never conceive the identity of itself in
the manifoldness of its representations (and this *a priori*) if it
did not clearly perceive the identity of its action, by which it
subjects all synthesis of apprehension (which is empirical) to a
transcendental unity, and thus renders its regular coherence *a*

priori possible. When we have clearly perceived this, we shall be able to determine more accurately our concept of an object in general. All representations have, as representations, their object, and can themselves in turn become objects of other representations. The only objects which can be given to us immediately are phenomena, and whatever in them refers immediately to the object is called intuition. These phenomena, however, are not things in themselves, but representations only which have their object, but an object that can no longer be seen by us, and may therefore be called the not-empirical, that is, the transcendental object, $= x$.

The pure concept of such a transcendental object (which in reality in all our knowledge is always the same $= x$) is that which alone can give to all our empirical concepts a relation to an object or objective reality. That concept cannot contain any definite intuition, and can therefore refer to that unity only, which must be found in the manifold of our knowledge, so far as it stands in relation to an object. That relation is nothing else but a necessary unity of consciousness, and therefore also of the synthesis of the manifold, by a common function of the mind, which unites it in one representation. As that unity must be considered as *a priori* necessary (because, without it, our knowledge would be without an object), we may conclude that the relation to a transcendental object, that is, the objective reality of our empirical knowledge, rests on a transcendental law, that all phenomena, if they are to give us objects, must be subject to rules *a priori* of a synthetical unity of these objects, by which rules alone their mutual relation in an empirical intuition becomes possible: that is, they must be subject, in experience, to the conditions of the necessary unity of apperception quite as much as, in mere intuition, to the formal conditions of space and time. Without this no knowledge is possible.

IV

Preliminary Explanation of the Possibility of the Categories as Knowledge a priori

There is but one experience in which all perceptions are represented as in permanent and regular connection, as there is but one space and one time in which all forms of phenomena and all relations of being or not being take place. If we speak of different experiences, we only mean different perceptions so far as they belong to one and the same general experience. It is the permanent and synthetical unity of perceptions that constitutes the form of experience, and experience is nothing but the synthetical unity of phenomena according to concepts.

Unity of synthesis, according to empirical concepts, would be purely accidental, nay, unless these were founded on a transcendental ground of unity, a whole crowd of phenomena might rush into our soul, without ever forming real experience. All relation between our knowledge and its objects would be lost at the same time, because that knowledge would no longer be held together by general and necessary laws; it would therefore become thoughtless intuition, never knowledge, and would be to us the same as nothing.

The conditions *a priori* of any possible experience in general are at the same time conditions of the possibility of any objects of our experience. Now I maintain that the categories of which we are speaking are nothing but the conditions of thought which make experience possible, as much as space and time contain the conditions of that intuition which forms experience. These categories therefore are also fundamental concepts by which we think objects in general for the phenomena, and have therefore *a priori* objective validity. This is exactly what we wish to prove.

The possibility, nay the necessity of these categories rests on the relation between our whole sensibility, and therefore all possible phenomena, and that original apperception in which everything must be necessarily subject to the conditions of the permanent unity of self-consciousness, that is, must submit to the general functions of that synthesis which we call synthesis according to concepts, by which alone our apperception can prove its permanent and necessary identity *a priori*. Thus the concept of cause is nothing but a synthesis of that which follows in temporal succession, with other phenomena, but a synthesis according to concepts: and without such a unity which rests on a rule *a priori*, and subjects all phenomena to itself, no permanent and general, and therefore necessary unity of consciousness would be formed in the manifold of our perceptions. Such perceptions would then belong to no experience at all, they would be without an object, a blind play of representations,—less even than a dream.

All attempts therefore at deriving those pure concepts of the understanding from experience, and ascribing to them a purely empirical origin, are perfectly vain and useless. I shall not dwell here on the fact that a concept of cause, for instance, contains an element of necessity, which no experience can ever supply, because experience, though it teaches us that after one phenomenon something else follows habitually, can never teach us that it follows necessarily, nor that we could *a priori*, and without any limitation, derive from it, as a condition, any conclusion as to what must follow. And thus I ask with reference to that empirical rule of association, which must always be admitted if we say that everything in the succession of events is so entirely subject to rules that nothing ever happens without something preceding it on which it always follows,— What does it rest on, if it is a law of nature, nay, how is that very association possible? You call the ground for the possibility of the association of the manifold, so far as it is contained in the objects themselves, the *affinity* of the manifold. I ask, therefore, how do you make that permanent affinity by which phenomena stand, nay, must stand, under permanent laws, conceivable to yourselves?

According to my principles it is easily conceivable. All possible phenomena belong, as representations, to the whole of our possible self-consciousness. From this, as a transcendental representation, numerical identity is inseparable and *a priori* certain, because nothing can become knowledge except by means of that original apperception. As this identity must necessarily enter into the synthesis of the whole of the manifold of phenomena, if that synthesis is to become empirical knowledge, it follows that the phenomena are subject to conditions *a priori* to which their synthesis (in apprehension) must always conform. The representation of a general condition according to which something manifold *can* be arranged (with uniformity) is called a *rule*, if it *must* be so arranged, a *law*. All phenomena therefore stand in a permanent connection according to necessary laws, and thus possess that transcendental affinity of which the empirical is a mere consequence.

It sounds no doubt very strange and absurd that nature should have to conform to our subjective ground of apperception, nay, be dependent on it, with respect to her laws. But if we consider that what we call nature is nothing but a whole of phenomena, not a thing by itself, but a number of representations in our soul, we shall no longer be surprised that we only see her through the fundamental faculty of all our knowledge, namely, the transcendental apperception, and in that unity without which it could not be called the object (or the whole) of all possible experience, that is, nature. We shall thus also understand why we can recognise this unity *a priori*, and therefore as necessary, which would be perfectly impossible if it were given by itself and independent of the first sources of our own thinking. In that case I could not tell whence we should take the synthetical propositions of such general unity of nature. They would have to be taken from the objects of nature themselves, and as this could be done empirically only, we could derive from it none but an accidental unity, which is very different from that necessary connection which we mean when speaking of nature.

DEDUCTION OF THE PURE CONCEPTS OF THE UNDERSTANDING

SECTION III

Of the Relation of the Understanding to Objects in General, and the Possibility of Knowing Them a priori

What in the preceding section we have discussed singly and separately we shall now try to treat in connection with each other and as a whole. We saw that there are three subjective sources of knowledge on which the possibility of all experience and of the knowledge of its objects depends, namely, *sense, imagination*, and *apperception*. Each of them may be considered as empirical in its application to given phenomena; all, however, are also elements or grounds *a priori* which render their empirical application possible. *Sense* represents phenomena empirically in *perception, imagination* in *association* (and reproduction), *apperception* in the *empirical consciousness* of the identity of these reproductive representations with the phenomena by which they were given; therefore in *recognition*.

The whole of our perception rests *a priori* on pure intuition (if the perception is regarded as representation, then on time, as the form of our internal intuition), the association of it (the whole) on the pure synthesis of imagination, and our empirical consciousness of it on pure apperception, that is, on the permanent identity of oneself in the midst of all possible representations.

If we wish to follow up the internal ground of this connection of representations to that point towards which they must all converge, and where they receive for the first time that unity of knowledge which is requisite for every possible experience, we must begin with pure apperception. Intuitions are nothing to us, and do not concern us in the least, if they cannot be received into our consciousness, into which they may enter either directly or indirectly. Knowledge is impossible in any other way. We are conscious *a priori* of our own permanent identity with regard to all representations that can ever belong to our knowledge, as forming a necessary condition of the possibility of all representations (because these could not represent anything in me, unless they belonged with everything else to one consciousness and could at least be connected within it). This principle stands firm *a priori*, and may be called the *transcendental principle of the unity* of all the manifold of our representations (therefore also of intuition). This unity of the manifold in one subject is synthetical; the pure apperception therefore supplies us with a principle of the synthetical unity of the manifold in all possible intuitions.*

This synthetical unity, however, presupposes or involves a synthesis, and if that unity is necessary *a priori*, the synthesis also must be *a priori*. The transcendental unity of apperception therefore refers to the pure synthesis of imagination as a con-

---

* This point is of great importance and should be carefully considered. All representations have a necessary relation to some possible empirical consciousness, for if they did not possess that relation, and if it were entirely impossible to become conscious of them, this would be the same as if they did not exist. All empirical consciousness has a necessary relation to a transcendental consciousness, which precedes all single experiences, namely, the consciousness of my own self as the original apperception. It is absolutely necessary therefore that in my knowledge all consciousness should belong to one consciousness of my own self. Here we have a synthetical unity of the manifold (consciousness) which can be known *a priori,* and which may thus supply a foundation for synthetical propositions *a priori* concerning pure thinking in the same way as space and time supply a foundation for synthetical propositions which concern the form of mere intuition.

The synthetical proposition that the different kinds of empirical consciousness must be connected in one self-consciousness, is the very first and synthetical foundation of all our thinking. It should be remembered that the mere representation of the Ego in reference to all other representations (the collective unity of which would be impossible without it) constitutes our transcendental consciousness. It does not matter whether that representation is clear (empirical consciousness) or confused, not even whether it is real; but the possibility of the logical form of all knowledge rests necessarily on the relation to this apperception *as a faculty.*

dition *a priori* of the possibility of the manifold being united in one knowledge. Now there can take place *a priori* the productive synthesis of imagination only, because the reproductive rests on conditions of experience. The principle therefore of the necessary unity of the pure (productive) synthesis of imagination, before all apperception, constitutes the ground of the possibility of all knowledge, nay, of all experience.

The synthesis of the manifold in imagination is called transcendental, if, without reference to the difference of intuitions, it affects only the *a priori* conjunction of the manifold; and the unity of that synthesis is called transcendental if, with reference to the original unity of apperception, it is represented as *a priori* necessary. As the possibility of all knowledge depends on the unity of that apperception, it follows that the transcendental unity of the synthesis of imagination is the pure form of all possible knowledge through which therefore all objects of possible experience must be represented *a priori*.

This unity of apperception with reference to the synthesis of imagination is the *understanding,* and the same unity with reference to the transcendental synthesis of the imagination, the *pure understanding*. It must be admitted therefore that there exist in the understanding pure forms of knowledge *a priori*, which contain the necessary unity of the pure synthesis of the imagination in reference to all possible phenomena. These are the categories, that is, the pure concepts of the understanding. The empirical faculty of knowledge of man contains therefore by necessity an understanding which refers to all objects of the senses, though by intuition only, and by its synthesis through imagination, and all phenomena, as data of a possible experience, must conform to that understanding. As this relation of phenomena to a possible experience is likewise necessary, (because, without it, we should receive no knowledge through them, and they would not in the least concern us), it follows that the pure understanding constitutes by the means of the categories a formal and synthetical principle of all experience, and that phenomena have thus a necessary relation to the understanding.

We shall now try to place the necessary connection of the understanding with the phenomena by means of the categories more clearly before the reader, by beginning with the beginning, namely, with the empirical.

The first that is given us is the *phenomenon,* which, if connected with consciousness, is called *perception*. (Without its relation to an at least possible consciousness, the phenomenon could never become to us an object of knowledge. It would therefore be nothing to us; and because it has no objective reality in itself, but exists only in being known, it would be nothing altogether.) As every phenomenon contains a manifold, and different perceptions are found in the mind singly and scattered, a connection of them is necessary, such as they cannot have in the senses by themselves. There exists therefore in us an active power for the synthesis of the manifold which we call imagination, and the function of which, as applied to perceptions, I call *apprehension*.* This imagination is meant to change the manifold of intuition into an image, it must therefore first receive the impressions into its activity, which I call *to apprehend*.

It must be clear, however, that even this apprehension of the manifold could not alone produce a coherence of impressions or an image, without some subjective power of calling one perception from which the mind has gone over to another back to that which follows, and thus forming whole series of perceptions. This is the reproductive faculty of imagination which is and can be empirical only.

If representations, as they happen to meet with one another, could reproduce each other at haphazard, they would have no definite coherence, but would form irregular agglomerations only, and never produce knowledge. It is necessary therefore that their reproduction should be subject to a rule by which one representation connects itself in imagination with a second and not with a third. It is this subjective and empirical ground of reproduction according to rules, which is called the *association* of representations.

If this unity of association did not possess an objective foundation also, which makes it impossible that phenomena should be apprehended by imagination in any other way but under the condition of a possible synthetical unity of that apprehension, it would be a mere accident that phenomena lend themselves to a certain connection in human knowledge. Though we might have the power of associating perceptions, it would still be a matter of uncertainty and chance whether they them-

---

* It has hardly struck any psychologist that this imagination is a necessary ingredient of perception. This was partly owing to their confining this faculty to reproduction, partly to our belief that the senses do not only give us impressions, but compound them also for us, thus producing pictures of objects. This, however, beyond our receptivity of impressions, requires something more, namely, a function for their synthesis.

selves are associable; and, in case they should not be so, a
number of perceptions, nay, the whole of our sensibility, might
possibly contain a great deal of empirical consciousness, but
in a separate state, nay, without belonging to the *one* consciousness of myself, which, however, is impossible. Only by ascribing all perceptions to one consciousness (the original apperception) can I say of all of them that I am conscious of them.
It must be therefore an objective ground, that is, one that
can be understood as existing *a priori,* and before all empirical
laws of imagination, on which alone the possibility, nay, even
the necessity of a law can rest, which pervades all phenomena,
and which makes us look upon them all, without exception,
as data of the senses, associable by themselves, and subject
to general rules of a permanent connection in their reproduction. This objective ground of all association of phenomena I
call their *affinity,* and this can nowhere be found except in the
principle of the unity of apperception applied to all knowledge
which is to belong to me. According to it all phenomena, without exception, must so enter into the mind or be apprehended
as to agree with the unity of apperception. This, without a
synthetical unity in their connection, which is therefore necessary objectively also, would be impossible.

We have thus seen that the objective unity of all (empirical)
consciousness in one consciousness (that of the original apperception) is the necessary condition even of all possible perception, while the affinity of all phenomena (near or remote) is a
necessary consequence of a synthesis in imagination which is
a priori founded on rules.

Imagination is therefore likewise the power of a synthesis
a priori which is the reason why we called it productive imagination, and so far as this aims at nothing but the necessary
unity in the synthesis of all the manifold in phenomena, it may
be called the transcendental function of imagination. However
strange therefore it may appear at first, it must nevertheless
have become clear by this time that the affinity of phenomena
and with it their association, and through that, lastly, their reproduction also according to laws, that is, the whole of our
experience, becomes possible only by means of that transcendental function of imagination, without which no concepts of
objects could ever come together in one experience.

It is the permanent and unchanging Ego (or pure apperception) which forms the correlative of all our representations,
if we are to become conscious of them, and all consciousness
belongs quite as much to such an all-embracing pure apper-

ception as all sensuous intuition belongs, as a representation, to a pure internal intuition, namely, time. This apperception it is which must be added to pure imagination, in order to render its function intellectual. For by itself, the synthesis of imagination, though carried out *a priori,* is always sensuous, and only connects the manifold as it appears in intuition, for instance, the shape of a triangle. But when the manifold is brought into relation with the unity of apperception, concepts which belong to the understanding become possible, but only as related to sensuous intuition through imagination.

We have therefore a pure imagination as one of the fundamental faculties of the human soul, on which all knowledge *a priori* depends. Through it we bring the manifold of intuition on one side in connection with the condition of the necessary unity of pure apperception on the other. These two extreme ends, sense and understanding, must be brought into contact with each other by means of the transcendental function of imagination, because, without it, the senses might give us phenomena, but no objects of empirical knowledge, therefore no experience. Real experience, which is made up of apprehension, association (reproduction), and lastly recognition of phenomena, contains in this last and highest (among the purely empirical elements of experience) concepts, which render possible the formal unity of experience, and with it, all objective validity (truth) of empirical knowledge. These grounds for the recognition of the manifold, so far as they concern the form only of experience in general, are our categories. On them is founded the whole formal unity in the synthesis of imagination and, through it, of[6] the whole empirical use of them (in recognition, reproduction, association, and apprehension) down to the very phenomena, because it is only by means of those elements of knowledge that the phenomena can belong to our consciousness and therefore to ourselves.

It is we therefore who carry into the phenomena which we call nature, order and regularity, nay, we should never find them in nature, if we ourselves, or the nature of our mind, had not originally placed them there. For the unity of nature is meant to be a necessary and *a priori* certain unity in the connection of all phenomena. And how should we *a priori* have arrived at such a synthetical unity, if the subjective grounds of such unity were not contained *a priori* in the original sources of our knowledge, and if those subjective conditions did not

[6] *Of* may be omitted, if we read *aller empirischer Gebrauch.*

at the same time possess objective validity, as being the grounds on which alone an object becomes possible in our experience?

We have before given various definitions of the understanding, by calling it the spontaneity of knowledge (as opposed to the receptivity of the senses), or the faculty of thinking, or the faculty of concepts or of judgments; all of these explanations, if more closely examined, coming to the same. We may now characterise it as *the faculty of rules.* This characteristic is more significant, and approaches nearer to the essence of the understanding. The senses give us forms (of intuition), the understanding rules, being always busy to examine phenomena, in order to discover in them some kind of rule. Rules, so far as they are objective (therefore necessarily inherent in our knowledge of an object), are called laws. Although experience teaches us many laws, yet these are only particular determinations of higher laws, the highest of them, to which all others are subject, springing *a priori* from the understanding; not being derived from experience, but, on the contrary, imparting to the phenomena their regularity, and thus making experience possible. The understanding therefore is not only a power of making rules by a comparison of phenomena, it is itself the lawgiver of nature, and without the understanding nature, that is, a synthetical unity of the manifold of phenomena, according to rules, would be nowhere to be found, because phenomena, as such, cannot exist without us, but exist in our sensibility only. This sensibility, as an object of our knowledge in any experience, with everything it may contain, is possible only in the unity of apperception, which unity of apperception is transcendental ground of the necessary order of all phenomena in an experience. The same unity of apperception with reference to the manifold of representations (so as to determine it out of one)[7] forms what we call the rule, and the faculty of these rules I call the understanding. As possible experience therefore, all phenomena depend in the same way *a priori* on the understanding, and receive their formal possibility from it as, when looked upon as mere intuitions, they depend on sensibility, and become possible through it, so far as their form is concerned.

However exaggerated therefore and absurd it may sound, that the understanding is itself the source of the laws of nature, and of its formal unity, such a statement is nevertheless correct and in accordance with experience. It is quite true,

[7] That is, out of one, or out of the unity of apperception.

no doubt, that empirical laws, as such, cannot derive their
origin from the pure understanding, as little as the infinite
manifoldness of phenomena could be sufficiently comprehended through the pure form of sensuous intuition. But all
empirical laws are only particular determinations of the pure
laws of the understanding, under which and according to
which the former become possible, and phenomena assume
a regular form, quite as much as all phenomena, in spite of
the variety of their empirical form, must always submit to the
conditions of the pure form of sensibility.

The pure understanding is therefore in the categories the
law of the synthetical unity of all phenomena, and thus makes
experience, so far as its form is concerned, for the first time
possible. This, and no more than this, we were called upon to
prove in the transcendental deduction of the categories,
namely, to make the relation of the understanding to our sensibility, and through it to all objects of experience, that is the
objective validity of the pure concepts *a priori* of the understanding, conceivable, and thus to establish their origin and
their truth.

Summary Representation

OF THE CORRECTNESS AND OF THE ONLY POSSIBILITY OF THIS DEDUCTION OF THE PURE CONCEPTS OF THE UNDERSTANDING

If the objects with which our knowledge has to deal were
things by themselves, we could have no concepts *a priori* of
them. For where should we take them? If we took them from
the object (without asking even the question, how that object
could be known to us) our concepts would be empirical only,
not concepts *a priori*. If we took them from within ourselves,
then that which is within us only, could not determine the
nature of an object different from our representations, that is,
supply a ground why there should be a thing to which something like what we have in our thoughts really belongs, and
why all this representation should not rather be altogether
empty. But if, on the contrary, we have to deal with phenomena only, then it becomes not only possible, but necessary,
that certain concepts *a priori* should precede our empirical
knowledge of objects. For being phenomena, they form an
object that is within us only, because a mere modification of

our sensibility can never exist outside us. The very idea that all these phenomena, and therefore all objects with which we have to deal, are altogether within me, or determinations of my own identical self, implies by itself the necessity of a permanent unity of them in one and the same apperception. In that unity of a possible consciousness consists also the form of all knowledge of objects, by which the manifold is thought as belonging to *one* object. The manner therefore in which the manifold of sensuous representation (intuition) belongs to our consciousness, precedes all knowledge of an object, as its intellectual form, and constitutes a kind of formal *a priori* knowledge of all objects in general, if they are to be thought (categories). Their synthesis by means of pure imagination, and the unity of all representations with reference to the original apperception, precede all empirical knowledge. Pure concepts of the understanding are therefore *a priori* possible, nay, with regard to experience, necessary, for this simple reason, because our knowledge has to deal with nothing but phenomena, the possibility of which depends on ourselves, and the connection and unity of which (in the representation of an object) can be found in ourselves only, as antecedent to all experience, nay, as first rendering all experience possible, so far as its form is concerned. On this ground, as the only possible one, our deduction of the categories has been carried out.]

TRANSCENDENTAL ANALYTIC

Book II

ANALYTIC OF PRINCIPLES

General logic is built up on a plan that coincides accurately with the division of the higher faculties of knowledge. These are, *Understanding, Judgment,* and *Reason.* Logic therefore treats in its analytical portion of *concepts, judgments,* and *syllogisms* corresponding with the functions and the order of the above-named faculties of the mind, which are generally comprehended under the vague name of the understanding.

As formal logic takes no account of the contents of our

knowledge (pure or empirical), but treats of the form of thought only (discursive knowledge), it may well contain in its analytical portion the canon of reason also, reason being, according to its form, subject to definite rules which, without reference to the particular nature of the knowledge to which they are applied, can be found out *a priori* by a mere analysis of the acts of reasoning into their component parts.

Transcendental logic, being limited to a certain content, namely, to pure knowledge *a priori,* cannot follow general logic in this division; for it is clear that the *transcendental use of reason* cannot be objectively valid, and cannot therefore belong to the *logic of truth,* that is, to Analytic, but must be allowed to form a separate part of our scholastic system, as a *logic of illusion,* under the name of *transcendental Dialectic.*

Understanding and judgment have therefore a canon of their objectively valid, and therefore true use in transcendental logic, and belong to its analytical portion. But reason, in its attempts to determine anything *a priori* with reference to objects, and to extend knowledge beyond the limits of possible experience, is altogether dialectical, and its illusory assertions have no place in a canon such as Analytic demands.

Our Analytic of principles therefore will be merely a canon of the faculty of judgment, teaching it how to apply to phenomena the concepts of the understanding, which contain the condition of rules *a priori.* For this reason, and in order to indicate my purpose more clearly, I shall use the name of *doctrine of the faculty of judgment,* while treating of the real *principles of the understanding.*

INTRODUCTION

OF THE TRANSCENDENTAL FACULTY OF JUDGMENT IN GENERAL

If the understanding is explained as the faculty of rules, the faculty of judgment consists in performing the subsumption under these rules, that is, in determining whether anything falls under a given rule (*casus datæ legis*) or not. General logic contains no precepts for the faculty of judgment and cannot contain them. For as it takes no account of the contents of our knowledge, it has only to explain analytically the mere form of knowledge in concepts, judgments, and syllogisms, and thus to establish formal rules for the proper employment of the understanding. If it were to attempt to show in general how anything should be arranged under these rules, and how we should determine whether something falls under them or not, this could only take place by means of a new rule. This, because it is a new rule, requires a new precept for the faculty of judgment, and we thus learn that, though the understanding is capable of being improved and instructed by means of rules, the faculty of judgment is a special talent which cannot be taught, but must be practised. This is what constitutes our so-called mother-wit, the absence of which cannot be remedied by any schooling. For although the teacher may offer, and as it were graft into a narrow understanding, plenty of rules borrowed from the experience of others, the faculty of using them rightly must belong to the pupil himself, and without that talent no precept that may be given is safe from abuse.* A physician, therefore, a judge, or a politician, may carry in his head many beautiful pathological, juridical, or political rules, nay, he may even become an accurate teacher of them, and he may yet in the application of these rules commit many a blunder, either because he is deficient in judgment, though not in understanding, knowing the general in the abstract, but unable to determine whether a concrete case falls under it; or, it may be, because his judgment has not been sufficiently trained by examples and practical experience. It is the one great advantage of examples that they sharpen the faculty of judgment, but they are apt to impair the accuracy and precision of the understanding, because they fulfil but rarely the conditions of the rule quite adequately (as *casus in terminis*). Nay, they often weaken the effort of the understanding in comprehending rules according to their general adequacy, and independent of the special circumstances of experience, and accustom us to use those rules in the end as formulas rather than as principles. Examples may

---

* Deficiency in the faculty of judgment is really what we call stupidity, and there is no remedy for that. An obtuse and narrow mind, deficient in nothing but a proper degree of understanding and correct concepts, may be improved by study, so far as to become even learned. But as even then there is often a deficiency of judgment (*secunda Petri*) we often meet with very learned men, who in handling their learning betray that original deficiency which can never be mended.

thus be called the go-cart of the judgment, which those who are deficient in that natural talent[1] can never do without.

But although general logic can give no precepts to the faculty of judgment, the case is quite different with transcendental logic, so that it even seems as if it were the proper business of the latter to correct and to establish by definite rules the faculty of the judgment in the use of the pure understanding. For as a doctrine and a means of enlarging the field of pure knowledge *a priori* for the benefit of the understanding, philosophy does not seem necessary, but rather hurtful, because, in spite of all attempts that have been hitherto made, hardly a single inch of ground has been gained by it. For critical purposes, however, and in order to guard the faculty of judgment against mistakes (*lapsus judicii*) in its use of the few pure concepts of the understanding which we possess, philosophy (though its benefits may be negative only) has to employ all the acuteness and penetration at its command.

What distinguishes transcendental philosophy is, that besides giving the rules (or rather the general condition of rules) which are contained in the pure concept of the understanding, it can at the same time indicate *a priori* the case to which each rule may be applied. The superiority which it enjoys in this respect over all other sciences, except mathematics, is due to this, that it treats of concepts which are meant to refer to their objects *a priori,* so that their objective validity cannot be proved *a posteriori,* because this would not affect their own peculiar dignity. It must show, on the contrary, by means of general but sufficient marks, the conditions under which objects can be given corresponding to those concepts; otherwise these would be without any contents, mere logical forms, and not pure concepts of the understanding.

Our transcendental doctrine of the faculty of judgment will consist of two chapters. The first will treat of the sensuous condition under which alone pure concepts of the understanding can be used. This is what I call the *schematism* of the pure understanding. The second will treat of the synthetical judgments, which can be derived *a priori* under these conditions from pure concepts of the understanding, and on which all knowledge *a priori* depends. It will treat, therefore, of the principles of the pure understanding.

[1] *Desselben* has been changed into *derselben* in later editions. *Desselben,* however, may be meant to refer to *Urtheil,* as contained in *Urtheilskraft.* The Second Edition has *desselben.*

THE TRANSCENDENTAL DOCTRINE OF THE FACULTY OF JUDGMENT OR ANALYTIC OF PRINCIPLES

CHAPTER I

OF THE SCHEMATISM OF THE PURE CONCEPTS OF THE UNDERSTANDING

In comprehending any object under a concept, the representation of the former must be homogeneous with the latter,[2] that is, the concept must contain that which is represented in the object to be comprehended under it, for this is the only meaning of the expression that an object is comprehended under a concept. Thus, for instance, the empirical concept of a plate is homogeneous with the pure geometrical concept of a circle, the roundness which is conceived in the first forming an object of intuition in the latter.

Now it is clear that pure concepts of the understanding, as compared with empirical or sensuous impressions in general, are entirely heterogeneous, and can never be met with in any intuition. How then can the latter be comprehended under the former, or how can the categories be applied to phenomena, as no one is likely to say that causality, for instance, could be seen through the senses, and was contained in the phenomenon? It is really this very natural and important question which renders a transcendental doctrine of the faculty of judgment necessary, in order to show how it is possible that any of the pure concepts of the understanding can be applied to phenomena. In all other sciences in which the concepts by which the object is thought in general are not so heterogeneous or different from those which represent it *in concreto,* and as it is given, there is no necessity to enter into any discussions as to the applicability of the former to the latter.

In our case there must be some third thing homogeneous on the one side with the category, and on the other with the phenomenon, to render the application of the former to the

---

[2] Read *dem letzteren,* as corrected by Rosenkranz, for *der letzteren.*

latter possible. This intermediate representation must be pure (free from all that is empirical) and yet intelligible on the one side, and sensuous on the other. Such a representation is the *transcendental schema.*

The concept of the understanding contains pure synthetical unity of the manifold in general. Time, as the formal condition of the manifold in the internal sense, consequently of the conjunction of all representations, contains a manifold *a priori* in pure intuition. A transcendental determination of time is so far homogeneous with the category (which constitutes its unity) that it is general and founded on a rule *a priori;* and it is on the other hand so far homogeneous with the phenomenon, that time must be contained in every empirical representation of the manifold. The application of the category to phenomena becomes possible therefore by means of the transcendental determination of time, which, as a *schema* of the concepts of the understanding, allows the phenomena to be comprehended under the category.

After what has been said in the deduction of the categories, we hope that nobody will hesitate in answering the question whether these pure concepts of the understanding allow only of an empirical or also of a transcendental application, that is, whether, as conditions of a possible experience, they refer *a priori* to phenomena only, or whether, as conditions of the possibility of things in general, they may be extended to objects by themselves (without restriction to our sensibility). For there we saw that concepts are quite impossible, and cannot have any meaning unless there be an object given either to them or, at least, to some of the elements of which they consist, and that they can never refer to things by themselves (without regard as to whether and how things may be given to us). We likewise saw that the only way in which objects can be given to us, consists in a modification of our sensibility, and lastly, that pure concepts *a priori* must contain, besides the function of the understanding in the category itself, formal conditions *a priori* of sensibility (particularly of the internal sense) which form the general condition under which alone the category may be applied to any object. We shall call this formal and pure condition of sensibility, to which the concept of the understanding is restricted in its application, its *schema;* and the function of the understanding in these schemata, the *schematism of the pure understanding.*

The schema by itself is no doubt a product of the imagination only, but as the synthesis of the imagination does not aim at a single intuition, but at some kind of unity alone in the determination of sensibility, the schema ought to be distinguished from the image. Thus, if I place five points, one after the other . . . . . , this is an image of the number five. If, on the contrary, I think of a number in general, whether it be five or a hundred, this thinking is rather the representation of a method of representing in one image a certain quantity (for instance a thousand) according to a certain concept, than the image itself, which, in the case of a thousand, I could hardly take in and compare with the concept. This representation of a general procedure of the imagination by which a concept receives its image, I call the schema of such concept.

The fact is that our pure sensuous concepts do not depend on images of objects, but on schemata. No image of a triangle in general could ever be adequate to its concept. It would never attain to that generality of the concept, which makes it applicable to all triangles, whether right-angled, or acute-angled, or anything else, but would always be restricted to one portion only of the sphere of the concept. The schema of the triangle can exist nowhere but in thought, and is in fact a rule for the synthesis of imagination with respect to pure forms in space. Still less does an object of experience or its image ever cover the empirical concept, which always refers directly to the schema of imagination as a rule for the determination of our intuitions, according to a certain general concept. The concept of dog means a rule according to which my imagination can always draw a general outline of the figure of a four-footed animal, without being restricted to any particular figure supplied by experience or to any possible image which I may draw in the concrete. This schematism of our understanding applied to phenomena and their mere form is an art hidden in the depth of the human soul, the true secrets of which we shall hardly ever be able to guess and reveal. So much only we can say, that the *image* is a product of the empirical faculty of the productive imagination, while the *schema* of sensuous concepts (such as of figures in space) is a product and so to say a monogram of the pure imagination *a priori*, through which and according to which images themselves become possible, though they are never fully adequate to the concept, and can be connected with it by means of their schema only. The schema of a pure concept of the understanding, on the contrary, is something which can never be made into an image; for it is nothing but the pure synthesis determined by a rule of unity, according to concepts, a synthesis as expressed by the category, and represents a transcendental product of the imagination, a product which concerns the determination of the internal sense in general, under the conditions of its form (time), with reference to all representations, so far as these are meant to be joined *a priori* in one concept, according to the unity of apperception.

Without dwelling any longer on a dry and tedious determination of all that is required for the transcendental schemata of the pure concepts of the understanding in general, we shall proceed at once to represent them according to the order of the categories, and in connection with them.

The pure image of all quantities (*quanta*) before the external sense, is space; that of all objects of the senses in general, time. The pure schema of quantity (*quantitas*), however, as a concept of the understanding, is *number,* a representation which comprehends the successive addition of one to one (homogeneous). Number therefore is nothing but the unity of the synthesis of the manifold (repetition) of a homogeneous intuition in general, I myself producing the time in the apprehension of the intuition.

Reality is, in the pure concept of the understanding, that which corresponds to a sensation in general: that, therefore, the concept of which indicates by itself being (in time), while negation is that the concept of which represents not-being (in time). The opposition of the two takes place therefore by a distinction of one and the same time, as either filled or empty. As time is only the form of intuition, that is, of objects as phenomena, that which in the phenomena corresponds to sensation, constitutes the transcendental matter of all objects, as things by themselves (reality, Sachheit). Every sensation, however, has a degree of quantity by which it can fill the same time (that is, the internal sense, with reference to the same representation of an object), more or less, till it vanishes into nothing (equal to nought or negation). There exists, therefore, a relation and connection, or rather a transition from reality to negation, which makes every reality representable as a quantum; and the schema of a reality, as the quantity of something which fills time, is this very continuous and uniform production of reality in time; while we either descend from the sensation which has a certain degree, to its vanishing in time, or ascend from the negation of sensation to some quantity of it.

The schema of substance is the permanence of the real in

time, that is, the representation of it as a substratum for the empirical determination of time in general, which therefore remains while everything else changes. (It is not time that passes, but the existence of the changeable passes in time. What corresponds therefore in the phenomena to time, which in itself is unchangeable and permanent, is the unchangeable in existence, that is, substance; and it is only in it that the succession and the coexistence of phenomena can be determined according to time.)

The schema of cause and of the causality of a thing in general is the real which, when once supposed to exist, is always followed by something else. It consists therefore in the succession of the manifold, in so far as that succession is subject to a rule.

The schema of community (reciprocal action) or of the reciprocal causality of substances, in respect to their accidents, is the coexistence, according to a general rule, of the determinations of the one with those of the other.

The schema of possibility is the agreement of the synthesis of different representations with the conditions of time in general, as, for instance, when opposites cannot exist at the same time in the same thing, but only one after the other. It is therefore the determination of the representation of a thing at any time whatsoever.

The schema of reality is existence at a given time.

The schema of necessity is the existence of an object at all times.

It is clear, therefore, if we examine all the categories, that the schema of quantity contains and represents the production (synthesis) of time itself in the successive apprehension of an object; the schema of quality, the synthesis of sensation (perception) with the representation of time or the filling-up of time; the schema of relation, the relation of perceptions to each other at all times (that is, according to a rule which determines time); lastly, the schema of modality and its categories, time itself as the correlative of the determination of an object as to whether and how it belongs to time. The schemata therefore are nothing but determinations of time *a priori* according to rules, and these, as applied to all possible objects, refer in the order of the categories to the *series of time*, the *contents of time*, the *order of time*, and lastly, the *comprehension of time*.

We have thus seen that the schematism of the understanding, by means of a transcendental synthesis of imagination, amounts to nothing else but to the unity of the manifold in the intuition of the internal sense, and therefore indirectly to the unity of apperception, as an active function corresponding to the internal sense (as receptive). These schemata therefore of the pure concepts of the understanding are the true and only conditions by which these concepts can gain a relation to objects, that is, a *significance,* and the categories are thus in the end of no other but a possible empirical use, serving only, on account of an *a priori* necessary unity (the necessary connection of all consciousness in one original apperception) to subject all phenomena to general rules of synthesis, and thus to render them capable of a general connection in experience.

All our knowledge is contained within this whole of possible experience, and transcendental truth, which precedes all empirical truth and renders it possible, consists in general relation of it to that experience.

But although the schemata of sensibility serve thus to realise the categories, it must strike everybody that they at the same time restrict them, that is, limit them by conditions foreign to the understanding and belonging to sensibility. Hence the schema is really the phenomenon, or the sensuous concept of an object in agreement with the category (numerus *est quantitas phaenomenon,* sensatio *realitas phaenomenon,* constans et perdurabile rerum *substantia phaenomenon—* aeternitas *necessitas phaenomenon,* etc.). If we omit a restrictive condition, it would seem that we amplify a formerly limited concept, and that therefore the categories in their pure meaning, free from all conditions of sensibility, should be valid of things in general, *as they are,* while their schemata represent them only *as they appear,* so that these categories might claim a far more extended power, independent of all schemata. And in truth we must allow to these pure concepts of the understanding, apart from all sensuous conditions, a certain significance, though a logical one only, with regard to the mere unity of representations produced by them, although these representations have no object and therefore no meaning that could give us a concept of an object. Thus substance, if we leave out the sensuous condition of permanence, would mean nothing but a something that may be conceived as a subject, without being the predicate of anything else. Of such a representation we can make nothing, because it does not teach us how that thing is determined which is thus to be considered as the first subject. Categories, therefore, without schemata are functions only of the understanding necessary for concepts, but do not themselves represent any object. This character is given to them by sensibility only, which realises the understanding by, at the same time, restricting it.

THE TRANSCENDENTAL DOCTRINE OF THE FACULTY OF JUDGMENT OR ANALYTIC OF PRINCIPLES

CHAPTER II

SYSTEM OF ALL PRINCIPLES OF THE PURE UNDERSTANDING

We have in the preceding chapter considered the transcendental faculty of judgment with reference to those general conditions only under which it is justified in using the pure concepts of the understanding for synthetical judgments. It now becomes our duty to represent systematically those judgments which, under that critical provision, the understanding, can really produce *a priori*. For this purpose our table of categories will be without doubt our natural and best guide. For it is the relation of the categories to all possible experience which must constitute all pure *a priori* knowledge of the understanding; and their relation to sensibility in general will therefore exhibit completely and systematically all the transcendental principles of the use of the understanding.[3]

Principles *a priori* are so called, not only because they contain the grounds for other judgments, but also because they themselves are not founded on higher and more general kinds of knowledge. This peculiarity, however, does not enable them to dispense with every kind of proof; for although this could not be given objectively, as all knowledge of any object really rests on it, this does not prevent us from attempting to produce a proof drawn from the subjective sources of the possibility of a knowledge of the object in general; nay, it may be necessary to do so, because, without it, our assertion might be suspected of being purely gratuitous.

We shall treat, however, of those principles only which relate to the categories. We shall have nothing to do with the

---

[3] The insertion of *man,* as suggested by Rosenkranz, is impossible.

principles of transcendental æsthetic, according to which space and time are the conditions of the possibility of all things as phenomena, nor with the limitation of those principles, prohibiting their application to things by themselves. Mathematical principles also do not belong to this part of our discussion, because they are derived from intuition, and not from the pure concept of the understanding. As they are, however, synthetical judgments *a priori,* their possibility will have to be discussed, not in order to prove their correctness and apodictic certainty, which would be unnecessary, but in order to make the possibility of such self-evident knowledge *a priori* conceivable and intelligible.

We shall also have to speak of the principle of analytical as opposed to synthetical judgments, the latter being the proper subject of our enquiries, because this very opposition frees the theory of the latter from all misunderstandings, and places them clearly before us in their own peculiar character.

SYSTEM OF THE PRINCIPLES OF THE PURE UNDERSTANDING

SECTION I

Of the Highest Principle of all Analytical Judgments

Whatever the object of our knowledge may be, and whatever the relation between our knowledge and its object, it must always submit to that general, though only negative condition of all our judgments, that they do not contradict themselves; otherwise these judgments, without any reference to their object, are in themselves nothing. But although there may be no contradiction in our judgment, it may nevertheless connect concepts in a manner not warranted by the object, or without there being any ground, whether *a priori* or *a posteriori,* to confirm such a judgment. A judgment may therefore be false or groundless, though in itself it is free from all contradiction.

The proposition that no subject can have a predicate which contradicts it, is called *the principle of contradiction.* It is a general though only negative criterion of all truth, and belongs to logic only, because it applies to knowledge as knowledge only, without reference to its object, and simply declares that such contradiction would entirely destroy and annihilate it.

Nevertheless, a positive use also may be made of that principle, not only in order to banish falsehood and error, so far as they arise from contradiction, but also in order to discover truth. For in an analytical judgment, whether negative or affirmative, its truth can always be sufficiently tested by the principle of contradiction, because the opposite of that which exists and is thought as a concept in our knowledge of an object, is always rightly negatived, while the concept itself is necessarily affirmed of it, for the simple reason that its opposite would be in contradiction with the object.

It must therefore be admitted that the principle of contradiction is the general and altogether sufficient principle of all analytical knowledge, though beyond this its authority and utility, as a sufficient criterion of truth, must not be allowed to extend. For the fact that no knowledge can run counter to that principle, without destroying itself, makes it no doubt a *conditio sine qua non,* but never the determining reason of the truth of our knowledge. Now, as in our present enquiry we are chiefly concerned with the synthetical part of our knowledge, we must no doubt take great care never to offend against that inviolable principle, but we ought never to expect from it any help with regard to the truth of this kind of knowledge.

There is, however, a formula of this famous principle—a principle merely formal and void of all contents—which contains a synthesis that has been mixed up with it from mere carelessness and without any real necessity. This formula is: It is impossible that anything should be and at the same time not be. Here, first of all, the apodictic certainty expressed by the word *impossible* is added unnecessarily, because it is understood by itself from the nature of the proposition; secondly, the proposition is affected by the condition of time, and says, as it were, something = A, which is something = B, cannot be at the same time not-B, but it can very well be both (B and not-B) in succession. For instance, a man who is young cannot be at the same time old, but the same man may very well be young at one time and not young, that is, old, at another. The principle of contradiction, however, as a purely logical principle, must not be limited in its application by time; and the before-mentioned formula runs therefore counter to its very nature. The misunderstanding arises from our first separating one predicate of an object from its concept, and by our afterwards joining its opposite with that predicate, which gives us a contradiction, not with the subject, but with its predicate only which was synthetically connected with it, and this again only on condition that the first and second predicate have both been applied at the same time. If I want to say that a man who is unlearned is not learned, I must add the condition 'at the same time,' for a man who is unlearned at one time may very well be learned at another. But if I say no unlearned man is learned, then the proposition is analytical, because the characteristic (unlearnedness) forms part now of the concept of the subject, so that the negative proposition becomes evident directly from the principle of contradiction, and without the necessity of adding the condition, 'at the same time.' This is the reason why I have so altered the wording of that formula that it displays at once the nature of an analytical proposition.

SYSTEM OF THE PRINCIPLES OF THE PURE UNDERSTANDING

SECTION II

Of the Highest Principle of all Synthetical Judgments

The explanation of the possibility of synthetical judgments is a subject of which general logic knows nothing, not even its name, while in a transcendental logic it is the most important task of all, nay, even the only one, when we have to consider the possibility of synthetical judgments *a priori,* their conditions, and the extent of their validity. For when that task is accomplished, the object of transcendental logic, namely, to determine the extent and limits of the pure understanding, will have been fully attained.

In forming an analytical judgment I remain within a given concept, while predicating something of it. If what I predicate is affirmative, I only predicate of that concept what is already contained in it; if it is negative, I only exclude from it the opposite of it. In forming synthetical judgments, on the contrary, I have to go beyond a given concept, in order to bring something together with it, which is totally different from what is contained in it. Here we have neither the relation of identity nor of contradiction, and nothing in the judgment itself by which we can discover its truth or its falsehood.

Granted, therefore, that we must go beyond a given concept in order to compare it synthetically with another, something else is necessary in which, as in a third, the synthesis of two concepts becomes possible. What then, is that third? What is the medium of all synthetical judgments? It can only be that in which all our concepts are contained, namely, the internal sense and its *a priori* form, time. The synthesis of representations depends on imagination, but their synthetical unity, which is necessary for forming a judgment, depends on the unity of apperception. It is here therefore that the possibility of synthetical judgments, and (as all the three contain the sources of representations *a priori*) the possibility of pure synthetical judgments also, will have to be discovered; nay, they will on these grounds be necessary, if any knowledge of objects is to be obtained that rests entirely on a synthesis of representations.

If knowledge is to have any objective reality, that is to say, if it is to refer to an object, and receive by means of it any sense and meaning, the object must necessarily be given in some way or other. Without that all concepts are empty. We have thought in them, but we have not, by thus thinking, arrived at any knowledge. We have only played with representations. To give an object, if this is not meant again as mediate only, but if it means to represent something immediately in intuition, is nothing else but to refer the representation of the object to experience (real or possible). Even space and time, however pure these concepts may be of all that is empirical, and however certain it is that they are represented in the mind entirely *a priori,* would lack nevertheless all objective validity, all sense and meaning, if we could not show the necessity of their use with reference to all objects of experience. Nay, their representation is a pure schema, always referring to that reproductive imagination which calls up the objects of experience, without which objects would be meaningless. The same applies to all concepts without any distinction.

It is therefore the *possibility of experience* which alone gives objective reality to all our knowledge *a priori.* Experience, however, depends on the synthetical unity of phenomena, that is, on a synthesis according to concepts of the object of phenomena in general. Without it, it would not even be knowledge, but only a rhapsody of perceptions, which would never grow into a connected text according to the rules of an altogether coherent (possible) consciousness, nor into a tran-

scendental and necessary unity of apperception. Experience
depends therefore on *a priori* principles of its form, that is,
on general rules of unity in the synthesis of phenomena, and
the objective reality of these (rules) can always be shown by
their being the necessary conditions in all experience; nay,
even in the possibility of all experience. Without such a relation synthetical propositions *a priori* would be quite impossible, because they have no third medium, that is, no object in
which the synthetical unity of their concepts could prove their
objective reality.

Although we know therefore a great deal *a priori* in synthetical judgments with reference to space in general, or to
the figures which productive imagination traces in it, without
requiring for it any experience, this our knowledge would
nevertheless be nothing but a playing with the cobwebs of
our brain, if space were not to be considered as the condition
of phenomena which supply the material for external experience. Those pure synthetical judgments therefore refer always,
though mediately only, to possible experience, or rather to
the possibility of experience, on which alone the objective
validity of their synthesis is founded.

As therefore experience, being an empirical synthesis, is in
its possibility the only kind of knowledge that imparts reality
to every other synthesis, this other synthesis, as knowledge *a
priori,* possesses truth (agreement with its object) on this
condition only, that it contains nothing beyond what is necessary for the synthetical unity of experience in general.

The highest principle of all synthetical judgments is therefore this, that every object is subject to the necessary conditions of a synthetical unity of the manifold of intuition in a
possible experience.

Thus synthetical judgments *a priori* are possible, if we refer the formal conditions of intuition *a priori,* the synthesis
of imagination, and the necessary unity of it in a transcendental apperception, to a possible knowledge in general, given
in experience, and if we say that the conditions of the possibility of experience in general are at the same time conditions of the possibility of the objects of experience themselves,
and thus possess objective validity in a synthetical judgment
a priori.

SYSTEM OF THE PRINCIPLES OF THE PURE UNDERSTANDING

SECTION III

*Systematical Representation of all Synthetical Principles
of the Pure Understanding*

That there should be principles at all is entirely due to the
pure understanding, which is not only the faculty of rules in
regard to all that happens, but itself the source of principles,
according to which everything (that can become an object
to us) is necessarily subject to rules, because, without such,
phenomena would never become objects corresponding to
knowledge. Even laws of nature, if they are considered as
principles of the empirical use of the understanding, carry
with them a character of necessity, and thus lead to the supposition that they rest on grounds which are valid *a priori*
and before all experience. Nay, all laws of nature without
distinction are subject to higher principles of the understanding, which they apply to particular cases of experience. They
alone therefore supply the concept which contains the condition, and, as it were, the exponent of a rule in general, while
experience furnishes each case to which the general rule
applies.

There can hardly be any danger of our mistaking purely
empirical principles for principles of the pure understanding
or *vice versa*, for the character of necessity which distinguishes the concepts of the pure understanding, and the
absence of which can easily be perceived in every empirical
proposition, however general it may seem, will always prevent
their confusion. There are, however, pure principles *a priori*
which I should not like to ascribe to the pure understanding,
because they are derived, not from pure concepts, but from
pure intuitions (although by means of the understanding); the
understanding being the faculty of the concepts. We find
such principles in mathematics, but their application to experience, and therefore their objective validity, nay, even the
possibility of such synthetical knowledge *a priori* (the deduction thereof) rests always on the pure understanding.

Hence my principles will not include the principles of
mathematics, but they will include those on which the possibil-

ity and objective validity *a priori* of those mathematical principles are founded, and which consequently are to be looked upon as the source of those principles, proceeding from concepts to intuitions, and not from intuitions to concepts.

When the pure concepts of the understanding are applied to every possible experience, their synthesis is either *mathematical* or *dynamical,* for it is directed partly to the *intuition* of a phenomenon only, partly to its *existence.* The conditions *a priori* of intuition are absolutely necessary with regard to every possible experience, while the conditions of the existence of the object of a possible empirical intuition are in themselves accidental only. The principles of the mathematical use of the categories will therefore be absolutely necessary, that is apodictic, while those of their dynamical use, though likewise possessing the character of necessity *a priori,* can possess such a character subject only to the condition of empirical thought in experience, that is mediately and indirectly, and cannot therefore claim that immediate evidence which belongs to the former, although their certainty with regard to experience in general remains unaffected by this. Of this we shall be better qualified to judge at the conclusion of this system of principles.

Our table of categories gives us naturally the best instructions for drawing up a table of principles, because these are nothing but rules for the objective use of the former.

All principles of the pure understanding are therefore,

I
Axioms of Intuition.

II	III
Anticipations of Perception.	Analogies of Experience.

IV
Postulates of Empirical Thought in General.

I have chosen these names not unadvisedly, so that the difference with regard to the evidence and the application of those principles should not be overlooked. We shall soon see that, both with regard to the evidence and the *a priori* determination of phenomena according to the categories of *quantity* and *quality* (if we attend to the form of them only) their principles differ considerably from those of the other two classes, inasmuch as the former are capable of an intuitive, the latter of a merely discursive, though both of a complete certainty. I shall therefore call the former *mathematical*, the latter *dynamical* principles.* It should be observed, however, that I do not speak here either of the principles of mathematics, or of those of general physical dynamics, but only of the principles of the pure understanding in relation to the internal sense (without any regard to the actual representations given in it). It is these through which the former become possible, and I have given them their name, more on account of their application than of their contents. I shall now proceed to consider them in the same order in which they stand in the table.

* All conjunction (conjunctio) *is either* composition (compositio) *or* connection (nexus). *The former is the synthesis of a manifold the parts of which do not* belong to each other necessarily. *The two triangles, for instance, into which a square is divided by a diagonal, do by themselves not necessarily belong to each other. Such is also the synthesis of the* homogeneous, *in everything that can be considered* mathematically, *and that synthesis can be divided again into* aggregation, *and* coalition, *the former referring to* extensive, *the latter to* intensive *qualities. The latter conjunction* (nexus) *is the synthesis of a manifold, in so far as its elements* belong to each other necessarily. *Thus the accident belonging to a substance, or the effect belonging to a cause, though* heterogeneous, *are yet represented as* a priori *connected, which connection, as it is not arbitrary, I call* dynamical, *because it concerns the connection of the* existence *of the manifold. This may again be divided into the* physical *connection of phenomena among each other, and their* metaphysical *connection in the faculty of cognition* a priori. (*This forms a note in the 2nd Edition.*)

I

[Of the Axioms of Intuition

'All phenomena are, with reference to their intuition, extensive quantities']

AXIOMS OF INTUITION

Their principle is: All intuitions are extensive quantities.

Proof

All phenomena contain, so far as their form is concerned, an intuition in space and time, which forms the a priori *foundation of all of them. They cannot, therefore, be apprehended, that is, received into empirical consciousness, except through the synthesis of the manifold, by which the representations of a definite space or time are produced, i.e. through the synthesis of the homogeneous, and the consciousness of the synthetical unity of that manifold (homogeneous). Now the consciousness of the manifold and homogeneous in intuition, so far as by it the representation of an object is first rendered possible, is the concept of quantity (quantum). Therefore even the perception of an object as a phenomenon is possible only through the same synthetical unity of the manifold of the given sensuous intuition, by which the unity of the composition of the manifold and homogeneous is conceived in the concept of a* quantity; *that is, phenomena are always quantities, and extensive quantities; because as intuitions in space and time, they must be represented through the same synthesis through which space and time in general are determined.*

I call an extensive quantity that in which the representation of the whole is rendered possible by the representation of its parts, and therefore necessarily preceded by it. I cannot represent to myself any line, however small it may be, without drawing it in thought, that is, without producing all its parts one after the other, starting from a given point, and thus, first of all, drawing its intuition. The same applies to every, even the smallest portion of time. I can only think in it the successive progress from one moment to another, thus producing in the end, by all portions of time and their addition, a definite quantity of time. As in all phenomena pure intuition is either space or time, every phenomenon, as an intuition, must be an extensive quantity, because it can be known in apprehension by a successive synthesis only (of part with part). All phenomena therefore, when perceived in intuition, are aggregates (collections) of previously given parts, which is not the case with every kind of quantities, but with those only which are represented to us and apprehended as *extensive*.

On this successive synthesis of productive imagination in elaborating figures are founded the mathematics of extension with their axioms (geometry), containing the conditions of sensuous intuition *a priori*, under which alone the schema of a pure concept of an external phenomenal appearance can be produced; for instance, between two points one straight line only is possible, or two straight lines cannot enclose a space, etc. These are the axioms which properly relate only to quantities (*quanta*) as such.

But with regard to quantity (*quantitas*), that is, with regard to the answer to the question, how large something may be, there are no axioms, in the proper sense of the word, though several of the propositions referring to it possess synthetical and immediate certainty (*indemonstrabilia*). The propositions that if equals be added to equals the wholes are equal, and if equals be taken from equals the remainders are equal, are really analytical, because I am conscious immediately of the identity of my producing the one quantity with my producing the other; axioms on the contrary must be synthetical propositions *a priori*. The self-evident propositions on numerical relation again are no doubt synthetical, but they are not general, like those of geometry, and therefore cannot be called axioms, but numerical formulas only. That $7 + 5 = 12$ is not an analytical proposition. For neither in the representation of 7, nor in that of 5, nor in that of the combination of both, do I think the number 12. (That I am meant to think it in the addition of the two, is not the question here, for in every analytical proposition all depends on this, whether the predicate is really thought in the representation of the subject.) Although the proposition is synthetical, it is a singular proposition only. If in this case we consider only the synthesis of the homogeneous unities, then the synthesis can here take place in one way only, although afterwards the *use* of these numbers becomes general. If I say, a triangle can be constructed with three lines, two of which together are greater than the third, I have before me the mere function of productive imagination, which may draw the lines greater or smaller, and bring them together at various angles. The number 7, on the contrary, is possible in one way only, and so likewise the number 12, which is produced by the synthesis of the former with 5. Such propositions therefore must not be called axioms (for their number would be endless) but numerical formulas.

This transcendental principle of phenomenal mathematics adds considerably to our knowledge *a priori*. Through it alone it becomes possible to make pure mathematics in their full precision applicable to objects of experience, which without that principle would by no means be self-evident, nay, has actually provoked much contradiction. Phenomena are not things in themselves. Empirical intuition is possible only through pure intuition (of space and time), and whatever geometry says of the latter is valid without contradiction of the former. All evasions, as if objects of the senses should not conform to the rules of construction in space (for instance, to the rule of the infinite divisibility of lines or angles) must cease, for one would thus deny all objective validity to space and with it to all mathematics, and would no longer know why and how far mathematics can be applied to phenomena. The synthesis of spaces and times, as the synthesis of the essential form of all intuition, is that which renders possible at the same time the apprehension of phenomena, that is, every external experience, and therefore also all knowledge of its objects, and whatever mathematics, in their pure use prove of that synthesis is valid necessarily also of this knowledge. All objections to this are only the chicaneries of a falsely guided reason, which wrongly imagines that it can separate the objects of the senses from the formal conditions of our sensibility, and represents them, though they are phenomena only, as objects by themselves, given to the understanding. In this case, however, nothing could be known of them *a priori,* nothing could be known synthetically through pure concepts of space, and the science which determines those concepts, namely, geometry, would itself become impossible.

II

Anticipations of Perception

[The principle which anticipates all perceptions as such, is this: In all phenomena sensation, and the Real which corresponds to it in the object (*realitas phaenomenon*), has an intensive quantity, that is, a degree]

Their principle is: In all phenomena *the* Real, *which is the* object of a sensation, has intensive quantity, *that is, a degree.*

Proof

Perception is empirical consciousness, that is, a consciousness in which there is at the same time sensation. Phenomena, as objects of perception, are not pure (merely formal) intuitions, like space and time (for space and time can never be perceived by themselves). They contain, therefore, over and above the intuition, the material for some one object in general (through which something existing in space and time is represented); that is, they contain the real of sensation, as a merely subjective representation, which gives us only the consciousness that the subject is affected, and which is referred to some object in general. Now there is a gradual transition possible from empirical to pure consciousness, till the real of it vanishes completely and there remains a merely formal consciousness (a priori) of the manifold in space and time; and, therefore, a synthesis also is possible in the production of the quantity of a sensation, from its beginning, that is, from the pure intuition = 0, onwards to any quantity of it. As sensation by itself is no objective representation, and as in it the intuition of neither space nor time can be found, it follows that though not an extensive, yet some kind of quantity must belong to it (and this through the apprehension of it, in which the empirical consciousness may grow in a certain time from nothing = 0 to any amount). That quantity must be intensive, and corresponding to it, an intensive quantity, i.e. a degree of influence upon the senses, must be attributed to all objects of perception, so far as it contains sensation.

All knowledge by means of which I may know and determine *a priori* whatever belongs to empirical knowledge, may be called an anticipation, and it is no doubt in this sense that Epicurus used the expression πρόληψις. But as there is always in phenomena something which can never be known *a priori*, and constitutes the real difference between empirical and *a priori* knowledge, namely, sensation (as matter of perception), it follows that this can never be anticipated. The pure determinations, on the contrary, in space and time, as regards both figure and quantity, may be called anticipations of phenomena, because they represent *a priori*, whatever may be given *a posteriori* in experience. If, however, there should be something in every sensation that could be known *a priori* as sensation in general, even if no particular sensation be given, this would, in a very special sense, deserve to be called anticipation, because it seems extraordinary that we should anticipate experience in that which concerns the matter of experience and can be derived from experience only. Yet such is really the case.

Apprehension, by means of sensation only, fills no more than one moment (if we do not take into account the succession of many sensations). Sensation, therefore, being that in the phenomenon the apprehension of which does not form a successive synthesis progressing from parts to a complete representation, is without any extensive quantity, and the absence of sensation in one and the same moment would represent it as empty, therefore = 0. What corresponds in every empirical intuition to sensation is reality (*realitas phaenomenon*), what corresponds to its absence is negation = 0. Every sensation, however, is capable of diminution, so that it may decrease, and gradually vanish. There is therefore a continuous connection between reality in phenomena and negation, by means of many possible intermediate sensations, the difference between which is always smaller than the difference between the given sensation and zero or complete negation. It thus follows that the real in each phenomenon has always a quantity, though it is not perceived in apprehension, because apprehension takes place by a momentary sensation, not by a successive synthesis of many sensations; it does not advance from the parts to the whole, and though it has a quantity, it has not an extensive quantity.

That quantity which can be apprehended as unity only, and in which plurality can be represented by approximation only to negation = 0, I call *intensive quantity*. Every reality therefore in a phenomenon has intensive quantity, that is, a degree.

If this reality is considered as a cause (whether of sensation, or of any other reality in the phenomenon, for instance, of change) the degree of that reality as a cause we call a momentum, for instance, the momentum of gravity: and this because the degree indicates that quantity only, the apprehension of which is not successive, but momentary. This I mention here in passing, because we have not yet come to consider causality.

Every sensation, therefore, and every reality in phenomena, however small it may be, has a degree, that is, an intensive quantity which can always be diminished, and there is between reality and negation a continuous connection of possible realities, and of possible smaller perceptions. Every colour, red, for instance, has a degree, which, however small, is never the smallest; and the same applies to heat, the momentum of gravity, etc.

This peculiar property of quantities that no part of them is the smallest possible part (no part indivisible) is called continuity. Time and space are *quanta continua,* because there is no part of them that is not enclosed between limits (points and moments), no part that is not itself again a space or a time. Space consists of spaces only, time of times. Points and moments are only limits, mere places of limitation, and as places presupposing always those intuitions which they are meant to limit or to determine. Mere places or parts that might be given before space or time, could never be compounded into space or time. Such quantities can also be called *flowing,* because the synthesis of the productive imagination which creates them is a progression in time, the continuity of which we are wont to express by the name of flowing, or passing away.

All phenomena are therefore continuous quantities, whether according to their intuition as extensive, or according to mere perception (sensation and therefore reality) as intensive quantities. When there is a break in the synthesis of the manifold of phenomena, we get only an aggregate of many phenomena, not a phenomenon, as a real quantum; for aggregate is called that what is produced, not by the mere continuation of productive synthesis of a certain kind, but by the repetition of a synthesis (beginning and) ending at every moment. If I call thirteen thalers a quantum of money, I am right, provided I understand by it the value of a mark of fine silver. This is a continuous quantity in which no part is the smallest, but every part may constitute a coin which contains material for still smaller coins. But if I understand by it thirteen round thalers, that is, so many coins (whatever their value in silver may be), then I should be wrong in speaking of a quantum of thalers, but should call it an aggregate, that is a number of coins. As every number must be founded on some unity, every phenomenon, as a unity, is a quantum, and, as such, a continuum.

If then all phenomena, whether considered as extensive or intensive, are continuous quantities, it might seem easy to prove with mathematical evidence that all change also (transition of a thing from one state into another) must be continuous, if the causality of the change did not lie quite outside the limits of transcendental philosophy, and presupposed empirical principles. For the understanding *a priori* tells us nothing of the possibility of a cause which changes the state of things, that is, determines them to the opposite of a given state, and this not only because it does not perceive the possibility of it (for such a perception is denied to us in several kinds of knowledge *a priori*), but because the changeability relates to certain determinations of phenomena to be taught by experience only, while their cause must lie in that which is unchangeable. But as the only materials which we may use at present are the pure fundamental concepts of every possible experience, from which all that is empirical is excluded, we cannot here, without injuring the unity of our system, anticipate general physical science which is based upon certain fundamental experiences.

Nevertheless, there is no lack of evidence of the great influence which our fundamental principle exercises in anticipating perceptions, nay, even in making up for their deficiency, in so far as it (that principle) stops any false conclusions that might be drawn from this deficiency.

If therefore all reality in perception has a certain degree, between which and negation there is an infinite succession of ever smaller degrees, and if every sense must have a definite degree of receptivity of sensations, it follows that no perception, and therefore no experience, is possible, that could prove, directly or indirectly, by any roundabout syllogisms, a complete absence of all reality in a phenomenon. We see therefore that experience can never supply a proof of empty space or empty time, because the total absence of reality in a sensuous intuition can itself never be perceived, neither can it be deduced from any phenomenon whatsoever and from the difference of degree in its reality; nor ought it ever to be admitted in explanation of it. For although the total intuition of a certain space or time is real all through, no part of it being empty,

yet as every reality has its degree which, while the extensive
quality of the phenomenon remains unchanged, may diminish
by infinite degrees down to the nothing or void, there must be
infinitely differing degrees in which space and time are filled,
and the intensive quantity in phenomena may be smaller or
greater, although the extensive quantity as given in intuition
remains the same.

We shall give an example. Almost all natural philosophers,
perceiving partly by means of the momentum of gravity or
weight, partly by means of the momentum of resistance
against other matter in motion, that there is a great difference
in the quantity of various kinds of matter though their volume
is the same, conclude unanimously that this volume (the extensive quantity of phenomena) must in all of them, though
in different degrees, contain a certain amount of empty space.
Who could have thought that these mathematical and mechanical philosophers should have based such a conclusion on a
purely metaphysical hypothesis, which they always profess to
avoid, by assuming that the real in space (I do not wish here
to call it impenetrability or weight, because these are empirical
concepts) must always be the same, and can differ only by its
extensive quantity, that is, by the number of parts. I meet this
hypothesis, for which they could find no ground in experience,
and which therefore is purely metaphysical, by a transcendental demonstration, which, though it is not intended to explain
the difference in the filling of spaces, will nevertheless entirely
remove the imagined necessity of their hypothesis which tries
to explain that difference by the admission of empty spaces,
and which thus restores, at least to the understanding, its liberty to explain to itself that difference in a different way, if any
such hypothesis be wanted in natural philosophy.

We can easily perceive that although the same spaces are
perfectly filled by two different kinds of matter, so that there
is no point in either of them where matter is not present, yet
the real in either, the quality being the same, has its own degrees (of resistance or weight) which, without any diminution
of its extensive quantity, may grow smaller and smaller in *infinitum*, before it reaches the void and vanishes. Thus a certain
expansion which fills a space, for instance, heat, and every
other kind of phenomenal reality, may, without leaving the
smallest part of space empty, diminish by degrees in *infinitum*,
and nevertheless fill space with its smaller, quite as much as another phenomenon with greater degrees. I do not mean to say
that this is really the case with different kinds of matter accord-

ing to their specific of gravity. I only want to show by a funda-mental principle of the pure understanding, that the nature of our perceptions renders such an explanation possible, and that it is wrong to look upon the real in phenomena as equal in degree, and differing only in aggregation and its extensive quantity, nay to maintain this on the pretended authority of an *a priori* principle of the understanding.

Nevertheless, this anticipation of perception is apt to startle[4] an enquirer accustomed to and rendered cautious by transcen-dental disquisitions, and we may naturally wonder that the understanding should be able to anticipate[5] a synthetical prop-osition with regard to the degree of all that is real in phenom-ena, and, therefore, with regard to the possibility of an internal difference of sensation itself, apart from its empirical quality; and it seems therefore a question well worthy of a solution, how the understanding can pronounce synthetically and *a priori* about phenomena, nay, anticipate them with regard to what, properly speaking, is empirical, namely, sensation.

The quality of sensation, colour, taste, etc., is always em-pirical, and cannot be conceived *a priori*. But the real that cor-responds to sensations in general, as opposed to negation $= 0$, does only represent something the concept of which implies being, and means nothing but the synthesis in any empirical consciousness. In the internal sense that empirical conscious-ness can be raised from 0 to any higher degree, so that an ex-tensive quantity of intuition (for instance, an illuminated plain) excites the same amount of sensation, as an aggregate of many other less illuminated plains. It is quite possible, there-fore, to take no account of the extensive quantity of a phenom-enon, and yet to represent to oneself in the mere sensation in any single moment a synthesis of a uniform progression from 0 to any given empirical consciousness. All sensations, as such, are therefore given *a posteriori*[6] only, but their quality, in so far as they must possess a degree, can be known *a priori*. It is remarkable that of quantities in general we can know one *quality* only *a priori*, namely, their continuity, while with re-

---

[4] Kant wrote, *etwas—etwas Auffallendes,* the second *etwas* being the adverb. Rosenkranz has left out one *etwas,* without necessity. It seems necessary, however, to add *Überlegung* after *transcenden-talen,* as done by Erdmann.

[5] *Anticipiren könne* must certainly be added, as suggested by Schopenhauer.

[6] The first and later editions have *a priori.* The correction is first made in the Seventh Edition, 1828.

gard to quality (the real of phenomena) nothing is known to us *a priori*, but their intensive *quantity*, that is, that they must have a degree. Everything else is left to experience.

III

[The Analogies of Experience

The general principle of them is: All phenomena, as far as their existence is concerned, are subject *a priori* to rules, determining their mutual relation in one and the same time]

ANALOGIES OF EXPERIENCE

Their principle is: Experience is possible only through the representation of a necessary connection of perceptions.

Proof

Experience is empirical knowledge, that is, knowledge which determines an object by means of perceptions. It is, therefore, a synthesis of perceptions, which synthesis itself is not contained in the perception, but contains the synthetical unity of the manifold of the perceptions in a consciousness, that unity constituting the essential of our knowledge of the objects of the senses, i.e. of experience (not only of intuition or of sensation of the senses). In experience perceptions come together contingently only, so that no necessity of their connection could be discovered in the perceptions themselves, apprehension being only a composition of the manifold of empirical intuition, but containing no representation of the necessity of the connected existence, in space and time, of the phenomena which it places together. Experience, on the contrary, is a knowledge of objects by perceptions, in which therefore the relation in the existence of the manifold is to be represented, not as it is put together in time, but as it is in time, objectively. Now, as time itself cannot be perceived, the determination of the existence of objects in time can take place only by their connection in time in general, that is, through concepts connecting them a priori. As these concepts always imply necessity, we are justified in saying that experience is possible only through a representation of the necessary connection of perceptions.

The three modi of time are *permanence, succession,* and *coexistence.* There will therefore be three rules of all relations of phenomena in time, by which the existence of every phenomenon with regard to the unity of time is determined, and these rules will precede all experience, nay, render experience possible.

The general principle of the three analogies depends on the necessary unity of apperception with reference to every possible empirical consciousness (perception) *at every time,* and, consequently, as that unity forms an *a priori* ground, on the synthetical unity of all phenomena, according to their relation in time. For the original apperception refers to the internal sense (comprehending all representations), and it does so *a priori* to its form, that is, to the relation of the manifold of the empirical consciousness in time. The original apperception is intended to combine all this manifold according to its relations in time, for this is what is meant by its transcendental unity *a priori,* to which all is subject which is to belong to my own and my uniform knowledge, and thus to become an object for me. This synthetical unity in the time relations of all perceptions, which is determined *a priori,* is expressed therefore in the law, that all empirical determinations of time must be subject to rules of the general determination of time; and the analogies of experience, of which we are now going to treat, are exactly rules of this kind.

These principles have this peculiarity, that they do not refer to phenomena and the synthesis of their empirical intuition, but only to the *existence* of phenomena and their mutual *relation* with regard to their existence. The manner in which something is apprehended as a phenomenon may be so determined *a priori* that the rule of its synthesis may give at the same time this intuition *a priori* in any empirical case, nay, may really render it possible. But the existence of phenomena can never be known *a priori,* and though we might be led in this way to infer some kind of existence, we should never be able to know it definitely, or to anticipate that by which the empirical intuition of one differs from that of others.

The principles which we considered before and which, as they enable us to apply mathematics to phenomena, I called mathematical, refer to phenomena so far only as they are possible, and showed how, with regard both to their intuition and to the real in their perception, they can be produced according to the rules of a mathematical synthesis, so that, in the one as well as in the other, we may use numerical quantities, and with them a determination of all phenomena as quantities. Thus I might, for example, compound the degree of sensations of the sunlight out of, say, 200,000 illuminations by the moon, and thus determine it *a priori* or construct it. Those former principles might therefore be called *constitutive*.

The case is totally different with those principles which are meant to bring the existence of phenomena under rules *a priori,* for as existence cannot be constructed, they can only refer to the relations of existence and become merely *regulative* principles. Here therefore we could not think of either axioms or anticipations, and whenever a perception is given us as related in time to some others (although undetermined), we could not say *a priori* what other perception or how great a perception is necessarily connected with it, but only how, if existing, it is necessarily connected with the other in a certain mode of time. In philosophy analogy means something very different to what it does in mathematics. In the latter they are formulas which state the equality of two quantitative relations, and they are always constitutive so that when three[7] terms of a proposition are given, the fourth also is given by it, that is, can be constructed out of it. In philosophy, on the contrary, analogy does not consist in the equality of two quantitative, but of two qualitative relations, so that when three terms are given I may learn from them *a priori* the relation to a fourth only, but not that fourth term itself. All I can thus gain is a rule according to which I may look in experience for the fourth term, or a characteristic mark by which I may find it. An analogy of experience can therefore be no more than a rule according to which a certain unity of experience may arise from perceptions (but not how perception itself, as an empirical intuition, may arise); it may serve as a principle for objects (as phenomena[8]) not in a constitutive, but only in a regulative capacity.

Exactly the same applies to the postulates of empirical thought in general, which relate to the synthesis of mere intuition (the form of phenomena), the synthesis of perception (the matter of them), and the synthesis of experience (the relation of these perceptions). They too are regulative principles only, and differ from the mathematical, which are constitutive, not in their certainty, which is established in both *a priori,* but

[7] The First and Second Editions read 'When two terms of a proposition are given, the third also.'
[8] Read *den Erscheinungen.*

in the character of their evidence, that is, in that which is intuitive in it, and therefore in their demonstration also.

What has been remarked of all synthetical principles and must be enjoined here more particularly is this, that these analogies have their meaning and validity, not as principles of the transcendent, but only as principles of the empirical use of the understanding. They can be established in this character only, nor can phenomena ever be comprehended under the categories directly, but only under their schemata. If the objects to which these principles refer were things by themselves, it would be perfectly impossible to know anything of them *a priori* and synthetically. But they are nothing but phenomena, and our whole knowledge of them, to which, after all, all principles *a priori* must relate, is only our possible experience of them. Those principles therefore can aim at nothing but the conditions of the unity of empirical knowledge in the synthesis of phenomena, which synthesis is represented only in the schema of the pure concepts of the understanding, while the category contains the function, restricted by no sensuous condition, of the unity of that synthesis as synthesis in general. Those principles will therefore authorise us only to connect phenomena, according to analogy, with the logical and universal unity of concepts, so that, though in using the principle we use the category, yet in practice (in the application to phenomena) we put the schema of the category, as a practical key, in its[9] place, or rather put it by the side of the category as a restrictive condition, or, as what may be called, a formula of the category.

A

First Analogy

[*Principle of Permanence*

All phenomena contain the permanent (substance) as the object itself, and the changeable as its determination only, that is, as a mode in which the object exists

[9] I read *deren,* and afterwards *der ersteren,* though even then the whole passage is very involved. Professor Noiré thinks that *dessen* may be referred to *Gebrauch,* and *des ersteren* to *Grundsatz.*

Proof of the First Analogy

All phenomena take place in time. Time can determine in two ways the relation in the existence of phenomena, so far as they are either successive or coexistent. In the first case time is considered as a series, in the second as a whole.]

Principle of the Permanence of Substance

In all changes of phenomena the substance is permanent, and its quantum is neither increased nor diminished in nature.

Proof

All phenomena exist in time, and in it alone, as the substratum (as permanent form of the internal intuition), can simultaneousness *as well as* succession *be represented. Time, therefore, in which all change of phenomena is to be thought, does not change, for it is that in which simultaneousness and succession can be represented only as determinations of it. As time by itself cannot be perceived, it follows that the substratum which represents time in general, and in which all change or simultaneousness can be perceived in apprehension, through the relation of phenomena to it, must exist in the objects of perception, that is, in the phenomena. Now the substratum of all that is real, that is, of all that belongs to the existence of things, is the* substance, *and all that belongs to existence can be conceived only as a determination of it. Consequently the permanent, in reference to which alone all temporal relations of phenomena can be determined, is the substance in phenomena, that is, what is real in them, and, as the substratum of all change, remains always the same. As therefore substance cannot change in existence, we were justified in saying that its quantum can neither be increased nor diminished in nature.*
Our apprehension of the manifold of phenomena is always successive, and therefore always changing. By it alone therefore we can never determine whether the manifold, as an object of experience, is coexistent or successive, unless there is something in it which exists always, that is, something constant and permanent, while change and succession are nothing but so many kinds (*modi*) of time in which the permanent exists. Relations of time are therefore possible in the permanent only (coexistence and succession being the only relations of time)

so that the permanent is the substratum of the empirical representation of time itself, and in it alone all determination of time is possible. Permanence expresses time as the constant correlative of all existence of phenomena, of all change and concomitancy. For change does not affect time itself, but only phenomena in time (nor is coexistence a mode of time itself, because in it no parts can be coexistent, but successive only). If we were to ascribe a succession to time itself, it would be necessary to admit another time in which such succession should be possible. Only through the permanent does *existence* in different parts of a series of time assume a *quantity* which we call *duration*. For in mere succession existence always comes and goes, and never assumes the slightest quantity. Without something permanent therefore no relation of time is possible. Time by itself, however, cannot be perceived, and it is therefore the permanent in phenomena that forms the substratum for all determination of time, and at the same time the condition of the possibility of all synthetical unity of perceptions, that is, of experience; while with regard to that permanent all existence and all change in time can only be taken as a mode of existence of what is permanent. In all phenomena therefore the permanent is the object itself, that is, the substance (phenomenon), while all that changes or can change belongs only to the mode in which substance or substances exist, therefore to their determinations.

I find that in all ages not only the philosopher, but also the man of common understanding has admitted this permanence as a substratum of all change of phenomena. It will be the same in future, only that a philosopher generally expresses himself somewhat more definitely by saying that in all changes in the world the substance remains, and only the accidents change. But I nowhere find even the attempt at a proof of this very synthetical proposition, and it occupies but seldom that place which it ought to occupy at the head of the pure and entirely *a priori* existing laws of nature. In fact the proposition that substance is permanent is tautological, because that permanence is the only ground why we apply the category of substance to a phenomenon, and it ought first to have been proved that there is in all phenomena something permanent, while the changeable is only a determination of its existence. But as such a proof can never be given dogmatically and as deduced from concepts, because it refers to a synthetical proposition *a priori,* and as no one ever thought that such propositions could be valid only in reference to possible experience, and could therefore be proved only by a deduction of the possibility of experience, we need not wonder that, though it served as the foundation of all experience (being felt to be indispensable for every kind of empirical knowledge), it has never been established by proof.

A philosopher was asked, What is the weight of smoke? He replied, Deduct from the weight of the wood burnt the weight of the remaining ashes, and you have the weight of the smoke. He was therefore convinced that even in fire matter (substance) does not perish, but that its form only suffers a change. The proposition also, from nothing comes nothing, was only another conclusion from the same principle of permanence, or rather of the constant presence of the real subject in phenomena. For if that which people call substance in a phenomenon is to be the true substratum for all determination in time, then all existence in the past as well as the future must be determined in it, and in it only. Thus we can only give to a phenomenon the name of substance because we admit its existence at all times, which is not even fully expressed by the word *permanence,* because it refers rather to future time only. The internal necessity however of permanence is inseparably connected with the necessity to have been always, and the expression may therefore stand. *Gigni de nihilo nihil, in nihilum nil posse reverti,* were two propositions which the ancients never separated, but which at present are sometimes parted, because people imagine that they refer to things by themselves, and that the former might contradict the dependence of the world on a Supreme Cause (even with regard to its substance), an apprehension entirely needless, as we are only speaking here of phenomena in the sphere of experience, the unity of which would never be possible, if we allowed that new things (new in substance) could ever arise. For in that case we should lose that which alone can represent the unity of time, namely, the identity of the substratum, in which alone all change retains complete unity. This permanence, however, is nothing but the manner in which we represent the existence of things (as phenomenal).

The different determinations of a substance, which are nothing but particular modes in which it exists, are called accidents. They are always real, because they concern the existence of a substance (negations are nothing but determinations which express the non-existence of something in the substance). If we want to ascribe a particular kind of existence to these real determinations of the substance, as, for instance, to motion, as an accident of matter, we call it *inherence,* in order to distinguish it from the existence of substance, which[10] we call *subsistence.* This, however, has given rise to many misunderstandings, and we shall express ourselves better and more correctly, if we define the accident through the manner only in which the existence of a substance is positively determined. It is inevitable, however, according to the conditions of the logical use of our understanding, to separate, as it were, whatever can change in the existence of a substance, while the substance itself remains unchanged, and to consider it in its relation to that which is radical and truly permanent. Hence a place has been assigned to this category under the title of relations, not so much because it contains itself a relation, as because it contains their condition.

On this permanence depends also the right understanding of the concept of *change.* To arise and to perish are not changes of that which arises or perishes. Change is a mode of existence, which follows another mode of existence of the same object. Hence whatever changes is permanent, and its condition only changes. As this alteration refers only to determinations which may have an end or a beginning, we may use an expression that seems somewhat paradoxical and say: the permanent only (substance) is changed, the changing itself suffers no change, but only an alteration, certain determinations ceasing to exist, while others begin.

It is therefore in substances only that change can be perceived. Arising or perishing absolutely, and not referring merely to a determination of the permanent can never become a possible perception, because it is the permanent only which renders the representations of a transition from one state to another, from not being to being, possible, which (changes) consequently can only be known empirically, as alternating determinations of what is permanent. If you suppose that something has an absolute beginning, you must have a moment of time in which it was not. But with what can you connect that moment, if not with that which already exists? An empty antecedent time cannot be an object of perception. But if you connect this beginning with things which existed already and continue to exist till the beginning of something new, then the latter is only a determination of

10 Read *das man.*

the former, as of the permanent. The same holds good with regard to perishing, for this would presuppose the empirical representation of a time in which a phenomenon exists no longer.

Substances therefore (as phenomena) are the true substrata of all determinations of time. If some substances could arise and others perish, the only condition of the empirical unity of time would be removed, and phenomena would then be referred to two different times, in which existence would pass side by side, which is absurd. For there is but one time in which all different times must be placed, not as simultaneous, but as successive.

Permanence, therefore, is a necessary condition under which alone phenomena, as things or objects, can be determined in a possible experience. What the empirical criterion of this necessary permanence, or of the substantiality of phenomena may be, we shall have to explain in the sequel.

B

Second Analogy

[Principle of Production

Everything that happens (begins to be), presupposes something on which it follows according to a rule]

Principle of the Succession of Time, according to the Law of Causality

All changes take place according to the law of connection between cause and effect.

Proof

(It has been shown by the preceding principle, that all phenomena in the succession of time are changes only, i.e. a successive being and not-being of the determinations of the substance, which is permanent, and consequently that the being of the substance itself, which follows upon its not-being, and its not-being, which follows on its being,—in other words, that an arising or perishing of the substance itself is inadmissible. The same principle might also have been expressed

thus: all change (succession) of phenomena consists in modi-fication only, *for arising and perishing are no modifications of the substance, because the concept of modification presupposes the same subject as existing with two opposite determinations, and therefore as permanent. After this preliminary remark, we shall proceed to the proof.*)

I perceive that phenomena succeed each other, that is, that there is a state of things at one time the opposite of which existed at a previous time. I am therefore really connecting two perceptions in time. That connection is not a work of the senses only and of intuition, but is here the product of a synthetical power of the faculty of imagination, which determines the internal sense with reference to relation in time. Imagination, however, can connect those two states in two ways, so that either the one or the other precedes in time: for time cannot be perceived by itself, nor can we determine in the object empirically and with reference to time, what precedes and what follows. I am, therefore, conscious only that my imagination places the one before, the other after, and not, that in the object the one state comes before the other. In other words, the objective relation of phenomena following upon each other remains undetermined by mere perception. In order that this may be known as determined, it is necessary to conceive the relation between the two states in such a way that it should be determined thereby with necessity, which of the two should be taken as coming first, and which as second, and not conversely. Such a concept, involving a necessity of synthetical unity, can be a pure concept of the understanding only, which is not supplied by experience, and this is, in this case, the concept of the relation of cause and effect, *the former determining the latter in time as the consequence, the cause not being something that might be antecedent in imagination only, or might not be perceived at all. Experience itself, therefore, that is, an empirical knowledge of phenomena, is possible only by our subjecting the succession of phenomena, and with it all change, to the law of causality, and phenomena themselves, as objects of experience, are consequently possible according to the same law only.*

The apprehension of the manifold of phenomena is always successive. The representations of the parts follow one upon another. Whether they also follow one upon the other in the object is a second point for reflection, not contained in the former. We may indeed call everything, even every representation, so far as we are conscious of it, an object; but it requires a more profound investigation to discover what this word may mean with regard to phenomena, not in so far as they (as representations) are objects, but in so far as they only signify an object. So far as they, as representations only, are at the same time objects of consciousness, they cannot be distinguished from our apprehension, that is from their being received in the synthesis of our imagination, and we must therefore say, that the manifold of phenomena is always produced in the mind successively. If phenomena were things by themselves, the succession of the representations of their manifold would never enable us to judge how that manifold is connected in the object. We have always to deal with our representations only; how things may be by themselves (without reference to the representations by which they affect us) is completely beyond the sphere of our knowledge. Since, therefore, phenomena are not things by themselves, and are yet the only thing that can be given to us to know, I am asked to say what kind of connection in time belongs to the manifold of the phenomena itself, when the representation of it in our apprehension is always successive. Thus, for instance, the apprehension of the manifold in the phenomenal appearance of a house that stands before me, is successive. The question then arises, whether the manifold of the house itself be successive by itself, which of course no one would admit. Whenever I ask for the transcendental meaning of my concepts of an object, I find that a house is not a thing by itself, but a phenomenon only, that is, a representation the transcendental object of which is unknown. What then can be the meaning of the question, how the manifold in the phenomenon itself (which is not a thing by itself) may be connected? Here that which is contained in our successive apprehension is considered as representation, and the given phenomenon, though it is nothing but the whole of those representations, as their object, with which my concept, drawn from the representations of my apprehension, is to accord. As the accord between knowledge and its object is truth, it is easily seen, that we can ask here only for the formal conditions of empirical truth, and that the phenomenon, in contradistinction to the representations of our apprehension, can only be represented as the object different from them, if it is subject to a rule distinguishing it from every other apprehension, and necessitating a certain kind of conjunction of the manifold. That which in the phenomenon contains the condition of this necessary rule of apprehension is *the object*.

Let us now proceed to our task. That something takes place, that is, that something, or some state, which did not exist before, begins to exist, cannot be perceived empirically, unless there exists antecedently a phenomenon which does not contain that state; for a reality, following on empty time, that is a beginning of existence, preceded by no state of things, can be apprehended as little as empty time itself. Every apprehension of an event is therefore a perception following on another perception. But as this applies to all synthesis of apprehension, as I showed before in the phenomenal appearance of a house, that apprehension would not thereby be different from any other. But I observe at the same time, that if in a phenomenon which contains an event I call the antecedent state of perception A, and the subsequent B, B can only follow A in my apprehension, while the perception A can never follow B, but can only precede it. I see, for instance, a ship gliding down a stream. My perception of its place below follows my perception of its place higher up in the course of the stream, and it is impossible in the apprehension of this phenomenon that the ship should be perceived first below and then higher up. We see therefore that the order in the succession of perceptions in our apprehension is here determined, and our apprehension regulated by that order. In the former example of a house my perceptions could begin in the apprehension at the roof and end in the basement, or begin below and end above: they could apprehend the manifold of the empirical intuition from right to left or from left to right. There was therefore no determined order in the succession of these perceptions, determining the point where I had to begin in apprehension, in order to connect the manifold empirically; while in the apprehension of an event there is always a rule, which makes the order of the successive perceptions (in the apprehension of this phenomenon) necessary.

In our case, therefore, we shall have to derive the subjective succession in our apprehension from the objective succession of the phenomena, because otherwise the former would be entirely undetermined, and unable to distinguish one phenomenon from another. The former alone proves nothing as to the connection of the manifold in the object, because it is quite arbitrary. The latter must therefore consist in the order of the manifold in a phenomenon, according to which the apprehension of what is happening follows upon the apprehension of what has happened, in conformity with a rule. Thus only can I be justified in saying, not only of my apprehension, but of the phenomenon itself, that there exists in it a succession, which is the same as to say that I cannot arrange the apprehension otherwise than in that very succession.

In conformity with this, there must exist in that which always precedes an event the condition of a rule, by which this event follows at all times, and necessarily; but I cannot go back from the event and determine by apprehension that which precedes. For no phenomenon goes back from the succeeding to the preceding point of time, though it is related to some preceding point of time, while the progress from a given time to a determined following time is necessary. Therefore, as there certainly is something that follows, I must necessarily refer it to something else which precedes, and upon which it follows by rule, that is, by necessity. So that the event, as being conditional, affords a safe indication of some kind of condition, while that condition itself determines the event.

If we supposed that nothing precedes an event upon which such event must follow according to rule, all succession of perception would then exist in apprehension only, that is, subjectively; but it would not thereby be determined objectively, what ought properly to be the antecedent and what the subsequent in perception. We should thus have a mere play of representations unconnected with any object, that is, no phenomenon would, by our perception, be distinguished in time from any other phenomenon, because the succession in apprehension would always be uniform, and there would be nothing in the phenomena to determine the succession, so as to render a certain sequence objectively necessary. I could not say therefore that two states follow each other in a phenomenon, but only that one apprehension follows another, which is purely subjective, and does not determine any object, and cannot be considered therefore as knowledge of anything (even of something purely phenomenal).

If therefore experience teaches us that something happens, we always presuppose that something precedes on which it follows by rule. Otherwise I could not say of the object that it followed, because its following in my apprehension only, without being determined by rule in reference to what precedes, would not justify us in admitting an objective following.[11] It is therefore always with reference to a rule by which phenomena as they follow, that is as they happen, are determined by an antecedent state, that I can give an objective character to my subjective synthesis (of apprehension); nay, it is under this supposition only that an experience of anything that happens becomes possible.

It might seem indeed as if this were in contradiction to all that has always been said on the progress of the human understanding, it having been supposed that only by a perception and comparison of many events, following in the same manner on preceding phenomena, we were led to the discovery of a rule according to which certain events always follow on certain phenomena, and that thus only we were enabled to form to ourselves the concept of a cause. If this were so, that concept would be empirical only, and the rule which it supplies, that everything which happens must have a cause, would be as accidental as experience itself. The universality and necessity of that rule would then be fictitious only, and devoid of any true and general validity, because not being *a priori,* but founded on induction only. The case is the same as with other pure representations *a priori* (for instance space and time), which we are only able to draw out as pure concepts from experience, because we have put them first into experience, nay, have rendered experience possible only by them. It is true, no doubt, that the logical clearness of this representation of a rule, determining the succession of events, as a concept of cause, becomes possible only when we have used it in experience, but, as the condition of the synthetical unity of phenomena in time, it was nevertheless the foundation of all experience, and consequently preceded it *a priori.*

It is necessary therefore to show by examples that we never, even in experience, ascribe the sequence or consequence (of an event or something happening that did not exist before) to the object, and distinguish it from the subjective sequence of our apprehension, except when there is a rule which forces us to observe a certain order of perceptions, and no other; nay, that it is this force which from the first renders the representation of a succession in the object possible.

We have representations within us, and can become conscious of them; but however far that consciousness may extend, and however accurate and minute it may be, yet the representations are always representations only, that is, internal

[11] Read *anzunehmen berechtigt.*

determinations of our mind in this or that relation of time. What right have we then to add to these representations an object, or to ascribe to these modifications, beyond their subjective reality, another objective one? Their objective character cannot consist in their relation to another representation (of that which one wished to predicate of the object), for thus the question would only arise again, how that representation could again go beyond itself, and receive an objective character in addition to the subjective one, which belongs to it, as a determination of our mind. If we try to find out what new quality or dignity is imparted to our representations by their relation to an *object,* we find that it consists in nothing but the rendering necessary the connection of representations in a certain way, and subjecting them to a rule; and that on the other hand they receive their objective character only because a certain order is necessary in the time relations of our representations.

In the synthesis of phenomena the manifold of our representations is always successive. No object can thus be represented, because through the succession which is common to all apprehensions, nothing can be distinguished from anything else. But as soon as I perceive or anticipate that there is in this succession a relation to an antecedent state from which the representation follows by rule, then something is represented as an event, or as something that happens: that is to say, I know an object to which I must assign a certain position in time, which, after the preceding state, cannot be different from what it is. If therefore I perceive that something happens, this representation involves that something preceded, because the phenomenon receives its position in time with reference to what preceded, that is, it exists after a time in which it did not exist. Its definite position in time can only be assigned to it, if in the antecedent state something is presupposed on which it always follows by rule. It thus follows that, first of all, I cannot invert the order, and place that which happens before that on which it follows; secondly, that whenever the antecedent state is there, the other event must follow inevitably and necessarily. Thus it happens that there arises an order among our representations, in which the present state (as having come to be), points to an antecedent state, as a correlative of the event that is given; a correlative which, though as yet indefinite, refers as determining to the event, as its result, and connects that event with itself by necessity, in the succession of time.

If then it is a necessary law of our sensibility, and therefore a *formal* condition of all perception, that a preceding necessarily determines a succeeding time (because I cannot arrive at the succeeding time except through the preceding), it is also an indispensable *law of the empirical representation* of the series of time that the phenomena of past time determine every existence in succeeding times, nay, that these, as events, cannot take place except so far as the former determine their existence in time, that is, determine it by rule. *For it is of course in phenomena only that we can know empirically this continuity in the coherence of times.*

What is required for all experience and renders it possible is the understanding, and the first that is added by it is not that it renders the representation of objects clear, but that it really renders the representation of any object for the first time possible. This takes place by the understanding transferring the order of time to the phenomena and their existence, and by assigning to each of them as to a consequence a certain *a priori* determined place in time, with reference to antecedent phenomena, without which place phenomena would not be in accord with time, which determines *a priori* their places to all its parts. This determination of place cannot be derived from the relation in which phenomena stand to absolute time (for that can never be an object of perception); but, on the contrary, phenomena must themselves determine to each other their places in time, and render them necessary in the series of time. In other words, what happens or follows must follow according to a general rule on that which was contained in a previous state. We thus get a series of phenomena which, by means of the understanding, produces and makes necessary in the series of possible perceptions the same order and continuous coherence which exists *a priori* in the form of internal intuition (time), in which all perceptions must have their place.

That something happens is therefore a perception which belongs to a possible experience, and this experience becomes real when I consider the phenomenon as determined with regard to its place in time, that is to say, as an object which can always be found, according to a rule, in the connection of perceptions. This rule, by which we determine everything according to the succession of time, is this: the condition under which an event follows at all times (necessarily) is to be found in what precedes. All possible experience therefore, that is, all objective knowledge of phenomena with regard to their relation in the succession of time, depends on 'the principle of sufficient reason.'

The proof of this principle rests entirely on the following considerations. All empirical knowledge requires synthesis of the manifold by imagination, which is always successive, one representation following upon the other. That succession, however, in the imagination is not at all determined with regard to the order in which something precedes and something follows, and the series of successive representations may be taken as retrogressive as well as progressive. If that synthesis, however, is a synthesis of apperception (of the manifold in a given phenomenon), then the order is determined in the object, or, to speak more accurately, there is then in it an order of successive synthesis which determines the object, and according to which something must necessarily precede, and, when it is once there, something else must necessarily follow. If therefore my perception is to contain the knowledge of an event, or something that really happens, it must consist of an empirical judgment, by which the succession is supposed to be determined, so that the event presupposes another phenomenon in time on which it follows necessarily and according to a rule. If it were different, if the antecedent phenomenon were there, and the event did not follow on it necessarily, it would become to me a mere play of my subjective imaginations, or if I thought it to be objective, I should call it a dream. It is therefore the relation of phenomena (as possible perceptions) according to which the existence of the subsequent (what happens) is determined in time by something antecedent necessarily and by rule, or, in other words, the relation of cause and effect, which forms the condition of the objective validity of our empirical judgments with regard to the series of perceptions, and therefore also the condition of the empirical truth of them, and of experience. The principle of the causal relation in the succession of phenomena is valid therefore for all objects of experience, also (under the conditions of succession), because that principle is itself the ground of the possibility of such experience.

Here, however, we meet with a difficulty that must first be removed. The principle of the causal connection of phenomena is restricted in our formula to their succession, while in practice we find that it applies also to their coexistence, because cause and effect may exist at the same time. There may be, for instance, inside a room heat which is not found in the open air. If I look for its cause, I find a heated stove. But that stove, as cause, exists at the same time with its effect, the heat of the room, and there is therefore no succession in time between cause and effect, but they are coexistent, and yet the law applies. The fact is, that the greater portion of the active causes[12] in nature is coexistent with its effects, and the succession of these effects in time is due only to this, that a cause cannot produce its whole effect in one moment. But at the moment in which an effect first arises it is always coexistent with the causality of its cause, because if that had ceased one moment before, the effect would never have happened. Here we must well consider that what is thought of is the *order*, not the *lapse* of time, and that the relation remains, even if no time had lapsed. The time between the causality of the cause and its immediate effect can be *vanishing* (they may be simultaneous), but the relation of the one to the other remains for all that determinable in time. If I look upon a ball that rests on a soft cushion, and makes a depression in it, as a cause, it is simultaneous with its effect. But I nevertheless distinguish the two through the temporal relation of dynamical connection. For if I place the ball on a cushion, its smooth surface is followed by a depression, while, if there is a depression in the cushion (I know not whence), a leaden ball does by no means follow from it.

The succession in time is therefore the only empirical criterion of an effect with regard to the causality of the cause which precedes it. The glass is the cause of the rising of the water above its horizontal surface, although both phenomena are simultaneous. For as soon as I draw water in a glass from a larger vessel, something follows, namely, the change of the horizontal state which it had before into a concave state which it assumes in the glass.

This causality leads to the concept of action, that to the concept of force, and lastly, to the concept of substance. As I do not mean to burden my critical task, which only concerns the sources of synthetical knowledge *a priori*, with analytical processes which aim at the explanation, and not at the expansion of our concepts, I leave a fuller treatment of these to a future system of pure reason; nay, I may refer to many well-known manuals in which such an analysis may be found. I cannot pass, however, over the empirical criterion of a substance, so far as it seems to manifest itself, not so much

[12] The reading of the First Edition is *Ursache; Ursachen* is a conjecture made by Rosenkranz and approved by others.

through the permanence of the phenomenon as through action.

Wherever there is action, therefore activity and force, there must be substance, and in this alone the seat of that fertile source of phenomena can be sought. This sounds very well, but if people are asked to explain what they mean by substance, they find it by no means easy to answer without reasoning in a circle. How can we conclude immediately from the action to the *permanence* of the agent, which nevertheless is an essential and peculiar characteristic of substance (*phaenomenon*)? After what we have explained before, however, the answer to this question is not so difficult, though it would be impossible, according to the ordinary way of proceeding analytically only with our concepts. Action itself implies the relation of the subject of the causality to the effect. As all effect consists in that which happens, that is, in the changeable, indicating time in succession, the last subject of it is the *permanent*, as the substratum of all that changes, that is substance. For, according to the principle of causality, actions are always the first ground of all change of phenomena, and cannot exist therefore in a subject that itself changes, because in that case other actions and another subject would be required to determine that change. Action, therefore, is a sufficient empirical criterion to prove substantiality, nor is it necessary that I should first establish its permanency by means of compared perceptions, which indeed would hardly be possible in this way, at least with that completeness which is required by the magnitude and strict universality of the concept. That the first subject of the causality of all arising and perishing cannot itself (in the field of phenomena) arise and perish, is a safe conclusion, pointing in the end to empirical necessity and permanency in existence, that is, the concept of a substance as a phenomenon.

If anything happens, the mere fact of something arising, without any reference to what it is, is in itself a matter for enquiry. The transition from the not-being of a state into that state, even though it contained no quality whatever as a phenomenon, must itself be investigated. This arising, as we have shown in No. A, does not concern the substance (because a substance never arises), but its state only. It is therefore mere change, and not an arising out of nothing. When such an arising is looked upon as the effect of a foreign cause, it is called creation. This can never be admitted as an event among phenomena, because its very possibility would destroy the unity of experience. If, however, we consider all things, not as phenomena, but as things by themselves and objects of the understanding only, then, though they are substances, they may be considered as dependent in their existence on a foreign cause. Our words would then assume quite a different meaning, and no longer be applicable to phenomena, as possible objects of experience.

How anything can be changed at all, how it is possible that one state in a given time is followed by another at another time, of that we have not the slightest conception a priori. We want for that a knowledge of real powers, which can be given empirically only: for instance, a knowledge of motive powers, or what is the same, a knowledge of certain successive phenomena (as movements) which indicate the presence of such forces. What can be considered a priori, according to the law of causality and the conditions of time, are the form of every change, the condition under which alone, as an arising of another state, it can take place (its contents, that is, the state, which is changed, being what it may), and therefore the succession itself of the states (that which has happened).*

When a substance passes from one state a into another b, the moment of the latter is different from the moment of the former state, and follows it. Again, that second state, as a reality (in phenomena), differs from the first in which that reality did not exist, as b from zero; that is, even if the state b differed from the state a in quantity only, that change is an arising of b − a, which in the former state was non-existent, and in relation to which that state is = 0.

The question therefore arises how a thing can pass from a state = a to another = b? Between two moments there is always a certain time, and between two states in these two moments there is always a difference which must have a certain quantity, because all parts of phenomena are always themselves quantities. Every transition therefore from one state into another takes place in a certain time between two moments, the first of which determines the state from which a thing arises, the second that at which it arrives. Both therefore are the temporal limits of a change or of an intermediate state between two states, and belong as such to the whole of the

* It should be remarked that I am not speaking here of the change of certain relations, but of the change of a state. Therefore when a body moves in a uniform way, it does not change its state of movement, but it does so when its motion increases or decreases.

change. Every change, however, has a cause which proves its causality during the whole of the time in which the change takes place. The cause therefore does not produce the change suddenly (in one moment), but during a certain time; so that, as the time grows from the initiatory moment a to its completion in b, the quantity of reality also $(b - a)$ is produced through all the smaller degrees between the first and the last. All change therefore is possible only through a continuous action of causality which, so far as it is uniform, is called a momentum. A change does not consist of such momenta, but is produced by them as their effect.

This is the law of continuity in all change, founded on this, that neither time nor a phenomenon in time consists of parts which are the smallest possible, and that nevertheless the state of a thing which is being changed passes through all these parts, as elements, to its new state. No difference of the real in phenomena and no difference in the quantity of times is ever the smallest; and thus the new state of reality grows from the first state in which that reality did not exist through all the infinite degrees thereof, the differences of which from one another are smaller than that between zero and a.

It does not concern us at present of what utility this principle may be in physical science. But how such a principle, which seems to enlarge our knowledge of nature so much, can be possible *a priori*, that requires a careful investigation, although we can see that it is real and true, and might thus imagine that the question how it was possible is unnecessary. For there are so many unfounded pretensions to enlarge our knowledge by pure reason that we must accept it as a general principle, to be always distrustful, and never to believe or accept anything of this kind without documents capable of a thorough deduction, however clear the dogmatical proof of it may appear.

All addition to our empirical knowledge and every advance in perception is nothing but an enlargement of the determinations of our internal sense, that is, a progression in time, whatever the objects may be, whether phenomena or pure intuitions. This progression in time determines everything, and is itself determined by nothing else, that is, the parts of that progression are only given in time, and through the synthesis of time, but not time before this synthesis. For this reason every transition in our perception to something that follows in time is really a determination of time through the production of that perception, and as time is always and in all its parts a quantity, the production of a perception as a quantity, through all degrees (none of them being the smallest), from zero up to its determined degree. This shows how it is possible to know *a priori* a law of changes, as far as their form is concerned. We are only anticipating our own apprehension, the formal condition of which, as it dwells in us before all given phenomena, may well be known *a priori*.

In the same manner therefore in which time contains the sensuous condition *a priori* of the possibility of a continuous progression of that which exists to that which follows, the understanding, by means of the unity of apperception, is a condition *a priori* of the possibility of a continuous determination of the position of all phenomena in that time, and this through a series of causes and effects, the former producing inevitably the existence of the latter, and thus rendering the empirical knowledge of the relations of time valid for all times (universally) and therefore objectively valid.

C

Third Analogy

[*Principle of Community*

All substances, in so far as they are coexistent, stand in complete community, that is, reciprocity one to another]

Principle of Coexistence, according to the Law of Reciprocity or Community

All substances, so far as they can be perceived as coexistent in space, are always affecting each other reciprocally.

Proof

Things are coexistent when, in empirical intuition, the perception of the one can follow upon the perception of the other, and vice versa, *which, as was shown in the second principle, is impossible in the temporal succession of phenomena. Thus I may first observe the moon and afterwards the earth, or, conversely also, first the earth and afterwards the moon, and because the perceptions of these objects can follow each other in both ways, I say that they are coexistent. Now co-*

*existence is the existence of the manifold in the same time.
Time itself, however, cannot be perceived, so that we might
learn from the fact that things exist in the same time that their
perceptions can follow each other reciprocally. The synthesis
of imagination in apprehension would, therefore, give us each
of these perceptions as existing in the subject, when the other
is absent, and vice versa: it would never tell us that the objects
are coexistent, that is, that if the one is there, the other also
must be there in the same time, and this by necessity, so that
the perceptions may follow each other reciprocally. Hence
we require a concept of understanding of the reciprocal sequence of determinations of things existing at the same time,
but outside each other, in order to be able to say, that the reciprocal sequence of the perceptions is founded in the object,
and thus to represent their coexistence as objective. The relation of substances, however, of which the first has determinations the ground of which is contained in the other, is the
relation of influence, and if, conversely also, the first contains
the ground of determinations in the latter, the relation is that
of community or reciprocity. Hence the coexistence of substances in space cannot be known in experience otherwise but
under the supposition of reciprocal action: and this is therefore the condition also of the possibility of things themselves
as objects of experience.*

Things are coexistent in so far as they exist at one and the
same time. But how can we know that they exist at one and
the same time? Only if the order in the synthesis of apprehension of the manifold is indifferent, that is, if I may advance from A through B, C, D, to E, or contrariwise from E
to A. For, if the synthesis were successive in time (in the order beginning with A and ending with E), it would be impossible to begin the apprehension with the perception of E and
to go backwards to A, because A belongs to past time, and
can no longer be an object of apprehension.

If we supposed it possible that in a number of substances,
as phenomena, each were perfectly isolated, so that none influenced another or received influences from another, then
the coexistence of them could never become an object of possible perception, nor could the existence of the one through
any process of empirical synthesis lead us on to the existence
of another. For if we imagined that they were separated by a
perfectly empty space, a perception, proceeding from the one
in time to the other might no doubt determine the existence

of it by means of a subsequent perception, but would never be able to determine whether that phenomenon followed objectively on the other or was coexistent with it.

There must therefore be something besides their mere existence by which *A* determines its place in time for *B*, and *B* for *A*, because thus only can these two substances be represented empirically as coexistent. Nothing, however, can determine the place of anything else in time, except that which is its cause or the cause of its determinations. Therefore every substance (since it can be effect with regard to its determinations only) must contain in itself the causality of certain determinations in another substance, and, at the same time, the effects of the causality of that other substance, that is, substances must stand in dynamical communion, immediately or mediately, with each other, if their coexistence is to be known in any possible experience. Now, everything without which the experience of any objects would be impossible, may be said to be necessary with reference to such objects of experience; from which it follows that it is necessary for all substances, so far as they are coexistent as phenomena, to stand in a complete communion of reciprocity with each other.

The word *communion* (Gemeinschaft) may be used in two senses, meaning either *communio* or *commercium*. We use it here in the latter sense: as a dynamical communion without which even the local *communio spatii* could never be known empirically. We can easily perceive in our experience, that continuous influences only can lead our senses in all parts of space from one object to another; that the light which plays between our eyes and celestial bodies produces a mediate communion between us and them, and proves the coexistence of the latter; that we cannot change any place empirically (perceive such a change) unless matter itself renders the perception of our own place possible to us, and that by means of its reciprocal influence only matter can evince its simultaneous existence, and thus (though mediately only) its coexistence, even to the most distant objects. Without this communion every perception (of any phenomenon in space) is separated from the others, and the chain of empirical representations, that is, experience itself, would have to begin *de novo* with every new object, without the former experience being in the least connected with it, or standing to it in any temporal relation. I do not want to say anything here against empty space. Empty space may exist where perception cannot reach, and where therefore no empirical knowledge of coexistence takes place, but, in that case, it is no object for any possible experience.

The following remarks may elucidate this. It is necessary that in our mind all phenomena, as being contained in a possible experience, must share a communion of apperception, and if the objects are to be represented as connected in coexistence, they must reciprocally determine their place in time, and thus constitute a whole. If this subjective communion is to rest on an objective ground, or is to refer to phenomena as substances, then the perception of the one as cause must render possible the perception of the other, and *vice versa:* so that the succession which always exists in perceptions, as apprehensions, may not be attributed to the objects, but that the objects should be represented as existing simultaneously. This is a reciprocal influence, that is a real *commercium* of substances, without which the empirical relation of coexistence would be impossible in our experience. Through this commercium, phenomena as being apart from each other and yet connected, constitute a compound (*compositum reale*), and such compounds become possible in many ways. The three dynamical relations, therefore, from which all others are derived, are *inherence, consequence,* and *composition.*

* * * * * * * *

These are the three analogies of experience. They are nothing but principles for determining the existence of phenomena in time, according to its three modes. First, the relation of time itself, as to a quantity (quantity of existence, that is duration). Secondly, the relation in time, as in a series (successively). And thirdly, likewise in time, as the whole of all existence (simultaneously). This unity in the determination of time is dynamical only, that is, time is not looked upon as that in which experience assigns immediately its place to every existence, for this would be impossible; because absolute time is no object of perception by which phenomena could be held together; but the rule of the understanding through which alone the existence of phenomena can receive synthetical unity in time determines the place of each of them in time, therefore *a priori* and as valid for all time.

By nature (in the empirical sense of the word) we mean the coherence of phenomena in their existence, according to necessary rules, that is, laws. There are therefore certain laws, and they exist *a priori,* which themselves make nature

possible, while the empirical laws exist and are discovered
through experience, but in accordance with those original laws
which first render experience possible. Our analogies therefore represent the unity of nature in the coherence of all phenomena, under certain exponents, which express the relation
of time (as comprehending all existence) to the unity of apperception, which apperception can only take place in the
synthesis according to rules. The three analogies, therefore,
simply say, that all phenomena exist in one nature, and must
so exist because, without such unity *a priori* no unity of experience, and therefore no determination of objects in experience, would be possible.

With regard to the mode of proof, by which we have arrived at these transcendental laws of nature and its peculiar
character, a remark must be made which will become important as a rule for any other attempt to prove intelligible, and
at the same time synthetical propositions *a priori.* If we had
attempted to prove these analogies dogmatically, that is from
concepts, showing that all which exists is found only in that
which is permanent, that every event presupposes something
in a previous state on which it follows by rule, and lastly, that
in the manifold which is coexistent, states coexist in relation
to each other by rule, all our labour would have been in vain.
For we may analyse as much as we like, we shall never arrive
from one object and its existence at the existence of another,
or at its mode of existence by means of the concepts of these
things only. What else then remained? There remained the
possibility of experience, as that knowledge in which all objects must in the end be capable of being given to us, if their
representation is to have any objective reality for us. In this,
namely in the synthetical unity of apperception of all phenomena, we discovered the conditions *a priori* of an absolute and
necessary determination in time of all phenomenal existence.
Without this even the empirical determinations in time would
be impossible, and we thus established the rules of the synthetical unity *a priori,* by which we might anticipate experience. It was because people were ignorant of this method, and
imagined that they could prove dogmatically synthetical propositions which the empirical use of the understanding follows
as its principles, that so many and always unsuccessful attempts have been made to prove the proposition of the 'sufficient reason.' The other two analogies have not even been

thought of, though everybody followed them unconsciously,* because the method of the categories was wanting, by which alone every gap in the understanding, both with regard to concepts and principles, can be discovered and pointed out.

IV

The Postulates of Empirical Thought in General

1. What agrees with the formal conditions of experience (in intuition and in concepts) is possible
2. What is connected with the material conditions of experience (sensation) is real
3. That which, in its connection with the real, is determined by universal conditions of experience, is (exists as) necessary

Explanation

The categories of modality have this peculiar character that, as determining an object, they do not enlarge in the least the concept to which they are attached as predicates, but express only a relation to our faculty of knowledge. Even when the concept of a thing is quite complete, I can still ask with reference to that object, whether it is possible only, or real also, and, if the latter, whether it is necessary? No new determinations of the object are thereby conceived, but it is only asked in what relation it (with all its determinations) stands to the understanding and its empirical employment, to the empirical faculty of judgment, and to reason, in its application to experience?

The principles of modality are therefore nothing but explanations of the concepts of possibility, reality, and necessity, in

---

* The unity of the universe, in which all phenomena are supposed to be connected, is evidently a mere deduction of the quietly adopted principle of the communion of all substances as coexistent; for if they were isolated, they would not form parts of a whole, and if their connection (the reciprocity of the manifold) were not necessary for the sake of their coexistence, it would be impossible to use the latter, which is a purely ideal relation, as a proof of the former, which is real. We have shown, however, that communion is really the ground of the possibility of an empirical knowledge of coexistence, and that really we can only conclude from this the existence of the former, as its condition.

their empirical employment, confining all categories to an empirical employment only, and prohibiting their transcendental[13] use. For if these categories are not to have a purely logical character, expressing the forms of thought analytically, but are to refer to things, their possibility, reality, or necessity, they must have reference to possible experience and its synthetical unity, in which alone objects of knowledge can be given.

The postulate of the possibility of things demands that the concept of these should agree with the formal conditions of experience in general. This, the objective form of experience in general, contains all synthesis which is required for a knowledge of objects. A concept is to be considered as empty, and as referring to no object, if the synthesis which it contains does not belong to experience, whether as borrowed from it (in which case it is called an empirical concept), or as a synthesis on which, as a condition *a priori,* all experience (in its form) depends, in which case it is a pure concept, but yet belonging to experience, because its object can only be found in it. For whence could the character of the possibility of an object, which can be conceived by a synthetical concept *a priori,* be derived, except from the synthesis which constitutes the form of all empirical knowledge of objects? It is no doubt a necessary logical condition, that such a concept must contain nothing contradictory, but this is by no means sufficient to establish the objective reality of a concept, that is, the possibility of such an object, as is conceived by a concept. Thus in the concept of a figure to be enclosed between two straight lines, there is nothing contradictory, because the concepts of two straight lines and their meeting contain no negation of a figure. The impossibility depends, not on the concept itself, but on its construction in space, that is, the conditions of space and its determinations, and it is these that have objective reality, or apply to possible things, because they contain *a priori* in themselves the form of experience in general.

And now we shall try to explain the manifold usefulness and influence of this postulate of possibility. If I represent to myself a thing that is permanent, while everything which changes belongs merely to its state, I can never know from such a concept by itself that a thing of that kind is possible. Or, if I represent to myself something so constituted that, when it is given, something else must at all times and inevitably fol-

---

[13] Here the same as *transcendent.*

low upon it, this may no doubt be conceived without contradiction, but we have as yet no means of judging whether such a quality, viz. causality, is to be met with in any possible object. Lastly, I can very well represent to myself different things (substances) so constituted, that the state of the one produces an effect on the state of the other, and this reciprocally; but whether such a relation can belong to any things cannot be learned from these concepts which contain a purely arbitrary synthesis. The objective reality of these concepts is only known when we see that they express *a priori* the relations of perceptions in every kind of experience; and this objective reality, that is, their transcendental truth, though independent of all experience, is nevertheless not independent of all relation to the form of experience in general, and to that synthetical unity in which alone objects can be known empirically.

But if we should think of framing new concepts of substances, forces, and reciprocal actions out of the material supplied to us by our perceptions, without borrowing from experience the instance of their connection, we should entangle ourselves in mere cobwebs of our brain, the possibility of which could not be tested by any criteria, because in forming them we were not guided by experience, nor had borrowed these concepts from it. Such purely imaginary concepts cannot receive the character of possibility, like the categories *a priori,* as conditions on which all experience depends, but only *a posteriori,* as concepts that must be given by experience, so that their possibility can either not be known at all, or *a posteriori,* and empirically only. Thus, for instance, a substance supposed to be present as permanent in space, and yet not filling it (like that something between matter and the thinking subject, which some have tried to introduce), or a peculiar faculty of our mind, by which we can see (not only infer) the future, or lastly, another faculty, by which we can enter into a community of thought with other men (however distant they may be), all these are concepts the possibility of which has nothing to rest on, because it is not founded on experience and its known laws. Without these they are and can only be arbitrary combinations of thought which, though they contain nothing contradictory in themselves, have no claim to objective reality, or to the possibility of such an object as is to be conceived by them. With regard to reality, it stands to reason that we cannot conceive it in the concrete without the aid of experience; for reality concerns sensation only, as the material of experience, and not the form of relations, which might to a certain extent allow us to indulge in mere fancies.

I here pass by everything the possibility of which can only be learned from its reality in experience, and I only mean to consider the possibility of things through concepts *a priori*. Of these (concepts) I persist in maintaining that they can never exist as such concepts by themselves alone, but only as formal and objective conditions of experience in general.[14]

It might seem indeed as if the possibility of a triangle could be known from its concept by itself (being independent of all experience), for we can give to it an object entirely *a priori,* that is, we can construct it. But as this is only the form of an object, it would always remain a product of the imagination only. The possibility of its object would remain doubtful, because more is wanted to establish it, namely, that such a figure should really be conceived under all those conditions on which all objects of experience depend. That which alone connects with this concept the representation of the possibility of such a thing, is the fact that space is a formal condition *a priori* of all external experiences, and that the same formative synthesis, by which we construct a triangle in imagination, should be identical with that which we exercise in the apprehension of a phenomenon, in order to make an empirical concept of it. And thus the possibility of continuous quantities, nay, of all quantities, the concepts of which are always synthetical, can never be deduced from the concepts themselves, but only from them, as formal conditions of the determination of objects in all experience. And where indeed should we look for objects, corresponding to our concepts, except in experience, by which alone objects are given us? If we are able to know and determine the possibility of things without any previous experience, this is only with reference to those formal conditions under which anything may become an object in experience. This takes place entirely *a priori,* but nevertheless in constant reference to experience, and within its limits.

The postulate concerning our knowledge of the *reality* of things, requires *perception,* therefore sensation and consciousness of it, not indeed immediately of the object itself, the existence of which is to be known, but yet of a connection between it and some real perception, according to the analogies of ex-

---

[14] I have adopted Erdmann's conjecture, *als solche Begriffe* instead of *aus solchen Begriffen.*

perience which determine in general all real combinations in experience.

In the *mere concept* of a thing no sign of its existence can be discovered. For though the concept be ever so perfect, so that nothing should be wanting in it to enable us to conceive the thing with all its own determinations, existence has nothing to do with all this. It depends only on the question whether such a thing be given us, so that its perception may even precede its concept. A concept preceding experience implies its possibility only, while perception, which supplies the material of a concept, is the only characteristic of reality. It is possible, however, even before the perception of a thing, and therefore, in a certain sense, *a priori,* to know its existence, provided it hang together with some other perceptions, according to the principles of their empirical connection (analogies). For in that case the existence of a thing hangs together at least with our perceptions in a possible experience, and guided by our analogies we can, starting from our real experience, arrive at some other thing in the series of possible perceptions. Thus we know the existence of some magnetic matter pervading all bodies from the perception of the attracted iron filings, though our organs are so constituted as to render an immediate perception of that matter impossible. According to the laws of sensibility and the texture of our perceptions, we ought in our experience to arrive at an immediate empirical intuition of that magnetic matter, if only our senses were more acute, for their actual obtuseness does not concern the form of possible experience. Wherever, therefore, perception and its train can reach, according to empirical laws, there our knowledge also of the existence of things can reach. But if we do not begin with experience, or do not proceed according to the laws of the empirical connection of phenomena, we are only making a vain display, as if we could guess and discover the existence of anything.

An important protest, however, against these rules for proving existence mediately is brought forward by Idealism, *and this is therefore the proper place for its refutation.*

Refutation of Idealism

Idealism (I mean material *idealism) is the theory which declares the existence of objects in space, without us, as either doubtful only and not demonstrable, or as false and impossi-*

ble. The former *is the* problematical *idealism of Descartes, who declares one empirical assertion only to be undoubted, namely, that of* I am; *the* latter *is the* dogmatical *idealism of Berkeley, who declares space and all things to which it belongs as an inseparable condition, as something impossible in itself, and, therefore, the things in space as mere imaginations. Dogmatic idealism is inevitable, if we look upon space as a property belonging to things by themselves, for in that case space and all of which it is a condition, would be a non-entity. The ground on which that idealism rests has been removed by us in the transcendental Æsthetic. Problematical idealism, which asserts nothing, but only pleads our inability of proving any existence except our own by means of immediate experience, is reasonable and in accordance with a sound philosophical mode of thought, which allows of no decisive judgment, before a sufficient proof has been found. The required proof will have to demonstrate that we may have not only an* imagination, *but also an* experience *of external things, and this it seems can hardly be effected in any other way except by proving that even our internal experience, which Descartes considers as undoubted, is possible only under the supposition of external experience.*

Theorem

The simple, but empirically determined Consciousness of my own existence, proves the Existence of objects in space outside myself.

Proof

I am conscious of my own existence as determined in time, and all determination in time presupposes something permanent *in the perception.*[15] *That* permanent, *however, cannot be an intuition within me, because all the causes which determine my existence, so far as they can be found within me, are representations, and as such require themselves something permanent, different from them, in reference to which their change, and therefore my existence in time in which they change, may be determined. The perception of this permanent, therefore, is possible only through a thing* outside *me, and not through the mere* representation *of a thing outside me, and the deter-*

---

[15] This passage has been translated as amended by Kant himself in the Preface to the Second Edition. (See p. xliv.)

mination of my existence in time is, consequently, possible only by the existence of real things, which I perceive outside me. Now, as the consciousness in time is necessarily connected with the consciousness of the possibility of that determination of time, it is also necessarily connected with the existence of things outside me, as the condition of the determination of time. In other words, the consciousness of my own existence is, at the same time, an immediate consciousness of the existence of other things.

Note 1.—It will have been perceived that in the foregoing proof the trick played by idealism has been turned against it, and with greater justice. Idealism assumed that the only immediate experience is the internal, and that from it we can no more than infer external things, though in an untrustworthy manner only, as always happens if from given effects we infer definite causes: it being quite possible that the cause of the representations, which are ascribed by us, it may be wrongly, to external things, may lie within ourselves. We, however, have proved that external experience is really immediate,* and that only by means of it, though not the consciousness of our own existence, yet its determination in time, that is, internal experience, becomes possible. No doubt the representation of I am, which expresses the consciousness that can accompany all thought, is that which immediately includes the existence of a subject: but it does not yet include a knowledge of it, and therefore no empirical knowledge, that is, experience. For that we require, besides the thought of something existing, intuition also, and in this case internal intuition in respect to which, that is, to time, the subject must be determined. For that purpose external objects are absolutely necessary, so that

---

* The immediate consciousness of the existence of external things is not simply assumed in the preceding theorem, but proved, whether we can understand the possibility of this consciousness or not. The question with regard to that possibility would come to this, whether we have an internal sense only, and no external sense, but merely an external imagination. It is clear, however, that, even in order to imagine only something as external, that is, to represent it to the senses in intuition, we must have an external sense, and thus distinguish immediately the mere receptivity of an external intuition from that spontaneity which characterizes every act of imagination. For merely to imagine an external sense would really be to destroy the faculty of intuition, which is to be determined by the faculty of imagination.

internal experience itself is possible, mediately only, and through external experience.

Note 2.—This view is fully confirmed by the empirical use of our faculty of knowledge, as applied to the determination of time. Not only are we unable to perceive any determination of time, except through a change in external relations (motion) with reference to what is permanent in space (for instance, the movement of the sun with respect to terrestrial objects), but we really have nothing permanent to which we could refer the concept of a substance, as an intuition, except matter *only: and even its permanence is not derived from external experience, but presupposed* a priori *as a necessary condition of all determination of time, and therefore also of*[16] *the determination of the internal sense with respect to our own existence through the existence of external things. The consciousness of myself, in the representation of the* ego, *is not an intuition, but a merely* intellectual *representation of the spontaneity of a thinking subject. Hence that* ego *has not the slightest predicate derived from intuition, which predicate, as* permanent, *might serve as the correlate of the determination of time in the internal sense: such as is, for instance,* impermeability *in matter, as an* empirical *intuition.*

Note 3.—Because the existence of external objects is required for the possibility of a definite consciousness of ourselves, it does not follow that every intuitional representation of external things involves, at the same time, their existence; for such a representation may well be the mere effect of the faculty of imagination (in dreams as well as in madness); but it can be such an effect only through the reproduction of former external perceptions, which, as we have shown, is impossible without the reality of external objects. What we wanted to prove here was only that internal experience in general is possible only through external experience in general. Whether this or that supposed experience be purely imaginary, must be settled according to its own particular determinations, and through a comparison with the criteria of all real experience.

With reference to the third postulate we find that it refers to the material necessity in existence, and not to the merely formal and logical necessity in the connection of concepts. As it is impossible that the existence of the objects of the senses

[16] Read *der* instead of *als.*

should ever be known entirely *a priori,* though it may be known to a certain extent *a priori,* namely, with reference to another already given existence, and as even in that case we can only arrive at such an existence as must somewhere be contained in the whole of the experience of which the given perception forms a part, it follows that the necessity of existence can never be known from concepts, but always from the connection only with what is actually perceived, according to general rules of experience.[17] Now, there is no existence that can be known as necessary under the condition of other given phenomena, except the existence of effects from given causes, according to the laws of causality. It is not therefore the existence of things (substances), but the existence of their state, of which alone we can know the necessity, and this from other states only, which are given in perception, and according to the empirical laws of causality. Hence it follows that the criterium of necessity can only be found in the law of possible experience, viz. that everything that happens is determined *a priori* by its cause in phenomena.[18] We therefore know in nature the necessity of those effects only of which the causes are given, and the character of necessity in existence never goes beyond the field of possible experience, and even there it does not apply to the existence of things, as substances, because such substances can never be looked upon as empirical effects or as something that happens and arises. Necessity, therefore, affects only the relations of phenomena according to the dynamical law of causality, and the possibility, dependent upon it, of concluding *a priori* from a given existence (of a cause) to another existence (that of an effect). Thus the principle that everything which happens is hypothetically necessary, subjects all the changes in the world to a law, that is, to a rule of necessary existence, without which there would not even be such a thing as nature. Hence the proposition that nothing happens by blind chance (*in mundo non datur casus*) is an *a priori* law of nature, and so is likewise the other, that no necessity in nature is a blind, but always a conditional and therefore an intelligible, necessity (*non datur fatum*). Both these are laws by which the mere play of changes is rendered subject to a *nature of things* (as phenomena), or what is the same, to that unity of the understanding in which alone they can belong to experience, as the synthetical unity of phenom-

[17] Insert *man* before *gleichwohl,* and leave out *können* at the end of the sentence.
[18] Read *seine Ursache* instead of *ihre.*

ena. Both are dynamical principles. The former is in reality a consequence of the principle of causality (the second of the analogies of experience). The latter is one of the principles of modality, which to the determination of causality adds the concept of necessity, which itself is subject to a rule of the understanding. The principle of continuity rendered every break in the series of phenomena (changes) impossible (*in mundo non datur saltus*), and likewise any gap between two phenomena in the whole of our empirical intuitions in space (*non datur hiatus*). For so we may express the proposition that nothing can enter into experience to prove a vacuum, or even to admit it as a possible part of empirical synthesis. For the vacuum, which one *may* conceive as outside the field of possible experience (the world), can never come before the tribunal of the understanding which has to decide on such questions only as concern the use to be made of given phenomena for empirical knowledge. It is in reality a problem of that ideal reason which goes beyond the sphere of a possible experience, and wants to form an opinion of that which surrounds and limits experience, and will therefore have to be considered in our transcendental Dialectic. With regard to the four propositions (*in mundo non datur hiatus, non datur saltus, non datur casus, non datur fatum*), it would be easy to represent each of them, as well as all principles of a transcendental origin, according to the order of the categories, and thus to assign its proper place to every one of them. But, after what has been said before, the versed and expert reader will find it easy to do this himself, and to discover the proper method for it. They all simply agree in this, that they admit nothing in our empirical synthesis that would in any way run counter to the understanding, and to the continuous cohesion of all phenomena, that is, to the unity of its concepts. For it is the understanding alone through which the unity of experience, in which all perceptions must have their place, becomes possible.

Whether the field of possibility be larger than the field which contains everything which is real, and whether this again be larger than the field of what is necessary, are curious questions and admitting of a synthetical solution, which questions however are to be brought before the tribunal of reason only. They really come to this, whether all things, as phenomena, belong to the sphere of one experience, of which every given perception forms a part, that could not be connected with any other phenomena, or whether my perceptions can ever belong to more than one possible experience (in its general connection). The understanding in reality does nothing but give to experience a rule *a priori,* according to the subjective and formal conditions of sensibility and apperception, which alone render experience possible. Other forms of intuition (different from space and time), and other forms of the understanding (different from the discursive forms of thought or conceptual knowledge), even if they were possible, we could in no wise render conceivable or intelligible to ourselves; and even if we could, they would never belong to experience, the only field of knowledge in which objects are given to us. Whether there be therefore other perceptions but those that belong to our whole possible experience, whether there be in fact a completely new field of matter, can never be determined by the understanding, which is only concerned with the synthesis of what is given.

The poverty of the usual arguments by which we construct a large empire of possibility of which all that is real (the objects of experience) forms but a small segment, is but too apparent. When we say that all that is real is possible, we arrive, according to the logical rules of inversion, at the merely particular proposition that some possible is real, and thus seem to imply that much is possible that is not real. Nay, it seems as if we might extend the number of things possible beyond that of things real, simply on the ground that something must be added to the possible to make it real. But this addition to the possible I cannot recognise, because what would thus be added to the possible, would be really the impossible. It is only to my understanding that anything can be added concerning the agreement with the formal conditions of experience, and what can be added is the connection with some perception; and whatever is connected with such a perception, according to empirical laws, is real, though it may not be perceived immediately. But that, in constant connection with what is given us in experience, there should be another series of phenomena, and therefore more than one all-embracing experience, cannot possibly be concluded from what is given us, and still less, if nothing is given us, because nothing can be thought without some kind of material. What is possible only under conditions which themselves are possible only, is not possible in the full sense of the word, not therefore in the sense in which we ask whether the possibility of things can extend beyond the limits of experience.

I have only touched on these questions in order to leave no gap in what are commonly supposed to be the concepts of the understanding. But absolute possibility (which has no regard for the formal conditions of experience) is really no concept of the understanding, and can never be used empirically, but belongs to reason alone, which goes beyond all possible empirical use of the understanding. We have therefore made these few critical remarks only, leaving the subject itself unexplained for the present.

And here, when I am on the point of concluding this fourth number and at the same time the system of all principles of the pure understanding, I think I ought to explain why I call the principles of modality *postulates*. I do not take this term in the sense which has been given to it by some modern philosophical writers, and which is opposed to the sense in which mathematicians take it, viz. that to postulate should mean to represent a proposition as certain without proof or justification; for if we were to admit with regard to synthetical propositions, however evident they may appear, that they should meet with unreserved applause, without any deduction, and on their own authority only, all criticism of the understanding would be at an end. And as there is no lack of bold assertions, which public opinion does not decline to accept, (this acceptance being, however, no credential), our understanding would be open to every fancy, and could not refuse its sanction to claims which demand admission as real axioms in the same confident tone, though without any substantial reasons. If therefore a condition *a priori* is to be synthetically joined to the concept of a thing, it will be indispensable that, if not a proof, at least a deduction of the legitimacy of such an assertion, should be forthcoming.

The principles of modality, however, are not objectively synthetical, because the predicates of possibility, reality, and necessity do not in the least increase the concept of which they are predicated, by adding anything to its representation. But as nevertheless they are synthetical, they are so subjectively only, i.e. they add to the concept of a (real) thing, without predicating anything new, the peculiar faculty of knowledge from which it springs and on which it depends, so that, if in the understanding the concept is only connected with the formal conditions of experience, its object is called *possible;* if it is connected with perception (sensation as the material of the senses), and through it determined by the understanding, its object is called *real;* while, if it is determined through the connection of perceptions, according to concepts, its object is called *necessary*. The principles of modality therefore predicate nothing of a concept except the act of the faculty of knowledge by which it is produced. In mathematics a postulate means a practical proposition, containing nothing but a synthesis by which we first give an object to ourselves and produce its concept, as if, for instance, we draw a circle with a given line from a given point in the plane. Such a proposition cannot be proved, because the process required for it is the very process by which we first produce the concept of such a figure. We may therefore with the same right postulate the principles of modality, because they never increase* the concept of a thing, but indicate the manner only in which the concept was joined with our faculty of knowledge.

General Note on the System of the Principles

It is something very remarkable that we cannot understand the possibility of anything from the category alone, but must always have an intuition in order to exhibit by it the objective reality of the pure concept of the understanding. Let us take, for instance, the categories of relation. It is impossible to understand, from mere concepts alone:—

First, *how something can exist as* subject *only, and not as a mere determination of other things, that is, how it can be a* substance: *or,*

Secondly, *how, because something is, something else must be, that is, how something can ever be a cause: or,*

Thirdly, *how, when there are several things, something could follow from the existence of one of them as affecting the rest, and* vice versa, *so that there should exist, in this way, a certain community of substances. The same applies to the other categories, as, for instance, how a thing could be of the same kind as many others, and thus be a quantity. So long as there is no intuition, we do not know whether by the categories we conceive an object, nay, whether any object can at all belong to them: and thus we see again that by themselves the categories are not* knowledge, *but mere* forms of thought, *by which given intuitions are turned into knowledge.*

It likewise follows from this, that no synthetical proposition

* No doubt by reality I assert more than by possibility, but not in the thing itself, which can never contain more in its reality than what is contained in its complete possibility. While possibility is only the positing of a thing in reference to the understanding (in its empirical use), reality is, at the same time, a connection of it with perception.

can be made out of mere categories, as, for instance, if it is said that in everything existing there is substance, i.e. something that can exist as subject only, and not as a mere predicate; or, everything is a quantum, etc. Here we have really nothing whatever which would enable us to go beyond a given concept, and to connect with it another. Hence no one has ever succeeded in proving a synthetical proposition by pure concepts of the understanding only: as, for instance, the proposition that everything which exists contingently, has a cause. All that could be proved was, that, without such a relation, we could not conceive the existence of what is contingent, that is, that we could not know a priori through the understanding the existence of such a thing; from which it does not follow in the least that the same condition applies to the possibility of things themselves. If the reader will go back to our proof of the principle of causality, he will perceive that we could prove it of objects of possible experience only, by saying that everything which happens (every event) presupposes a cause. We could prove it only as the principle of the possibility of experience, that is, of the knowledge of an object, given in empirical intuition, but not by means of mere concepts. It is perfectly true, that nevertheless this proposition, that everything contingent must have a cause, carries conviction to everybody from mere concepts: but it should be observed, that in this case the concept of the contingent contains no longer the category of modality (as something the non-existence of which can be conceived), but that of relation (as something which can only exist as the consequence of something else). It thus becomes in reality an identical proposition, namely, that that which can exist as a consequence only has its cause. And thus, when we have to give examples of contingent existence, we have always recourse to changes, and not only to the possibility of conceiving the opposite.* Change, however, is an

---

* It is easy enough to conceive the non-existence of matter, but the ancients did not infer from this its contingency. Not even the change of being and not-being of any given state of a thing, which constitutes all change, can prove the contingency of that state, as if from the reality of its opposite. The rest of a body, for instance, following on its motion, does not yet prove the contingency of that motion, because the former is the opposite of the latter. The opposite here is opposed to the other, not realiter, but logically only. In order to prove the contingency of the motion of a body, we should have to prove that instead of the motion at the antecedent point of time, it would have been possible for the body to

event which, as such, is possible through a cause only, and the non-existence of which is therefore possible in itself. We thus mean by contingency, that something can exist as the effect of a cause only; and if therefore a thing is assumed to be contingent, it becomes a merely analytical proposition to say that it has a cause.

It is still more remarkable, however, that, in order to understand the possibility of things according to the categories, and thus to establish the objective reality *of the latter, we require not only intuitions, but always* external intuitions. *Thus, if we take, for instance, the pure concepts of* relation, *we find that:—*

First, in order to give something permanent *in intuition, corresponding to the concept of* substance *(and thus to show the objective reality of that concept), we require an intuition in space (of matter), because space alone can determine anything as permanent, while time, and therefore everything that exists in the internal sense, is in a constant flux.*

Secondly, that in order to exhibit change, *as the intuition corresponding to the concept of* causality, *we must use motion as change in space for our example, nay, can thus only gain an intuition of changes the possibility of which no pure understanding can ever conceive. Change is the connection of contradictory opposites in the existence of one and the same thing. Now, how it is possible that from a given state another state, opposed to it, should arise in the same thing, no reason can comprehend without an example; nay, without an intuition, cannot even render it intelligible to itself. That intuition, however, is that of the motion of a point in space, the presence of which in different places (as a consequence of opposite determinations) gives us, for the first time, an intuition of change: so that, in order to make even internal changes afterwards conceivable to ourselves, we must make time, as the form of the internal sense, figuratively comprehensible to ourselves by means of a line, and the internal change by means of the drawing of that line (motion): in other words, the successive existence of ourselves in different states, by means of an external intuition. The real reason of this lies in the fact that all change presupposes something permanent in intuition, in order that it may itself be perceived as change, while no permanent intuition is to be found in the internal sense.*

Thirdly, and lastly, the category of community *cannot, so*

---

have been at rest at that very time, *not that it is at rest afterwards; for in this case both opposites are quite consistent with each other.*

far as its possibility is concerned, be conceived by mere reason alone: and the objective reality of that concept cannot therefore be possibly understood without intuition, and without external intuition in space. For how should we conceive the possibility that, when several substances exist, something (as an effect) could follow from the existence of one of them as affecting reciprocally the existence of the other, and that, therefore, because there is something in the former, something must also be in the latter, which, from the existence of the latter alone, could not be understood? For this is necessary to establish community, though it is utterly inconceivable among things, each of which completely isolates itself through its substantiality. Leibniz, therefore, as he attributed community to the substances of the world, as conceived by the understanding alone, required the interference of a Deity; because, as he justly perceived, such community would have been inconceivable from the existence of such substances only. We, on the contrary, can render the possibility of such a communion (of substances as phenomena) perfectly conceivable to ourselves, if we represent them to ourselves in space, that is, in external intuition. For space contains, even a priori, formal external relations, as conditions of the possibility of the real relations of action and reaction, that is, of community.

It is easy to show, in the same manner, that the possibility of things as quanta, and therefore, the objective reality of the category of quantity, can be exhibited in external intuition only, and, by means of it alone, be afterwards applied to the internal sense. But, in order to avoid prolixity, I must leave it to the reflection of the reader to find the examples of this.

The whole of these notes is of great importance, not only as confirming our previous refutation of idealism, but even more, when we come to treat of self-knowledge by mere internal consciousness, and the determination of our own nature, without the help of external empirical intuitions, in order to show us the limits of the possibility of such knowledge.

The last result of the whole of this section is therefore this: All principles of the pure understanding are nothing more than a priori principles of the possibility of experience; and to experience alone do all synthetical propositions a priori relate: nay, their possibility itself rests entirely on that relation.

THE TRANSCENDENTAL DOCTRINE OF THE FACULTY OF JUDGMENT OR ANALYTIC OF PRINCIPLES

CHAPTER III

ON THE GROUND OF DISTINCTION OF ALL SUBJECTS INTO PHENOMENA AND NOUMENA

We have now not only traversed the whole domain of the pure understanding, and carefully examined each part of it, but we have also measured its extent, and assigned to everything in it its proper place. This domain, however, is an island and enclosed by nature itself within limits that can never be changed. It is the country of truth (a very attractive name), but surrounded by a wide and stormy ocean, the true home of illusion, where many a fog bank and ice that soon melts away tempt us to believe in new lands, while constantly deceiving the adventurous mariner with vain hopes, and involving him in adventures which he can never leave, and yet can never bring to an end. Before we venture ourselves on this sea, in order to explore it on every side, and to find out whether anything is to be hoped for there, it will be useful to glance once more at the map of that country which we are about to leave, and to ask ourselves, first, whether we might not be content with what it contains, nay, whether we must not be content with it, supposing that there is no solid ground anywhere else on which we could settle; secondly, by what title we possess even that domain, and may consider ourselves safe against all hostile claims. Although we have sufficiently answered these questions in the course of the analytic, a summary recapitulation of their solutions may help to strengthen our conviction, by uniting all arguments in one point.

We have seen that the understanding possesses everything which it draws from itself, without borrowing from experience, for no other purpose but for experience. The principles of the pure understanding, whether constitutive *a priori* (as the mathematical) or simply relative (as the dynamical), contain nothing but, as it were, the pure schema of possible experience; for that experience derives its unity from that synthetical unity alone which the understanding originally and spontaneously imparts to the synthesis of imagination, with reference to apperception, and to which all phenomena, as data of a possible knowledge, must conform *a priori*. But although these rules of the understanding are not only true *a priori,* but the very source of all truth, that is, of the agreement of our knowledge with objects, because containing the conditions of the possibility of experience, as the complete sphere of all knowledge in which objects can be given to us, nevertheless we do not seem to be content with hearing only what is true, but want to know a great deal more. If therefore this critical investigation does not teach us any more than what, even without such subtle researches, we should have practised ourselves in the purely empirical use of the understanding, it would seem as if the advantages derived from it were hardly worth the labour. One might reply that nothing would be more prejudicial to the enlargement of our knowledge than that curiosity which, before entering upon any researches, wishes to know beforehand the advantages likely to accrue from them, though quite unable as yet to form the least conception of such advantages, even though they were placed before our eyes. There is, however, one advantage in this transcendental investigation which can be rendered intelligible, nay, even attractive to the most troublesome and reluctant apprentice, namely this, that the understanding confined to its empirical use only and unconcerned with regard to the sources of its own knowledge, may no doubt fare very well in other respects, but can never determine for itself the limits of its own use and know what is inside or outside its own sphere. It is for that purpose that such profound investigations are required as we have just instituted. If the understanding cannot decide whether certain questions lie within its own horizon or not, it can never feel certain with regard to its claims and possessions, but must be prepared for many humiliating corrections, when constantly transgressing, as it certainly will, the limits of its own domain, and losing itself in follies and fancies.

That the understanding cannot make any but an empirical, and never a transcendental, use of all its principles *a priori,* nay, of all its concepts, is a proposition which, if thoroughly understood, leads indeed to most important consequences. What we call the transcendental use of a concept in any proposition is its being referred to things in general and to things by themselves, while its empirical use refers to phenomena only, that is, to objects of a possible experience. That the latter use alone is admissible will be clear from the following considerations. What is required for every concept is, first, the logical form of a concept (of thought) in general; and, secondly, the possibility of an object to which it refers. Without the latter, it has no sense, and is entirely empty, though it may still contain the logical function by which a concept can be formed out of any data. The only way in which an object can be given to a concept is in intuition, and though a pure intuition is possible *a priori* and before the object, yet even that pure intuition can receive its object, and with it its objective validity, by an empirical intuition only, of which it is itself nothing but the form. All concepts, therefore, and with them all principles, though they may be possible *a priori,* refer nevertheless to empirical intuitions, that is, to data of a possible experience. Without this, they can claim no objective validity, but are a mere play, whether of the imagination or of the understanding with their respective representations. Let us take the concepts of mathematics as an example, and, first, with regard to pure intuitions. Although such principles as 'space has three dimensions,' 'between two points there can be only one straight line,' as well as the representation of the object with which that science is occupied, may be produced in the mind *a priori,* they would have no meaning, if we were not able at all times to show their meaning as applied to phenomena (empirical objects). It is for this reason that an abstract concept is required to be made *sensuous,* that is, that its corresponding object is required to be shown in intuition, because, without this, the concept (as people say) is without *sense,* that is, without meaning. Mathematics fulfil this requirement by the construction of the figure, which is a phenomenon present to the senses (although constructed *a priori*). In the same science the concept of quantity finds its support and sense in number; and this in turn in the fingers, the beads of the abacus, or in strokes and points which can be presented to the eyes. The concept itself was produced *a priori,* together with all the synthetical principles or formulas which can be derived from such concepts; but their use and their relation to objects can nowhere be found except in experience, of which those concepts contain *a priori* the (formal) possibility only.

That this is the case with all categories and with all the principles drawn from them, becomes evident from the fact that we could not define any one of them (really, that is, make conceivable the possibility of their object),[19] without at once having recourse to the conditions of sensibility or the form of phenomena, to which, as their only possible objects, these categories must necessarily be restricted, it being impossible, if we take away these conditions, to assign to them any meaning, that is, any relation to an object, or to make it intelligible to ourselves by an example what kind of thing could be intended by such concepts.

[When representing the table of the categories, we dispensed with the definition of every one of them, because at that time it seemed unnecessary for our purpose, which concerned their synthetical use only, and because entailing responsibilities which we were not bound to incur. This was not a mere excuse, but a very important prudential rule, viz. not to rush into definitions, and to attempt or pretend completeness or precision in the definition of a concept, when one or other of its characteristic marks is sufficient without a complete enumeration of all that constitute the whole concept. Now, however, we can perceive that this caution had even a deeper ground, namely, that we could not have defined them, even if we had wished;* for, if we remove all conditions of sensibility, which distinguish them as the concepts of a possible empirical use, and treat them as concepts of things in general (therefore as of transcendental use), nothing remains but to regard the logical function in judgments as the condition of the possibility of the things themselves, without the slightest indication as to where they could have their application and their object, or how they could have any meaning or objective validity in the pure understanding, apart from sensibility.][20]

No one can explain the concept of quantity in general, except, it may be, by saying that it is the determination of an object, by which we may know how many times the one is supposed to exist in it. But this 'how many times' is based on

---

[19] Additions of the Second Edition.

* I am treating here of the real definition, which not only puts in place of the name of a thing other and more intelligible words, but that which contains a clear mark by which the object (*definitum*) can at all times be safely recognised, and by which the defined concept becomes fit for practical use. A real definition (*Realarklärung*) must therefore render clear the concept itself, and its objective reality also. Of this kind are the mathematical explanations which represent an object in intuition, according to its concept.

[20] Read *nimmt* instead of *nehmen*, and *können* instead of *könne*.

successive repetition, that is on time, and on the synthesis in it of the homogeneous.

Reality, again, can only be explained in opposition to a negation, if we think of time (as containing all being) being either filled or empty.

Were I to leave out permanence (which means existence at all times), nothing would remain of my concept of substance but the logical representation of a subject which I think I can realise by imagining something which is a subject only, without being a predicate of anything. But in this case we should not only be ignorant of all conditions under which this logical distinction could belong to anything, but we should be unable to make any use of it or draw any conclusions from it, because no object is thus determined for the use of this concept, and no one can tell whether such a concept has any meaning at all.

Of the concept of cause also (if I leave out time, in which something follows on something else by rule) I should find no more in the pure category than that it is something which enables us to conclude the existence of something else, so that it would not only be impossible to distinguish cause and effect from each other, but the concept of cause would possess no indication as to how it can be applied to any object, because, in order to form any such conclusion, certain conditions require to be known of which the concept itself tells us nothing. The so-called principle that everything contingent has a cause, comes no doubt before us with great solemnity and self-assumed dignity. But, if I ask what you understand by contingent and you answer, something of which the non-existence is possible, I should be glad to know how you can recognise this possibility of non-existence, if you do not represent to yourselves, in the series of phenomena, some kind of succession, and in it an existence that follows upon non-existence (or *vice versa*), and consequently a change? To say that the non-existence of a thing is not self-contradictory is but a lame appeal to a logical condition which, though it is necessary for the concept, yet is by no means sufficient for its real possibility. I can perfectly well remove in thought every existing substance, without contradicting myself, but I can by no means conclude from this as to its objective contingency in its existence, that is, the possibility of its non-existence in itself.

As regards the concept of community, it is easy to see that, as the pure categories of substance and causality admit of no explanation that would determine their object, neither could such an explanation apply to the reciprocal causality in the relation of substances to each other (*commercium*).

As to possibility, existence, and necessity, no one has yet been able to explain them, except by a manifest tautology, so long as their definition is to be exclusively drawn from the pure understanding. To substitute the transcendental possibility of things (when an object corresponds to a concept) for the logical possibility of the concept (when the concept does not contradict itself) is a quibble such as could deceive and satisfy the inexperienced only.*

[It seems to be something strange and even illogical that there should be a concept which must have a meaning, and yet is incapable of any explanation. But the case of these categories is peculiar, because it is only by means of the general sensuous condition that they can acquire a definite meaning, and a reference to any objects. That condition being left out in the pure category, it follows that it can contain nothing but the logical function by which the manifold is brought into a concept. By means of this function, that is, the pure form of the concept, nothing can be known nor distinguished as to the object belonging to it, because the sensuous condition, under which alone objects can belong to it, has been removed. Thus we see that the categories require, besides the pure concept of the understanding, certain determinations of their application to sensibility in general (schemata). Without them, they would not be concepts by which an object can be known and distinguished from other objects, but only so many ways of thinking an object for possible intuitions, and giving to it, according to one of the functions of the understanding, its meaning (certain requisite conditions being given). They are needed to define an object, and cannot therefore be defined themselves. The logical functions of judgments in general, namely, unity and plurality, assertion and negation, subject and predicate, cannot be defined without arguing in a circle, because the definition would itself be a judgment and contain these very functions. The pure categories are nothing but representations of things in general, so far as the manifold in

---

* *In one word, none of these concepts admit of being* authenticated, *nor can their real possibility be proved, if all sensuous intuition (the only one which we possess) is removed, and there remains in that case a* logical *possibility only, that is, that a concept (a thought) is possible. This, however, does not concern us here, but only whether the concept refers to an object and does therefore signify anything.*

intuition must be thought by one or the other of these functions. Thus, magnitude is the determination which can only be thought by a judgment possessing quantity (*judicium commune*); reality, the determination which can only be thought by an affirmative judgment; while substance is that which, in regard to intuition, must be the last subject of all other determinations. With all this it remains perfectly undetermined, what kind of things they may be with regard to which we have to use one rather than another of these functions, so that, without the condition of sensuous intuition, for which they supply the synthesis, the categories have no relation to any definite object, cannot define any object, and consequently have not in themselves the validity of objective concepts.]

From this it follows incontestably, that the pure concepts of the understanding never admit of a transcendental, but only of an empirical use, and that the principles of the pure understanding can only be referred, as general conditions of a possible experience, to objects of the senses, never to things by themselves (without regard to the manner in which we have to look at them).

Transcendental Analytic has therefore yielded us this important result, that the understanding *a priori* can never do more than anticipate the form of a possible experience; and as nothing can be an object of experience except the phenomenon, it follows that the understanding can never go beyond the limits of sensibility, within which alone objects are given to us. Its principles are principles for the exhibition of phenomena only; and the proud name of Ontology, which presumes to supply in a systematic form different kinds of synthetical knowledge *a priori* of things by themselves (for instance the principle of causality), must be replaced by the more modest name of a mere Analytic of the pure understanding.

Thought is the act of referring a given intuition to an object. If the mode of such intuition is not given, the object is called transcendental, and the concept of the understanding admits then of a transcendental use only, in producing a unity in the thought of the manifold in general. A pure category therefore, in which every condition of sensuous intuition, the only one that is possible for us, is left out, cannot determine an object, but only the thought of an object in general, according to different modes. Now, if we want to use a concept, we require in addition some function of the faculty of judgment, by which an object is subsumed under a concept, consequently the at least formal condition under which something can be given in intuition. If this condition of the faculty of judgment (schema) is wanting, all subsumption is impossible, because nothing is given that could be subsumed under the concept. The purely transcendental use of categories therefore is in reality of no use at all, and has no definite or even, with regard to its form only, definable object. Hence it follows that a pure category is not fit for any synthetical *a priori* principle, and that the principles of the pure understanding admit of empirical only, never of transcendental application, nay, that no synthetical principles *a priori* are possible beyond the field of possible experience.

It might therefore be advisable to express ourselves in the following way: the pure categories, without the formal conditions of sensibility, have a transcendental character only, but do not admit of any transcendental use, because such use in itself is impossible, as the categories are deprived of all the conditions of being used in judgments, that is, of the formal conditions of the subsumption of any possible object under these concepts. As therefore (as pure categories) they are not meant to be used empirically, and cannot be used transcendentally, they admit, if separated from sensibility, of no use at all; that is, they cannot be applied to any possible object, and are nothing but the pure form of the use of the understanding with reference to objects in general, and of thought, without ever enabling us to think or determine any object by their means alone.

[Appearances, so far as they are thought as objects under the unity of the categories, are called *phenomena*. But if I admit things which are objects of the understanding only, and nevertheless can be given as objects of an intuition, though not of sensuous intuition (as *coram intuitu intellectuali*), such things would be called *Noumena* (*intelligibilia*).

One might feel inclined to think that the concept of *Phenomena*, as limited by the transcendental æsthetic, suggested by itself the objective reality of the *Noumena*, and justified a division of objects into phenomena and noumena, and consequently of the world into a *sensible* and *intelligible* world (*mundus sensibilis et intelligibilis*); and this in such a way that the distinction between the two should not refer to the logical form only of a more or less clear knowledge of one and the same object, but to a difference in their original presentation to our knowledge, which makes them to differ in themselves from each other in kind. For if the senses only represent to us something as it appears, that something must by itself also be a thing, and an object of a non-sensuous intuition, i.e. of the understanding. That is, there must be a kind of knowledge in which there is no sensibility, and which alone possesses absolute objective reality, representing objects as they are, while through the empirical use of our understanding we know things only as they appear. Hence it would seem to follow that, beside the empirical use of the categories (limited by sensuous conditions), there was another one, pure and yet objectively valid, and that we could not say, as we have hitherto done, that our knowledge of the pure understanding contained nothing but principles for the exhibition of phenomena, which, even *a priori,* could not apply to anything but the formal possibility of experience. Here, in fact, quite a new field would seem to be open, a world, as it were, realised in thought (nay, according to some, even in intuition), which would be a more, and not a less, worthy object for the pure understanding.

All our representations are no doubt referred by the understanding to some sort of object, and as phenomena are nothing but representations, the understanding refers them to a *something,* as the object of our sensuous intuition, this something being however the transcendental object only. This means a something equal to *x,* of which we do not, nay, with the present constitution of our understanding, cannot know anything, but which[21] can only serve, as a correlatum of the unity of apperception, for the unity of the manifold in sensuous intuition, by means of which the understanding unites the manifold into the concept of an object. This transcendental object cannot be separated from the sensuous data, because in that case nothing would remain by which it could be thought. It is not therefore an object of knowledge in itself, but only the representation of phenomena, under the concept of an object in general, which can be defined by the manifold of sensuous intuition.

For this very reason the categories do not represent a peculiar object, given to the understanding only, but serve only to define the transcendental object (the concept of something in general) by that which is given us through the senses, in order thus to know empirically phenomena under the concepts of objects.

What then is the cause why people, not satisfied with the substratum of sensibility, have added to the phenomena the

[21] Read *welches* instead of *welcher.*

noumena, which the understanding only is supposed to be able to realise? It is this, that sensibility and its sphere, that is the sphere of phenomena, is so limited by the understanding itself that it should not refer to things by themselves, but only to the mode in which things appear to us, in accordance with our own subjective qualification. This was the result of the whole transcendental æsthetic, and it really follows quite naturally from the concept of a phenomenon in general, that something must correspond to it, which in itself is not a phenomenon, because a phenomenon cannot be anything by itself, apart from our mode of representation. Unless therefore we are to move in a constant circle, we must admit that the very word *phenomenon* indicates a relation to something the immediate representation of which is no doubt sensuous, but which nevertheless, even without this qualification of our sensibility (on which the form of our intuition is founded) must be something by itself, that is an object independent of our sensibility.

Hence arises the concept of a noumenon, which however is not positive, nor a definite knowledge of anything, but which implies only the thinking of something, without taking any account of the form of sensuous intuition. But in order that a noumenon may signify a real object that can be distinguished from all phenomena, it is not enough that I should free my thought of all conditions of sensuous intuition, but I must besides have some reason for admitting another kind of intuition besides the sensuous, in which such an object can be given; otherwise my thought would be empty, however free it may be from contradictions. It is true that we were not able to prove that the sensuous is the only possible intuition, though it is so for us: but neither could we prove that another kind of intuition was possible; and although our thought may take no account of any sensibility, the question always remains whether, after that, it is not a mere form of a concept, and whether any real object would thus be left.

The object to which I refer the phenomenon in general is the transcendental object, that is, the entirely indefinite thought of something in general. This cannot be called the noumenon, for I know nothing of what it is by itself, and have no conception of it, except as the object of sensuous intuition in general, which is therefore the same for all phenomena. I cannot lay hold of it by any of the categories, for these are valid for empirical intuitions only, in order to bring them under the concept of an object in general. A pure use of the categories is no doubt possible, that is, not self-contradictory, but it has no kind of objective validity, because it refers to no intuition to which it is meant to impart the unity of an object. The categories remain for ever mere functions of thought by which no object can be given to me, but by which I can only think whatever may be given to me in intuition.]

We are met here by an illusion which is difficult to avoid. The categories do not depend in their origin on sensibility, like the forms of intuition, space, and time, and seem, therefore, to admit of an application extending beyond the objects of the senses. But, on the other side, they are nothing but forms of thought, containing the logical faculty only of comprehending a priori in one consciousness the manifold that is given in intuition, and they would therefore, if we take away the only intuition which is possible to us, have still less significance than those pure sensuous forms by which at least an object is given, while a peculiar mode of our understanding of connecting the manifold (unless that intuition, in which the manifold alone can be given, is added), signifies nothing at all.

Nevertheless, it seems to follow from our very concept, if we call certain objects, as phenomena, beings of the senses, by distinguishing between the mode of our intuition and the nature of those objects by themselves, that we may take either the same objects in that latter capacity, though they cannot as such come before our intuition, or other possible things, which are not objects of our senses at all, and place them, as objects thought only by the understanding, in opposition to the former, calling them beings of the understanding (noumena). The question then arises, whether our pure concepts of the understanding do not possess some significance with regard to these so-called beings of the understanding, and constitute a mode of knowing them?

At the very outset, however, we meet with an ambiguity which may cause great misapprehension. The understanding, by calling an object in one aspect a phenomenon only, makes to itself, apart from that aspect, another representation of an object by itself, and imagines itself able to form concepts of such an object. As, then, the understanding yields no other concepts but the categories, it supposes that the object in the latter aspect can be thought at least by those pure concepts of the understanding, and is thus induced to take the entirely indefinite concept of a being of the understanding, as of a some-thing in general outside our sensibility, as a definite *concept of a being which we might know to a certain extent through the understanding.*

If by noumenon we mean a thing so far as it is not an object of our sensuous intuition, *and make abstraction of our mode of intuition, it may be called a noumenon in a* negative *sense. If, however, we mean by it an* object *of a* non-sensuous intuition, *we admit thereby a peculiar mode of intuition, namely, the intellectual, which, however, is not our own, nor one of which we can understand even the possibility. This would be the noumenon in a* positive *sense.*

The doctrine of sensibility is at the same time the doctrine of noumena in their negative sense; that is, of things which the understanding must think without reference to our mode of intuition, and therefore, not as phenomena only, but as things by themselves, but to which, after it has thus separated them, the understanding knows that it must not, in this new aspect, apply its categories; because these categories have significance only with reference to the unity of intuitions in space and time, and can therefore a priori *determine that unity, on account of the mere ideality of space and time only, by means of general connecting concepts. Where that unity in time cannot be found, i.e. in the noumenon, the whole use, nay, the whole significance of categories comes to an end: because even the possibility of things that should correspond to the categories, would be unintelligible. On this point I may refer the reader to what I have said at the very beginning of the general note to the previous chapter (p. 183 ff.) The possibility of a thing can never be proved from the fact that its concept is not self-contradictory, but only by being authenticated by an intuition corresponding to it. If, therefore, we attempted to apply the categories to objects which are not considered as phenomena, we should have to admit an intuition other than the sensuous, and thus the object would become a noumenon in a* positive sense. *As, however, such an intuition, namely, an intellectual one, is entirely beyond our faculty of knowledge, the use of the categories also can never reach beyond the limits of the objects of experience. Beings of the understanding correspond no doubt to beings of the senses, and there may be beings of the understanding to which our faculty of sensuous intuition has no relation at all; but our concepts of the understanding, being forms of thought for our sensuous intuition only, do not reach so far, and what is called by us a noumenon must be understood as such in a* negative sense *only.*

If all thought (by means of categories) is taken away from empirical knowledge, no knowledge of any object remains, because nothing can be thought by mere intuition, and the mere fact that there is within me an affection of my sensibility, establishes in no way any relation of such a representation to any object. If, on the contrary, all intuition is taken away, there always remains the form of thought, that is, the mode of determining an object for the manifold of a possible intuition. In this sense the categories may be said to extend further than sensuous intuition, because they can think objects in general without any regard to the special mode of sensibility in which they may be given; but they do not thus prove a larger sphere of objects, because we cannot admit that such objects can be given, without admitting the possibility of some other but sensuous intuition, for which we have no right whatever.

I call a concept problematic, if it is not self-contradictory, and if, as limiting other concepts, it is connected with other kinds of knowledge, while its objective reality cannot be known in any way. Now the concept of a noumenon, that is of a thing which can never be thought as an object of the senses, but only as a thing by itself (by the pure understanding), is not self-contradictory, because we cannot maintain that sensibility is the only form of intuition. That concept is also necessary, to prevent sensuous intuition from extending to things by themselves; that is, in order to limit the objective validity of sensuous knowledge (for all the rest to which sensuous intuition does not extend is called noumenon, for the very purpose of showing that sensuous knowledge cannot extend its domain over everything that can be thought by the understanding). But, after all, we cannot understand the possibility of such noumena, and whatever lies beyond the sphere of phenomena is (to us) empty; that is, we have an understanding which *problematically* extends beyond that sphere, but no intuition, nay not even the conception of a possible intuition, by which, outside the field of sensibility, objects could be given to us, and our understanding could extend beyond that sensibility in its assertory use. The concept of a noumenon is therefore merely *limitative,* and intended to keep the claims of sensibility within proper bounds, therefore of negative use only. But it is not a mere arbitrary fiction, but closely connected with the limitation of sensibility, though incapable of adding anything positive to the sphere of the senses.

A real division of objects into phenomena and noumena, and of the world into a sensible and intelligible world *in a positive sense,* is therefore quite inadmissible, although concepts may very well be divided into sensuous and intellectual. For no objects can be assigned to these intellectual concepts, nor can they be represented as objectively valid. If we drop the senses, how are we to make it conceivable that our categories (which would be the only remaining concepts for noumena) have any meaning at all, considering that, in order to refer them to any object, something more must be given than the mere unity of thought, namely, a possible intuition, to which the categories could be applied? With all this the concept of a noumenon, if taken as problematical only, remains not only admissible, but, as a concept to limit the sphere of sensibility, indispensable. In this case, however, it is not a particular *intelligible object* for *our* understanding, but an understanding to which it could belong is itself a problem, if we ask how it could know an object, not discursively by means of categories, but intuitively, and yet in a non-sensuous intuition,—a process of which we could not understand even the bare possibility. Our understanding thus acquires a kind of negative extension, that is, it does not become itself limited by sensibility, but, on the contrary, limits it, by calling things by themselves (not considered as phenomena) noumena. In doing this, it immediately proceeds to prescribe limits to itself, by admitting that it cannot know these noumena by means of the categories, but can only think of them under the name of something unknown.

In the writings of modern philosophers, however, I meet with a totally different use of the terms of *mundus sensibilis* and *intelligibilis,** totally different from the meaning assigned to these terms by the ancients. Here all difficulty seems to disappear. But the fact is, that there remains nothing but mere word-mongery. In accordance with this, some people have been pleased to call the whole of phenomena, so far as they are seen, the world of sense; but so far as their connection, according to general laws of the understanding, is taken into account, the world of the understanding. Theoretical astronomy, which only teaches the actual observation of the starry heavens, would represent the former; contemplative astronomy, on the contrary (taught according to the Copernican

* *We must not speak, as is often done, of an intellectual world, for intellectual and sensitive apply to knowledge only. That, however, to which the one or the other mode of intuition applies, that is, the objects themselves, must, however harsh it may sound, be called intelligible or sensible. (Note in 2nd Edition.)*

system, or, it may be, according to Newton's laws of gravitation), the latter, namely, a purely intelligible world. But this twisting of words is a mere sophistical excuse, in order to avoid a troublesome question, by changing its meaning according to one's own convenience. Understanding and reason may be applied to phenomena, but it is very questionable whether they can be applied at all to an object which is not a phenomenon, but a noumenon; and it is this, when the object is represented as purely intelligible, that is, as given to the understanding only, and not to the senses. The question therefore is whether, besides the empirical use of the understanding (even in the Newtonian view of the world), a transcendental use is possible, referring to the noumenon, as its object; and that question we have answered decidedly in the negative.

When *we* therefore say that the senses represent objects to us as they *appear,* and the understanding as they *are,* the latter is not to be taken in a transcendental, but in a purely empirical meaning, namely, as to how they, as objects of experience, must be represented, according to the regular connection of phenomena, and not according to what they may be, as objects of the pure understanding, apart from their relation to possible experience, and therefore to our senses. This will always remain unknown to us; nay, we shall never know whether such a transcendental and exceptional knowledge is possible at all, at least as comprehended under our ordinary categories. With us understanding and sensibility cannot determine objects, unless they are joined together. If we separate them, we have intuitions without concepts, or concepts without intuitions, in both cases representations which we cannot refer to any definite object.

If, after all these arguments, anybody should still hesitate to abandon the purely transcendental use of the categories, let him try an experiment with them for framing any synthetical proposition. An analytical proposition does not in the least advance the understanding, which, as in such a proposition it is only concerned with what is already thought in the concept, does not ask whether the concept in itself has any reference to objects, or expresses only the unity of thought in general (this completely ignoring the manner in which an object may be given). The understanding in fact is satisfied if it knows what it contained in the concept of an object; it is indifferent as to the object to which the concept may refer. But let him try the experiment with any synthetical and so-called transcendental proposition, as for instance, 'Everything that exists, exists as a substance, or as a determination inherent in it,' or 'Everything contingent exists as an effect of some other thing, namely, its cause,' etc. Now I ask, whence can the understanding take these synthetical propositions, as the concepts are to apply, not to some possible experience, but to things by themselves (noumena)? Where is that third term to be found which is always required for a synthetical proposition, in order thus to join concepts which have no logical (analytical) relation with each other? It will be impossible to prove such a proposition, nay even to justify the possibility of any such pure assertion, without appealing to the empirical use of the understanding, and thus renouncing entirely the so-called pure and non-sensuous judgment. There are no principles therefore according to which the concepts of pure and merely intelligible objects could ever be applied, because we cannot imagine any way in which they could be given, and the problematic thought, which leaves a place open to them, serves only, like empty space, to limit the sphere of empirical principles, without containing or indicating any other object of knowledge, lying beyond that sphere.

APPENDIX

OF THE AMPHIBOLY OF REFLECTIVE CONCEPTS, OWING TO THE CONFUSION OF THE EMPIRICAL WITH THE TRANSCENDENTAL USE OF THE UNDERSTANDING

Reflection (*reflexio*) is not concerned with objects themselves, in order to obtain directly concepts of them, but is a state of the mind in which we set ourselves to discover the subjective conditions under which we may arrive at concepts. It is the consciousness of the relation of given representations to the various sources of our knowledge by which alone their mutual relation can be rightly determined. Before saying any more of our representations, the first question is, to which faculty of knowledge they may all belong; whether it is the understanding or the senses by which they are connected and compared. Many a judgment is accepted from mere habit, or made from inclination, and as no reflection precedes or even follows it critically, the judgment is supposed to have had its origin in the understanding. It is not all judgments that require an investigation, that is, a careful attention with regard to the grounds of their truth; for if they are immediately certain, as for instance, that between two points there can be only one straight line, no more immediately certain marks of their truth than that which they themselves convey could be discovered. But all judgments, nay, all comparisons, require reflection, that is, a discrimination of the respective faculty of knowledge to which any given concepts belong. The act by which I place in general the comparison of representations by the side of the faculty of knowledge to which that comparison belongs, and by which I determine whether these representations are compared with each other as belonging to the pure understanding or to sensuous intuition, I call *transcendental reflection*. The relation in which the two concepts may stand to each other in one state of the mind is that of *identity* and *difference*, of *agreement* and *opposition*, of the *internal* and *external*, and finally of the *determinable* and the *determination* (matter and form). The right determination of that relation depends on the question in which faculty of knowledge they *subjectively* belong to each other, whether in sensibility or in the understanding. For the proper distinction of the latter is of great importance with regard to the manner in which the former must be considered.

Before proceeding to form any objective judgments, we have to compare the concepts with regard to the *identity* (of many representations under one concept) as the foundation of general judgments, or with regard to their *difference* as the foundation of particular judgments, or with regard to their *agreement* and *opposition* serving as the foundations of affirmative and negative judgments, etc. For this reason it might seem that we ought to call these concepts concepts of comparison (*conceptus comparationis*). But as, when the contents of concepts and not their logical form must be considered, that is, whether the things themselves are identical or different, in agreement or in opposition, etc., all things may have a two-fold relation to our faculty of knowledge, namely, either to sensibility or to the understanding, and as the manner in which they belong to one another depends on the place to which they belong, it follows that the transcendental reflection, that is the power of determining the relation of given representations to one or the other class of knowledge, can alone determine their mutual relation. Whether the things are identical or different, in agreement or opposition, etc., cannot be established at once by the concepts themselves by means of a mere comparison (*comparatio*), but first of all by a proper discrimination of that class of knowledge to which they belong, that is, by transcendental reflection. It might therefore be said, that *logical reflection* is a mere comparison, because it takes no account of the faculty of knowledge to which any given representations belong, and treats them, so far as they are all found in the mind, as homogeneous, while *transcendental reflection* (which refers to the objects themselves) supplies the possibility of an objective comparison of representations among themselves, and is therefore very different from the other, the faculty of knowledge to which they belong not being the same. This transcendental reflection is a duty from which no one can escape who wishes to form judgments *a priori*. We shall now take it in hand, and may hope thus to throw not a little light on the real business of the understanding.

I. *Identity and Difference*

When an object is presented to us several times, but each time with the same internal determinations (*qualitas et quantitas*), it is, so long as it is considered as an object of the pure understanding, always one and the same, one thing, not many (*numerica identitas*). But if it is a phenomenon, a comparison of the concepts is of no consequence, and though everything may be identical with regard to the concepts, yet the difference of the places of this phenomenon at the same time is a sufficient ground for admitting the *numerical difference* of the object (of the senses). Thus, though there may be no internal difference whatever (either in quality or quantity) between two drops of water, yet the fact that they may be seen at the same time in different places is sufficient to establish their numerical difference. Leibniz took phenomena to be things by themselves, *intelligibilia,* that is, objects of the pure understanding (though, on account of the confused nature of their representations, he assigned to them the name of phenomena), and from that point of view his principle of their *indiscernibility* (*principium identitas indiscernibilium*) could not be contested. As, however, they are objects of sensibility, and the use of the understanding with regard to them is not pure, but only empirical, their plurality and numerical diversity are indicated by space itself, as the condition of external phenomena. For one part of space, though it may be perfectly similar and equal to another, is still outside it, and for this very reason a part of space different from the first which, added to it, makes a larger space: and this applies to all things which exist at the same time in different parts of space, however similar or equal they may be in other respects.

II. *Agreement and Opposition*

When reality is represented by the pure understanding only (*realitas noumenon*), no opposition can be conceived between realities, that is, no such relation that, if connected in one subject, they should annihilate the effects one of the other, as for instance $3 - 3 = 0$. The real in the phenomena, on the contrary (*realitas phenomenon*), may very well be in mutual opposition, and if connected in one subject, one may annihilate completely or in part the effect of the other, as in the case of two forces moving in the same straight line, either drawing or impelling a point in opposite directions, or in the case of pleasure, counterbalancing a certain amount of pain.

III. *The Internal and the External*

In an object of the pure understanding that only is internal which has no relation whatever (as regards its existence) to anything different from itself. The inner relations, on the contrary, of a *substantia phenomenon* in space are nothing but relations, and the substance itself a complex of mere relations. We only know substances in space through the forces which are active in a certain space, by either drawing others near to it (attraction) or by preventing others from penetrating into it (repulsion and impenetrability). Other properties constituting the concept of a substance appearing in space, and which we call matter, are unknown to us. As an object of the pure understanding, on the contrary, every substance must have internal determinations and forces bearing on the internal reality. But what other internal accidents can I think, except those which my own internal sense presents to me, namely, something which is either itself *thought*, or something analogous to it? Hence Leibniz represented all substances (as he conceived them as noumena), even the component parts of matter (after having in thought removed from them everything implying external relation, and therefore composition also), as simple subjects endowed with powers of representation, in one word, as *monads*.

IV. *Matter and Form*

These are two concepts which are treated as the foundation of all other reflection, so inseparably are they connected with every act of the understanding. The former denotes the determinable in general, the latter its determination (both in a purely transcendental meaning, all differences in that which is given and the mode in which it is determined being left out of consideration). Logicians formerly called the universal, *matter;* the specific difference, *form.* In every judgment the given concepts may be called the logical matter (for a judgment); their relation, by means of the copula, the form of a judgment. In every being its component parts (*essentialia*) are the matter; the mode in which they are connected in it, the essential form. With respect to things in general, unlimited reality was regarded as the matter of all possibility, and the limitation thereof (negation) as that form by which one thing is distinguished from another, according to transcendental concepts. The understanding demands first that something should be given (at least in concept) in order to be able afterwards to determine it in a certain manner. In the concept of the pure understanding therefore, matter comes before form, and Leibniz in consequence first assumed things (monads), and within them an internal power of representation, in order afterwards to found thereon their external relation, and the community of their states, that is, of their representations. In this way space and time were possible only, the former through the relation of substances, the latter through the connection of their determinations among themselves, as causes and effects. And so it would be indeed, if the pure understanding could be applied immediately to objects, and if space and time were determinations of things by themselves. But if they are sensuous intuitions only, in which we determine all objects merely as phenomena, then it follows that the form of intuition (as a subjective quality of sensibility) comes before all matter (sensations), that space and time therefore come before all phenomena, and before all data of experience, and render in fact all experience possible. As an intellectual philosopher Leibniz could not endure that this form should come before things and determine their possibility: a criticism quite just when he assumed that we see things as they are (though in a confused representation). But as sensuous intuition is a peculiar subjective condition on which all perception *a priori* depends, and the form of which is original and independent, the form must be given by itself, and so far from matter (or the things themselves which appear) forming the true foundation (as we might think, if we judged according to mere concepts), the very possibility of matter presupposes a formal intuition (space and time) as given.

NOTE ON THE AMPHIBOLY OF REFLECTIVE CONCEPTS

I beg to be allowed to call the place which we assign to a concept, either in sensibility or in the pure understanding, its *transcendental place*. If so, then the determination of this position which belongs to every concept, according to the difference of its use, and the directions for determining according to rules that place for all concepts, would be called *transcendental topic;* a doctrine which would thoroughly protect us against the subreptitious claims of the pure understanding and the errors arising from it, by always distinguishing to what faculty of knowledge each concept truly belongs. Every concept, or every *title* to which many kinds of knowledge belong, may be called a *logical place.* Upon this is based the logical topic of Aristotle, of which orators and schoolmasters avail themselves in order to find under certain titles of thought what would best suit the matter they have in hand, and thus to be able, with a certain appearance of thoroughness, to argue and wrangle to any extent.

Transcendental topic, on the contrary, contains no more than the above-mentioned four titles of all comparison and distinction, which differ from the categories because they do not serve to represent the object according to what constitutes its concept (quantity, reality, etc.), but only the comparison of representations, in all its variety, which precedes the concept of things. This comparison, however, requires first a reflection, that is, a determination of the place to which the representations of things which are to be compared belong, namely, whether they are thought by the pure understanding or given as phenomena by sensibility.

Concepts may be logically compared without our asking any questions as to what place their objects belong, whether as noumena to the understanding, or to sensibility as phenomena. But if with these concepts we wish to proceed to the objects themselves, a transcendental reflection is necessary first of all, in order to determine whether they are meant to be objects for the pure understanding or for sensibility. Without this reflection our use of these concepts would be very uncertain, and synthetical propositions would spring up which critical reason cannot acknowledge, and which are simply founded on transcendental amphiboly, that is, on our con-

founding an object of the pure understanding with a phenomenon.

For want of such a transcendental topic, and deceived by
the amphiboly of reflective concepts, the celebrated Leibniz
erected an *intellectual system of the world,* or believed at
least that he knew the internal nature of things by comparing
all objects with the understanding only and with the abstract
formal concepts of his thought. Our table of reflective concepts gives us the unexpected advantage of being able to exhibit clearly the distinctive features of his system in all its
parts, and at the same time the leading principle of this
peculiar view which rested on a simple misunderstanding. He
compared all things with each other by means of concepts
only, and naturally found no other differences but those by
which the understanding distinguishes its pure concepts from
each other. The conditions of sensuous intuition, which carry
their own differences, are not considered by him as original
and independent; for sensibility was with him a confused
mode of representation only, and not a separate source of
representations. According to him a phenomenon was the
representation of a thing by itself, though different, in its logical form, from knowledge by means of the understanding,
because the phenomenon, in the ordinary absence of analysis,
brings a certain admixture of collateral representations into
the concept of a thing which the understanding is able to
separate. In one word, Leibniz *intellectualised* phenomena,
just as Locke, according to his system of Noogony (if I may
use such an expression), *sensualised* all concepts of the understanding, that is, represented them as nothing but empirical,
though abstract, reflective concepts. Instead of regarding the
understanding and sensibility as two totally distinct sources
of representations, which however can supply objectively valid
judgments of things only in conjunction with each other, each
of these great men recognised but one of them, which in their
opinion applied immediately to things by themselves, while
the other did nothing but to produce either disorder or order
in the representations of the former.

Leibniz accordingly compared the objects of the senses
with each other as things in general and in the understanding
only. He did this,

First, so far as they are judged by the understanding to be
either identical or different. As he considers their concepts
only and not their place in intuition, in which alone objects
can be given, and takes no account of the transcendental

place of these concepts (whether the object is to be counted among phenomena or among things by themselves), it could not happen otherwise than that he should extend his principle of indiscernibility, which is valid with regard to concepts of things in general only, to objects of the senses also (*mundus phaenomenon*), and imagine that he thus added no inconsiderable extension to our knowledge of nature. No doubt, if I know a drop of water as a thing by itself in all its internal determinations, I cannot allow that one is different from the other, when their whole concepts are identical. But if the drop of water is a phenomenon in space, it has its place not only in the understanding (among concepts), but in the sensuous external intuition (in space), and in this case the physical place is quite indifferent with regard to the inner determinations of things, so that a place B can receive a thing which is perfectly similar or identical with another in place A, quite as well as if it were totally different from it in its internal determinations. Difference of place by itself and without any further conditions renders the plurality and distinction of objects as phenomena not only possible, but also necessary. That so-called law of Leibniz therefore is no law of nature, but only an analytical rule, or a comparison of things by means of concepts only.

Secondly. The principle that realities (as mere assertions) never logically contradict each other, is perfectly true with regard to the relation of concepts, but has no meaning whatever either as regards nature or as regards anything by itself (of which we can have no concept whatever).[22] The real opposition, as when $A - B = 0$, takes place everywhere wherever one reality is united with another in the same subject and one annihilates the effect of the other. This is constantly brought before our eyes in nature by all impediments and reactions which, as depending on forces, must be called *realitates phaenomena*. General mechanics can even give us the empirical condition of that opposition in an *a priori* rule, by attending to the opposition of directions; a condition of which the transcendental concept of reality knows nothing. Although Leibniz himself did not announce this proposition with all the pomp of a new principle, he yet made use of it for new assertions, and his followers expressly inserted it in their system of the Leibniz-Wolfian philosophy. According to this principle all evils, for example, are nothing but the con-

[22] 'Whatever' is omitted in the Second Edition.

sequences of the limitations of created beings, that is, they are negations, because these can be the only opposites of reality (which is perfectly true in the mere concept of the thing in general, but not in things as phenomena). In like manner the followers of Leibniz consider it not only possible, but even natural, to unite all reality, without fearing any opposition, in one being; because the only opposition they know is that of contradiction (by which the concept of a thing itself is annihilated), while they ignore that of reciprocal action and reaction, when one real cause destroys the effect of another, a process which we can only represent to ourselves when the conditions are given in sensibility.

Thirdly. The Leibnizian monadology has really no other foundation than that Leibniz represented the difference of the internal and the external in relation to the understanding only. Substances must have something *internal,* which is free from all external relations, and therefore from composition also. The simple, therefore, or uncompounded, is the foundation of the internal of things by themselves. This internal in the state of substances cannot consist in space, form, contact, or motion (all these determinations being external relations), and we cannot therefore ascribe to substances any other internal state but that which belongs to our own internal sense, namely, the *state of representations.* This is the history of the monads, which were to form the elements of the whole universe, and the energy of which consists in representations only, so that properly they can be active within themselves only.

For this reason, his principle of a possible community of substances could only be a pre-established harmony, and not a physical influence. For, as everything is actively occupied internally only, that is, with its own representations, the state of representations in one substance could not be in active connection with that of another; but it became necessary to admit a third cause, exercising its influence on all substances, and making their states to correspond with each other, not indeed by occasional assistance rendered in each particular case (*systema assistentiae*), but through the unity of the idea of a cause valid for all, and in which all together must receive their existence and permanence, and therefore also their reciprocal correspondence according to universal laws.

Fourthly. Leibniz's celebrated doctrine of space and time, in which he intellectualised these forms of sensibility, arose entirely from the same delusion of transcendental reflection.

If by means of the pure understanding alone I want to represent the external relations of things, I can do this only by means of the concept of their reciprocal action; and if I want to connect one state with another state of the same thing, this is possible only in the order of cause and effect. Thus it happened that Leibniz conceived space as a certain order in the community of substances, and time as the dynamical sequence of their states. That which space and time seem to possess as proper to themselves and independent of things, he ascribed to the confusion of these concepts, which made us mistake what is a mere form of dynamical relations for a peculiar and independent intuition, antecedent to things themselves. Thus space and time became with him the intelligible form of the connection of things (substances and their states) by themselves, and things were intelligible substances (*substantiae noumena*). Nevertheless he tried to make these concepts valid for phenomena, because he would not concede to sensibility any independent kind of intuition, but ascribed all, even the empirical representation of objects, to the understanding, leaving to the senses nothing but the contemptible work of confusing and mutilating the representations of the understanding.

But, even if we could predicate anything synthetically by means of the pure understanding of things by themselves (which however is simply impossible), this could never be referred to phenomena, because these do not represent things by themselves. We should therefore in such a case have to compare our concepts in a transcendental reflection under the conditions of sensibility only, and thus space and time would never be determinations of things by themselves, but of phenomena. What things may be by themselves we know not, nor need we care to know, because, after all, a thing can never come before me otherwise than as a phenomenon.

The remaining reflective conceptions have to be treated in the same manner. Matter is *substantia phenomenon*. What may belong to it internally, I seek for in all parts of space occupied by it, and in all effects produced by it, all of which, however, can be phenomena of the external senses only. I have therefore nothing that is absolutely, but only what is relatively internal, and this consists itself of external relations. Nay, what according to the pure understanding should be the absolutely internal of matter is a mere phantom, for matter is never an object of the pure understanding, while the transcendental object which may be the ground of the phenomenon which we call matter, is a mere something of which we could not even understand what it is, though somebody should tell us. We cannot understand anything except what carries with it in intuition something corresponding to our words. If the complaint 'that we do not understand the internal of things,' means that we do not comprehend by means of the pure understanding what the things which appear to us may be of themselves, it seems totally unjust and unreasonable; for it means that without senses we should be able to know and therefore to see things, that is, that we should possess a faculty of knowledge totally different from the human, not only in degree, but in kind and in intuition, in fact, that we should not be men, but beings of whom we ourselves could not say whether they are even possible, much less what they would be like. Observation and analysis of phenomena enter into the internal of nature, and no one can say how far this may go in time. Those transcendental questions, however, which go beyond nature, would nevertheless remain unanswerable, even if the whole of nature were revealed to us, for it is not given to us to observe even our own mind with any intuition but that of our internal sense. In it lies the mystery of the origin of our sensibility. Its relation to an object, and the transcendental ground of that unity, are no doubt far too deeply hidden for us, who can know even ourselves by means of the internal sense only, that is, as phenomena, and we shall never be able to use the same imperfect instrument of investigation in order to find anything but again and again phenomena, the non-sensuous, and non-phenomenal cause of which we are seeking in vain.

What renders this criticism of the conclusions by means of the acts of mere reflection extremely useful is, that it shows clearly the nullity of all conclusions with regard to objects compared with each other in the understanding only, and that it confirms at the same time what we have so strongly insisted on, namely, that phenomena, though they cannot be comprehended as things by themselves among the objects of the pure understanding, are nevertheless the only objects in which our knowledge can possess objective reality, i.e. where intuition corresponds to concepts.

When we reflect logically only, we only compare in our understanding concepts among themselves, trying to find out whether both have exactly the same contents, whether they contradict themselves or not, whether something belongs to a concept, or is added to it, and which of the two may be given, while the other may be a mode only of thinking the given concept. But if I refer these concepts to an object in general (in a transcendental sense), without determining whether it be an object of sensuous or intellectual intuition, certain limitations appear at once, warning us not to go beyond the concept, and upsetting all empirical use of it, thus proving that a representation of an object, as of a thing in general, is not only insufficient, but, if without sensuous determination, and independent of empirical conditions, self-contradictory. It is necessary therefore either to take no account at all of the object (as we do in logic) or, if not, then to think it under the conditions of sensuous intuition, because the intelligible would require a quite peculiar intuition which we do not possess, and, without it, would be nothing to us, while on the other side phenomena also could never be things by themselves. For if I represent to myself things in general only, the difference of external relations cannot, it is true, constitute a difference of the things themselves, but rather presupposes it; and, if the concept of one thing does not differ at all internally from that of another, I only have one and the same thing placed in different relations. Furthermore, by adding a mere affirmation (reality) to another, the positive in it is indeed augmented, and nothing is taken away or removed, so that we see that the real in things can never be in contradiction with itself, etc.

* * * * * * * *

A certain misunderstanding of these reflective concepts has, as we showed, exercised so great an influence on the use of the understanding, as to mislead even one of the most acute philosophers to the adoption of a so-called system of intellectual knowledge, which undertakes to determine objects without the intervention of the senses. For this reason the exposition of the cause of the misunderstanding, which lies in the amphiboly of these concepts, as the origin of false principles, is of great utility in determining and securing the true limits of the understanding.

It is no doubt true, that what can be affirmed or denied of a concept in general, can also be affirmed or denied of any part of it (*dictum de omni et nullo*); but it would be wrong so to change this logical proposition as to make it say that whatever is not contained in a general concept, is not contained either in the particular concepts comprehended under it; for these are particular concepts for the very reason that they contain more than is conceived in the general concept.

Nevertheless the whole intellectual system of Leibniz is built up on this fallacy, and with it falls necessarily to the ground, together with all equivocation in the use of the understanding, that had its origin in it.

Leibniz's principle of discernibility is really based on the supposition that, if a certain distinction is not to be found in the general concept of a thing, it could not be met with either in the things themselves, and that therefore all things were perfectly the same (*numero eadem*), which are not distinguished from each other in their concept also, as to quality or quantity. And because in the mere concept of a thing, no account has been taken of many a necessary condition of its intuition, it has rashly been concluded that that which, in forming an abstraction, has been intentionally left out of account, did really not exist anywhere, and nothing has been allowed to a thing except what is contained in its concept.

The concept of a cubic foot of space, wherever and how many times soever I may think it, is in itself perfectly the same. But two cubic feet are nevertheless distinguished in space, by their places alone (*numero diversa*), and these places are conditions of the intuition in which the object of our concept is given, and which, though they do not belong to the concept, belong nevertheless to the whole of sensibility. In a similar manner there is no contradiction in the concept of a thing, unless something negative has been connected with something affirmative; and simply affirmative concepts, if joined together, cannot neutralise each other. But in sensuous intuition, where we have to deal with reality (for instance motion), there exist conditions (opposite directions) of which in the concept of motion in general no account was taken, and which render possible an opposition (not however a logical one), and from mere positives produce zero $= 0$, so that it would be wrong to say that all reality must be in perfect agreement, if there is no opposition between its concepts.*
If we keep to concepts only, that which we call internal is

---

* If one wished to use here the usual subterfuge that *realitates noumena*, at least, cannot oppose each other, it would be necessary to produce an example of such pure and non-sensuous reality, to enable us to see whether it was something or nothing. No example, however, can be produced, except from experience, which never offers us anything but phenomena; so that this proposition means really nothing but that a concept, which contains affirmatives only, contains no negative, a proposition which we at least have never doubted.

the substratum of all relations or external determinations. If therefore I take no account of any of the conditions of intuition, and confine myself solely to the concept of a thing, then I may drop no doubt all external relations, and yet there must remain the concept of something which implies no relation, but internal determinations only. From this it might seem to follow that there exists in everything something (substance) which is absolutely internal, preceding all external determinations, nay, rendering them possible. It might likewise seem to follow that this substratum, as no longer containing any external relations, must be *simple* (for corporeal things are always relations only, at least of their parts existing side by side); and as we know of no entirely internal determinations beyond those of our own internal sense, that substratum might be taken, not only as simple, but likewise (according to the analogy of our own internal sense) as determined by representations, so that all things would be really *monads,* or simple beings endowed with representations. All this would be perfectly true, unless something more than the concept of a thing in general were required in order to give us objects of external intuition, although the pure concept need take no account of it. But we see, on the contrary, that a permanent phenomenon in space (impenetrable extension) may contain mere relations without anything that is absolutely internal, and yet be the first substratum of all external perception. It is true that if we think by concepts only, we cannot think something external without something internal, because conceptions of relations presuppose things given, and are impossible without them. But as in intuition something is contained which does not exist at all in the mere concept of a thing, and as it is this which supplies the substratum that could never be known by mere concepts, namely, a space which, with all that is contained in it, consists of purely formal, or real relations also, I am not allowed to say, that, because nothing can be represented by mere concepts without something absolutely internal, there could not be in the real things themselves, comprehended under those concepts, and in their *intuition,* anything external, without a foundation of something absolutely internal. For, if we take no account of all conditions of intuition, then no doubt nothing remains in the mere concept but the internal in general, with its mutual relations, through which alone the external is possible. This necessity, however, which depends on abstraction alone, does not apply to things, if they are given in intuition with determinations expressive of mere relations, and without having for their foundation anything internal, for the simple reason that they are phenomena only, and not things in themselves. Whatever we may know of matter are nothing but relations (what we call internal determinations are but relatively internal); but there are among these relations some which are independent and permanent, and by which a certain object is given us. That I, when abstraction is made of these relations, have nothing more to think, does not do away with the concept of a thing, as a phenomenon, nor with the concept of an object *in abstracto*. It only shows the impossibility of such an object as could be determined by mere concepts, that is of a noumenon. It is no doubt startling to hear, that a thing should consist entirely of relations, but such a thing as we speak of is merely a phenomenon, and can never be thought by means of the categories only; nay, it consists itself of the mere relation of something in general to our senses. In the same manner, it is impossible for us to represent the relations of things *in abstracto* as long as we deal with concepts only, in any other way than that one should be the cause of determinations in the other, this being the very concept of our understanding, with regard to relations. But as in this case we make abstraction of all intuition, a whole class of determinations, by which the manifold determines its place to each of its component parts, that is, the form of sensibility (space), disappears, though in truth it precedes all empirical causality.

If by purely intelligible objects we understand things which, without all schemata of sensibility, are thought by mere categories, such objects are simply impossible. It is our sensuous intuition by which objects are given to us that forms the condition of the objective application of all the concepts of our understanding, and without that intuition the categories have no relation whatever to any object. Nay, even if we admitted a kind of intuition different from the sensuous, our functions of thought would have no meaning with regard to it. If we only mean objects of a non-sensuous intuition, to which our categories do not apply, and of which we can have no knowledge whatever (either intuitional or conceptual), there is no reason why noumena, in this merely negative meaning, should not be admitted, because in this case we mean no more than this, that our intuition does not embrace all things, but objects of our senses only; that, consequently, its objective validity is limited, and space left for some other kind of intuition, and consequently for things as objects of it. But in that sense the concept of a noumenon is *problematical,* that is, the representation of a thing of which we can neither say that it is possible or that it is impossible, because we have no conception of any kind of intuition but that of our senses, or of any kind of concepts but of our categories, neither of them being applicable to any extrasensuous object. We cannot therefore extend in a positive sense the field of the objects of our thought beyond the conditions of our sensibility, or admit, besides phenomena, objects of pure thought, that is, noumena, simply because they do not possess any positive meaning that could be pointed out. For it must be admitted that the categories by themselves are not sufficient for a knowledge of things, and that, without the data of sensibility, they would be nothing but subjective forms of unity of the understanding, and without an object. We do not say that thought is a mere product of the senses, and therefore limited by them, but it does not follow that therefore thought, without sensibility, has its own pure use, because it would really be without an object. Nor would it be right to call the noumenon such an object of the pure understanding, for the noumenon means the problematical concept of an object, intended for an intuition and understanding totally different from our own, and therefore themselves mere problems. The concept of the noumenon is not therefore the concept of an object, but only a problem, inseparable from the limitation of our sensibility, whether there may not be objects independent of its intuition. This is a question that can only be answered in an uncertain way, by saying that as sensuous intuition does not embrace all things without exception, there remains a place for other objects, that cannot therefore be absolutely denied, but cannot be asserted either as objects of our understanding, because there is no definite concept for them (our categories being unfit for that purpose).

The understanding therefore limits the sensibility without enlarging thereby its own field, and by warning the latter that it can never apply to things by themselves, but to phenomena only, it forms the thought of an object by itself, but as transcendental only, which is the cause of phenomena, and therefore never itself a phenomenon: which cannot be thought as quantity, nor as reality, nor as substance (because these concepts require sensuous forms in which to determine an object), and of which therefore it must always remain unknown, whether it is to be found within us only, or also without us; and whether, if sensibility were removed, it would vanish or remain. If we like to call this object noumenon, because the representation of it is not sensuous, we are at liberty to do so. But as we cannot apply to it any of the concepts of our understanding, such a representation remains to us empty, serving no purpose but that of indicating the limits of our sensuous knowledge, and leaving at the same time an empty space which we cannot fill either by possible experience, or by the pure understanding.

The critique of the pure understanding does not therefore allow us to create a new sphere of objects beyond those which can come before it as phenomena, or to stray into intelligible worlds, or even into the concept of such. The mistake which leads to this in the most plausible manner, and which, though excusable, can never be justified, consists in making the use of the understanding, contrary to its very intention, transcendental, so that objects, that is, possible intuitions, are made to conform to concepts, not concepts to possible intuitions, on which alone their objective validity can rest. The cause of this is again, that apperception, and with it thought, precedes every possible determinate arrangement of representations. We are thinking something in general, and determine it on one side sensuously, but distinguish at the same time the general object, represented in abstraction, from this particular mode of sensuous intuition. Thus there remains to us a mode of determining the object by thought only, which, though it is a mere logical form without any contents, seems to us nevertheless a mode in which the object by itself exists (*noumenon*), without regard to the intuition which is restricted to our senses.

*   *   *   *   *   *   *   *

Before leaving this transcendental Analytic, we have to add something which, though in itself of no particular importance, may yet seem to be requisite for the completeness of the system. The highest concept of which all transcendental philosophy generally begins, is the division into the *possible* and the *impossible*. But, as all division presupposes a divisible concept, a higher concept is required, and this is the concept of an object in general, taken as problematical, it being left uncertain whether it be something or nothing. As the categories are the only concepts which apply to objects in general, the distinction whether an object is something or nothing must proceed according to the order and direction of the categories.

I. Opposed to the concepts of *all, many,* and *one,* is the concept which annihilates everything, that is, *none;* and thus the object of a concept, to which no intuition can be found to correspond, is = 0, that is, a concept without an object, like the noumena, which cannot be counted as possibilities, though not as impossibilities either (*ens rationis*); or like certain fundamental forces, which have been newly invented, and have been conceived without contradiction, but at the same time without any example from experience, and must not therefore be counted among possibilities.

II. Reality is *something,* negation is *nothing;* that is, it is the concept of the absence of an object, as shadow or cold (*nihil privativum*).

III. The mere form of intuition (without substance) is in itself no object, but the merely formal condition of it (as a phenomenon), as pure space and pure time (*ens imaginarium*), which, though they are something, as forms of intuition, are not themselves objects of intuition.

IV. The object of a concept which contradicts itself, is nothing, because the concept is nothing; it is simply the impossible, as a figure composed of two straight lines (*nihil negativum*).

A table showing this division of the concept of nothing (the corresponding division of the concept of something follows by itself) would have to be arranged as follows.

NOTHING,
as
I
Empty concept without an object.
Ens rationis.

II
Empty object
of a concept.
Nil privativum.

III
Empty intuition
without an object.
Ens imaginarium.

IV
Empty object without a concept.
Nihil negativum.

We see that the *ens rationis* (No. 1) differs from the *ens negativum* (No. 4), because the former cannot be counted among the possibilities, being the result of fancy, though not self-contradictory, while the latter is opposed to possibility, the concept annihilating itself. Both, however, are empty concepts. The *nihil privativum* (No. 2) and the *ens imaginar-*

ium (No. 3) are, on the contrary, empty data for concepts. It would be impossible to represent to ourselves darkness, unless light had been given to the senses, or space, unless extended beings had been perceived. The negation, as well as the pure form of intuition are, without something real, no objects.

TRANSCENDENTAL LOGIC

SECOND DIVISION

Transcendental Dialectic

INTRODUCTION

1. OF TRANSCENDENTAL APPEARANCE (ILLUSION)

We call Dialectic in general a logic of *illusion* (eine Logik des Scheins). This does not mean that it is a doctrine of *probability* (Wahrscheinlichkeit), for probability is a kind of truth, known through insufficient causes, the knowledge of which is therefore deficient, but not deceitful, and cannot properly be separated from the analytical part of logic. Still less can *phenomenon* (Erscheinung) and *illusion* (Schein) be taken as identical. For truth or illusion is not to be found in the objects of intuition, but in the judgments upon them, so far as they are thought. It is therefore quite right to say, that the senses never err, not because they always judge rightly, but because they do not judge at all. Truth therefore and error, and consequently illusory appearance also, as the cause of error, exist in our judgments only, that is, in the relation of an object to our understanding. No error exists in our knowledge, if it completely agrees with the laws of our understanding, nor can there be an error in a representation of the senses, because they involve no judgment, and no power of nature can, of its own accord, deviate from its own laws. Therefore neither the understanding by itself (without the influence of another cause), nor the senses by themselves could ever err. The understanding could not err, because as long as it acts according to its own laws, the effect (the judgment) must necessarily agree with those laws, and the formal test of all truth consists in this agreement with the laws of the understanding. The senses cannot err, because there is in them no judgment at all, whether true or false. Now as we have no other sources of knowledge but these two, it follows that error can only arise through the unperceived influence of the sensibility on the understanding, whereby it happens that subjective grounds of judgment are mixed up with the objective, and cause them to deviate from their destination;* just as a body in motion would, if left to itself, always follow a straight line in the same direction, which is changed however into a curvilinear motion, as soon as another force influences it at the same time in a different direction. In order to distinguish the proper action of the understanding from that other force which is mixed up with it, it will be necessary to look on an erroneous judgment as the diagonal between two forces, which determine the judgment in two different directions, forming as it were an angle, and to dissolve that composite effect into the simple ones of the understanding and of the sensibility, which must be effected in pure judgments *a priori* by transcendental reflection, whereby, as we tried to show, the right place is assigned to each representation in the faculty of knowledge corresponding to it, and the influence of either faculty upon such representation is determined.

It is not at present our business to treat of empirical, for instance, optical appearance or illusion, which occurs in the empirical use of the otherwise correct rules of the understanding, and by which, owing to the influence of imagination, the faculty of judgment is misled. We have to deal here with nothing but the *transcendental illusion,* which touches principles never even intended to be applied to experience, which might give us a test of their correctness,—an illusion which, in spite of all the warnings of criticism, tempts us far beyond the empirical use of the categories, and deludes us with the mere dream of an extension of the pure understanding. All principles the application of which is entirely confined within the limits of possible experience, we shall call *immanent;* those, on the contrary, which tend to transgress those limits, *transcendent.* I do not mean by this the transcendental use or abuse of the categories, which is a mere fault of the faculty of the judgment, not being as yet sufficiently

---

* Sensibility, if subjected to the understanding as the object on which it exercises its function, is the source of real knowledge, but sensibility, if it influences the action of the understanding itself and leads it on to a judgment, is the cause of error.

subdued by criticism nor sufficiently attentive to the limits of the sphere within which alone the pure understanding has full play, but real principles which call upon us to break down all those barriers, and to claim a perfectly new territory, which nowhere recognises any demarcation at all. Here *transcendental* and *transcendent* do not mean the same thing. The principles of the pure understanding, which we explained before, are meant to be only of empirical, and not of transcendental application, that is, they cannot transcend the limits of experience. A principle, on the contrary, which removes these landmarks, nay, insists on our transcending them, is called *transcendent*. If our critique succeeds in laying bare the illusion of those pretended principles, the other principles of a purely empirical use may, in opposition to the former, be called *immanent*.

Logical illusion, which consists in a mere imitation of the forms of reason (the illusion of sophistic syllogisms), arises entirely from want of attention to logical rules. It disappears at once, when our attention is roused. Transcendental illusion, on the contrary, does not disappear, although it has been shown up, and its worthlessness rendered clear by means of transcendental criticism, as, for instance, the illusion inherent in the proposition that the world must have a beginning in time. The cause of this is that there exists in our reason (considered subjectively as a faculty of human knowledge) principles and maxims of its use, which have the appearance of objective principles, and lead us to mistake the subjective necessity of a certain connection of our concepts in favour of the understanding for an objective necessity in the determination of things by themselves. This illusion is as impossible to avoid as it is to prevent the sea from appearing to us higher at a distance than on the shore, because we see it by higher rays of light; or to prevent the moon from appearing, even to an astronomer, larger at its rising, although he is not deceived by that illusion.

Transcendental Dialectic must, therefore, be content to lay bare the illusion of transcendental judgments and guarding against its deceptions—but it will never succeed in removing the transcendental illusion (like the logical), and putting an end to it altogether. For we have here to deal with a natural and inevitable illusion, which itself rests on subjective principles, representing them to us as objective, while logical Dialectic, in removing sophisms, has to deal merely with a mistake in applying the principles, or with an artificial illusion produced by an imitation of them. There exists, therefore, a natural and inevitable Dialectic of pure reason, not one in which a mere bungler might get entangled from want of knowledge, or which a sophist might artificially devise to confuse rational people, but one that is inherent in, and inseparable from human reason, and which, even after its illusion has been exposed, will never cease to fascinate our reason, and to precipitate it into momentary errors, such as require to be removed again and again.

2. OF PURE REASON, AS THE SEAT OF TRANSCENDENTAL ILLUSION

A. *Of Reason in General*

All our knowledge begins with the senses, proceeds thence to the understanding, and ends with reason. There is nothing higher than reason, for working up the material of intuition, and comprehending it under the highest unity of thought. As it here becomes necessary to give a definition of that highest faculty of knowledge, I begin to feel considerable misgivings. There is of reason, as there is of the understanding, a purely formal, that is logical use, in which no account is taken of the contents of knowledge; but there is also a real use, in so far as reason itself contains the origin of certain concepts and principles, which it has not borrowed either from the senses or from the understanding. The former faculty has been long defined by logicians as the faculty of mediate conclusions, in contradistinction to immediate ones (*consequentiae immediatae*); but this does not help us to understand the latter, which itself produces concepts. As this brings us face to face with the division of reason into a logical and a transcendental faculty, we must look for a higher concept for this source of knowledge, to comprehend both concepts: though, according to the analogy of the concepts of the understanding, we may expect that the logical concept will give us the key to the transcendental, and that the table of the functions of the former will give us the genealogical outline of the concepts of reason.

In the first part of our transcendental logic we defined the understanding as the *faculty of rules*, and we now distinguish reason from it, by calling it the *faculty of principles*.

The term *principle* is ambiguous, and signifies commonly

some kind of knowledge only that may be used as a principle, though in itself, and according to its origin, it is no principle at all. Every general proposition, even though it may have been derived from experience (by induction), may serve as a major in a syllogism of reason; but it is not on that account a principle. Mathematical axioms, as, for instance, that between two points there can be only one straight line, constitute even general knowledge *a priori,* and may therefore, with reference to the cases which can be brought under them, rightly be called principles. Nevertheless it would be wrong to say, that this property of a straight line, in general and by itself, is known to us from principles, for it is known from pure intuition only.

I shall therefore call it knowledge from principles, whenever we know the particular in the general, by means of concepts. Thus every syllogism of reason is a form of deducing some kind of knowledge from a principle, because the major always contains a concept which enables us to know, according to a principle, everything that can be comprehended under the conditions of that concept. As every general knowledge may serve as a major in such a syllogism, and as the understanding supplies such general propositions *a priori,* these no doubt may, with reference to their possible use, be called principles.

But, if we consider these principles of the pure understanding in themselves, and according to their origin, we find that they are anything rather than knowledge from concepts. They would not even be possible *a priori,* unless we relied on pure intuition (in mathematics) or on conditions of a possible experience in general. That everything which happens has a cause, can by no means be concluded from the concept of that which happens; on the contrary, that very principle shows in what manner alone we can form a definite empirical concept of that which happens.

It is impossible therefore for the understanding to supply us with synthetical knowledge from concepts, and it is really that kind of knowledge which I call principles absolutely; while all general propositions may be called principles relatively.

It is an old desideratum, which at some time, however distant, may be realised, that, instead of the endless variety of civil laws, their principles might be discovered, for thus alone the secret might be found of what is called simplifying legislation. Such laws, however, are only limitations of our freedom under conditions by which it always agrees with itself; they refer to something which is entirely our own work, and of which we ourselves can be the cause, by means of these concepts. But that objects in themselves, as for instance material nature, should be subject to principles, and be determined according to mere concepts, is something, if not impossible, at all events extremely contradictory. But be that as it may (for on this point we have still all investigations before us), so much at least is clear, that knowledge from principles (by itself) is something totally different from mere knowledge of the understanding, which, in the form of a principle, may no doubt precede other knowledge, but which by itself (in so far as it is synthetical) is not based on mere thought, nor contains anything general, according to concepts.

If the understanding is a faculty for producing unity among phenomena, according to rules, reason is the faculty for producing unity among the rules of the understanding, according to principles. Reason therefore never looks directly to experience, or to any object, but to the understanding, in order to impart *a priori* through concepts to its manifold kinds of knowledge a unity that may be called the unity of reason, and is very different from the unity which can be produced by the understanding.

This is a general definition of the faculty of reason, so far as it was possible to make it intelligible without the help of illustrations, which are to be given hereafter.

B. *Of the Logical Use of Reason*

A distinction is commonly made between what is immediately known and what is only inferred. That in a figure bounded by three straight lines there are three angles, is known immediately, but that these angles together are equal to two right angles, is only inferred. As we are constantly obliged to infer, we grow so accustomed to it, that in the end we no longer perceive this difference, and as in the case of the so-called deceptions of the senses, often mistake what we have only inferred for something perceived immediately. In every syllogism there is first a fundamental proposition; secondly, another deduced from it; and lastly, the conclusion (consequence), according to which the truth of the latter is indissolubly connected with the truth of the former. If the judgment or the conclusion is so clearly contained in the first that it can be inferred from it without the mediation or intervention of a third representation, the conclusion is called immediate (*consequentia immediata*): though I should prefer to call it a conclusion of the understanding. But if, besides the fundamental knowledge, another judgment is required to bring out the consequence, then the conclusion is called a conclusion of reason. In the proposition '*all men are mortal*,' the following propositions are contained: some men are mortal; or some mortals are men; or nothing that is immortal is a man. These are therefore immediate inferences from the first. The proposition, on the contrary, all the learned are mortal, is not contained in the fundamental judgment, because the concept of learned does not occur in it, and can only be deduced from it by means of an intervening judgment.

In every syllogism I first think a rule (the major) by means of the understanding. I then bring some special knowledge under the condition of the rule (the minor) by means of the faculty of judgment, and I finally determine my knowledge through the predicate of the rule (*conclusio*), that is, *a priori*, by means of reason. It is therefore the relation represented by the major proposition, as the rule, between knowledge and its condition, that constitutes the different kinds of syllogism. Syllogisms are therefore threefold, like all judgments, differing from each other in the manner in which they express the relation of knowledge in the understanding, namely, categorical, hypothetical, and disjunctive.

If, as often happens, the conclusion is put forward as a judgment, in order to see whether it does not follow from other judgments by which a perfectly different object is conceived, I try to find in the understanding the assertion of that conclusion, in order to see whether it does not exist in it, under certain conditions, according to a general rule. If I find such a condition, and if the object of the conclusion can be brought under the given condition, then that conclusion follows from the rule *which is valid for other objects of knowledge also*. Thus we see that reason, in forming conclusions, tries to reduce the great variety of the knowledge of the understanding to the smallest number of principles (general conditions), and thereby to produce in it the highest unity.

C. *Of the Pure Use of Reason*

The question to which we have at present to give an answer, though a preliminary one only, is this, whether reason can be isolated and thus constitute by itself an independent source of concepts and judgments, which spring from it alone, and through which it has reference to objects, or whether it is only a subordinate faculty for imparting a certain form to any given knowledge, namely, a logical form, a faculty whereby the cognitions of the understanding are arranged among themselves only, and lower rules placed under higher ones (the condition of the latter comprehending in its sphere the condition of the former) so far as all this can be done by their comparison. Variety of rules with unity of principles is a requirement of reason for the purpose of bringing the understanding into perfect agreement with itself, just as the understanding brings the variety of intuition under concepts, and thus imparts to intuition a connected form. Such a principle however prescribes no law to the objects themselves, nor does it contain the ground on which the possibility of knowing and determining objects depends. It is merely a subjective law of economy, applied to the stores of our understanding; having for its purpose, by means of a comparison of concepts, to reduce the general use of them to the smallest possible number, but without giving us a right to demand of the objects themselves such a uniformity as might conduce to the comfort and the extension of our understanding, or to ascribe to that maxim any objective validity. In one word, the question is, whether reason in itself, that is pure reason, contains synthetical principles and rules *a priori,* and what those principles are?

The merely formal and logical procedure of reason in syllogisms gives us sufficient hints as to the ground on which the transcendental principle of synthetical knowledge, by means of pure reason, is likely to rest.

First, a syllogism, as a function of reason, does not refer to intuitions in order to bring them under rules (as the understanding does with its categories), but to concepts and judgments. Although pure reason refers in the end to objects, it has no immediate relation to them and their intuition, but only to the understanding and its judgments, these having a direct relation to the senses and their intuition, and determining their objects. Unity of reason is therefore never the unity of a possible experience, but essentially different from it, as the unity of the understanding. That everything which happens has a cause, is not a principle discovered or prescribed by reason, it only makes the unity of experience possible, and borrows nothing from reason, which without this relation to possible experience could never, from mere concepts, have prescribed such a synthetical unity.

Secondly. Reason, in its logical employment, looks for the general condition of its judgment (the conclusion), and the syllogism produced by reason is itself nothing but a judgment by means of bringing its condition under a general rule (the major). But as this rule is again liable to the same experiment, reason having to seek, as long as possible, the condition of a condition (by means of a prosyllogism), it is easy to see that it is the peculiar principle of reason (in its logical use) to find for every conditioned knowledge of the understanding the unconditioned, whereby the unity of that knowledge may be completed.

This logical maxim, however, cannot become a principle of *pure reason,* unless we admit that, whenever the condition is given, the whole series of conditions, subordinated to one another, a series, which consequently is itself unconditioned, is likewise given (that is, is contained in the object and its connection).

Such a principle of pure reason, however, is evidently synthetical; for analytically the conditioned refers no doubt to some condition, but not to the unconditioned. From this principle several other synthetical propositions also must arise of which the pure understanding knows nothing; because it has to deal with objects of a possible experience only, the knowledge and synthesis of which are always conditioned. The unconditioned, if it is really to be admitted, has to be especially considered with regard to all the determinations which distinguish it from whatever is conditioned, and will thus supply material for many a synthetical proposition *a priori.*

The principles resulting from this highest principle of pure reason will however be *transcendent,* with regard to all phenomena; that is to say, it will be impossible ever to make any adequate empirical use of such a principle. It will thus be completely different from all principles of the understanding, the use of which is entirely *immanent* and directed to the possibility of experience only. The task that is now before us in the transcendental Dialectic which has to be developed from sources deeply hidden in the human reason, is this: to discover the correctness or otherwise the falsehood of the principle that the series of conditions (in the synthesis of phenomena, or of objective thought in general) extends to the unconditioned, and what consequences result therefrom with regard to the empirical use of the understanding:—to find out whether there is really such an objectively valid principle of reason, and not only, in place of it, a logical rule which requires us, by ascending to ever higher conditions, to approach their completeness, and thus to bring the highest unity of reason, which is possible to us, into our knowledge: to find out, I say, whether, by some misconception, a mere tendency of reason has not been mistaken for a transcendental principle of pure reason, postulating, without sufficient reflection, absolute completeness in the series of conditions in the objects themselves, and what kind of misconceptions and illusions may in that case have crept into the syllogisms of reason, the major proposition of which has been taken over from pure reason (being perhaps a *petitio* rather than a *postulatum*), and which ascend from experience to its conditions. We shall divide it into two parts, of which the first will treat of the *transcendent concepts* of pure reason, the second of *transcendent and dialectical syllogisms*.

TRANSCENDENTAL DIALECTIC

BOOK I

OF THE CONCEPTS OF PURE REASON

Whatever may be thought of the possibility of concepts of pure reason, it is certain that they are not simply obtained by reflection, but by inference. Concepts of the understanding exist *a priori,* before experience, and for the sake of it, but they contain nothing but the unity of reflection applied to phenomena, so far as they are necessarily intended for a possible empirical consciousness. It is through them alone that knowledge and determination of an object become possible. They are the first to give material for conclusions, and they are not preceded by any concepts *a priori* of objects from which they could themselves be deduced. Their objective reality however depends on this, that because they constitute the intellectual form of all experience, it is necessary that their application should always admit of being exhibited in experience.

The very name, however, of a *concept of reason* gives a kind of intimation that it is not intended to be limited to experience, because it refers to a kind of knowledge of which every empirical knowledge is a part only (it may be, the whole of possible experience or of its empirical synthesis): and to which all real experience belongs, though it can never fully attain to it. Concepts of reason serve for conceiving or comprehending; concepts of the understanding for understanding (perceptions). If they contain the unconditioned, they refer to something to which all experience may belong, but which itself can never become an object of experience;— something to which reason in its conclusions from experience leads up, and by which it estimates and measures the degree of its own empirical use, but which never forms part of empirical synthesis. If such concepts possess, notwithstanding, objective validity, they may be called *conceptus ratiocinati* (concepts legitimately formed); if they have only been surreptitiously obtained, by a kind of illusory conclusion, they may be called *conceptus ratiocinantes* (sophistical concepts). But as this subject can only be fully treated in the chapter on the dialectical conclusions of pure reason, we shall say no more of it now, but shall only, as we gave the name of categories to the pure concepts of the understanding, give a new name to the concepts of pure reason, and call them *transcendental ideas,* a name that has now to be explained and justified.

TRANSCENDENTAL DIALECTIC

Book I

FIRST SECTION

Of Ideas in General

In spite of the great wealth of our languages, a thoughtful mind is often at a loss for an expression that should square exactly with its concept; and for want of which he cannot make himself altogether intelligible, either to others or to himself. To coin new words is to arrogate to oneself legislative power in matters of language, a proceeding which seldom succeeds, so that, before taking so desperate a step, it is always advisable to look about, in dead and learned languages, whether they do not contain such a concept and its adequate expression. Even if it should happen that the original meaning of the word had become somewhat uncertain, through carelessness on the part of its authors, it is better nevertheless to determine and fix the meaning which principally belonged to it (even if it should remain doubtful whether it was originally used exactly in that meaning), than to spoil our labour by becoming unintelligible.

Whenever therefore there exists one single word only for a certain concept, which, in its received meaning, exactly covers that concept, and when it is of great consequence to keep that concept distinct from other related concepts, we ought not to be lavish in using it nor employ it, for the sake of variety only, as a synonyme in the place of others, but carefully preserve its own peculiar meaning, as otherwise it may easily happen that the expression ceases to attract special attention, and loses itself in a crowd of other words of very different import, so that the thought, which that expression alone could have preserved, is lost with it.

From the way in which Plato uses the term *idea*, it is easy to see that he meant by it something which not only was never borrowed from the senses, but which even far transcends the concepts of the understanding, with which Aristotle occupied himself, there being nothing in experience corresponding to the ideas. With him the ideas are archetypes of things themselves, not only, like the categories, keys to possible experiences. According to his opinion they flowed out from the highest reason, which however exists no longer in its original state, but has to recall, with difficulty, the old but now very obscure ideas, which it does by means of reminiscence, commonly called philosophy. I shall not enter here on any literary discussions in order to determine the exact meaning which the sublime philosopher himself connected with that expression. I shall only remark, that it is by no means unusual, in ordinary conversations, as well as in written works, that by carefully comparing the thoughts uttered by an author on his own subject, we succeed in understanding him better than he understood himself, because he did not sufficiently define his concept, and thus not only spoke, but sometimes even thought, in opposition to his own intentions.

Plato knew very well that our faculty of knowledge was filled with a much higher craving than merely to spell out phenomena according to a synthetical unity, and thus to read and understand them as experience. He knew that our reason, if left to itself, tries to soar up to knowledge to which no object that experience may give can ever correspond; but which nevertheless is real, and by no means a mere cobweb of the brain.

Plato discovered his ideas principally in what is practical,* that is, in what depends on freedom, which again belongs to a class of knowledge which is a peculiar product of reason. He who would derive the concept of virtue from experience, and would change what at best could only serve as an example or an imperfect illustration, into a type and a source of knowledge (as many have really done), would indeed transform virtue into an equivocal phantom, changing according to times and circumstances, and utterly useless to serve as a rule. Everybody can surely perceive that, when a person is held up to us as a model of virtue, we have always in our own mind the true original with which we compare this so-called model, and estimate it accordingly. The true original is the idea of virtue, in regard to which all possible objects of experience may serve as examples (proofs of the practicability, in a certain degree, of that which is required by the concept of reason), but never as archetypes. That no man can ever act up to the pure idea of virtue does not in the least prove the chimerical nature of that concept; for every judgment as to the moral worth or unworth of actions is possible by means of that idea only, which forms, therefore, the necessary foundation for every approach to moral perfection, however far the impediments inherent in human nature, the extent of which it is difficult to determine, may keep us removed from it.

The Platonic Republic has been supposed to be a striking example of purely imaginary perfection. It has become a by-word, as something that could exist in the brain of an idle thinker only, and Brucker thinks it ridiculous that Plato could have said that no prince could ever govern well, unless he participated in the ideas. We should do better, however, to follow up this thought and endeavour (where that excellent philosopher leaves us without his guidance) to place it in a clearer light by our own efforts, rather than to throw it aside

---

* It is true, however, that he extended his concept of ideas to speculative knowledge also, if only it was pure, and given entirely *a priori*. He extended it even to mathematics, although they can have their object nowhere but in possible experience. In this I cannot follow him, nor in the mystical deduction of his ideas, and in the exaggerations which led him, as it were, to hypostasise them, although the high-flown language which he used, when treating of this subject, may well admit of a milder interpretation, and one more in accordance with the nature of things.

as useless, under the miserable and very dangerous pretext of its impracticability. A constitution founded on the greatest possible human freedom, according to laws which enable the freedom of each individual to exist by the side of the freedom of others (without any regard to the highest possible human happiness, because that must necessarily follow by itself), is, to say the least, a necessary idea, on which not only the first plan of a constitution or a state, but all laws must be based, it being by no means necessary to take account from the beginning of existing impediments, which may owe their origin not so much to human nature itself as to the actual neglect of true ideas in legislation. For nothing can be more mischievous and more unworthy a philosopher than the vulgar appeal to what is called adverse experience, which possibly might never have existed, if at the proper time institutions had been framed according to those ideas, and not according to crude concepts, which, because they were derived from experience only, have marred all good intentions. The more legislation and government are in harmony with that idea, the rarer, no doubt, punishments would become; and it is therefore quite rational to say (as Plato did), that in a perfect state no punishments would be necessary. And though this can never be realised, yet the idea is quite correct which sets up this maximum as an archetype, in order thus to bring our legislative constitutions nearer and nearer to the greatest possible perfection. Which may be the highest degree where human nature must stop, and how wide the chasm may be between the idea and its realisation, no one can or ought to determine, because it is this very freedom that may be able to transcend any limits hitherto assigned to it.

It is not only, however, where human reason asserts its free causality and ideas become operative agents (with regard to actions and their objects), that is to say, in the sphere of ethics, but also in nature itself, that Plato rightly discovered clear proofs of its origin from ideas. A plant, an animal, the regular plan of the cosmos (most likely therefore the whole order of nature), show clearly that they are possible according to ideas only; and that though no single creature, under the singular conditions of its existence, can fully correspond with the idea of what is most perfect of its kind (as little as any individual man with the idea of humanity, which, for all that, he carries in his mind as the archetype of all his actions), those ideas are nevertheless determined throughout in the highest understanding each by itself as unchangeable, and are in fact the original causes of things, although it can only be said of the whole of them, connected together in the universe, that it is perfectly adequate to the idea. If we make allowance for the exaggerated expression, the effort of the philosopher to ascend from the mere observing and copying of the physical side of nature to an architectonic system of it, teleologically, that is according to ideas, deserves respect and imitation, while with regard to the principles of morality, legislation, and religion, where it is the ideas themselves that make experience of the good possible, though they can never be fully realised in experience, such efforts are of very eminent merit, which those only fail to recognise who attempt to judge it according to empirical rules, the very validity of which, as principles, was meant to be denied by Plato. With regard to nature, it is experience no doubt which supplies us with rules, and is the foundation of all truth: with regard to moral laws, on the contrary, experience is, alas! but the source of illusion; and it is altogether reprehensible to derive or limit the laws of what we ought to do according to our experience of what has been done.

Instead of considering these subjects, the full development of which constitutes in reality the peculiar character and dignity of philosophy, we have to occupy ourselves at present with a task less brilliant, though not less useful, of building and strengthening the foundation of that majestic edifice of morality, which at present is undermined by all sorts of moletracks, the work of our reason, which thus vainly, but always with the same confidence, is searching for buried treasures. It is our duty at present to acquire an accurate knowledge of the transcendental use of the pure reason, its principles and ideas, in order to be able to determine and estimate correctly their influence and value. But before I leave this preliminary introduction, I beg those who really care for philosophy (which means more than is commonly supposed) if they are convinced by what I have said and shall still have to say, to take the term *idea*, in its original meaning, under their special protection, so that it should no longer be lost among other expressions, by which all sorts of representations are loosely designated, to the great detriment of philosophy. There is no lack of names adequate to express every kind of representation, without our having to encroach on the property of others. I shall give a graduated list of them. The whole class may be called *representation* (*repraesentatio*). Under it stands conscious representation, *perception* (*perceptio*). A *perception* referring to the subject only, as a modification of his state, is *sensation* (*sensatio*), while an objective sensation is called *knowledge, cognition* (*cognitio*). Cognition is either *intuition* or *concept* (*intuitus vel conceptus*). The former refers immediately to an object and is singular, the latter refers to it mediately, that is, by means of a characteristic mark that can be shared by several things in common. A concept is either *empirical* or *pure,* and the pure concept, so far as it has its origin in the understanding only (not in the pure image of sensibility) is called *notion* (*notio*). A concept formed of notions and transcending all possible experience is an *idea,* or a concept of reason. To any one who has once accustomed himself to these distinctions, it must be extremely irksome to hear the representation of red colour called an idea, though it could not even be rightly called a notion (a concept of the understanding).

TRANSCENDENTAL DIALECTIC

Book I

SECOND SECTION

Of Transcendental Ideas

We had an instance in our transcendental Analytic, how the mere logical form of our knowledge could contain the origin of pure concepts *a priori,* which represent objects antecedently to all experience, or rather indicate a synthetical unity by which alone an empirical knowledge of objects becomes possible. The form of judgments (changed into a concept of the synthesis of intuitions) gave us the categories that guide and determine the use of the understanding in every experience. We may expect, therefore, that the form of the syllogisms, if referred to the synthetical unity of intuitions, according to the manner of the categories, will contain the origin of certain concepts *a priori,* to be called concepts of pure reason, or *transcendental ideas,* which ought to determine the use of the understanding within the whole realm of experience, according to principles.

The function of reason in its syllogisms consists in the universality of cognition, according to concepts, and the syllogism itself is in reality a judgment, determined *a priori* in the whole extent of its condition. The proposition 'Caius is mortal,' might be taken from experience, by means of the understanding only. But what we want is a concept, containing the condition under which the predicate (assertion in general) of that judgment is given (here the concept of man), and after I have arranged it under this condition, taken in its whole extent (all men are mortal), I proceed to determine accordingly the knowledge of my object (Caius is mortal).

What we are doing therefore in the conclusion of a syllogism is to restrict the predicate to a certain object, after we have used it first in the major, in its whole extent, under a certain condition. This completeness of its extent, in reference to such a condition, is called universality (*universalitas*); and to this corresponds, in the synthesis of intuitions, the totality (*universitas*) of conditions. The transcendental concept of reason is, therefore, nothing but the concept of the totality of the conditions of anything given as conditioned. As therefore the unconditioned alone renders a totality of conditions possible, and as conversely the totality of conditions must always be unconditioned, it follows that a pure concept of reason in general may be explained as a concept of the unconditioned, so far as it contains a basis for the synthesis of the conditioned.

As many kinds of relations as there are, which the understanding represents to itself by means of the categories, so many pure concepts of the reason we shall find, that is, first, the *unconditioned* of the *categorical* synthesis in a subject; secondly, the *unconditioned* of the *hypothetical* synthesis of the members of a series; thirdly, the *unconditioned* of the *disjunctive* synthesis of the parts of a system.

There are exactly as many kinds of syllogisms, each of which tries to advance by means of prosyllogisms to the unconditioned: the first to the subject, which itself is no longer a predicate; the second to the presupposition, which presupposes nothing else; and the third to an aggregate of the members of a division, which requires nothing else, in order to render the division of the concept complete. Hence the pure concepts of reason implying totality in the synthesis of the conditions are necessary, at least as problems, in order to carry the unity of the understanding to the unconditioned, if that is possible, and they are founded in the nature of human reason, even though these transcendental concepts may be without any proper application *in concreto,* and thus have no utility beyond bringing the understanding into a direction where its application, being extended as far as possible, is brought throughout in harmony with itself.

Whilst speaking here of the totality of conditions, and of the unconditioned, as the common title of all the concepts of reason, we again meet with a term which we cannot do without, but which, by long abuse, has become so equivocal that we cannot employ it with safety. The term *absolute* is one of those few words which, in their original meaning, were fitted to a concept, which afterwards could not be exactly fitted with any other word of the same language, and the loss of which, or what is the same, the loose employment of which, entails the loss of the concept itself, and that of a concept with which reason is constantly occupied, and cannot dispense with without real damage to all transcendental investigations. At present the term *absolute* is frequently used simply in order to indicate that something applies to an object, considered in itself, and thus as it were internally. In this way *absolutely possible* would mean that something is possible in itself (interné), which in reality is the least that could be said of it. It is sometimes used also to indicate that something is valid in all respects (without limitation), as people speak of absolute sovereignty. In this way *absolutely possible* would mean that which is possible in all respects, and this is again the utmost that could be said of the possibility of a thing. It is true that these two significations sometimes coincide, because something that is internally impossible is impossible also in every respect, and therefore absolutely impossible. But in most cases they are far apart, and I am by no means justified in concluding that, because something is possible in itself, it is possible also in every respect, that is, absolutely possible. Nay, with regard to absolute necessity, I shall be able to show hereafter that it by no means always depends on internal necessity, and that the two cannot therefore be considered synonymous. No doubt, if the opposite of a thing is intrinsically impossible, that opposite is also impossible in every respect, and the thing itself therefore absolutely necessary. But I cannot conclude conversely, that the opposite of what is absolutely necessary is internally impossible, or that the absolute necessity of things is the same as an internal necessity. For in certain cases that internal necessity is an entirely empty expression, with which we cannot connect the least concept, while that of the necessity of a thing in every respect (with regard to all that is possible) implies very peculiar determinations. As therefore the loss of a concept which has acted a great part in speculative philosophy can never be indifferent to philosophers, I hope they will also take some interest in the definition and careful preservation of the term with which that concept is connected.

I shall therefore use the term *absolute* in this enlarged meaning only, in opposition to that which is valid relatively and in particular respects only, the latter being restricted to conditions, the former free from any restrictions whatsoever.

It is then the absolute totality in the synthesis of conditions at which the transcendental concept of reason aims, nor does it rest satisfied till it has reached that which is unconditioned absolutely and in every respect. Pure reason leaves everything to the understanding, which has primarily to do with the objects of intuition, or rather their synthesis in imagination. It is only the absolute totality in the use of the concepts of the understanding, which reason reserves for itself, while trying to carry the synthetical unity, which is realised in the category, to the absolutely unconditioned. We might therefore call the latter the unity of the phenomena in reason, the former, which is expressed by the category, the unity in the understanding. Hence reason is only concerned with the use of the understanding, not so far as it contains the basis of possible experience (for the absolute totality of conditions is not a concept that can be used in experience, because no experience is unconditioned), but in order to impart to it a direction towards a certain unity of which the understanding knows nothing, and which is meant to comprehend all acts of the understanding, with regard to any object, into an absolute whole. On this account the objective use of the pure concepts of reason must always be *transcendent:* while that of the pure concepts of the understanding must always be *immanent,* being by its very nature restricted to possible experience.

By idea I understand the necessary concept of reason, to which the senses can supply no corresponding object. The concepts of reason, therefore, of which we have been speaking, are *transcendental ideas.* They are concepts of pure reason, so far as they regard all empirical knowledge as determined by an absolute totality of conditions. They are not mere fancies, but supplied to us by the very nature of reason, and referring by necessity to the whole use of the understanding. They are, lastly, transcendent, as overstepping the limits of all experience which can never supply an object adequate to the transcendental idea. If we speak of an idea, we say a great deal with respect to the object (as the object of the pure understanding) but very little with respect to the subject, that is, with respect to its reality under empirical conditions, because an idea, being the concept of a maximum, can never be adequately given *in concreto*. As the latter is really the whole aim in the merely speculative use of reason, and as the mere approaching a concept, which in reality can never be reached, is the same as if the concept were missed altogether, people, when speaking of such a concept, are wont to say, it is an idea only. Thus one might say, that the absolute whole of all phenomena is an idea only, for as we can never form a representation of such a whole, it remains a problem without a solution. In the practical use of the understanding, on the contrary, where we are only concerned with practice, according to rules, the idea of practical reason can always be realised *in concreto*, although partially only; nay, it is the indispensable condition of all practical use of reason. The practical realisation of the idea is here always limited and deficient, but these limits cannot be defined, and it always remains under the influence of a concept, implying absolute completeness and perfection. The practical idea is therefore in this case truly fruitful, and, with regard to practical conduct, indispensable and necessary. In it pure reason becomes a cause and active power, capable of realising what is contained in its concept. Hence we cannot say of wisdom, as if contemptuously, that it is an idea only, but for the very reason that it contains the idea of the necessary unity of all possible aims, it must determine all practical acts, as an original and, at least, limitative condition.

Although we must say that all transcendental concepts of reason are ideas only, they are not therefore to be considered as superfluous and useless. For although we cannot by them determine any object, they may nevertheless, even unobserved, supply the understanding with a canon or rule of its extended and consistent use, by which, though no object can be better known than it is according to its concepts, yet the understanding may be better guided onwards in its knowledge, not to mention that they may possibly render practicable a transition from physical to practical concepts, and thus impart to moral ideas a certain strength and connection with the speculative knowledge of reason. On all this more light will be thrown in the sequel.

For our present purposes we are obliged to set aside a consideration of these practical ideas, and to treat of reason in its speculative, or rather, in a still more limited sense, its purely transcendental use. Here we must follow the same road which we took before in the deduction of the categories; that is, we must consider the logical form of all knowledge of reason, and see whether, perhaps, by this logical form, reason may become a source of concepts also, which enable us to regard objects in themselves, as determined synthetically *a priori* in relation to one or other of the functions of reason.

Reason, if considered as a faculty of a certain logical form of knowledge, is the faculty of concluding, that is, of judging mediately, by bringing the condition of a possible under the condition of a given judgment. The given judgment is the general rule (*major*). Bringing the condition of another possible judgment under the condition of the rule, which may be called subsumption, is the *minor,* and the actual judgment, which contains the assertion of the rule in the subsumed case, is the conclusion. We know that the rule asserts something as general under a certain condition. The condition of the rule is then found to exist in a given case. Then that which, under that condition, was asserted as generally valid, has to be considered as valid in that given case also, which complies with that condition. It is easy to see therefore that reason arrives at knowledge by acts of the understanding, which constitute a series of conditions. If I arrive at the proposition that all bodies are changeable, only by starting from a more remote knowledge (which does not yet contain the concept of body, but a condition of such a concept only), namely, that all which is composite is changeable; and then proceed to something less remotely known, and depending on the former, namely, that bodies are composite; and, lastly, only advance to a third proposition, connecting the more remote knowledge (changeable) with the given case, and conclude that bodies therefore are changeable, we see that we have passed through a series of conditions (premisses) before we arrived at knowledge (conclusion). Every series, the exponent of which (whether of a categorical or hypothetical judgment) is given, can be continued, so that this procedure of reason leads to *ratiocinatio polysyllogistica,* a series of conclusions which, either on the side of the conditions (*per prosyllogismos*) or of the conditioned (*per episyllogismos*), may be continued indefinitely.

It is soon perceived, however, that the chain or series of prosyllogisms, that is, of knowledge deduced on the side of reasons or conditions of a given knowledge, in other words, the *ascending series* of syllogisms, must stand in a very different relation to the faculty of reason from that of the *descending series,* that is, of the progress of reason on the side of the conditioned, by means of episyllogisms. For, as in the former case the knowledge embodied in the conclusion is given as conditioned only, it is impossible to arrive at it by means of reason in any other way except under the supposition at least that all the members of the series on the side of the conditions are given (totality in the series of premisses), because it is under that supposition only that the contemplated judgment *a priori* is possible; while on the side of the conditioned, or of the inferences, we can only think of a growing series, not of one presupposed as complete or given, that is, of a potential progression only. Hence, when our knowledge is considered as conditioned, reason is constrained to look upon the series of conditions in the ascending line as complete, and given in their totality. But if the same knowledge is looked upon at the same time as a condition of other kinds of knowledge, which constitute among themselves a series of inferences in a descending line, it is indifferent to reason how far that progression may go *a parte posteriori,* or whether a totality of the series is possible at all, because such a series is not required for the conclusion in hand, which is sufficiently determined and secured on grounds *a parte priori.* Whether the series of premisses on the side of the conditions have a something that stands first as the highest condition, or whether it be without limits *a parte priori,* it must at all events contain a totality of conditions, even though we should never succeed in comprehending it; and the whole series must be unconditionally true, if the conditioned, which is considered as a consequence resulting from it, is to be accepted as true. This is a demand of reason which pronounces its knowledge as determined *a priori* and as necessary, either in itself, and in that case it requires no reasons, or, if derivative, as a member of a series of reasons, which itself is unconditionally true.

TRANSCENDENTAL DIALECTIC

BOOK I

THIRD SECTION

System of Transcendental Ideas

We are not at present concerned with logical Dialectic, which takes no account of the contents of knowledge, and has only to lay bare the illusions in the form of syllogisms, but with transcendental Dialectic, which is supposed to contain entirely *a priori* the origin of certain kinds of knowledge, arising from pure reason, and of certain deduced concepts, the object of which can never be given empirically, and which therefore lie entirely outside the domain of the pure understanding. We gathered from the natural relation which must exist between the transcendental and the logical use of our knowledge, in syllogisms as well as in judgments, that there must be three kinds of dialectic syllogisms, and no more, corresponding to the three kinds of conclusion by which reason may from principles arrive at knowledge, and that in all of these it is the object of reason to ascend from the conditioned synthesis, to which the understanding is always restricted, to an unconditioned synthesis, which the understanding can never reach.

The relations which all our representations share in common are, 1st, relation to the subject; 2ndly, the relation to objects, either as phenomena, or as objects of thought in general. If we connect this subdivision with the former division, we see that the relation of the representations of which we can form a concept or an idea can only be threefold: 1st, the relation to the subject; 2ndly, the relation to the manifold of the phenomenal object; 3rdly, the relation to all things in general.

All pure concepts in general aim at a synthetical unity of representations, while concepts of pure reason (transcendental ideas) aim at unconditioned synthetical unity of all conditions. All transcendental ideas therefore can be arranged in three classes: the *first* containing the absolute (unconditioned) *unity of the thinking subject;* the *second* the absolute *unity of the series of conditions of phenomena;* the *third* the absolute *unity of the condition of all objects of thought in general.*

The thinking subject is the object-matter of *psychology,* the system of all phenomena (the world) the object-matter of *cosmology,* and the being which contains the highest condition of the possibility of all that can be thought (the Being of all beings), the object-matter of *theology.* Thus it is pure reason which supplies the idea of a transcendental science of the soul (*psychologia rationalis*), of a transcendental science of the world (*cosmologia rationalis*), and, lastly, of a transcendental science of God (*theologia transcendentalis*). Even the mere plan of any one of these three sciences does not come from the understanding, even if connected with the highest logical use of reason, that is, with all possible conclusions, leading from one of its objects (phenomenon) to all others, and on to the most remote parts of any possible empirical synthesis,—but is altogether a pure and genuine product or rather problem of pure reason.

What kinds of pure concepts of reason are comprehended under these three titles of all transcendental ideas will be fully explained in the following chapter. They follow the thread of the categories, for pure reason never refers direct to objects, but to the concepts of objects framed by the understanding. Nor can it be rendered clear, except hereafter in a detailed explanation, how first, reason simply by the synthetical use of the same function which it employs for categorical syllogisms is necessarily led on to the concept of the absolute unity of the thinking subject; secondly, how the logical procedure in hypothetical syllogisms leads to the idea of something absolutely unconditioned, in a series of given conditions, and how, thirdly, the mere form of the disjunctive syllogism produces necessarily the highest concept of reason, that of a Being of all beings; a thought which, at first sight, seems extremely paradoxical.

No objective deduction, like that given of the categories, is possible with regard to these transcendental ideas; they are ideas only, and for that very reason they have no relation to any object corresponding to them in experience. What we could undertake to give was a subjective deduction[1] of them from the nature of reason, and this has been given in the present chapter.

We can easily perceive that pure reason has no other aim but the absolute totality of synthesis *on the side of conditions*

---

[1] Instead of *Anleitung* read *Ableitung.*

(whether of inherence, dependence, or concurrence), and that it has nothing to do with the absolute completeness *on the part of the conditioned*. It is the former only which is required for presupposing the whole series of conditions, and thus presenting it *a priori* to the understanding. If once we have a given condition, complete and unconditioned itself, no concept of reason is required to continue the series, because the understanding takes by itself every step downward from the condition to the conditioned. The transcendental ideas therefore serve only for *ascending* in the series of conditions till they reach the unconditioned, that is, the principles. With regard to *descending* to the conditioned, there is no doubt a widely extended logical use which our reason may make of the rules of the understanding, but no transcendental one; and if we form an idea of the absolute totality of such a synthesis (by *progressus*), as, for instance, of the whole series of all future changes in the world, this is only a thought (*ens rationis*) that may be thought if we like, but is not presupposed as necessary by reason. For the possibility of the conditioned, the totality of its conditions only, but not of its consequences, is presupposed. Such a concept therefore is not one of the transcendental ideas, with which alone we have to deal.

Finally, we can perceive, that there is among the transcendental ideas themselves a certain connection and unity by which pure reason brings all its knowledge into one system. There is in the progression from our knowledge of ourselves (the soul) to a knowledge of the world, and through it to a knowledge of the Supreme Being, something so natural that it looks like the logical progression of reason from premises to a conclusion.* Whether there exists here a real though hidden

---

* *Metaphysic has for the real object of its investigations three ideas only, God, Freedom, and Immortality; the second concept connected with the first leading by necessity to the third as conclusion. Everything else treated by that science is a means only in order to establish those ideas and their reality. Metaphysic does not require these ideas for the sake of natural science; but in order to go beyond nature. A right insight into them would make theology, morality, and, by the union of both, religion also, therefore the highest objects of our existence, dependent on the speculative faculty of reason only, and on nothing else. In a systematical arrangement of those ideas the above order, being synthetical, would be the most appropriate; but in their elaboration, which must necessarily come first, the analytical or inverse order is more practical, enabling us, by starting from what is given us by experience, namely, the study of the soul (psychology), and proceeding thence*

relationship, such as we saw before between the logical and transcendental use of reason, is also one of the questions the answer to which can only be given in the progress of these investigations. For the present we have achieved what we wished to achieve, by removing the transcendental concepts of reason, which in the systems of other philosophers are generally mixed up with other concepts, without being distinguished even from the concepts of the understanding, out of so equivocal a position; by being able to determine their origin and thereby at the same time their number, which can never be exceeded, and by thus bringing them into a systematic connection, marking out and enclosing thereby a separate field for pure reason.

TRANSCENDENTAL DIALECTIC

Book II

OF THE DIALECTICAL CONCLUSIONS OF PURE REASON

One may say that the object of a purely transcendental idea is something of which we have no concept, although the idea is produced with necessity according to the original laws of reason. Nor is it possible indeed to form of an object that should be adequate to the demands of reason, a concept of the understanding, that is, a concept which could be shown in any possible experience, and rendered intuitive. It would be better, however, and less liable to misunderstandings, to say that we can have no knowledge of an object corresponding to an idea, but a problematic concept only.

The transcendental (subjective) reality, at least of pure concepts of reason, depends on our being led to such ideas by a necessary syllogism of reason. There will be syllogisms therefore which have no empirical premisses, and by means of which we conclude from something which we know to something else of which we have no concept, and to which, constrained by an inevitable illusion, we nevertheless attribute objective reality. As regards their result, such syllogisms are

to the study of the world (*cosmology*), *and lastly, to a* knowledge of God (*theology*), *to carry out the whole of our great plan in its entirety.*

rather to be called sophistical than rational, although, as regards their origin, they may claim the latter name, because they are not purely fictitious or accidental, but products of the very nature of reason. They are sophistications, not of men, but of pure reason itself, from which even the wisest of men cannot escape. All he can do is, with great effort, to guard against error, though never able to rid himself completely of an illusion which constantly torments and mocks him.

Of these dialectical syllogisms of reason there are therefore three classes only, that is as many as the ideas to which their conclusions lead. In the syllogism of the *first* class, I conclude from the transcendental concept of the subject, which contains nothing manifold, the absolute unity of the subject itself, of which however I have no concept in this regard. This dialectical syllogism I shall call the transcendental *paralogism*.

The *second* class of the so-called sophistical syllogisms aims at the transcendental concept of an absolute totality in the series of conditions to any given phenomenon; and I conclude from the fact that my concept of the unconditioned synthetical unity of the series is always self-contradictory on one side, the correctness of the opposite unity, of which nevertheless I have no concept either. The state of reason in this class of dialectical syllogisms, I shall call the *antinomy* of pure reason.

Lastly, according to the *third* class of sophistical syllogisms, I conclude from the totality of conditions, under which objects in general, so far as they can be given to me, must be thought, the absolute synthetical unity of all conditions of the possibility of things in general; that is to say, I conclude from things which I do not know according to their mere transcendental[1] concept, a Being of all beings, which I know still less through a transcendental concept, and of the unconditioned necessity of which I can form no concept whatever. This dialectical syllogism of reason I shall call the *ideal* of pure reason.

[1] *Transcendent* is a misprint.

TRANSCENDENTAL DIALECTIC

Book II

Chapter I

OF THE PARALOGISMS OF PURE REASON

The logical paralogism consists in the formal faultiness of a conclusion, without any reference to its contents. But a transcendental paralogism arises from a transcendental cause, which drives us to a formally false conclusion. Such a paralogism, therefore, depends most likely on the very nature of human reason, and produces an illusion which is inevitable, though not insoluble.

We now come to a concept which was not inserted in our general list of transcendental concepts, and yet must be reckoned with them, without however changing that table in the least, or proving it to be deficient. This is the concept, or, if the term is preferred, the judgment, *I think*. It is easily seen, however, that this concept is the vehicle of all concepts in general, therefore of transcendental concepts also, being always comprehended among them, and being itself transcendental also, though without any claim to a special title, inasmuch as it serves only to introduce all thought, as belonging to consciousness. However free that concept may be from all that is empirical (impressions of the senses), it serves nevertheless to distinguish two objects within the nature of our faculty of representation. *I,* as thinking, am an object of the internal sense, and am called soul. That which is an object of the external senses is called body. The term *I,* as a thinking being, signifies the object of psychology, which may be called the rational science of the soul, supposing that we want to know nothing about the soul except what, independent of all experience (which determines the I more especially and *in concreto*), can be deduced from the concept of I, so far as it is present in every act of thought.

Now the rational science of the soul is really such an undertaking; for if the smallest empirical element of my thought or any particular perception of my internal state were mixed up with the sources from which that science derives its materials, it would be an empirical, and no longer a purely rational science of the soul. There is therefore a pretended science, founded on the single proposition of *I think,* and the soundness or unsoundness of which may well be examined in this place, according to the principles of transcendental philosophy. It should not be objected that even in that proposition, which expresses the perception of oneself, I have an internal experience, and that therefore the rational science of the soul, which is founded on it, can never be quite pure, but rests, to a certain extent, on an empirical principle. For this inner perception is nothing more than the mere apperception, *I think,* without which even all transcendental concepts would be impossible, in which we really say, I think the substance, I think the cause, etc. This internal experience in general and its possibility, or perception in general and its relation to other perceptions, there being no special distinction or empirical determination of it, cannot be regarded as empirical knowledge, but must be regarded as knowledge of the empirical in general, and falls therefore under the investigation of the possibility of all experience, which investigation is certainly transcendental. The smallest object of perception (even pleasure and pain), if added to the general representation of self-consciousness, would at once change rational into empirical psychology.

I think is, therefore, the only text of rational psychology, out of which it must evolve all its wisdom. It is easily seen that this thought, if it is to be applied to any object (my self), cannot contain any but transcendental predicates, because the smallest empirical predicate would spoil the rational purity of the science, and its independence of all experience.

We shall therefore follow the threat of the categories, with this difference, however, that as here the first thing which is given is a thing, the I, a thinking being, we must begin with the category of substance, by which a thing in itself is represented, and then proceed backwards, though without changing the respective order of the categories, as given before in our table. The topic of the rational science of the soul, from which has to be derived whatever else that science may contain, is therefore the following.

I

The Soul is *substance*.

<table>
<tr><td>

II

As regards its quality, *simple*.

</td><td>

III

As regards the different times in which it exists, numerically identical, that is *unity* (not plurality).

</td></tr>
</table>

IV

It is in relation to *possible* objects in space.*

All concepts of pure psychology arise from these elements, simply by way of combination, and without the admixture of any other principle. This substance, taken simply as the object of the internal sense, gives us the concept of *immateriality;* and as simple substance, that of *incorruptibility;* its identity, as that of an intellectual substance, gives us *personality;* and all these three together, *spirituality;* its relation to objects in space gives us the concept of *commercium* (intercourse) with *bodies;* the pure psychology thus representing the thinking substance as the principle of life in matter, that is, as soul (*anima*), and as the ground of *animality;* which again, as restricted by spirituality, gives us the concept of *immortality*.

To these concepts refer four paralogisms of a transcendental psychology, which is falsely supposed to be a science of pure reason, concerning the nature of our thinking being. We can, however, use as the foundation of such a science nothing but the single, and in itself perfectly empty, representation of the *I,* of which we cannot even say that it is a concept, but merely a consciousness that accompanies all concepts. By this *I,* or *he,* or *it* (the thing), which thinks, nothing is represented beyond a transcendental subject of thoughts $= x,$ which is known only through the thoughts that are its predicates, and

* The reader, who may not guess at once the psychological purport of these transcendental and abstract terms, or understand why the latter attribute of the soul belongs to the category of existence, will find their full explanation and justification in the sequel. Moreover, I have to apologise for the many Latin expressions which, contrary to good taste, have crept in instead of their native equivalents, not only here, but throughout the whole of the work. My only excuse is, that I thought it better to sacrifice something of the elegance of language, rather than to throw any impediments in the way of real students, by the use of inaccurate and obscure expressions.

of which, apart from them, we can never have the slightest concept, so that we are really turning round it in a perpetual circle, having already to use its representation, before we can form any judgment about it. And this inconvenience is really inevitable, because consciousness in itself is not so much a representation, distinguishing a particular object, but really a form of representation in general, in so far as it is to be called knowledge, of which alone I can say that I think something by it.

It must seem strange, however, from the very beginning, that the condition under which I think, and which therefore is a property of my own subject only, should be valid at the same time for everything which thinks, and that, depending on a proposition which seems to be empirical, we should venture to found the apodictical and general judgment, namely, that everything which thinks is such as the voice of my own consciousness declares it to be within me. The reason of it is, that we are constrained to attribute *a priori* to things all the qualities which form the conditions, under which alone we are able to think them. Now it is impossible for me to form the smallest representation of a thinking being by any external experience, but I can do it through self-consciousness only. Such objects therefore are nothing but a transference of my own consciousness to other things, which thus, and thus only, can be represented as thinking beings. The proposition *I think* is used in this case, however, as problematical only; not so far as it may contain the perception of an existence (the Cartesian, *cogito, ergo sum*), but with regard to its mere possibility, in order to see what properties may be deduced from such a simple proposition with regard to its subject, whether such subject exists or not.

If our knowledge of thinking beings in general, so far as it is derived from pure reason, were founded on more than the *cogito,* and if we made use at the same time of observations on the play of our thoughts and the natural laws of the thinking self, derived from them, we should have before us an empirical psychology, which would form a kind of physiology of the internal sense, and perhaps explain its manifestations, but would never help us to understand such properties as do not fall under any possible experience (as, for instance, simplicity), or to teach apodictically anything touching the nature of thinking beings in general. It would not therefore be a rational psychology.

As the proposition *I think* (taken problematically) contains the form of every possible judgment of the understanding, and accompanies all categories as their vehicle, it must be clear that the conclusions to be drawn from it can only contain a transcendental use of the understanding, which declines all admixture of experience, and of the achievements of which, after what has been said before, we cannot form any very favourable anticipations. We shall therefore follow it, with a critical eye, through all the predicaments of pure psychology.

[The First Paralogism of Substantiality

That the representation of which is the absolute subject of our judgments, and cannot be used therefore as the determination of any other thing, is the *substance*.

I, as a thinking being, am the absolute subject of all my possible judgments, and this representation of myself can never be used as the predicate of any other thing.

Therefore I, as a thinking being (Soul), am *Substance*.

Criticism of the First Paralogism of Pure[1] Psychology

We showed in the analytical portion of transcendental logic, that pure categories, and among them that of substance, have in themselves no objective meaning, unless they rest on some intuition, and are applied to the manifold of such intuitions as functions of synthetical unity. Without this they are merely functions of a judgment without contents. I may say of everything, that it is a substance, so far as I distinguish it from what are mere predicates and determinations. Now in all our thinking the I is the subject, in which thoughts are inherent as determinations only; nor can that I ever be used as a determination of any other thing. Thus everybody is constrained to look upon himself as the substance, and on thinking as the accidents only of his being, and determinations of his state.

But what use are we to make of such a concept of a substance? That I, as a thinking being, *continue* for myself, and naturally neither *arise* nor *perish,* is no legitimate deduction from it; and yet this conclusion would be the only advantage that could be gained from the concept of the substantiality of my own thinking subject, and, but for that, I could do very well without it.

So far from being able to deduce these properties from the pure category of substance, we have on the contrary to observe the permanency of an object in our experience and then

[1] Afterwards *transcendental* instead of *pure*.

lay hold of this permanency, if we wish to apply to it the empirically useful concept of substance. In this case, however, we had no experience to lay hold of, but have only formed a deduction from the concept of the relation which all thinking has to the I, as the common subject to which it belongs. Nor should we, whatever we did, succeed by any certain observation in proving such permanency. For though the I exists in all thoughts, not the slightest intuition is connected with that representation, by which it might be distinguished from other objects of intuition. We may very well perceive therefore that this representation appears again and again in every act of thought, but not that it is a constant and permanent intuition, in which thoughts, as being changeable, come and go.

Hence it follows that in the first syllogism of transcendental psychology reason imposes upon us an apparent knowledge only, by representing the constant logical subject of thought as the knowledge of the real subject in which that knowledge inheres. Of that subject, however, we have not and cannot have the slightest knowledge, because consciousness is that which alone changes representations into thoughts, and in which therefore, as the transcendental subject, all our perceptions must be found. Beside this logical meaning of the I, we have no knowledge of the subject in itself, which forms the substratum and foundation of it and of all our thoughts. In spite of this, the proposition that the soul is a substance may well be allowed to stand, if only we see that this concept cannot help us on in the least or teach us any of the ordinary conclusions of rationalising psychology, as, for instance, the everlasting continuance of the soul amid all changes and even in death, and that it therefore signifies a substance in idea only, and not in reality.

The Second Paralogism of Simplicity

Everything, the action of which can never be considered as the concurrence of several acting things, is simple.
Now the Soul, or the thinking I, is such a thing:—
Therefore, etc.

Criticism of the Second Paralogism of Transcendental Psychology

This is the strong (yet not invulnerable) syllogism among all dialectical syllogisms of pure psychology, not a mere sophism contrived by a dogmatist in order to impart a certain plausibility to his assertions, but a syllogism which seems able to stand the sharpest examination and the gravest doubts of the philosopher. It is this:—

Every composite substance is an aggregate of many substances, and the action of something composite, or that which is inherent in it as such, is an aggregate of many actions or accidents distributed among many substances. An effect due to the concurrence of many acting substances is no doubt possible, if that effect is external only (as, for instance, the motion of a body is the combined motion of all its parts). The case is different however with thoughts, if considered as accidents belonging to a thinking being within. For suppose it is the composite which thinks, then every part of it would contain a part of the thought, and all together only the whole of it. This however is self-contradictory. For as representations, distributed among different beings (like the single words of a verse), never make a whole thought (a verse), it is impossible that a thought should be inherent in something composite, as such. Thought therefore is possible only in a substance which is not an aggregate of many, and therefore absolutely simple.*

What is called the *nervus probandi* in this argument lies in the proposition that, in order to constitute a thought, the many representations must be comprehended under the absolute unity of the thinking subject. Nobody however can prove this proposition from concepts. For how would he undertake to do it? The proposition that a thought can only be the effect of the absolute unity of a thinking being, cannot be considered as analytical. For the unity of thought, consisting of many representations, is collective, and may, so far as mere concepts are concerned, refer to the collective unity of all co-operating substances (as the movement of a body is the compound movement of all its parts) quite as well as to the absolute unity of the subject. According to the rule of identity it would be impossible therefore to establish the necessity of the presupposition of a simple substance, the thought being composite. That, on the other hand, such a proposition might be established synthetically and entirely *a priori* from mere concepts, no one will venture to affirm who has once understood the grounds on which the possibility of synthetical propositions *a priori* rests, as explained by us before.

It is likewise impossible, however, to derive this necessary

* It would be very easy to give to this argument the ordinary scholastic dress. But for my purposes it is sufficient to have clearly exhibited, even in a popular form, the ground on which it rests.

unity of the subject, as the condition of the possibility of the unity of every thought, from experience. For experience never supplies any necessity of thought, much less the concept of absolute unity. Whence then do we take that proposition on which the whole psychological syllogism of reason rests?

It is manifest that if we wish to represent to ourselves a thinking being, we must put ourselves in its place, and supplant as it were the object which has to be considered by our own subject (which never happens in any other kind of investigation). The reason why we postulate for every thought absolute unity of the subject is because otherwise we could not say of it, I think (the manifold in one representation). For although the whole of a thought may be divided and distributed under many subjects, the subjective I can never thus be divided and distributed, and it is this I which we presuppose in every thought.

As in the former paralogism therefore, so here also, the formal proposition of apperception, I think, remains the sole ground on which rational psychology ventures to undertake the extension of its knowledge. That proposition, however, is no experience, but only the form of apperception inherent in, and antecedent to, every experience, that is a *purely subjective condition,* having reference to a possible experience only, but by no means the condition of the possibility of the knowledge of objects, and by no means necessary to the concept of a thinking being in general; although it must be admitted that we cannot represent to ourselves another intelligent being without putting ourselves in its place with that formula of our consciousness.

Nor is it true that the simplicity of my self (as a soul) is really deduced from the proposition, I think, for it is already involved in every thought itself. The proposition *I am simple* must be considered as the immediate expression of apperception, and the so-called syllogism of Cartesius, *cogito, ergo sum,* is in reality tautological, because *cogito* (*sum cogitans*) predicates reality immediately. *I am simple* means no more than that this representation of I does not contain the smallest trace of manifoldness, but is absolute (although merely logical) unity.

Thus we see that the famous psychological argument is founded merely on the indivisible unity of a representation, which only determines the verb with reference to a person; and it is clear that the subject of inherence is designated transcendentally only by the I, which accompanies the thought, without our perceiving the smallest quality of it, in fact, without our knowing anything about it. It signifies a something in general (a transcendental subject) the representation of which must no doubt be simple, because nothing is determined in it, and nothing can be represented more simple than by the concept of a mere something. The simplicity however of the representation of a subject is not therefore a knowledge of the simplicity of the subject, because no account whatever is taken of its qualities when it is designated by the entirely empty expression I, an expression that can be applied to every thinking subject.

So much is certain therefore that though I always represent by the I an absolute, but only logical, unity of the subject (simplicity), I never know thereby the real simplicity of my subject. We saw that the proposition, I am a substance, signified nothing but the mere category of which I must not make any use (empirically) *in concreto*. In the same manner, I may well say, I am a simple substance, that is, a substance the representation of which contains no synthesis of the manifold; but that concept, or that proposition also, teaches us nothing at all with reference to myself, as an object of experience, because the concept of substance itself is used as a function of synthesis only, without any intuition to rest on, and therefore without any object, valid with reference to the condition of our knowledge only, but not with reference to any object of it. We shall test the usefulness of this proposition by an experiment.

Everybody must admit that the assertion of the simple nature of the soul can only be of any value in so far as it enables me to distinguish the soul from all matter, and thus to except it from that decay to which matter is at all times subject. It is for that use that our proposition is really intended, and it is therefore often expressed by, the soul is not corporeal. If then I can show that, although we allow to this cardinal proposition of rational psychology (as a mere judgment of reason from pure categories) all objective validity (everything that thinks is simple substance), we cannot make the least use of it, in order to establish the homogeneousness or non-homogeneousness of soul and matter, this will be the same as if I had relegated this supposed psychological truth to the field of mere ideas, without any real or objective use.

We have irrefutably proved in the transcendental Æsthetic that bodies are mere phenomena of our external sense, not things by themselves. We are justified therefore in saying that our thinking subject is not a body, i.e. that, because it is represented by us as an object of the internal sense, it is, so far as it thinks, no object of our external senses, and no phenomenon in space. This means the same as that among external phenomena we can never have thinking beings as such, or ever see their thoughts, their consciousness, their desires, etc., externally. All this belongs to the internal sense. This argument seems indeed so natural and popular that even the commonest understanding has always been led to it, the distinction between souls and bodies being of very early date.

But although extension, impermeability, cohesion, and motion, in fact everything that the external senses can give us, cannot be thoughts, feeling, inclination, and determination, or contain anything like them, being never objects of external intuition, it might be possible, nevertheless, that that something which forms the foundation of external phenomena, and which so affects our sense as to produce in it the representations of space, matter, form, etc., if considered as a noumenon (or better as a transcendental object) might be, at the same time, the subject of thinking, although by the manner in which it affects our external sense it produces in us no intuitions of representations, will, etc., but only of space and its determinations. This something, however, is not extended, not impermeable, not composite, because such predicates concern sensibility only and its intuition, whenever we are affected by these (to us otherwise unknown) objects. These expressions, however, do not give us any information what kind of object it is, but only that, if considered by itself, without reference to the external senses, it has no right to these predicates, peculiar to external appearance. The predicates of the internal sense, on the contrary, such as representation, thinking, etc., are by no means contradictory to it, so that really, even if we admit the simplicity of its nature, the human soul is by no means sufficiently distinguished from matter, so far as its substratum is concerned, if (as it ought to be) matter is considered as a phenomenon only.

If matter were a thing by itself, it would, as a composite being, be totally different from the soul, as a simple being. But what we call matter is an external phenomenon only, the substratum of which cannot possibly be known by any possible predicates. I can therefore very well suppose that that substratum is simple, although in the manner in which it affects our senses it produces in us the intuition of something extended, and therefore composite, so that the substance which, with reference to our external sense, possesses extension, might very well by itself possess thoughts which can be represented consciously by its own internal sense. In such wise the same thing which in one respect is called corporeal, would in another respect be at the same time a thinking being, of which though we cannot see its thoughts, we can yet see the signs of them phenomenally. Thus the expression that souls only (as a particular class of substances) think, would have to be dropped, and we should return to the common expression that men think, that is, that the same thing which, as an external phenomenon, is extended, is internally, by itself, a subject, not composite, but simple and intelligent.

But without indulging in such hypotheses, we may make this general remark, that if I understand by soul a being by itself, the very question would be absurd, whether the soul be homogeneous or not with matter which is not a thing by itself, but only a class of representations within us; for so much at all events must be clear, that a thing by itself is of a different nature from the determinations which constitute its state only.

If, on the contrary, we compare the thinking I, not with matter, but with that object of the intellect that forms the foundation of the external phenomena which we call matter, then it follows, as we know nothing whatever of the matter, that we have no right to say that the soul by itself is different from it in any respect.

The simple consciousness is not therefore a knowledge of the simple nature of our subject, so that we might thus distinguish the soul from matter, as a composite being.

If therefore, in the only case where that concept might be useful, namely, in comparing myself with objects of external experience, it is impossible to determine the peculiar and distinguishing characteristics of its nature, what is the use, if we pretend to know that the thinking I, or the soul (a name for the transcendental object of the internal sense), is simple? Such a proposition admits of no application to any real object, and cannot therefore enlarge our knowledge in the least.

Thus collapses the whole of rational psychology, with its fundamental support, and neither here nor elsewhere can we hope by means of mere concepts (still less through the mere subjective form of all our concepts, that is, through our consciousness) and without referring these concepts to a possible experience, to extend our knowledge, particularly as even the fundamental concept of a *simple nature* is such that it can never be met with in experience, so that no chance remains of arriving at it as a concept of objective validity.

The Third Paralogism of Personality

Whatever is conscious of the numerical identity of its own self at different times, is in so far a person.

Now the Soul, etc.

Therefore the Soul is a person.

Criticism of the Third Paralogism of Transcendental Psychology

Whenever I want to know by experience the numerical identity of an external object, I shall have to attend to what is permanent in that phenomenon to which, as the subject, everything else refers as determination, and observe the identity of the former during the time that the latter is changing. I myself, however, am an object of the internal sense, and all time is but the form of the internal sense. I therefore refer each and all of my successive determinations to the numerically identical self; and this in all time, that is, in the form of the inner intuition of myself. From this point of view, the personality of the soul should not even be considered as inferred, but as an entirely identical proposition of self-consciousness in time, and that is indeed the reason why it is valid *a priori*. For it really says no more than this: that during the whole time, while I am conscious of myself, I am conscious of that time as belonging to the unity of myself; and it comes to the same thing whether I say that this whole time is within me as an individual unity, or that I with numerical identity am present in all that time.

In my own consciousness, therefore, the identity of person is inevitably present. But if I consider myself from the point of view of another person (as an object of his external intuition), then that external observer considers me, first of all, in time, for in the apperception time is really represented in *me* only. Though he admits, therefore, the I, which at all times accompanies all representations in *my* consciousness, and with entire identity, he will not yet infer from it the objective permanence of myself. For as in that case the time in which the observer places me is not the time of my own, but of his sensibility, it follows that the identity which is connected with my consciousness is not therefore connected with his, that is, with the external intuition of my subject.

The identity of my consciousness at different times is therefore a formal condition only of my thoughts and their coherence, and proves in no way the numerical identity of my subject, in which, in spite of the logical identity of the I, such a change may have passed as to make it impossible to retain its identity, though we may still attribute to it the same name of I, which in every other state, and even in the change of the subject, might yet retain the thought of the preceding and hand it over to the subsequent subject.*

Although the teaching of some old schools that everything is in a flux, and nothing in the world permanent, cannot be admitted, if we admit substances, yet it must not be supposed that it can be refuted by the unity of self-consciousness. For we ourselves cannot judge from our own consciousness whether, as souls, we are permanent or not, because we reckon as belonging to our own identical self that only of which we are conscious, and therefore are constrained to admit that, during the whole time of which we are conscious, we are one and the same. From the point of view of a stranger, however, such a judgment would not be valid, because, perceiving in the soul no permanent phenomena, except the representation of the I, which accompanies and connects them all, we cannot determine whether that I (being a mere thought) be not in the same state of flux as the other thoughts which are chained together by the I.

It is curious, however, that the personality and what is presupposed by it, namely, the permanence and substantiality of the soul, has now to be proved first. For if we could presuppose these, there would follow, if not the permanence of consciousness, yet the possibility of a permanent consciousness in one and the same subject, and this is sufficient to establish personality which does not cease at once, because its effect is interrupted at the time. This permanence, however, is by no means given us before the numerical identity of ourself, which

* An elastic ball, which impinges on another in a straight line, communicates to it its whole motion, and therefore (if we only consider the places in space) its whole state. If then, in analogy with such bodies, we admit substances of which the one communicates to the other representations with consciousness, we could imagine a whole series of them, in which the first communicates its state and its consciousness to the second, the second its own state with that of the first substance to a third, and this again all the states of the former, together with its own, and a consciousness of them, to another. That last substance would be conscious of all the states of the previously changed substances, as of its own, because all of them had been transferred to it with the consciousness of them; but for all that it would not have been the same person in all those states.

we infer from identical apperception, but is itself inferred from it, so that, according to rule, the concept of substance, which alone is empirically useful, would have to follow first upon it. But as the identity of person follows by no means from the identity of the I, in the consciousness of all time in which I perceive myself, it follows that we could not have founded upon it the substantiality of the soul.

Like the concept of substance and of the simple, however, the concept of personality also may remain, so long as it is used as transcendental only, that is, as a concept of the unity of the subject which is otherwise unknown to us, but in the determinations of which there is an uninterrupted connection by apperception. In this sense such a concept is necessary for practical purposes and sufficient, but we can never pride ourselves on it as helping to expand our knowledge of our self by means of pure reason, which only deceives us if we imagine that we can conclude an uninterrupted continuance of the subject from the mere concept of the identical self. That concept is only constantly turning round itself in a circle, and does not help us as with respect to any question which aims at synthetical knowledge. What matter may be as a thing by itself (a transcendental object) is entirely unknown to us; though we may observe its permanence as a phenomenon, since it is represented as something external. When however I wish to observe the mere I during the change of all representations, I have no other correlative for my comparisons but again the I itself, with the general conditions of my consciousness. I cannot therefore give any but tautological answers to all questions, because I put my concept and its unity in the place of the qualities that belong to me as an object, and thus really take for granted what was wished to be known.

The Fourth Paralogism of Ideality (with Regard to External Relations)

That, the existence of which can only be inferred as a cause of given perceptions, has a doubtful existence only:—

All external phenomena are such that their existence cannot be perceived immediately, but that we can only infer them as the cause of given perceptions:—

Therefore the existence of all objects of the external senses is doubtful. This uncertainty I call the ideality of external phenomena, and the doctrine of that ideality is called *idealism;* in comparison with which the other doctrine, which maintains a possible certainty of the objects of the external senses, is called *dualism*.

Criticism of the Fourth Paralogism of Transcendental Psychology

We shall first have to examine the premises. We are perfectly justified in maintaining that that only which is within ourselves can be perceived immediately, and that my own existence only can be the object of a mere perception. The existence of a real object therefore outside me (taking this word in its intellectual meaning) can never be given directly in perception, but can only be added in thought to the perception, which is a modification of the internal sense, and thus inferred as its external cause. Hence Cartesius was quite right in limiting all perception, in the narrowest sense, to the proposition, I (as a thinking being) am. For it must be clear that, as what is without is not within me, I cannot find it in my apperception; nor hence in any perception which is in reality a determination of apperception only.

In the true sense of the word, therefore, I can never perceive external things, but only from my own internal perception infer their existence, taking the perception as an effect of which something external must be the proximate cause. An inference, however, from a given effect to a definite cause is always uncertain, because the effect may be due to more than one cause. Therefore in referring a perception to its cause, it always remains doubtful whether that cause be internal or external; whether in fact all so-called external perceptions are not a mere play of our external sense, or point to real external objects as their cause. At all events the existence of the latter is inferential only, and liable to all the dangers of inferences, while the object of the internal sense (I myself with all my representations) is perceived immediately, and its existence cannot be questioned.

It must not be supposed, therefore, that an idealist is he who denies the existence of external objects of the senses; all he does is to deny that it is known by immediate perception, and to infer that we can never become perfectly certain of their reality by any experience whatsoever.

Before I expose the deceptive illusion of our paralogism, let me remark that we must necessarily distinguish two kinds of idealism, the transcendental and the empirical. *Transcendental idealism* teaches that all phenomena are representations only, not things by themselves, and that space and time therefore are only sensuous forms of our intuition, not determinations given independently by themselves or conditions of objects, as things by themselves. Opposed to this transcendental idealism, is a *transcendental realism,* which considers space and time as something in itself (independent of our sensibility). Thus the transcendental realist represents all external phenomena (admitting their reality) as things by themselves, existing independently of us and our sensibility, and therefore existing outside us also, if regarded according to pure concepts of the understanding. It is this transcendental realist who afterwards acts the empirical idealist, and who, after wrongly supposing that the objects of the senses, if they are to be external, must have an existence by themselves, and without our senses, yet from this point of view considers all our sensuous representations insufficient to render certain the reality of their objects.

The transcendental idealist, on the contrary, may well be an empirical realist, or, as he is called, a dualist; that is, he may admit the existence of matter, without taking a step beyond mere self-consciousness, or admitting more than the certainty of representations within me, that is the *cogito, ergo sum.* For as he considers matter, and even its internal possibility, as a phenomenon only, which, if separated from our sensibility, is nothing, matter with him is only a class of representations (intuition) which are called external, not as if they referred to objects external by themselves, but because they refer perceptions to space, in which everything is outside everything else, while space itself is inside us.

We have declared ourselves from the very beginning in favour of this transcendental idealism. In our system, therefore, we need not hesitate to admit the existence of matter on the testimony of mere self-consciousness, and to consider it as established by it (i.e. the testimony), in the same manner as the existence of myself, as a thinking being. I am conscious of my representations, and hence they exist as well as I myself, who has these representations. External objects, however (bodies), are phenomena only, therefore nothing but a class of my representations, the objects of which are something by means of these representations only, and apart from them nothing. External things, therefore, exist by the same right as I myself, both on the immediate testimony of my self-consciousness, with this difference only, that the representation of myself, as a thinking subject, is referred to the internal sense only, while the representations which indicate extended beings are referred to the external sense also. With reference to the reality of external objects, I need as little trust to inference, as with reference to the reality of the object of my internal sense (my thoughts), both being nothing but representations, the immediate perception (consciousness) of which is at the same time a sufficient proof of their reality.

The transcendental idealist is, therefore, an empirical realist, and allows to matter, as a phenomenon, a reality which need not be inferred, but may be immediately perceived. The transcendental realism, on the contrary, is necessarily left in doubt, and obliged to give way to empirical idealism, because it considers the objects of the external senses as something different from the senses themselves, taking mere phenomena as independent beings, existing outside us. And while with the very best consciousness of our representation of these things, it is far from certain that, if a representation exists, its corresponding object must exist also, it is clear that in our system external things, that is, matter in all its shapes and changes, are nothing but mere phenomena, that is, representations within us, of the reality of which we are immediately conscious.

As, so far as I know, all psychologists who believe in empirical idealism are transcendental realists, they have acted no doubt quite consistently, in ascribing great importance to empirical idealism, as one of the problems from which human reason could hardly extricate itself. For indeed, if we consider external phenomena as representations produced inside us by their objects, as existing as things by themselves outside us, it is difficult to see how their existence could be known otherwise but through a syllogism from effect to cause, where it must always remain doubtful, whether the cause be within or without us. Now we may well admit that something which, taken transcendentally, is outside us, may be the cause of our external intuitions, but this can never be the object which we mean by the representations of matter and material things; for these are phenomena only, that is, certain kinds of representations existing always within us, and the reality of which depends on our immediate consciousness, quite as much as the consciousness of my own thoughts. The transcendental object is unknown equally in regard to internal and external intuition.

Of this, however, we are not speaking at present, but only of the empirical object, which is called external, if represented in space, and internal, when represented in temporal relations only, both space and time being to be met with nowhere except in ourselves.

The expression, *outside us,* involves however an inevitable ambiguity, because it may signify either, something which, as a thing by itself, exists apart from us, or what belongs to outward appearance only. In order, therefore, to remove all uncertainty from that concept, taken in the latter meaning (which alone affects the psychological question as to the reality of our external intuition) we shall distinguish *empirically external* objects from those that may be called so in a transcendental sense, by calling the former simply *things occurring in space.*

Space and time are no doubt representations *a priori,* which dwell in us as forms of our sensuous intuition, before any real object has determined our senses by means of sensation, enabling them to represent the object under those sensuous conditions. But this something, material or real, that is to be seen in space, presupposes necessarily perception, and cannot be fancied or produced by means of imagination without that perception, which indicates the reality of something in space. It is sensation, therefore, that indicates reality in space and time, according as it is related to the one or the other mode of sensuous intuition. If sensation is once given (which, if referring to an object in general, and not specialising it, is called perception), many an object may be put together in imagination from the manifold materials of perception, which has no empirical place in space or time, but in imagination only. This admits of no doubt, whether we take the sensations of pain and pleasure, or the external ones of colour, heat, etc.; it is always perception by which the material for thinking of any objects of external intuition must be first supplied. This perception, therefore (to speak at present of external intuitions only), represents something real in space. For, first, perception is the representation of a reality, while space is the representation of a mere possibility of coexistence. Secondly, this reality is represented before the external sense, that is, in space. Thirdly, space itself is nothing but mere representation, so that nothing in it can be taken as real, except what is represented in it;* or, *vice versa,* whatever is

* We must well master this paradoxical, but quite correct proposition, that nothing can be in space, except what is represented in it. For space itself is nothing but representation, and whatever is in it must therefore be contained in that representation. There is

given in it, that is, whatever is represented in it by perception, is also real in it, because, if it were not real in it, that is, given immediately by empirical intuition, it could not be created by fancy, the real of intuition being unimaginable *a priori*.

Thus we see that all external perception proves immediately something real in space, or rather is that real itself. Empirical realism is therefore perfectly true, that is, something real in space always corresponds to our external intuitions. Space itself, it is true, with all its phenomena, as representations, exists within me only, but the real or the material of all objects of intuition is nevertheless given in that space, independent of all fancy or imagination; nay, it is impossible that *in that space* anything *outside us* (in a transcendental sense) could be given, because space itself is nothing outside our sensibility. The strictest idealist, therefore, can never require that we should prove that the object without us (in its true meaning) corresponds to our perception. For granted there are such objects, they could never be represented and seen, as outside us, because this presupposes space, and the reality in space, as a mere representation, is nothing but the perception itself. It thus follows, that what is real in external phenomena, is real in perception only, and cannot be given in any other way.

From such perceptions, whether by mere play of fancy or by experience, knowledge of objects can be produced, and here no doubt deceptive representations may arise, without truly corresponding objects, the deception being due, either to illusions of imagination (in dreams), or to a fault of judgment (the so-called deceptions of the senses). In order to escape from these false appearances, one has to follow the rule that, *whatever is connected according to empirical laws with a perception, is real.* This kind of illusion, however, and its prevention, concerns idealism as well as dualism, since it affects the form of experience only. In order to refute empirical idealism and its unfounded misgivings as to the objective reality of our external perceptions, it is sufficient to consider 1) that external perception proves immediately a reality in space, which space, though in itself a mere form of representations, possesses nevertheless objective reality with respect to all external

---

nothing whatever in space, except so far as it is really represented in it. That a thing can exist only in the representation of it, may no doubt sound strange; but will lose its strangeness if we consider that the things with which we have to deal, are not things by themselves, but phenomena only, that is, representations.

phenomena (which themselves are mere representations only);
2) that without perception, even the creations of fancy and
dreams would not be possible, so that our external senses, with
reference to the data from which experience can spring, must
have real objects corresponding to them in space.

There are two kinds of idealists, the *dogmatic,* who denies
the existence of matter, and the *sceptical,* who doubts it, because he thinks it impossible to prove it. At present we have
nothing to do with the former, who is an idealist, because he
imagines he finds contradictions in the possibility of matter in
general. This is a difficulty which we shall have to deal with in
the following section on dialectical syllogisms, treating of reason in its internal struggle with reference to the concepts of
the possibility of all that belongs to the connection of experience. The sceptical idealist, on the contrary, who attacks only
the ground of our assertion, and declares our conviction of the
existence of matter, which we founded on immediate perception, as insufficient, is in reality a benefactor of human reason,
because he obliges us, even in the smallest matter of common
experience, to keep our eyes well open, and not to consider as
a well-earned possession what may have come to us by mistake only. We now shall learn to understand the great advantage of these idealistic objections. They drive us by main force,
unless we mean to contradict ourselves in our most ordinary
propositions, to consider all perceptions, whether we call them
internal or external, as a consciousness only of what affects
our sensibility, and to look on the external objects of them,
not as things by themselves, but only as representations of
which, as of every other representation, we can become immediately conscious, and which are called external, because
they depend on what we call the external sense with its intuition of space, space being itself nothing but an internal kind of
representation in which certain perceptions become associated.

If we were to admit external objects to be things by themselves, it would be simply impossible to understand how we
can arrive at a knowledge of their reality outside us, considering that we always depend on representations which are inside
us. It is surely impossible that we should feel outside us, and
not inside us, and the whole of our self-consciousness cannot
give us anything but our own determinations. Thus sceptical
idealism forces us to take refuge in the only place that is left
to us, namely, in the ideality of all phenomena: the very ideality which, though as yet unprepared for its consequences, we
established in our own transcendental Æsthetic. If then we

ask whether, consequently, dualism only must be admitted in psychology, we answer, certainly, but only in its empirical acceptation. In the connection of experience matter, as the substance of phenomena, is really given to the external sense in the same manner as the thinking I, likewise as the substance of phenomena, is given to the internal sense; and it is according to the rules which this category introduces into the empirical connection of our external as well as internal perceptions, that phenomena on both sides must be connected among themselves. If, on the contrary, as often happens, we were to extend the concept of dualism and take it in its transcendental acceptation, then neither it, nor on one side the *pneumatism*, or on the other side the *materialism*, which are opposed to dualism, would have the smallest foundation; we should have missed the determination of our concepts, and have mistaken the difference in our mode of representing objects, which, with regard to what they are in themselves, remain always unknown to us, for a difference of the things themselves. No doubt I, as represented by the internal sense in time, and objects in space outside me, are two specifically different phenomena, but they are not therefore conceived as different things. The transcendental object, which forms the foundation of external phenomena, and the other, which forms the foundation of our internal intuition, is therefore neither matter, nor a thinking being by itself, but simply an unknown cause of phenomena which supply to us the empirical concept of both.

If therefore, as evidently forced to do by this very criticism, we remain faithful to the old rule, never to push questions beyond where possible experience can supply us with an object, we shall never dream of going beyond the objects of our senses and asking what they may be by themselves, that is, without any reference to our senses. But if the psychologist likes to take phenomena for things by themselves, then, whether he admit into his system, as a materialist, matter only, or, as a spiritualist, thinking beings only (according to the form of our own internal sense), or, as a dualist, both, as things existing in themselves, he will always be driven by his mistake to invent theories as to how that which is not a thing by itself, but a phenomenon only, could exist by itself.

CONSIDERATION

on the Whole of Pure Psychology, as affected by these
Paralogisms

If we compare the science of the soul, as the physiology of the internal sense, with the science of the body, as a physiology of the objects of external senses, we find, besides many things which in both must be known empirically, this important difference, that in the latter many things can be known *a priori* from the mere concept of an extended and impermeable being, while in the former nothing can be known *a priori* and synthetically from the concept of a thinking being. The cause is this. Though both are phenomena, yet the phenomena of the external sense have something permanent, which suggests a substratum of varying determinations, and consequently a synthetical concept, namely, that of space, and of a phenomenon in space; while time, the only form of our internal intuition, has nothing permanent, and makes us to know the change of determinations only, but not the determinable object. For in what we call soul there is a continuous flux, and nothing permanent, except it may be (if people will so have it) the simple *I,* so simple because this representation has no contents, consequently nothing manifold, so that it seems to represent, or more accurately to indicate, a simple object. This I or Ego would have to be an intuition, which, being presupposed in all thought (before all experience), might as an intuition *a priori* supply synthetical propositions, if it should be possible to get any knowledge by pure reason of the nature of a thinking being in general. But this I is neither an intuition nor a concept of any object, but the mere form of consciousness which can accompany both classes of representations, and impart to them the character of knowledge, provided something else be given in intuition which supplies matter for a representation of an object. Thus we see that the whole of rational psychology is impossible as transcending the powers of human reason, and nothing remains to us but to study our soul under the guidance of experience, and to keep ourselves within the limits of questions which do not go beyond the line where the material can be supplied by possible internal experience.

But although rational psychology is of no use in extending our knowledge, but as such is made up of paralogisms only, we cannot deny to it an important negative utility, if it does not pretend to be more than a critical investigation of our dialectical syllogisms, as framed by our common and natural reason.

What purpose can be served by psychology founded on pure principles of reason? Its chief purpose is meant to be to guard our thinking self against the danger of materialism. This purpose however is answered, as we have shown, by the concept which reason gives of our thinking self. For, so far from there being any fear lest, if matter be taken away, all thought, and even the existence of thinking beings might vanish, it has been on the contrary clearly shown that, if we take away the thinking subject, the whole material world would vanish, because it is nothing but a phenomenon in the sensibility of our own subject, and a certain class of its representations.

It is true that I do not know thus this thinking self any better according to its qualities, nor can I perceive its permanence, or even the independence of its existence from the problematical transcendental substratum of external phenomena, both being necessarily unknown to us. But as it is nevertheless possible that I may find reason, from other than purely speculative causes, to hope for an independent, and, during every possible change of my states, permanently abiding existence of my thinking nature, much is gained if, though I freely confess my own ignorance, I can nevertheless repel the dogmatical attacks of a speculative opponent, showing to him that he can never know more of the nature of the subject, in order to deny the possibility of my expectations, than I can know, in order to cling to them.

Three dialectical questions, which form the real object of all rational psychology, are founded on this transcendental illusion of our psychological concepts, and cannot be answered except by means of the considerations in which we have just been engaged, namely, (1) the question of the possibility of the association of the soul with an organic body, that is, of animality and the state of the soul in the life of man; (2) the question of the beginning of that association of the soul at the time and before the time of our birth; (3) the question of the end of that association of the soul at and after the time of death (immortality).

What I maintain is, that all the difficulties which we imagine to exist in these questions, and with which, as dogmatical objections, people wish to give themselves an air of deeper insight into the nature of things than the common understanding can ever claim, rest on a mere illusion, which leads us to hypostatize what exists in thought only, and to accept it in the same quality in which it is thought as a real object, outside the thinking subject, taking in fact extension, which is phenomenal only, for a quality of external things, existing without our sensibility also, and movement as their effect, taking place by itself also, and independently of our senses. For matter, the association of which with the soul causes so much misgiving, is nothing but a mere orm, or a certain mode of representing an unknown object by that intuition which we call the external sense. There may, therefore, well be something outside us to which the phenomenon which we call matter corresponds; though in its quality of phenomenon it cannot be outside us, but merely as a thought within us, although that thought represents it through the external sense as existing outside us. Matter, therefore, does not signify a class of substances totally heterogeneous and different from the object of the internal sense (the soul), but only the different nature of the phenomenal appearance of objects (in themselves unknown to us), the representations of which we call external, as compared with those which we assign to the internal sense, although, like other thoughts, those external representations also belong to the thinking subject only. They possess however this illusion that, as they represent objects in space, they seem to separate themselves from the soul and to move outside it, although even the space, in which they are seen, is nothing but a representation of which no homogeneous original can ever be found outside the soul. The question therefore is no longer as to the possibility of an association of the soul with other known and foreign substances outside us, but only as to the connection of the representations of the internal sense with the modifications of our external sensibility, and how these can be connected with each other according to constant laws, and acquire cohesion in experience.

So long as we connect internal and external phenomena with each other as mere representations in our experience, there is nothing irrational, nor anything to make the association of both senses to appear strange. As soon however as we hypostatize the external phenomena, looking upon them no longer as representations, but *as things existing by themselves and outside us, with the same quality in which they exist inside us,* and referring to our own thinking subject their acts which they, as phenomena, show in their mutual relation, the effective causes outside us assume a character which will not harmonise with their effects within us, because that character refers to the external senses only, but the effects to the internal sense, both being entirely unhomogeneous, though united in the same subject. We then have no other external effects but changes of place, and no forces but tendencies, which have for their effects relations in space only. Within us, on the contrary, those effects are mere thoughts, without any relations of space, movement, shape, or local determination between them; and we entirely lose the thread of the causes in the effects which ought to show themselves in the internal sense. We ought to consider therefore that bodies are not objects by themselves which are present to us, but a mere appearance of we do not know what unknown object, and that movement likewise is not the effect of that unknown cause, but only the appearance of its influence on our senses. Both are not something outside us, but only representation within us, and consequently it is not the movement of matter which produces representations within us, but that motion itself (and matter also, which makes itself known through it) is representation only. Our whole self-created difficulty turns on this, how and why the representations of our sensibility are so connected with each other that those which we call external intuitions can, according to empirical laws, be represented as objects outside us; a question which is entirely free from the imagined difficulty of explaining the origin of our representations from totally heterogeneous efficient causes, existing outside us, the confusion arising from our mistaking the phenomenal appearance of an unknown cause for the very cause outside us. In judgments in which there is a misapprehension confirmed by long habit, it is impossible to bring its correction at once to that clearness which can be produced in other cases, where no inevitable illusion confuses our concept. Our attempt therefore at freeing reason from these sophistical theories can hardly claim as yet that perspicuity which would render it perfectly satisfactory. I hope however to arrive at greater lucidity in the following manner.

All *objections* may be divided into *dogmatical, critical,* and *sceptical.* The dogmatical attacks the *proposition,* the critical the *proof* of a proposition. The former presupposes an insight into the peculiar nature of the object in order to be able to assert the contrary of what the proposition asserts. It is therefore itself dogmatical, and pretends to know the peculiar nature of the object in question better than the opponent. The critical objection, as it says nothing about the worth or worthlessness of the proposition, and attacks the proof only, need not know the object itself better, or claim a better knowledge of it. All it wants to show is, that a proposition is not well grounded, not that it is false. The sceptical objection, lastly, places assertion and denial side by side, as of equal value, taking one or the other now as dogma, and now as denial; and being thus in appearance dogmatical on both sides, it renders every judgment on the object impossible. Both the dogmatical and sceptical objections must pretend to so much knowledge of their object as is necessary in order to assert or deny anything about it. The critical objection, on the contrary, wishes only to show that something purely futile and fanciful has been used in support of a proposition, and thus upsets a theory by depriving it of its pretended foundation, without wishing to establish itself anything else about the nature of the object.

According to the ordinary concepts of our reason with regard to the association between our thinking subject and the things outside us, we are dogmatical, and look upon them as real objects, existing independently of ourselves, in accordance with a certain transcendental dualism which does not reckon external phenomena as representations belonging to the subject, but places them, as they are given us in sensuous intuition, as objects outside us and entirely separated from the thinking subject. This mere assumption is the foundation of all theories on the association between soul and body. It is never asked whether this objective reality of phenomena is absolutely true, but it is taken for granted, and the only question seems to be, how it is to be explained and understood. The three systems which are commonly suggested, and which in fact are alone possible, are those, 1st, of *physical influence*, 2nd, of *preestablished harmony*, and 3rd, of *supernatural assistance*.

The second and third explanations of the association between soul and matter arise from objections to the first, which is that of the ordinary understanding, the objection being, that what appears as matter cannot by its immediate influence be the cause of representations, these being a totally heterogeneous class of effects. Those who start this objection cannot understand by the objects of the external senses matter, conceived as phenomenon only, and therefore itself a mere representation produced by whatever external objects. For in that case they would really say that the representations of external objects (phenomena) cannot be the external causes of the representations in our mind, which would be a meaningless objection, because nobody would think of taking for an external cause what he knows to be a mere representation. According to our principles the object of their theory can only be, that that which is the true (transcendental) object of our external senses cannot be the cause of those representations (phenomena) which we mean by the name of matter. As no one has any right to say that he knows anything of the transcendental cause of the representations of our external senses, their assertion is entirely groundless. And if the pretended reformers of the doctrine of physical influence represent, according to the ordinary views of transcendental dualism, matter, as such, as a thing by itself (not simply as a mere phenomenal appearance of an unknown thing), and then proceed in their objections to show that such an external object, which shows no causality but that of movements, can never be the efficient cause of representations, but that a third being must intervene in order to produce, if not reciprocal action, at least correspondence and harmony between the two, they would really begin their refutation by admitting in their dualism the πρῶτον ψεῦδος of a physical influence, and thus refute by their objection, not so much the physical influence as their own dualistic premisses. For all the difficulties with regard to a possible connection between a thinking nature and matter arise, without exception, from that too readily admitted dualistic representation, namely, that matter, as such, is not phenomenal, that is, a mere representation of the mind to which an unknown object corresponds, but the object itself, such as it exists outside us, and independent of all sensibility.

It is impossible, therefore, to start a dogmatical objection against the commonly received theory of a physical influence. For if the opponent were to say that matter and its movements are purely phenomenal and therefore mere representations, the only difficulty remaining to him would be that the unknown object of our senses could not be the cause of our representations, and this he has no right to say, because no one is able to determine what an unknown object may or may not be able to effect; and, according to our former arguments, he must necessarily admit this transcendental idealism, unless he wishes to hypostatize mere representations and place them outside himself as real things.

What is quite possible, however, is to raise a well-founded *critical objection* to the commonly received opinion of a physical influence. For the pretended association between two kinds of substances, the one thinking, the other extended, rests on a coarse dualism, and changes the latter, though they are nothing but representations of the thinking subject, into things existing by themselves. Thus the misunderstood physical influence may be entirely upset by showing that the proof which was to establish it, was surreptitiously obtained, and therefore, valueless.

The notorious problem, therefore, as to a possible association between the thinking and the extended, would, when all that is purely imaginative is deducted, come to this, *how external intuition,* namely, that of space (or what fills space, namely, form and movement), *is possible in any thinking subject?* To this question, however, no human being can return an answer, and instead of attempting to fill this gap in our knowledge, all we can do is to indicate it by ascribing external phenomena to a transcendental object as the cause of this class of representations, but which we shall never know, nor be able to form any concept of. In all practical questions we treat phenomena as objects by themselves, without troubling ourselves about the first cause of their possibility (as phenomena). But as soon as we go beyond, the concept of a transcendental object becomes inevitable.

The decision of all the discussions on the state of a thinking being, before this association with matter (life) or after the ceasing of such association (death), depends on the remarks which we have just made on the association between the thinking and the extended. The opinion that the thinking subject was able to think before any association with bodies, would assume the following form, that before the beginning of that kind of sensibility through which something appears to us in space, the same transcendental objects, which in our present state appear as bodies, could have been seen in a totally different way. The other opinion that, after the cessation of its association with the material world, the soul could continue to think, would be expressed as follows: that, if that kind of sensibility through which transcendental and, for the present, entirely unknown objects appear to us as a material world, should cease, it would not follow that thereby all intuition of them would be removed: it being quite possible that the same unknown objects should continue to be known by the thinking subject, although no longer in the quality of bodies.

Now it is quite true that no one can produce from speculative principles the smallest ground for such an assertion, or do more than presuppose its possibility, but neither can any valid dogmatical objection be raised against it. For whoever would attempt to do so, would know neither more nor less than I myself, or anybody else, about the absolute and internal cause of external and material phenomena. As he cannot pretend to know on what the reality of external phenomena in our present state (in life) really rests, neither can he know that the condition of all external intuition, or the thinking subject itself, will cease after this state (in death).

We thus see that all the wrangling about the nature of a thinking being, and its association with the material world, arises simply from our filling the gap, due to our ignorance, with paralogisms of reason, and by changing thoughts into things and hypostatizing them. On this an imaginary science is built up, both by those who assert and by those who deny, some pretending to know about objects of which no human being has any conception, while others make their own representations to be objects, all turning round in a constant circle of ambiguities and contradictions. Nothing but a sober, strict, and just criticism can free us of this dogmatical illusion, which, through theories and systems, deceives so many by an imaginary happiness. It alone can limit our speculative pretensions to the sphere of possible experience, and this not by a shallow scoffing at repeated failures or by pious sighs over the limits of our reason, but by a demarcation made according to well-established principles, writing the *nihil ulterius* with perfect assurance on those Herculean columns which Nature herself has erected, in order that the voyage of our reason should be continued so far only as the continuous shores of experience extend—shores which we can never forsake without being driven upon a boundless ocean, which, after deceiving us again and again, makes us in the end cease all our laborious and tedious endeavours as perfectly hopeless.

*　　*　　*　　*　　*　　*　　*　　*

We have yet to give a general and clear investigation of the transcendental, and yet natural illusion, produced by the paralogisms of pure reason, and the justification of our systematical arrangement of them, which ran parallel with the table of the categories. We could not have done this at the beginning of this section, without running the risk of becoming obscure, or inconveniently anticipating our arguments. We shall now try to fulfil our duty.

All illusion may be explained as mistaking the subjective condition of thought for the knowledge of the object. In the introduction to the transcendental Dialectic, we showed that pure reason is occupied exclusively with the totality of the synthesis of conditions belonging to anything conditioned.

Now as the dialectical illusion of pure reason cannot be an empirical illusion, such as occurs in certain empirical kinds of knowledge, it can refer only to the conditions of thought in general, so that there can only be three cases of the dialectical use of pure reason:—

1. The synthesis of the conditions of a thought in general.
2. The synthesis of the conditions of empirical thought.
3. The synthesis of the conditions of pure thought.

In every one of these three cases pure reason is occupied only with the absolute totality of that synthesis, that is, with that condition, which is itself unconditioned. It is on this division also that the threefold transcendental illusion is founded which leads to three subdivisions of the Dialectic, and to as many pretended sciences flowing from pure reason, namely, transcendental psychology, cosmology, and theology. We are at present concerned with the first only.

As, in thinking in general, we take no account of the relation of our thoughts to any object (whether of the senses or of the pure understanding), what is called (1) the synthesis of the conditions of a thought in general, is not objective at all, but only a synthesis of thought with the subject, which synthesis is wrongly taken for the synthetical representation of an object.

It follows from this that the dialectical conclusion as to the condition of all thought in general, which condition itself is unconditioned, does not involve a fault in its contents (for it ignores all contents or objects), but only a fault in form, and must therefore be called a paralogism.

As, moreover, the only condition which accompanies all thought is the *I,* in the general proposition *I think,* reason has really to deal with this condition, so far as that condition is itself unconditioned. It is however a formal condition only, namely, the logical unity of every thought, no account being taken of any object; but it is represented nevertheless as an object which I think, namely, as the I itself and its unconditioned unity.

If I were asked what is the nature of a thing which thinks, I could not give any answer *a priori,* for the answer ought to be synthetical, as an analytical answer might explain perhaps the meaning of the term "thought," but could never add any real knowledge of that on which the possibility of thought depends. For a synthetical solution, however, we should require intuition, and this has been entirely left out of account in the general form given to our problem. It is equally impossible to answer the general question, what is the nature of a thing which is moveable, because in that case the impermeable extension (matter) is not given. But although I have no answer to return to that question in general, it might seem that I could answer it in a special case, namely, in the proposition which expresses the self-consciousness, I think. For this I is the first subject, i.e. substance, it is simple, etc. These, however, ought then to be propositions of experience, which nevertheless, without a general rule containing the conditions of the possibility of thought in general and *a priori,* could not contain such predicates (which are not empirical). This consideration makes our knowledge of the nature of a thinking being derived from pure concepts, which seemed at first so plausible, extremely suspicious, though we have not yet discovered the place where the fault really lies.

A further investigation, however, of the origin of the attributes which I predicate of myself as a thinking being in general, may help us to discover the fault. They are no more than pure categories by which I can never think a definite object, but only the unity of the representations which is requisite in order to determine an object. Without a previous intuition, no category by itself can give me a concept of an object, for by intuition alone the object is given, which afterwards is thought in accordance with a category. In order to declare a thing to be a substance in phenomenal appearance, predicates of its intuition must first be given to me, in which I may distinguish the permanent from the changeable, and the substratum (the thing in itself) from that which is merely inherent in it. If I call a thing simple as a phenomenon, what I mean is that its intuition is a part of phenomenal appearance, but cannot itself be divided into parts, etc. But if I know something to be simple by a concept only, and not by phenomenal appearance, I have really no knowledge whatever of the object, but only of my concept which I make to myself of something in general, that is incapable of any real intuition. I only say that I think something as perfectly simple, because I have really nothing to say of it except that it is something.

Now the mere apperception (the I) is substance in concept, simple in concept, etc., and so far all the psychological propositions of which we spoke before are incontestably true. Nevertheless what we really wish to know of the soul, becomes by no means known to us in that way, because all those predicates

are with regard to intuition non-valid, entailing no consequences with regard to objects of experience, and therefore
entirely empty. For that concept of substance does not teach
me that the soul continues by itself, or that it is a part of external intuitions, which itself cannot be resolved into parts, and
cannot therefore arise or perish by any changes of nature.
These are qualities which would make the soul known to us in
its connection with experience, and might give us an insight
into its origin and future state. But if I say, by means of the
category only, that the soul is a simple substance, it is clear
that the bare rational concept of substance contains nothing
beyond the thought that a thing should be represented as a
subject in itself, without becoming in turn a predicate of anything else. Nothing can be deduced from this, with regard to
the permanence (of the I), nor can the attribute of simplicity
add that of permanence, nor can we thus learn anything
whatsoever as to the fate of the soul in the revolutions of
the world. If anybody could tell us that the soul is a *simple
part of matter,* we might, with the help of experience, deduce
from this the permanence and, on account of its simple nature,
the indestructibility of the soul. But of all this, the concept of
the I, in the psychological proposition of *I think,* tells us nothing.

The reason why that being which thinks within us imagines
that it knows itself by means of pure categories, and especially
by that which expresses absolute unity under each head, is
this. The apperception itself is the ground of the possibility of
the categories, and these represent nothing but the synthesis of
the manifold in intuition, so far as it has unity in apperception. Self-consciousness therefore is the representation of that
which forms the condition of all unity, and is itself unconditioned. One may therefore say of the thinking I (the soul),
which represents itself as substance, simple, numerically identical in all time, and as the correlative of all existence, from
which in fact all other existence must be concluded, that it
does not know itself through the categories, but knows the
categories only, and through them all objects, in the absolute
unity of apperception, *that is, through itself.* It may seem no
doubt self-evident that I cannot know as an object that which
is presupposed in order to enable me to know an object, and
that the determining self (thought) differs from the self that is
to be determined (the thinking subject), like knowledge from
its object. Nevertheless nothing is more natural or at least

more tempting than the illusion which makes us look upon the unity in the synthesis of thoughts as a perceived unity in the subject of thoughts. One might call it the surreptitious admission of an hypostatized consciousness (*apperceptionis substantiatae*).

If we want to have a logical term for the paralogism in the dialectical syllogisms of rational psychology, based on perfectly correct premisses, it might be called a *sophisma figurae dictionis*. In the major we use the category, with reference to its condition, transcendentally only; in the minor and in the conclusion, we use the same category, with reference to the soul which is to be comprehended under that condition, empirically. Thus, in the paralogism of substantiality,[2] the concept of substance is a purely intellectual concept which, without the conditions of sensuous intuition, admits of a transcendental use only, that is, of no use at all. In the minor, however, we refer the same concept to the object of all internal experience, though without having previously established the condition of its application *in concreto,* namely, its permanence. We thus are making an empirical, and therefore entirely inadmissible use of it.

Lastly, in order to show the systematical connection of all these dialectical propositions of a rationalising psychology, according to their connection in pure reason, and thus to establish their completeness, it should be remarked that the apperception is carried through all the classes of the categories, but only with reference to those concepts of the understanding, which in each of them formed a foundation of unity for the others in a possible perception, namely subsistence, reality, unity (not plurality), and existence, all of which are here represented by reason, as conditions (themselves unconditioned) of the possibility of a thinking being. Thus the soul knows in itself:—

I

The unconditioned unity
of the relation,
that is,
itself, not as inherent,
but as
subsisting.

[2] *Simplicität* was a misprint for *substantialität.*

II

The unconditioned unity
of quality,
that is,
not as a real whole,
but as
simple.*

III

The unconditioned unity
in the manifoldness of time,
that is,
not as at different times
numerically different,
but as
one and the same subject.

IV

The unconditioned unity
of existence in space,
that is,
not as the consciousness of many things outside it,
but as the consciousness of the existence of itself only,
and of other things, merely
as its representations.

Reason is the faculty of principles. The statements of pure psychology do not contain empirical predicates of the soul, but such as, if they exist, are meant to determine the object by itself, independent of all experience, and therefore by a pure reason only. They ought therefore to rest on principles and on general concepts of thinking beings. Instead of this we find that a single representation, I think,[3] governs them all, a representation which, for the very reason that it expresses the pure formula of all my experience (indefinitely), claims to be a general proposition, applicable to all thinking beings, and, though single in all respects, has the appearance of an absolute unity of the conditions of thought in general, thus stretching far beyond the limits of possible experience.]

We shall therefore follow it with a critical eye through all the predicaments of pure psychology; but we shall, for the sake of brevity, let their examination proceed uninterruptedly.

The following general remark may at the very outset make us more attentive to this mode of syllogism. I do not know any object by merely thinking, but only by determining a given intuition with respect to that unity of consciousness in which all thought consists; therefore, I do not know myself by being

* How the simple can again correspond to the category of reality cannot yet be explained here; but will be shown in the following chapter, when another use has to be discussed which reason makes of the same concept.
[3] *Ich bin* was a mistake, it can only be meant for *Ich denke.*

conscious of myself, as thinking, but only if I am conscious of the intuition of myself as determined with respect to the function of thought. All modes of self-consciousness in thought are therefore by themselves not yet concepts of understanding of objects (categories), but mere logical functions, which present no object to our thought to be known, and therefore do not present myself either as an object. It is not a consciousness of the determining, but only that of the determinable self, that is, of my internal intuition (so far as the manifold in it can be connected in accordance with the general condition of the unity of apperception in thought) which forms the object.

1. In all judgments I am always the determining subject only of the relation which constitutes the judgment. That I, who think, can be considered in thinking as subject only, and as something not simply inherent in the thinking, as predicate, is an apodictical and even identical proposition; but it does not mean that, as an object, I am a self-dependent being or a substance. The latter would be saying a great deal, and requires for its support data which are not found in the thinking, perhaps (so far as I consider only the thinking subject as such) more than I shall ever find in it.

2. That the Ego of apperception, and therefore the Ego in every act of thought, is a singular which cannot be dissolved into a plurality of subjects, and that it therefore signifies a logically simple subject, follows from the very concept of thinking, and is consequently an analytical proposition. But this does not mean that a thinking Ego is a simple substance, which would indeed be a synthetical proposition. The concept of substance always relates to intuitions which, with me, cannot be other but sensuous, and which therefore lie completely outside the field of the understanding and its thinking, which alone is intended here, when we say that the Ego, in thinking, is simple. It would indeed be strange, if what elsewhere requires so great an effort, namely, to distinguish in what is given by intuition what is substance, and still more, whether that substance can be simple (as in the case of the component parts of matter), should in our case be given to us so readily in what is really the poorest of all representations, and, as it were, by an act of revelation.

3. The proposition of the identity of myself amidst the manifold of which I am conscious, likewise follows from the concepts themselves, and is therefore analytical; but the identity of the subject of which, in all its representations, I may become conscious, does not refer to the intuition by which it is given

*as an object, and cannot therefore signify the identity of the
person, by which is understood the consciousness of the identity of one's own substance, as a thinking being, in all the
changes of circumstances. In order to prove this, the mere
analysis of the proposition, I think, would avail nothing: but
different synthetical judgments would be required, which are
based on the given intuition.*

*4. To say that I distinguish my own existence, as that of a
thinking being, from other things outside me (one of them being my body) is likewise an analytical proposition; for other
things are things which I conceive as* different *from myself.
But, whether such a consciousness of myself is even possible
without things outside me, whereby representations are given
to me, and whether I could exist merely as a thinking being
(without being a man), I do not know at all by that proposition.*

*Nothing therefore is gained by the analysis of the conscious-
ness of myself, in thought in general, towards the knowledge
of myself as an object. The logical analysis of thinking in general is simply mistaken for a metaphysical determination of the
object.*

*It would be a great, nay, even the only objection to the
whole of our critique, if there were a possibility of proving
a priori that all thinking beings are by themselves simple substances, that as such (as a consequence of the same argument)
personality is inseparable from them, and that they are conscious of their existence as distinct from all matter. For we
should thus have made a step beyond the world of sense and
entered into the field of noumena, and after that no one could
dare to question our right of advancing further, of settling in
it, and, as each of us is favoured by luck, taking possession of
it. The proposition that every thinking being is, as such, a simple substance, is synthetical a priori, because, first, it goes beyond the concept on which it rests, and adds to act of thinking
in general the* mode *of* existence; *and secondly, because it
adds to that concept a predicate (simplicity) which cannot be
given in any experience. Hence synthetical propositions a
priori would be not only admissible, as we maintained, in reference to objects of possible experience, and then only as
principles of the possibility of that experience, but could be
extended to things in general and to things by themselves, a
result which would put an end to the whole of our critique,
and bid us to leave everything as we found it. However, the*

danger is not so great, if only we look more closely into the matter.

In this process of rational psychology, there lurks a paralogism, which may be represented by the following syllogism.

That which cannot be conceived otherwise than as a subject, does not exist otherwise than as a subject, and is therefore a substance.

A thinking being, considered as such, cannot be conceived otherwise than as a subject.

Therefore it exists also as such only, that is, as a substance.

In the major they speak of a being that can be thought in every respect, and therefore also as it may be given in intuition. In the minor, however, they speak of it only so far as it considers itself, as subject, with respect to the thinking and the unity of consciousness only, but not at the same time in respect to the intuition whereby this unity is given as an object of thinking. The conclusion, therefore, has been drawn by a sophism, and more especially by sophisma figurae dictionis.*

That we are perfectly right in thus resolving that famous argument into a paralogism, will be clearly seen by referring to the general note on the systematical representation of the principles, and to the section on the noumena, for it has been proved there that the concept of a thing, which can exist by itself as a subject, and not as a mere predicate, carries as yet no objective reality, that is, that we cannot know whether any object at all belongs to it, it being impossible for us to understand the possibility of such a mode of existence. It yields us therefore no knowledge at all. If such a concept is to indicate, under the name of a substance, an object that can be given, and thus become knowledge, it must be made to rest on a

* The thinking is taken in each of the two premisses in a totally different meaning:—in the major, as it refers to an object in general (and therefore also as it may be given in intuition), but in the minor, only as it exists in its relation to self-consciousness, where no object is thought of, but where we only represent the relation to the self as the subject (as the form of thought). In the former, things are spoken of that cannot be conceived otherwise than as subjects; while in the second we do not speak of things, but of the thinking (abstraction being made of all objects), wherein the Ego always serves as the subject of consciousness. The conclusion, therefore, ought not to be that I cannot exist otherwise than as a subject, but only, that in thinking my existence I can use myself as the subject of a judgment only. This is an identical proposition, and teaches us nothing whatever as to the mode of our existence.

permanent intuition, as the indispensable condition of the objective reality of a concept, that is, as that by which alone the
object can be given. In internal intuition, however, we have
nothing permanent, for the Ego is only the consciousness of
my thinking; and if we do not go beyond this thinking, we are
without the necessary condition for applying the concept of
substance, that is, of an independent subject, to the self, as a
thinking being. Thus the simplicity of the substance entirely
disappears with the objective reality of the concept: and is
changed into a purely logical qualitative unity of self-consciousness in thinking in general, whether the subject be composite or not.

Refutation of Mendelssohn's Proof of the Permanence of the Soul

This acute philosopher perceived very quickly how the ordinary argument that the soul (if it is once admitted to be a
simple being) cannot cease to exist by decomposition, was insufficient to prove its necessary continuance, because it might
cease to exist by simply vanishing. He therefore tried, in his
Phædon, to prove that the soul was not liable to that kind of
perishing which would be a real annihilation, by endeavouring
to show that a simple being cannot cease to exist, because as
it could not be diminished, and thus gradually lose something
of its existence, and be changed, by little and little, into nothing (it having no parts, and therefore no plurality in itself),
there could be no time between the one moment in which it
exists, and the other in which it exists no longer; and this
would be impossible.

He did not consider, however, that, though we might allow
to the soul this simple nature, namely, that it contains nothing
manifold, nothing by the side of each other, and therefore no
extensive quantity, yet we could not deny to it, as little as to
any other existing thing, intensive quantity, i.e. a degree of
reality with respect to all its faculties, nay, to all which constitutes its existence. Such a degree of reality might diminish
by an infinite number of smaller degrees, and thus the supposed substance (the thing, the permanence of which has not
yet been established), might be changed into nothing, not indeed through decomposition, but through a gradual remission
of its powers, or, if I may say so, through elanguescence. For
even consciousness has always a degree, which admits of being

diminished,* and therefore also the faculty of being conscious of oneself, as well as all other faculties.

The permanence of the soul, therefore, considered merely as an object of the internal sense, remains undemonstrated and undemonstrable, though its permanence in life, while the thinking being (as man) is at the same time to itself an object of the external senses, is clear by itself. But this does not satisfy the rational psychologist, who undertakes to prove, from mere concepts, the absolute permanence of the soul, even beyond this life.†

* *Clearness is not, as the Logicians maintain, the consciousness of a representation; for a certain degree of consciousness, though insufficient for recollection, must exist, even in many dark representations, because without all consciousness we should make no distinction in the connection of dark representations, which yet we are able to do with the* notae *of many concepts (such as those of right and justice, or as the musician does who in improvising strikes several keys at once). A representation is clear in which the consciousness is sufficient for a consciousness of its difference from others. If the consciousness is sufficient for distinguishing, but not for a consciousness of the difference, the representation would still have to be called dark. There is, therefore, an infinite number of degrees of consciousness, down to its complete vanishing.*

† *Those who, in establishing the possibility of a new theory, imagine that they have done enough if they can show triumphantly that no one can show a contradiction in their premises (as do those who believe that they understand the possibility of thinking, of which they have an example in the empirical intuitions of human life only, even after the cessation of life) can be greatly embarrassed by other possible theories, which are not a whit bolder than their own. Such is, for instance, the possibility of a division of* simple substance *into several, or of the coalition of several substances into one simple substance. For although divisibility presupposes a composite, it does not necessarily require a composite of substances, but of degrees only (of the manifold faculties) of one and the same substance. As, then, we may conceive all powers and faculties of the soul, even that of consciousness, as diminished by one-half, the substance still remaining, we may also represent to ourselves, without any contradiction, that extinguished half as preserved, though not within it, but outside it, so that as the whole of what is real in it and has a degree, and therefore the whole existence of it, without any rest, has been halved, another separate substance would arise apart from it. For the plurality, which has been divided, existed before, though not as a plurality of substances, yet of every reality as a quantum of existence in it, and the unity of substance was only a mode of existence, which by mere division has been changed into a plurality of substantiality. In the*

*If now we take the above propositions in synthetical con-
nection, as indeed they must be taken, as valid for all thinking
beings, in a system of rational psychology, and proceed from
the category of relation, with the proposition, all thinking beings, as such, are substances, backwards through the series
till the circle is completed, we arrive in the end at their existence, and this, according to that system, they are not only
conscious of, independently of external things, but are supposed to be able to determine it even of themselves (with
respect to that permanence which necessarily belongs to the
character of substance). Hence it follows, that in this ration-
alistic system idealism is inevitable, at least problematical
idealism, because, if the existence of external things is not required at all for the determination of one's own existence in
time, their existence is really a gratuitous assumption of which
no proof can ever be given.*

*If, on the contrary, we proceed analytically, taking the
proposition, I think, which involves existence (according to the
category of modality) as given, and analyse it, in order to find
out whether, and how, the Ego determines its existence in
space and time by it alone, the propositions of rational psy-*

---

same manner several simple substances might coalesce again into
one, nothing being lost thereby, but merely the plurality of substantiality; so that one substance would contain in itself the degree
of reality of all former substances together. We might suppose that
the simple substances which give us matter as a phenomenon (not
indeed through a mechanical or chemical influence upon each
other, but yet, it may be, by some unknown influence, of which the
former is only a manifestation), produce by such a dynamical division of parental souls, taken as intensive quantities, what may
be called child-souls, while they themselves repair their loss again
through a coalition with new matter of the same kind. I am far
from allowing the slightest value of validity to such vague speculations, and I hope that the principles of our Analytic have given a
sufficient warning against using the categories (as, for instance,
that of substance) for any but empirical purposes. But if the ra-
tionalist is bold enough to create an independent being out of the
mere faculty of thought, without any permanent intuition, by which
an object can be given, simply because the unity of apperception
in thought does not allow him to explain it as something composite, instead of simply confessing that he cannot explain the possibility of a thinking nature, why should not a materialist, though
he can as little appeal to experience in support of his theories, be
entitled to use the same boldness, and use his principle for the
opposite purpose, though retaining the formal unity on which his
opponent relied?

chology would not start from the concept of a thinking being, in general, but from a reality, and the inference would consist in determining from the manner in which that reality is thought, after everything that is empirical in it has been removed, what belongs to a thinking being in general. This may be shown by the following Table.

1.

I think,

2.   *3.*

as Subject,   *as simple Subject,*

4.

as identical Subject,
in every state of my thought.

As it has not been determined in the second proposition, whether I can exist and be conceived to exist as a subject only, and not also as a predicate of something else, the concept of subject is here taken as logical only, and it remains undetermined whether we are to understand by it a substance or not. In the third proposition, however, the absolute unity of apperception, the simple I, being the representation to which all connection or separation (which constitute thought) relate, assumes its own importance, although nothing is determined as yet with regard to the nature of the subject, or its subsistence. The apperception is something real, and it is only possible, if it is simple. In space, however, there is nothing real that is simple, for points (the only simple in space) are limits only, and not themselves something which, as a part, serves to constitute space. From this follows the impossibility of explaining the nature of myself, as merely a thinking subject, from the materialistic *point of view. As, however, in the first proposition, my existence is taken for granted, for it is not said in it that every thinking being exists (this would predicate too much, namely, absolute necessity of them), but only, I exist, as thinking, the proposition itself is empirical, and contains only the determinability of my existence, in reference to my representations in time. But as for that purpose again I require, first of all, something permanent, such as is not given to me at all in internal intuition, so far as I think myself, it is really impossible by that simple self-consciousness to determine the manner in which I exist, whether as a substance or as an accident. Thus, if* materialism *was inadequate to explain my existence,* spiritualism *is equally insufficient for that purpose, and the conclusion is, that, in no way whatsoever can we know anything of the nature of our soul, so far as the possibility of its separate existence is concerned.*

And how indeed should it be possible by means of that unity of consciousness which we only know because it is indispensable to us for the very possibility of experience, to get beyond experience (our existence in life), and even to extend our knowledge to the nature of all thinking beings in general, by the empirical, but, with reference to every kind of intuition, undetermined proposition, I think.

There is, therefore, no rational psychology, as a doctrine, *furnishing any addition to our self-knowledge, but only as a* discipline, *fixing unpassable limits to speculative reason in this field, partly to keep us from throwing ourselves into the arms of a soulless materialism, partly to warn us against losing ourselves in a vague, and, with regard to practical life, baseless spiritualism. It reminds us at the same time to look upon this refusal of our reason to give a satisfactory answer to such curious questions, which reach beyond the limits of this life, as a hint to turn our self-knowledge away from fruitless speculations to a fruitful practical use—a use which, though directed always to objects of experience only, derives its principle from a higher source, and so regulates our conduct, as if our destination reached far beyond experience, and therefore far beyond this life.*

We see from all this, that rational psychology owes its origin to a mere misunderstanding. The unity of consciousness, on which the categories are founded, is mistaken for an intuition of the subject as object, and the category of substance applied to it. But that unity is only the unity in thought, *by which alone no object is given, and to which, therefore, the category of substance, which always presupposes a given in-* tuition, *cannot be applied, and therefore the subject cannot be known. The subject of the categories, therefore, cannot, by thinking them, receive a concept of itself, as an object of the categories; for in order to think the categories, it must presuppose its pure self-consciousness, the very thing that had to be explained. In like manner the subject, in which the representation of time has its original source, cannot determine by it its own existence in time; and if the latter is impossible, the former, as a determination of oneself (as of a thinking being in general) by means of the categories, is equally so.**

* *The 'I think' is, as has been stated, an empirical proposition, and contains within itself the proposition, I exist. I cannot say, how-*

*   *   *   *   *   *   *   *

Thus vanishes, as an idle dream, that knowledge which was to go beyond the limits of possible experience, and was connected no doubt with the highest interests of humanity, so far at least as speculative philosophy was to supply it. Yet no unimportant service has thus been rendered to reason by the severity of our criticism, in proving, at the same time, the impossibility of settling anything dogmatically with reference to an object of experience, beyond the limits of experience, and thus securing it against all possible assertions to the contrary. This can only be done in two ways, either by proving one's own proposition apodictically, or, if that does not succeed, by trying to discover the causes of that failure, which, if they lie in the necessary limits of our reason, must force every opponent to submit to exactly the same law of renunciation with reference to any claims to dogmatic assertion.

Nothing is lost, however, by this with regard to the right, nay, the necessity of admitting a future life, according to the principles of practical, as connected with the speculative employment of reason. It is known besides, that a purely specula-

---

ever, everything which thinks exists; for in that case the property of thinking would make all beings which possess it necessary beings. Therefore, my existence cannot, as Descartes supposed, be considered as derived from the proposition, I think (for in that case the major, everything that thinks exists, ought to have preceded), but is identical with it. It expresses an indefinite empirical intuition, that is, a perception (and proves, therefore, that this proposition, asserting existence, is itself based on sensation, which belongs to sensibility), but it precedes experience, which is meant to determine the object of perception through the categories in respect to time. Existence, therefore, is here not yet a category, which never refers to an indefinitely given object, but only to one of which we have a concept, and of which we wish to know whether it exists also apart from that conception or no. An indefinite perception signifies here something real only that has been given merely for thinking in general, not therefore as a phenomenon, nor as a thing by itself (noumenon), but as something that really exists and is designated as such in the proposition, I think. For it must be observed, that if I have called the proposition, I think, an empirical proposition, I did not mean to say thereby, that the ego in that proposition is an empirical representation; it is rather purely intellectual, because it belongs to thought in general. Without some empirical representation, however, which supplies the matter for thought, the act, I think, would not take place, and the empirical is only the condition of the application or of the use of the pure intellectual faculty.

tive proof has never been able to exercise any influence on the ordinary reason of men. It stands so entirely upon the point of a hair, that even the schools can only keep it from falling so long as they keep it constantly spinning round like a top, so that, even in their own eyes, it yields no permanent foundation upon which anything could be built. The proofs which are useful for the world at large retain their value undiminished, nay, they gain in clearness and natural power, by the surrender of those dogmatical pretensions, placing reason in its own peculiar domain, namely, the system of ends, which is, however, at the same time the system of nature; so that reason, as a practical faculty by itself, without being limited by the conditions of nature, becomes justified in extending the system of ends, and with it, our own existence, beyond the limits of experience and of life. According to the analogy with the nature of living beings in this world, in which reason must necessarily admit the principle that no organ, no faculty, no impulse, can be found, as being either superfluous or disproportionate to its use, and therefore purposeless, but that everything is adequate to its destination in life, man, who alone can contain in himself the highest end of all this, would be the only creature excepted from it. For, his natural dispositions, not only so far as he uses them according to his talents and impulses, but more especially the moral law within him, go so far beyond all that is useful and advantageous in this life, that he is taught thereby, in the absence of all advantages, even of the shadowy hope of posthumous fame, to esteem the mere consciousness of righteousness beyond everything else, feeling an inner call, by his conduct in this world and a surrender of many advantages, to render himself fit to become the citizen of a better world, which exists in his idea only. This powerful and incontrovertible proof, accompanied by our constantly increasing recognition of a design pervading all that we see around us, and by a contemplation of the immensity of creation, and therefore also by the consciousness of an unlimited possibility in the extension of our knowledge, and a desire commensurate therewith, all this remains and always will remain, although we must surrender the hope of ever being able to understand, from the mere theoretical knowledge of ourselves, the necessary continuance of our existence.

Conclusion of the Solution of the Psychological Paralogism

The dialectical illusion in rational psychology arises from our confounding an idea of reason (that of a pure intelligence) with the altogether indefinite concept of a thinking being in general. What we are doing is, that we conceive ourselves for the sake of a possible experience, taking no account, as yet, of any real experience, and thence conclude that we are able to become conscious of our existence, independently of experience and of its empirical conditions. We are, therefore, confounding the possible abstraction of our own empirically determined existence with the imagined consciousness of a possible separate existence of our thinking self, and we bring ourselves to believe that we know the substantial within us as the transcendental subject, while what we have in our thoughts is only the unity of consciousness, on which, as on the mere form of knowledge, all determination is based.

The task of explaining the community of the soul with the body does not properly fall within the province of that psychology of which we are here speaking, because that psychology tries to prove the personality of the soul, apart also from that community (after death), being therefore transcendent, in the proper sense of that word, inasmuch as, though dealing with an object of experience, it deals with it only so far as it has ceased to be an object of experience. According to our doctrine, however, a sufficient answer may be returned to that question also. The difficulty of the task consists, as is well known, in the assumed heterogeneousness of the object of the internal sense (the soul), and the objects of the external senses, the formal condition of the intuition with regard to the former being time only, with regard to the latter, time and space. If we consider, however, that both kinds of objects thus differ from each other, not internally, but so far only as the one appears externally to the other, and that possibly what is at the bottom of phenomenal matter, as a thing by itself, may not be so heterogeneous after all as we imagine, that difficulty vanishes, and there remains that one difficulty only, how a community of substances is possible at all; a difficulty which it is not the business of psychology to solve, and which, as the reader will easily understand, after what has been said in the Analytic of fundamental powers and faculties, lies undoubtedly beyond the limits of all human knowledge.

General Note on the Transition from Rational Psychology to Cosmology

The proposition, I think, or, I exist thinking, is an empirical proposition. Such a proposition is based on an empirical intuition, and its object is phenomenal: so that it might seem as if, according to our theory, the soul was changed altogether, even in thinking, into something phenomenal, and our consciousness itself, as merely phenomenal, would thus indeed refer to nothing.

Thinking, taken by itself, is a logical function only, and therefore pure spontaneity, in connecting the manifold of a merely possible intuition. It does not represent the subject of consciousness, as phenomenal, for the simple reason, that it takes no account whatsoever of the manner of intuition, whether it be sensuous or intellectual. I do not thereby represent myself to myself, either as I am, or as I appear to myself, but I only conceive of myself, as of any other object, without taking account of the manner of intuition. If thereby I represent myself as the subject of my thoughts, or as the ground of thinking, these modes of representation are not the categories of substance or cause, because these are functions of thought (judgment) as applied already to our sensuous intuition, such sensuous intuition being necessary, if I wish to know myself. But I only wish to become conscious of myself as thinking, and as I take no account of what my own self may be as a phenomenon, it is quite possible that it might be a phenomenon only to me, who thinks, but not to me, so far as I am thinking. In the consciousness of myself in mere thinking I am the substance itself, but of that substance nothing is thus given me for thinking.

The proposition I think, if it means I exist thinking, is not merely logical function, but determines the subject (which then is at the same time object) with reference to its existence, and is impossible without the internal sense, the intuition of which always supplies the object, not as a thing by itself, but as phenomenal only. Here, therefore, we have no longer mere spontaneity of thinking, but also receptivity of intuition, that is, the thinking of myself applied to the empirical intuition of the same subject. In that empirical intuition the thinking self would have to look for the conditions under which its logical functions can be employed as categories of substance, cause, etc., in order not only to distinguish itself as an object by itself, through the Ego, but to determine the mode of its existence also, that is, to know itself as a noumenon. This, as we know, is impossible, because the internal empirical intuition is sensuous, and supplies us with phenomenal data only, which furnish nothing to the object of the pure consciousness for *the knowledge of its own separate existence, but can serve the purpose of experience only.*

Supposing, however, that we should hereafter discover, not indeed in experience, but in certain (not only logical rules, but) a priori established laws of pure reason, concerning our existence, some ground for admitting ourselves, entirely a priori, as determining and ruling our own existence, there would then be a spontaneity by which our reality would be determinable without the conditions of empirical intuition, and we should then perceive that in the consciousness of our existing there is contained a priori something which may serve to determine with respect to some inner faculty, our existence, which otherwise can be determined sensuously only with reference to an intelligible, though, of course, an ideal world only.

This, however, would not in the least benefit the attempts of rational psychology. For though through that wonderful faculty, which becomes first revealed to myself by the consciousness of a moral law, I should have a principle, purely intellectual, for a determination of my existence, what would be its determining predicates? No other but those which must be given to me in sensuous intuition; and I should therefore find myself again in the same situation where I was before in rational psychology, requiring sensuous intuitions in order to give significance to the concepts of my understanding, such as substance, cause, etc., by which alone I can gain a knowledge of myself; and these intuitions can never carry me beyond the field of experience. Nevertheless, for practical purposes, which always concern objects of experience, I should be justified in applying these concepts, in analogy with their theoretical employment, to liberty also and to the subject of liberty, by taking them only as logical functions of subject and predicate,[4] of cause and effect. According to them, acts or effects, as following those (moral) laws, would be so determined that they may together with the laws of nature be explained in accordance with the categories of substance and cause; though arising in reality from a totally different principle. All this is only meant to prevent a misunderstanding to which our doctrine, which represents self-intuition as purely phenomenal, might easily be exposed. In what follows we shall have occasion to make good use of it.

[4] It is necessary to put a comma after *Prädicats*.

TRANSCENDENTAL DIALECTIC

Book II

Chapter II

THE ANTINOMY OF PURE REASON

In the Introduction to this part of our work we showed that all the transcendental illusion of pure reason depended on three dialectical syllogisms, the outline of which is supplied to us by logic in the three formal kinds of the ordinary syllogism, in about the same way in which the logical outline of the categories was derived from the four functions of all judgments. *The first class* of these rationalising syllogisms aimed at the unconditioned unity of the subjective conditions of all representations (of the subject or the soul) as corresponding to the *categorical* syllogisms of reason, the major of which, as the principle, asserts the relation of a predicate to a subject. *The second class* of the dialectical arguments will, therefore, in analogy with the *hypothetical* syllogisms, take for its object the unconditioned unity of the objective conditions in phenomenal appearance, while the *third class*, which has to be treated in the following chapter, will be concerned with the unconditioned unity of the objective conditions of the possibility of objects in general.

It is strange, however, that a transcendental paralogism caused a one-sided illusion only, with regard to our idea of the subject of our thought; and that it is impossible to find in mere concepts of reason the slightest excuse for maintaining the contrary. All the advantage is on the side of pneumatism, although it cannot hide the hereditary taint by which it evaporates into nought, when subjected to the ordeal of our critique.

The case is totally different when we apply reason to the *objective synthesis* of phenomena; here reason tries at first, with great plausibility, to establish its principle of unconditioned unity, but becomes soon entangled in so many contradictions, that it must give up its pretensions with regard to cosmology also.

For here we are met by a new phenomenon in human reason, namely, a perfectly natural Antithetic, which is not produced by any artificial efforts, but into which reason falls by itself, and inevitably. Reason is no doubt preserved thereby from the slumber of an imaginary conviction, which is often produced by a purely one-sided illusion; but it is tempted at the same time, either to abandon itself to sceptical despair, or to assume a dogmatical obstinacy, taking its stand on certain assertions, without granting a hearing and doing justice to the arguments of the opponent. In both cases, a death-blow is dealt to sound philosophy, although in the former we might speak of the *Euthanasia* of pure reason.

Before showing the scenes of discord and confusion produced by the conflict of the laws (antinomy) of pure reason, we shall have to make a few remarks in order to explain and justify the method which we mean to follow in the treatment of this subject. I shall call all transcendental ideas, so far as they relate to the absolute totality in the synthesis of phenomena, *cosmical concepts,* partly, because of even this unconditioned totality on which the concept of the cosmical universe also rests (which is itself an idea only), partly, because they refer to the synthesis of phenomena only, which is empirical, while the absolute totality in the synthesis of the conditions of all possible things must produce an ideal of pure reason, totally different from the cosmical concept, although in a certain sense related to it. As therefore the paralogisms of pure reason formed the foundation for a dialectical psychology, the antinomy of pure reason will place before our eyes the transcendental principles of a pretended pure (rational) cosmology, not in order to show that it is valid and can be accepted, but, as may be guessed from the very name of the antinomy of reason, in order to expose it as an idea surrounded by deceptive and false appearances, and utterly irreconcilable with phenomena.

THE ANTINOMY OF PURE REASON

SECTION I

System of Cosmological Ideas

Before we are able to enumerate these ideas according to a principle and with systematic precision, we must bear in mind,

1st, That pure and transcendental concepts arise from the understanding only, and that reason does not in reality produce any concept, but only *frees,* it may be, the *concept of the understanding* of the inevitable limitation of a possible experience, and thus tries to enlarge it, beyond the limits of experience, yet in connection with it. Reason does this by demanding for something that is given as conditioned, absolute totality on the side of the conditions (under which the understanding subjects all phenomena to the synthetical unity). It thus changes the category into a transcendental idea, in order to give absolute completeness to the empirical synthesis, by continuing it up to the unconditioned (which can never be met with in experience, but in the idea only). In doing this, reason follows the principle that, *if the conditioned is given, the whole sum of conditions, and therefore the absolutely unconditioned must be given likewise,* the former being impossible without the latter. Hence the transcendental ideas are in reality nothing but categories, enlarged till they reach the unconditioned, and those ideas must admit of being arranged in a table, according to the titles of the categories.

2ndly, Not all categories will lend themselves to this, but those only in which the synthesis constitutes a *series,* and a series of subordinated (not of co-ordinated) conditions. Absolute totality is demanded by reason, with regard to an ascending series of conditions only, not therefore when we have to deal with a descending line of consequences, or with an aggregate of co-ordinated conditions. For, with reference to something given as conditioned, conditions are presupposed and considered as given with it, while, on the other hand, as consequences do not render their conditions possible, but rather presuppose them, we need not, in proceeding to the consequences (or in descending from any given condition to the conditioned), trouble ourselves whether the series comes to an end or not, the question as to their totality being in fact no presupposition of reason whatever.

Thus we necessarily conceive time past up to a given moment, as given, even if not determinable by us. But with regard to time future, which is not a condition of arriving at time present, it is entirely indifferent, if we want to conceive the latter, what we may think about the former, whether we take it, as coming to an end somewhere, or as going on to infinity. Let us take the series, *m, n, o,* where *n* is given as conditioned by *m,* and at the same time as a condition of *o.* Let that series ascend from the conditioned *n* to its condition *m* (*l, k, i,* etc.), and descend from the condition *n* to the conditioned *o* (*p, q, r,* etc.). I must then presuppose the former series, in order to take *n* as given, and according to reason (the totality of conditions) *n* is possible only by means of that series, while its possibility depends in no way on the subsequent series, *o, p, q, r,* which therefore cannot be considered as given, but only as *dabilis,* capable of being given.

I shall call the synthesis of a series on the side of the conditions, beginning with the one nearest to a given phenomenon, and advancing to the more remote conditions, *regressive;* the other, which on the side of the conditioned advances from the nearest effect to the more remote ones, *progressive.* The former proceeds in *antecedentia,* the second in *consequentia.* Cosmological ideas therefore, being occupied with the totality of regressive synthesis, proceed in *antecedentia,* not in *consequentia.* If the latter should take place, it would be a gratuitous, not a necessary problem of pure reason, because for a complete comprehension of what is given us in experience we want to know the causes, but not the effects.

In order to arrange a table of ideas in accordance with the table of the categories, we must take, *first,* the two original *quanta* of all our intuition, time and space. Time is in itself a series (and the formal condition of all series), and in it, therefore, with reference to any given present, we have to distinguish *a priori* the *antecedentia* as conditions (the past) from the *consequentia* (the future). Hence the transcendental idea of the absolute totality of the series of conditions of anything conditioned refers to time past only. The whole of time past is looked upon, according to the idea of reason, as a necessary condition of the given moment. With regard to space there is in it no difference between *progressus* and *regressus,* because all its parts exist together and form an aggregate, but *no series.* We can look upon the present moment, with reference to time past, as conditioned only, but never as condition, because this moment arises only through time past (or rather through the passing of antecedent time). But as the parts of space are not subordinate to one another, but co-ordinate, no part of it is in the condition of the possibility of another, nor does it, like time, constitute a series in itself. Nevertheless the synthesis by which we apprehend the many parts of space is successive, takes place in time, and contains a series. And as in that series of aggregated spaces (as, for instance, of feet in a rood) the spaces added to a given space are always the *condition of the limit* of the preceding spaces, we ought to consider the *measuring* of a space also as a synthesis of a series of conditions of something given as conditioned, with this difference only, that the side of the conditions is by itself not different from the other side which comprehends the conditioned, so that *regressus* and *progressus* seem to be the same in space. As however every part of space is limited only, and not given by another, we must look upon every limited space as conditioned also, so far as it presupposes another space as the condition of its limit, and so on. With reference to limitation therefore *progressus* in space is also *regressus*, and the transcendental idea of the absolute totality of the synthesis in the series of conditions applies to space also. I may ask then for the absolute totality of phenomena in space, quite as well as in time past, though we must wait to see whether an answer is ever possible.

Secondly, reality in space, that is, matter, is something conditioned, the parts of which are its internal conditions, and the parts of its parts, its remoter conditions. We have therefore here a regressive synthesis the absolute totality of which is demanded by reason, but which cannot take place except by a complete division, whereby the reality of matter dwindles away into nothing, or into that at least which is no longer matter, namely, the simple; consequently we have here also a series of conditions, and a progress to the unconditioned.

Thirdly, when we come to the categories of the real relation between phenomena, we find that the category of substance with its accidents does not lend itself to a transcendental idea; that is, reason has here no inducement to proceed regressively to conditions. We know that accidents, so far as they inhere in one and the same substance, are co-ordinated with each other, and do not constitute a series; and with reference to the substance, they are not properly subordinate to it, but are the mode of existence of the substance itself. The concept of the *substantial* might seem to be here an idea of transcendental reason. This, however, signifies nothing but the concept of the object in general, which *subsists,* so far as we think in it the transcendental subject only, without any predicates; and, as we are here speaking only of the unconditioned in the series of phenomena, it is clear that the substantial cannot be a part of it. The same applies to substances in community, which are aggregates only, without having an exponent of a series, since they are not subordinate to each other, as conditions of their possibility, in the same way as spaces were, the limits of which can never be determined by itself, but always through another space. There remains therefore only the category of *causality,* which offers a series of causes to a given effect, enabling us to ascend from the latter, as the conditioned, to the former as the conditions, and thus to answer the question of reason.

Fourthly, the concepts of the possible, the real, and the necessary do not lead to any series, except so far as the *accidental* in existence must always be considered as conditioned, and point, according to a rule of the understanding, to a condition which makes it necessary to ascend to a higher condition, till reason finds at last, only, in the totality of that series, the unconditioned *necessity* which it requires.

If therefore we select those categories which necessarily imply a series in the synthesis of the manifold, we shall have no more than four cosmological ideas, according to the four titles of the categories.

I

Absolute completeness
of the composition
of the given whole of all phenomena.

II

Absolute completeness
of the division
of a given whole
in phenomenal appearance.

III

Absolute completeness
of the origination
of a phenomenon
in general.

IV

Absolute completeness
of the dependence of the existence
of the changeable in phenomenal appearance.

It should be remarked, *first,* that the idea of absolute totality refers to nothing else but the exhibition of phenomena, and not therefore to the pure concept, formed by the understanding, of a totality of things in general. Phenomena, therefore, are considered here as given, and reason postulates the absolute completeness of the conditions of their possibility, so far as these conditions constitute a series, that is, an absolutely (in every respect) complete synthesis, whereby phenomena could be exhibited according to the laws of the understanding.

Secondly, it is in reality the unconditioned alone which reason is looking for in the synthesis of conditions, continued regressively and serially, as it were a completeness in the series of premisses, which taken together require no further premisses. This *unconditioned* is always contained in *the absolute totality of a series,* as represented in imagination. But this absolutely complete synthesis is again an idea only, for it is impossible to know beforehand, whether such a synthesis be possible in phenomena. If we represent everything by means of pure concepts of the understanding only, and without the conditions of sensuous intuition, we might really say that of everything given as conditioned the whole series also of conditions, subordinated to each other, is given, for the conditioned is given through the conditions only. When we come to phenomena, however, we find a particular limitation of the mode in which conditions are given, namely, through the successive synthesis of the manifold of intuition which should become complete by the *regressus.* Whether this completeness, however, is possible, with regard to sensuous phenomena, is still a question. But the idea of that completeness is no doubt contained in reason, without reference to the possibility or impossibility of connecting with it adequate empirical concepts. As therefore in the absolute totality of the regressive synthesis of the manifold in intuition (according to the categories which represent that totality as a series of conditions of something given as conditioned) the unconditioned is necessarily contained without attempting to determine whether and how such a totality be possible, reason here takes the road to start from the idea of totality, though her final aim is the *unconditioned,* whether of the whole series or of a part thereof.

This unconditioned may be either conceived as existing in the whole series only, in which all members without exception are conditioned and the whole of them only absolutely unconditioned—and in this case the *regressus* is called infinite— or the absolutely unconditioned is only a part of the series, the other members being subordinate to it, while it is itself conditioned by nothing else.* In the former case the series is with-

* The absolute total of a series of conditions of anything given as conditioned, is itself always unconditioned; because there are no

out limits *a parte priori* (without a beginning), that is infinite; given however as a whole in which the *regressus* is never complete, and can therefore be called infinite potentially only. In the latter case there is something that stands first in the series, which, with reference to time past, is called the *beginning of the world;* with reference to space, the *limit of the world;* with reference to the parts of a limited given whole, the *simple;* with reference to causes, absolute *spontaneity* (liberty); with reference to the existence of changeable things, the absolute *necessity of nature.*

We have two expressions, *world* and *nature,* which frequently run into each other. The first denotes the mathematical total of all phenomena and the totality of their synthesis of large and small in its progress whether by composition or division. That world, however, is called nature* if we look upon it as a dynamical whole, and consider not the aggregation in space and time, in order to produce a quantity, but the unity in the *existence* of phenomena. In this case the condition of that which happens is called *cause,* the unconditioned causality of the cause as phenomenal, *liberty,* while the conditioned causality, in its narrower meaning, is called *natural cause.* That of which the existence is conditioned is called *contingent,* that of which it is unconditioned, *necessary.* The unconditioned necessity of phenomena may be called *natural necessity.*

I have called the ideas, which we are at present discussing, cosmological, partly because we understand by *world* the totality of all phenomena, our ideas being directed to that only which is unconditioned among the phenomena; partly, because world, in its transcendental meaning, denotes the totality of all existing things, and we are concerned only with the com-

---

conditions beyond on which it could depend. Such an absolute total of a series is, however, an idea only, or rather a problematical concept, the possibility of which has to be investigated with reference to the mode in which the unconditioned, that is, in reality, the transcendental idea with which we are concerned, may be contained in it.

* Nature, if taken *adjective* (*formaliter*), is meant to express the whole complex of the determinations of a thing, according to an inner principle of causality; while, if taken *substantive* (*materialiter*), it denotes the totality of phenomena, so far as they are all held together by an internal principle of causality. In the former meaning we speak of the nature of liquid matter, of fire, etc., using the word *adjective;* while, if we speak of the objects of nature, or of natural objects, we have in our mind the idea of a subsisting whole.

pleteness of the synthesis (although properly only in the *regressus* to the conditions). Considering, therefore, that all these ideas are transcendent because, though not transcending in kind their object, namely, phenomena, but restricted to the world of sense (and excluded from all noumena) they nevertheless carry synthesis to a *degree* which transcends all possible experience, they may, according to my opinion, very properly be called *cosmical concepts.* With reference to the distinction, however, between the mathematically or the dynamically unconditioned at which the *regressus* aims, I might call the two former, in a narrower sense, *cosmical concepts* (macrocosmically or microcosmically) and the remaining two *transcendent concepts of nature.* This distinction, though for the present of no great consequence, may become important hereafter.

THE ANTINOMY OF PURE REASON

Section II

Antithetic of Pure Reason

If every collection of dogmatical doctrines is called *Thetic,* I may denote by *Antithetic,* not indeed dogmatical assertions of the opposite, but the conflict between different kinds of apparently dogmatical knowledge (*thesis cum antithesi*), to none of which we can ascribe a superior claim to our assent. This antithetic, therefore, has nothing to do with one-sided assertions, but considers general knowledge of reason with reference to the conflict only that goes on in it, and its causes. The transcendental antithetic is in fact an investigation of the antinomy of pure reason, its causes and its results. If we apply our reason, not only to objects of experience, in order to make use of the principles of the understanding, but venture to extend it beyond the limit of experience, there arise rationalising or sophistical propositions, which can neither hope for confirmation nor need fear refutation from experience. Every one of them is not only in itself free from contradiction, but can point to conditions of its necessity in the nature of reason itself, only that, unfortunately, its opposite can produce equally valid and necessary grounds for its support.

The questions which naturally arise in such a Dialectic of pure reason are the following. 1. In what propositions is pure reason inevitably subject to an antinomy? 2. On what causes does this antinomy depend? 3. Whether, and in what way, reason may, in spite of this contradiction, find a way to certainty?

A dialectical proposition of pure reason must have this characteristic to distinguish it from all purely sophistical propositions, *first,* that it does not refer to a gratuitous question, but to one which human reason in its natural progress must necessarily encounter, and, *secondly,* that it, as well as its opposite, carries with itself not a merely artificial illusion, which when once seen through disappears, but a natural and inevitable illusion, which, even when it deceives us no longer, always remains, and though rendered harmless, cannot be annihilated.

This dialectical doctrine will not refer to the unity of the understanding in concepts of experience, but to the unity of reason in mere ideas, the condition of which, as it is meant to agree, as a synthesis according to rules, with the understanding, and yet at the same time, as the absolute unity of that synthesis, with reason, must either, if it is adequate to the unity of reason, be too great for the understanding, or, if adequate to the understanding, too small for reason. Hence a conflict must arise, which cannot be avoided, do what we will.

These apparently rational, but really sophistical assertions open a dialectical battle-field, where that side always obtains the victory which is allowed to make the attack, and where those must certainly succumb who are obliged to keep on the defensive. Hence doughty knights, whether fighting for the good or the bad cause, are sure to win their laurels, if only they take care that they have the right to make the last attack, and are not obliged to stand a new onslaught of the enemy. We can easily imagine that this arena has often been entered, and many victories have been won on both sides, the last decisive victory being always guarded by the defender of the good cause maintaining his place, his opponent being forbidden ever to carry arms again. As impartial judges we must take no account of whether it be the good or the bad cause which the two champions defend. It is best to let them fight it out between themselves in the hope that, after they have rather tired out than injured each other, they may themselves perceive the uselessness of their quarrel, and part as good friends.

This method of watching or even provoking such a conflict of assertions, not in order to decide in favour of one or the other side, but in order to find out whether the object of the struggle be not a mere illusion, which everybody tries to grasp in vain, and which never can be of any use to any one, even if no resistance were made to him, this method, I say, may be called the *sceptical method*. It is totally different from *scepticism*, or that artificial and scientific agnosticism which undermines the foundations of all knowledge, in order if possible to leave nothing trustworthy and certain anywhere. The sceptical method, on the contrary, aims at certainty, because, while watching a contest which on both sides is carried on honestly and intelligently, it tries to discover the point where the misunderstanding arises, in order to do what is done by wise legislators, namely, to derive from the embarrassments of judges in law-suits information as to what is imperfectly, or not quite accurately, determined in their laws. The antinomy which shows itself in the application of laws, is, considering our limited wisdom, the best criterion of the original legislation (nomothetic), and helps to attract the attention of reason, which in abstract speculations does not easily become aware of its errors, to the important points in the determination of its principles.

This sceptical method is essential in transcendental philosophy only, while it may be dispensed with in other fields of investigation. It would be absurd in mathematics, for no false assertions can there be hidden or rendered invisible, because the demonstrations must always be guided by pure intuition, and proceed by evident synthesis. In experimental philosophy a doubt, which causes delay, may be useful, but at least no misunderstanding is possible that could not be easily removed, and the final means for deciding a question, whether found sooner or later, must always be supplied by experience. Moral philosophy too can always produce its principles and their practical consequences in the concrete also, or at least in possible experience, and thus avoid the misunderstandings inherent in abstraction. Transcendental assertions, on the contrary, pretending to knowledge far beyond the field of possible experience, can never produce their abstract synthesis in any intuition *a priori*, nor can their flaws be discovered by means of any experience. Transcendental reason, therefore, admits of no other criterion but an attempt to combine its conflicting assertions, and therefore, previous to this, unrestrained conflict between them. This is what we shall now attempt to do.*

* The antinomies follow each other, according to the order of the transcendental ideas mentioned before [p. 300 ff.]

THESIS

THE ANTINOMY

FIRST CONFLICT OF THE

THESIS

The world has a beginning in time, and is limited also with regard to space.

Proof

For if we assumed that the world had no beginning in time, then an eternity must have elapsed up to every given point of time, and therefore an infinite series of successive states of things must have passed in the world. The infinity of a series, however, consists in this, that it never can be completed by means of a successive synthesis. Hence an infinite past series of worlds is impossible, and the beginning of the world a necessary condition of its existence. This was what had to be proved first.

With regard to the second, let us assume again the opposite. In that case the world would be given as an infinite whole of co-existing things. Now we cannot conceive in any way the extension of a quantum, which is not given within certain limits to every intuition,* except through the synthesis of its parts, nor the totality of such a quantum in any way, except through a completed synthesis, or by the repeated addition of unity to itself.† In order therefore to conceive the world, which fills all space, as a whole, the successive synthesis of the parts of an infinite world would have to be looked upon as completed; that is, an infinite time would have to be looked upon as

---

* We may perceive an indefinite quantum as a whole, if it is included in limits, without having to build up its totality by means of measuring, that is, by the successive synthesis of its parts. The limits themselves determine its completeness, by cutting off everything beyond.
† The concept of totality is in this case nothing but the representation of the completed synthesis of its parts, because, as we cannot deduce the concept from the intuition of the whole (this being in this case impossible), we can conceive it only through the synthesis of its parts, up to the completion of the infinite, at least in the idea.

ANTITHESIS

OF PURE REASON

TRANSCENDENTAL IDEAS

ANTITHESIS

The world has no beginning and no limits in space, but is infinite, in respect both to time and space.

Proof

For let us assume that it has a beginning. Then, as beginning is an existence which is preceded by a time in which the thing is not, it would follow that antecedently there was a time in which the world was not, that is, an empty time. In an empty time, however, it is impossible that anything should take its beginning, because of such a time no part possesses any condition as to existence rather than non-existence, which condition could distinguish that part from any other (whether produced by itself or through another cause). Hence, though many a series of things may take its beginning in the world, the world itself can have no beginning, and in reference to time past is infinite.

With regard to the second, let us assume again the opposite, namely, that the world is finite and limited in space. In that case the world would exist in an empty space without limits. We should therefore have not only a relation of things *in space*, but also of things *to space*. As however the world is an absolute whole, outside of which no object of intuition, and therefore no correlate of the world can be found, the relation of the world to empty space would be a relation to *no object*. Such a relation, and with it the limitation of the world by empty space, is nothing, and therefore the world is not limited with regard to space, that is, it is infinite in extension.*

* Space is merely the form of external intuition (formal intuition) and not a real object that can be perceived by external intuition. Space, as prior to all things which determine it (fill or limit it), or rather which give an empirical intuition determined by its form, is, under the name of absolute space, nothing but a mere possibility of external phenomena, so far as they either exist already, or can be added to given phenomena. Empirical intuition, therefore, is not a compound of phenomena and of space (perception and empty in-

THESIS

elapsed, during the enumeration of all co-existing things. This is impossible. Hence an infinite aggregate of real things cannot be regarded as a given whole, nor, therefore, as given at the same time. Hence it follows that the world is not infinite, as regards extension in space, but enclosed in limits. This was the second that had to be proved.

OBSERVATIONS ON THE

I

ON THE THESIS

In exhibiting these conflicting arguments I have not tried to avail myself of mere sophisms for the sake of what is called special pleading, which takes advantage of the want of caution of the opponent, and gladly allows his appeal to a misunderstood law, in order to establish his own illegitimate claims on its refutation. Every one of our proofs has been deduced from the nature of the case, and no advantage has been taken of the wrong conclusions of dogmatists on either side.

I might have apparently proved my thesis too by putting forward, as is the habit of dogmatists, a wrong definition of the infinity of a given quantity. I might have said that the quantity is *infinite,* if no greater quantity (that is, greater than the number of given units contained in it) is possible. As no number is the greatest, because one or more units can always be added to it, I might have argued that an infinite given quantity, and therefore also an infinite world (infinite as regards both the past series of time and extension in space) is impossible, and therefore the world limited in space and time. I might have done this, but, in that case, my definition would not have agreed with the true concept of an infinite whole. We do not represent by it how large it is, and the concept of it is not therefore the concept of a *maximum,* but we conceive by it its relation only to any possible unit, in regard to which it is greater than any number. According as this unit is either greater or smaller, the infinite would be greater or smaller, while infinity, consisting in the relation only to this given unit,

FIRST ANTINOMY

II

ON THE ANTITHESIS

The proof of the infinity of the given series of world, and of the totality of the world, rests on this, that in the opposite case an empty time, and likewise an empty space, would form the limits of the world. Now I am quite aware that people have tried to escape from this conclusion by saying that a limit of the world, both in time and space, is quite possible, without our having to admit an absolute time before the beginning of the world or an absolute space outside the real world, which is impossible. I have nothing to say against the latter part of this opinion, held by the philosophers of the school of Leibniz. Space is only the form of external intuition, and not a real object that could be perceived externally, nor is it a correlate of phenomena, but the form of phenomena themselves. Space, therefore, cannot exist absolutely (by itself) as something determining the existence of things, because it is no object, but only the form of possible objects. Things, therefore, as phenomenal, may indeed determine space, that is, impart reality to one or other of its predicates (quantity and relation); but space, on the other side, as something existing by itself, can-

---

tuition). The one is not a correlate of the other in a synthesis, but the two are only connected as matter and form in one and the same empirical intuition. If we try to separate one from the other, and to place space outside all phenomena, we arrive at a number of empty determinations of external intuition, which, however, can never be possible perceptions; for instance, motion or rest of the world in an infinite empty space, i.e. a determination of the mutual relation of the two, which can never be perceived, and is therefore nothing but the predicate of a mere idea.

THESIS

would always remain the same, although the absolute quantity of the whole would not be known by it. This, however, does not concern us at present.

The true transcendental concept of infinity is, that the successive synthesis of units in measuring a quantum, can never be completed.* Hence it follows with perfect certainty, that an eternity of real and successive states cannot have elapsed up to any given (the present) moment, and that the world therefore must have a beginning.

With regard to the second part of the thesis, the difficulty of an endless and yet past series does not exist; for the manifold of a world, infinite in extension, is given at *one and the same time*. But, in order to conceive the totality of such a multitude of things, as we cannot appeal to those limits which in intuition produce that totality by themselves, we must render an account of our concept, which in our case cannot proceed from the whole to the determined multitude of the parts, but has to demonstrate the possibility of a whole by the successive synthesis of the parts. As such a synthesis would constitute a series that would never be completed, it is impossible to conceive a totality either before it, or through it. For the concept of totality itself is in this case the representation of a completed synthesis of parts, and such a completion, and therefore its concept also, is impossible.

* This quantum contains therefore a multitude (of given units) which is greater than any number; this is the mathematical concept of the infinite.

ANTITHESIS

not determine the reality of things in regard to quantity or form, because it is nothing real in itself. Space therefore (whether full or empty* may be limited by phenomena, but phenomena cannot be limited *by empty space* outside them. The same applies to time. But, granting all this, it cannot be denied that we should be driven to admit these two monsters, empty space outside, and empty time before the world, if we assumed the limit of the world, whether in space or time.

For as to the plea by which people try to escape from the conclusion, that if the world has limits in time or space, the infinite void would determine the existence of real things, so far as their dimensions are concerned, it is really no more than a covered attempt at putting some unknown *intelligible* world in the place of our *sensuous* world, and an existence in general, which *presupposes no other condition* in the world, in the place of a first beginning (an existence preceded by a time of non-existence), and *boundaries* of the universe in place of the limits of extension,—thus getting rid of time and space. But we have to deal here with the *mundus phaenomenon* and its quantity, and we could not ignore the conditions of sensibility, without destroying its very essence. The world of sense, if it is limited, lies necessarily within the infinite void. If we ignore this, and with it, space in general, as an *a priori* condition of the possibility of phenomena, the whole world of sense vanishes, which alone forms the object of our enquiry. The *mundus intelligibilis* is nothing but the general concept of any world, which takes no account of any of the conditions of intuition, and which therefore admits of no synthetical proposition, whether affirmative or negative.

* It is easily seen that what we wish to say is that empty space, so far as limited *by phenomena,* that is, space *within* the world, does not at least contradict transcendental principles, and may be admitted, therefore, so far as they are concerned, though by this its possibility is not asserted.

THESIS

THE ANTINOMY

SECOND CONFLICT OF THE

THESIS

Every compound substance in the world consists of simple parts, and nothing exists anywhere but the simple, or what is composed of it.

Proof

For let us assume that compound substances did not consist of simple parts, then, if all composition is removed in thought, there would be no compound part, and (as no simple parts are admitted) no simple part either, that is, there would remain nothing, and there would therefore be no substance at all. Either, therefore, it is impossible to remove all composition in thought, or, after its removal, there must remain something that exists without composition, that is the simple. In the former case the compound could not itself consist of substances (because with them composition is only an accidental relation of substances, which substances, as permanent beings, must subsist without it). As this contradicts the supposition, there remains only the second view, namely, that the substantial compounds in the world consist of simple parts.

It follows as an immediate consequence that all the things in the world are simple beings, that their composition is only an external condition, and that, though we are unable to remove these elementary substances from their state of composition and isolate them, reason must conceive them as the first subjects of all composition, and therefore, antecedently to it, as simple beings.

ANTITHESIS

OF PURE REASON

TRANSCENDENTAL IDEAS

ANTITHESIS

No compound thing in the world consists of simple parts,
and there exists nowhere in the world anything simple.

Proof

Assume that a compound thing, a substance, consists of
simple parts. Then as all external relation, and therefore all
composition of substances also, is possible in space only, it follows that space must consist of as many parts as the parts of
the compound that occupies the space. Space, however, does
not consist of simple parts, but of spaces. Every part of a compound, therefore, must occupy a space. Now the absolutely
primary parts of every compound are simple. It follows therefore that the simple occupies a space. But as everything real,
which occupies a space, contains a manifold, the parts of
which are by the side of each other, and which therefore is
compounded, and, as a real compound, compounded not of
accidents (for these could not exist by the side of each other,
without a substance), but of substances, it would follow that
the simple is a substantial compound, which is self-contradictory.

The second proposition of the antithesis, that there exists
nowhere in the world anything simple, is not intended to mean
more than that the existence of the absolutely simple cannot
be proved from any experience or perception, whether external or internal, and that the absolutely simple is a mere idea,
the objective reality of which can never be shown in any possible experience, so that in the explanation of phenomena it
is without any application or object. For, if we assumed that
an object of this transcendental idea might be found in experience, the empirical intuition of some one object would have
to be such as to contain absolutely nothing manifold by the
side of each other, and combined to a unity. But as, from our
not being conscious of such a manifold, we cannot form any

THESIS

OBSERVATIONS ON THE

I

ON THE THESIS

If I speak of a whole as necessarily consisting of separate parts, I understand by it a substantial whole only, as a real compound, that is, that contingent unity of the manifold, which, given as *separate* (at least in thought), is brought into a mutual connection, and thus constitutes one whole. We ought not to call space a compositum, but a totum, because in it its parts are possible only in the whole, and not the whole by its parts. It might therefore be called a *compositum ideale,* but not *reale.* But this is an unnecessary distinction. As space is no compound of substances, not even of real accidents, nothing remains of it, if I remove all composition in it, not even the point, for a point is possible only as the limit of a space, and therefore of a compound. Space and time do not therefore consist of simple parts. What belongs only to the condition of a substance, even though it possesses quantity (as, for instance, change), does not consist of the simple; that is to say, a certain degree of change does not arise through the accumulation of many simple changes. We can infer the simple from the compound in self-subsisting objects only. Acci-

ANTITHESIS

valid conclusion as to the entire impossibility of it in any objective intuition, and as without this no absolute simplicity can be established, it follows that such simplicity cannot be inferred from any perception whatsoever. As, therefore, an absolutely simple object can never be given in any possible experience, while the world of sense must be looked upon as the sum total of all possible experience, it follows that nothing simple exists in it.

This second part of the antithesis goes far beyond the first, which only banished the simple from the intuition of the composite, while the second drives it out of the whole of nature. Hence we could not attempt to prove it out of the concept of any given object of external intuition (of the compound), but from its relation to a possible experience in general.

SECOND ANTINOMY

II

ON THE ANTITHESIS

Against the theory of the infinite divisibility of matter, the proof of which is mathematical only, objections have been raised by the *Monadists,* which become suspicious by their declining to admit the clearest mathematical proofs as founded on a true insight into the quality of space, so far as space is indeed the formal condition of the possibility of all matter, but treating them only as conclusions derived from abstract but arbitrary concepts, which ought not to be applied to real things. But how is it possible to conceive a different kind of intuition from that given in the original intuition of space, and how can its determinations *a priori* not apply to everything, since it becomes possible only by its filling that space? If we were to listen to them, we should have to admit, beside the mathematical point, which is simple, but no part, but only the limit of a space, other physical points, simple likewise, but possessing this privilege that, as parts of space, they are able, by mere aggregation, to fill space. Without repeating here the many clear refutations of this absurdity, it being quite futile to attempt to reason away by purely discursive concepts the evidence of mathematics, I only remark, that if philosophy in this

THESIS

dents of a state, however, are not self-subsisting. The proof of
the necessity of the simple, as the component parts of all that
is substantially composite, can therefore easily be injured, if it
is extended too far, and applied to all compounds without distinction, as has often been the case.

I am, however, speaking here of the simple only so far as
it is necessarily given in the composite, which can be dissolved
into the former, as its component parts. The true meaning of
the word *Monas* (as used by Leibniz) should refer to that
simple only, which is given *immediately* as simple substance
(for example in self-consciousness), and not as an element of
the composite, in which case it is better called an *Atomus*.[1] As
I wish to prove the existence of simple substances, as the elements of the composite only, I might call the thesis[2] of the
second antinomy transcendental *Atomistic*. But as this word
has long been used as the name of a particular explanation of
material phenomena (*moleculae*) and presupposes, therefore,
empirical concepts, it will be better to call it the dialectic principle of *monadology*.

[1] Rosenkranz thinks that *atomus* is here used intentionally by Kant
as a *masculine*, to distinguish it from the *atomon*, translated by
scholastic philosophers as *inseparable, indiscernible, simplex*, etc.,
while with the Greek philosophers *atomus* is feminine. Erdmann,
however, has shown that Kant has used *atomus* elsewhere also as
masculine.
[2] *Antithesis* is a misprint.

ANTITHESIS

case seems to play tricks with mathematics, it does so because it forgets that in this discussion we are concerned with *phenomena* only, and their conditions. Here, however, it is not enough to find for the pure *concept*, produced by the understanding, of the composite the concept of the simple, but we must find for the *intuition* of the composite (matter) the intuition of the simple; and this, according to the laws of sensibility, and therefore with reference to the objects of the senses, is totally impossible. Though it may be true, therefore, with regard to a whole, consisting of substances, which is conceived by the pure understanding only, that before its composition there must be the simple, this does not apply to the *totum substantiale phaenomenon* which, as an empirical intuition in space, carries with it the necessary condition that no part of it is simple, because no part of space is simple. The monadists, however, have been clever enough to try to escape from this difficulty, by not admitting space as a condition of the possibility of the objects of external intuition (bodies), but by presupposing these and the dynamical relation of substances in general as the condition of the possibility of space. But we have no concept of bodies, except as phenomena, and, as such, they presuppose space as the necessary condition of the possibility of all external phenomena. The argument of the monadists, therefore, is futile, and has been sufficiently answered in the transcendental Æsthetic. If the bodies were things by themselves, then, and then only, the argument of the monadists would be valid.

The second dialectical assertion possesses this peculiarity, that it is opposed by dogmatical assertion which, among all sophistical assertions, is the only one which undertakes to prove palpably in an object of experience the reality of that which we counted before as belonging only to transcendental ideas, namely, the absolute simplicity of a substance,—I mean the assertion that the object of the internal sense, or the thinking I, is an absolutely simple substance. Without entering upon this question (as it has been fully discussed before), I only remark, that if something is conceived as an object only, without adding any synthetical determination of its intuition (and this is the case in the bare representation of the I), it would no doubt be impossible that anything manifold or composite could be perceived in such a representation. Besides, as the

THESIS

THE ANTINOMY

THIRD CONFLICT OF THE

THESIS

Causality, according to the laws of nature, is not the only causality from which all the phenomena of the world can be deduced. In order to account for these phenomena it is necessary also to admit another causality, that of freedom.

Proof

Let us assume that there is no other causality but that according to the laws of nature. In that case everything that *takes place*, presupposes an anterior state, on which it follows inevitably according to a rule. But that anterior state must itself be something which has taken place (which has come to be in time, and did not exist before), because, if it had always existed, its effect too would not have only just arisen, but have existed always. The causality, therefore, of a cause, through which something takes place, is itself an *event*, which again, according to the law of nature, presupposes an anterior state and its causality, and this again an anterior state, and so on. If, therefore, everything takes place according to mere laws of nature, there will always be a secondary only, but never a primary beginning, and therefore no completeness of the series, predicates through which I conceive this object are only intuitions of the internal sense, nothing can occur in them to prove a manifold (one by the side of another), and therefore a real composition. It follows, therefore, from the nature of self-consciousness that, as the thinking subject is at the same time its own object, it cannot divide itself (though it might divide its inherent determinations); for in regard to itself every object is absolute unity. Nevertheless, when this subject is looked upon externally, as an object of intuition, it would most likely exhibit some kind of composition as a phenomenon, and it must always be looked upon in this light, if we wish to know whether its manifold constituent elements are *by the side* of each other or not.

OF PURE REASON

TRANSCENDENTAL IDEAS

ANTITHESIS

There is no freedom, but everything in the world takes place entirely according to the laws of nature.

Proof

If we admit that there is *freedom,* in the transcendental sense, as a particular kind of causality, according to which the events in the world could take place, that is a faculty of absolutely originating a state, and with it a series of consequences, it would follow that not only a series would have its absolute beginning through this spontaneity, but the determination of that spontaneity itself to produce the series, that is, the causality, would have an absolute beginning, nothing preceding it by which this act is determined according to permanent laws. Every beginning of an act, however, presupposes a state in which the cause is not yet active, and a dynamically primary beginning of an act presupposes a state which has no causal connection with the preceding state of that cause, that is, in no wise follows from it. Transcendental freedom is therefore opposed to the law of causality, and represents such a connection of successive states of effective causes, that no unity of experi-

THESIS

on the side of successive causes. But the law of nature consists in this, that nothing takes place without a cause sufficiently determined *a priori*. Therefore the proposition, that all causality is possible according to the laws of nature only, contradicts itself, if taken in unlimited generality, and it is impossible, therefore, to admit that causality as the only one.

We must therefore admit another causality, through which something takes place, without its cause being further determined according to necessary laws by a preceding cause, that is, an *absolute spontaneity* of causes, by which a series of phenomena, proceeding according to natural laws, begins by itself; we must consequently admit transcendental freedom, without which, even in the course of nature, the series of phenomena on the side of causes, can never be perfect.

OBSERVATIONS ON THE

I

ON THE THESIS

The transcendental idea of freedom is far from forming the whole content of the psychological concept of that name, which is chiefly empirical, but only that of the absolute spontaneity of action, as the real ground of imputability; it is, however, the real stone of offence in the eyes of philosophy, which finds its unsurmountable difficulties in admitting this kind of unconditioned causality. That element in the question of the freedom of the will, which has always so much embarrassed speculative reason, is therefore in reality *transcendental* only, and refers merely to the question whether we must admit a faculty of *spontaneously* originating a series of successive things or states. How such a faculty is possible need not be answered, because, with regard to the causality, according to the laws of nature also, we must be satisfied to know *a priori*

ANTITHESIS

ence is possible with it. It is therefore an empty fiction of the mind, and not to be met with in any experience.

We have, therefore, nothing but *nature,* in which we must try to find the connection and order of cosmical events. Freedom (independence) from the laws of nature is no doubt a *deliverance* from restraint, but also from the *guidance* of all rules. For we cannot say that, instead of the laws of nature, laws of freedom may enter into the causality of the course of the world, because, if determined by laws, it would not be freedom, but nothing else but nature. Nature, therefore, and transcendental freedom differ from each other like legality and lawlessness. The former, no doubt, imposes upon the understanding the difficult task of looking higher and higher for the origin of events in the series of causes, because their causality is always conditioned. In return for this, however, it promises a complete and well-ordered unity of experience; while, on the other side, the fiction of freedom promises, no doubt, to the enquiring mind, rest in the chain of causes, leading him up to an unconditioned causality, which begins to act by itself, but which, as it is blind itself, tears the thread of rules by which alone a complete and coherent experience is possible.

THIRD ANTINOMY

II

ON THE ANTITHESIS

He who stands up for the omnipotence of nature (transcendental *physiocracy*), in opposition to the doctrine of freedom, would defend his position against the sophistical conclusions of that doctrine in the following manner. *If you do not admit something mathematically the first in the world with reference to time, there is no necessity why you should look for something dynamically the first with reference to causality.* Who has told you to invent an absolutely first state of the world, and with it an absolute beginning of the gradually progressing series of phenomena, and to set limits to unlimited nature in order to give to your imagination something to rest on? As substances have always existed in the world, or as the unity of experience renders at least such a supposition necessary, there is no difficulty in assuming that a change of their states, that

THESIS

that such a causality has to be admitted, though we can in no
wise understand the possibility how, through one existence, the
existence of another is given, but must for that purpose appeal to experience alone. The necessity of a first beginning of a
series of phenomena from freedom has been proved so far
only as it is necessary in order to comprehend an origin of
the world, while all successive states may be regarded as a
result in succession according to mere laws of nature. But as
thus the faculty of originating a series in time by itself has
been proved, though by no means understood, it is now permitted also to admit, within the course of the world, different
series, beginning by themselves, with regard to their causality,
and to attribute to their substances a faculty of acting with
freedom. But we must not allow ourselves to be troubled by a
misapprehension, namely that, as every successive series in the
world can have only a relatively primary beginning, some
other state of things always preceding in the world, therefore
no absolutely primary beginning of different series is possible
in the course of the world. For we are speaking here of the
absolutely first beginning, not according to time, but according
to causality. If, for instance, at this moment I rise from my
chair with perfect freedom, without the necessary determining
influence of natural causes, a new series has its absolute beginning in this event, with all its natural consequences *ad infinitum*, although, with regard to time, this event is only the
continuation of a preceding series. For this determination
and this act do not belong to the succession of merely natural
effects, nor are they a mere continuation of them, but the
determining natural causes completely stop before it, so far
as this event is concerned, which no doubt follows them, and
does not *result* from them, and may therefore be called an
absolutely first beginning in a series of phenomena, not with
reference to time, but with reference to causality.

This requirement of reason to appeal in the series of natural
causes to a first and free beginning is fully confirmed if we see
that, with the exception of the Epicurean school, all philosophers of antiquity have felt themselves obliged to admit, for
the sake of explaining all cosmical movements, a *prime mover,*
that is, a freely acting cause which, first and by itself, started
this series of states. They did not attempt to make a first beginning comprehensible by an appeal to nature only.

ANTITHESIS

is, a series of their changes, has always existed also, so that there is no necessity for looking for a first beginning either mathematically or dynamically. It is true we cannot render the possibility of such an infinite descent comprehensible without the first member to which everything else is subsequent. But, if for this reason you reject this riddle of nature, you will feel yourselves constrained to reject many synthetical fundamental properties (natural forces), which you cannot comprehend any more, nay, the very possibility of change in general would be full of difficulties. For if you did not know from experience that change exists, you would never be able to conceive *a priori* how such a constant succession of being and not being is possible.

And, even if the transcendental faculty of freedom might somehow be conceded to start the changes of the world, such faculty would at all events have to be outside the world (though it would always remain a bold assumption to admit, outside the sum total of all possible intuitions, an object that cannot be given in any possible experience). But to attribute in the world itself a faculty to substances can never be allowed, because in that case the connection of phenomena determining each other by necessity and according to general laws, which we call nature, and with it the test of empirical truth, which distinguishes experience from dreams, would almost entirely disappear. For by the side of such a lawless faculty of freedom, nature could hardly be conceived any longer, because the laws of the latter would be constantly changed through the influence of the former, and the play of phenomena which, according to nature, is regular and uniform, would become confused and incoherent.

THESIS

THE ANTINOMY

FOURTH CONFLICT OF THE

THESIS

There exists an absolutely necessary Being belonging to the world, either as a part or as a cause of it.

Proof

The world of sense, as the sum total of all phenomena, contains a series of changes without which even the representation of a series of time, which forms the condition of the possibility of the world of sense, would not be given us.* But every change has its condition which precedes it in time, and renders it necessary. Now, everything that is given as conditional presupposes, with regard to its existence, a complete series of conditions, leading up to that which is entirely unconditioned, and alone absolutely necessary. Something absolutely necessary therefore must exist, if there exists a change as its consequence. And this absolutely necessary belongs itself to the world of sense. For if we supposed that it existed outside that world, then the series of changes in the world would derive its origin from it, while the necessary cause itself would not belong to the world of sense. But this is impossible. For as the beginning of a temporal series can be determined only by that which precedes it in time, it follows that the highest condition of the beginning of a series of changes must exist in the time when that series was not yet (because the beginning is an existence, preceded by a time in which the thing which begins was not yet). Hence the causality of the necessary cause of changes and that cause itself belong to time and therefore to phenomena (in which alone time, as their form, is possible), and it cannot therefore be conceived as separated from the

---

* As formal condition of the possibility of changes, time is no doubt objectively prior to them (read *dissen* instead of *disser*); subjectively, however, and in the reality of our consciousness the representation of time, like every other, is occasioned solely by perceptions.

ANTITHESIS

OF PURE REASON

TRANSCENDENTAL IDEAS

ANTITHESIS

There nowhere exists an absolutely necessary Being, either within or without the world, as the cause of it.

Proof

If we supposed that the world itself is a necessary Being, or that a necessary Being exists in it, there would then be in the series of changes either a beginning, unconditionally necessary, and therefore without a cause, which contradicts the dynamical law of the determination of all phenomena in time; or the series itself would be without any beginning, and though contingent and conditioned in all its parts, yet entirely necessary and unconditioned as a whole. This would be self-contradictory, because the existence of a multitude cannot be necessary, if no single part of it possesses necessary existence.

If we supposed, on the contrary, that there exists an absolutely necessary cause of the world, outside the world, then that cause, as the highest member in *the series of causes* of cosmical changes, would begin the existence of the latter and their series.* In that case, however, that cause would have to begin to act, and its causality would belong to time, and therefore to the sum total of phenomena. It would belong to the world, and would therefore not be outside the world, which is contrary to our supposition. Therefore, neither in the world, nor outside the world (yet in causal connection with it), does there exist anywhere an absolutely necessary Being.

---

* The word *to begin* is used in two senses. The first is active when the cause begins, or starts (infit), a series of states as its effect. The second is passive (or neuter) when the causality begins in the cause itself (fit). I reason here from the former to the latter meaning.

world of sense, as the sum total of all phenomena. It follows, therefore, that something absolutely necessary is contained in the world, whether it be the whole cosmical series itself, or only a part of it.

OBSERVATIONS ON THE

I

ON THE THESIS

In order to prove the existence of a necessary Being, I ought not, in this place, to use any but the *cosmological* argument, which ascends from what is conditioned in the phenomena to what is unconditioned in concept, that being considered as the necessary condition of the absolute totality of the series. To undertake that proof from the mere idea of a Supreme Being belongs to another principle of reason, and will have to be treated separately.

The pure cosmological proof cannot establish the existence of a necessary Being, without leaving it open, whether that Being be the world itself, or a Being distinct from it. In order to settle this question, principles are required which are no longer cosmological, and do not proceed in the series of phenomena. We should have to introduce concepts of contingent beings in general (so far as they are considered as objects of the understanding only), and also a principle according to which we might connect them, by means of concepts only, with a necessary Being. All this belongs to a *transcendent* philosophy, for which this is not yet the place.

If, however, we once begin our proof cosmologically, taking for our foundation the series of phenomena, and the regressus in it, according to the empirical laws of causality, we cannot afterwards suddenly leave this line of argument and pass over to something which does not belong as a member to this series. For the condition must be taken in the same meaning in which the relation of the condition to that condition was taken in the series which, by continuous progress, was to lead to that highest condition. If therefore that relation is sensuous and intended for a possible empirical use of the under-

ANTITHESIS

FOURTH ANTINOMY

II

ON THE ANTITHESIS

If, in ascending the series of phenomena, we imagine we meet with difficulties militating against the existence of an absolutely necessary supreme cause, such difficulties ought not to be derived from mere concepts of the necessary existence of a thing in general. They ought not to be ontological, but ought to arise from the causal connection with a series of phenomena for which a condition is required which is itself unconditioned, that is, they ought to be cosmological, and dependent on empirical laws. It must be shown that our ascending in the series of causes (in the world of sense) can never end with a condition empirically unconditioned, and that the cosmological argument, based on the contingency of cosmical states, as proved by their changes, ends in a verdict against the admission of a first cause, absolutely originating the whole series.

A curious contrast however meets us in this antinomy. From the same ground on which, in the thesis, the existence of an original Being was proved, its non-existence is proved in the antithesis with equal stringency. We were first told, that *a necessary Being exists,* because the whole of time past comprehends the series of all conditions, and with it also the unconditioned (the necessary). We are now told *there is no necessary Being,* for the very reason that the whole of past time comprehends the series of all conditions (which therefore altogether are themselves conditioned). The explanation is this. The first argument regards only the *absolute totality* of the series of conditions determining each other in time, and thus arrives at something unconditioned and necessary. The second, on the contrary, regards the *contingency* of all that is determined *in the temporal series* (everything being preceded

THESIS

standing, the highest condition or cause can close the regressus according to the laws of sensibility only, and therefore as belonging to that temporal series itself. The necessary Being must therefore be regarded as the highest member of the cosmical series.

Nevertheless, certain philosophers have taken the liberty of making such a salto (μετάβασις εἰς ἄλλο γένος). From the changes in the world they concluded their empirical contingency, that is, their dependence on empirically determining causes, and they thus arrived at an ascending series of empirical conditions. This was quite right. As, however, in this way they could not find a first beginning, or any highest member, they suddenly left the empirical concept of contingency, and took to the pure category. This led to a purely intelligible series, the completeness of which depended on the existence of an absolutely necessary cause, which cause, as no longer subject to any sensuous conditions, was freed also from the temporal condition of itself beginning its causality. Such a proceeding is entirely illegitimate, as may be seen from what follows.

In the pure sense of the category we call contingent that the contradictory opposite of which is possible. Now we cannot conclude that intelligible contingency from empirical contingency. Of what is being changed we may say that the opposite (of its state) is real, and therefore possible also at another time. But this is not the contradictory opposite of the preceding state. In order to establish that, it is necessary that, at the same time, when the previous state existed, its opposite could have existed in its place, and this can never be concluded from change. A body, for instance, which, when in motion, was A, comes to be, when at rest, = non A. From the fact that the state opposite to the state A follows upon it, we can in no wise conclude that the contradictory opposite of A is possible, and therefore A contingent only. In order to establish this, it would be necessary to prove that, at the same time when there was motion, there might have been, instead of it, rest. But we know no more than that, at a subsequent time, such rest was real, and therefore possible also. Motion at one time, and rest at another, are not contradictory opposites. Therefore the succession of opposite determinations, that is, change, in no way proves contingency, according to the

ANTITHESIS

by a time in which the condition itself must again be determined as conditioned), in which case everything unconditioned, and every absolute necessity, must absolutely vanish.
In both, the manner of concluding is quite in conformity with
ordinary human reason, which frequently comes into conflict
with itself, from considering its object from two different
points of view. Herr von Mairan considered the controversy
between two famous astronomers, which arose from a similar
difficulty, as to the choice of the true standpoint, as something
sufficiently important to write a separate treatise on it. The
one reasoned thus, the *moon revolves on its own axis,* because
it always turns the same side towards the earth. The other
concluded, the *moon does not revolve on its own axis,* because
it always turns the same side towards the earth. Both conclusions were correct, according to the point of view from
which one chose to consider the motion of the moon.

concepts of the pure understanding, and can therefore never lead us on to the existence of a necessary Being, according to the pure concepts of the understanding. Change proves empirical contingency only; it proves that the new state could not have taken place according to the law of causality by itself, and without a cause belonging to a previous time. This cause, even if it is considered as absolutely necessary, must, as we see, exist in time, and belong to the series of phenomena.

THE ANTINOMY OF PURE REASON

Section III

Of the Interest of Reason in these Conflicts

We have thus watched the whole dialectical play of the cosmological ideas, and have seen that they do not even admit of any adequate object being supplied to them in any possible experience, nay, not even of reason treating them in accordance with the general laws of experience. Nevertheless these ideas are not arbitrary fictions, but reason in the continuous progress of empirical synthesis is necessarily led on to them, whenever it wants to free what, according to the rules of experience, can be determined as conditioned only, from all conditions, and comprehend it in its unconditioned totality. These rationalising or dialectical assertions are so many attempts at solving four perfectly natural and inevitable problems of reason. There cannot be either more or less of them, because there are neither more nor less series of synthetical hypotheses, which limit empirical synthesis *a priori*.

We have represented the brilliant pretensions of reason, extending its domain beyond all the limits of experience, in dry formulas only, containing nothing but the grounds of its claims; and, as it befits transcendental philosophy, divested them of everything empirical, although it is only in connection with this that the whole splendour of the assertions of reason can be fully seen. In their application, and in the progressive extension of the employment of reason, beginning from the field of experience, and gradually soaring up to those sublime ideas, philosophy displays a grandeur which, if it could only establish its pretensions, would leave all other kinds of human knowledge far behind, promising to us a safe foundation for our highest expectations and hopes for the attainment of the highest aims, towards which all the exertions of reason must finally converge. The questions, whether the world has a beginning and any limit of its extension in space; whether there is anywhere, and it may be in my own thinking self, an indivisible and indestructible unity, or whether there exists nothing but what is divisible and perishable; whether in my acts I am free, or, like other beings, led by the hand of nature and of fate; whether, finally, there exists a supreme cause of the world, or whether the objects of nature and their order form the last object which we can reach in all our speculations,—these are questions for the solution of which the mathematician would gladly sacrifice the whole of his science, which cannot give him any satisfaction with regard to the highest and dearest aspirations of mankind. Even the true dignity and worth of mathematics, that pride of human reason, rest on this, that they teach reason how to understand nature in what is great and what is small in her, in her order and regularity, and likewise in the admirable unity of her moving powers, far above all expectations of a philosophy restricted to common experience, and thus encourage reason to extend its use far beyond experience, nay, supply philosophy with the best materials intended to support its investigations, so far as their nature admits of it, by adequate intuitions.

Unfortunately for mere speculation (but fortunately perhaps for the practical destinies of men), reason, in the very midst of her highest expectations, finds herself so hemmed in by a press of reasons and counter reasons, that, as neither her honour nor her safety admit of her retreating and becoming an indifferent spectator of what might be called a mere passage of arms, still less of her commanding peace in a strife in which she is herself deeply interested, nothing remains to her but to reflect on the origin of this conflict, in order to find out whether it may not have arisen from a mere misunderstanding. After such an enquiry proud claims would no doubt have to be surrendered on both sides, but a permanent and tranquil rule of reason over the understanding and the senses might then be inaugurated.

For the present we shall defer this thorough enquiry, in order to consider which side we should like to take, if it should become necessary to take sides at all. As in this case we do not consult the logical test of truth, but only our own interest, such an enquiry, though settling nothing as to the contested rights of both parties, will have this advantage, that it makes us understand why those who take part in this contest embrace one rather than the other side, without being guided by any special insight into the subject. It may also explain some other things, as, for instance, the zelotic heat of the one and the calm assurance of the other party, and why the world greets one party with rapturous applause, and entertains towards the other an irreconcilable prejudice.

There is something which in this preliminary enquiry determines the right point of view, from which alone it can be carried on with proper completeness, and this is the comparison of the principles from which both parties start. If we look at the propositions of the antithesis, we shall find in it a perfect uniformity in the mode of thought and a complete unity of principle, namely, the principle of pure empiricism, not only in the explanation of the phenomena of the world, but also in the solution of the transcendental ideas of the cosmical universe itself. The propositions of the thesis, on the contrary, rest not only on the empirical explanation within the series of phenomena, but likewise on intelligible beginnings, and its maxim is therefore not simple. With regard to its essential and distinguishing characteristic, I shall call it the *dogmatism* of pure reason.

On the side of *dogmatism* we find in the determination of the cosmological ideas, or in the *Thesis:*—

First, A certain *practical interest,* which every right-thinking man, if he knows his true interests, will heartily share. That the world has a beginning; that my thinking self is of a simple and therefore indestructible nature; that the same self is free in all his voluntary actions, and raised above the compulsion of nature; that, finally, the whole order of things, or the world, derives its origin from an original Being, whence everything receives both unity and purposeful connection—these are so many foundation stones on which morals and religion are built up. The antithesis robs us, or seems to rob us, of all these supports.

Secondly, Reason has a certain *speculative interest* on the same side. For, if we take and employ the transcendental ideas as they are in the thesis, one may quite *a priori* grasp the whole chain of conditions and comprehend the derivation of the conditioned by beginning with the unconditioned. This cannot be done by the antithesis, which presents itself in a very unfavourable light, because it cannot return to the question as to the conditions of its synthesis any answer which does not lead to constantly new questions. According to it one has always to ascend from a given beginning to a higher one, every part leads always to a still smaller part, every event has always before it another event as its cause, and the conditions of existence in general always rest on others, without ever receiving unconditioned strength and support from a self-subsisting thing, as the original Being.

Thirdly, This side has also the advantage of *popularity,* which is by no means its smallest recommendation. The common understanding does not see the smallest difficulty in the idea of the unconditioned beginning of all synthesis, being accustomed rather to descend to consequences, than to ascend to causes. It finds comfort in the ideas of the absolutely first (the possibility of which does not trouble it), and at the same time a firm point to which the leading strings of its life may be attached, while there is no pleasure in a restless ascent from condition to condition, and keeping one foot always in the air.

On the side of *empiricism,* so far as it determines the cosmological ideas, or the *antithesis,* there is:—

First, No such practical interest, arising from the pure principles of reason, as morality and religion possess. On the contrary, empiricism seems to deprive both of their power and influence. If there is no original Being, different from the world; if the world is without a beginning, and therefore without a Creator; if our will is not free, and our soul shares the same divisibility and perishableness with matter, *moral ideas* also and principles lose all validity, and fall with the *transcendental* ideas, which formed their theoretic support.

But, on the other side, empiricism offers advantages to the speculative interests of reason, which are very tempting, and far exceed those which the dogmatical teacher can promise. With the empiricist the understanding is always on its own proper ground, namely, the field of all possible experience, the laws of which may be investigated and serve to enlarge certain and intelligible knowledge without end. Here every object can and ought to be represented to intuition, both in itself and in its relations, or at least in concepts, the images of which can be clearly and distinctly represented in given similar intuitions. Not only is there no necessity for leaving the chain of the order of nature in order to lay hold of ideas, the objects of which are not known, because, as mere products of thought, they can never be given, but the understanding is not even allowed to leave its proper business and, under pretence of its being finished, to cross into the domain of idealising reason and transcendental concepts, where it need no longer observe and investigate according to the laws of nature, but only *think* and *dream,* without any risk of being contradicted by the facts of nature, not being bound by their evidence, but justified in passing them by, or in even subordinating them to a higher authority, namely, that of pure reason.

Hence the empiricist will never allow that any epoch of nature should be considered as the absolutely first, or any limit of his vision into the extent of nature should be considered as the last. He will not approve of a transition from the objects of nature, which he can analyse by observation and mathematics and determine synthetically in intuition (the extended), to those which neither sense nor imagination can ever represent *in concreto* (the simple); nor will he concede that a faculty be presupposed, even in nature, to act independent of the laws of nature (freedom), thus narrowing the operations of the understanding in investigating, according to the necessary rules, the origin of phenomena. Lastly, he will never tolerate that the cause of anything should be looked for anywhere outside of nature (in the original Being), because we know nothing but nature, which alone can offer us objects and instruct us as to their laws.

If the empirical philosopher had no other purpose with his antithesis but to put down the rashness and presumption of reason in mistaking her true purpose, while boasting of *insight* and *knowledge,* where insight and knowledge come to an end, nay, while representing, what might have been allowed to pass on account of practical interests, as a real advancement of speculative enquiry, in order, when it is so disposed, either to tear the thread of physical enquiry, or to fasten it, under the pretence of enlarging our knowledge, to those transcendental ideas, which really teach us only *that we know nothing;* if, I say, the empiricist were satisfied with this, then his principle would only serve to teach moderation in claims, modesty in assertions, and encourage the greatest possible enlargement of our understanding through the true teacher given to us, namely, experience. For in such a case we should not be deprived of our own intellectual *presumptions* or of our *faith* in their influence on our practical interests. They would only have lost the pompous titles of science and rational insight, because true speculative *knowledge* can never have any other object but experience; and, if we transcend its limits, our synthesis, which attempts new kinds of knowledge independent of experience, lacks that substratum of intuition to which alone it could be applied.

As it is, empiricism becomes often itself dogmatical with regard to ideas, and boldly denies what goes beyond the sphere of its intuitive knowledge, and thus becomes guilty itself of a want of modesty, which here is all the more reprehensible, because an irreparable injury is thereby inflicted on the practical interests of reason.

This constitutes the opposition of *Epicureanism** to *Platonism*.

Either party says more than it knows; but, while the *former* encourages and advances knowledge, although at the expense of practical interests, the *latter* supplies excellent practical principles, but with regard to everything of which speculative knowledge is open to us, it allows reason to indulge in ideal explanations of natural phenomena and to neglect physical investigation.

With regard to the *third* point which has to be considered in a preliminary choice between the two opposite parties, it is very strange that empiricism should be so unpopular, though it might be supposed that the common understanding would readily accept a theory which promises to satisfy it by experimental knowledge and its rational connection, while transcendental dogmatism forces it to ascend to concepts which far surpass the insight and rational faculties of the most practised thinkers. But here is the real motive;—the man of ordinary

---

* It is, however, doubtful whether Epicurus did ever teach these principles as objective assertions. If he meant them to be no more than maxims for the speculative use of reason, he would have shown thereby a truer philosophical spirit than any of the philosophers on antiquity. The principles that in explaining phenomena we must proceed as if the field of investigation were enclosed by no limit or beginning of the world; that the material of the world should be accepted as it must be, if we want to learn anything about it from experience; that there is no origination of events except as determined by invariable laws of nature; and, lastly, that we must not appeal to a cause distinct from the world, all these are still perfectly true, though seldom observed in enlarging the field of speculative philosophy, or in discovering the principles of morality, independently of foreign aid. It is not permissible that those who wish only to *ignore* those dogmatical propositions, while still engaged in mere speculation, should be accused of wishing to *deny* them.

understanding is so placed thereby that even the most learned can claim no advantage over him. If he knows little or nothing, no one can boast of knowing much more, and though he may not be able to employ such scholastic terms as others, he can argue and subtilise infinitely more, because he moves about among mere ideas, about which it is easy to be eloquent, because *no one knows anything about them.* The same person would have to be entirely silent, or would have to confess his ignorance with regard to scientific enquiries into nature. Indolence, therefore, and vanity are strongly in favour of those principles. Besides, although a true philosopher finds it extremely hard to accept the principle of which he can give no reasonable account, still more to introduce concepts the objective reality of which cannot be established, nothing comes more natural to the common understanding that wants something with which it can operate securely. The difficulty of comprehending such a supposition does not disquiet a person of common understanding, because not knowing what comprehending really means, it never enters into his mind, and he takes everything for known that has become familiar to him by frequent use. At last all speculative interest disappears before the practical, and he imagines that he understands and knows what his fears and hopes impel him to accept or to believe. Thus the empiricism of a transcendentally idealising reason loses all popularity and, however prejudicial it may be to the highest practical principles, there is no reason to fear that it will ever pass the limits of the school and obtain in the commonwealth any considerable authority, or any favour with the multitude.

Human reason is by its nature architectonic, and looks upon all knowledge as belonging to a possible system. It therefore allows such principles only which do not render existing knowledge incapable of being associated with other knowledge in some kind of system. The propositions of the antithesis, however, are of such a character that they render the completion of any system of knowledge quite impossible. According to them there is always beyond every state of the world, an older state; in every part, other and again divisible parts; before every event, another event which again is produced from elsewhere, and everything in existence is conditioned, without an unconditioned and first existence anywhere. As therefore the antithesis allows of nothing that is first, and of no beginning which could serve as the foundation of an edifice, such an edifice of knowledge is entirely impossible with such premisses. Hence the architectonic interest of reason (which demands not empirical, but pure rational unity *a priori*) serves as a natural recommendation of the propositions of the thesis.

But if men could free themselves from all such interests, and consider the assertions of reason, unconcerned about their consequences, according to the value of their arguments only, they would find themselves, if they knew of no escape from the press except adhesion to one or the other of the opposite doctrines, in a state of constant oscillation. To-day they would be convinced that the human will is free; to-morrow, when considering the indissoluble chain of nature, they would think that freedom is nothing but self-deception, and *nature* all in all. When afterwards they come to act, this play of purely speculative reason would vanish like the shadows of a dream, and they would choose their principles according to practical interests only. But, as it well befits a reflecting and enquiring being to devote a certain time entirely to the examination of his own reason, divesting himself of all partiality, and then to publish his observations for the judgment of others, no one ought to be blamed, still less be prevented, if he wishes to produce the thesis as well as the antithesis, so that they may defend themselves, terrified by no menace, before a jury of his peers, that is, before a jury of weak mortals.

THE ANTINOMY OF PURE REASON

SECTION IV

Of the Transcendental Problems of Pure Reason, and the Absolute Necessity of their Solution

To attempt to solve all problems, and answer all questions, would be impudent boasting, and so extravagant a self-conceit, that it would forfeit all confidence. Nevertheless there are sciences the very nature of which requires that every question which can occur in them should be answerable at once from what is known, because the answer must arise from the same sources from which the question springs. Here it is not allowed to plead inevitable ignorance, but a solution can be demanded. We must be able, for instance, to know, according to a rule, what in every possible case is *right* or *wrong,* because this touches our obligation, and we cannot have any obligation to that which *we cannot know*. In the explanation, however, of the phenomena of nature, many things must remain uncertain, and many a question insoluble, because what we know of nature is by no means sufficient, in all cases, to explain what has to be explained. It has now to be considered, whether there exists in transcendental philosophy any question relating to any object of reason which, by that pure reason, is unanswerable, and whether we have a right to decline its decisive answer by treating the object as absolutely uncertain (from all that we are able to know), and as belonging to that class of objects of which we may form a sufficient conception for starting a question, without having the power or means of ever answering it.

Now I maintain that transcendental philosophy has this peculiarity among all speculative knowledge, that no question, referring to an object of pure reason, can be insoluble for the same human reason; and that no excuse of inevitable ignorance on our side, or of unfathomable depth on the side of the problem, can release us from the obligation to answer it thoroughly and completely; because the same concept, which enables us to ask the question, must qualify us to answer it, considering that, as in the case of right and wrong, the object itself does not exist, except in the concept.

There are, however, in transcendental philosophy no other questions but the cosmological, with regard to which we have a right to demand a satisfactory answer, touching the *quality* of the object; nor is the philosopher allowed here to decline an answer by pleading impenetrable obscurity. These questions can refer to cosmological ideas only, because the object must be given empirically, and the question only refers to the adequateness of it to an idea. If the object is transcendental and therefore itself unknown, as, for instance, whether that something the phenomenal appearance of which (within ourselves) is the thinking (soul), be in itself a simple being, whether there be an absolutely necessary cause of all things, etc., we are asked to find an object for our idea of which we may well confess that it is unknown to us, though not therefore impossible.* The cosmological ideas alone possess this peculiarity

---

* Though we cannot answer the question, what kind of quality a transcendental object may possess, or *what it is*, we are well able to answer that the question itself *is nothing*, because it is without an object. All questions, therefore, of transcendental psychology are answerable, and have been answered, for they refer to the transcendental subject of all internal phenomena, which itself is not

that they may presuppose their object, and the empirical synthesis required for the object, as given, and the question
which they suggest refers only to the progress of that synthesis,
so far as it is to contain absolute totality, such absolute totality
being no longer empirical, because it cannot be given in any
experience. As we are here concerned solely with a thing, as
an object of possible experience, not as a thing by itself, it is
impossible that the answer of the transcendent cosmological
question can be anywhere but in the idea, because it refers to
no object by itself; and in respect to possible experience we do
not ask for that which can be given *in concreto* in any experience, but for that which lies in the idea, to which the empirical
synthesis can no more than approach. Hence that question can
be solved from the idea only, and being a mere creation of
reason, reason cannot decline her responsibility and put it on
the unknown object.

It is in reality not so strange as it may seem at first, that a
science should demand and expect definite answers to all the
questions belonging to it (*quaestiones domesticae*), although
at present these answers have not yet been discovered. There
are, in addition to transcendental philosophy, two other sciences of pure reason, the one speculative, the other practical,
pure mathematics, and *pure ethics.* Has it ever been alleged
that, it may be on account of our necessary ignorance of the
conditions, it must remain uncertain what exact relation the
diameter bears to a circle, in rational or irrational numbers?
As by the former the relation cannot be expressed adequately,
and by the latter has not yet been discovered, it was judged
rightly that the impossibility at least of the solution of such a
problem can be known with certainty, and Lambert gave even
a demonstration of this. In the general principles of morality
there can be nothing uncertain, because its maxims are either
entirely null and void, or derived from our own rational concepts only. In natural science, on the contrary, we have an
infinity of conjectures with regard to which certainty can never
be expected, because natural phenomena are objects given to

---

phenomenal, and not *given* as an object, and possesses none of the
conditions which make any of the categories (and it is to them
that the question really refers) applicable to it. We have, therefore,
here a case where the common saying applies, that no answer is as
good as an answer, that is, that the question regarding the quality
of something which cannot be conceived by any definite predicates,
being completely beyond the sphere of objects, is entirely null and
void.

us independent of our concepts, and the key to them cannot be found within our own mind, but in the world outside us. For that reason it cannot in many cases be found at all, and a satisfactory answer must not be expected. The questions of the transcendental Analytic, referring to the deduction of our pure knowledge, do not belong to this class, because we are treating at present of the certainty of judgments with reference to their objects only, and not with reference to the origin of our concepts themselves.

We shall not, therefore, be justified in evading the obligation of a critical solution, at least of the questions of reason, by complaints on the narrow limits of our reason, and by confessing, under the veil of humble self-knowledge, that it goes beyond the powers of our reason to determine whether the world has existed from eternity, or has had a beginning; whether cosmical space is filled with beings *ad infinitum,* or enclosed within certain limits; whether anything in the world is simple, or everything can be infinitely divided; lastly, whether there is a Being entirely unconditioned and necessary in itself, or whether the existence of everything is conditioned, and therefore externally dependent, and in itself contingent. For all these questions refer to an object which can be found nowhere except in our own thoughts, namely, the absolutely unconditioned totality of the synthesis of phenomena. If we are not able to say and establish anything certain about this from our own concepts, we must not throw the blame on the object itself as obscure, because such an object (being nowhere to be found, except in our ideas) can never be given to us; but we must look for the real cause of obscurity in our idea itself, which is a problem admitting of no solution, though we insist obstinately that a real object must correspond to it. A clear explanation of the dialectic within our own concept, would soon show us, with perfect certainty, how we ought to judge with reference to such a question.

If people put forward a pretext of being unable to arrive at certainty with regard to these problems, the first question which we ought to address to them, and which they ought to answer clearly, is this, Whence do you get those ideas, the solution of which involves you in such difficulty? Are they phenomena, of which you require an explanation, and of which you have only to find, in accordance with those ideas, the principles, or the rule of their explanation? Suppose the whole of nature were spread out before you, and nothing were hid to your senses and to the consciousness of all that is presented to your intuition, yet you would never be able to know by one single experience the object of your ideas *in concreto* (because, in addition to that complete intuition, what is required is a completed synthesis, and the consciousness of its absolute totality, which is impossible by any empirical knowledge). Hence your question can never be provoked for the sake of explaining any given phenomenon, and as it were suggested by the object itself. Such an object can never come before you, because it can never be given by any possible experience. In all possible perceptions you always remain under the sway of *conditions,* whether in space or in time; you never come face to face with anything unconditioned, in order thus to determine whether the unconditioned exists in an absolute beginning of the synthesis, or in an absolute totality of the series without any beginning. The whole, in its empirical meaning, is always relative only. The absolute whole of quantity (the universe), of division, of origination, and of the condition of existence in general, with all the attendant questions as to whether it can be realised by a finite synthesis or by a synthesis to be carried on *ad infinitum,* has nothing to do with any possible experience. You would, for instance, never be able to explain the phenomena of a body in the least better, or even differently, whether you assume that it consists of simple or throughout of composite parts: for neither a simple phenomenon, nor an infinite composition can ever meet your senses. Phenomena require to be explained so far only as the conditions of their explanation are given in perception; but whatever may exist in them, if comprehended as an *absolute whole,* can[3] never be a perception. Yet it is this very whole the explanation of which is required in the transcendental problems of reason.

As therefore the solution of these problems can never be supplied by experience, you cannot say that it is uncertain what ought to be predicated of the object. For your object is in your brain only, and cannot possibly exist outside it; so that you have only to take care to be at one with yourselves, and to avoid the amphiboly, which changes your idea into a pretended representation of an object empirically given, and therefore to be known according to the laws of experience. The dogmatical solution is therefore not only uncertain, but impossible; while the critical solution, which may become per-

---

[3] Read *keine* in original, not *eine.*

fectly certain, does not consider the question objectively, but only with reference to the foundation of the knowledge on which it is based.

THE ANTINOMY OF PURE REASON

SECTION V

Sceptical Representation of the Cosmological Questions in the Four Transcendental Ideas

We should no doubt gladly desist from wishing to have our questions answered dogmatically, if we understood beforehand that, whatever the answer might be, it would only increase our ignorance, and throw us from one incomprehensibility into another, from one obscurity into a still greater obscurity, or it may be even into contradictions. If our question can only be answered by yes or no, it would seem to be prudent to take no account at first of the probable grounds of the answer, but to consider before, what we should gain, if the answer was yes, and what, if the answer was no. If we should find that in either case nothing comes of it but mere nonsense, we are surely called upon to examine our question critically, and to see whether it does not rest on a groundless supposition, playing only with an idea which betrays its falsity in its application and its consequences better than when represented by itself. This is the great advantage of the sceptical treatment of questions which pure reason puts to pure reason. We get rid by it, with a little effort, of a great amount of dogmatical rubbish, in order to put in its place sober criticism which, as a true cathartic, removes successfully all illusion with its train of omniscience.

If, therefore, I could know beforehand that a cosmological idea, in whatever way it might try to realise the unconditioned of the regressive synthesis of phenomena (whether in the manner of the thesis or in that of the antithesis), that, I say, the cosmological idea would always be either *too large* or *too small* for any *concept of the understanding,* I should understand that, as that cosmological idea refers only to an object of experience which is to correspond to a possible concept of the understanding, it must be empty and without meaning, because the object does not fit into it, whatever I may do to adapt it. And this must really be the case with all cosmical concepts, which on that very account involve reason, so long as it remains attached to them, in inevitable antinomy. For suppose:—

First, That the *world has no beginning,* and you will find that it is too large for your concept, which, as it consists in a successive regressus, can never reach the whole of past eternity. Or, suppose, *that the world has a beginning,* then it is again too small for the concept of your understanding engaged in the necessary empirical regressus. For as a beginning always presupposes a time preceding, it is not yet unconditioned; and the law of the empirical use of the understanding obliges you to look for a higher condition of time, so that, with reference to such a law, the world (as limited in time) is clearly too small.

The same applies to the twofold answer to the question regarding the extent of the world in space. For if *it is infinite* and unlimited, it is *too large* for every possible empirical concept. If *it is finite* and limited, you have a perfect right to ask what determines that limit. Empty space is not an independent correlate of things, and cannot be a final condition, still less an empirical condition forming a part of a possible experience; —for how can there be experience of what is absolutely void? But, in order to produce an absolute totality in an empirical synthesis, it is always requisite that the unconditioned should be an empirical concept. Thus it follows that a *limited world* would be *too small* for your concept.

Secondly, If every phenomenon in space (matter) consists of an *infinite number of parts,* the regressus of a division will always be too large for your concept, while if the *division* of space is to *stop* at any member (the simple), it would be *too small* for the idea of the unconditioned, because that member always admits of a regressus to more parts contained in it.

Thirdly, If you suppose that everything that happens in the world is nothing but the *result* of the laws of *nature,* the causality of the cause will always be something that happens, and that necessitates a regressus to a still higher cause, and therefore a continuation of the series of conditions *a parte priori* without end. Mere active *nature,* therefore, is *too large* for any concept in the synthesis of cosmical events.

If you admit, on the contrary, *spontaneously* produced events, therefore generation from *freedom,* you have still, according to an inevitable law of nature, to ask why, and you are forced by the empirical law of causality beyond that point, so that you find that any such totality of connection is too small for your necessary empirical concept.

Fourthly, If you admit an *absolutely necessary* Being (whether it be the world itself or something in the world, or the cause of the world), you place it at a time infinitely remote from any given point of time, because otherwise it would be dependent on another and antecedent existence. In that case, however, such an existence would be unapproachable by your empirical concept, and *too large* even to be reached by any continued regressus.

But if, according to your opinion, everything which belongs to the world (whether as conditioned or as condition) is *contingent,* then every given existence is *too small* for your concept, because compelling you to look still for another existence, on which it depends.

We have said that in all these cases, the *cosmical idea* is either too large or too small for the empirical regressus, and therefore for every possible concept of the understanding. But why did we not take the opposite view and say that in the former case the empirical concept is always too small for the idea, and in the latter too large, so that blame should attach to the empirical regressus, and not to the cosmological idea, which we accused of deviating from its object, namely, possible experience, either by its too-much or its too-little? The reason was this. It is possible experience alone that can impart reality to our concepts; without this, a concept is only an idea without truth, and without any reference to an object. Hence the possible empirical concept was the standard by which to judge the idea, whether it be an idea and fiction only, or whether it has an object in the world. For we then only say that anything is relatively to something else either too large or too small, if it is required for the sake of the other and ought to be adapted to it. One of the playthings of the old dialectical school was the question, whether we should say that the ball is too large or the hole too small, if a ball cannot pass through a hole. In this case it is indifferent what expression we use, because we do not know which of the two exists for the sake of the other. But you would never say that the man is too large for his coat, but that the coat is too small for the man.

We have thus been led at least to a well-founded suspicion that the cosmological ideas, and with them all the conflicting sophistical assertions, may rest on an empty and merely imaginary conception of the manner in which the object of those ideas can be given, and this suspicion may lead us on the right track to discover the illusion which has so long led us astray.

THE ANTINOMY OF PURE REASON

SECTION VI

Transcendental Idealism as the Key to the Solution of Cosmological Dialectic

It has been sufficiently proved in the transcendental Æsthetic that everything which is perceived in space and time, therefore all objects of an experience possible to us, are nothing but phenomena, that is, mere representations which, such as they are represented, namely, as extended beings, or series of changes, have no independent existence outside our thoughts. This system I call *Transcendental Idealism*.* Transcendental realism changes these modifications of our sensibility into self-subsistent things, that is, it changes *mere representations* into things by themselves.

It would be unfair to ask us to adopt that long-decried empirical idealism which, while it admits the independent reality of space, denies the existence of extended beings in it, or at all events considers it as doubtful and does not admit that there is in this respect a sufficiently established difference between dream and reality. It sees no difficulty with regard to the phenomena of the internal sense in time, being real things; nay, it even maintains that this internal experience alone sufficiently proves the real existence of its object (by itself), with all the determinations in time.

Our own transcendental idealism, on the contrary, allows that the objects of external intuition may be real, as they are perceived in space, and likewise all changes in time, as they are represented by the internal sense. For as space itself is a form of that intuition which we call external, and as there would be no empirical representation at all, unless there were objects in space, we can and must admit the extended beings

* *I have sometimes called it* formal *idealism also, in order to distinguish it from the* material *or common idealism, which doubts or denies the very existence of external things. In some cases it seems advisable to use these terms rather than those in the text, in order to prevent all misunderstanding.*

in it as real; and the same applies to time. Space itself, however, as well as time, and with them all phenomena, are not
things by themselves, but representations, and cannot exist outside our mind; and even the internal sensuous intuition of our
mind (as an object of consciousness) which is represented as
determined by the succession of different states in time, is not a
real self, as it exists by itself, or what is called the transcendental subject, but a phenomenon only, given to the sensibility of
this to us unknown being. It cannot be admitted that this internal phenomenon exists as a thing by itself, because it is
under the condition of time, which can never be the determination of anything by itself. In space and time, however, the empirical truth of phenomena is sufficiently established, and kept
quite distinct from a dream, if both are properly and completely connected together in experience, according to empirical laws.

The objects of experience are therefore *never given by
themselves,* but in our experience only, and do not exist outside it. That there may be inhabitants in the moon, though no
man has ever seen them, must be admitted; but it means no
more than that, in the possible progress of our experience, we
may meet with them; for everything is real that hangs together
with a perception, according to the laws of empirical progress.
They are therefore real, if they are empirically connected with
any real consciousness, although they are not therefore real
by themselves, that is, apart from that progress of experience.

Nothing is really given to us but perception, and the empirical progress from this to other possible perceptions. For by
themselves phenomena, as mere representations, are real in
perception only, which itself is nothing but the reality of an
empirical representation, that is, phenomenal appearance. To
call a phenomenon a real thing, before it is perceived, means
either, that in the progress of experience we must meet with
such a perception, or it means nothing. For that it existed by
itself, without any reference to our senses and possible experience, might no doubt be said when we speak of a thing by
itself. We here are speaking, however, of a phenomenon only
in space and time, which are not determinations of things by
themselves, but only of our sensibility. Hence that which exists
in them (phenomena) is not something by itself, but consists
in representations only, which, unless they are given in us (in
perception), exist nowhere.

The faculty of sensuous intuition is really some kind of receptivity only, according to which we are affected in a certain

way by representations the mutual relation of which is a pure intuition of space and time (mere forms of our sensibility), and which, if they are connected and determined in that relation of space and time, according to the laws of the unity of experience, are called objects. The non-sensuous cause of these representations is entirely unknown to us, and we can never perceive it as an object, for such a cause would have to be represented neither in space nor in time, which are conditions of sensuous representations only, and without which we cannot conceive any intuition. We may, however, call that purely intelligible cause of phenomena in general, the transcendental object, in order that we may have something which corresponds to sensibility as a kind of receptivity. We may ascribe to that transcendental object the whole extent and connection of all our possible perceptions, and we may say that it is given by itself antecedently to all experience. Phenomena, however, are given accordingly, not by themselves, but in experience only, because they are mere representations which as perceptions only, signify a real object, provided that the perception is connected with all others, according to the rules of unity in experience. Thus we may say that the real things of time past are given in the transcendental object of experience, but they only are objects to me, and real in time past, on the supposition that I conceive that a regressive series of possible perceptions (whether by the light of history, or by the vestiges of causes and effects), in one word, the course of the world, leads, according to empirical laws, to a past series of time, as a condition of the present time. It is therefore represented as real, not by itself, but in connection with a possible experience, so that all past events from time immemorial and before my own existence mean after all nothing but the possibility of an extension of the chain of experience, beginning with present perception and leading upwards to the conditions which determine it in time.

If, therefore, I represent to myself all existing objects of the senses, at all times and in all spaces, I do not place them before experience into space and time, but the whole representation is nothing but the idea of a possible experience, in its absolute completeness. In that alone those objects (which are nothing but mere representations) are given; and if we say that they exist before my whole experience, this only means that they exist in that part of experience to which, starting from perception, I have first to advance. The cause of empirical conditions of that progress, and consequently with what members, or how far I may meet with certain members in that regressus, is transcendental, and therefore entirely unknown to me. But that cause does not concern us, but only the rule of the progress of experience, in which objects, namely phenomena, are given to me. In the end it is just the same whether I say, that in the empirical progress in space I may meet with stars a hundred times more distant than the most distant which I see, or whether I say that such stars are perhaps to be met with in space, though no human being did ever or will ever see them. For though, as things by themselves, they might be given without any relation to possible experience, they are nothing to me, and therefore no objects, unless they can be comprehended in the series of the empirical regressus. Only in another relation, when namely these phenomena are meant to be used for the cosmological idea of an absolute whole, and when we have to deal with a question that goes beyond the limits of possible experience, the distinction of the mode in which the reality of those objects of the senses is taken becomes of importance, in order to guard against a deceptive error that would inevitably arise from a misinterpretation of our own empirical concepts.

THE ANTINOMY OF PURE REASON

SECTION VII

Critical Decision of the Cosmological Conflict of Reason with Itself

The whole antinomy of pure reason rests on the dialectical argument that, if the conditioned is given, the whole series of conditions also is given. As therefore the objects of the senses are given us as conditioned, it follows, etc. Through this argument, the major of which seems so natural and self-evident, cosmological ideas have been introduced corresponding in number to the difference of conditions (in the synthesis of phenomena) which constitute a series. These cosmological ideas postulate the absolute totality of those series, and thus place reason in inevitable contradiction with itself. Before, however, we show what is deceptive in this sophistical argument, we must prepare ourselves for it by correcting and defining certain concepts occurring in it.

First, the following proposition is clear and admits of no doubt, that if the conditioned is given, it imposes on us the regressus in the series of all conditions of it; for it follows from the very concept of the conditioned that through it something is referred to a condition, and, if that condition is again conditioned, to a more distant condition, and so on through all the members of the series. This proposition is really analytical, and need not fear any transcendental criticism. It is a logical postulate of reason to follow up through the understanding, as far as possible, that connection of a concept with its conditions, which is inherent in the concept itself.

Further, if the conditioned as well as its conditions are things by themselves, then, if the former be given, the regressus to the latter is not only *required,* but is really *given;* and as this applies to all the members of the series, the complete series of conditions and with it the unconditioned also is given, or rather it is presupposed that the conditioned, which was possible through that series only, is given. Here the synthesis of the conditioned with its condition is a synthesis of the understanding only, which represents things *as they are,* without asking whether and how we can arrive at the knowledge of them. But if I have to deal with phenomena, which, as mere representations, are not given at all, unless I attain to a knowledge of them (that is, to the phenomena themselves, for they are nothing but empirical knowledge), then I cannot say in the same sense that, if the conditioned is given, all its conditions (as phenomena) are also given, and can therefore by no means conclude the absolute totality of the series. For *phenomena* in their apprehension are themselves nothing but an empirical synthesis (in space and time), and are given therefore in *that* synthesis only. Now it follows by no means that, if the conditioned (as phenomenal) is given, the synthesis also that constitutes its empirical condition should thereby be given at the same time and presupposed; for this takes place in the regressus only, and never without it. What we may say in such a case is this, that a regressus to the conditions, that is, a continued empirical synthesis in that direction is required, and that conditions cannot be wanting that are given through that regressus.

Hence we see that the major of the cosmological argument takes the conditioned in the transcendental sense of a pure category, while the minor takes it in the empirical sense of a concept of the understanding, referring to mere phenomena, so that it contains that dialectical deceit which is called *Sophisma figurae dictionis.* That deceit, however, is not artificial, but a perfectly natural illusion of our common reason. It is owing to it that, in the major, we presuppose the conditions and their series as it were *on trust,* if anything is given as conditioned, because this is no more than the logical postulate to assume complete premisses for any given conclusion. Nor does there exist in the connection of the conditioned with its condition any order of time, but they are presupposed in themselves as given *together.* It is equally natural also in the minor to look on phenomena as things by themselves, and as objects given to the understanding only in the same manner as in the major, as no account was taken of all the conditions of intuition under which alone objects can be given. But there is an important distinction between these concepts, which has been overlooked. The synthesis of the conditioned with its condition, and the whole series of conditions in the major, was in no way limited by time, and was free from any concept of succession. The empirical synthesis, on the contrary, and the series of conditions in phenomena, which was subsumed in the minor, is necessarily successive and given as such in time only. Therefore I had no right to assume the absolute *totality* of the synthesis and of the series represented by it in this case as well as in the former. For in the former all the members of the series are given by themselves (without determination in time), while here they are possible through the successive regressus only, which cannot exist unless it is actually carried out.

After convicting them of such a mistake in the argument adopted by both parties as the foundation of their cosmological assertions, both might justly be dismissed as not being able to produce any good title in support of their claims. But even thus their quarrel is not yet ended, as if it had been proved that both parties, or one of them, were wrong in the matter contended for (in the conclusion), though they had failed to support it by valid proof. Nothing seems clearer than that, if one maintains that the world has a beginning, and the other that it has no beginning, but exists from all eternity, one or the other must be right. But if this were so, as the arguments on both sides are equally clear, it would still remain impossible ever to find out on which side the truth lies, and the suit continues, although both parties have been ordered to keep the peace before the tribunal of reason. Nothing remains therefore in order to settle the quarrel once for all, and to the satisfaction of both parties, but to convince them that, though they can refute each other so eloquently, they are really quarrelling about nothing, and that a certain transcendental illusion has mocked them with a reality where no reality exists. We shall now enter upon this way of adjusting a dispute, which cannot be adjudicated.

*   *   *   *   *   *   *   *

The Eleatic philosopher Zeno, a subtle dialectician, was severely reprimanded by Plato as a heedless Sophist who, in order to display his skill, would prove a proposition by plausible arguments and subvert the same immediately afterwards by arguments equally strong. He maintained, for instance, that God (which to him was probably nothing more than the universe) is neither finite nor infinite, neither in motion nor at rest, neither similar nor dissimilar to any other thing. It seemed to his critics as if he had intended to deny completely both of the two self-contradictory propositions which would be absurd. But I do not think that he can be rightly charged with this. We shall presently consider the first of these propositions more carefully. With regard to the others, if by the word *God* he meant the universe, he could not but say that it is neither permanently present in its place (at rest) nor that it changes it (in motion), because all places exist in the universe only, while the universe exists in no place. If the universe comprehends in itself everything that exists, it follows that it cannot be similar or dissimilar to any other thing, because there is no other thing besides it with which it could be compared. If two opposite judgments presuppose an inadmissible condition, they both, in spite of their contradiction (which, however, is no real contradiction), fall to the ground, because the condition fails under which alone either of the propositions was meant to be valid.

If somebody were to say that every body has either a good or a bad smell, a third case is possible, namely, that it has no smell at all, in which case both contradictory propositions would be false. If I say that it is either good smelling or not good smelling (*vel suaveolens vel non suaveolens*), in that case the two judgments are contradictory, and the former only is wrong, while its contradictory opposite, namely, that some bodies are not good smelling, comprehends those bodies also which have no smell at all. In the former opposition (*per disparata*) the contingent condition of the concept of a body (smell) still remained in the contradictory judgment and was not eliminated by it, so that the latter could not be called the contradictory opposite of the former.

If I say therefore that the world is either infinite in space or is not infinite (*non est infinitus*), then, if the former proposition is wrong, its contradictory opposite, that the world is not infinite, must be true. I should thus only eliminate an infinite world without affirming another, namely, the finite. But if I had said the world is either infinite or finite (not-infinite), both statements may be false. For I then look upon the world, as by itself, determined in regard to its extent, and I do not only eliminate in the opposite statement the infinity, and with it, it may be, its whole independent existence, but I add a determination to the world as a thing existing by itself, which may be false, because the world may not be a thing by itself, and therefore, with regard to extension, neither infinite nor finite. This kind of opposition I may be allowed to call *dialectical,* that the real contradiction, the *analytical opposition.* Thus then of two judgments opposed to each other dialectically both may be false, because the one does not only contradict the other, but says something more than is requisite for a contradiction.

If we regard the two statements that the world is infinite in extension, and that the world is finite in extension, as contradictory opposites, we assume that the world (the whole series of phenomena) is a thing by itself; for it remains, whether I remove the infinite or the finite regressus in the series of its phenomena. But if we remove this supposition, or this transcendental illusion, and deny that it is a thing by itself, then the contradictory opposition of the two statements becomes purely dialectical, and as the world does not exist by itself (independently of the regressive series of my representations), it exists neither as a whole *by itself infinite,* nor as a whole *by itself finite.* It exists only in the empirical regressus in the series of phenomena, and nowhere by itself. Hence, if that series is always conditioned, it can never exist as complete, and the world is therefore not an inconditioned whole, and does not exist as such, either with infinite or finite extension.

What has here been said of the first cosmological idea, namely, that of the absolute totality of extension in phenomena, applies to the others also. The series of conditions is to be found only in the regressive synthesis, never by itself, as complete, in phenomenon as an independent thing, existing prior to every regressus. Hence I shall have to say that the number of parts in any given phenomenon is by itself neither finite nor infinite, because a phenomenon does not exist by itself, and its parts are only found through the regressus of the decomposing synthesis through and in the regressus, and that regressus can never be given as absolutely complete, whether as finite or as infinite. The same applies to the series of causes, one being prior to the other, and to the series leading from conditioned to unconditioned necessary existence, which can never be regarded either by itself finite in its totality or infinite, because, as a series of subordinated representations, it forms a dynamical regressus only, and cannot exist prior to it, by itself, as a self-subsistent series of things.

The antinomy of pure reason with regard to its cosmological ideas is therefore removed by showing that it is dialectical only, and a conflict of an illusion produced by our applying the idea of absolute totality, which exists only as a condition of things by themselves, to phenomena, which exist in our representation only, and if they form a series, in the successive regressus, but nowhere else. We may, however, on the other side, derive from that antinomy a true, if not dogmatical, at least critical and doctrinal advantage, namely, by proving through it indirectly the transcendental ideality of phenomena, in case anybody should not have been satisfied by the direct proof given in the transcendental Æsthetic. The proof would consist in the following dilemma. If the world is a whole existing by itself, it is either finite or infinite. Now the former as well as the latter proposition is false, as has been shown by the proofs given in the antithesis on one and in the thesis on the other side. It is false, therefore, that the world (the sum total of all phenomena) is a whole existing by itself. Hence it follows that phenomena in general are nothing outside our representations, which was what we meant by their transcendental ideality.

This remark is of some importance, because it shows that our proofs of the fourfold antinomy were not mere sophistry, but honest and correct, always under the (wrong) supposition that phenomena, or a world of sense which comprehends them all, are things by themselves. The conflict of the conclusions drawn from this shows, however, that there is a flaw in the supposition, and thus leads us to the discovery of the true nature of things, as objects of the senses. This transcendental Dialectic therefore does not favour scepticism, but only the sceptical method, which can point to it as an example of its great utility, if we allow the arguments of reason to fight against each other with perfect freedom, from which something useful and serviceable for the correction of our judg—ments will always result, though it may not be always that which we were looking for.

THE ANTINOMY OF PURE REASON

Section VIII

The Regulative Principle of Pure Reason with Regard to the Cosmological Ideas

As through the cosmological principle of totality no real maximum is *given* of the series of conditions in the world of sense, as a thing by itself, but can only be *required* in the regressus of that series, that principle of pure reason, if thus amended, still retains its validity, not indeed as an *axiom,* requiring us to think the totality in the object as real, but as a *problem* for the understanding, and therefore for the subject, encouraging us to undertake and to continue, according to the completeness in the idea, the regressus in the series of conditions of anything given as conditioned. In our sensibility, that is, in space and time, every condition which we can reach in examining given phenomena is again conditioned, because these phenomena are not objects by themselves, in which something absolutely unconditioned might possibly exist, but empirical representations only, which always must have their condition in intuition, whereby they are determined in space and time. The principle of reason is therefore properly a rule only, which in the series of conditions of given phenomena postulates a regressus which is never allowed to stop at anything absolutely unconditioned. It is therefore no principle of the possibility of experience and of the empirical knowledge of the objects of the senses, and not therefore a principle of the understanding, because every experience is (according to a given intuition) within its limits; nor is it a *constitutive principle* of reason, enabling us to extend the concept of the world of sense beyond all possible experience, but it is merely a principle of the greatest possible continuation and extension of our experience, allowing no empirical limit to be taken as an absolute limit. It is therefore a principle of reason, which, as a *rule,* postulates what we ought to do in the regressus, but does *not anticipate* what may be given in the *object,* before such regressus. I therefore call it a *regulative* principle of reason, while, on the contrary, the principle of the absolute totality of the series of conditions, as given in the object (the phenomena) by itself, would be a constitutive cosmological principle, the hollowness of which I have tried to indicate by this very distinction, thus preventing what otherwise would have inevitably happened (through a transcendental surreptitious proceeding), namely, an idea, which is to serve as a rule only, being invested with objective reality.

In order properly to determine the meaning of this rule of pure reason it should be remarked, first of all, that it cannot tell us what *the object is,* but only *how the empirical regressus is to be carried out,* in order to arrive at the complete concept of the object. If we attempted the first, it would become a constitutive principle, such as pure reason can never supply. It cannot therefore be our intention to say through this principle, that a series of conditions of something, given as conditioned, is by itself either finite or infinite; for in that case a mere idea of absolute totality, produced in itself only, would represent in thought an object such as can never be given in experience, and an objective reality, independent of empirical synthesis, would have been attributed to a series of phenomena. This idea of reason can therefore do no more than prescribe a rule to the regressive synthesis in the series of conditions, according to which that synthesis is to advance from the conditioned, through all subordinate conditions, towards the unconditioned, though it can never reach it, for the absolutely unconditioned can never be met with in experience.

To this end it is necessary, first of all, to define accurately the synthesis of a series, so far as it never is complete. People are in the habit of using for this purpose two expressions which are meant to establish a difference, though they are unable clearly to define the ground of the distinction. Mathematicians speak only of a *progressus in infinitum.* Those who enquire into concepts (philosophers) will admit instead the expression of a *progressus in indefinitum* only. Without losing any time in the examination of the reasons which may have suggested such a distinction, and of its useful or useless application, I shall at once endeavour to define these concepts accurately for my own purpose.

Of a straight line it can be said correctly that it may be produced to infinity; and here the distinction between an infinite and an indefinite progress (*progressus in indefinitum*) would be mere subtilty. No doubt, if we are told to carry on a line, it would be more correct to add *in indefinitum*, than *in infinitum*, because the former means no more than, produce it as far as *you wish*, but the second, *you shall* never cease producing it (which can never be intended). Nevertheless, if we speak only of what is possible, the former expression is quite correct, because we can always make it longer, if we like, without end. The same applies in all cases where we speak only of the progressus, that is, of our proceeding from the condition to the conditioned, for such progress proceeds in the series of phenomena without end. From a given pair of parents we may, in the descending line of generation, proceed without end, and conceive quite well that that line should so continue in the world. For here reason never requires an absolute totality of the series, because it is not presupposed as a condition, and as it were given (*datum*), but only as something conditioned, that is, capable only of being given (*dabile*), and can be added to without end.

The case is totally different with the problem, how far the regressus from something given as conditioned may ascend in a series to its conditions; whether I may call it *a regressus into the infinite*, or only into the *indefinite* (*in indefinitum*); and whether I may ascend, for instance, from the men now living, through the series of their ancestors, *in infinitum;* or whether I may only say that, so far as I have gone back, I have never met with an empirical ground for considering the series limited anywhere, so that I feel justified, and at the same time obliged to search for an ancestor of every one of these ancestors, though not to presuppose them.

I say, therefore, that where the whole is given in empirical intuition, the regressus in the series of its internal conditions proceeds *in infinitum*, while if a member only of a series is given, from which the regressus to the absolute totality has first to be carried out, the regressus is only *in indefinitum*. Thus we must say that the division of matter, as given between its limits (a body), goes on *in infinitum*, because that matter is complete and therefore, with all its possible parts, given in empirical intuition. As the condition of that whole consists in its part, and the condition of that part in the part of that part, and so on, and as in this regressus of decomposition we never meet with an unconditioned (indivisible) member of that series of conditions, there is nowhere an empirical ground for stopping the division; nay, the further members of that continued division are themselves empirically given before the continuation of the division, and therefore the division goes on *in infinitum*. The series of ancestors, on the contrary, of any given man, exists nowhere in its absolute totality, in any possible experience, while the regressus goes on from every link in the generation to a higher one, so that no empirical limit can be found which should represent a link as absolutely unconditioned. As, however, the links too, which might supply the condition, do not exist in the empirical intuition of the whole, prior to the regressus, that regressus does not proceed *in infinitum* (by a division of what is given), but to an indefinite distance, in its search for more links in addition to those which are given, and which themselves are again always conditioned only.

In neither case—the *regressus in infinitum* nor the *regressus in indefinitum*—is the series of conditions to be considered as given as infinite in the object. They are not things by themselves, but phenomena only, which, as conditions of each other, are given only in the regressus itself. Therefore the question is no longer how great this series of conditions may be by itself, whether finite or infinite, for it is nothing by itself, but only how we are to carry out the empirical regressus, and how far we may continue it. And here we see a very important difference with regard to the rule of that progress. If the whole is given empirically, it is possible to go back in the series of its conditions *in infinitum*. But if the whole is not given, but has first to be given through an empirical regressus, I can only say that it is possible to proceed to still higher conditions of the series. In the former case I could say that more members exist and are empirically given than I can reach through the regressus (of decomposition); in the latter I can only say that I may advance still further in the regressus, because no member is empirically given as absolutely unconditioned, and a higher member therefore always possible, and therefore the enquiry for it necessary. In the former case it was necessary to *find* more members of the series, in the latter it is necessary to *enquire* for more, because no experience is absolutely limiting. For either you have no perception which absolutely limits your empirical regressus, and in that case you cannot consider that regressus as complete, or you have a perception which limits your series, and in that case it cannot be a part of your finished series (because what *limits* must be different from that which is *limited by it*), and you must therefore continue your regressus to that condition also, and so on for ever.

The following section, by showing their application, will place these observations in their proper light.

THE ANTINOMY OF PURE REASON

SECTION IX

Of the Empirical Use of the Regulative Principle of Reason with Regard to all Cosmological Ideas

No transcendental use, as we have shown on several occasions, can be made of the concepts either of the understanding or of reason; and the absolute totality of the series of conditions in the world of sense is due entirely to a transcendental use of reason, which demands this unconditioned completeness from what presupposes as a thing by itself. As no such thing is contained in the world of sense, we can never speak again of the absolute quantity of different series in it, whether they be limited or in themselves unlimited; but the question can only be, how far, in the empirical regressus, we may go back in tracing experience to its conditions, in order to stop, according to the rule of reason, at no other answer of its questions but such as is in accordance with the object.

What therefore remains to us is only the *validity of the principle of reason,* as a rule for the continuation and for the extent of a possible experience, after its invalidity, as a constitutive principle of things by themselves, has been sufficiently established. If we have clearly established that invalidity, the conflict of reason with itself will be entirely finished, because not only has the illusion which led to that conflict been removed through critical analysis, but in its place the sense in which reason agrees with itself, and the misapprehension of which was the only cause of conflict, has been clearly exhibited, and a principle formerly *dialectical* changed into a *doctrinal* one. In fact, if that principle, according to its subjective meaning, can be proved fit to determine the greatest possible use of the understanding in experience, as adequate to its objects, this would be the same as if it determined, as an axiom (which is impossible from pure reason), the objects themselves *a priori:* for this also could not, with reference to the objects of experience, exercise a greater influence on the extension and correction of our knowledge, than proving itself efficient in the most extensive use of our understanding, as applied to experience.

I

Solution of the Cosmological Idea of the Totality of the Composition of Phenomena in an Universe

Here, as well as in the other cosmological problems, the regulative principle of reason is founded on the proposition that, in the empirical regressus, *no experience of an absolute limit*, that is, of any condition as such, which *empirically is absolutely unconditioned*, can exist. The ground of this is that such an experience would contain a limitation of phenomena by nothing or by the void, on which the continued regressus by means of experience must abut; and this is impossible.

This proposition, which says that in an empirical regressus I can only arrive at the condition which itself must be considered empirically conditioned, contains the rule *in terminis*, that however far I may have reached in the ascending series, I must always enquire for a still higher member of that series, whether it be known to me by experience or not.

For the solution, therefore, of the first cosmological problem, nothing more is wanted than to determine whether, in the regressus to the unconditioned extension of the universe (in time and in space), this nowhere limited ascent is to be called a *regressus in infinitum*, or a *regressus in indefinitum*.

The mere general representation of the series of all past states of the world, and of the things which exist together in space, is itself nothing but a possible empirical regressus, which I represent to myself, though as yet as indefinite, and through which alone the concept of such a series of conditions of the perception given to me can arise.* Now the universe exists for me as a concept only, and never (as a whole) as an intuition. Hence I cannot from its quantity conclude the quantity of the regressus, and determine the one by the other; but I must first frame to myself a concept of the quantity of the world through the quantity of the empirical regressus. Of this, however, I never know anything more than that, empirically, I must go on

---

* This cosmical series can therefore be neither greater nor smaller than the possible empirical regressus on which alone its concept rests. And as this can give neither a definite infinite, nor a definite finite (absolutely limited), it becomes clear that we cannot accept the quantity of the world, either as finite or as infinite, because the regressus (by which it is represented) admits of neither the one nor the other.

from every given member of the series of conditions to a higher and more distant member. Hence the quantity of the whole of phenomena is not absolutely determined, and we cannot say therefore that it is a *regressus in infinitum,* because this would anticipate the members which the regressus has not yet reached, and represent its number as so large that no empirical synthesis could ever reach it. It would therefore (though negatively only) determine the quantity of the world prior to the regressus, which is impossible, because it is not given to me by any intuition (in its totality), so that its quantity cannot be given prior to the regressus. Hence we cannot say anything of the quantity or extension of the world by itself, not even that there is in it a *regressus in infinitum;* but we must look for the concept of its quantity according to the rule that determines the empirical regressus in it. This rule, however, says no more than that, however far we may have got in the series of empirical conditions, we ought never to assume an absolute limit, but subordinate every phenomenon, as conditioned, to another, as its condition, and that we must proceed further to that condition. This is the *regressus in indefinitum,* which, as it fixes no quantity in the object, can clearly enough be distinguished from the *regressus in infinitum.*

I cannot say therefore that, as to time past or as to space, the world is infinite. For such a concept of quantity, as a given infinity, is empirical, and therefore, with reference to the world as an object of the senses, absolutely impossible. Nor shall I say that the regressus, beginning with a given perception, and going on to everything that limits it in a series, both in space and in time past, goes on *in infinitum,* because this would presuppose an infinite quantity of the world. Nor can I say again that it is *finite,* for the absolute limit is likewise empirically impossible. Hence it follows that I shall not be able to say anything of the whole object of experience (the world of sense), but only of the rule, according to which experience can take place and be continued in accordance with its object.

To the cosmological question, therefore, respecting the quantity of the world, the first and negative answer is, that the world has no first beginning in time, and no extreme limit in space.

For, in the contrary case, the world would be limited by empty time and empty space. As however, as a phenomenon, it cannot, by itself, be either,—a phenomenon not being a thing by itself,—we should have to admit the perception of a limitation by means of absolute empty time or empty space, by which these limits of the world could be given in a possible experience. Such an experience, however, would be perfectly void of contents, and therefore impossible. Consequently an absolute limit of the world is impossible empirically, and therefore absolutely also.*

From this follows at the same time the affirmative answer, that the regressus in the series of the phenomena of the world, intended as a determination of the quantity of the world, goes on *in indefinitum,* which is the same as if we say that the world of sense has no absolute quantity, but that the empirical regressus (through which alone it can be given on the side of its conditions) has its own rule, namely, to advance from every member of the series, as conditioned, to a more distant member, whether by our own experience, or by the guidance of history, or through the chain of causes and their effects; and never to dispense with the extension of the possible empirical use of the understanding, this being the proper and really only task of reason and its principles.

We do not prescribe by this a definite empirical regressus advancing without end in a certain class of phenomena; as, for instance, that from a living person one ought always to ascend in a series of ancestors, without ever expecting a first pair; or, in the series of cosmical bodies, without admitting in the end an extremest sun. All that is demanded is a progressus from phenomena to phenomena, even if they should not furnish us with a real perception (if it is too weak in degree to become experience in our consciousness), because even thus they belong to a possible experience.

Every beginning is in time, and every limit of extension in space. Space and time, however, exist in the world of sense only. Hence phenomena only are limited *in the world* conditionally; the *world* itself, however, is limited neither conditionally nor unconditionally.

For the same reason, and because the world can never be given *complete,* and even the series of conditions of something

---

* It will have been observed that the argument has here been carried on in a very different way from the dogmatical argument, which was presented before, in the antithesis of the first antinomy. There we took the world of sense, according to the common and dogmatical view, as a thing given by itself, in its totality, before any regressus: and we had denied to it, if it did not occupy all time and all space, any place at all in both. Hence the conclusion also was different from what it is here, for it went to the real infinity of the world.

given as conditioned cannot, as a cosmical series, *be given as complete,* the concept of the quantity of the world can be given through the regressus only, and not before it in any collective intuition. That regressus, however, consists only in the *determining* of the quantity, and does not give, therefore, any *definite* concept, nor the concept of any quantity which, with regard to a certain measure, could be called infinite. It does not therefore proceed to the infinite (as if given), but only into an indefinite distance, in order to give a quantity (of experience) which has first to be realised by that very regressus.

II

Solution of the Cosmological Idea of the Totality of the Division of a Whole Given in Intuition

If I divide a whole, given in intuition, I proceed from the conditioned to the conditions of its possibility. The division of the parts (*subdivisio* or *decompositio*) is a regressus in the series of those conditions. The absolute totality of *this series* could only be given, if the regressus could reach the *simple* parts. But if all parts in a continuously progressing decomposition are always divisible again, then the division, that is, the regressus from the condition to its conditions, goes on *in infinitum;* because the conditions (the parts) are contained in the conditioned itself, and as that is given as complete in an intuition enclosed within limits, are all given with it. The regressus must therefore not be called a *regressus in indefinitum,* such as was alone allowed by the former cosmological idea, where from the conditioned we had to proceed to conditions outside it, and therefore not given at the same time through it, but first to be added in the empirical regressus. It is not allowed, however, even in the case of a whole that is divisible *in infinitum,* to say, *that it consists of infinitely many parts.* For although all parts are contained in the intuition of the whole, yet the *whole division* is not contained in it, because it consists in the continuous decomposition, or in the regressus itself, which first makes that series real. As this regressus is infinite, all members (parts) at which it arrives are contained, no doubt, in the given whole as *aggregates;* but not so the *whole series of the division,* which is successively infinite and never complete, and cannot, therefore, represent an infinite number, or any comprehension of it as a whole.

It is easy to apply this remark to space. Every space, perceived within its limits, is such a whole the parts of which, in spite of all decomposition, are always spaces again, and therefore divisible *in infinitum*.

From this follows, quite naturally, the second application to an external phenomenon, enclosed within its limits (body). The divisibility of this is founded on the divisibility of space, which constitutes the possibility of the body, as an extended whole. This is therefore divisible *in infinitum*, without consisting, however, of an infinite number of parts.

It might seem indeed, as a body must be represented as a substance in space, that, with regard to the law of the divisibility of space, it might differ from it, for we might possibly concede, that in the latter case decomposition could never do away with all composition, because in that case all space, which besides has nothing independent of its own, would cease to be (which is impossible), while, even if all composition of matter should be done away with in thought, it would not seem compatible with the concept of a substance that nothing should remain of it, because substance is meant to be the subject of all composition, and ought to remain in its elements, although their connection in space, by which they become a body, should have been removed. But, what applies to a thing by itself, represented by a pure concept of the understanding, does not apply to what is called substance, as a phenomenon. This is not an absolute subject, but only a permanent image of sensibility, nothing in fact but intuition, in which nothing unconditioned can ever be met with.

But although this rule of the progress *in infinitum* applies without any doubt to the subdivision of a phenomenon, as a mere occupant of space, it does not apply to the number of the parts, separated already in a certain way in a given whole, which thus constitute a *quantum discretum*. To suppose that in every organised whole every part is again organised, and that by thus dissecting the parts *in infinitum* we should meet again and again with new organised parts, in fact that the whole is organised *in infinitum*, is a thought difficult to think, though it is possible to think that the parts of matter decomposed *in infinitum* might become organised. For the infinity of the division of a given phenomenon in space is founded simply on this, that by it *divisibility* only, that is, an entirely indefinite number of parts, is given, while the parts themselves can only be given and determined through the subdivision, in short, that the whole is not itself already divided. Thus the division can determine a number in it, which goes so far as we like to go, in the regressus of a division. In an organic body, on the contrary, organised *in infinitum* the whole is by that very concept represented as divided, and a number of parts, definite in itself, and yet infinite, is found in it, before every regressus of division. This would be self-contradictory, because we should have to consider this infinite convolute as a never-to-be-completed series (infinite), and yet as complete in its (organised) comprehension. Infinite division takes the phenomenon only as a *quantum continuum,* and is inseparable from the occupation of space, because in this very occupation lies the ground of endless divisibility. But as soon as anything is taken as a *quantum discretum,* the number of units in it is determined, and therefore at all times equal to a certain number. How far the organisation in an organised body may go, experience alone can show us; but though it never arrived with certainty at any unorganised part, they would still have to be admitted as lying within possible experience. It is different with the transcendental division of a phenomenon. How far that may extend is not a matter of experience, but a principle of reason, which never allows us to consider the empirical regressus in the decomposition of extended bodies, according to the nature of these phenomena, as at any time absolutely completed.

*   *   *   *   *   *   *   *

Concluding Remarks on the Solution of the Transcendental-mathematical Ideas, and Preliminary Remark for the Solution of the Transcendental-dynamical Ideas

When exhibiting in a tabular form the antinomy of pure reason, through all the transcendental ideas, and indicating the ground of the conflict and the only means of removing it, by declaring both contradictory statements as false, we always represented the conditions as belonging to that which they conditioned, according to relations of space and time, this being the ordinary supposition of the common understanding, and in fact the source from which that conflict arose. In that respect all dialectical representations of the totality in a series of conditions of something given as conditioned were always of the *same character.* It was always a series in which the condition was connected with the conditioned, as members of the same series, both being thus *homogeneous.* In such a series the regressus was never conceived as completed, or, if that had to be done, one of the members, being in itself conditioned, had wrongly to be accepted as the first, and therefore as unconditioned. If not always the object, that is, the conditioned, yet the series of its conditions was always considered according to quantity only, and then the difficulty arose (which could not be removed by any compromise, but only by cutting the knot), that reason made it either *too long or too short* for the understanding, which could in neither case come up to the idea.

But in this we have overlooked an essential distinction between the objects, that is, the concepts of the understanding, which reason tries to raise into ideas. Two of them, according to the above table of the categories, imply a *mathematical,* the remaining two a *dynamical* synthesis of phenomena. Hitherto this overlooking was of no great importance, because, in the general representation of all transcendental ideas, we always remained under *phenomenal* conditions, and with regard to the two transcendental-mathematical ideas also, we had to do with no object but the phenomenal only. Now, however, as we have come to consider the *dynamical* concepts of the understanding, so far as they should be rendered adequate to the idea of reason, that distinction becomes important, and opens to us an entirely new insight into the character of the suit in which reason is implicated. That suit had before been dismissed, as resting on both sides on wrong presuppositions. Now, however, as there seems to be in the dynamical antinomy such a presupposition as may be compatible with the pretensions of reason, and as the judge himself supplies perhaps the deficiency of legal grounds, which had been misunderstood on both sides, the suit may possibly be adjusted, from this point of view, to the satisfaction of both parties, which was impossible in the conflict of the mathematical antinomy.

If we merely look to the extension of the series of conditions, and whether they are adequate to the idea, or whether the idea is too large or too small for them, the series are no doubt all homogeneous. But the concept of the understanding on which these ideas are founded contains either a *synthesis* of the *homogeneous* only (which is presupposed in the composition as well as the decomposition of every quantity), or of the *heterogeneous* also, which must at least be admitted as possible in the dynamical synthesis, both in a causal connection, and in the connection of the necessary with the contingent.

Thus it happens that none but sensuous conditions can enter into the mathematical connection of the series of phenomena, that is, conditions which themselves are part of the series;

while the dynamical series of sensuous conditions admits also of a heterogeneous condition, which is not a part of the series, but, as merely intelligible, outside it; so that a certain satisfaction is given to reason by the unconditioned being placed before the phenomena, without disturbing the series of the phenomena, which must always be conditioned, or breaking it off, contrary to the principles of the understanding.

Owing to the dynamical ideas admitting of a condition of the phenomena outside their series, that is, a condition which itself is not a phenomenon, something arises which is totally different from the result of the mathematical[4] antinomy. The result of that antinomy was, that both the contradictory dialectical statements had to be declared false. The throughout conditioned character, however, of the dynamical series, which is inseparable from them as phenomena, if connected with the empirically unconditioned, but at the same time *not sensuous* condition, may give satisfaction to the *understanding* on one, and the *reason* on the other side,* because the dialectical arguments which, in some way or other, required unconditioned totality in mere phenomena, vanish; while the propositions of reason, if thus amended, may *both be true.* This cannot be the case with the cosmological ideas, which refer only to a mathematically unconditioned unity, because with them no condition can be found in the series of phenomena which is not itself a phenomenon, and as such constitutes one of the links of the series.

III

Solution of the Cosmological Ideas with Regard to the Totality of the Derivation of Cosmical Events from their Causes

We can conceive two kinds of causality only with reference to events, causality either of *nature* or of *freedom.* The former is the connection of one state in the world of sense with a pre-

---

[4] Mathematical, omitted in the First and Second Editions.
* The understanding admits of no condition *among phenomena,* which should itself be empirically unconditioned. But if we might conceive an *intelligible condition,* that is to say, a condition, not belonging itself as a link to the series of phenomena, of something conditioned (as a phenomenon) without in the least interrupting the series of empirical conditions, such a condition might be admitted as *empirically unconditioned,* without interfering with the empirical continuous regressus.

ceding state, on which it follows according to a rule. As the *causality* of phenomena depends on conditions of time, and as the preceding state, if it had always existed, could not have produced an effect, which first takes place in time, it follows that the causality of the cause of that which happens or arises must, according to the principle of the understanding, have itself *arisen* and require a cause.

By freedom, on the contrary, in its cosmological meaning, I understand the faculty of beginning a state *spontaneously*. Its causality, therefore, does not depend, according to the law of nature, on another cause, by which it is determined in time. In this sense freedom is a purely transcendental idea, which, first, contains nothing derived from *experience*, and, secondly, the object of which cannot be determined in any *experience*; because it is a general rule, even of the possibility of all *experience*, that everything which happens has a cause, and that therefore the causality also of the cause, which *itself has happened* or arisen, must again have a cause. In this manner the whole field of experience, however far it may extend, has been changed into one great whole of nature. As, however, it is impossible in this way to arrive at an absolute totality of the conditions in causal relations, reason creates for itself the idea of spontaneity, or the power of beginning by itself, without an antecedent cause determining it to action, according to the law of causal connection.

It is extremely remarkable, that the practical concept of freedom is founded on the *transcendental idea of freedom*, which constitutes indeed the real difficulty which at all times has surrounded the question of the possibility of freedom. *Freedom*, in its *practical sense*, is the independence of our (arbitrary) will from the *coercion* through sensuous impulses. Our (arbitrary) will is *sensuous*, so far as it is *affected pathologically* (by sensuous impulses); it is called animal (*arbitrium brutum*), if *necessitated* pathologically. The human will is certainly sensuous, an *arbitrium sensitivum*, but not *brutum*, but *liberum*, because sensuous impulses do not necessitate its action, but there is in man a faculty of determination, independent of the necessitation through sensuous impulses.

It can easily be seen that, if all causality in the world of sense belonged to nature, every event would be determined in time through another, according to necessary laws. As therefore the phenomena, in determining the will, would render every act necessary as their natural effect, the annihilation of transcendental freedom would at the same time destroy all practical freedom. Practical freedom presupposes that, although something has not happened, it *ought* to have happened, and that its cause therefore had not that determining force among phenomena, which could prevent the causality of our will from producing, independently of those natural causes, and even contrary to their force and influence, something determined in the order of time, according to empirical laws, and from originating *entirely by itself* a series of events.

What happens here is what happens generally in the conflict of reason venturing beyond the limits of possible experience, namely, that the problem is not *physiological,* but *transcendental.* Hence the question of the possibility of freedom concerns no doubt psychology; but its solution, as it depends on dialectical arguments of pure reason, belongs entirely to transcendental philosophy. In order to enable that philosophy to give a satisfactory answer, which it cannot decline to do, I must first try to determine more accurately its proper procedure in this task.

If phenomena were things by themselves, and therefore space and time forms of the existence of things by themselves, the conditions together with the conditioned would always belong, as members, to one and the same series, and thus in our case also, the antinomy which is common to all transcendental ideas would arise, namely, that that series is inevitably too large or too small for the understanding. The dynamical concepts of reason, however, which we have to discuss in this and the following section, have this peculiarity that, as they are not concerned with an object, considered as a quantity, but only with its *existence,* we need take no account of the quantity of the series of conditions. All depends here only on the dynamical relation of conditions to the conditioned, so that in the question on nature and freedom we at once meet with the difficulty, whether freedom is indeed possible, and whether, if it is possible, it can exist together with the universality of the natural law of causality. The question in fact arises, whether it is a proper disjunctive proposition to say, that every effect in the world must arise, *either* from nature, *or* from freedom, or whether *both* cannot coexist in the same event in different relations. The correctness of the principle of the unbroken connection of all events in the world of sense, according to unchangeable natural laws, is firmly established by the transcendental Analytic, and admits of no limitation. The question, therefore, can only be whether, in spite of it, freedom also can be found in the same effect which is determined by nature; or whether freedom is entirely excluded by that inviolable rule? Here the common but fallacious supposition of the *absolute reality* of phenomena shows at once its pernicious influence in embarrassing reason. For if phenomena are things by themselves, freedom cannot be saved. Nature in that case is the complete and sufficient cause determining every event, and its condition is always contained in that series of phenomena only which, together with their effect, are necessary under the law of nature. If, on the contrary, phenomena are taken for nothing except what they are in reality, namely, not things by themselves, but representations only, which are connected with each other according to empirical laws, they must themselves have causes, which are not phenomenal. Such an intelligible cause, however, is not determined with reference to its causality by phenomena, although its effects become phenomenal, and can thus be determined by other phenomena. That intelligible cause, therefore, with its causality, is outside the series, though its effects are to be found in the series of empirical conditions. The effect therefore can, with reference to its intelligible cause, be considered as free, and yet at the same time, with reference to phenomena, as resulting from them according to the necessity of nature; a distinction which, if thus represented, in a general and entirely abstract form, may seem extremely subtle and obscure, but will become clear in its practical application. Here I only wished to remark that, as the unbroken *connection* of all phenomena in the context (woof) of nature, is an unalterable law, it would necessarily destroy all freedom, if we were to defend obstinately the reality of phenomena. Those, therefore, who follow the common opinion on this subject, have never been able to reconcile nature and freedom.

Possibility of a Causality through Freedom, in Harmony with the Universal Law of Natural Necessity

Whatever in an object of the senses is not itself phenomenal, I call *intelligible*. If, therefore, what in the world of sense must be considered as phenomenal, possesses in itself a faculty which is not the object of sensuous intuition, but through which it can become the cause of phenomena, the *causality* of that being may be considered from *two sides*, as *intelligible* in its *action*, as the causality of a thing by itself, and as *sensible* in the *effects* of the action, as the causality of a phenomenon in the world of sense. Of the faculty of such a being we should have to form both an *empirical* and an *intellectual concept* of its causality, both of which consist together in one and the same effect. This twofold way of conceiving the faculty of an object of the senses does not contradict any of the concepts which we have to form of phenomena and of a possible experience. For as all phenomena, not being things by themselves, must have for their foundation a transcendental object, determining them as mere representations, there is nothing to prevent us from attributing to that transcendental object, besides the quality through which it becomes phenomenal, a *causality* also which is not phenomenal, although its *effect* appears in the phenomenon. Every efficient cause, however, must have a *character*, that is, a rule according to which it manifests its causality, and without which it would not be a cause. According to this we should have in every subject of the world of sense, first, an *empirical character*, through which its acts, as phenomena, stand with other phenomena in an unbroken connection, according to permanent laws of nature, and could be derived from them as their conditions, and in connection with them form the links of one and the same series in the order of nature. Secondly, we should have to allow to it an *intelligible character* also, by which, it is true, it becomes the cause of the same acts as phenomena, but which itself is not subject to any conditions of sensibility, and never phenomenal. We might call the former the character of such a thing as a phenomenon, in the latter the character of the thing by itself.

According to its intelligible character, this active subject would not depend on conditions of time, for time is only the condition of phenomena, and not of things by themselves. In it no *act* would *arise* or *perish*, neither would it be subject therefore to the law of determination in time and of all that is changeable, namely, that everything *which happens* must have its cause in *the phenomena* (of the previous state). In one word its causality, so far as it is intelligible, would not have a place in the series of empirical conditions by which the event is rendered necessary in the world of sense. It is true that that intelligible character could never be known immediately, because we cannot perceive anything, except so far as it appears, but it would nevertheless have to be conceived, according to the empirical character, as we must always admit in thought a transcendental object, as the foundation of phenomena, though we know nothing of what it is by itself.

In its empirical character, therefore, that subject, as a phenomenon, would submit, according to all determining laws, to a causal nexus, and in that respect it would be nothing but a part of the world of sense, the effects of which, like every other phenomenon, would arise from nature without fail. As soon as external phenomena began to influence it, and as soon as its empirical character, that is the law of its causality, had been known through experience, all its actions ought to admit of explanation, according to the laws of nature, and all that is requisite for its complete and necessary determination would be found in a possible experience.

In its intelligible character, however (though we could only have a general concept of it), the same subject would have to be considered free from all influence of sensibility, and from all determination through phenomena: and as in it, so far as it is a *noumenon*, nothing *happens*, and no change which requires dynamical determination of time, and therefore no connection with phenomena as causes, can exist, that active being would so far be quite independent and free in its acts from all natural necessity, which can exist in the world of sense only. One might say of it with perfect truth that it originates its effects in the world of sense *by itself*, though the act does not begin *in itself*. And this would be perfectly true, though the effects in the world of sense need not therefore originate by themselves, because in it they are always determined previously through empirical conditions in the previous time, though only by means of the empirical character (which is the phenomenal appearance of the intelligible character), and therefore impossible, except as a continuation of the series of natural causes. In this way freedom and nature, each in its complete signification, might exist together and without any conflict in the same action, according as we refer it to its intelligible or to its sensible cause.

Explanation of the Cosmological Idea of Freedom in Connection with the General Necessity of Nature

I thought it best to give first this sketch of the solution of our transcendental problem, so that the course which reason has to adopt in its solution might be more clearly surveyed. We shall now proceed to explain more fully the points on which the decision properly rests, and examine each by itself.

The law of nature, that everything which happens has a cause,—that the causality of that cause, that is, its *activity* (as it is anterior in time, and, with regard to an effect which has *arisen,* cannot itself have always existed, but must have *happened* at some time), must have its cause among the phenomena by which it is determined, and that therefore all events in the order of nature are empirically determined, this law, I say, through which alone phenomena become *nature* and objects of experience, is a law of the understanding, which can on no account be surrendered, and from which no single phenomenon can be exempted; because in doing this we should place it outside all possible experience, separate from all objects of possible experience, and change it into a mere fiction of the mind or a cobweb of the brain.

But although this looks merely like a chain of causes, which in the regressus to its conditions admits of no *absolute totality,* this difficulty does not detain us in the least, because it has already been removed in the general criticism of the antinomy of reason when, starting from the series of phenomena, it aims at the unconditioned. Were we to yield to the illusion of transcendental realism, we should have neither nature nor freedom. The question therefore is, whether, if we recognise in the whole series of events nothing but natural necessity, we may yet regard the same event which on one side is an effect of nature only, on the other side, as an effect of freedom; or whether there is a direct contradiction between these two kinds of causality?

There can certainly be nothing among phenomenal causes that could originate a series absolutely and by itself. Every action, as a phenomenon, so far as it produces an event, is itself an event, presupposing another state, in which its cause can be discovered; and thus everything that happens is only a continuation of the series, and no beginning, happening by itself, is possible in it. Actions of natural causes in the succession of time are therefore themselves effects, which likewise presuppose causes in the series of time. A *spontaneous* and original action by which something takes place, which did not exist before, cannot be expected from the causal nexus of phenomena.

But is it really necessary that, if effects are phenomena, the causality of their cause, which cause itself is phenomenal, could be nothing but empirical; or is it not possible, although for every phenomenal effect a connection with its cause, according to the laws of empirical causality, is certainly required, that empirical causality itself could nevertheless, without breaking in the least its connection with the natural causes, represent an effect of a non-empirical and intelligible causality, that is, of a caused action, original in respect to phenomena, and in so far not phenomenal; but, with respect to this faculty, intelligible, although, as a link in the chain of nature, to be regarded as entirely belonging to the world of sense?

We require the principle of the causality of phenomena among themselves, in order to be able to look for and to produce natural conditions, that is, phenomenal causes of natural events. If this is admitted and not weakened by any exceptions, the understanding, which in its empirical employment recognises in all events nothing but nature, and is quite justified in doing so, has really all that it can demand, and the explanations of physical phenomena may proceed without let or hindrance. The understanding would not be wronged in the least, if we assumed, though it be a mere fiction, that some among the natural causes have a faculty which is intelligible only, and whose determination to activity does not rest on empirical conditions, but on mere grounds of the intellect, if only the *phenomenal activity* of that cause is in accordance with all the laws of empirical causality. For in this way the active subject, as *causa phaenomenon*, would be joined with nature through the indissoluble dependence of all its actions, and the noumenon[5] only of that subject (with all its phenomenal causality) would contain certain conditions which, if we want to ascend from the empirical to the transcendental object, would have to be considered as intelligible only. For, if only we follow the rule of nature in that which may be the cause among phenomena, it is indifferent to us what kind of ground of those phenomena, and of their connection, may be conceived to exist in the transcendental subject, which is empirically unknown to us. This intelligible ground does not touch the empirical questions, but concerns only, as it would seem, the thought in the pure understanding; and although the effects of that thought and action of the pure understanding may be discovered in the phenomena, these have nevertheless to be completely explained from their phenomenal cause, according to the laws of nature, by taking their empirical character as the highest ground of explanation, and passing by the intelligible character, which is the transcendental cause of the other, as entirely unknown, except so far as it is indicated by the empirical, as its sensuous sign. Let us apply this to experience. Man is one among the phenomena of the world of sense, and in so far one of the natural causes the causality of which must be subject to empirical laws. As such he must therefore

[5] It seems better to read *noumenon* instead of *phenomenon*.

have an empirical character, like all other objects of nature. We perceive it through the forces and faculties which he shows in his actions and effects. In the lifeless or merely animal nature we see no ground for admitting any faculty, except as sensuously conditioned. Man, however, who knows all the rest of nature through his senses only, knows himself through mere apperception also, and this in actions and internal determinations, which he cannot ascribe to the impressions of the senses. Man is thus to himself partly a phenomenon, partly, however, namely with reference to certain faculties, a purely intelligible object, because the actions of these faculties cannot be ascribed to the receptivity of sensibility. We call these faculties understanding and reason. It is the latter, in particular, which is entirely distinguished from all empirically conditioned forces or faculties, because it weighs its objects according to ideas, and determines the understanding accordingly, which then makes an empirical use of its (by themselves, however pure) concepts.

That our reason possesses causality, or that we at least represent to ourselves such a causality in it, is clear from the *imperatives* which, in all practical matters, we impose as rules on our executive powers. The *ought* expresses a kind of necessity and connection with causes, which we do not find elsewhere in the whole of nature. The understanding can know in nature only what is present, past, or future. It is impossible that anything in it *ought to be* different from what it is in reality, in all these relations of time. Nay, if we only look at the course of nature, the ought has no meaning whatever. We cannot ask, what ought to be in nature, as little as we can ask, what qualities a circle ought to possess. We can only ask what happens in it, and what qualities that which happens has.

This ought expresses a possible action, the ground of which cannot be anything but a mere concept; while in every merely natural action the ground must always be a phenomenon. Now it is quite true that the action to which the ought applies must be possible under natural conditions, but these natural conditions do not affect the determination of the will itself, but only its effects and results among phenomena. There may be ever so many natural grounds which impel me to *will* and ever so many sensuous temptations, but they can never produce the *ought,* but only a willing which is always conditioned, but by no means necessary, and to which the ought, pronounced by reason, opposes measure, ay, prohibition and authority. Whether it be an object of the senses merely (pleas-

ure), or of pure reason (the good), reason does not yield to
the impulse that is given empirically, and does not follow the
order of things, as they present themselves as phenomena, but
frames for itself, with perfect spontaneity, a new order according to ideas to which it adapts the empirical conditions,
and according to which it declares actions to be necessary,
even though they *have not taken place,* and, maybe, never will
take place. Yet it is presupposed that reason may have causality with respect to them, for otherwise no effects in experience
could be expected to result from these ideas.

Now let us take our stand here and admit it at least as possible, that reason really possesses causality with reference to
phenomena. In that case, reason though it be, it must show
nevertheless an empirical character, because every cause presupposes a rule according to which certain phenomena follow
as effects, and every rule requires in the effects a homogeneousness, on which the concept of cause (as a faculty) is
founded. This, so far as it is derived from mere phenomena,
may be called the empirical character, which is *permanent,*
while the effects, according to a diversity of concomitant, and
in part, restraining conditions, appear in *changeable* forms.

Every man therefore has an empirical character of his (arbitrary) will, which is nothing but a certain causality of his
reason, exhibiting in its phenomenal actions and effects a rule,
according to which one may infer the motives of reason and
its actions, both in kind and in degree, and judge of the subjective principles of his will. As that empirical character itself
must be derived from phenomena, as an effect, and from their
rule which is supplied by experience, all the acts of a man, so
far as they are phenomena, are determined from his empirical
character and from the other concomitant causes, according
to the order of nature; and if we could investigate all the manifestations of his will to the very bottom, there would be not a
single human action which we could not predict with certainty
and recognise from its preceding conditions as necessary.
There is no freedom therefore with reference to this empirical
character, and yet it is only with reference to it that we can
consider man, when we are merely *observing,* and, as is the
case in anthropology, trying to investigate the motive causes
of his actions physiologically.

If, however, we consider the same actions with reference to
reason, not with reference to speculative reason, in order to
explain their origin, but solely so far as reason is the cause
which *produces* them; in one word, if we compare actions

with reason, with reference to *practical* purposes, we find a rule and order, totally different from the order of nature. For, from this point of view, everything, it may be, *ought not to have happened*, which according to the course of nature *has happened*, and according to its empirical grounds, was inevitable. And sometimes we find, or believe at least that we find, that the ideas of reason have really proved their causality with reference to human actions as phenomena, and that these actions have taken place, not because they were determined by empirical causes, but by the causes of reason.

Now supposing one could say that reason possesses causality in reference to phenomena, could the action of reason be called free in that case, as it is accurately determined by the empirical character (the disposition) and rendered necessary by it? That character again is determined in the intelligible character (way of thinking). The latter, however, we do not know, but signify only through phenomena, which in reality give us immediately a knowledge of the disposition (empirical character) only.* An action, so far as it is to be attributed to the way of thinking as its cause, does nevertheless not result from it according to empirical laws, that is, it is not *preceded* by the conditions of pure reason, but only by its effects in the phenomenal form of the internal sense. Pure reason, as a simple intelligible faculty, is not subject to the form of time, or to the conditions of the succession of time. The causality of reason in its intelligible character does *not arise* or begin at a certain time in order to produce an effect; for in that case it would be subject to the natural law of phenomena, which determines all causal series in time, and its causality would then be nature and not freedom. What, therefore, we can say is, that if reason can possess causality with reference to phenomena, it is a faculty *through which* the sensuous condition of an empirical series of effects first begins. For the condition that lies in reason is not sensuous, and therefore does itself not begin. Thus we get what we missed in all empirical series, namely, that the *condition* of a successive series of events should itself be empirically unconditioned. For here the condi-

---

* The true morality of actions (merit or guilt), even that of our own conduct, remains therefore entirely hidden. Our imputations can refer to the empirical character only. How much of that may be the pure effect of freedom, how much should be ascribed to nature only, and to the faults of temperament, for which man is not responsible, or its happy constitution (*merito fortunae*), no one can discover, and no one can judge with perfect justice.

tion is really *outside* the series of phenomena (in the intelligible), and therefore not subject to any sensuous condition, nor to any temporal determination through preceding causes.

Nevertheless the same cause belongs also, in another respect, to the series of phenomena. Man himself is a phenomenon. His will has an empirical character, which is the (empirical) cause of all his actions. There is no condition, determining man according to this character, that is not contained in the series of natural effects and subject to their law, according to which there can be no empirically unconditioned causality of anything that happens in time. No given action therefore (as it can be perceived as a phenomenon only) can begin absolutely by itself. Of pure reason, however, we cannot say that the state in which it determines the will is preceded by another in which that state itself is determined. For as reason itself is not a phenomenon, and not subject to any of the conditions of sensibility, there exists in it, even in reference to its causality, no succession of time, and the dynamical law of nature, which determines the succession of time according to rules, cannot be applied to it.

Reason is therefore the constant condition of all free actions by which man takes his place in the phenomenal world. Every one of them is determined beforehand in his empirical character, before it becomes actual. With regard to the intelligible character, however, of which the empirical is only the sensuous schema, there is neither *before* nor *after;* and every action, without regard to the temporal relation which connects it with other phenomena, is the immediate effect of the intelligible character of pure reason. That reason therefore acts freely, without being determined dynamically, in the chain of natural causes, by external or internal conditions, anterior in time. That freedom must then not only be regarded negatively, as independence of empirical conditions (for in that case the faculty of reason would cease to be a cause of phenomena), but should be determined positively also, as the faculty of beginning spontaneously a series of events. Hence nothing begins in reason itself, and being itself the unconditioned condition of every free action, reason admits of no condition antecedent in time above itself, while nevertheless its effect takes its beginning in the series of phenomena, though it can never constitute in that series an *absolutely* first beginning.

In order to illustrate the regulative principle of reason by an example of its empirical application, not in order to confirm it (for such arguments are useless for transcendental propositions), let us take a voluntary action, for example, a malicious lie, by which a man has produced a certain confusion in society, and of which we first try to find out the motives, and afterwards try to determine how far it and its consequences may be imputed to the offender. With regard to the first point, one has first to follow up his empirical character to its very sources, which are to be found in wrong education, bad society, in part also in the viciousness of a natural disposition, and a nature insensible to shame, or ascribed to frivolity and heedlessness, not omitting the occasioning causes at the time. In all this the procedure is exactly the same as in the investigation of a series of determining causes of a given natural effect. But although one believes that the act was thus determined, one nevertheless blames the offender, and not on account of his unhappy natural disposition, not on account of influencing circumstances, not even on account of his former course of life, because one supposes one might leave entirely out of account what that course of life may have been, and consider the past series of conditions as having never existed, and the act itself as totally unconditioned by previous states, as if the offender had begun with it a new series of effects, quite by himself. This blame is founded on a law of reason, reason being considered as a cause which, independent of all the before-mentioned empirical conditions, would and should have determined the behaviour of the man otherwise. Nay, we do not regard the causality of reason as a concurrent agency only, but as complete in itself, even though the sensuous motives did not favour, but even oppose it. The action is imputed to a man's intelligible character. At the moment when he tells the lie, the guilt is entirely his; that is, we regard reason, in spite of all empirical conditions of the act, as completely free, and the act has to be imputed entirely to a fault of reason.

Such an imputation clearly shows that we imagine that reason is not affected at all by the influences of the senses, and that it does not change (although its manifestations, that is the mode in which it shows itself by its effects, do change): that in it no state precedes as determining a following state, in fact, that reason does not belong to the series of sensuous conditions which render phenomena necessary, according to laws of nature. Reason, it is supposed, is present in all the actions of man, in all circumstances of time, and always the same; but it is itself never in time, never in a new state in which it was not before; it is *determining,* never *determined.*

We cannot ask, therefore, why reason has not determined itself differently, but only why it has not differently determined the *phenomena* by its causality. And here no answer is really possible. For a different intelligible character would have given a different empirical character, and if we say that, in spite of the whole of his previous course of life, the offender could have avoided the lie, this only means that it was in the power of reason, and that reason, in its causality, is subject to no phenomenal and temporal conditions, and lastly, that the difference of time, though it makes a great difference in phenomena and their relation to each other, can, as these are neither things nor causes by themselves, produce no difference of action in reference to reason.

We thus see that, in judging of voluntary actions, we can, so far as their causality is concerned, get only so far as the intelligible cause, but not beyond. We can see that that cause is free, that it determines as independent of sensibility, and therefore is capable of being the sensuously unconditioned condition of phenomena. To explain why that intelligible character should, under present circumstances, give these phenomena and this empirical character, and no other, transcends all the powers of our reason, nay, all its rights of questioning, as if we were to ask why the transcendental object of our external sensuous intuition gives us intuition in *space* only and no other. But the problem which we have to solve does not require us to ask or to answer such questions. Our problem was, whether freedom is contradictory to natural necessity in one and the same action: and this we have sufficiently answered by showing that freedom may have relation to a very different kind of conditions from those of nature, so that the law of the latter does not affect the former, and both may exist independent of, and undisturbed by, each other.

*　　*　　*　　*　　*　　*　　*　　*

It should be clearly understood that, in what we have said, we had no intention of establishing the *reality* of freedom, as one of the faculties which contain the cause of the phenomenal appearances in our world of sense. For not only would this have been no transcendental consideration at all, which is concerned with concepts only, but it could never have succeeded, because from experience we can never infer anything but what must be represented in thought according to the laws of experience. It was not even our intention to prove the *possibility* of freedom, for in this also we should not have succeeded, because from mere concepts *a priori* we can never know the possibility of any real ground or any causality. We have here treated freedom as a transcendental idea only, which makes reason imagine that it can absolutely begin the series of phenomenal conditions through what is sensuously unconditioned, but by which reason becomes involved in an antinomy with its own laws, which it had prescribed to the empirical use of the understanding. That this antinomy rests on a mere illusion, and that nature does *not contradict* the causality of freedom, that was the only thing which we could prove, and cared to prove.

IV

Solution of the Cosmological Idea of the Totality of the Dependence of Phenomena, with Regard to their Existence in General

In the preceding article we considered the changes in the world of sense in their dynamical succession, every one being subordinate to another as its cause. Now, however, the succession of states is to serve only as our guide in order to arrive at an existence that might be the highest condition of all that is subject to change, namely, the *necessary Being*. We are concerned here, not with the unconditioned causality, but with the unconditioned existence of the substance itself. Therefore the succession which we have before us is properly one of concepts and not of intuitions, so far as the one is the condition of the other.

It is easy to see, however, that as everything comprehended under phenomena is changeable, and therefore conditioned in its existence, there cannot be, in the whole series of dependent existence, any unconditioned link the existence of which might be considered as absolutely necessary, and that therefore, if phenomena were things by themselves, and their condition accordingly belonged with the conditioned always to one and the same series of intuitions, a necessary being, as the condition of the existence of the phenomena of the world of sense, could never exist.

The dynamical regressus has this peculiar distinction as compared with the mathematical, that, as the latter is only concerned with the composition of parts in forming a whole or the division of a whole into its parts, the conditions of that series must always be considered as parts of it, and therefore as homogeneous and as phenomena, while in the dynamical regressus, where we are concerned, not with the possibility of an unconditioned whole, consisting of a number of given parts, or of an unconditioned part belonging to a given whole, but with the derivation of a state from its cause, or of the contingent existence of the substance itself from the necessary substance, it is not required that the condition should form one and the same empirical series with the conditioned.

There remains therefore to us another escape from this apparent antinomy: because both conflicting propositions might, under different aspects, be true at the same time. That is, all things of the world of sense might be entirely contingent, and have therefore an empirically conditioned existence only, though there might nevertheless be a non-empirical condition of the whole series, that is, an unconditionally necessary being. For this, as an intelligible condition, would not belong to the series, as a link of it (not even as the highest link), nor would it render any link of that series empirically unconditioned, but would leave the whole world of sense, in all its members, in its empirically conditioned existence. This manner of admitting an unconditioned existence as the ground of phenomena would differ from the empirically unconditioned causality (freedom), treated of in the preceding article, because, with respect to freedom, the thing itself, as cause (*substantia phaenomenon*), belonged to the series of conditions, and its causality only was represented as intelligible, while here, on the contrary, the necessary being has to be conceived as lying outside the series of the world of sense (as *ens extramundanum*), and as purely intelligible, by which alone it could be guarded against itself becoming subject to the law of contingency and dependence applying to all phenomena.

The *regulative principle* of reason, with regard to our present problem, is therefore this, that everything in the world of sense has an empirically conditioned existence, and that in it there is never any unconditioned necessity with reference to any quality; that there is no member in the series of conditions of which one ought not to expect, and as far as possible to seek, the empirical condition in some possible experience; and that we are never justified in deriving any existence from a condition outside the empirical series, or in considering it as independent and self-subsistent in the series itself; without however denying in the least that the whole series may depend on some intelligible being, which is free therefore from all empirical conditions, and itself contains rather the ground of the possibility of all those phenomena.

By this we by no means intend to prove the unconditionally necessary existence of such a being, or even to demonstrate the possibility of a purely intelligible condition of the existence of the phenomena of the world of sense. But as on the one side we limit reason, lest it should lose the thread of the empirical condition and lose itself in *transcendent* explanations incapable of being represented *in concreto,* thus, on the other side, we want to limit the law of the purely empirical use of the understanding, lest it should venture to decide on the possibility of things in general, and declare the intelligible to be *impossible,* because it has been shown to be useless for the explanation of phenomena. What is shown by this is simply this, that the complete contingency of all things in nature and of all their (empirical) conditions, may well coexist with the arbitrary presupposition of a necessary, though purely intelligible condition, and that, as there is no real contradiction between these two views, they *may well both be true.* Granted even that such an absolutely necessary being, as postulated by the understanding, is impossible in itself, we still maintain that this cannot be concluded from the general contingency and dependence of all that belongs to the world of sense, nor from the principle that we ought not to stop at any single member so far as it is contingent, and appeal to a cause outside the world. Reason follows its own course in its empirical, and again a peculiar course in its transcendental use.

The world of sense contains nothing but phenomena, and these are mere representations which are always sensuously conditioned. As our objects are never things by themselves, we need not be surprised that we are never justified in making a jump from any member of the several empirical series, beyond the connection of sensibility, as if they were things by themselves, existing apart from their transcendental ground, and which we might leave behind in order to seek for the cause of their existence outside them. This, no doubt, would have to be done in the end with contingent *things,* but not with mere *representations* of things, the contingency of which is itself a phenomenon, and cannot lead to any other regressus but that which determines the phenomena, that is, which is empirical. To conceive, however, an intelligible ground of phenomena, that is, of the world of sense, and to conceive it as freed from the contingency of the latter, does not run counter

either to the unlimited empirical regressus in the series of phenomena, nor to their general contingency. And this is really
the only thing which we had to do in order to remove this
apparent antinomy, and which could be done in this wise only.
For if every condition of everything conditioned (according to
its existence) is sensuous, and therefore belongs to the series,
that series is again conditioned (as shown in the antithesis of
the fourth antinomy). Either therefore there would remain a
conflict with reason, which postulates the unconditioned, or
this would have to be placed outside the series, i.e. in the intelligible, the necessity of which neither requires nor admits of
any empirical condition, and is therefore, as regards phenomena, unconditionally necessary.

The empirical use of reason (with regard to the conditions
of existence in the world of sense) is not affected by the admission of a purely intelligible being, but ascends, according
to the principle of a general contingency, from empirical conditions to higher ones, which again are empirical. This regulative principle, however, does not exclude the admission of
an intelligible cause not comprehended in the series, when we
come to the pure use of reason (with reference to ends or
aims). For in this case, an intelligible cause only means the
transcendental, and, to us, unknown ground of the possibility
of the sensuous series in general, and the existence of this,
independent of all conditions of the sensuous series, and, in
reference to it, unconditionally, necessary, is by no means opposed to the unlimited contingency of the former, nor to the
never-ending regressus in the series of empirical conditions.

Concluding Remark on the Whole Antinomy of Pure Reason

So long as it is only the totality of the conditions in the
world of sense and the interest it can have to reason, that form
the object of the concepts of our reason, our ideas are no
doubt transcendental, but yet *cosmological.* If, however, we
place the unconditioned (with which we are chiefly concerned) in that which is entirely outside the world of sense,
therefore beyond all possible experience, our ideas become
transcendent: for they serve not only for the completion of the
empirical use of the understanding (which always remains an
idea that must be obeyed, though it can never be fully carried
out), but they separate themselves entirely from it, and create
to themselves objects the material of which is not taken from

experience, and the objective reality of which does not rest on the completion of the empirical series, but on pure concepts *a priori*. Such transcendent ideas have a merely intelligible object, which may indeed be admitted as a transcendental object, of which, for the rest, we know nothing, but for which, if we wish to conceive it as a thing determined by its internal distinguishing predicates, we have neither grounds of possibility (as independent of all concepts of experience) nor the slightest justification on our side in admitting it as an object, and which, therefore, is a mere creation of our thoughts. Nevertheless that cosmological idea, which owes its origin to the fourth antinomy, urges us on to take that step. For the conditioned existence of all phenomena, not being founded in itself, requires us to look out for something different from all phenomena, that is, for an intelligible object in which there should be no more contingency. As, however, if we have once allowed ourselves to admit, outside the field of the whole of sensibility, a reality existing by itself, phenomena can only be considered as contingent modes of representing intelligible objects on the part of beings which themselves are intelligences,[6] nothing remains to us, in order to form some kind of concept of intelligible things, of which in themselves we have not the slightest knowledge, but analogy, applied to the concepts of experience. As we know the contingent by experience only, but have here to deal with things which are not meant to be objects of experience, we shall have to derive our knowledge of them from what is necessary in itself, that is, from pure concepts of things in general. Thus the first step which we take outside the world of sense, obliges us to begin our new knowledge with the investigation of the absolutely necessary Being, and to derive from its concepts the concepts of all things, so far as they are intelligible only; and this we shall attempt to do in the next chapter.

[6] After anzusehen, *sind* may be added for the sake of clearness, but it is often omitted in Kant's style.

TRANSCENDENTAL DIALECTIC

Chapter III

THE IDEAL OF PURE REASON

Section I

Of the Ideal in General

We have seen that without the conditions of sensibility, it is impossible to represent objects by means of the pure *concepts of the understanding,* because the conditions of their objective reality are absent, and they contain the mere form of thought only. If, however, we apply these concepts to phenomena, they can be represented *in concreto,* because in the phenomena they have the material for forming concepts of experience, which are nothing but concepts of the understanding *in concreto. Ideas,* however, are still further removed from objective reality than the *categories,* because they can meet with no phenomenon in which they could be represented *in concreto.* They contain a certain completeness unattainable by any possible empirical knowledge, and reason aims in them at a systematical unity only, to which the empirically possible unity is to approximate, without ever fully reaching it.

Still further removed from objective reality than the Idea, would seem to be what I call the *Ideal,* by which I mean the idea, not only *in concreto,* but *in individuo,* that is, an individual thing determinable or even determined by the idea alone.

Humanity (as an idea), in its complete perfection, implies not only all essential qualities belonging to human nature, which constitute our concept of it, enlarged to a degree of complete agreement with the highest aims that would represent our idea of perfect humanity, but everything also which, beside this concept, is required for the complete determination of the idea. For of all contradictory predicates one only can agree with the idea of the most perfect man. What to us is an ideal, was in Plato's language an *Idea of a divine mind,* an individual object present to its pure intuition, the most perfect of every kind of possible beings, and the archetype of all phenomenal copies.

Without soaring so high, we have to admit that human reason contains not only ideas, but ideals also, which though they have not, like those of Plato, creative, yet have certainly *practical* power (as regulative principles), and form the basis of the possible perfection of certain *acts*. Moral concepts are not entirely pure concepts of reason, because they rest on something empirical, pleasure or pain. Nevertheless, with regard to the principle by which reason imposes limits on freedom, which in itself is without laws, these moral concepts (with regard to their form at least) may well serve as examples of pure concepts of reason. Virtue and human wisdom in its perfect purity are ideas, while the wise man (of the Stoics) is an ideal, that is, a man existing in thought only, but in complete agreement with the idea of wisdom. While the idea gives *rules,* the ideal serves as the *archetype* for the permanent determination of the copy; and we have no other rule of our actions but the conduct of that divine man within us, with which we compare ourselves, and by which we judge and better ourselves, though we can never reach it. These ideals, though they cannot claim objective reality (existence), are not therefore to be considered as mere chimeras, but supply reason with an indispensable standard, because it requires the concept of that which is perfect of its kind, in order to estimate and measure by it the degree and the number of the defects in the imperfect. To attempt to realise the ideal in an example, that is, as a real phenomenon, as we might represent a perfectly wise man in a novel, is impossible, nay, absurd, and but little encouraging, because the natural limits, which are constantly interfering with the perfection in the idea, make all illusion in such an experiment impossible, and thus render the good itself in the idea suspicious and unreal.

This is the case with the ideal of reason, which must always rest on definite concepts, and serve as rule and model, whether for imitation or for criticism. The case is totally different with those creations of our imagination of which it is impossible to give an intelligible concept, or say anything,—which are in fact a kind of *monogram*, consisting of single lines without any apparent rule, a vague outline rather of different experiences than a definite image, such as painters and physiognomists pretend to carry in their heads, and of which they speak as a kind of vague shadow only of their creations and criticisms that can never be communicated to others. They may be termed, though improperly, ideals of sensibility, because they are meant to be the never-attainable model of possible empirical intuitions, and yet furnish no rule capable of being explained or examined.

In its ideal, on the contrary, reason aims at a perfect determination, according to rules *a priori,* and it conceives an object throughout determinable according to principles, though without the sufficient conditions of experience, so that the concept itself is transcendent.

THE IDEAL OF PURE REASON

SECTION II

Of the Transcendental Ideal
(*Prototypon Transcendentale*)

Every concept is, with regard to that which is not contained in it, undetermined and subject to the principle of *determinability,* according to which of *every two* contradictorily opposite predicates, one only can belong to it. This rests on the principle of contradiction, and is therefore a purely logical principle, taking no account of any of the contents of our knowledge, and looking only to its logical form.

Besides this everything is subject, in its possibility, to the principle of complete determination, according to which one of all the possible predicates of things, as compared with their opposites, must be applicable to it. This does not rest only on the principle of contradiction, for it regards everything, not only in relation to two contradictory predicates, but in relation to the *whole possibility,* that is, to the whole of all predicates of things, and, presupposing these as a condition *a priori,* it represents everything as deriving its own possibility from the share which it possesses in that whole possibility.* This princi-

---

* According to this principle, therefore, everything is referred to a common correlate, that is, the whole possibility, which, if it (that is, the matter for all possible predicates) could be found in the idea of any single thing, would prove an affinity of all possible things, through the identity of the ground of their complete determination. The determinability of any concept is subordinate to the *universality* (*universalitas*) of the principle of the excluded middle,

ple of complete determination relates therefore to the content, and not only to the logical form. It is the principle of the synthesis of all predicates which are meant to form the complete concept of a thing, and not the principle of analytical representation only, by means of one of two contradictory predicates; and it contains a transcendental presupposition, namely, that of the material for all possibility which is supposed to contain *a priori* the data for the particular possibility of everything.

The proposition, that *everything which exists is completely determined,* does not signify only that one of every pair of *given* contradictory predicates, but that one of all possible predicates must always belong to a thing, so that by this proposition predicates are not only compared with each other logically, but the thing itself is compared transcendentally with the sum total of all possible predicates. The proposition really means that, in order to know a thing completely, we must know everything that is possible, and thereby determine it either affirmatively or negatively. This complete determination is therefore a concept which *in concreto* can never be represented in its totality, and is founded therefore on an idea which belongs to reason only, reason prescribing to the understanding the rule of its complete application.

Now although this idea of the *sum total of all possibility,* so far as it forms the condition of the complete determination of everything, is itself still undetermined with regard to its predicates, and is conceived by us merely as a sum total of all possible predicates, we find nevertheless on closer examination that this idea, as a fundamental concept, excludes a number of predicates which, being derivative, are given by others, or cannot stand one by the side of the other, and that it is raised to a completely *a priori* determined concept, thus becoming the concept of an individual object which is completely determined by the mere idea, and must therefore be called an ideal of pure reason.

If we consider all possible predicates not only logically, but transcendentally, that is, according to their content, which may be thought in them *a priori,* we find that through some we represent being, through others a mere not-being. The logical negation, which is merely indicated through the small word *not,* does in reality never apply to a concept, but only to its

---

while the determination of a thing is subordinate to the *totality* (*universitas*), or the sum total of all possible predicates.

relation to another in a judgment, and is very far therefore from being sufficient to determine a concept with regard to its content. The expression, *not-mortal,* can in no wise indicate that mere not-being if thereby represented in an object, but leaves the content entirely untouched. A transcendental negation, on the contrary, signifies not-being by itself, and is opposed to transcendental affirmation, or a something the concept of which in itself expresses being. It is called, therefore, reality (from *res,* a thing), because through it alone, and so far only as it reaches, are objects something, while the opposite negation indicates a mere want, and, if it stands by itself, represents the absence of everything.

No one can definitely think a negation, unless he founds it on the opposite affirmation. A man born blind cannot frame the smallest conception of darkness, because he has none of light. The savage knows nothing of poverty, because he does not know ease, and the ignorant has no conception of his ignorance,* because he has none of knowledge, etc. All negative concepts are therefore derivative, and it is the realities which contain the data and, so to speak, the material, or the transcendental content, by which a complete determination of all things becomes possible.

If, therefore, our reason postulates a transcendental substratum for all determinations, a substratum which contains, as it were, the whole store of material whence all possible predicates of things may be taken, we shall find that such a substratum is nothing but the idea of the sum total of reality (*omnitudo realitatis*). In that case all true negations are nothing but *limitations* which they could not be unless there were the substratum of the unlimited (the All).

By this complete possession of all reality we represent the concept of a *thing by itself* as completely determined, and the concept of an *ens realissimum* is the concept of individual being, because of all possible opposite predicates one, namely, that which absolutely belongs to being, is found in its determination. It is therefore a transcendental *ideal* which forms the foundations of the complete determination which is necessary for all that exists, and which constitutes at the same time the

---

* The observations and calculations of astronomers have taught us much that is wonderful; but the most important is, that they have revealed to us the abyss of our *ignorance,* which otherwise human reason could never have conceived so great. To meditate on this must produce a great change in the determination of the aims of our reason.

highest and complete condition of its possibility, to which all thoughts of objects, with regard to their content, must be traced back. It is at the same time the only true ideal of which human reason is capable, because it is in this case alone that a concept of a thing, which in itself is general, is completely determined by itself, and recognised as the representation of an individual.

The logical determination of a concept by reason is based upon a disjunctive syllogism in which the major contains a logical division (the division of the sphere of a general concept), while the minor limits that sphere to a certain part, and the conclusion determines the concept by that part. The general concept of a reality in general cannot be divided *a priori,* because without experience we know no definite kinds of reality contained under that genus. Hence the transcendental major of the complete determination of all things is nothing but a representation of the sum total of all reality, and not only a concept which comprehends all predicates, according to their transcendental content, *under itself,* but *within itself;* and the complete determination of everything depends on the limitation of this total of reality, of which some part is ascribed to the thing, while the rest is excluded from it, a procedure which agrees with the *aut aut* of a disjunctive major, and with the determination of the object through one of the members of that division in the minor. Thus the procedure of reason by which the transcendental ideal becomes the basis of the determination of all possible things, is analogous to that which reason follows in disjunctive syllogisms, a proposition on which I tried before to base the systematical division of all transcendental ideas, and according to which they are produced, as corresponding to the three kinds of the syllogisms of reason.

It is self-evident that for that purpose, namely, in order simply to represent the necessary and complete determination of things, reason does not presuppose the existence of a being that should correspond to the ideal, but its idea only, in order to derive from an unconditioned totality of complete determination the conditioned one, that is the totality of something limited. Reason therefore sees in the ideal the prototypon of all things which, as imperfect copies (*ectypa*), derive the material of their possibility from it, approaching more or less nearly to it, yet remaining always far from reaching it.

Thus all the possibility of things (or of the synthesis of the manifold according to their content) is considered as derivative, and the possibility of that only which includes in itself all reality as original. For all negations (which really are the only predicates by which everything else is distinguished from the truly real being) are limitations only of a greater and, in the last instance, of the highest reality, presupposing it, and, according to their content, derived from it. All the manifoldness of things consist only of so many modes of limiting the concept of the highest reality that forms their common substratum, in the same way as all figures are only different modes of limiting endless space. Hence the object of its ideal which exists in reason only is called the *original Being* (*ens originarium*), and so far as it has nothing above it, the *highest Being* (*ens summum*), and so far as everything as conditioned is subject to it, the *Being of all beings* (*ens entium*). All this however does not mean the objective relation of any real thing to other things, but of the *idea to concepts,* and leaves us in perfect ignorance as to the existence of a being of such superlative excellence.

Again, as we cannot say that an original being consists of so many derivative beings, because these in reality presuppose the former, and cannot therefore constitute it, it follows that the ideal of the original being must be conceived as simple.

The derivation of all other possibility from that original being cannot therefore, if we speak accurately, be considered as a *limitation* of its highest reality, and, as it were, a *division* of it—for in that case the original being would become to us a mere aggregate of derivative beings, which, according to what we have just explained, is impossible, though we represented it so in our first rough sketch. On the contrary, the highest reality would form the basis of the possibility of all things as a *cause,* and not as a *sum total.* The manifoldness of things would not depend on the limitation of the original being, but on its complete effect, and to this also would belong all our sensibility, together with all reality in phenomenal appearance, which could not, as an ingredient, belong to the idea of a supreme being.

If we follow up this idea of ours and hypostasise it, we shall be able to determine the original being by means of the concept of the highest reality as one, simple, all sufficient, eternal, etc., in one word, determine it in its unconditioned completeness through all predicaments. The concept of such a being is the concept *of God* in its transcendental sense, and thus, as I indicated above, the ideal of pure reason is the object of a transcendental *theology*.

By such an employment of the transcendental idea, however, we should be overstepping the limits of its purpose and admissibility. Reason used it only, as being the *concept* of all reality, for a foundation of the complete determination of things in general, without requiring that all this reality should be given objectively and constitute itself a thing. This is a mere fiction by which we comprehend and realise the manifold of our idea in one ideal, as a particular being. We have no right to do this, not even to assume the possibility of such an hypothesis; nor do all the consequences which flow from such an ideal concern the complete determination of things in general, for the sake of which alone the idea was necessary, or influence it in the least.

It is not enough to describe the procedure of our reason and its dialectic, we must try also to discover its sources, in order to be able to explain that illusion itself as a phenomenon of the understanding. The ideal of which we are speaking is founded on a natural, not on a purely arbitrary idea. I ask, therefore, how does it happen that reason considers all the possibility of things as derived from one fundamental possibility, namely, that of the highest reality, and then presupposes it as contained in a particular original being?

The answer is easily found in the discussions of the transcendental Analytic. The possibility of the objects of our senses is their relation to our thought, by which something (namely, the empirical form) can be thought *a priori,* while what constitutes the matter, the reality in the phenomena (all that corresponds to sensation) must be given, because without it it could not even be thought, nor its possibility be represented. An object of the senses can be completely determined only when it is compared with all phenomenal predicates, and represented by them either affirmatively or negatively. As, however, that which constitutes the thing itself (as a phenomenon), namely, the real, must be given, and as without this the thing could not be conceived at all, and as that in which the real of all phenomena is given is what we call the one and all comprehending experience, it is necessary that the material for the possibility of all objects of our senses should be presupposed as given in one whole, on the limitation of which alone the possibility of all empirical objects, their difference from each other, and their complete determination can be founded. And since no other objects can be given us but those of the senses, and nowhere but in the context of a possible experience, nothing can be an object to us, if it does not presuppose that whole of all empirical reality, as the condition of its possibility. Owing to a natural illusion, we are led to consider a principle which applies only to the objects of *our* senses, as a principle valid for all things, and thus to take the empirical principle of our concepts of the possibility of things as phenomena, by omitting this limitation, as a transcendental principle of the possibility of things in general.

If afterwards we hypostasise this idea of the whole of all reality, this is owing to our changing dialectically the distributive unity of the empirical use of our understanding into the collective unity of an empirical whole, and then represent to ourselves this whole of phenomena as an individual thing, containing in itself all empirical reality. Afterwards, by means of the aforementioned transcendental subreption, this is taken for the concept of a thing standing at the head of the possibility of all things, and supplying the real conditions for their complete determination.*

THE IDEAL OF PURE REASON

SECTION III

Of the Arguments of Speculative Reason in Proof of the Existence of a Supreme Being

Notwithstanding this urgent want of reason to presuppose something, as a foundation for the complete determination of the concepts of the understanding, reason nevertheless becomes too soon aware of the purely ideal and factitious character of such a supposition to allow itself to be persuaded by it alone to admit a mere creation of thought as a real being, unless it were forced by something else to seek for some rest in its regressus from the conditioned, which is given, to the uncon-

---

* This ideal of the most real of all things, although merely a representation, is first *realised,* that is, changed into an object, then *hypostasised,* and lastly, by the natural progress of reason towards unity, as we shall presently show, *personified;* because the regulative unity of experience does not rest on the phenomena themselves (sensibility alone), but on the connection of the manifold, through the *understanding* (in an *apperception*), so that the unity of the highest reality, and the complete determinability (possibility) of all things, seem to reside in a supreme understanding, and therefore in an intelligence.

ditioned which, though in itself and according to its mere concept not given as real, can alone complete the series of conditions followed up to their causes. This is the natural course, taken by the reason of every, even the most ordinary, human being, although not every one can hold out in it. It does not begin with concepts, but with common experience, and thus has something really existing for its foundation. That foundation however sinks, unless it rests upon the immoveable rock of that which is absolutely necessary; and this itself hangs without a support, if without and beneath it there be empty space, and everything be not filled by it, so that no room be left for a *why*,—in fact, if it be not infinite in reality.

If we admit the existence of something, whatever it may be, we must also admit that something exists by *necessity*. For the contingent exists only under the condition of something else as its cause, and from this the same conclusion leads us on till we reach a cause which is not contingent, and therefore unconditionally necessary. This is the argument on which reason founds its progress towards an original being.

Now reason looks out for the concept of a being worthy of such a distinction as the unconditioned necessity of its existence, not in order to conclude *a priori* its existence from its concept (for if it ventured to do this, it might confine itself altogether to mere concepts, without looking for a given existence as their foundation), but only in order to find among all concepts of possible things one which has nothing incompatible with absolute necessity. For that something absolutely necessary must exist, is regarded as certain after the first conclusion. And after discarding everything else, as incompatible with that necessity, reason takes the one being that remains for the absolutely necessary being, whether its necessity can be comprehended, that is, derived from its concept alone, or not. Now the being the concept of which contains a therefore for every wherefore, which is in no point and no respect defective, and is sufficient as a condition everywhere, seems, on that account, to be most compatible with absolute necessity, because, being in possession of all conditions of all that is possible, it does not require, nay, is not capable of any condition, and satisfies at least in this one respect the concept of unconditioned necessity more than any other concept which, because it is deficient and in need of completion, does not exhibit any such characteristic of independence from all further conditions. It is true that we ought not to conclude that what does not contain the highest and in every respect complete condition, must therefore be conditioned even in its existence; yet it does not exhibit the only characteristic of unconditioned existence, by which reason is able to know any being as unconditioned by means of a concept *a priori*.

The concept of a being of the highest reality (*ens realissimum*) would therefore seem of all concepts of all possible things to be the most compatible with the concept of an unconditionally necessary Being, and though it may not satisfy that concept altogether, yet no choice is left to us, and we are forced to keep to it, because we must not risk the existence of a necessary Being, and, if we admit it, can, in the whole field of possibility, find nothing that could produce better founded claims on such a distinction in existence.

This therefore is the natural course of human reason. It begins by persuading itself of the existence of some necessary Being. In this being it recognises unconditioned existence. It then seeks for the concept of that which is independent of all condition, and finds it in that which is itself the sufficient condition of all other things, that is, in that which contains all reality. Now as the unlimited all is absolute unity, and implies the concept of a being, one and supreme, reason concludes that the Supreme Being, as the original cause of all things, must exist by absolute necessity.

We cannot deny that this argument possesses a certain foundation, when we must come to a decision, that is, when, after having once admitted the existence of some one necessary Being, we agree that we must decide where to place it; for in that case we could not make a better choice, or we have really no choice, but are forced to vote for the absolute unity of complete reality, as the source of all possibility. If, however, we are not forced to come to a decision, but prefer to leave the question open till our consent has been forced by the full weight of arguments, that is, if we only have to form a *judgment* of what we really do know, and what we only seem to know, then our former conclusion does by no means appear in so favourable a light, and must appeal to favour in order to make up for the defects of its legal claims.

For, if we accept everything as here stated, namely, *first,* that we may infer rightly from any given existence (perhaps even my own only) the existence of an unconditionally necessary Being, *secondly,* that I must consider a being which contains all reality and therefore also all condition, as absolutely unconditioned, and that therefore the concept of the thing which is compatible with absolute necessity has thus been found, it follows by no means from this, that a concept of a limited being, which does not possess the highest reality, is therefore contradictory to absolute necessity. For, though I do not find in its concept the unconditioned which carries the whole of conditions with it, this does not prove that, for the same reason, its existence must be conditioned; for I cannot say in a hypothetical argument, that if a certain condition is absent (here the completeness according to concepts), the conditioned also is absent. On the contrary, it will be open to us to consider all the rest of limited beings as equally unconditioned, although we cannot from the general concept which we have of them deduce their necessity. Thus this argument would not have given us the least concept of the qualities of a necessary Being, in fact it would not have helped us in the least.

Nevertheless this argument retains a certain importance and authority, of which it cannot be at once deprived on account of this objective insufficiency. For suppose that there existed certain obligations, quite correct in the idea of reason, but without any reality in their application to ourselves, that is without any motives, unless we admitted a Supreme Being to give effect to practical laws, we should then be bound to follow the concepts which, though not objectively sufficient, are yet, according to the standard of our reason, preponderant, and more convincing than any others. The duty of deciding would here turn the balance against the hesitation of speculation by an additional practical weight; nay, reason would not be justified, even before the most indulgent judge, if, under such urgent pleas, though with deficient insight, it had not followed its judgment, of which we can say at least, that we know no better.

This argument, though it is no doubt transcendental, as based on the internal insufficiency of the contingent, is nevertheless so simple and natural, that the commonest understanding accepts it, if once led up to it. We see things change, arise and perish, and these, or at least their state, must therefore have a cause. Of every cause, however, that is given in experience, the same question must be asked. Where, therefore, could we more fairly place the *last* causality, except where there exists also the *supreme* causality, that is in that Being, which originally contains in itself the sufficient cause for every possible effect, and the concept of which can easily be realised by the one trait of an all-comprehending perfection? That supreme cause we afterwards consider as absolutely necessary, because we find it absolutely necessary to ascend to it, while there is no ground for going beyond it. Thus among all nations, even when still in a state of blind polytheism, we always see some sparks of monotheism, to which they have been led, not by meditation and profound speculation, but by the natural bent of the common understanding, which they gradually followed and comprehended.

There are only three kinds of proofs of the existence of God from speculative reason.

All the paths that can be followed to this end begin either from definite experience and the peculiar nature of the world of sense, known to us through experience, and ascend from it, according to the laws of causality, to the highest cause, existing outside the world; or they rest on indefinite experience only, that is, on any existence which is empirically given; or lastly, they leave all experience out of account, and conclude, entirely *a priori* from mere concepts, the existence of a supreme cause. The first proof is the *physico-theological,* the second the *cosmological,* the third the *ontological* proof. There are no more, and there can be no more.

I shall show that neither on the one path, the empirical, nor on the other, the transcendental, can reason achieve anything, and that it stretches its wings in vain, if it tries to soar beyond the world of sense by the mere power of speculation. With regard to the order in which these three arguments should be examined, it will be the opposite of that, followed by reason in its gradual development, in which we placed them also at first ourselves. For we shall be able to show that, although experience gives the first impulse, it is the transcendental concept only which guides reason in its endeavours, and fixes the last goal which reason wishes to retain. I shall therefore begin with the examination of the transcendental proof, and see afterwards how far it may be strengthened by the addition of empirical elements.

THE IDEAL OF PURE REASON

SECTION IV

Of the Impossibility of an Ontological Proof of the Existence of God

It is easily perceived, from what has been said before, that the concept of an absolutely necessary Being is a concept of pure reason, that is, a mere idea, the objective reality of which is by no means proved by the fact that reason requires it. That idea does no more than point to a certain but unattainable completeness, and serves rather to limit the understanding, than to extend its sphere. It seems strange and absurd, however, that a conclusion of an absolutely necessary existence from a given existence in general should seem urgent and correct, and that yet all the conditions under which the understanding can form a concept of such a necessity should be entirely against us.

People have at all times been talking of an *absolutely necessary* Being, but they have tried, not so much to understand whether and how a thing of that kind could even be conceived, as rather to prove its existence. No doubt a verbal definition of that concept is quite easy, if we say that it is something the non-existence of which is impossible. This, however, does not make us much wiser with reference to the conditions that make it necessary[1] to consider the non-existence of a thing as absolutely inconceivable. It is these conditions which we want to know, and whether by that concept we are thinking anything or not. For to use the word *unconditioned,* in order to get rid of all the conditions which the understanding always requires, when wishing to conceive something as necessary, does not render it clear to us in the least whether, after that, we are still thinking anything or perhaps nothing, by the concept of the unconditionally necessary.

Nay, more than this, people have imagined that by a number of examples they had explained this concept, at first risked at haphazard, and afterwards become quite familiar, and that therefore all further inquiry regarding its intelligibility were

[1] Read *nothwendig* instead of *unmöglich*. Noiré.

unnecessary. It was said that every proposition of geometry, such as, for instance, that a triangle has three angles, is absolutely necessary, and people began to talk of an object entirely outside the sphere of our understanding, as if they understood perfectly well what, by that concept, they wished to predicate of it.

But all these pretended examples are taken without exception from *judgments* only, not from *things,* and their existence. Now the unconditioned necessity of judgments is not the same thing as an absolute necessity of things. The absolute necessity of a judgment is only a conditioned necessity of the thing, or of the predicate in the judgment. The above proposition did not say that three angles were absolutely necessary, but that under the condition of the existence of a triangle, three angles are given (in it) by necessity. Nevertheless, this pure logical necessity has exerted so powerful an illusion, that, after having formed of a thing a concept *a priori* so constituted that it seemed to include existence in its sphere, people thought they could conclude with certainty that, because existence necessarily belongs to the object of that concept, provided always that I accept the thing as given (existing), its existence also must necessarily be accepted (according to the rule of identity), and that the Being therefore must itself be absolutely necessary, because its existence is implied in a concept, which is accepted voluntarily only, and always under the condition that I accept the object of it as given.

If in an identical judgment I reject the predicate and retain the subject, there arises a contradiction, and hence, I say, that the former belongs to the latter necessarily. But if I reject the subject as well as the predicate, there is no contradiction, because there is nothing left that can be contradicted. To accept a triangle and yet to reject its three angles is contradictory, but there is no contradiction at all in admitting the non-existence of the triangle and of its three angles. The same applies to the concept of an absolutely necessary Being. Remove its existence, and you remove the thing itself, with all its predicates, so that a contradiction becomes impossible. There is nothing external to which the contradiction could apply, because the thing is not meant to be externally necessary; nor is there anything internal that could be contradicted, for in removing the thing out of existence, you have removed at the same time all its internal qualities. If you say, God is almighty, that is a necessary judgment, because almightiness cannot be removed, if you accept a deity, that is, an infinite Being, with the concept of which that other concept is identical. But if you say, God is not, then neither his almightiness, nor any other of his predicates is given; they are all, together with the subject, removed out of existence, and therefore there is not the slightest contradiction in that sentence.

We have seen therefore that, if I remove the predicate of a judgment together with its subject, there can never be an internal contradiction, whatever the predicate may be. The only way of evading this conclusion would be to say that there are subjects which cannot be removed out of existence, but must always remain. But this would be the same as to say that there exist absolutely necessary subjects, an assumption the correctness of which I have called in question, and the possibility of which you had undertaken to prove. For I cannot form to myself the smallest concept of a thing which, if it had been removed together with all its predicates, should leave behind a contradiction; and except contradiction, I have no other test of impossibility by pure concepts *a priori*. Against all these general arguments (which no one can object to) you challenge me with a case, which you represent as a proof by a fact, namely, that there is one, and this one concept only, in which the non-existence or the removal of its object would be self-contradictory, namely, the concept of the most real Being (*ens realissimum*). You say that it possesses all reality, and you are no doubt justified in accepting such a Being as possible. This for the present I may admit, though the absence of self-contradictoriness in a concept is far from proving the possibility of its object.* Now reality comprehends existence, and therefore existence is contained in the concept of a thing possible. If that thing is removed, the internal possibility of the thing would be removed, and this is self-contradictory.

I answer:—Even in introducing into the concept of a thing, which you wish to think in its possibility only, the concept of its existence, under whatever disguise it may be, you have been

---

* A concept is always possible, if it is not self-contradictory. This is the logical characteristic of possibility, and by it the object of the concept is distinguished from the *nihil negativum*. But it may nevertheless be an empty concept, unless the objective reality of the synthesis, by which the concept is generated, has been distinctly shown. This, however, as shown above, must always rest on principles of possible experience, and not on the principle of analysis (the principle of contradiction). This is a warning against inferring at once from the possibility of concepts (logical) the possibility of things (real).

guilty of a contradiction. If you were allowed to do this, you would apparently have carried your point; but in reality you have achieved nothing, but have only committed a tautology. I simply ask you, whether the proposition, that *this or that thing* (which, whatever it may be, I grant you as possible) *exists,* is an analytical or a synthetical proposition? If the former, then by its existence you add nothing to your thought of the thing; but in that case, either the thought within you would be the thing itself, or you have presupposed existence, as belonging to possibility, and have according to your own showing deduced existence from internal possibility, which is nothing but a miserable tautology. The mere word *reality,* which in the concept of a thing sounds different from existence in the concept of the predicate, can make no difference. For if you call all accepting or positing (without determining what it is) reality, you have placed a thing, with all its predicates, within the concept of the subject, and accepted it as real, and you do nothing but repeat it in the predicate. If, on the contrary, you admit, as every sensible man must do, that every proposition involving existence is synthetical, how can you say that the predicate of existence does not admit of removal without contradiction, a distinguishing property which is peculiar to analytical propositions only, the very character of which depends on it?

I might have hoped to put an end to this subtle argumentation, without many words, and simply by an accurate definition of the concept of existence, if I had not seen that the illusion, in mistaking a logical predicate for a real one (that is the predicate which determines a thing), resists all correction. Everything can become a *logical predicate,* even the subject itself may be predicated of itself, because logic takes no account of any contents of concepts. *Determination,* however, is a predicate, added to the concept of the subject, and enlarging it, and it must not therefore be contained in it.

Being is evidently not a real predicate, or a concept of something that can be added to the concept of a thing. It is merely the admission of a thing, and of certain determinations in it. Logically, it is merely the copula of a judgment. The proposition, *God is almighty,* contains two concepts, each having its object, namely, God and almightiness. The small word *is,* is not an additional predicate, but only serves to put the predicate *in relation* to the subject. If, then, I take the subject (God) with all its predicates (including that of almightiness), and say, *God is,* or there is a God, I do not put a new predicate to the concept of God, but I only put the subject by itself, with all its predicates, in relation to my concept, as its object. Both must contain exactly the same kind of thing, and nothing can have been added to the concept, which expresses possibility only, by my thinking its object as simply given and saying, it is. And thus the real does not contain more than the possible. A hundred real dollars do not contain a penny more than a hundred possible dollars. For as the latter signify the concept, the former the object and its position by itself, it is clear that, in case the former contained more than the latter, my concept would not express the whole object, and would not therefore be its adequate concept. In my financial position no doubt there exists more by one hundred real dollars, than by their concept only (that is their possibility), because in reality the object is not only contained analytically in my concept, but is added to my concept (which is a determination of my state), synthetically; but the conceived hundred dollars are not in the least increased through the existence which is outside my concept.

By whatever and by however many predicates I may think a thing (even in completely determining it), nothing is really added to it, if I add that the thing exists. Otherwise, it would not be the same that exists, but something more than was contained in the concept, and I could not say that the exact object of my concept existed. Nay, even if I were to think in a thing all reality, except one, that one missing reality would not be supplied by my saying that so defective a thing exists, but it would exist with the same defect with which I thought it; or what exists would be different from what I thought. If, then, I try to conceive a being, as the highest reality (without any defect), the question still remains, whether it exists or not. For though in my concept there may be wanting nothing of the possible real content of a thing in general, something is wanting in its relation to my whole state of thinking, namely, that the knowledge of that object should be possible *a posteriori* also. And here we perceive the cause of our difficulty. If we were concerned with an object of our senses, I could not mistake the existence of a thing for the mere concept of it; for by the concept the object is thought as only in harmony with the general conditions of a possible empirical knowledge, while by its existence it is thought as contained in the whole content of experience. Through this connection with the content of the whole experience, the concept of an object is not in the least increased; our thought has only received through it one more possible perception. If, however, we are thinking existence through the pure category alone, we need not wonder that we cannot find any characteristic to distinguish it from mere possibility.

Whatever, therefore, our concept of an object may contain, we must always step outside it, in order to attribute to it existence. With objects of the senses, this takes place through their connection with any one of my perceptions, according to empirical laws; with objects of pure thought, however, there is no means of knowing their existence, because it would have to be known entirely *a priori,* while our consciousness of every kind of existence, whether immediately by perception, or by conclusions which connect something with perception, belongs entirely to the unity of experience, and any existence outside that field, though it cannot be declared to be absolutely impossible, is a presupposition that cannot be justified by anything.

The concept of a Supreme Being is, in many respects, a very useful idea, but, being an idea only, it is quite incapable of increasing, by itself alone, our knowledge with regard to what exists. It cannot even do so much as to inform us any further as to its possibility. The analytical characteristic of possibility, which consists in the absence of contradiction in mere positions (realities), cannot be denied to it; but the connection of all real properties in one and the same thing is a synthesis the possibility of which we cannot judge *a priori* because these realities are not given to us as such, and because, even if this were so, no judgment whatever takes place, it being necessary to look for the characteristic of the possibility of synthetical knowledge in experience only, to which the object of an idea can never belong. Thus we see that the celebrated Leibniz is far from having achieved what he thought he had, namely, to understand *a priori* the possibility of so sublime an ideal Being.

Time and labour therefore are lost on the famous ontological (Cartesian) proof of the existence of a Supreme Being from mere concepts; and a man might as well imagine that he could become richer in knowledge by mere ideas, as a merchant in capital, if, in order to improve his position, he were to add a few noughts to his cash account.

SECTION V

Of the Impossibility of a Cosmological Proof of the Existence of God

It was something quite unnatural, and a mere innovation of scholastic wisdom, to attempt to pick out of an entirely arbitrary idea the existence of the object corresponding to it. Such an attempt would never have been made, if there had not existed beforehand a need of our reason of admitting for existence in general something necessary, to which we may ascend and in which we may rest; and if, as that necessity must be unconditioned and *a priori* certain, reason had not been forced to seek a concept which, if possible, should satisfy such a demand and give us a knowledge of an existence entirely *a priori*. Such a concept was supposed to exist in the idea of an *ens realissimum,* and that idea was therefore used for a more definite knowledge of that, the existence of which one had admitted or been persuaded of independently, namely, of the necessary Being. This very natural procedure of reason was carefully concealed, and instead of ending with that concept, an attempt was made to begin with it, and thus to derive from it the necessity of existence, which it was only meant to supplement. Hence arose that unfortunate ontological proof, which satisfies neither the demands of our natural and healthy understanding, nor the requirements of the schools.

The *cosmological proof,* which we have now to examine, retains the connection of absolute necessity with the highest reality, but instead of concluding, like the former, from the highest reality necessity in existence, it concludes from the given unconditioned necessity of any being, its unlimited reality. It thus brings everything at least into the groove of a natural, though I know not whether of a really or only apparently rational syllogism, which carries the greatest conviction, not only for the common, but also for the speculative understanding, and has evidently drawn the first outline of all proofs of natural theology, which have been followed at all times, and will be followed in future also, however much they may be hidden and disguised. We shall now proceed to exhibit and to examine this cosmological proof which Leibniz calls also the proof *a contingentia mundi*.

It runs as follows: If there exists anything, there must exist an absolutely necessary Being also. Now I, at least, exist; therefore there exists an absolutely necessary Being. The minor contains an experience, the major the conclusion from experience in general to the existence of the necessary.* This proof therefore begins with experience, and is not entirely *a priori*, or ontological; and, as the object of all possible experience is called the world, this proof is called the *cosmological proof*. As it takes no account of any peculiar property of the objects of experience, by which this world of ours may differ from any other possible world, it is distinguished, in its name also, from the physico-theological proof, which employs as arguments, observations of the peculiar property of this our world of sense.

The proof then proceeds as follows: The necessary Being can be determined in one way only, that is, by one only of all possible opposite predicates; it must therefore be determined completely by its own concept. Now, there is only one concept of a thing possible, which *a priori* completely determines it, namely, that of the *ens realissimum*. It follows, therefore, that the concept of the *ens realissimum* is the only one by which a necessary Being can be thought, and therefore it is concluded that a highest Being exists by necessity.

There are so many sophistical propositions in this cosmological argument, that it really seems as if speculative reason had spent all her dialectical skill in order to produce the greatest possible transcendental illusion. Before examining it, we shall draw up a list of them, by which reason has put forward an old argument disguised as a new one, in order to appeal to the agreement of two witnesses, one supplied by pure reason, the other by experience, while in reality there is only one, namely, the first, who changes his dress and voice in order to be taken for a second. In order to have a secure foundation, this proof takes its stand on experience, and pretends to be different from the ontological proof, which places its whole confidence in pure concepts *a priori* only. The cos-

---

* This conclusion is too well known to require detailed exposition. It rests on the apparently transcendental law of causality in nature, that everything *contingent* has its cause, which, if contingent again, must likewise have a cause, till the series of subordinate causes ends in an absolutely necessary cause, without which it could not be complete.

mological proof, however, uses that experience only in order to make one step, namely, to the existence of a necessary Being in general. What properties that Being may have, can never be learnt from the empirical argument, and for that purpose reason takes leave of it altogether, and tries to find out, from among concepts only, what properties an absolutely necessary Being ought to possess, i.e. which among all possible things contains in itself the requisite conditions (*requisita*) of absolute necessity. This requisite is believed by reason to exist in the concept of an *ens realissimum* only, and reason concludes at once that this must be the absolutely necessary Being. In this conclusion it is simply assumed that the concept of a being of the highest reality is perfectly adequate to the concept of absolute necessity in existence; so that the latter might be concluded from the former. This is the same proposition as that maintained in the ontological argument, and is simply taken over into the cosmological proof, nay, made its foundation, although the intention was to avoid it. For it is clear that absolute necessity is an existence from mere concepts. If, then, I say that the concept of the *ens realissimum* is such a concept, and is the only concept adequate to necessary existence, I am bound to admit that the latter may be deduced from the former. The whole conclusive strength of the so-called cosmological proof rests therefore in reality on the ontological proof from mere concepts, while the appeal to experience is quite superfluous, and, though it may lead us on to the concept of absolute necessity, it cannot demonstrate it with any definite object. For as soon as we intend to do this, we must at once abandon all experience, and try to find out which among the pure concepts may contain the conditions of the possibility of an absolutely necessary Being. But if in this way the possibility of such a Being has been perceived, its existence also has been proved: for what we are really saying is this, that under all possible things there is one which carries with it absolute necessity, or that this Being exists with absolute necessity.

Sophisms in arguments are most easily discovered, if they are put forward in a correct scholastic form. This we shall now proceed to do.

If the proposition is right, that every absolutely necessary Being is, at the same time, the most real Being (and this is the *nervus probandi* of the cosmological proof), it must, like all affirmative judgments, be capable of conversion, at least *per accidens*. This would give us the proposition that some *entia realissima* are at the same time absolutely necessary beings. One *ens realissimum*, however, does not differ from any other on any point, and what applies to one, applies also to all. In this case, therefore, I may employ absolute conversion, and say, that every *ens realissimum* is a necessary Being. As this proposition is determined by its concepts *a priori* only, it follows that the mere concept of the *ens realissimum* must carry with it its absolute necessity; and this, which was maintained by the ontological proof, and not recognised by the cosmological, forms really the foundation of the conclusions of the latter, though in a disguised form.

We thus see that the second road taken by speculative reason, in order to prove the existence of the highest Being, is not only as illusory as the first, but commits in addition an *ignoratio elenchi*, promising to lead us by a new path, but after a short circuit bringing us back to the old one, which we had abandoned for its sake.

I said before that a whole nest of dialectical assumptions was hidden in that cosmological proof, and that transcendental criticism might easily detect and destroy it. I shall here enumerate them only, leaving it to the experience of the reader to follow up the fallacies and remove them.

We find, first, the transcendental principle of inferring a cause from the accidental. This principle, that everything contingent must have a cause, is valid in the world of sense only, and has not even a meaning outside it. For the purely intellectual concept of the contingent cannot produce a synthetical proposition like that of causality, and the principle of causality has no meaning and no criterion of its use, except in the world of sense, while here it is meant to help us beyond the world of sense.

Secondly. The inference of a first cause, based on the impossibility of an infinite ascending series of given causes in this world of sense,—an inference which the principles of the use of reason do not allow us to draw even in experience, while here we extend that principle beyond experience, whither that series can never be prolonged.

Thirdly. The false self-satisfaction of reason with regard to the completion of that series, brought about by removing in the end every kind of condition, without which, nevertheless, no concept of necessity is possible, and by then, when any definite concepts have become impossible, accepting this as a completion of our concept.

Fourthly. The mistaking the logical possibility of a concept of all united reality (without any internal contradiction) for the transcendental, which requires a principle for the practicability of such a synthesis, such principle however being applicable to the field of possible experience only, etc.

The trick of the cosmological proof consists only in trying to avoid the proof of the existence of a necessary Being *a priori* by mere concepts. Such a proof would have to be ontological, and of this we feel ourselves quite incapable. For this reason we take a real existence (of any experience whatever), and conclude from it, as well as may be, some absolutely necessary condition of it. In that case there is no necessity for explaining its possibility, because, if it has been proved that it exists, the question as to its possibility is unnecessary. If then we want to determine that necessary Being more accurately, according to its nature, we do not seek what is sufficient to make us understand from its concept the necessity of its existence. If we could do this, no empirical presupposition would be necessary. No, we only seek the negative condition (*conditio sine qua non*), without which a Being would not be absolutely necessary. Now, in every other kind of syllogisms leading from a given effect to its cause, this might well be feasible. In our case, however, it happens unfortunately that the condition which is required for absolute necessity exists in one single Being only, which, therefore, would have to contain in its concept all that is required for absolute necessity, and that renders a conclusion *a priori*, with regard to such necessity, possible. I ought therefore to be able to reason conversely, namely, that everything is absolutely necessary, if that concept (of the highest reality) belongs to it. If I cannot do this (and I must confess that I cannot, if I wish to avoid the ontological proof), I have suffered shipwreck on my new course, and have come back again from where I started. The concept of the highest Being may satisfy all questions *a priori* which can be asked regarding the internal determinations of a thing, and it is therefore an ideal, without an equal, because the general concept distinguishes it at the same time as an individual being among all possible things. But it does not satisfy the really important question regarding its own existence; and if some one who admitted the existence of a necessary Being were to ask us which of all things in the world could be regarded as such, we could not answer: This here is the necessary Being.

It may be allowable to *admit* the existence of a Being entirely sufficient to serve as the cause of all possible effects, simply in order to assist reason in her search for unity of causes. But to go so far as to say that *such a Being exists necessarily,* is no longer the modest language of an admissible hypothesis, but the bold assurance of apodictic certainty; for the knowledge of that which is absolutely necessary must itself possess absolute necessity.

The whole problem of the transcendental Ideal is this, either to find a concept compatible with absolute necessity, or to find the absolute necessity compatible with the concept of anything. If the one is possible, the other must be so also, for reason recognises that only as absolutely necessary which is necessary according to its concept. Both these tasks baffle our attempts at *satisfying* our understanding on this point, and likewise our endeavours to comfort it with regard to its impotence.

That unconditioned necessity, which we require as the last support of all things, is the true abyss of human reason. Eternity itself, however terrible and sublime it may have been depicted by Haller, is far from producing the same giddy impression, for it only *measures* the duration of things, but does not *support* them. We cannot put off the thought, nor can we support it, that a Being, which we represent to ourselves as the highest among all possible beings, should say to himself, I am from eternity to eternity, there is nothing beside me, except that which is something through my will,—*but whence am I?* Here all sinks away from under us, and the highest perfection, like the smallest, passes without support before the eyes of speculative reason, which finds no difficulty in making the one as well as the other to disappear without the slightest impediment.

Many powers of nature, which manifest their existence by certain effects, remain perfectly inscrutable to us, because we cannot follow them up far enough by observation. The transcendental object, which forms the foundation of all phenomena, and with it the ground of our sensibility having this rather than any other supreme conditions, is and always will be inscrutable. The thing no doubt is given, but it is incomprehensible. An ideal of pure reason, however, cannot be called inscrutable, because it cannot produce any credentials of its reality beyond the requirement of reason to perfect all synthetical unity by means of it. As, therefore, it is not even given as an object that can be thought, it cannot be said to be, as such, inscrutable; but, being a mere idea, it must find in the nature of reason its place and its solution, and in that sense be capable of scrutiny. For it is the very essence of reason that we are able to give an account of all our concepts, opinions, and assertions either on objective or, if they are a mere illusion, on subjective grounds.

Discovery and Explanation of the Dialectical Illusion in all Transcendental Proofs of the Existence of a Necessary Being

Both proofs, hitherto attempted, were transcendental, that is, independent of empirical principles. For although the cosmological proof assumes for its foundation an experience in general, it does not rest on any particular quality of it, but on pure principles of reason, with reference to an existence given by the empirical consciousness in general, and abandons even that guidance in order to derive its support from pure concepts only. What then in these transcendental proofs is the cause of the dialectical, but natural, illusion which connects the concepts of necessity and of the highest reality, and realises and hypostasises that which can only be an idea? What is the cause that renders it inevitable to admit something as necessary in itself among existing things, and yet makes us shrink back from the existence of such a Being as from an abyss? What is to be done that reason should understand itself on this point, and, escaping from the wavering state of hesitatingly approving or disapproving, acquire a calm insight into the matter?

It is surely extremely strange that, as soon as we suppose that something exists, we cannot avoid the conclusion that something exists necessarily. On this quite natural, though by no means, therefore, certain conclusion, rests the whole cosmological argument. On the other side, I may take any concept of anything, and I find that its existence has never to be represented by me as absolutely necessary, nay, that nothing prevents me, whatever may exist, from thinking its non-existence. I may, therefore, have to admit something necessary as the condition of existing things in general, but I need not think any single thing as necessary in itself. In other words I can never *complete* the regressus to the conditions of existence without admitting a necessary Being, but I can never *begin* with such a Being.

If, therefore, I am obliged to think something necessary for all existing things, and at the same time am not justified in thinking of anything as in itself necessary, the conclusion is inevitable: that necessity and contingency do not concern things themselves, for otherwise there would be a contradiction, and that therefore neither of the two principles can be objective; but that they may possibly be subjective principles of reason only, according to which, on one side, we have to find for all that is given as existing, something that is necessary, and thus never to stop except when we have reached an *a priori* complete explanation; while on the other we must never hope for that completion, that is, never admit anything empirical as unconditioned, and thus dispense with its further derivation. In that sense both principles as purely heuristic and *regulative*, and affecting the formal interests of reason only, may well stand side by side. For the one tells us that we ought to philosophise on nature as if there was a necessary first cause for everything that exists, if only in order to introduce systematical unity into our knowledge, by always looking for such an idea as an imagined highest cause. The other warns us against mistaking any single determination concerning the existence of things for such a highest cause, i.e. for something absolutely necessary, and bids us to keep the way always open for further derivation, and to treat it always as conditioned. If, then, everything that is perceived in things has to be considered by us as only conditionally necessary, nothing that is empirically given can ever be considered as absolutely necessary.

It follows from this that the absolutely necessary must be accepted as *outside the world,* because it is only meant to serve as a principle of the greatest possible unity of phenomena, of which it is the highest cause, and that it can never be reached *in the world,* because the second rule bids you always to consider all empirical causes of that unity as derived.

The philosophers of antiquity considered all form in nature as contingent, but matter, according to the judgment of common reason, as primitive and necessary. If, however, they had considered matter, not relatively as the substratum of phenomena, but as existing *by itself,* the idea of absolute necessity would have vanished at once, for there is nothing that binds reason absolutely to that existence, but reason can at any time and without contradiction remove it in thought, and it was in thought only that it could claim absolute necessity. The ground of this persuasion must therefore have been a certain regulative principle. And so it is; for extension and impermeability (which together constitute the concept of matter) furnish the highest empirical principle of the unity of phenomena, and possess, so far as this principle is empirically unconditioned, the character of a regulative principle. Nevertheless, as every determination of matter, which constitutes its reality, and hence the impermeability of matter also, is an effect (action) which must have a cause, and therefore be itself derived, matter is not adequate to the idea of a necessary Being, as a principle of all derived unity, because every one of its real qualities is derived and, therefore, conditionally necessary only, so that it could be removed, and with it would be removed the whole existence of matter. If this were not so, we should have reached the highest cause of unity, empirically, which is forbidden by the second regulative principle. It follows from all this that matter and everything in general that belongs to the world are not fit for the idea of a necessary original Being, as a mere principle of the greatest empirical unity, but that we must place it outside the world. In that case there is no reason why we should not simply derive the phenomena of the world and their existence from other phenomena, as if there were no necessary Being at all, while at the same time we might always strive towards the completeness of that derivation, just as if such a Being, as the highest cause, were presupposed.

The ideal of the Supreme Being is therefore, according to these remarks, nothing but a *regulative principle* of reason, which obliges us to consider all connection in the world as if it arose from an all-sufficient necessary cause, in order to found on it the rule of a systematical unity necessary according to general laws for the explanation of the world; it does not involve the assertion of an existence necessary by itself. It is impossible, however, at the same time, to escape from a transcendental *subreptio,* which leads us to represent that formal principle as constitutive, and to think that unity as hypostasised. It is the same with space. Space, though it is only a principle of sensibility, yet serves originally to make all forms possible, these being only limitations of it. For that very reason, however, it is mistaken for something absolutely necessary and independent, nay, for an object *a priori* existing in itself. It is the same here, and as this systematical unity of nature can in no wise become the principle of the empirical use of our reason, unless we base it on the idea of an *ens realissimum* as the highest cause, it happens quite naturally that we thus represent that idea as a real object, and that object again, as it is the highest condition, as necessary. Thus a *regulative* principle has been changed into a *constitutive* principle, which substitution becomes evident at once because, as soon as I consider that highest Being, which with regard to the world was absolutely (unconditionally) necessary, as a thing by itself, that necessity cannot be conceived, and can therefore have existed in my reason as a formal condition of thought only, and not as a material and substantial condition of existence.

THE IDEAL OF PURE REASON

Section VI

Of the Impossibility of the Physico-theological Proof

If, then, neither the concept of things in general, nor the experience of any *existence in general,* can satisfy our demands, there still remains one way open, namely, to try whether any *definite experience,* and consequently that of things in the world as it is, their constitution and disposition, may not supply a proof which could give us the certain conviction of the existence of a Supreme Being. Such a proof we should call *physico-theological.* If that, however, should prove impossible too, then it is clear that no satisfactory proof whatever, from merely speculative reason, is possible, in support of the existence of a Being, corresponding to our transcendental idea.

After what has been said already, it will be easily understood that we may expect an easy and complete answer to this question. For how could there ever be an experience that should be adequate to an idea? It is the very nature of an idea that no experience can ever be adequate to it. The transcendental idea of a necessary and all-sufficient original Being is so overwhelming, so high above everything empirical, which is always conditioned, that we can never find in experience enough material to fill such a concept, and can only grope about among things conditioned, looking in vain for the unconditioned, of which no rule of any empirical synthesis can ever give us an example, or even show the way towards it.

If the highest Being should stand itself in that chain of conditions, it would be a link in the series, and would, exactly like the lower links, above which it is placed, require further investigation with regard to its own still higher cause. If, on the contrary, we mean to separate it from that chain, and, as a purely intelligible Being, not comprehend it in the series of natural causes, what bridge is then open for reason to reach it, considering that all rules determining the transition from effect to cause, nay, all synthesis and extension of our knowledge in general, refer to nothing but possible experience, and therefore to the objects of the world of sense only, and are valid nowhere else?

This present world presents to us so immeasurable a stage of variety, order, fitness, and beauty, whether we follow it up in the infinity of space or in its unlimited division, that even with the little knowledge which our poor understanding has been able to gather, all language, with regard to so many and inconceivable wonders, loses its vigour, all numbers their power of measuring, and all our thoughts their necessary determination; so that our judgment of the whole is lost in a speechless, but all the more eloquent astonishment. Everywhere we see a chain of causes and effects, of means and ends, of order in birth and death, and as nothing has entered by itself into the state in which we find it, all points to another thing as its cause. As that cause necessitates the same further enquiry, the whole universe would thus be lost in the abyss of nothing, unless we admitted something which, existing by itself, original and independent, outside the chain of infinite contingencies, should support it, and, as the cause of its origin, secure to it at the same time its permanence. Looking at all the things in the world, what greatness shall we attribute to that highest cause? We do not know the whole contents of the world, still less can we measure its magnitude by a comparison with all that is possible. But, as with regard to causality, we cannot do without a last and highest Being, why should we not fix the degree of its perfection *beyond everything else that is possible?* This we can easily do, though only in the faint outline of an abstract concept, if we represent to ourselves all possible perfections united in it as in one substance. Such a concept would agree with the demand of our reason, which requires parsimony in the number of principles; it would have no contradictions in itself, would be favourable to the extension of the employment of reason in the midst of experience, by guiding it towards order and system, and lastly, would never be decidedly opposed to any experience.

This proof will always deserve to be treated with respect. It is the oldest, the clearest, and most in conformity with human reason. It gives life to the study of nature, deriving its own existence from it, and thus constantly acquiring new vigour.

It reveals aims and intention, where our own observation would not by itself have discovered them, and enlarges our knowledge of nature by leading us towards that peculiar unity the principle of which exists outside nature. This knowledge reacts again on its cause, namely, the transcendental idea, and thus increases the belief in a supreme Author to an irresistible conviction.

It would therefore be not only extremely sad, but utterly vain to attempt to diminish the authority of that proof. Reason, constantly strengthened by the powerful arguments that come to hand by themselves, though they are no doubt empirical only, cannot be discouraged by any doubts of subtle and abstract speculation. Roused from every inquisitive indecision, as from a dream, by one glance at the wonders of nature and the majesty of the cosmos, reason soars from height to height till it reaches the highest, from the conditioned to conditions, till it reaches the supreme and unconditioned Author of all.

But although we have nothing to say against the reasonableness and utility of this line of argument, but wish, on the contrary, to commend and encourage it, we cannot approve of the claims which this proof advances to apodictic certainty, and to an approval on its own merits, requiring no favour, and no help from any other quarter. It cannot injure the good cause, if the dogmatical language of the overweening sophist is toned down to the moderate and modest statements of a faith which does not require unconditioned submission, yet is sufficient to give rest and comfort. I therefore maintain that the physico-theological proof can never establish by itself alone the existence of a Supreme Being, but must always leave it to the ontological proof (to which it serves only as an introduction), to supply its deficiency; so that, after all, it is the ontological proof which contains the *only possible argument* (supposing always that any speculative proof is possible), and human reason can never do without it.

The principal points of the physico-theological proof are the following. 1st. There are everywhere in the world clear indications of an intentional arrangement carried out with great wisdom, and forming a whole indescribably varied in its contents and infinite in extent.

2ndly. The fitness of this arrangement is entirely foreign to the things existing in the world, and belongs to them contingently only; that is, the nature of different things could never spontaneously, by the combination of so many means, cooperate towards definite aims, if these means had not been selected and arranged on purpose by a rational disposing principle, according to certain fundamental ideas.

3rdly. There exists, therefore, a sublime and wise cause (or many), which must be the cause of the world, not only as a blind and all-powerful nature, by means of unconscious *fecundity*, but as an intelligence, by *freedom*.

4thly. The unity of that cause may be inferred with certainty from the unity of the reciprocal relation of the parts of the world, as portions of a skilful edifice, so far as our experience reaches, and beyond it, with plausibility, according to the principles of analogy.

Without wishing to argue, for the sake of argument only, with natural reason, as to its conclusion in inferring from the analogy of certain products of nature with the works of human art, in which man does violence to nature, and forces it not to follow its own aims, but to adapt itself to ours (that is, from the similarity of certain products of nature with houses, ships, and watches), in inferring from this, I say, that a similar causality, namely, understanding and will, must be at the bottom of nature, and in deriving the internal possibility of a freely acting nature (which, it may be, renders all human art and even human reason possible) from another though superhuman art—a kind of reasoning, which probably could not stand the severest test of transcendental criticism; we are willing to admit, nevertheless, that if we have to name such a cause, we cannot do better than to follow the analogy of such products of human design, which are the only ones of which we know completely both cause and effect. There would be no excuse, if reason were to surrender a causality which it knows, and have recourse to obscure and indemonstrable principles of explanation, which it does not know.

According to this argument, the fitness and harmony existing in so many works of nature might prove the contingency of the form, but not of the matter, that is, the substance in the world, because, for the latter purpose, it would be necessary to prove in addition, that the things of the world were in themselves incapable of such order and harmony, according to general laws, unless there existed, even in their *substance,* the product of a supreme wisdom. For this purpose, very different arguments would be required from those derived from the analogy of human art. The utmost, therefore, that could be established by such a proof would be an *architect of the world,* always very much hampered by the quality of the material with which he has to work, not a *creator,* to whose idea everything is subject. This would by no means suffice for the purposed aim of proving an all-sufficient original Being. If we wished to prove the contingency of matter itself, we must have recourse to a transcendental argument, and this is the very thing which was to be avoided.

The inference, therefore, really proceeds from the order and design that can everywhere be observed in the world, as an entirely contingent arrangement, to the existence of a cause, *proportionate to it*. The concept of that cause must therefore teach us something quite *definite* about it, and can therefore be no other concept but that of a Being which possesses all might, wisdom, etc., in one word, all perfection of an all-sufficient Being. The predicates of a *very great,* of an astounding, of an immeasurable might and virtue give us no definite concept, and never tell us really what the thing is by itself. They are only relative representations of the magnitude of an object, which the observer (of the world) compares with himself and his own power of comprehension, and which would be equally grand, whether we magnify the object, or reduce the observing subject to smaller proportions in reference to it. Where we are concerned with the magnitude (of the perfection) of a thing in general, there exists no definite concept, except that which comprehends all possible perfection, and only the all (*omnitudo*) of reality is thoroughly determined in the concept.

Now I hope that no one would dare to comprehend the relation of that part of the world which he has observed (in its extent as well as in its contents) to omnipotence, the relation of the order of the world to the highest wisdom, and the relation of the unity of the world to the absolute unity of its author, etc. Physico-theology, therefore, can never give a definite concept of the highest cause of the world, and is insufficient, therefore, as a principle of theology, which is itself to form the basis of religion.

The step leading to absolute totality is entirely impossible on the empirical road. Nevertheless, that step is taken in the physico-theological proof. How then has this broad abyss been bridged over?

The fact is that, after having reached the stage of admiration of the greatness, the wisdom, the power, etc. of the Author of the world, and seeing no further advance possible, one suddenly leaves the argument carried on by empirical proofs, and lays hold of that contingency which, from the very first, was inferred from the order and design of the world. The next step from that contingency leads, by means of transcendental concepts only, to the existence of something absolutely necessary, and another step from the absolute necessity of the first cause to its completely determined or determining concept, namely, that of an all-embracing reality. Thus we see that the physico-theological proof, baffled in its own undertaking, takes suddenly refuge in the cosmological proof, and as this is only the ontological proof in disguise, it really carries out its original intention by means of pure reason only; though it so strongly disclaimed in the beginning all connection with it, and professed to base everything on clear proofs from experience.

Those who adopt the physico-theological argument have no reason to be so very coy towards the transcendental mode of argument, and with the conceit of enlightened observers of nature to look down upon them as the cobwebs of dark speculators. If they would only examine themselves, they would find that, after they had advanced a good way on the soil of nature and experience, and found themselves nevertheless as much removed as ever from the object revealed to their reason, they suddenly leave that soil, to enter into the realm of pure possibilities, where on the wings of ideas they hope to reach that which had withdrawn itself from all their empirical investigations. Imagining themselves to be on firm ground after that desperate leap, they now proceed to expand the definite concept which they have acquired, they do not know how, over the whole field of creation; and they explain the ideal, which was merely a product of pure reason, by experience, though in a very poor way, and totally beneath the dignity of the object, refusing all the while to admit that they have arrived at that knowledge or supposition by a very different road from that of experience.

Thus we have seen that the physico-theological proof rests on the cosmological, and the cosmological on the ontological proof of the existence of one original Being as the Supreme Being; and, as besides these three, there is no other path open to speculative reason, the ontological proof, based exclusively on pure concepts of reason, is the only possible one, always supposing that any proof of a proposition, so far transcending the empirical use of the understanding, is possible at all.

THE IDEAL OF PURE REASON

Section VII

Criticism of all Theology based on Speculative Principles of Reason

If by *Theology* we understand the knowledge of the original Being, it is derived either from reason only (*theologia rationalis*), or from revelation (*revelata*). The former thinks its object either by pure reason and through transcendental concepts only (*ens originarium, realissimum, ens entium*), and is then called *transcendental* theology, or by a concept, borrowed from the nature (of our soul), as the highest intelligence, and ought then to be called *natural* theology. Those who admit a transcendental theology only are called *Deists,* those who admit also a *natural* theology *Theists.* The former admit that we may know the existence of an original Being by mere reason, but that our concept of it is transcendental only, as of a Being which possesses all reality, but a reality that cannot be further determined. The latter maintain that reason is capable of determining that object more accurately in analogy with nature, namely, as a Being which, through understanding and freedom, contains within itself the original ground of all other things. The former admits a *cause of the world* only (whether through the necessity of its nature or through freedom, remains undecided), the latter an *author of the world*.

Transcendental theology, again, either derives the existence of the original Being from an experience in general (without saying anything about the world, to which it belongs), and is then called *Cosmotheology;* or it believes that it can know its existence, without the help of any experience whatsoever, and by mere concepts, and is then called *Ontotheology*.

Natural theology infers the qualities and the existence of an author of the world from the constitution, the order, and the unity, which are seen in this world, in which two kinds of causality with their rules must be admitted, namely, nature and freedom. It ascends from this world to the highest intelligence as the principle either of all natural or of all moral order and perfection. In the former case it is called *Physico-theology,* in the other *Ethico-theology.**

As we are accustomed to understand by the concept of God, not only a blindly working eternal nature, as the root of all things, but a Supreme Being, which, through understanding and freedom, is supposed to be the author of all things, and as it is this concept alone in which we really take an interest, one might strictly deny to the *Deist* all belief in God, and allow him only the maintaining of an original Being, or a supreme cause. But as no one, simply because he does not dare to assert, ought to be accused of denying a thing, it is kinder and juster to say, that the *Deist* believes in a God, but the *Theist* in a *living God* (*summa intelligentia*). We shall now try to discover the possible sources of all these attempts of reason.

I shall not do more, at present, than define theoretical knowledge as one by which I know what *there is,* practical knowledge as one by which I represent to myself what *ought to be.* Hence the theoretical use of reason is that by which I know *a priori* (as necessary) that something is, while the practical use of reason is that by which I know *a priori* what ought to be. If then it is certain, beyond the possibility of doubt, that something is, or that something ought to be, though both are conditioned, then a certain definite condition of it may be either absolutely necessary or presupposed only as possible and contingent. In the former case, the condition is postulated (*per thesin*), in the latter supposed (*per hypothesin*). As there are practical laws, which are absolutely necessary (the moral laws), it follows, if they necessarily presuppose any existence as the condition of the possibility of their *obligatory* power, that the existence of that condition must be *postulated,* because the conditioned, from which we infer that condition, has been recognised *a priori* as absolutely necessary. On a future occasion we shall show that the moral laws not only presuppose the existence of a Supreme Being, but that, as they are in other respects absolutely necessary, they postulate it by right, though of course practically only. For the present we leave this mode of argument untouched.

If we only speak of that which is, not of that which ought to be, the conditioned given to us in experience is always conceived as contingent, and the condition belonging to it can

* Not theological Ethics; for these contain moral laws, which *presuppose* the existence of a supreme ruler of the world, while Ethico-theology is the conviction of the existence of a Supreme Being, founded on moral laws.

therefore not be known as absolutely necessary, but serves only as a relatively necessary, or rather *needful,* though in itself an *a priori* arbitrary supposition for a rational understanding of the conditioned. If, therefore, we wish to know in our theoretical knowledge the absolute necessity of a thing, this could only be done from concepts *a priori,* and never as of a cause in reference to an existence which is given in experience.

I call a theoretical knowledge *speculative,* if it relates to an object, or such concepts of an object, which we can never reach in any experience. It is opposed to our *knowledge of nature,* which relates to no other objects or predicates of them except those that can be given in a possible experience.

From something that happens (the empirically contingent) as an effect, to infer a cause, is a principle of natural, though not of speculative knowledge. For if we no longer use it as a principle involving the condition of possible experience, and, leaving out everything that is empirical, try to apply it to the contingent in general, there does not remain the smallest justification of such a synthetical proposition, showing how from something which is, there can be a transition to something totally different, which we call cause; nay, in such purely speculative application, the concepts both of cause and of the contingent lose all meaning, the objective reality of which would be made intelligible in the concrete.

If from the existence of *things* in the world we infer their cause, we are using reason not *naturally,* but *speculatively.* Naturally, reason refers not the things themselves (substances), but only that which *happens,* their *states,* as empirically contingent, to some cause; but it could know speculatively only that a substance itself (matter) is contingent in its existence. And even if we were thinking only of the form of the world, the manner of its composition and the change of this composition, and tried to infer from this a cause totally different from the world, this would be again a judgment of speculative reason only; because the object here is not an object of any possible experience. In this case the principle of causality, which is valid within the field of experience only, and utterly useless, nay, even meaningless, outside it, would be totally diverted from its proper destination.

What I maintain then is, that all attempts at a purely speculative use of reason, with reference to theology, are entirely useless and intrinsically null and void, while the principles of their natural use can never lead to any theology, so that unless we depend on moral laws, or are guided by them, there cannot be any theology of reason. For all synthetical principles of the understanding are applicable immanently only, i.e. within its own sphere, while, in order to arrive at the knowledge of a Supreme Being, we must use them transcendentally, and for this our understanding is not prepared. If the empirically valid law of causality is to conduct us to the original Being, that Being must belong to the chain of objects of experience, and in that case it would, like all phenomena, be itself conditioned. And even if that sudden jump beyond the limits of experience, according to the dynamical law of the relation of effects to their causes, could be allowed, what concept could we gain by this proceeding? Certainly no concept of a Supreme Being, because experience never presents to us the greatest of all possible effects, to bear witness of its cause. If we claim to be allowed, only in order to leave no void in our reason, to supply this defect in the complete determination of that cause by the mere idea of the highest perfection and of original necessity, this may possibly be granted as a favour, but can never be demanded on the strength of an irresistible proof. The physico-theological proof, as connecting speculation with intuition, might possibly therefore be used in support of other proofs (if they existed); it cannot, however, finish the task for itself, but can only prepare the understanding for theological knowledge, and impart to it the right and natural direction.

It must have been seen from this that transcendental questions admit of transcendental answers only, that is, of such which consist of mere concepts *a priori* without any empirical admixture. Our question, however, is clearly synthetical, and requires an extension of our knowledge beyond all limits of experience, till it reaches the existence of a Being which is to correspond to our pure idea, though no experience can ever be adequate to it. According to our former proofs, all synthetical knowledge *a priori* is possible only, if it conforms to the formal conditions of a possible experience. All these principles therefore are of immanent validity only, that is, they must remain within the sphere of objects of empirical knowledge, or of phenomena. Nothing, therefore, can be achieved by a transcendental procedure with reference to the theology of a purely speculative reason.

If people, however, should prefer to call in question all the former proofs of the Analytic, rather than allow themselves to be robbed of their persuasion of the value of the proofs on which they have rested so long, they surely cannot decline my request, when I ask them to justify themselves, at least on this point, in what manner, and by what kind of illumination they trust themselves to soar above all possible experience, on the wings of pure ideas. I must ask to be excused from listening to new proofs, or to the tinkered workmanship of the old. No doubt the choice is not great, for all speculative proofs end in the one, namely, the ontological; nor need I fear to be much troubled by the inventive fertility of the dogmatical defenders of that reason which they have delivered from the bondage of the senses; nor should I even, without considering myself a very formidable antagonist, decline the challenge to detect the fallacy in every one of their attempts, and thus to dispose of their pretensions. But I know too well that the hope of better success will never be surrendered by those who have once accustomed themselves to dogmatical persuasion, and I therefore restrict myself to the one just demand, that my opponents should explain in general, from the nature of the human understanding, or from any other sources of knowledge, what we are to do in order to extend our knowledge entirely *a priori,* and to carry it to a point where no possible experience, and therefore no means whatever, is able to secure to a concept invented by ourselves its objective reality. In whatever way the understanding may have reached that concept, it is clearly impossible that the *existence* of its object could be found in it through analysis, because the very knowledge of the existence of the object implies that it exists *outside our thoughts*. We cannot in fact go beyond concepts, nor, unless we follow the empirical connection by which nothing but phenomena can be given, hope to discover new objects and imaginary beings.

Although then reason, in its purely speculative application, is utterly insufficient for this great undertaking, namely, to prove the existence of a Supreme Being, it has nevertheless this great advantage of being able to *correct* our knowledge of it, if it can be acquired from elsewhere, to make it consistent with itself and every intelligible view, and to purify it from everything incompatible with the concept of an original Being, and from all admixture of empirical limitations.

In spite of its insufficiency, therefore, transcendental theology has a very important negative use, as a constant test of our reason, when occupied with pure ideas only, which, as such, admit of a transcendental standard only. For suppose that on practical grounds the *admission* of a highest and all-sufficient Being, as the highest intelligence, were to maintain its validity without contradiction, it would be of the greatest importance that we should be able to determine that concept accurately on its transcendental side, as the concept of a necessary and most real Being, to remove from it what is contradictory to that highest reality and purely phenomenal (anthropomorphic in the widest sense), and at the same time to put an end to all opposite assertions, whether *atheistic, deistic,* or *anthropomorphistic.* Such a critical treatment would not be difficult, because the same arguments by which the insufficiency of human reason in asserting the existence of such a Being has been proved, must be sufficient also to prove the invalidity of opposite assertions. For whence can anybody, through pure speculation of reason, derive his knowledge that there is no Supreme Being, as the cause of all that exists, or that it can claim none of those qualities which we, to judge from their effects, represent to ourselves as compatible with the dynamical realities of a thinking Being, or that, in the latter case, they would be subject to all those limitations which sensibility imposes inevitably on all the intelligences known to us by experience?

For the purely speculative use of reason, therefore, the Supreme Being remains, no doubt, an ideal only, but an ideal *without a flaw,* a concept which finishes and crowns the whole of human knowledge, and the objective reality of which, though it cannot be proved, can neither be disproved in that way. If then there should be an Ethico-theology to supply that deficiency, transcendental theology, which before was problematical only, would prove itself indispensable in determining its concept, and in constantly testing reason, which is so often deceived by sensibility, and not even always in harmony with its own ideas. Necessity, infinity, unity, extramundane existence (not as a world-soul), eternity, free from conditions of time, omnipresence, free from conditions of space, omnipotence, etc., all these are transcendental predicates, and their purified concepts, which are so much required for every theology, can therefore be derived from transcendental theology only.

APPENDIX

TO THE TRANSCENDENTAL DIALECTIC

Of the Regulative Use of the Ideas of Pure Reason

The result of all the dialectical attempts of pure reason does not only confirm what we proved in the transcendental Analytic, namely, that all our conclusions, which are to lead us beyond the field of possible experience, are fallacious and groundless, but teaches us also this in particular, that human reason has a natural inclination to overstep these limits, and that transcendental ideas are as natural to it as categories to the understanding, with this distinction, however, that while the latter convey truth, that is, agreement of our concepts with their objects, the former produce merely an irresistible illusion, against which we can defend ourselves by the severest criticism only.

Everything that is founded in the nature of our faculties must have some purpose, and be in harmony with the right use of them, if only we can guard against a certain misunderstanding and discover their proper direction. The transcendental ideas, therefore, will probably possess their own proper and, therefore, *immanent* use, although, if their object is misunderstood, and they are mistaken for the concepts of real things, they may become transcendent in their application, and hence deceptive. For not the idea in itself, but its use only can, in regard to the whole of possible experience, be either *transcendent* or *immanent*, according as we direct them either immediately to objects wrongly supposed to correspond to them, or only to the use of the understanding in general with reference to objects with which it has a right to deal. All the faults of *subreptio* are to be attributed to a want of judgment, never to the understanding or to reason themselves.

Reason never refers immediately to an object, but to the understanding only, and through it to its own empirical use. It does not *form*, therefore, concepts of objects, but *arranges* them only, and imparts to them that unity which they can have in their greatest possible extension, that is, with reference to the totality of different series; while the understanding does not concern itself with this totality, but only with that connection through which such series of conditions become possible according to concepts. Reason has therefore for its object the understanding only and its *fittest* employment; and, as the understanding brings unity into the manifold of the objects by means of concepts, reason brings unity into the manifold of concepts by means of ideas, making a certain collective unity the aim of the operations of the understanding, which otherwise is occupied with distributive unity only.

I maintain, accordingly, that transcendental ideas ought never to be employed as constitutive, so that by them concepts of certain objects should be given, and that, if they are so employed, they are merely sophistical (dialectic concepts). They have, however, a most admirable and indispensably necessary regulative use, in directing the understanding to a certain aim, towards which all the lines of its rules converge and which, though it is an idea only (*focus imaginarius*), that is, a point from which, as lying completely outside the limits of possible experience, the concepts of the understanding do not in reality proceed, serves nevertheless to impart to them the greatest unity and the greatest extension. Hence there arises, no doubt, the illusion, as if those lines sprang[2] from an object itself, outside the field of empirically possible experience (as objects are seen behind the surface of a mirror); but this illusion (by which we need not allow ourselves to be deceived) is nevertheless indispensably necessary, if, besides the objects which lie before our eyes, we want to see those also which lie far away at our back, that is to say, if, as in our case, we wish to direct the understanding beyond every given experience (as a part of the whole of possible experience), and thus to its greatest possible, or extremest extension.

If we review the entire extent of our knowledge supplied to us by the understanding, we shall find that it is the *systematising* of that knowledge, that is, its coherence according to one principle, which forms the proper province of reason. This unity of reason always presupposes an idea, namely, that of the form of a whole of our knowledge, preceding the definite knowledge of its parts, and containing the conditions according to which we are to determine *a priori* the place of every part and its relation to the rest. Such an idea accordingly demands the complete unity of the knowledge of our understanding, by which that knowledge becomes not only a mere aggregate but a system, connected according to necessary

---

[2] Read *ausgeschossen*.

laws. We ought not to say that such an idea is a concept of an object, but only of the complete unity of concepts, so far as that unity can serve as a rule of the understanding. Such concepts of reason are not derived from nature, but we only interrogate nature, according to these ideas, and consider our knowledge as defective so long as it is not adequate to them. We must confess that *pure earth, pure water, pure air,* etc., are hardly to be met with. Nevertheless we require the concepts of them (which, so far as their perfect purity is concerned, have their origin in reason only) in order to be able to determine properly the share which belongs to every one of these natural causes in phenomena. Thus every kind of matter is referred to earths (as mere weight), to salts and inflammable bodies (as force), and lastly, to water and air as vehicles (or, as it were, machines, by which the former exercise their operations), in order thus, according to the idea of a mechanism, to explain the mutual chemical workings of matter. For, although not openly acknowledged in these terms, such an influence of reason on the classifications of natural philosophers can easily be discovered.

If reason is the faculty of deducing the particular from the general, the general is either *certain in itself* and given, or not. In the former case nothing is required but *judgment* in subsuming, the particular being thus necessarily determined by the general. This I shall call the apodictic use of reason. In the latter case, when the general is admitted as *problematical* only, and as a mere idea, while the particular is certain, but the universality of the rule applying to it is still a problem, several particular cases, which are all certain, are tested by the rule, whether they submit to it; and in this case, when it appears that all particular cases which can be produced are subjected to it, the rule is concluded to be universal, and from that universality of the rule conclusions are drawn afterwards with regard to all cases, even those that are not given by themselves. This I shall call the hypothetical use of reason.

The hypothetical use of reason, resting on ideas as problematical concepts, ought not to be used *constitutively,* as if we could prove by it, judging strictly, the truth of the universal rule, which has been admitted as an hypothesis. For how are we to know all possible cases, which, as subject to the same principle, should prove its universality? The proper hypothetical use of reason is regulative only, and intended to introduce, as much as possible, unity into the particulars of knowledge, and thus to *approximate* the rule to universality.

The hypothetical use of reason aims therefore at the systematical unity of the knowledge of the understanding, and that unity is the *touchstone* of the truth of the rules. On the other hand, that systematical unity (as a mere idea) is only a *projected* unity, to be considered, not as given in itself, but as a problem only, though helping us to discover a principle for the manifold and particular exercise of the understanding, and thus to lead the understanding to cases also which are not given, and to render it more systematical.

We have learnt, therefore, that the systematical unity, introduced by reason into the manifold knowledge of the understanding, is a logical principle, intended to help the understanding by means of ideas, where by itself it is insufficient to establish rules, and at the same time to impart to the variety of its rules a certain harmony (or system according to principles), and by it a certain coherence, so far as that is possible. To say, however, whether the nature of the objects or the nature of the understanding which recognises them as objects, were in themselves intended for systematical unity, and whether to a certain extent we may postulate real unity *a priori,* without any reference to the peculiar interest of reason, maintaining that all possible kinds of knowledge of the understanding (therefore the empirical also) possess such unity and are subject to such general principles from which, in spite of their differences, they can all be derived, would be to apply a *transcendental* principle of reason, and to render systematical unity necessary, not only subjectively and logically as a method, but objectively also.

We shall try to illustrate this use of reason by an example. One of the different kinds of unity, according to the concepts of the understanding, is that of the causality of a substance, which we call power. The different manifestations of one and the same substance display at first so much diversity that one feels constrained to admit at first almost as many powers as there are effects. Thus we see, for instance, in the human mind sensation, consciousness, imagination, memory, wit, discrimination, pleasure, desire, etc. At first a simple logical maxim tells us to reduce this apparent diversity as much as possible by discovering, through comparison, hidden identity, and finding out, for instance, whether imagination connected with consciousness, be not memory, wit, discrimination, or, it may be, understanding and reason. The idea of a *fundamental power,* of which logic knows nothing as to its existence, is thus at least the problem of a systematical representation of the existing diversity of powers. The logical principle of reason requires us to produce this unity as far as possible, and the more we find that manifestations of one or the other power are identical, the more probable does it become that they are only different expressions of one and the same power which, relatively speaking, may be called their *fundamental power*. The same is done with the others.

These relatively fundamental powers must again be compared with each other, in order, if possible, by discovering their harmony, to bring them nearer to one only radical, that is, absolute fundamental power. Such a unity, however, is only an hypothesis of reason. It is not maintained that such a unity must really exist, but only that we must look for it in the interest of reason, that is, for the establishment of certain principles for the various rules supplied to us by experience, and thus introduce, if it is possible, systematical unity into our knowledge.

If, however, we watch the transcendental use of the understanding, we find that the idea of a fundamental power is not only meant as a problem, and for hypothetical use, but claims for itself objective reality, postulating the systematical unity of the diverse powers of a substance, and thus establishing an apodictic principle of reason. For without even having tested the harmony of those diverse powers, nay, even if failing to discover it, after repeated experiments, we still suppose that such a unity exists, and this not only, as in our example, on account of the unity of the substance, but even in cases where very many, though to a certain degree homogeneous, powers are seen, as in matter in general. Here, too, reason presupposes a systematical unity of diverse powers, because particular laws of nature are subject to more general laws, and parsimony in principles is not only considered as an economical rule of reason, but as an essential law of nature.

And, indeed, it is difficult to understand how a logical principle by which reason demands the unity of rules can exist without a transcendental principle, by which such a systematical unity is admitted as inherent in the objects themselves, and as *a priori* necessary. For how could reason in its logical application presume to treat the diversity of powers which we see in nature as simply a disguised unity, and to deduce it, as far as possible, from some fundamental power, if it were open to reason to admit equally the diversity of all powers, and to look upon the systematical unity in their derivation as contrary to nature? In doing this reason would run counter to its own destination, and propose as its aim an idea contrary to the constitution of nature. Nor could we say that reason had previously, according to its principles, deduced that unity from the contingent character of nature, because this law of reason, compelling her to look for unity, is necessary, and without it we should have no reason at all, and, in the absence of reason, no coherent use of the understanding, and, in the absence of that, no sufficient test of empirical truth;—on which account we must admit the systematical unity of nature as objectively valid and necessary.

We find this transcendental presupposition concealed in the cleverest way in the principles of philosophers, though they are not aware of it, nor have confessed it to themselves. That all the diversities of particular things do not exclude identity of species, that the various species must be treated as different determinations (varieties) of a few *genera,* and these again of still *higher genera;* that therefore we ought to look for a certain systematical unity of all possible empirical concepts, as derivable from higher and more general concepts, this is a rule of the schools or a logical principle without which no use of the understanding would be possible; for we can only conclude the particular from the general, if the general qualities of things form the foundation on which the particular qualities rest.

That, however, there exists in nature such a unity, is only a supposition of the philosophers, embodied in their well-known scholastic rule, *'entia praeter necessitatem non esse multiplicanda,'* 'beginnings or principles should not be multiplied beyond necessity.' It is implied in this, that the nature of things itself offers material for the postulated unity of reason, and that the apparent infinite variety ought not to prevent us from supposing behind it the existence of unity in fundamental properties, from which all diversity is derived by mere determination only. That unity, though it is an idea only, has been at all times so zealously pursued, that there was more ground for moderating than for encouraging the desire for it. It was something when chemists succeeded in reducing all salts to two genera, namely, acids and alkalies; but they tried to consider even this distinction as a variety only, or as a different manifestation of one and the same fundamental element. Different kinds of earths (the material of stones and even of metals) have been reduced gradually to three, at last to two; but not content with this, chemists cannot get rid of the idea that there is behind those varieties but one genus, nay, that there may be even a common principle for the earths and the salts. It might be supposed that this is only an economical trick of reason, for the purpose of saving itself trouble, and a purely hypothetical attempt which, if successful, would impart by that very unity a certain amount of probability to the presupposed principle of explanation. Such a selfish purpose, however, can easily be distinguished from the idea according to which we all presuppose that this unity of reason agrees with nature, and that in this case reason does not beg but bids, although we may be quite unable, as yet, to determine the limits of that unity.

If there existed among phenomena so great a diversity, not of form, for in this they may be similar, but of contents, that even the sharpest human understanding could not, by a comparison of the one with the other, discover the slightest similarity among them (a case which is quite conceivable), the logical law of genera would have no existence at all, there would be no concept of genus, nor any general concept, nay, no understanding at all, considering that the understanding has to do with concepts only. The logical principle of genera presupposes, therefore, a transcendental one, if it is to be applied to nature, that is, to all objects presented to our senses. According to it, in the manifoldness of a possible experience, some homogeneousness is necessarily supposed (although it may be impossible to determine its degree *a priori*), because without it, no empirical concepts, and consequently no experience, would be possible.

The logical principle of genera, which postulates identity, is balanced by another principle, namely, that of species, which requires manifoldness and diversity in things, in spite of their agreement as belonging to the same genus, and which prescribes to the understanding that it should pay no less attention to the one than to the other. This principle, depending on acute observation or on the faculty of distinction, checks the generalising flights of fancy, and reason thus exhibits a twofold and conflicting interest, namely, on the one hand, the interest in the *extent* (generality) of genera, on the other hand, the interest in the *contents* (distinction) of the manifoldness of species. In the former case the understanding thinks more *under* its concepts, in the latter, more *in* its concepts. This distinction shows itself in the different manner of thought among students of nature, some of them (who are pre-eminently speculative) being almost averse to heterogeneousness, and always intent on the unity of genera; while others, pre-eminently empirical, are constantly striving to divide nature into so much variety that one might lose almost all hope of being able to judge its phenomena according to general principles.

This latter tendency of thought is likewise based on a logical principle which aims at the systematical completeness of all knowledge, so that, beginning with the genus and descending to the manifold that may be contained in it, we try to impart extension to our system, as we tried to impart unity to it, when ascending to a genus. For if we only know the sphere of a concept which determines a genus, we can no more judge how far its subdivision may be carried than we can judge how far the divisibility of matter may be carried, by knowing the space it occupies. Hence every *genus* requires *species,* and these again *sub-species,* and as none even of these sub-species is without a sphere (extent as *conceptus communis*), reason in its utmost extension requires that no species or sub-species should in itself be considered as the lowest. Every species is always a concept containing that only which is common to different things, and as it cannot be completely determined, it cannot be directly referred to an individual, but must always comprehend other concepts, that is, sub-species. This principle of specification might be expressed by *entium varietates non temere esse minuendas.*

It is easily seen that this logical law also would be without meaning and incapable of application, unless it were founded on a transcendental *law of specification* which, though it cannot demand a real *infinity* of variety in things that are to become our objects (for this would not be justified by the logical principle, which only asserts the *indeterminability* of the logical sphere with regard to a possible division), yet imposes on the understanding the duty of looking for sub-species under every species, and for smaller varieties for every variety. If there were no lower concepts, there could not be higher concepts. Now the understanding knows all that it knows by concepts only, and hence, however far it may carry the division, never by means of intuition alone, but again and again by lower concepts. In order to know phenomena in their complete determination (which is possible by the understanding only) it is necessary to carry on without stopping the specification of its concepts, and always to proceed to still remaining differences or varieties of which abstraction had been made in forming the concept of the species, and still more in forming that of the genus.

Nor can this law of specification have been derived from experience, which can never give so far-reaching a prospect.

Empirical specification very soon comes to a standstill in the distinction of the manifold, unless it is led by the antecedent transcendental law of specification, as a principle of reason, and impelled to look for and to conjecture still differences, even where they do not appear to the senses. That absorbent earths are of different kinds (chalk and muriatic earths) could only be discovered by an antecedent rule of reason, which required the understanding to look for diversity, because it presupposed such wealth in nature as to feel justified in anticipating such diversity. For it is only under a presupposition of a diversity in nature, and under the condition that its objects should be homogeneous, that we have understanding, because it is this very diversity of all that can be comprehended under a concept which constitutes the use of that concept, and the occupation of the understanding.

Reason thus prepares the field for the understanding—

1st. Through the principle of the *homogeneousness* of the manifold, as arranged under higher genera.

2ndly. Through the principle of the *variety* of the homogeneous in lower species; to which,

3rdly, it adds a law of the *affinity* of all concepts, which requires a continual transition from every species to every other species, by a gradual increase of diversity. We may call these the principles of *homogeneousness*, of *specification*, and of *continuity* of forms. The last arises from the union of the two former, after both in ascending to higher genera, and in descending to lower species, the systematical connection in the idea has been completed; so that all diversities are related to each other, because springing from one highest genus, through all degrees of a more and more extended determination.

We may represent to ourselves the systematical unity under these three logical principles, in the following manner. Every concept may be regarded as a point which, as the standpoint of the spectator, has its own horizon, enclosing a number of things that may be represented, and, as it were, surveyed from that point. Within that horizon, an infinite number of points must exist, each of which has again its own narrower horizon; that is, every species contains sub-species, according to the principle of specification, and the logical horizon consists of smaller horizons (sub-species only), but not of points, which possess no extent (individuals). But for all these different horizons, that is genera, determined by as many concepts, a common horizon may be imagined, in which they may all be surveyed, as from a common centre. This would be the higher

genus, while the highest genus would be the universal and true
horizon, determined from the standpoint of the highest concept, and comprehending all variety as genera, species, and
sub-species.

That highest standpoint is reached by the law of homogeneousness, and all the lower standpoints in their greatest variety,
by the law of specification. As in this way there is no void in
the whole extent of all possible concepts, and as nothing can
be met with outside it, there arises from the presupposition of
that universal horizon and its complete division, the principle
of *non datur vacuum formarum.* According to this principle
there are no different original and first *genera,* as it were
isolated and separated from each other (by an intervening
void), but all diverse *genera* are divisions only of one supreme
and general *genus.* From that principle springs its immediate
consequence, *datur continuum formarum;* that is, all the diversities of species touch each other and admit of no transition from one to another *per saltum,* but only by small
degrees of difference, by which from one we arrive at the
other. In one word, there are neither species nor sub-species,
which (in the view of reason) are the nearest possible to each
other, but there always remain possible intermediate species,
differing from the first and the second by smaller degrees than
those by which these differ from each other.

The first law, therefore, keeps us from admitting an extravagant variety of different original genera, and recommends
attention to homogeneousness. The second, on the contrary,
checks that tendency to unity, and prescribes distinction of
sub-species before applying any general concept to individuals.
The third unites both, by prescribing, even with the utmost
variety, homogeneousness, through the gradual transition from
the one species to another: thus indicating a kind of relationship of the different branches, as having all sprung from the
same stem.

This logical law, however, of the *continuum specierum*
(*formarum logicarum*) presupposes a transcendental law (*lex
continui in natura*), without which the understanding would
only be misled by following, it may be, a path contrary to
nature. That law must therefore rest on purely transcendental,
and not on empirical grounds. For in the latter case, it would
come later than the systems, while in fact the systematical
character of our knowledge of nature is produced by it. Nor
are these laws intended only for tests to be carried out experi-
mentally by their aid, although such a connection, if it is found

in nature, forms a powerful argument in support of that unity which was conceived as hypothetical only. These laws have therefore a certain utility in this respect also, yet it is easily seen that they regard the parsimony of causes, the manifoldness of effects, and an affinity between the parts of nature arising from thence, as both rational and natural, so that these principles carry their recommendation direct, and not only as aids towards a proper method of studying nature.

It is easy to see, however, that this continuity of forms is a mere idea, and that no object corresponding to it can be pointed out in experience, *not only* because the species in nature are actually divided, and must form, each by itself, a *quantum discretum,* while, if the gradual progression of their affinity were continuous, nature would contain a real infinity of intermediate links between every two given species, which is impossible; *but also,* because we cannot make any definite empirical use of that law, considering that not the smallest criterion of affinity is indicated by it to tell us how and how far we ought to seek for grades of affinity, it telling us only that we ought to seek for them.

If we now arrange these principles of systematical *unity* in the order required for their *empirical employment,* they might stand thus: *manifoldness, variety,* and *unity,* each of them as ideas taken in the highest degree of their completeness. Reason presupposes the cognitions of the understanding in their direct relation to experience, and looks for their unity according to ideas which go far beyond the possibility of experience. The affinity of the manifold, in spite of its diversity, under one principle of unity, refers not only to things, but even more to the qualities and powers of things. Thus if, for example, our imperfect experience represents to us the orbits of the planets as circular, and we find deviations from that course, we look for them in that which is able to change the circle according to a fixed law, through infinite intervening degrees, into one of these deviating courses; that is, we suppose that the movements of the planets which are not circular will approximate more or less to the properties of a circle, and thus are led on to the ellipse. The comets display a still greater deviation in their courses, because, so far as our experience goes, they do not return in a circle, and we then conjecture a parabolic course which, at all events, is allied to the ellipse, and if its longer axis is widely extended, cannot be distinguished from it in our observations. We thus arrive, under the guidance of these principles, at a unity of the different genera or kinds in the forms of these orbits, and, proceeding still further, at a unity of the cause of all the laws of their movements, namely, gravitation. Here we take our stand and extend our conquests, trying to explain all varieties and seeming deviations from those rules from the same principle, nay, adding more than experience can ever affirm, namely, imaginary hyperbolic courses of comets constructed according to the rules of affinity, in which courses these heavenly bodies may entirely leave our solar system, and, moving from sun to sun, unite in their course the most distant parts of a universe unlimited to our minds, but yet held together by one and the same moving power.

What is most remarkable in these principles, and is, in fact, their chief interest for us is, that they seem to be transcendental, and, although containing mere ideas for the guidance of the empirical use of reason, ideas which our reason can only follow as it were asymptotically, that is, approximately and without our reaching them, they nevertheless possess, as synthetical propositions *a priori*, an objective, though an undefined validity, serving as a rule for possible experience, nay, as heuristic principles in the elaboration of experience. With all this a transcendental deduction of them cannot be produced, and is, in fact, as we have proved before, always impossible with regard to ideas.

In the transcendental Analytic we distinguished the *dynamical* principles of the understanding, as purely regulative principles of the *intuition*, from the *mathematical*, which, in regard to intuition, are constitutive. In spite of this, these dynamical laws are constitutive with regard to *experience*, because they render the *concepts*, without which there can be no experience, *a priori* possible. The principles of pure reason, however, cannot be constitutive, even with reference to empirical *concepts*, because we cannot assign to them any corresponding schema of sensibility; they cannot, consequently, have any object *in concreto*. If, then, I give up an empirical use of them as constitutive principles, how can I yet secure to them a regulative employment, and with it some objective validity, and what can be the meaning of it?

The understanding forms an object for reason in the same manner as sensibility for the understanding. It is the proper business of reason to render the unity of all possible empirical acts of the understanding systematical, in the same manner as the understanding connects the manifold of phenomena by concepts, and brings it under empirical laws. The acts of the understanding, however, without the schemata of sensibility, are *undefined,* and in the same manner the *unity of reason* is in itself undefined with reference to the conditions under which, and the extent to which, the understanding may connect its concepts systematically. But although no schema of *intuition* can be discovered for the perfect systematical unity of all the concepts of the understanding, it is possible and necessary that there should be an *analogon* of such a schema, and this is the idea of the *maximum,* both of the division and of the combination of the knowledge of the understanding under one single principle. It is quite possible to form a definite thought of what is greatest and absolutely complete, when all restrictive conditions that lead to an undefined manifoldness have been omitted. In this sense the idea of reason forms an analogon of the schema of sensibility, but with this difference, that the application of the concepts of the understanding to the schema of reason is not a knowledge of the object itself, as in the case of the application of the categories to sensuous schemata, but only a rule or principle for the systematical unity in the whole use of the understanding. Now, as every principle which fixes *a priori* a perfect unity of its use for the understanding is valid, though indirectly only, for the object of experience also, it follows that the principles of pure reason have objective reality with reference to that object also, not, however, in order to *determine* anything therein, but only in order to indicate the procedure by which the empirical and definite use of the understanding may throughout remain in complete harmony with itself, by being brought into connection, *as much as possible,* with the principle of systematical unity, and being deduced from it.

I call all subjective principles which are derived, not from the quality of an object, but from the interest which reason takes in a certain possible perfection of our knowledge of an object, *maxims* of reason. Thus there are maxims of speculative reason, which rest entirely on its speculative interest, though they may seem to be objective principles.

When purely regulative principles are taken for constitutive, they may become contradictory, as objective principles. If, however, they are taken for *maxims* only, there is no real contradiction, but it is only the different interest of reason which causes different modes of thought. In reality, reason has one interest only, and the conflict of its maxims arises only from a difference and a mutual limitation of the methods in which that interest is to be satisfied.

In this manner one philosopher is influenced more by the interest of *diversity* (according to the principle of specification), another by the interests of *unity* (according to the principle of aggregation). Each believes that he has derived his judgment from his insight into the object, and yet founds it entirely on the greater or smaller attachment to one of the two principles, neither[3] of which rests on objective grounds, but only on an interest of reason, and should therefore be called maxims rather than principles. I often see even intelligent men quarrelling with each other about the characteristic distinctions of men, animals, or plants, nay, even of minerals, the one admitting the existence of certain tribal characteristics, founded on descent, or decided and inherited differences of families, races, etc., while others insist that nature has made the same provision for all, and that all differences are due to accidental environment. But they need only consider the nature of the object, in order to understand that it is far too deeply hidden for both of them to enable them to speak from a real insight into the nature of the object. It is nothing but the two-fold interest of reason, one party cherishing the one, another party the other, or pretending to do so. But this difference of the two maxims of manifoldness or unity in nature may easily be adjusted, though as long as they are taken for objective knowledge they cause not only disputes, but actually create impediments which hinder the progress of truth, until a means is found of reconciling the contradictory interests, and thus giving satisfaction to reason.

The same applies to the assertion or denial of the famous law of the *continuous scale* of created beings, first advanced by Leibniz, and so cleverly trimmed up by Bonnet. It is nothing but a carrying out of the principle of affinity, resting on the interest of reason; for neither observation nor insight into the constitution of nature could ever have supplied it as an objective assertion. The steps of such a ladder, as far as they can be supplied by experience, are too far apart from each other, and the so-called small differences are often in nature itself such wide gaps that no value can be attached to such observations as revealing the intentions of nature, particularly as it must always be easy to discover in the great variety of things certain similarities and approximations. The method, on the contrary, of looking for order in nature, according to such a principle, and the maxim of admitting such order (though it

---

[3] Read *keiner* instead of *keine*.

may be uncertain where and how far) as existing in nature in general, form certainly a legitimate and excellent regulative principle of reason, only that, as such, it goes far beyond where experience or observation could follow it. It only indicates the way which leads to systematical unity, but does not determine anything beyond.

Of the Ultimate Aim of the Natural Dialectic of Human Reason

The ideas of pure reason can never be dialectical in themselves, but it must be due to their misemployment, if a deceptive illusion arise from them. They are given to us by the nature of our reason, and this highest tribunal of all the rights and claims of speculation cannot possibly itself contain original fallacies and deceits. We must suppose, therefore, that they had a good and legitimate intention in the natural disposition of our reason. The mob of sophists, however, cry out as usual about absurdities and contradictions, and blame the government the secret plans of which they cannot even understand, while it is to its beneficent influence that they owe their protection and that amount of intelligence which enables them to blame and condemn the government.

We cannot use a concept *a priori* with any safety, without having first established its transcendental deduction. It is true the ideas of pure reason do not allow of a deduction in the same manner as the categories; but if they are to claim any, though only an undefined objective validity, and are not to represent mere fictions of thought only (*entia rationis ratiocinantis*), a deduction of them must be possible, even though it may differ from that which we were able to give of the categories. This will form the completion of the critical task of pure reason, and it is this which we now mean to undertake.

It makes a great difference whether something is represented to our reason as an *object absolutely,* or merely as an *object in the idea.* In the former case my concepts are meant to determine the object, in the latter there is only a schema to which no object, not even a hypothetical one, corresponds directly, but which only serves to represent to ourselves indirectly other objects through their relation to that idea, and according to their systematical unity. Thus I say that the concept of a highest intelligence is a mere idea, that is, that its objective reality is not to consist in its referring directly to any object (for in that sense we should not be able to justify its objective validity); but that it is only a schema, arranged according to the conditions of the highest unity of reason, of the concept of a thing in general, serving only to obtain the greatest systematical unity in the empirical use of our reason, by helping us, as it were, to deduce the object of experience from the imagined object of that idea as its ground or cause. Thus we are led to say, for instance, that the things of the world must be considered *as if* they owed their existence to some supreme intelligence; and the idea is thus a heuristic only, not an ostensive concept, showing us not how an object is really constituted, but how we, under the guidance of that concept, should look for the constitution and connection of the objects of experience in general. If, then, it can be shown that the three transcendental ideas (the *psychological, cosmological,* and *theological*), although they cannot be used directly to *determine* any object corresponding to them, yet as rules[4] of the empirical use of reason will lead, under the presupposition of such an *object* in the *idea,* to a systematical unity, and to an extension of our empirical knowledge, without ever running counter to this knowledge, it becomes a necessary *maxim* of reason to act in accordance with such ideas. And this is really the transcendental deduction of all ideas of speculative reason, considered not as *constitutive* principles for extending our knowledge to more objects than can be given by experience, but as *regulative* principles for the systematical unity of the manifold of empirical knowledge in general, which knowledge, within its own limits, can thus be better arranged and improved than it would be possible without such ideas, and by the mere use of the principles of the understanding.

I shall try to make this clearer. Following these ideas as principles, we shall first (in psychology) connect all phenomena, all the activity and receptivity of our mind, according to our internal experience, as if our mind were a simple substance, existing permanently, and with personal identity (in this life at least), while its states, to which those of the body belong as external conditions, are changing continually. Secondly (in cosmology), we are bound to follow up the conditions both of internal and external natural phenomena in an investigation that can never become complete, looking upon this investigation as infinite, and without any first or supreme member; but we ought not therefore to deny the purely intelligible first grounds of these phenomena, as outside of them,

4 Instead of *alle* read *als.*

though not allowed to bring them ever into connection with our explanations of nature, for the simple reason that we do not know them. Thirdly, and lastly (in theology), we must consider everything that may belong to the whole of possible experience as if that experience formed one absolute but thoroughly dependent, and always, within the world of sense, conditioned unity; but, at the same time, as if it, the whole of phenomena (the world of sense itself), had one supreme and all-sufficient ground, outside its sphere, namely, an independent, original, creative reason, in reference to which we direct all empirical use of *our* reason in its widest extension in such a way as if the objects themselves had sprung from that archetype of all reason. In other words, we ought not to derive the internal phenomena of the soul as if from a simple thinking substance, but derive them from each other, according to the idea of a simple being; we ought not to derive the order and systematical unity of the world from a supreme intelligence, but borrow from the idea of a supremely wise cause the rule according to which reason may best be used for her own satisfaction in the connection of causes and effects in this world.

Now there is nothing that could in the least prevent us from admitting these ideas as objective and hypostatical also, except in the case of the cosmological idea, where reason, when trying to carry it out objectively, is met by an antinomy. There is no such antinomy in the psychological and theological ideas, and how could anybody contest their objective reality, as he knows as little how to deny, as we how to assert, their possibility?

It is true nevertheless that, in order to admit anything, it is not enough that there should be no positive impediment to it, nor are we allowed to introduce fictions of our thoughts, transcending all our concepts, though contradicting none, as real and definite objects, on the mere credit of our somewhat perfunctory speculative reason. They should not therefore be admitted as real in themselves, but their reality should only be considered as the reality of a schema of a regulative principle for the systematical unity of all natural knowledge. Hence they are to be admitted as analoga only of real things, and not as real things in themselves. We remove from the object of an idea the conditions which limit the concepts of our understanding, and which alone enable us to have a definite concept of anything; and then we represent to ourselves a something of which we know not in the least what it is by itself, but which, nevertheless, we represent to ourselves in a relation to the whole of phenomena, analogous to that relation which phenomena have among themselves.

If therefore we admit such ideal beings, we do not really enlarge our knowledge beyond the objects of possible experience, but only the empirical unity of those objects, by means of that systematical unity of which the idea furnishes us the schema, and which therefore cannot claim to be a constitutive, but only a regulative principle. For if we admit a something, or a real being, corresponding to the idea, we do not intend thereby to enlarge our knowledge of things by means of transcendental[5] concepts; for such a being is admitted in the idea only, and not by itself, and only in order to express that systematical unity which is to guide the empirical use of our reason, without stating anything as to what is the ground of that unity or the internal nature of such a being on which, as its cause, that unity depends.

Thus the transcendental and the only definite concept which purely speculative reason gives us of God is in the strictest sense *deistic;* that is, reason does not even supply us with the objective validity of such a concept, but only with the idea of something on which the highest and necessary unity of all empirical reality is founded, and which we cannot represent to ourselves except in analogy with a real substance, being, according to the laws of nature, the cause of all things; always supposing that we undertake to think it at all as a particular object, and, satisfied with the mere idea of the regulative principle of reason, do not rather put aside the completion of all the conditions of our thought, as too much for the human understanding, which, however, is hardly compatible with that perfect systematical unity of our knowledge to which reason at least imposes no limits.

Thus it happens that, if we admit a Divine Being, we have not the slightest conception either of the internal possibility of its supreme perfection, nor of the necessity of its existence, but are able at least thus to satisfy all other questions relating to contingent things, and give the most perfect satisfaction to reason with reference to that highest unity in its empirical application that has to be investigated, but not in reference to that hypothesis itself. This proves that it is the speculative interest of reason, and not its real insight, which justifies it in starting

[5] The early editions read *transcendenten,* instead of *transcendentalen,* which is given in the corrigenda of the Fifth Edition; it is not impossible, however, that Kant may have meant to write *transcendenten,* in order to indicate the illegitimate use of these concepts.

from a point so far above its proper sphere, in order to survey from thence its objects, as belonging to a complete whole.

Here we meet with a distinction in our mode of thought, the premisses remaining the same, a distinction which is somewhat subtle, but of great importance in transcendental philosophy. I may have sufficient ground for admitting something relatively (*suppositio relativa*), without having a right to admit it absolutely (*suppositio absoluta*). This distinction comes in when we have to deal with a regulative principle, of which we know the necessity by itself, but not the source of this necessity, and where we admit a supreme cause, only in order to think the universality of the principle with greater definiteness. Thus, if I think of a being as existing which corresponds to a mere idea, and to a transcendental one, I ought not to admit the existence of such a being by itself, because no concepts through which I can conceive any object definitely, can reach it, and the conditions of the objective validity of my concepts are excluded by the idea itself. The concepts of reality, of substance, even of causality, and those of necessity in existence, have no meaning that could determine any object, unless they are used to make the empirical knowledge of an object possible. They may be used, therefore, to explain the possibility of things in the world of sense, but not to explain the possibility of a *universe itself,* because such an hypothesis is outside the world and could never be an object of possible experience. I can, however, admit perfectly well such an inconceivable Being, being the object of a mere idea, relative to the world of sense, though not as existing by itself. For if the greatest possible empirical use of my reason depends on an idea (on the systematically complete unity of which I shall soon speak more in detail), which by itself can never be adequately represented in experience, though it is indispensably necessary in order to bring the empirical unity as near as possible to the highest perfection, I shall not only have the right, but even the duty, to realise such an idea, that is, to assign to it a real object, though only as a something in general, which by itself I do not know at all, and to which, as the cause of that systematical unity, I ascribe, in reference to it, such qualities as are analogous to the concepts employed by the understanding in dealing with experience. I shall, therefore, according to the analogy of realities in the world, of substances, of causality, and of necessity, conceive a Being possessing all these in the highest perfection, and, as this idea rests on my reason only, conceive that Being as *self-subsistent reason,* being, through the ideas of the greatest harmony and unity, the cause of the universe. In doing this I omit all conditions which could limit the idea, simply in order to render, with the help of such a fundamental càuse, the systematical unity of the manifold in the universe, and, through it, the greatest possible empirical use of reason, possible. I then look upon all connections in the world as if they were ordered by a supreme reason, of which our own reason is but a faint copy, and I represent to myself that Supreme Being through concepts which, properly speaking, are applicable to the world of sense only. As, however, I make none but a relative use of that transcendental hypothesis, as the substratum of the greatest possible unity of experience, I may perfectly well represent a Being which I distinguish from the world, by qualities which belong to the world of sense only. For I demand by no means, nor am I justified in demanding, that I should know that object of my idea, according to what it may be by itself. I have no concepts whatever for it, and even the concepts of reality, substance, causality, ay, of the necessity in existence, lose all their meaning, and become mere titles of concepts, void of contents, as soon as I venture with them outside the field of the senses. I only present to myself the relation of a Being, utterly unknown to me as existing by itself, to the greatest possible systematical unity of the universe, in order to use it as a schema of the regulative principle of the greatest possible empirical use of my reason.

If now we glance at the transcendental object of our idea, we find that we cannot, according to the concepts of reality, substance, causality, etc., presuppose its reality *by itself,* because such concepts are altogether inapplicable to something totally distinct from the world of sense. The supposition, therefore, which reason makes of a Supreme Being, as the highest cause, is relative only, devised for the sake of the systematical unity in the world of sense, and a mere Something in the idea, while we have no concept of what it may be by itself. Thus we are able to understand why we require the idea of an original Being, *necessary by itself,* with reference to all that is given to the senses as existing, but can never have the slightest conception of it and of its absolute *necessity.*

At this point we are able to place the results of the whole transcendental Dialectic clearly before our eyes, and to define accurately the final aim of the ideas of pure reason, which could become dialectical through misapprehension and carelessness only. Pure reason is, in fact, concerned with nothing but itself, nor can it have any other occupation, because what is given to it are not the objects intended for the unity of an empirical concept, but the knowledge supplied by the understanding for the unity of the concept of reason, that is, of its connection according to a principle. The unity of reason is the unity of a system, and that systematical unity does not serve objectively as a principle of reason to extend its sway over objects, but subjectively as a maxim to extend its sway over all possible empirical knowledge of objects. Nevertheless, the systematical connection which reason can impart to the understanding in its empirical use helps not only to extend that use, but confirms at the same time its correctness; nay, the principle of such systematical unity is objective also, though in an indefinite manner (*principium vagum*), not as a constitutive principle, determining something in its direct object, but only as a regulative principle and maxim, advancing and strengthening infinitely (indefinitely), the empirical use of reason by the opening of new paths unknown to the understanding, without ever running counter to the laws of its practical use.

Reason, however, cannot think this systematical unity, without attributing to its idea an object, which, as experience has never given an example of complete systematical unity, can never be given in any experience. This Being, demanded by reason (*ens rationis ratiocinatae*), is no doubt a mere idea, and not therefore received as something absolutely real and real *by itself*. It is only admitted problematically (for we cannot reach it by any concepts of the understanding), in order to enable us to look upon the connection of things in the world of sense, *as if* they had their ground in that being, the real intention being to found upon it that systematical unity which is indispensable to reason, helpful in every way to the empirical knowledge of the understanding, and never a hindrance to it.

We misapprehend at once the true meaning of that idea, if we accept it as the assertion, or even as the hypothesis of a real thing to which the ground of the systematical construction of the world should be ascribed. What we ought to do is to leave it entirely uncertain, what that ground which escapes all our concepts may be by itself, and to use the idea only as a point of view from which alone we may expand that unity which is as essential to reason as beneficial to the understanding. In one word, that transcendental thing is only the schema of the regulative principle with which reason spreads systematical unity, as far as possible, over all experience.

The first object of such an idea is the *ego*, considered merely as a thinking nature (soul). Now if I want to know the qualities with which a thinking being exists in itself, I have to consult experience: but of all the categories, I cannot apply a single one to that object, unless its schema is given in sensuous intuition. Thus, however, I can never arrive at a systematical unity of all the phenomena of the internal sense. Reason, therefore, instead of taking from experience the concept of that which the soul is in reality, which would not lead us very far, prefers the concept of the empirical unity of all thought, and by representing that unity as unconditioned and original, it changes it into a concept of reason, or an idea of a simple substance, a substance unchangeable in itself (personally identical), and in communication with other real things outside it; in one word, into a simple self-subsistent intelligence. In doing this, its object is merely to find principles of systematical unity for the explanation of the phenomena of the soul, so that all determinations may be received as existing in one subject, all powers, as much as possible, as derived from one fundamental power, and all changes as belonging to the states of one and the same permanent being, while all *phenomena* in space are represented as totally different from the acts of *thought*. That simplicity of substance, etc., was only meant to be the schema of this regulative principle; it is not assumed to be the real ground of all the properties of the soul. These properties may rest on quite different grounds, of which we know nothing; nor could we know the soul even by these assumed predicates by itself, even if we regarded them as absolutely valid with regard to it, for they really constitute a mere idea which cannot be represented *in concreto*. Nothing but good can spring from such a psychological idea, if only we take care not to take it for more than an idea, that is, if we apply it only in relation to the systematical use of reason, with reference to the phenomena of our soul. For in that case no empirical laws of corporeal phenomena, which are of a totally different kind, are mixed up with the explanation of what belongs to the *internal sense;* and no windy hypothesis of generation, extinction, and palingenesis of souls are admitted. The consideration of this object of the internal sense remains pure and unmixed with heterogeneous matters, while reason in its investigations is directed towards tracing all the grounds of explanation, as far as possible, to one single principle; and this can best be achieved, nay, cannot be achieved otherwise but by such a schema which attributes to the soul hypothetically the character of a real being. The psychological idea cannot be anything but such a schema of a regulative concept. The very question, for instance, whether the soul by itself be of a spiritual nature, would have no meaning, because, by such a concept, I should take away not only corporeal, but all nature, that is, all predicates of any possible experience, and therefore all the conditions under which the object of such a concept could be thought; and, in that case, the concept would have no meaning at all.

The second regulative idea of speculative reason is the concept of the universe. For nature is really the only object given to us in regard to which reason requires regulative principles. Nature, however, is twofold, either thinking or corporeal. In order to think the internal possibility of the latter, that is, in order to determine the application of the categories to it, we require no idea, that is, no representation which transcends experience. Nor is such an idea possible in regard to it, because we are here guided by sensuous intuition only, different from what it was in the case of the psychological fundamental concept of the I, which contains *a priori* a certain form of thought, namely, the unity of the I. There remains therefore for pure reason nothing to deal with but nature in general, and the completeness of its conditions according to some principle. The absolute totality of the series of these conditions determining the derivation of all their members, is an idea which, though never brought to perfection in the empirical use of reason, may yet become a rule, telling us how to proceed in the explanation of given phenomena (whether in an ascending or descending line), namely, as if the series were in themselves infinite, that is, *in indefinitum;* while, when reason itself is considered as the determining cause (in freedom), in the case of practical principles therefore, we must proceed as if we had to deal, not with an object of the senses, but with one of the pure understanding. Here the conditions are no longer placed within the series of phenomena, but outside it, and the series of states considered, as if it had an absolute beginning through an intelligible cause. All this proves that cosmological ideas are nothing but regulative principles, and by no means constitutive, as establishing a real totality of such series. The remainder of this argument may be seen in its place, namely, in the chapter on the Antinomy of Pure Reason.

The third idea of pure reason, containing a merely relative

hypothesis of a Being which is the only and all-sufficient cause of all cosmological series, is the idea of God. We have not the slightest ground to admit absolutely the object of that idea (to suppose it in itself); for what could enable, or even justify us in believing or asserting a Being of the highest perfection, and absolutely necessary from its very nature, on the strength of its concept only, except the world with reference to which alone such an hypothesis may be called necessary? We then perceive that the idea of it, like all speculative ideas, means no more than that reason requires us to consider all connection in the world according to the principles of a systematical unity, and, therefore, as if the whole of it had sprung from a single all-embracing Being, as its highest and all-sufficient cause. We see, therefore, that reason can have no object here but its own formal rule in the extension of its empirical use, but can never aim at extension beyond *all limits of its empirical application.* This idea, therefore, does not involve a constitutive principle of its use as applied to possible experience.

The highest formal unity, which is based on concepts of reason alone, is the systematical and purposeful unity of things, and it is the speculative interest of reason which makes it necessary to regard all order in the world as if it had originated in the purpose of a supreme wisdom. Such a principle opens to our reason in the field of experience quite new views, how to connect the things of the world according to teleological laws, and thus to arrive at their greatest systematical unity. The admission of a highest intelligence, as the only cause of the universe, though in the idea only, can therefore always benefit reason, and yet never injure it. For if, with regard to the figure of the earth (which is round, though somewhat flattened*), of mountains, and seas, etc., we admit at once nothing but wise intentions of their author, we are enabled to make in this wise a number of important discoveries. If we

---

* The advantage which arises from the circular shape of the earth is well known; but few only know that its flattening, which gives it the form of a spheroid, alone prevents the elevations of continents, or even of smaller volcanically raised mountains, from continuously and, within no very great space of time, considerably altering the axis of the earth. The protuberance of the earth at the equator forms however so considerable a mountain, that the impetus of every other mountain can never drive it perceptibly out of its position with reference to the axis of the earth. And yet people do not hesitate to explain this wise arrangement simply from the equilibrium of the once fluid mass.

keep to this hypothesis as a purely regulative principle, even error cannot hurt us much; for the worst that could happen would be that, when we expected a teleological connection (*nexus finalis*), we only find a mechanical or physical (*nexus effectivus*), in which case we merely lose an additional unity, but we do not destroy the unity of reason in its empirical application. And even this failure could not affect the law itself, in its general and teleological character. For although an anatomist may be convicted of error, if referring any member of an animal body to a purpose of which it can clearly be shown that it does not belong to it, it is entirely impossible in any given case to *prove* that an arrangement of nature, be it what it may, has no purpose at all. Medical physiology, therefore, enlarges its very limited empirical knowledge of the purposes of the members of an organic body by a principle inspired by pure reason only, so far as to admit confidently, and with the approbation of all intelligent persons, that everything in an animal has its purpose and advantage. Such a supposition, if used constitutively, goes far beyond where our present observation would justify us in going, which shows that it is nothing but a regulative principle of reason, leading us on to the highest systematical unity, by the idea of an intelligent causality in the supreme cause of the world, and by the supposition that this, as the highest intelligence, is the cause of everything, according to the wisest design.

But if we remove this restriction of the idea to a merely regulative use, reason is led away in many ways. It leaves the ground of experience, which ought always to show the vestiges of its progress, and ventures beyond it to what is inconceivable and unsearchable, becoming giddy from the very height of it, and from seeing itself on that high standpoint entirely cut off from its proper work in agreement with experience.

The first fault which arises from our using the idea of a Supreme Being, not regulatively only, but (contrary to the nature of an idea) constitutively, is what I call the indolence of reason (*ignava ratio**). We may so term every principle which causes us to look on our investigation of nature, wher-

---

* This was a name given by the old dialecticians to a sophistical argument, which ran thus: If it is your fate that you should recover from this illness, you will recover, whether you send for a doctor or not. Cicero says that this argument was called *ignava ratio*, because, if we followed it, reason would have no use at all in life. It is for this reason that I apply the same name to this sophistical argument of pure reason.

ever it may be, as absolutely complete, so that reason may rest as if her task were fully accomplished. Thus the task of reason is rendered very easy even by the psychological idea, if that idea is used as a constitutive principle for the explanation of the phenomena of our soul, and afterwards even for the extension of our knowledge of this subject beyond all possible experience (its state after death); but the natural use of reason, under the guidance of experience, is thus entirely ruined and destroyed. The dogmatical spiritualist finds no difficulty in explaining the unchanging unity of the person, amidst all the changes of condition, from the unity of the thinking substance, which he imagines he perceives directly in the I;—or the interest which we take in things that are to happen after death, from the consciousness of the immaterial nature of our thinking subject, and so on. He dispenses with all investigations of the origin of these internal phenomena from physical causes, passing by, as it were, by a decree of transcendent reason, the immanent sources of knowledge given by experience. This may be convenient to himself, but involves a sacrifice of all real insight. These detrimental consequences become still more palpable in the dogmatism involved in our idea of a supreme intelligence, and of the theological system of nature, erroneously based on it (physicotheology). For here all the aims which we observe in nature, many of which we only imagined ourselves, serve to make the investigation of causes extremely easy, if, instead of looking for them in the general mechanical laws of matter, we appeal directly to the unsearchable counsel of the supreme wisdom, imagining the efforts of our reason as ended, when we have really dispensed with its employment, which nowhere finds its proper guidance, except where the order of nature and the succession of changes, according to their own internal and general laws, supply it. This error may be avoided, if we do not merely consider certain parts of nature, such as the distribution of land, its structure, the constitution and direction of certain mountains, or even the organisation of plants and animals, from the standpoint of final aims, but look upon this systematical unity of nature as something *general,* in relation to the idea of a supreme intelligence. For, in this case, we look upon nature as founded on intelligent purposes, according to general laws, no particular arrangement of nature being exempt from them, but only exhibiting them more or less distinctly. We have then, in fact, a regulative principle of the systematical unity in a teleological connection, though we do not determine it beforehand, but only look forward to it expectantly, while following up the physico-mechanical connection according to general laws. In this way alone can the principle of systematical and intelligent unity enlarge the use of reason with reference to experience, without at any time being prejudicial to it.

The second error, arising from the misapprehension of the principle of systematical unity, is that of perverted reason (*perversa ratio*, ὕστερον πρότερον *rationis*). The idea of systematic unity was only intended as a regulative principle for discovering that unity, according to general laws, in the connection of things, believing that we have approached the completeness of its use by exactly so much as we have discovered of it empirically, though never able to reach it fully. Instead of this, the procedure is reversed; the reality of a principle of systematical unity is at once admitted and hypostasised, the concept of such a supreme intelligence, though being in itself entirely inscrutable, is determined anthropomorphically, and aims are afterwards imposed on nature violently and dictatorially, instead of looking for them by means of physical investigation. Thus teleology, which was meant to supplement the unity of nature according to general laws, contributes only to destroy it, and reason deprives itself of its own aim, namely, that of proving the existence of such an intelligent supreme cause from nature. For, if we may not presuppose *a priori* the most perfect design in nature as belonging to its very essence, what should direct us to look for it, and to try to approach by degrees to the highest perfection of an author, that is, to an absolutely necessary and *a priori* intelligible perfection? The regulative principle requires us to admit absolutely, and as following from the very nature of things, systematical unity as an *unity of nature,* which has not only to be known empirically, but must be admitted *a priori,* though as yet in an indefinite form only. But if I begin with a supreme ordaining Being, as the ground of all things, the unity of nature is really surrendered as being quite foreign to the nature of things, purely contingent, and not to be known from its own general laws. Thus arises a vicious circle by our presupposing what, in reality, ought to have been proved.

To mistake the regulative principle of the systematical unity of nature for a constitutive principle, and to presuppose hypostatically as cause, what is only in the idea made the foundation for the consistent use of reason, is simply to confound reason. The investigation of nature pursues its own course, guided by the chain of natural causes only, according to general laws. It knows the idea of an author, but not in order to derive from it that system of purposes which it tries to discover everywhere, but in order to recognise his existence from those purposes, which are sought in the essence of the things of nature, and, if possible, also in the essence of all things in general, and consequently to recognise his existence as absolutely necessary. Whether this succeeds or not, the idea itself remains always true, as well as its use, if only it is restricted to the conditions of a merely regulative principle.

Complete unity of design constitutes perfection (absolutely considered). If we do not find such perfection in the nature of the things which form the object of experience, that is, of all our objectively valid knowledge; if we do not find it in the general and necessary laws of nature, how shall we thence infer the idea of a supreme and absolutely necessary perfection of an original Being, as the origin of all causality? The greatest systematical and, therefore, well-planned unity teaches us, and first enables us, to make the widest use of human reason, and that idea is, therefore, inseparably connected with the very nature of our reason. That idea becomes, in fact, to us a law, and hence it is very natural for us to assume a corresponding law-giving reason (*intellectus archetypus*) from which, as the object of our reason, all systematical unity of nature should be derived.

When discussing the antinomy of pure reason, we remarked that all questions raised by pure reason must admit of an answer, and that the excuse derived from the natural limits of our knowledge, which in many questions concerning nature is as inevitable as it is just, cannot be admitted here, because questions are here placed before us through the very nature of our reason, referring entirely to its own natural constitution, and not to the nature of things. We have now an opportunity of confirming this assertion of ours, which at first sight may have appeared rash, with regard to the two questions in which pure reason takes the greatest interest, and of thus bringing to perfection our considerations on the Dialectic of pure reason.

If, then, we are asked the question (with reference to a transcendental theology),* *First,* whether there is something

* After what I have said before about the psychological idea, and its proper destination to serve as a regulative principle only for the use of reason, there is no necessity for my discussing separately and in full detail the transcendental illusion which leads us to rep-

different from the world, containing the ground of the order of the world and of its connection according to general laws? our answer is, *Certainly there is*. For the world is a sum of phenomena, and there must, therefore, be some transcendental ground of it, that is, a ground to be thought by the pure understanding only. If, *secondly*, we are asked whether that Being is a substance of the greatest reality, necessary, etc.? our answer is, *that such a question has no meaning at all*. For all the categories by which I can try to frame to myself a concept of such an object admit of none but an empirical use, and have no meaning at all, unless they are applied to objects of possible experience, that is, to the world of sense. Outside that field they are mere titles of concepts, which we may admit, but by which we can understand nothing. If, *thirdly*, the question is asked, whether we may not at least conceive this Being, which is different from the world, in *analogy* with the objects of experience? our answer is, *Certainly we may*, but only as an object in the idea, and not in the reality, that is, in so far only as it remains a substratum, unknown to us, of the systematic unity, order, and design of the world, which reason is obliged to adopt as a regulative principle in the investigation of nature. Nay, more, we need not be afraid to admit certain anthropomorphisms in that idea, which favour the regulative principle of our investigations. For it always remains an idea only, which is never referred directly to a Being, different from the world, but only to the regulative principle of the systematical unity of the world, and this by some schema of it, namely, that of a supreme intelligence, being the author of it, for the wisest purposes. It was not intended that by it we should try to form a conception of what that original cause of the unity of the world may be by itself; it was only meant to teach us how to use it, or rather its idea, with reference to the systematical use of reason, applied to the things of the world.

But, surely, people will proceed to ask, we *may*, according to this, admit a wise and omnipotent Author of the world? *Certainly*, we answer, and not only we may, but we *must*. In that case, therefore, we surely extend our knowledge beyond the field of possible experience? *By no means*. For we have only presupposed a something of which we have no concep-

---

resent hypostatically that systematical unity of the manifold phenomena of the internal sense. The procedure would here be very similar to that which we are following in our criticism of the theological ideal.

tion whatever as to what it is by itself (as a purely transcendental object). We have only, with reference to the systematical and well-designed order of the world, which we must presuppose, if we are to study nature at all, presented to ourselves that unknown Being in *analogy* with what is an empirical concept, namely, an intelligence; that is, we have, with reference to the purposes and the perfection which depend on it, attributed to it those very qualities on which, according to the conditions of our reason, such a systematical unity may depend. That idea, therefore, is entirely founded on the *employment* of our reason *in the world,* and if we were to attribute to it absolute and objective validity, we should be forgetting that it is only a Being in the idea which we think: and as we should then be taking our start from a cause, that cannot be determined by mundane considerations, we should no longer be able to employ that principle in accordance with the empirical use of reason.

But people will go on to ask, May we not then in this way use that concept, and the supposition of a Supreme Being in a rational consideration of the world? No doubt we may, and it was for that very purpose that that idea of reason was established. And if it be asked whether we may look upon arrangements in nature which have all the appearance of design, as real designs, and trace them back to a divine will, though with the intervention of certain arrangements in the world, we answer again, Yes, but only on condition that it be the same to you whether we say that the divine wisdom has arranged everything for the highest purposes, or whether we take the idea of the supreme wisdom as our rule in the investigation of nature, and as the principle of its systematical and well-planned unity according to general laws, even when we are not able to perceive that unity. In other words, it must be the same to you, when you do perceive it, whether we say, God has wisely willed it so, or nature has wisely arranged it so. For it was that greatest systematical and well-planned unity, required by your reason as the regulative principle of all investigation of nature, which gave you the right to admit the idea of a supreme intelligence as the schema of that regulative principle. As much of design, therefore, as you discover in the world, according to that principle, so much of confirmation has the legitimacy of your idea received. But as that principle was only intended for finding the necessary and greatest possible unity in nature, we shall, no doubt, owe that unity, so far as we may find it, to our idea of a Supreme Being; but we cannot, without contradicting ourselves, ignore the general laws of nature for which that idea was adopted, or look upon the designs of nature as contingent and hyperphysical in their origin. For we were not justified in admitting a Being endowed with those qualities as above nature (hyperphysical), but only in using the idea of it in order to be able to look on all phenomena[6] as being systematically connected among themselves, in analogy with a causal determination.

For the same reason we are justified, not only in representing to ourselves the cause of the world in our idea according to a subtle kind of anthropomorphism (without which we can think nothing of it), as a Being endowed with understanding, the feelings of pleasure and displeasure, and accordingly with desire and will, but also in attributing to it infinite perfection, which therefore far transcends any perfection known to us from the empirical knowledge of the order of the world. For the regulative law of systematical unity requires that we should study nature as if there existed in it everywhere, with the greatest possible variety, an infinitely systematical and well-planned unity. And although we can discover but little of that perfection of the world, it is nevertheless a law of our reason, always to look for it and to expect it; and it must be beneficial, and can never be hurtful, to carry on the investigation of nature according to this principle. But in admitting this fundamental idea of a Supreme Author, it is clear that I do not admit the existence and knowledge of such a Being, but its idea only, and that in reality I do not derive anything from that Being, but only from the idea of it, that is, from the nature of the things of the world, according to such an idea. It seems also, as if a certain, though undeveloped consciousness of the true use of this concept of reason had dictated the modest and reasonable language of philosophers of all times, when they use such expressions as the wisdom and providence of nature as synonymous with divine wisdom, nay, even prefer the former expression, when dealing with speculative reason only, as avoiding the pretension of a greater assertion than we are entitled to make, and at the same time restricting reason to its proper field, namely, nature.

Thus we find that pure reason, which at first seemed to promise nothing less than extension of our knowledge beyond all limits of experience, contains, if properly understood,

[6] Instead of *der Erscheinungen* read *die Erscheinungen*.

nothing but regulative principles, which indeed postulate greater unity than the empirical use of the understanding can ever achieve, but which, by the very fact that they place the goal which has to be reached at so great a distance, carry the agreement of the understanding with itself by means of systematical unity to the highest possible degree; while, if they are misunderstood and mistaken for constitutive principles of transcendent knowledge, they produce, by a brilliant but deceptive illusion, some kind of persuasion and imaginary knowledge, but, at the same time, constant contradictions and disputes.

*   *   *   *   *   *   *   *

Thus all human knowledge begins with intuitions, advances to concepts, and ends with ideas. Although with reference to every one of these three elements, it possesses *a priori* sources of knowledge, which at first sight seemed to despise the limits of all experience, a perfect criticism soon convinces us, that reason, in its speculative use, can never get with these elements beyond the field of possible experience, and that it is the true destination of that highest faculty of knowledge to use all methods and principles of reason with one object only, namely, to follow up nature into her deepest recesses, according to every principle of unity, the unity of design being the most important, but never to soar above its limits, outside of which there is for us nothing but empty space. No doubt, the critical examination of all propositions which seemed to be able to enlarge our knowledge beyond real experience, as given in the transcendental Analytic, has fully convinced us that they could never lead to anything more than to a possible experience; and, if people were not suspicious even of the clearest, but abstract and general doctrines, and charming and specious prospects did not tempt us to throw off the restraint of those doctrines, we might indeed have dispensed with the laborious examination of all the dialectical witnesses which a transcendent reason brings into court in support of her pretensions. We knew beforehand with perfect certainty that all these pretensions, though perhaps honestly meant, were absolutely untenable, because they relate to a kind of knowledge to which man can never attain. But we know that there is no end of talk, unless the true cause of the illusion, by which even the wisest are deceived, has been clearly exhibited. We also know that the analysis of all our transcendent knowledge into its elements (as a study of our own internal nature) has no little value in itself, and to a philosopher is really a matter of duty. We therefore thought that it was not only necessary to follow up the whole of this vain treatment of speculative reason to its first sources, but considered it advisable also, as the dialectical illusion does here not only deceive the judgment, but, owing to the interest which we take in the judgment, possesses and always will possess a certain natural and irresistible charm, to write down the records of this lawsuit in full detail, and to deposit them in the archives of human reason, to prevent for the future all errors of a similar kind.

CRITIQUE OF PURE REASON

II

METHOD OF TRANSCENDENTALISM

THE METHOD OF TRANSCENDENTALISM

If we look upon the whole knowledge of pure and speculative reason as an edifice of which we possess at least the
idea within ourselves, we may say that in the Elements of
Transcendentalism we made an estimate of the materials and
determined for what kind of edifice and of what height and
solidity they would suffice. We found that although we had
thought of a tower that would reach to the sky, the supply of
materials would suffice for a dwelling-house only, sufficiently
roomy for all our business on the level plain of experience,
and high enough to enable us to survey it: and that the original
bold undertaking could not but fail for want of materials, not
to mention the confusion of tongues which inevitably divided
the labourers in their views of the building, and scattered them
over all the world, where each tried to erect his own building
according to his own plan. At present, however, we are concerned not so much with the material as with the plan, and
though we have been warned not to venture blindly on a plan
which may be beyond our powers, we cannot altogether give
up the erection of a solid dwelling, but have to make the plan
for a building in proportion to the material which we possess,
and sufficient for all our real wants. This determination of the
formal conditions of a complete system of pure reason I call
the Method of Transcendentalism. We shall here have to treat
of a *discipline,* a *canon,* an *architectonic,* and lastly, a *history*
of pure reason, and shall have to do, from a transcendental
point of view, what the schools attempt, but fail to carry out
properly, with regard to the use of the understanding in general, under the name of *practical logic.* The reason of this
failure is that general logic is not limited to any particular kind
of knowledge, belonging to the understanding (not for instance to its pure knowledge), nor to certain objects. It cannot,
therefore, without borrowing knowledge from other sciences,
do more than produce titles of *possible methods* and technical

terms which are used in different sciences in reference to their systematical arrangement, so that the pupil becomes acquainted with names only, the meaning and application of which he has to learn afterwards.

METHOD OF TRANSCENDENTALISM

CHAPTER I

THE DISCIPLINE OF PURE REASON

Negative judgments, being negative not only in their logical form, but in their contents also, do not enjoy a very high reputation among persons desirous of increasing human knowledge. They are even looked upon as jealous enemies of our never-ceasing desire for knowledge, and we have almost to produce an apology, in order to secure for them toleration, or favour and esteem.

No doubt, all propositions may *logically* be expressed as negative: but when we come to the question whether the contents of our knowledge are enlarged or restricted by a judgment, we find that the proper object of negative judgments is solely to *prevent error*. Hence negative propositions, intended to prevent erroneous knowledge in cases where error is never possible, may no doubt be very true, but they are empty, they do not answer any purpose, and sound therefore often absurd; like the well-known utterance of a rhetorician, that Alexander could not have conquered any countries without an army.

But in cases where the limits of our possible knowledge are very narrow, where the temptation to judge is great, the illusion which presents itself very deceptive, and the evil consequences of error very considerable, the *negative* element, though it teaches us only how to avoid errors, has even more value than much of that positive instruction which adds to the stock of our knowledge. The *restraint* which checks our constant inclination to deviate from certain rules, and at last destroys it, is called *discipline*. It is different from *culture,* which is intended to form a certain kind of skill, without destroying another kind which is already present. In forming a talent, therefore, which has in itself an impulse to manifest itself, discipline will contribute a negative,* culture and doctrine a positive, influence.

* I am well aware that in the language of the schools, *discipline* is used as synonymous with instruction. But there are so many

That our temperament and various talents which like to indulge in free and unchecked exercise (such as imagination and wit) require some kind of discipline, will easily be allowed by everybody. But that reason, whose proper duty it is to prescribe a discipline to all other endeavours, should itself require such discipline, may seem strange indeed. It has in fact escaped that humiliation hitherto, because, considering the solemnity and thorough self-possession in its behaviour, no one has suspected it of thoughtlessly putting imaginations in the place of concepts, and words in the place of things.

In its empirical use reason does not require such criticism, because its principles are constantly subject to the test of experience. Nor is such criticism required in mathematics, where the concepts of reason must at once be represented *in concreto* in pure intuition, so that everything unfounded and arbitrary is at once discovered. But when neither empirical nor pure intuition keeps reason in a straight groove, that is, when it is used transcendently and according to mere concepts, the discipline to restrain its inclination to go beyond the narrow limits of possible experience, and to keep it from extravagance and error is so necessary, that the whole philosophy of pure reason is really concerned with that one negative discipline only. Single errors may be corrected by *censure,* and their causes removed by *criticism.* But when, as in pure reason, we are met by a whole system of illusions and fallacies, well connected among themselves and united by common principles, a separate negative code seems requisite, which, under the name of a *discipline,* should erect a system of caution and self-examination, founded on the nature of reason and of the objects of its use, before which no false sophistical illusion could stand, but should at once betray itself in spite of all excuses.

It should be well borne in mind, however, that in this second division of the transcendental critique, I mean to direct the discipline of pure reason not to its contents, but only to the method of its knowledge. The former task has been performed in the Elements of Transcendentalism. There is so much similarity in the use of reason, whatever be the subject to which it is applied, and yet, so far as this use is to be transcendental, it is so essentially different from every other, that, without the

cases in which the former term, in the sense of *restraint,* is carefully distinguished from the latter in the sense of *teaching,* and the nature of things makes it so desirable to preserve the only suitable expressions for that distinction, that I hope that the former term may never be allowed to be used in any but a negative meaning.

warning voice of a discipline, especially devised for that purpose, it would be impossible to avoid errors arising necessarily from the improper application of methods, which are suitable to reason in other spheres, only not quite here.

DISCIPLINE OF PURE REASON

SECTION I

The Discipline of Pure Reason in its Dogmatical Use

The science of mathematics presents the most brilliant example of how pure reason may successfully enlarge its domain without the aid of experience. Such examples are always contagious, particularly when the faculty is the same, which naturally flatters itself that it will meet with the same success in other cases which it has had in one. Thus pure reason hopes to be able to extend its domain as successfully and as thoroughly in its transcendental as in its mathematical employment; particularly if it there follows the same method which has proved of such decided advantage elsewhere. It is, therefore, of great consequence for us to know whether the method of arriving at apodictic certainty, which in the former science was called *mathematical,* be identical with that which is to lead us to the same certainty in philosophy, and would have to be called *dogmatic.*

Philosophical knowledge is that which reason gains from *concepts,* mathematical, that which it gains from the *construction* of concepts. By *constructing* a concept I mean representing *a priori* the intuition corresponding to it. For the construction of a concept, therefore, a *non-empirical* intuition is required which, as an intuition, is a *single* object, but which, nevertheless, as the construction of a concept (of a general representation) must express in the representation something that is generally valid for all possible intuitions which fall under the same concept. Thus I construct a triangle by representing the object corresponding to that concept either by mere imagination, in the pure intuition, or, afterwards on paper also in the empirical intuition, and in both cases entirely *a priori* without having borrowed the original from any experience. The particular figure drawn on the paper is empirical, but serves nevertheless to express the concept without any detriment to its generality, because, in that empirical intuition, we consider always the act of the construction of the concept only, to which many determinations, as, for instance, the magnitude of the sides and the angles, are quite indifferent, these differences, which do not change the concept of a triangle, being entirely ignored.

Philosophical knowledge, therefore, considers the particular in the general only, mathematical, the general in the particular, nay, even in the individual, all this, however, *a priori,* and by means of reason; so that, as an individual figure is determined by certain general conditions of construction, the object of the concept, of which this individual figure forms only the schema, must be thought of as universally determined.

The essential difference between these two modes of the knowledge of reason consists, therefore, in the form, and does not depend on any difference in their matter or objects. Those who thought they could distinguish philosophy from mathematics by saying that the former was concerned with *quality* only, the latter with *quantity* only, mistook effect for cause. It is owing to the form of mathematical knowledge that it can refer to *quanta* only, because it is only the concept of quantities that admits of construction, that is, of *a priori* representation in intuition, while qualities cannot be represented in any but empirical intuition. Hence reason can gain a knowledge of qualities by concepts only. No one can take an intuition corresponding to the concept of reality from anywhere except from experience; we can never lay hold of it *a priori* by ourselves, and before we have had an empirical consciousness of it. We can form to ourselves an intuition of a cone, from its concept alone, and without any empirical assistance, but the colour of this cone must be given before, in some experience or other. I cannot represent in intuition the concept of a cause in general in any way except by an example supplied by experience, etc. Besides, philosophy treats of quantities quite as much as mathematics; for instance, of totality, infinity, etc., and mathematics treats also of the difference between lines and planes, as spaces of different quality, it treats further of the continuity of extension as one of its qualities. But, though in such cases both have a common object, the manner in which reason treats it is totally different in philosophy and mathematics. The former is concerned with general concepts only, the other can do nothing with the pure concept, but proceeds at once to intuition, in which it looks upon the concept *in concreto;* yet not in an empirical intuition, but in an intuition which it represents *a priori*, that is, which it has constructed and in which, whatever follows from the general conditions of the construction, must be valid in general of the object of the constructed concept also.

Let us give to a philosopher the concept of a triangle, and let him find out, in his own way, what relation the sum of its angles bears to a right angle. Nothing is given him but the concept of a figure, enclosed within three straight lines, and with it the concept of as many angles. Now he may ponder on that concept as long as he likes, he will never discover anything new in it. He may analyse the concept of a straight line or of an angle, or of the number three, and render them more clear, but he will never arrive at other qualities which are not contained in those concepts. But now let the geometrician treat the same question. He will begin at once with constructing a triangle. As he knows that two right angles are equal to the sum of all the contiguous angles which proceed from one point in a straight line, he produces one side of his triangle, thus forming two adjacent angles which together are equal to two right angles. He then divides the exterior of these angles by drawing a line parallel with the opposite side of the triangle, and sees that an exterior adjacent angle has been formed, which is equal to an interior, etc. In this way he arrives, through a chain of conclusions, though always guided by intuition, at a thoroughly convincing and general solution of the question.

In mathematics, however, we construct not only quantities (*quanta*) as in geometry, but also mere quantity (*quantitas*) as in algebra, where the quality of the object, which has to be thought according to this quantitative concept, is entirely ignored. We then adopt a certain notation for all constructions of quantities (numbers), such as addition, subtraction, extraction of roots, etc., and, after having denoted also the general concept of quantities according to their different relations, we represent in intuition according to general rules, every operation which is produced and modified by quantity. Thus when one quantity is to be divided by another, we place the signs of both together according to the form denoting division, etc., and we thus arrive, by means of a symbolical construction in algebra, quite as well as by an ostensive or geometrical construction of the objects themselves in geometry, at results which our discursive knowledge could never have reached by the aid of mere conceptions.

What may be the cause of this difference between two persons, the philosopher and the mathematician, both practising the art of reason, the former following his path according to concepts, the latter according to intuitions, which he represents *a priori* according to concepts? If we remember what has been said before in the Elements of Transcendentalism, the cause is clear. We are here concerned not with analytical propositions, which can be produced by a mere analysis of concepts (here the philosopher would no doubt have an advantage over the mathematician), but with synthetical propositions, and synthetical propositions that can be known *a priori*. We are not intended here to consider what we are really thinking in our concept of the triangle (this would be a mere definition), but we are meant to go beyond that concept, in order to arrive at properties which are not contained in the concept, but nevertheless belong to it. This is impossible, except by our determining our object according to the conditions either of empirical, or of pure intuition. The former would give us an empirical proposition only, through the actual measuring of the three angles. Such a proposition would be without the character of either generality or necessity, and does not, therefore, concern us here at all. The second procedure consists in the mathematical and here the geometrical construction, by means of which I add in a pure intuition, just as I may do in the empirical intuition, everything that belongs to the schema of a triangle in general and, therefore, to its concept, and thus arrive at general synthetical propositions.

I should therefore in vain philosophise, that is, reflect discursively on the triangle, without ever getting beyond the mere definition with which I ought to have begun. There is no doubt a transcendental synthesis, consisting of mere concepts, and in which the philosopher alone can hope to be successful. Such a synthesis, however, never relates to more than a thing in general, and to the conditions under which its perception could be a possible experience. In the mathematical problems, on the contrary, all this, together with the question of existence, does not concern us, but the properties of objects in themselves only (without any reference to their existence), and those properties again so far only as they are connected with their concept.

We have tried by this example to show how great a difference there is between the discursive use of reason, according to concepts, and its intuitive use, through the construction of concepts. The question now arises what can be the cause that makes this twofold use of reason necessary, and how can we discover whether in any given argument the former only, or the latter use also, takes place?

All our knowledge relates, in the end, to possible intuitions, for it is by them alone that an object can be given. A concept *a priori* (or a non-empirical concept) contains either a pure intuition, in which case it can be constructed, or it contains nothing but the synthesis of possible intuitions, which are not given *a priori,* and in that case, though we may use it for synthetical and *a priori* judgments, such judgments can only be discursive, according to concepts, and never intuitive, through the construction of the concept.

There is no intuition *a priori* except space and time, the mere forms of phenomena. A concept of them, as *quanta,* can be represented *a priori* in intuition, that is, can be constructed either at the same time with their quality (figure), or as quantity only (the mere synthesis of the manifold-homogeneous), by means of number. The matter of phenomena, however, by which *things* are given us in space and time, can be represented in perception only, that is *a posteriori.* The one concept which *a priori* represents the empirical contents of phenomena is the concept of a *thing* in general, and the synthetical knowledge which we may have *a priori* of a thing in general, can give us nothing but the mere rule of synthesis, to be applied to what perception may present to us *a posteriori,* but never an *a priori* intuition of a real object, such an intuition being necessarily empirical.

Synthetical propositions with regard to *things* in general, the intuition of which does not admit of being given *a priori,* are called transcendental. Transcendental propositions, therefore, can never be given through a construction of concepts, but only according to concepts *a priori.* They only contain the rule, according to which we must look empirically for a certain synthetical unity of what cannot be represented in intuition *a priori* (perceptions). They can never represent any one of their concepts *a priori,* but can do this only *a posteriori,* that is, by means of experience, which itself becomes possible according to those synthetical principles only.

If we are to form a synthetical judgment of any concept, we must proceed beyond that concept to the intuition in which it is given. For if we kept within that which is given in the concept, the judgment could only be analytical and an explanation of the concept, in accordance with what we have conceived in it. I may, however, pass from the conception to the pure or empirical intuition which corresponds to it, in order thus to consider it *in concreto,* and thus to discover what belongs to the object of the concept, whether *a priori* or *a posteriori.* The former consists in rational or mathematical knowledge, arrived at by the construction of the concept, the latter in the purely empirical (mechanical) knowledge which can never supply us with necessary and apodictic propositions. Thus I might analyse my empirical concept of gold, without gaining anything beyond being able to enumerate everything that I can really think by this word. This might yield a logical improvement of my knowledge, but no increase or addition. If, however, I take the material which is known by the name of gold, I can make observations on it, and these will yield me different synthetical, but empirical propositions. Again, I might construct the mathematical concept of a triangle, that is, give it *a priori* in intuition, and gain in this manner a synthetical but rational knowledge of it. But when the transcendental concept of a reality, a substance, a power, etc., is given me, that concept denotes neither an empirical nor a pure intuition, but merely the synthesis of empirical intuitions, which, being empirical, cannot be given *a priori.* No determining synthetical proposition therefore can spring from it, because the synthesis cannot *a priori* pass beyond to the intuition that corresponds to it, but only a principle of the synthesis* of possible empirical intuitions.

A transcendental proposition, therefore, is synthetical knowledge acquired by reason, according to mere concepts; and it is discursive, because through it alone synthetical unity of empirical knowledge becomes possible, while it cannot give us any intuition *a priori.*

We see, therefore, that reason is used in two ways which, though they share in common the generality of their knowledge and its production *a priori,* yet diverge considerably afterwards, because in each phenomenon (and no object can be given us, except as a phenomenon), there are two elements, the form of intuition (space and time), which can be

* In the concept of cause I really pass beyond the empirical concept of an event, but not to the intuition which represents the concept of cause *in concreto,* but to the conditions of time in general, which in experience might be found in accordance with the concept of cause. I therefore proceed here, according to concepts only, but cannot proceed by means of the construction of concepts, because the concept is only a rule for the synthesis of perceptions, which are not pure intuitions, and therefore cannot be given *a priori.*

known and determined entirely *a priori,* and the matter (the physical) or the contents, something which exists in space and time, and therefore contains an existence corresponding to sensation. As regards the latter, which can never be given in a definite form except empirically, we can have nothing *a priori* except indefinite concepts of the synthesis of possible sensations, in so far as they belong to the unity of apperception (in a possible experience). As regards the former, we can determine *a priori* our concepts in intuition, by creating to ourselves in space and time, through a uniform synthesis, the objects themselves, considering them simply as *quanta.* The former is called the use of reason according to concepts; and here we can do nothing more than to bring phenomena under concepts, according to their real contents, which therefore can be determined empirically only, that is *a posteriori* (though in accordance with those concepts as rules of an empirical synthesis). The latter is the use of reason through the construction of concepts, which, as they refer to an intuition *a priori,* can for that reason be given *a priori,* and defined in pure intuition, without any empirical *data.* To consider everything which exists (everything in space or time) whether, and how far, it is a *quantum* or not; to consider that we must represent in it either existence, or absence of existence; to consider how far this something which fills space or time is a primary substratum, or merely determination of it; to consider again whether its existence is related to something else as cause or effect, or finally, whether it stands isolated or in reciprocal dependence on others, with reference to existence, —this and the possibility, reality, and necessity of its existence, or their opposites, all belong to that *knowledge of reason,* derived from concepts, which is called *philosophical.* But to determine *a priori* an intuition in space (figure), to divide time (duration), or merely to know the general character of the synthesis of one and the same thing in time and space, and the quantity of an intuition in general which arises from it (number), all this is the *work of reason* by means of the construction of concepts, and is called *mathematical.*

The great success which attends reason in its mathematical use produces naturally the expectation that it, or rather its method, would have the same success outside the field of quantities also, by reducing all concepts to intuitions which may be given *a priori,* and by which the whole of nature might be conquered, while pure philosophy, with its discursive concepts *a priori,* does nothing but bungle in every part of nature, without being able to render the reality of those concepts intuitive *a priori,* and thereby legitimatised. Nor does there seem to be any lack of confidence on the part of those who are masters in the art of mathematics, or of high expectations on the part of the public at large, as to their ability of achieving success, if only they would try it. For as they have hardly ever philosophised on mathematics (which is indeed no easy task), they never think of the specific difference between the two uses of reason which we have just explained. Current and empirical rules, borrowed from the ordinary operations of reason, are then accepted instead of axioms. From what quarter the concepts of space and time with which alone (as the original *quanta*) they have to deal, may have come to them, they do not care to enquire, nor do they see any use in investigating the origin of the pure concepts of the understanding, and with it the extent of their validity, being satisfied to use them as they are. In all this no blame would attach to them, if only they did not overstep their proper limits, namely, those of nature. But as it is, they lose themselves, without being aware of it, away from the field of sensibility on the uncertain ground of pure and even transcendental concepts (*instabilis tellus, innabilis unda*) where they are neither able to stand nor to swim, taking only a few hasty steps, the vestiges of which are soon swept away, while their steps in mathematics become a highway, on which the latest posterity may march on with perfect confidence.

We have chosen it as our duty to determine with accuracy and certainty the limits of pure reason in its transcendental use. These transcendental efforts, however, have this peculiar character that, in spite of the strongest and clearest warnings, they continue to inspire us with new hopes, before the attempt is entirely surrendered at arriving beyond the limits of experience at the charming fields of an intellectual world. It is necessary therefore to cut away the last anchor of that fantastic hope, and to show that the employment of the mathematical method cannot be of the slightest use for this kind of knowledge, unless it be in displaying its own deficiencies; and that the art of measuring and philosophy are two totally different things, though they are mutually useful to each other in natural science, and that the method of the one can never be imitated by the other.

The exactness of mathematics depends on definitions, axioms, and demonstrations. I shall content myself with showing that none of these can be achieved or imitated by the philosopher in the sense in which they are understood by the mathematician. I hope to show at the same time that the art of measuring, or geometry, will by its method produce nothing in philosophy but card-houses, while the philosopher with his method produces in mathematics nothing but vain babble. It is the very essence of philosophy to teach the limits of knowledge, and even the mathematician, unless his talent is limited already by nature and restricted to its proper work, cannot decline the warnings of philosophy or altogether defy them.

I. Of definitions. To *define,* as the very name implies, means only to represent the complete concept of a thing within its limits and in its primary character.* From this point of view, an empirical concept cannot be *defined,* but can be *explained* only. For, as we have in an empirical concept some predicates only belonging to a certain class of sensuous objects, we are never certain whether by the word which denotes one and the same object, we do not think at one time a greater, at another a smaller number of predicates. Thus one man may by the concept of gold think, in addition to weight, colour, malleability, the quality of its not rusting, while another may know nothing of the last. We use certain predicates so long only as they are required for distinction. New observations add and remove certain predicates, so that the concept never stands within safe limits. And of what use would it be to define an empirical concept, as for instance that of water, because, when we speak of water and its qualities, we do not care much what is thought by that word, but proceed at once to experiments? the word itself with its few predicates being a *designation* only and not a concept, so that a so-called definition would be no more than a determination of the word. Secondly, if we reasoned accurately, no *a priori* given concept can be defined, such as substance, cause, right, equity, etc. For I can never be sure that the clear representation of a given but still confused concept has been completely analysed, unless I know that such representation is adequate to the object. As its concept, however, such as it is given, may

* *Completeness* means clearness and sufficiency of predicates; *limits* mean precision, no more predicates being given than belong to the complete concept; *in its primary character* means that the determination of these limits is not derived from anything else, and therefore in need of any proof, because this would render the so-called definition incapable of standing at the head of all the judgments regarding its object.

contain many obscure representations which we pass by in our analysis, although we use them always in the practical application of the concept, the completeness of the analysis of my concept must always remain doubtful, and can only be rendered *probable* by means of apt examples, although never apodictically certain. I should therefore prefer to use the term *exposition* rather than definition, as being more modest, and more likely to be admitted to a certain extent by a critic who reserves his doubts as to its completeness. As therefore it is impossible to define either empirically or *a priori* given concepts, there remain arbitrary concepts only on which such an experiment may be tried. In such a case I can always define my concept, because I ought certainly to know what I wish to think, the concept being made intentionally by myself, and not given to me either by the nature of the understanding or by experience. But I can never say that I have thus defined a real object. For if the concept depends on empirical conditions, as, for instance, a ship's chronometer, the object itself and its possibility are not given by this arbitrary concept; it does not even tell us whether there is an object corresponding to it, so that my explanation should be called a declaration (of my project) rather than a definition of an object. Thus there remain no concepts fit for definition except those which contain an arbitrary synthesis that can be constructed *a priori*. It follows, therefore, that mathematics only can possess definitions, because it is in mathematics alone that we represent *a priori* in intuition the object which we think, and that object cannot therefore contain either more or less than the concept, because the concept of the object was given by the definition in its primary character, that is, without deriving the definition from anything else. The German language has but the one word *Erklärung* (literally clearing up) for the terms *exposition, explication, declaration,* and *definition;* and we must not therefore be too strict in our demands, when denying to the different kinds of a philosophical *clearing up* the honourable name of definition. What we really insist on is this, that philosophical definitions are possible only as expositions of given concepts, mathematical definitions as constructions of concepts, originally framed by ourselves, the former therefore analytically (where completeness is never apodictically certain), the latter synthetically. Mathematical definitions *make* the concept, philosophical definitions explain it only. Hence it follows,

   a. That we must not try in philosophy to imitate mathematics by beginning with definitions, except it be by way of experiment. For as they are meant to be an analysis of given concepts, these concepts themselves, although as yet confused only, must come first, and the incomplete exposition must precede the complete one, so that we are able from some characteristics, known to us from an, as yet, incomplete analysis, to infer many things before we come to a complete exposition, that is, the definition of the concept. In philosophy, in fact, the definition in its complete clearness ought to conclude rather than begin our work,* while in mathematics we really have no concept antecedent to the definition by which the concept itself is first given, so that in mathematics no other beginning is necessary or possible.

b. Mathematical definitions can never be erroneous, because, as the concept is first given by the definition, it contains neither more nor less than what the definition wishes should be conceived by it. But although there can be nothing wrong in it, so far as its contents are concerned, mistakes may sometimes, though rarely, occur in the form or wording, particularly with regard to perfect precision. Thus the common definition of a circle, that it is a *curved* line, every point of which is equally distant from one and the same point (namely, the centre), is faulty, because the determination of *curved* is introduced unnecessarily. For there must be a particular theorem, derived from the definition, and easily proved, viz. that every line, all points of which are equidistant from one and the same point, must be curved (no part of it being straight). Analytical definitions, however, may be erroneous in many respects, either by introducing characteristics which do not really exist in the concept, or by lacking that completeness which is essential to a definition, because we can never be quite certain of the completeness of our analysis. It is on these ac-

---

* Philosophy swarms with faulty definitions, particularly such as contain some true elements of a definition, but not all. If, therefore, it were impossible to use a concept until it had been completely defined, philosophy would fare very ill. As, however, we may use a definition with perfect safety, so far at least as the elements of the analysis will carry us, imperfect definitions also, that is, propositions which are not yet properly definitions, but are yet true, and, therefore, approximations to a definition, may be used with great advantage. In mathematics definitions belong *ad esse,* in philosophy *ad melius esse.* It is desirable, but it is extremely difficult to construct a proper definition. Jurists are without a definition of right to the present day.

counts that the method of mathematics cannot be imitated in the definitions of philosophy.

II. Of Axioms. These, so far as they are immediately certain, are synthetical principles *a priori*. One concept cannot, however, be connected synthetically and yet immediately with another, because, if we wish to go beyond a given concept, a third connecting knowledge is required; and, as philosophy is the knowledge of reason based on concepts, no principle can be found in it deserving the name of an axiom. Mathematics, on the other hand, may well possess axioms, because here, by means of the construction of concepts in the intuition of their object, the predicates may always be connected *a priori* and immediately; for instance, that three points always lie in a plane. A synthetical principle, on the contrary, made up of concepts only, can never be immediately certain, as, for example, the proposition that everything which happens has its cause. Here I require something else, namely, the condition of the determination by time in a given experience, it being impossible for me to know such a principle, directly and immediately, from the concepts. Discursive principles are, therefore, something quite different from intuitive principles or axioms. The former always require, in addition, a deduction, not at all required for the latter, which, on that very account, are evident, while philosophical principles, whatever their certainty may be, can never pretend to be so. Hence it is very far from true to say that any synthetical proposition of pure and transcendental reason is so evident (as people sometimes emphatically maintain) as the statement that *twice two are four*. It is true that in the Analytic, when giving the table of the principles of the pure understanding, I mentioned also certain axioms of intuition; but the principle there mentioned was itself no axiom, but served only to indicate the principle of the possibility of axioms in general, being itself no more than a principle based on concepts. It was necessary in our transcendental philosophy to show the possibility even of mathematics. Philosophy, therefore, is without axioms, and can never put forward its principles *a priori* with absolute authority, but must first consent to justify its claims by a thorough deduction.

III. Of Demonstrations. An apodictic proof only, so far as it is intuitive, can be called demonstration. Experience may teach us what is, but never that it cannot be otherwise. Empirical arguments, therefore, cannot produce an apodictic proof. From concepts *a priori*, however (in discursive knowledge), it is impossible that intuitive certainty, that is, evidence, should ever arise, however apodictically certain the judgment may otherwise seem to be. Demonstrations we get in mathematics only, because here our knowledge is derived not from concepts, but from their construction, that is, from intuition, which can be given *a priori,* in accordance with the concepts. Even the proceeding of algebra, with its equations, from which by reduction both the correct result and its proof are produced, is a construction by characters, though not geometrical, in which, by means of signs, the concepts, particularly those of the relation of quantities, are represented in intuition, and (without any regard to the heuristic method) all conclusions are secured against errors by submitting each of them to intuitive evidence. Philosophical knowledge cannot claim this advantage, for here we must always consider the general in the abstract (by concepts), while in mathematics we may consider the general in the concrete, in each single intuition, and yet through pure representation *a priori,* where every mistake becomes at once manifest. I should prefer, therefore, to call the former *acroamatic,* or audible (discursive) *proofs,* because they can be carried out by words only (the object in thought), rather than *demonstrations,* which, as the very term implies, depend on the intuition of the object.

It follows from all this that it is not in accordance with the very nature of philosophy to boast of its dogmatical character, particularly in the field of pure reason, and to deck itself with the titles and ribands of mathematics, an order to which it can never belong, though it may well hope for co-operation with that science. All those attempts are vain pretensions which can never be successful, nay, which can only prove an obstacle in the discovery of the illusions of reason, when ignoring its own limits, and which must mar our success in calling back, by means of a sufficient explanation of our concepts, the conceit of speculation to the more modest and thorough work of self-knowledge. Reason ought not, therefore, in its transcendental endeavours, to look forward with such confidence, as if the path which it has traversed must lead straight to its goal, nor depend with such assurance on its premises as to consider it unnecessary to look back from time to time, to find out whether, in the progress of its conclusions, errors may come to light, which were overlooked in the principles, and which render it necessary either to determine those principles more accurately or to change them altogether.

I divide all apodictic propositions, whether demonstrable

or immediately certain, into *Dogmata* and *Mathemata*. A directly synthetical proposition, based on concepts, is a *Dogma;* a proposition of the same kind, arrived at by the construction of concepts, is a *Mathema.* Analytical judgments teach us really no more of an object than what the concept which we have of it contains in itself. They cannot enlarge our knowledge beyond the concept, but only clear it. They cannot, therefore, be properly called dogmas (a word which might perhaps best be translated by *precepts, Lehrsprüche*). According to our ordinary mode of speech, we could apply that name to that class only of the two above-mentioned classes of synthetical propositions *a priori* which refers to philosophical knowledge, and no one would feel inclined to give the name of Dogma to the propositions of arithmetic or geometry. In this way the usage of language confirms our explanation that those judgments only which are based on conceptions, and not those which are arrived at by the construction of concepts, can be called dogmatic.

Now in the whole domain of pure reason, in its purely speculative use, there does not exist a single directly synthetical judgment based on concepts. We have shown that reason, by means of ideas, is incapable of any synthetical judgments which could claim objective validity, while by means of the concepts of our understanding it establishes no doubt some perfectly certain principles, but not directly from concepts, but indirectly only, by referring such concepts to something purely contingent, namely, *possible experience.* When such experience (anything as an object of possible experience) is presupposed, these principles are, no doubt, apodictically certain, but in themselves (directly) they cannot even be known *a priori.* Thus the proposition that everything which happens has its cause, can never be thoroughly understood by means of the concepts alone which are contained in it; hence it is no dogma in itself, although, from another point of view, that is, in the only field of its possible use, namely, in experience, it may be proved apodictically. It should be called, therefore, a *principle,* and not a *precept* or a dogma (though it is necessary that it should itself be proved), because it has this peculiarity that it first renders its own proof, namely, experience, possible, and has always to be presupposed for the sake of experience.

If, therefore, there are no *dogmata* whatever in the speculative use of pure reason, with regard to their contents also, all *dogmatical* methods, whether borrowed from mathematics or invented on purpose, are alike inappropriate. They only serve to hide mistakes and errors, and thus deceive philosophy, whose true object is to shed the clearest light on every step which reason takes. The method may, however, well be *systematical;* for our reason (subjectively) is itself a system, though in its pure use, by means of mere concepts, a system intended for investigation only, according to principles of unity, to which *experience* alone can supply the material. We cannot, however, dwell here on the method of transcendental philosophy, because all we have to do at present is to take stock in order to find out whether we are able to build at all, and how high the edifice may be which we can erect with the materials at our command (the pure concepts *a priori*).

DISCIPLINE OF PURE REASON

Section II

The Discipline of Pure Reason in its Polemical Use

Reason in all her undertakings must submit to criticism, and cannot attempt to limit the free exercise of such criticism without injury to herself, and without exposing herself to dangerous suspicion. There is nothing so important with reference to its usefulness, nothing so sacred, that it could withdraw itself from that searching examination which has no respect of persons. The very existence of reason depends on that freedom; for reason can claim no dictatorial authority, but its decrees are rather like the votes of free citizens, every one of whom may freely express, not only his doubts, but even his veto.

But, though reason can never refuse to submit to criticism, it does not follow that she need always be *afraid* of it, while pure reason in her dogmatical (not mathematical) use is not so thoroughly conscious of having herself obeyed her own supreme laws as not to appear with a certain shyness, nay, without any of her assumed dogmatical authority, before the tribunal of a *higher* judicial reason.

The case is totally different when reason has to deal, not with the verdicts of a judge, but with the claims of her fellow-citizens, and has to defend itself only against these claims. For as these mean to be as dogmatical in their negations as reason is in her affirmations, reason may justify herself κατ' ἄνθρωπον, so as to be safe against all damages, and with a good title to her own property that need not fear any foreign claims, although κατ' ἀλήθειαν it could not itself be established with sufficient evidence.

By the polemical use of pure reason I mean the defence of her own propositions against dogmatical negations. Here the question is not, whether her own assertions may not themselves be false, but it is only to be shown that no one is ever able to prove the opposite with apodictic certainty, nay, even with a higher degree of plausibility. For we are not on sufferance in our possession, when, though our own title may not be sufficient, it is nevertheless quite certain that no one can ever prove its insufficiency.

It is sad, no doubt, and discouraging, that there should be an antithetic of pure reason, and that reason, being the highest tribunal for all conflicts, should be in conflict with herself. We had on a former occasion to treat of such an apparent antithetic, but we saw that it arose from a misunderstanding, phenomena, according to the common prejudice, being taken for things in themselves, and an absolute completeness of their synthesis being demanded in one way or other (being equally impossible in either way), a demand entirely unreasonable with regard to phenomena. There was, therefore, no real *contradiction* in *reason* herself when making the two propositions, *first*, that the series of phenomena *given by themselves* has an absolutely first beginning; and, *secondly*, that the series is absolutely and *by itself* without any beginning; for both propositions are perfectly consistent with each other, because *phenomena*, with regard to their existence as phenomena, are *by themselves* nothing, that is, something self-contradictory, so that their hypothesis must naturally lead to contradictory inferences.

We cannot, however, appeal to a similar misunderstanding, in order to remove the conflict of reason, when it is said, for instance, on one side, theistically, *that there is a Supreme Being,* and on the other, atheistically, *that there is no Supreme Being;* or if in psychology it is maintained that everything which thinks possesses an absolute and permanent unity and is different, therefore, from all perishable material unity, while others maintain that a soul is not an immaterial unity, and not exempt, therefore, from perishableness. For here the object of the question is free from anything heterogeneous or contradictory to its own nature, and our understanding has to deal with things *by themselves only* and not with phenomena. Here, therefore, we should have a real conflict, if only on the negative side pure reason could advance anything like the ground of an assertion. We may well admit the criticism of the arguments advanced by those who dogmatically assert, without therefore having to surrender these assertions, which are supported at least by the interest of reason, to which the opposite party cannot appeal.

I cannot share the opinion so frequently expressed by excellent and thoughtful men (for instance Sulzer) who, being fully conscious of the weakness of the proofs hitherto advanced, indulge in a hope that the future would supply us with evident demonstrations of the two cardinal propositions of pure reason, namely, that there is a God, and that there is a future life. I am certain, on the contrary, that this will never be the case, for whence should reason take the grounds for such synthetical assertions, which do not refer to objects of experience and their internal possibility? But there is the same apodictic certainty that no man will ever arise to assert the *contrary* with the smallest plausibility, much less dogmatically. For, as he could prove it by means of pure reason only, he would have to prove that a Supreme Being, and that a thinking subject within us, as pure intelligence, is *impossible*. But whence will he take the knowledge that would justify him in thus judging synthetically on things far beyond all possible experience? We may, therefore, rest so completely assured that no one will ever really prove the opposite, that there is no need to invent any scholastic arguments. We may safely accept those propositions which agree so well with the speculative interests of our reason in its empirical use, and are besides the only means of reconciling them with our practical interests. As against our opponent, who must not be considered here as a critic only, we are always ready with our *Non liquet*. This must inevitably confound our adversary, while we need not mind his retort, because we can always fall back on the subjective maxim of reason, which our adversary cannot, and can thus, protected by it, look upon all his vain attacks with calmness and indifference.

Thus we see that there is really no antithetic of pure reason, for the only arena for it would be the field of pure theology and psychology, and on that field it is not able to support a champion in full armour and with weapons which we need be afraid of. He can only use ridicule and boasting, and these we may laugh at as mere child's play. This ought to be a real comfort and inspire reason with new courage; for what else could she depend on, if she herself, who is called upon to remove all errors, were divided against herself, without any hope of peace and quiet possession?

Whatever has been ordained by nature is good for some purpose or other. Even poisons serve to counteract other poisons which are in our own blood, and they must not be absent therefore in a complete collection of medicines. The objections against the vain persuasions and the conceit of our own purely speculative reason are inspired by the very nature of that reason, and must therefore have their own good purpose, which must not be lightly cast aside. Why has Providence placed certain things, which concern our highest interests, so far beyond our reach that we are only able to apprehend them very indistinctly and dubiously, and our enquiring gaze is more excited than satisfied by them? It is very doubtful whether it is useful to venture on any bold answers with regard to such obscure questions, nay, whether it may not be detrimental. But one thing is quite certain, namely, that it is useful to grant to reason the fullest freedom, both of enquiry and of criticism, so that she may consult her own interest without let or hindrance. And this is done quite as much by limiting her insight as by enlarging it, while nothing but mischief must arise from any foreign interference or any attempt to direct reason, against her own natural inclination, towards objects forced upon her from without.

Allow, therefore, your adversary to speak reason, and combat him with weapons of reason only. As to any practical interests you need not be afraid, for in purely speculative discussions they are not involved at all. What comes to light in these discussions is only a certain antinomy of reason which, as it springs from the very nature of reason, must needs be listened to and examined. Reason is thus improved only by a consideration of both sides of her subject. Her judgment is corrected by the very limitations imposed upon her. What people may differ about is not the matter so much as the tone and manner of these discussions. For, though you have to surrender the language of *knowledge,* it is perfectly open to you to retain the language of the firmest faith, which need not fear the severest test of reason.

If we could ask that dispassionate philosopher, David Hume, who seemed made to maintain the most perfect equilibrium of judgment, what induced him to undermine by carefully elaborated arguments the persuasion, so useful and so full of comfort for mankind, as that reason is sufficient to assert and to form a definite concept of a Supreme Being, he would answer, Nothing but a wish to advance reason in self-knowledge, and at the same time a certain feeling of indignation at the violence which people wish to inflict on reason by boasting of her powers, and yet at the same time preventing her from openly confessing her weakness of which she has become conscious by her own self-examination. If, on the contrary, you were to ask Priestley, who was guided by the principles of the empirical use of reason only and opposed to all transcendental speculation, what could have induced him to pull down two such pillars of religion as the freedom and immortality of our soul (for the hope of a future life is with him an expectation only of the miracle of a resuscitation), he, who was himself so pious and zealous a teacher of religion, could answer nothing but that he was concerned for reason, which must suffer if certain subjects are withdrawn from the laws of material nature, the only laws which we can accurately know and fix. It would be most unjust to decry the latter, who was able to combine his paradoxical assertions with the interests of religion, and to inflict pain on a well-intentioned man, simply because he could not find his way, the moment he strayed away from the field of natural science. And the same favour must be extended to the equally well-intentioned, and in his moral character quite blameless, Hume, who could not and would not leave his abstract speculations, because he was rightly convinced that their object lies entirely outside the limits of natural science, and within the sphere of pure ideas.

What then is to be done, especially with regard to the danger which is believed to threaten the commonwealth from such speculations? Nothing is more natural, nothing more fair than the decision which you have to come to. Let these people go! If they show talent, if they produce new and profound investigations, in one word, if they show reason, reason can only gain. If you have recourse to anything else but untrammelled reason, if you raise the cry of high treason, and call together the ignorant mob as it were to extinguish a conflagration—you simply render yourself ridiculous. For here the question is not what may be useful or dangerous to the commonwealth, but merely how far reason may advance in her speculations, which are independent of all practical interests; in fact, whether these speculations are to count for anything, or are to be surrendered entirely for practical considerations.

Instead of rushing in, sword in hand, it is far wiser to watch the struggle from the safe seat of the critic. That struggle is very hard for the combatants themselves, while to you it need not be anything but entertaining, and, as the issue is sure to be without bloodshed, it may become highly improving to your own intellect. For it is extremely absurd to expect to be enlightened by reason, and yet to prescribe to her beforehand on which side she must incline. Besides, reason is naturally so subdued and checked by reason, that you need not send out patrols in order to bring the civil law to bear on that party whose victory you fear. In this dialectical war no victory is gained that need disturb your peace of mind.

Reason really stands in need of such dialectical strife, and it is much to be wished that it had taken place sooner, and with the unlimited sanction of the public, for, in that case, criticism would sooner have reached complete maturity, and disputes would have come to an end by each party becoming aware of the illusions and prejudices which caused their differences.

There is in human nature a certain disingenuousness which, however, like everything that springs from nature, must contain a useful germ, namely, a tendency to conceal one's own true sentiments, and to give expression to adopted opinions which are supposed to be good and creditable. There is no doubt that this tendency to conceal oneself and to assume a favourable appearance has helped towards the progress of civilisation, nay, to a certain extent, of morality, because others, who could not see through the varnish of respectability, honesty, and correctness, were led to improve themselves by seeing everywhere these examples of goodness which they believed to be genuine. This tendency, however, to show oneself better than one really is, and to utter sentiments which one does not really share, can only serve provisionally to rescue men from a rude state, and to teach them to assume at least the appearance of what they know to be good. Afterwards, when genuine principles have once been developed and become part of our nature, that disingenuousness must be gradually conquered, because it will otherwise deprave the heart and not allow the good seeds of honest conviction to grow up among the tares of fair appearances.

I am sorry to observe the same disingenuousness, concealment, and hypocrisy even in the utterances of speculative thought, though there are here fewer hindrances in uttering our convictions openly and freely as we ought, and no advantage whatever in our not doing so. For what can be more mischievous to the advancement of knowledge than to communicate even our thoughts in a falsified form, to conceal doubts which we feel in our own assertions, and to impart an appearance of conclusiveness to arguments which we know ourselves to be inconclusive? So long as those tricks arise from personal vanity only (which is commonly the case with speculative arguments, as touching no particular interests, nor easily capable of apodictic certainty) they are mostly counteracted by the vanity of others, with the full approval of the public at large, and thus the result is generally the same as what would or might have been obtained sooner by means of pure ingenuousness and honesty. But where the public has once persuaded itself that certain subtle speculators aim at nothing less than to shake the very foundations of the common welfare of the people, it is supposed to be not only prudent, but even advisable and honourable, to come to the succour of what is called the good cause, by sophistries, rather than to allow to our supposed antagonists the satisfaction of having lowered our tone to that of a purely practical conviction, and having forced us to confess the absence of all speculative and apodictic certainty. I cannot believe this, nor can I admit that the intention of serving a good cause can ever be combined with trickery, misrepresentation, and fraud. That in weighing the arguments of a speculative discussion we ought to be honest, seems the least that can be demanded; and if we could at least depend on this with perfect certainty, the conflict of speculative reason with regard to the important questions of God, the immortality of the soul, and freedom, would long ago have been decided, or would soon be brought to a conclusion. Thus it often happens that the purity of motives and sentiments stands in an inverse ratio to the goodness of the cause, and that its supposed assailants are more honest and more straightforward than its defenders.

Supposing that I am addressing readers who never wish to see a just cause defended by unjust means, I may say that, according to our principles of criticism, and looking not at what commonly happens, but at what in all common fairness ought to happen, there ought to be no polemical use of reason at all. For how can two persons dispute on a subject the reality of which neither of them can present either in real, or even in possible experience, while they brood on the mere idea of it with the sole intention of eliciting something more than the idea, namely, the reality of the object itself? How can they ever arrive at the end of their dispute, as neither of them can make his view comprehensible and certain, or do more than attack and refute the view of his opponent? For this is the fate of all assertions of pure reason. They go beyond the conditions of all possible experience, where no proof of truth is to be found anywhere, but they have to follow, nevertheless, the laws of the understanding, which are intended for empirical use only, but without which no step can be made in synthetical thought. Thus it happens that each side lays open its own weaknesses, and each can avail itself of the weaknesses of the other.

The critique of pure reason may really be looked upon as the true tribunal for all disputes of reason; for it is not concerned in these disputes which refer to objects immediately, but is intended to fix and to determine the rights of reason in general, according to the principles of its original institution.

Without such a critique, reason may be said to be in a state of nature, and unable to establish and defend its assertions and claims except by war. The critique of pure reason, on the contrary, which bases all its decisions on the indisputable principles of its own original institution, secures to us the peace of a legal status, in which disputes are not to be carried on except in the proper form of a *lawsuit*. In the former state such disputes generally end in both parties claiming *victory*, which is followed by an uncertain peace, maintained chiefly by the civil power, while in the latter state a *sentence* is pronounced which, as it goes to the very root of the dispute, must secure an eternal peace. These never-ceasing disputes of a purely dogmatical reason compel people at last to seek for rest and peace in some criticism of reason itself, and in some sort of legislation founded upon such criticism. Thus Hobbes maintains that the state of nature is a state of injustice and violence, and that we must needs leave it and submit ourselves to the constraint of law, which alone limits our freedom in such a way that it may consist with the freedom of others and with the common good.

It is part of that freedom that we should be allowed openly to state our thoughts and our doubts which we cannot solve ourselves, without running the risk of being decried on that account as turbulent and dangerous citizens. This follows from the inherent rights of reason, which recognises no other judge but universal human reason itself. Here everybody has a vote; and, as all improvements of which our state is capable must spring from thence, such rights are sacred and must never be minished. Nay, it would really be foolish to proclaim certain bold assertions, or reckless attacks upon assertions which enjoy the approval of the largest and best portion of the commonwealth, as dangerous; for that would be to impart to them an importance which they do not possess. Whenever I hear that some uncommon genius has demonstrated away the freedom of the human will, the hope of a future life, or the existence of God, I am always desirous to read his book, for I expect that his talent will help me to improve my own insight into these problems. Of one thing I feel quite certain, even without having seen his book, that he has not disproved any single one of these doctrines; not because I imagine that I am myself in possession of irrefragable proofs of them, but because the transcendental critique, by revealing to me the whole apparatus of our pure reason, has completely convinced me that, as reason is insufficient to establish affirmative propositions in this sphere of thought, it is equally, nay, even more powerless to establish the negative on any of these points. For where is this so-called freethinker to take the knowledge that, for instance, there exists no Supreme Being? This proposition lies outside the field of possible experience and, therefore, outside the limits of all human cognition. The dogmatical defender of the good cause I should not read at all, because I know beforehand that he will attack the sophistries of the other party simply in order to recommend his own. Besides, a mere defence of the common opinion does not supply so much material for new remarks as a strange and ingeniously contrived theory. The opponent of religion, himself dogmatical in his own way, would give me a valuable opportunity for amending here and there the principles of my own critique of pure reason, while I should not be at all afraid of any danger arising from his theories.

But it may be argued that the youth at least, entrusted to our academical teaching, should be warned against such writings, and kept away from a too early knowledge of such dangerous propositions, before their faculty of judgment, or we should rather say, before the doctrines which *we* wish to inculcate on them, have taken root, and are able to withstand all persuasion and pressure, from whatever quarter it may proceed.

Yes, if the cause of pure reason is always to be pleaded dogmatically, and if opponents are to be disposed of polemically, i.e. simply by taking up arms against them and attacking them by means of proofs of opposite opinions, nothing might seem for the moment more advisable, but nothing would prove in the long run more vain and inefficient than to keep the reason of youth in temporary tutelage, and to guard it against temptation for a time at least. If, however, curiosity or the fashion of the age should afterwards make them acquainted with such writings, will their youthful persuasion then hold good? He who is furnished with dogmatical weapons only in order to resist the attacks of his opponent, and is not able to analyse that hidden dialectic which is concealed in his own breast quite as much as in that of his opponent, sees sophistries which at all events have the charm of novelty, opposed to other sophistries which possess that charm no longer, and excite the suspicion of having imposed on the natural credulity of youth. He sees no better way of showing that he is no longer a child than by ignoring all well-meant warnings, and, accustomed as he is to dogmatism, he swallows the poison which destroys his principles by a new dogmatism.

The very opposite of this is the right course for academical instruction, provided always that it is founded on a thorough training in the principles of the criticism of pure reason. For, in order to practically apply these principles as soon as possible, and to show their sufficiency even when faced by the strongest dialectical illusion, it is absolutely necessary to allow the attacks, which seem so formidable to the dogmatist, to be directed against the young mind whose reason, though weak as yet, has been enlightened by criticism, so as to let him test by its principles the groundless assertions of his opponents one after the other. He cannot find it very difficult to dissolve them all into mere vapour, and thus alone does he early begin to feel his own power and is able to secure himself against all dangerous illusions which in the end lose all their fascination on him. It is true, the same blows which destroy the stronghold of his opponent must prove fatal also to his own speculative structures, if he should wish to erect such. But this need not disturb him, because he does not wish to shelter himself beneath them, but looks out for the fair field of practical philosophy, where he may hope to find firmer ground for erecting his own rational and beneficial system.

There is, therefore, no room for real polemic in the sphere of pure reason. Both parties beat the air and fight with their own shadows, because they go beyond the limits of nature, where there is nothing that they could lay hold of with their dogmatical grasp. They may fight to their hearts' content, the shadows which they are cleaving grow together again in one moment, like the heroes in Valhalla, in order to disport themselves once more in these bloodless contests.

Nor can we admit a sceptical use of pure reason, which might be called the principle of *neutrality* in all its disputes. Surely, to stir up reason against itself, to supply it with weapons on both sides, and then to look on quietly and scoffingly while the fierce battle is raging, does not look well from a dogmatical point of view, but has the appearance of a mischievous and malevolent disposition. If, however, we consider the invincible obstinacy and the boasting of the dogmatical sophists, who are deaf to all the warnings of criticism, there really seems nothing left but to meet the boasting on one side by an equally justified boasting on the other, in order at least to startle reason by a display of opposition, and thus to shake her confidence and make her willing to listen to the voice of criticism. But to stop at this point, and to look upon the conviction and confession of ignorance, not only as a remedy against dogmatical conceit, but as the best means of settling the conflict of reason with herself, is a vain attempt that will never give rest and peace to reason. The utmost it can do is to rouse reason from her sweet dogmatical dreams, and to induce her to examine more carefully her own position. As, however, the sceptical manner of avoiding a troublesome business seems to be the shortest way out of all difficulties, and promises to lead to a permanent peace in philosophy, or is chosen at least as the highroad by all who, under the pretence of a scornful dislike of all investigations of this kind, try to give themselves the air of philosophers, it seems necessary to exhibit this mode of thought in its true light.

The Impossibility of a Sceptical Satisfaction of Pure Reason in Conflict with itself

The consciousness of my ignorance (unless we recognise at the same time its necessity) ought, instead of forming the end of my investigations, to serve, on the contrary, as their strongest impulse. All ignorance is either an ignorance of things, or an ignorance of the limits of our cognition. If ignorance is accidental, it should incite us, in the former case, to investigate things *dogmatically,* in the latter to investigate the limits of possible knowledge *critically*. That my ignorance is absolutely necessary and that I am absolved from the duty of all further investigation, can never be established *empirically* by mere observation, but *critically* only, by a thorough examination of the first sources of our knowledge. The determination of the true limits of our reason, therefore, can be made on *a priori* grounds only, while its limitation, which consists in a general recognition of our never entirely removable ignorance, may be realised *a posteriori* also, by seeing how much remains to be known in spite of all that can be known. The former knowledge of our ignorance, possible only by criticism of reason, is truly *scientific,* the latter is merely matter of experience, where it is never possible to say how far the inferences drawn from it may reach. If I regard the earth, according to the evidence of my senses, as a flat surface, I cannot tell how far it may extend. But what experience teaches me is, that wheresoever I go, I always see before me a space in which I can proceed further. Thus I am conscious of the limits of my actual knowledge of the earth at any given moment, but not of the limits of all possible geography. But if I have got so far as to know that the earth is a sphere and its surface spherical, I am able from any small portion of it, for instance, from a degree, to know definitely and according to principles *a priori,* the diameter, and through it, the complete periphery of the earth; and, though I am ignorant with regard to the objects which are contained in that surface, I am not so with regard to its extent, its magnitude, and its limits.

In a similar manner the whole of the objects of our knowledge appears to us like a level surface, with its apparant horizon which encircles its whole extent, and was called by us the idea of unconditioned totality. To reach this limit empirically is impossible, and all attempts have proved vain to determine it *a priori* according to a certain principle. Nevertheless, all questions of pure reason refer to what lies outside of that horizon, or, it may be, on its boundary line.

The celebrated David Hume was one of those geographers of human reason who supposed that all those questions were sufficiently disposed of by being relegated outside that horizon, which, however, he was not able to determine. He was chiefly occupied with the principle of causality, and remarked quite rightly, that the truth of this principle (and even the objective validity of the concept of an efficient cause in general) was based on no knowledge, i.e. on no cognition *a priori,* and that its authority rested by no means on the necessity of such a law, but merely on its general usefulness in experience, and on a kind of subjective necessity arising from thence, which he called *habit.* From the inability of reason to employ this principle beyond the limits of experience he inferred the nullity of all the pretensions of reason in her attempts to pass beyond what is empirical.

This procedure of subjecting the *facts* of reason to examination, and, if necessary, to blame, may be termed the *censorship* of reason. There can be no doubt that such a censorship must inevitably lead to *doubts* against all the transcendental employment of such principles. But this is only the second and by no means the last step in our enquiry. The first step in matters of pure reason, which marks its infancy, is *dogmatism.* The second, which we have just described, is *scepticism,* and marks the stage of caution on the part of reason, when rendered wiser by experience. But a third step is necessary, that of the maturity and manhood of judgment, based on firm and universally applicable maxims, when not the facts of reason, but reason itself in its whole power and fitness for pure knowledge *a priori* comes to be examined. This is not the *censura* merely, but the true *criticism* of reason, by which not the *barrier* only, but the fixed *frontiers* of reason, not ignorance only on this or that point, but ignorance with reference to all possible questions of a certain kind, must be proved from principles, instead of being merely guessed at. Thus *scepticism* is a resting-place of reason, where it may reflect for a time on its dogmatical wanderings and gain a survey of the region where it happens to be, in order to choose its way with greater certainty for the future: but it can never be its permanent dwelling-place. That can only be found in perfect certainty, whether of our knowledge of the objects themselves or of the limits within which all our knowledge of objects is enclosed.

Our reason is not to be considered as an indefinitely extended plain, the limits of which are known in a general way only, but ought rather to be compared to a sphere the radius of which may be determined from the curvature of the arc of its surface (corresponding to the nature of synthetical propositions *a priori*), which enables us likewise to fix the extent and periphery of it with perfect certainty. Outside that sphere (the field of experience) nothing can become an object to our reason, nay, questions even on such imaginary objects relate to the subjective principles only for a complete determination of all the relations which may exist between the concepts of the understanding within that sphere.

It is a fact that we are in possession of different kinds of synthetical knowledge *a priori*, as shown by the principles of the understanding which anticipate experience. If anybody finds it quite impossible to understand the possibility of such principles, he may at first have some doubts as to whether they really dwell within us *a priori;* but he cannot thus, by the mere powers of the understanding, prove their impossibility, and declare all the steps which reason takes under their guidance as null and void. All he can say is that, if we could understand their origin and genuineness, we should be able to determine the extent and limits of our reason, and that, until that is done, all the assertions of reason are made at random. And in this way a complete scepticism with regard to all dogmatical philosophy, which is not guided by a criticism of reason, is well grounded, though we could not therefore deny to reason such further advance, after the way has once been prepared and secured on firmer ground. For all these concepts, nay, all the questions which pure reason places before us, have their origin, not in experience, but in reason itself, and must therefore be capable of being solved and tested as to their validity or invalidity. Nor are we justified, while pretending that the solution of these problems is really to be found in the nature of things, to decline their consideration and further investigation, under the pretext of our weakness, for reason alone begets all these ideas by itself, and is bound therefore to give an account of their validity or their dialectical vanity.

All sceptical polemic should properly be directed against the dogmatist only who, without any misgivings about his own fundamental objective principles, that is, without criticism, continues his course with undisturbed gravity, and should be intended only to unsettle his brief and to bring him thus to a proper self-knowledge. With regard to what we know or what we cannot know, that polemic is of no consequence whatever. All the unsuccessful dogmatical attempts of reason are *facta,* and it is always useful to submit them to the *censura* of the sceptic. But this can decide nothing as to the expectations of reason in her hopes and claims of a better success in future attempts; and no mere *censura* can put an end to the disputes regarding the rights of human reason.

Hume is, perhaps, the most ingenious of all sceptics, and without doubt the most important with regard to the influence which the sceptical method may exercise in awakening reason to a thorough examination of its rights. It will therefore be worth our while to make clear to ourselves the course of his reasoning and the errors of an intelligent and estimable man, who at the outset of his enquiries was certainly on the right track of truth.

Hume was probably aware, though he never made it quite

clear to himself, that in judgments of a certain kind we pass beyond our concept of the object. I have called this class of judgments *synthetical.* There is no difficulty as to how I may, by means of experience, pass beyond the concept which I have hitherto had. Experience is itself such a synthesis of perceptions through which a concept, which I have by means of one perception, is increased by means of other perceptions. But we imagine that we are able also *a priori* to pass beyond our concept and thus to enlarge our knowledge. This we attempt to do either by the pure understanding, in relation to that which can at least be an *object of experience,* or even by means of pure reason, in relation to such qualities of things, or even the existence of such things, as can never occur in experience. Hume in his scepticism did not distinguish between these two kinds of judgments as he ought to have done, but regarded this augmentation of concepts by themselves, and, so to say, the spontaneous generation of our understanding (and of our reason), without being impregnated by experience, as perfectly impossible. Considering all principles *a priori* as imaginary, he arrived at the conclusion that they were nothing but a habit arising from experience and its laws; that they were therefore merely empirical, that is, in themselves, contingent rules to which we wrongly ascribe necessity and universality. In order to establish this strange proposition, he appealed to the generally admitted principle of the relation between cause and effect. For as no faculty of the understanding could lead us from the concept of a thing to the existence of something else that should follow from it universally and necessarily, he thought himself justified in concluding that, without experience, we have nothing that could augment our concept and give us a right to form a judgment that extends itself *a priori.* That the light of the sun which shines on the wax should melt the wax and at the same time harden the clay, no understanding, he maintained, could guess from the concepts which we had before of these things, much less infer, according to a law, experience only being able to teach us such a law. We have seen, on the contrary, in the transcendental logic that, though we can never pass *immediately* beyond the content of a concept that is given us, we are nevertheless able, entirely *a priori,* but yet in reference to something else, namely, possible experience, to know the law of its connection with other things. If, therefore, wax, which was formerly hard, melts, I can know *a priori* that *something* else must have preceded (for instance the heat of the sun) upon which this melting has followed according to a permanent law, although without experience I could never know *a priori* definitely either from the effect the cause, or from the cause the effect. Hume was therefore wrong in inferring from the mere contingency of our being determined according to the law of causality, the contingency of that law itself, and he mistook our passing beyond the concept of a thing to some possible experience (which is entirely *a priori* and constitutes the objective reality of it) for the synthesis of the objects of real experience which, no doubt, is always empirical. He thus changed a principle of affinity which resides in the understanding and predicates necessary connection, into a rule of association residing in the imitative faculty of imagination, which can only represent contingent, but never objective connections.

The sceptical errors of that otherwise singularly acute thinker arose chiefly from a defect, which he shared, however, in common with all dogmatists, namely, of not having surveyed systematically all kinds of synthesis *a priori* of the understanding. For in doing this he would, without mentioning others, have discovered, for instance, the *principle of permanency* as one which, like causality, anticipates experience. He would thus have been able also to fix definite limits to the understanding in its attempts at expansion *a priori* and to pure reason. He only *narrows* the sphere of our understanding, without definitely *limiting* it, and produces a general mistrust, but no definite knowledge of that ignorance which to us is inevitable. He only subjects certain principles of the understanding to his *censura,* but does not place the understanding, with reference to all its faculties, on the balance of criticism. He is not satisfied with denying to the understanding what in reality it does not possess, but goes on to deny to it all power of expanding *a priori,* though he has never really tested all its powers. For this reason, what always defeats scepticism has happened to Hume also, namely, that he himself becomes subject to scepticism, because his objections rest on facts only which are contingent, and not on principles which alone can force a surrender of the right of dogmatical assertion.

As, besides this, he does not sufficiently distinguish between the well-grounded claims of the understanding and the dialectical pretensions of reason, against which, however, his attacks are chiefly directed, it so happens that reason, the peculiar tendency of which has not in the least been destroyed, but only checked, does not at all consider itself shut out from its attempts at expansion, and can never be entirely turned away from them, although it may be punished now and then. Mere attacks only provoke counter attacks, and make us more obstinate in enforcing our own views. But a complete survey of all that is really our own, and the conviction of a certain though a small possession, make us perceive the vanity of higher claims, and induce us, after surrendering all disputes, to live contentedly and peacefully within our own limited, but undisputed domain.

These sceptical attacks are not only dangerous, but even destructive to the uncritical dogmatist who has not measured the sphere of his understanding, and has not, therefore, determined, according to principles, the limits of his own possible knowledge, and does not know beforehand how much he is really able to achieve, but thinks that he is able to find all this out by a purely tentative method. For if he has been found out in one single assertion of his, which he cannot justify, or the fallacy of which he cannot evolve according to principles, suspicion falls on all his assertions, however plausible they may appear.

And thus the sceptic is the true schoolmaster to lead the dogmatic speculator towards a sound criticism of the understanding and of reason. When he has once been brought there, he need fear no further attacks, for he has learnt to distinguish his own possession from that which lies completely beyond it, and on which he can lay no claim, nor become involved in any disputes regarding it. Thus the sceptical method, though it *cannot* in itself *satisfy* with regard to the problems of reason, is nevertheless an excellent preparation in order to awaken its circumspection, and to indicate the true means whereby the legitimate possessions of reason may be secured against all attacks.

DISCIPLINE OF PURE REASON

SECTION III

The Discipline of Pure Reason with Regard to Hypotheses

As then the criticism of our reason has at last taught us so much at least, that with its pure and speculative use we can arrive at no knowledge at all, would not this seem to open a wide field for *hypotheses,* as, where we cannot assert with certainty, we are at all events at liberty to form guesses and opinions?

If the faculty of imagination is not simply to indulge in dreams, but to invent and compose under the strict surveillance of reason, it is necessary that there should always be something perfectly certain, and not only invented or resting on opinion, and that is the *possibility* of the object itself. If that is once given, it is then allowable, so far as its reality is concerned, to have recourse to opinion, which opinion, however, if it is not to be utterly groundless, must be brought in connection with what is really given and therefore certain, as its ground of explanation. In that case, and in that case only, can we speak of an *hypothesis.*

As we cannot form the least conception of the possibility of a dynamical connection *a priori,* and as the categories of the pure understanding are not intended to invent any such connection, but only, when it is given in experience, to understand it, we cannot by means of these categories invent one single object as endowed with a new quality not found in experience, or base any permissible hypothesis on such a quality; otherwise we should be supplying our reason with empty chimeras, and not with concepts of things. Thus it is not permissible to invent any new and original powers, as, for instance, an understanding capable of perceiving objects without the aid of the senses; or a force of attraction without any contact; a new kind of substances that should exist, for instance, in space, without being impenetrable, and consequently, also, any connection of substances, different from that which is supplied by experience; no presence, except in space, no duration, except in time. In one word, our reason can only use the conditions of possible experience as the conditions of the possibility of things; it cannot invent them independently, because such concepts, although not self-contradictory, would always be without an object.

The concepts of reason, as was said before, are mere ideas, and it is true that they have no object corresponding to them in experience; but they do not, for all that, refer to purely imaginary objects, which are supposed to be possible. They are purely problematical, in order to supply (as heuristic fictions) regulative principles for the systematical employment of the understanding in the sphere of experience. If they are not that, they would become mere fictions the possibility of which is quite indemonstrable, and which, therefore, can never be employed as hypotheses for the explanation of real phenomena. It is quite permissible to represent the soul to ourselves as simple, in order, according to this idea, to use the complete and necessary unity of all the faculties of the soul, although we cannot understand it *in concreto,* as the principle of all our enquiries into its internal phenomena. But to *assume* the soul as a simple substance (which is a transcendent concept) would be a proposition, not only indemonstrable (this is the case with several physical hypotheses), but purely arbitrary and rash: because the simple can never occur in any experience, and if by substance we understand the permanent object of sensuous intuition, the very possibility of a *simple phenomenon* is perfectly inconceivable. Reason has no right whatever to assume, as an opinion, purely intelligible beings, or purely intelligible qualities of the objects of the senses; although, on the other side, as we have no concepts whatever, either of their possibility or impossibility, we cannot claim any truer insight enabling us to deny dogmatically their possibility.

In order to explain given phenomena, no other things or reasons can be adduced but those which, according to the already known laws of phenomena, have been put in connection with them. A transcendental hypothesis, adducing a mere idea of reason for the explanation of natural things, would therefore be no explanation at all, because it would really be an attempt at explaining what, according to known empirical principles, we do not understand sufficiently by something which we do not understand at all. Nor would the principle of such an hypothesis serve to help the understanding with regard to its objects, but only to satisfy our reason. Order and design in nature must themselves be explained on natural grounds and according to natural laws; and for this purpose even the wildest hypotheses, if only they are physical, are more tolerable than a hyperphysical one,—that is, the appeal to the Divine Author, who is called in for that very purpose. This would be a principle of *ratio ignava,* to pass by all causes the objective reality of which, in their possibility at least, may be known by continued experience, in order to rest on a mere idea, which no doubt is very agreeable to our reason. With regard to the absolute totality of the ground of explanation in the series of causes, there can be no difficulty, considering that all mundane objects are nothing but phenomena, in which we can never hope to find absolute completeness in the synthesis of the series of conditions.

It is impossible to allow transcendental hypotheses in the

speculative use of reason, or the use of hyperphysical instead of physical explanations; partly, because reason is not in the least advanced in that way, but, on the contrary, cut off from its own proper employment, partly because such a licence would in the end deprive reason of all the fruits that spring from the cultivation of its own proper soil, namely, experience. It is true, no doubt, that whenever the explanation of nature seems difficult to us, we should thus always have a transcendent explanation ready to hand, which relieves us of all investigation; but in that case we are led in the end, not to an understanding, but to a complete incomprehensibility of the principle which, from the very beginning, was so designed that it must contain the concept of something which is the absolutely First.

What is, secondly, required in order to render an hypothesis acceptable, is its adequacy for determining *a priori,* by means of it, all the consequences that are given. If, for that purpose, we have to call in the aid of supplementary hypotheses, they rouse the suspicion of a mere fiction, because each of them requires for itself the same justification as the fundamental idea, and cannot serve therefore as a sufficient witness. No doubt, if we once admit an absolutely perfect cause, there is no difficulty in accounting for all the order, magnitude, and design which are seen in the world. But if we consider what seem to us at least deviations and evils in nature, new hypotheses will be required in order to save the first hypothesis from the objections which it has to encounter. In the same manner, whenever the simple independence of the human soul, which has been admitted in order to account for all its phenomena, is called into question on account of the difficulties arising from phenomena similar to the changes of matter (growth and decay), new hypotheses have to be called in, which may seem plausible, but possess no authority, except what they derive from the opinion which was to yield the chief explanation, and which they themselves were called upon to defend.

If the two hypotheses which we have just mentioned as examples of the assertions of reason (the incorporeal unity of the soul, and the existence of a Supreme Being) are to be accepted, not as hypotheses, but as dogmas proved *a priori,* we have nothing to say to them. Great care, however, should be taken in that case that they should be proved with the apodictic certainty of a demonstration. It would be as absurd to try to make the reality of such ideas plausible only, as to try to make a geometrical proposition plausible. Reason, independent of all experience, knows everything either *a priori,* and as necessary, or not at all. Its judgment, therefore, is never opinion, but either an abstaining from all judgments, or apodictic certainty. Opinions and guesses as to what belongs to things can be admitted in explanation only of what is really given, or as resulting, according to empirical laws, from something that is really given. They belong, therefore, to the series of the objects of experience only. Outside that field to opine is the same as to play with thoughts, unless we suppose that even a doubtful and uncertain way of judging might lead us perhaps on to the truth.

But although, when dealing with the purely speculative questions of pure reason, no hypotheses are admissible in order to found on them any propositions, they are perfectly admissible in order, if possible, to defend them; that is to say, they may be used for polemical, but not for dogmatical purposes. Nor do I understand by defending the strengthening of the proofs in support of our assertions, but only the refutation of the dialectical arguments of the opponent which are intended to invalidate our assertions. All synthetical propositions of pure reason have this peculiarity that, although the philosopher who maintains the reality of certain ideas never possesses sufficient knowledge in order to render his own propositions certain, his opponent is equally unable to prove the opposite. It is true, no doubt, that this equality of fortune, which is peculiar to human reason, favours neither of the two parties with regard to their speculative knowledge, and hence the never-ending feuds in this arena. But we shall see nevertheless that, in relation to its practical employment, reason has the right of admitting what, in the sphere of pure speculation, it would not be allowed to admit without sufficient proof. Such admissions, no doubt, detract from the perfection of speculation, but practical interests take no account of this. Here, therefore, reason is in possession, without having to prove the legitimacy of its title, which, indeed, it would be difficult to do. The burden of proof rests, therefore, on the opponent; and as he knows as little of the point in question, to enable him to prove its non-existence, as the other who maintains its reality, it is evident that there is an advantage on the side of him who maintains something as a practically necessary supposition (*melior est conditio possidentis*). He is clearly entitled, as it were in self-defence, to use the same weapons in support of his own good cause, which the opponent uses against it, that is, to employ hypotheses, which are not intended to strengthen the arguments in favour of his own view, but only to show that the opponent knows far too little of the subject under discussion to flatter himself that he possesses any advantage over us, so far as speculative insight is concerned.

In the field of pure reason, therefore, hypotheses are admitted as weapons of defence only, not in order to establish a right, but simply in order to defend it; and it is our duty at all times to look for a real opponent within ourselves. Speculative reason in its transcendental employment is by its very nature dialectical. The objections which we have to fear lie in ourselves. We must look for them as we look for old, but never superannuated claims, if we wish to destroy them, and thus to establish a permanent peace. External tranquillity is a mere illusion. It is necessary to root up the very germ of these objections which lies in the nature of human reason; and how can we root it up, unless we allow it freedom, nay, offer it nourishment, so that it may send out shoots, and thus discover itself to our eyes, so that we may afterwards destroy it with its very root? Try yourselves therefore to discover objections of which no opponent has ever thought; nay, lend him your weapons, and grant him the most favourable position which he could wish for. You have nothing to fear in all this, but much to hope for, namely, that you may gain a possession which no one will ever again venture to contest.

In order to be completely equipped you require the hypotheses of pure reason also, which, although but leaden weapons (because not steeled by any law of experience), are yet quite as strong as those which any opponent is likely to use against you. If, therefore (for any not speculative reason), you have admitted the immaterial nature of the soul, which is not subject to any corporeal changes, and you are met by the difficulty that nevertheless experience seems to prove both the elevation and the decay of our mental faculties as different modifications of our organs, you can weaken the force of this objection by saying that you look upon the body as a fundamental phenomenon only, which, in our present state (in this life), forms the condition of all the faculties of our sensibility, and hence of our thought. In that case the separation from the body would be the end of the sensuous employment and the beginning of the intelligible employment of our faculty of knowledge. The body would thus have to be considered, not as the cause of our thinking, but only as a restrictive condition of it, and, therefore, if on one side as a support of our sensuous and animal life, on the other, all the more, as an impediment of our pure and spiritual life, so that the dependence of the animal life on the constitution of the body would in no wise prove the dependence of our whole life on the state of our organs. You may go even further and discover new doubts which have either not been raised at all before, or at all events have not been carried far enough.

Generation in the human race, as well as among irrational creatures, depends on so many accidents, on occasion, on sufficient sustenance, on the views and whims of government, nay, even on vice, that it is difficult to believe in the eternal existence of a being whose life has first begun under circumstances so trivial, and so entirely dependent on our own choice. As regards the continuance (here on earth) of the whole race, there is less difficulty, because the accidents in individual cases are subject nevertheless to a rule with regard to the whole. With regard to each individual, however, to expect so important an effect from such insignificant causes seems very strange. But even against this you may adduce the following transcendental hypothesis, namely, that all life is really intelligible only, not subject to the changes of time, and neither beginning in birth, nor ending in death. You may say that this life is phenomenal only, that is, a sensuous representation of the pure spiritual life, and that the whole world of sense is but an image passing before our present mode of knowledge, but, like a dream, without any objective reality in itself; nay, that if we could see ourselves and other objects also *as they really are,* we should see ourselves in a world of spiritual natures, our community with which did neither begin at our birth nor will end with the death of the body, both being purely phenomenal.

Although it is true that we do not know anything about what we have here been pleading hypothetically against our opponents, and that we ourselves do not even seriously maintain it, it being simply an idea *invented* for self-defence and not even an idea of reason, yet we are acting throughout quite rationally. In answer to our opponent who imagines that he has exhausted all possibilities, and who wrongly represents the absence of empirical conditions as a proof of the total impossibility of our own belief, we are simply showing him that he can no more, by mere laws of experience, comprehend the whole field of possible things by themselves than we are able, outside of experience, to establish anything for our reason on a really secure foundation. Because we bring forward such hypothetical defences against the pretensions of our boldly denying opponent, we must not be supposed to have adopted these opinions as our own. We abandon them so soon as we have disposed of the dogmatical conceit of our opponent. It seems no doubt very modest and moderate to maintain a simple negative position with regard to the assertions of other people; but to attempt to represent objections as proofs of the opposite opinion is quite as arrogant as to assume the position of the affirming party and its opinions.

It is easy to see, therefore, that in the speculative employment of reason hypotheses are of no value by themselves, but relatively only, as opposed to the transcendental pretensions of the opposite party. For to extend the principles of possible experience to the possibility of things in general is quite as transcendent as to ascribe objective reality to concepts which cannot have an object except outside the limits of all possible experience. The assertory judgments of pure reason must (like everything known by reason) be either necessary or nothing at all. Reason, in fact, knows of no opinions. The hypotheses, however, which we have just been discussing are problematical judgments only, which, at least, cannot be refuted, though they can neither be proved by anything. They are nothing but private[1] opinions, but (for our own satisfaction) we cannot well do without them to counteract misgivings that may arise in our minds. In this character they should be maintained, but we must take great care lest they should assume independent authority and a certain absolute validity, and drown our reason beneath fictions and phantoms.

THE DISCIPLINE OF PURE REASON

SECTION IV

The Discipline of Pure Reason with Regard to its Proofs

What distinguishes the proofs of transcendental and synthetical propositions from all other proofs of a synthetical knowledge *a priori* is this, that reason is not allowed here to apply itself directly to an object through its concepts, but has first to prove the objective validity of those concepts and the pos-

[1] Read *reine* instead of *keine*.

sibility of their synthesis *a priori*. This rule is not suggested by prudence only, but refers to the very nature and the possibility of such proofs. If I am to go beyond the concept of an object *a priori*, this is impossible without some special guidance coming to me from without that concept. In mathematics it is intuition *a priori* which thus guides my synthesis, so that all our conclusions may be drawn immediately from pure intuition. In transcendental knowledge the same guidance, so long as we are dealing with concepts of the understanding only, is to be found in possible experience. For here the proof does not show that the given concept (for instance, the concept of that which happens) leads directly to another concept (that of a cause). This would be a saltus which nothing could justify. What our proof really shows is, that experience itself and therefore the object of experience would be impossible without such a (causal) connection. The proof, therefore, had at the same time to indicate the possibility of arriving synthetically and *a priori* at a certain knowledge of things which was not contained in our concept of them. Unless we attend to this point, our proofs, like streams which have broken their banks, run wildly across the fields wherever the inclination of some hidden association may chance to lead them. The semblance of a conviction, based on subjective causes of association and mistaken for the preception of a natural affinity, cannot balance the misgivings which are justly roused by such bold proceedings. Hence all attempts at proving the principle of sufficient reason have, according to the universal admission of all competent judges, been vain; and before the appearance of transcendental criticism it was thought better, as that principle could never be surrendered, to make a sturdy appeal to the common sense of mankind (an expedient which always shows that the cause of reason is desperate) than to attempt new dogmatical proofs of it.

But, if the proposition that has to be proved is an assertion of pure reason, and if I even intend by means of pure ideas to go beyond my empirical concepts, it would be all the more necessary that the proof should contain the justification of such a step of synthesis (if it were possible) as a necessary condition of its own validity. The so-called proof of the simple nature of our thinking substance (soul), derived from the unity of apperception, seems very plausible; but it is confronted by an inevitable difficulty, because, as the absolute unity is not a concept that can be immediately referred to a perception, but, as an idea, can only be inferred, it is difficult to understand how the mere consciousness which is, or at least may be, contained in *all thought,* though it may be so far a simple representation, can lead me on to the consciousness and the knowledge of a thing, *in which* thought alone is contained. For if I represent to myself the power of my body, as in motion, it is then to me an absolute unity, and my representation of it is a simple one. I can, therefore, very well express this representation by the motion of a point; because the volume of the body is here of no consequence, and can, without any diminution of its power, be conceived as small as one likes, and, therefore, even as existing in one point. But I should never conclude from this that, if nothing is given to me but the motive power of a body, that body can be conceived as a simple substance, because its representation is independent of the quantity of its volume, and, therefore, simple. I thus detect a paralogism, because the simple in the abstract is totally different from the simple as an object, and the *ego* which, conceived in the abstract, contains nothing manifold, can, as an object, when signifying the soul, become a very complex concept, comprehending and implying many things. In order to be prepared for such a paralogism (for unless we suspected it, the proof might excite no suspicion), it is absolutely necessary to be always in possession of a criterion of such synthetical propositions, which are meant to prove more than experience can ever supply. This criterion consists in our demanding that the proof should not be carried directly to the predicate in question, but that, first, the principle of the possibility of expanding our given concept *a priori* into ideas and realising them, should be established. If we always exercised this caution, and, before attempting any such proof, wisely considered ourselves, how, and with what degree of confidence, we might expect such an expansion through pure reason, and whence we might take, in such cases, knowledge which cannot be evolved from concepts nor anticipated with reference to possible experience, we might spare ourselves many difficult, and yet fruitless endeavours, by not asking of reason what evidently is beyond its power, or rather, by subjecting reason, which when once under the influence of this passion for speculative conquest, is not easily checked, to a thorough discipline of moderation.

The first rule, therefore, is to attempt no transcendental proofs before having first considered from whence we should take the principles on which such proofs are to be based, and by what right we may expect our conclusions to be successful.

If they are principles of the understanding (for instance of causality), it is useless to attempt to arrive, by means of them, at ideas of pure reason; because they are valid only with regard to objects of experience. If they are principles of pure reason, it is again labour lost, because, though reason possesses such principles, they are all, as objective principles, dialectical and cannot be valid, except perhaps as regulative principles, for the empirical use of reason, in order to make it systematically coherent. If such so-called proofs exist already, we ought to meet their deceptive pleadings with the *non liquet* of a mature judgment; and although we may be unable to expose their sophisms, we have a perfect right to demand a deduction of the principles employed, which, if these principles are to have their origin in reason alone, will never be forthcoming. You may thus dispense with the analysis and refutation of every one of these sophisms, and dispose in a lump of the endless fallacies of Dialectic, by appealing to the tribunal of critical reason, which insists on laws.

The second peculiarity of transcendental proofs is this, that for every transcendental proposition *one* proof *only* can be found. If I have to draw conclusions, not from concepts, but from the intuition which corresponds to a concept, whether it be pure intuition, as in mathematics, or empirical, as in physical science, the intuition on which my conclusions are to rest supplies me with manifold material for synthetical propositions, which I may connect in more than one way, so that, by starting from different points, I can arrive at the same conclusion by different paths.

Every transcendental proposition, on the contrary, starts from *one* concept only, and predicates the synthetical condition of the possibility of the object, according to that concept. There can therefore be but one proof, because beside that concept there is nothing else whereby that object could be determined. The proof therefore can contain nothing more but the determination of an object in general according to that concept, which is itself one only. In the transcendental Analytic, for instance, we had deduced the principle, that everything which happens has a cause, from the single condition of the objective possibility of the concept of an event in general, namely, that the determination of any event in time, and therefore the event itself also, as belonging to experience, would be impossible, unless it were subject to such a dynamical rule. This is therefore the only possible proof; for the event which we represent to ourselves has objective validity, that is, truth, on this condition only, that an object is determined as belonging to that concept by means of the law of causality. It is true that other arguments in support of this proposition have been attempted, for instance, one derived from contingency; but if that argument is examined more carefully, we can discover no characteristic sign of contingency, except the *happening,* that is, existence preceded by the non-existence of the object, which leads us back to the same argument as before. If the proposition has to be proved that everything which thinks is simple, no attention is paid to what is manifold in thought, and the concept of the *ego* only is kept in view, which is simple, and to which all thinking is referred. The same applies to the transcendental proof of the existence of God, which rests entirely on the reciprocability of the two concepts of a most real and a necessary Being, and cannot be found anywhere else.

By this caution the criticism of the assertions of reason is much simplified. Wherever reason operates with concepts only, only one proof is possible, if any. If therefore we see the dogmatist advance with his ten proofs, we may be sure that he has none. For if he had one which (as it ought to be in all matters of pure reason) had apodictic power, what need would he have of others? His object can only be the same as that of the parliamentary lawyer who has one argument for one person, and another for another. He wants to take advantage of the weakness of the judges, who, without enquiring more deeply, and in order to get away as soon as possible, lay hold of the first argument that catches their attention, and decide accordingly.

The third peculiar rule of pure reason, if it is once subjected to a proper discipline with regard to transcendental proofs, is this, that such proofs must never be *apagogical* or circumstantial, but always *ostensive* or direct. The direct or ostensive proof combines, with regard to every kind of knowledge, a conviction of its truth with an insight into its sources; the apagogical proof, on the contrary, though it may produce certainty, cannot help us to comprehend the truth in its connection with the grounds of its possibility. It is therefore a mere expedient, and cannot satisfy all the requirements of reason. The apagogical proofs have, however, this advantage with regard to their evidence over direct proofs, that contradiction always carries with it more clearness in the representation than the best combination, and thus approaches more to the intuitional character of a demonstration.

The real reason why apagogical proofs are so much employed in different sciences, seems to be this. If the grounds from which some knowledge is to be derived are too numerous or too deeply hidden, one tries whether they may not be reached through their consequences. Now it is quite true that this *modus ponens,* that is, this inferring of the truth of some knowledge from the truth of its consequences, is only permitted, if all possible consequences flowing from it are true. In that case they have only one possible ground, which therefore is also the true one. This procedure, however, is impracticable, because to discover all possible consequences of any given proposition exceeds our powers. Nevertheless, this mode of arguing is employed, though under a certain indulgence, whenever something is to be established as a hypothesis only, in which case a conclusion, according to analogy, is admitted, namely, that if as many consequences as one has tested agree with an assumed ground, all others will also agree with it. To change in this way a hypothesis into a demonstrated truth, is clearly impossible. The *modus tollens* of reasoning, from consequences to their grounds, is not only perfectly strict, but also extremely easy. For if one single false consequence only can be drawn from a proposition, that proposition is wrong. Instead, therefore, of examining, for the sake of an ostensive proof, the whole series of grounds that may lead us to the truth of a cognition by means of a perfect insight into its possibility, we have only to prove that one single consequence, resulting from the opposite, is false, in order to show that the opposite itself is false, and therefore the cognition, which we had to prove, true.

This apagogical method of proof, however, is admissible in those sciences only where it is impossible to *foist* the subjective elements of our representations into the place of what is objective, namely, the knowledge of that which exists in the object. When this is not impossible, it must often happen that the opposite of any proposition contradicts the subjective conditions of thought only, but not the object itself, or, that both propositions contradict each other under a subjective condition, which is mistaken as objective, so that, as the condition is false, both may be false, without our being justified in inferring the truth of the one from the falseness of the other.

In mathematics such subreptions are impossible; and it is true, therefore, that the apagogical proof has its true place there. In natural science, in which everything is based on empirical intuitions, that kind of subreption can generally be guarded against by a repeated comparison of observations; but even thus, this mode of proof is of little value there. The transcendental endeavours of pure reason, however, are all made within the very sphere of dialectical illusion, where what is subjective presents itself, nay, forces itself upon reason in its premisses as objective. Here, therefore, it can never be allowed, with reference to synthetical propositions, to justify one's assertions by refuting their opposite. For, either this refutation may be nothing but the mere representation of the conflict of the opposite opinion with the subjective conditions under which our reason could alone comprehend it, and this would be of no avail for rejecting the proposition itself,— (thus we see, for instance, that the unconditioned necessity of the existence of a Being cannot possibly be comprehended by us, which *subjectively* bars every speculative proof of a necessary Supreme Being but by no means, the possibility of such a Being by *itself*),—or, on the other hand, it may be that both the affirmative and the negative party have been deceived by the transcendental illusion, and base their arguments on an impossible concept of an object. In that case the rule applies, *non entis nulla sunt praedicata,* that is, everything that has been asserted with regard to an object, whether affirmatively or negatively, is wrong, and we cannot therefore arrive apagogically at the knowledge of truth by the refutation of its opposite. If, for example, we assume that the world of sense is given *by itself* in its totality, it is wrong to conclude that it must be *either* infinite in space, *or* finite and limited; for either is wrong, because phenomena (as mere representations) which nevertheless are to be things *by themselves* (as objects) are something impossible, and the infinitude of this imaginary whole, though it might be unconditioned, would (because everything in phenomena is conditioned) contradict that very unconditioned quantity which is presupposed in its concept.

The apagogical mode of proof is also the blind by which the admirers of our dogmatical philosophy have always been deceived. It may be compared to a prizefighter who is willing to prove the honour and the incontestable rights of his adopted party by offering battle to all and every one who should dare to doubt them. Such brawling, however, settles nothing, but only shows the respective strength of the two parties, and even this on the part of those only who take the offensive. The spectators, seeing that each party is alternately conqueror and conquered, are often led to regard the very object of the dispute with a certain amount of scepticism. In this, however, they are wrong, and it is sufficient to remind them of *non defensoribus istis tempus eget*. It is absolutely necessary that every one should plead his cause directly by means of a legitimate proof based on a transcendental deduction of the grounds of proof. Thus only can we see what he may have to say himself in favour of his own claims of reason. If his opponent relies on subjective grounds only, it is easy, no doubt, to refute him; but this does not benefit the dogmatist, who generally depends quite as much on the subjective grounds of his judgment, and can be quite as easily driven into a corner by his opponent. If, on the contrary, both parties employ only the direct mode of proof, they will either themselves perceive the difficulty, nay, the impossibility of finding any title for their assertions, and appeal in the end to prescription only, or, our criticism will easily discover the dogmatical illusion, and compel pure reason to surrender its exaggerated pretensions in the sphere of speculative thought, and to retreat within the limits of its own domain,—that of practical principles.

METHOD OF TRANSCENDENTALISM

Chapter II

THE CANON OF PURE REASON

It is humiliating, no doubt, for human reason that it can achieve nothing by itself, nay, that it stands in need of a discipline to check its vagaries, and to guard against the illusions arising from them. But, on the other hand, it elevates reason and gives it self-confidence, that it can and must exercise that discipline itself, and allows no censorship to any one else. The bounds, moreover, which it is obliged to set to its own speculative use check at the same time the sophistical pretensions of all its opponents, and thus secure everything that remains of its formed exaggerated pretensions against every possible attack. The greatest and perhaps the only advantage of all philosophy of pure reason seems therefore to be negative only; because it serves, not as an organon for the extension, but as a discipline for the limitation of its domain, and instead of discovering truth, it only claims the modest merit of preventing error.

Nevertheless, there must be somewhere a source of positive cognitions which belong to the domain of pure reason, and which perhaps, owing to some misunderstanding only, may lead to error, while they form in reality the true goal of all the efforts of reason. How else could we account for that inextinguishable desire to gain a footing by any means somewhere beyond the limits of experience? Reason has a presentiment of objects which possess a great interest for it. It enters upon the path of pure speculation in order to approach them, but they fly before it. May we not suppose that on the only path which is still open to it, namely, that of its *practical* employments, reason may hope to meet with better success?

I understand by a canon a system of principles *a priori* for the proper employment of certain faculties of knowledge in general. Thus general logic, in its analytical portion, is a canon for the understanding and reason in general, but only so far as the form is concerned, for it takes no account of any contents. Thus we saw that the transcendental analytic is the canon of the pure *understanding,* and that it alone is capable of true synthetical knowledge *a priori.* When no correct use of a faculty of knowledge is possible, there is no canon, and as all synthetical knowledge of pure *reason* in its speculative employment is, according to all that has been hitherto said, totally impossible, there exists no canon of the speculative employment of reason (for that employment is entirely dialectical), but all transcendental logic is, in this respect, disciplinary only. Consequently, if there exists any correct use of pure reason at all, and, therefore, a canon relating to it, that canon will refer not to the speculative, but to the *practical use of reason,* which we shall now proceed to investigate.

THE CANON OF PURE REASON

SECTION I

Of the Ultimate Aim of the Pure Use of our Reason

Reason is impelled by a tendency of its nature to go beyond the field of experience, and to venture in its pure employment and by means of mere ideas to the utmost limits of all knowledge; nay, it finds no rest until it has fulfilled its course and established an independent and systematic whole of all knowledge. The question is, whether this endeavour rests on the speculative, or rather, exclusively on the practical interests of reason?

I shall say nothing at present of the success which has attended pure reason in its speculative endeavours, and only ask which are the problems, the solution of which forms its ultimate aim (whether that object be really reached or not), and in relation to which all other problems are only means to an end. These highest aims must again, according to the nature of reason, possess a certain unity in order to advance by their union that interest of humanity which is second to no other.

The highest aim to which the speculation of reason in its transcendental employment is directed comprehends three objects: the freedom of the will, the immortality of the soul, and the existence of God. The purely speculative interest of reason in every one of these three questions is very small, and, for its sake alone, this fatiguing and ceaseless labour of transcendental investigation would hardly have been undertaken, because whatever discoveries may be made, they could never be used in a way that would be advantageous *in concreto,* that is, in the investigation of nature.

Our will may be free, but this would only refer to the intelligible cause of our volition. With regard to the phenomena in which that will manifests itself, that is, our actions, we have to account for them (according to an inviolable maxim without which reason could not be employed for empirical purposes at all), in no other way than for all other phenomena of nature, that is, according to her unchangeable laws.

Secondly, the spiritual nature of the soul, and with it its immortality, may be understood by us, yet we could not base upon this any explanation, either with regard to the phenomena of this life, or the peculiar nature of a future state, because our concept of an incorporeal nature is purely negative and does not expand our knowledge in the least, nor does it offer any fit material for drawing consequences, except such as are purely fictitious, and could never be countenanced by philosophy.

Thirdly, even admitting that the existence of a highest intelligence had been proved, we might, no doubt, use it in order to make the design in the constitution of the world and its order in general intelligible, but we should never be justified in deriving from it any particular arrangement, or disposition, or in boldly inferring it where it cannot be perceived. For it is a necessary rule for the speculative employment of reason, never to pass by natural causes, and, abandoning what we may learn from experience, to derive something which we know, from something which entirely transcends all our knowledge.

In one word, these three propositions remain always transcendent for speculative reason, and admit of no immanent employment, that is, an employment admissible for objects of experience, and therefore of some real utility to ourselves, but are by themselves entirely valueless and yet extremely difficult exertions of our reason.

If, therefore, these three cardinal propositions are of no use to us, so far as *knowledge* is concerned, and are yet so strongly recommended to us by our reason, their true value will probably be connected with our *practical* interests only.

I call practical whatever is possible through freedom. When the conditions of the exercise of our free-will are empirical, reason can have no other but a regulative use, serving only to bring about the unity of empirical laws. Thus, for instance, in the teaching of prudence, the whole business of reason consists in concentrating all the objects of our desires in one, namely, *happiness,* and in co-ordinating the means for obtaining it. Reason, therefore, can give us none but *pragmatic* laws of free action for the attainment of the objects recommended to us by the senses, and never pure laws, determined entirely *a priori.* Pure practical laws, on the contrary, the object of which is given by reason entirely *a priori,* and which convey commands, not under empirical conditions, but absolutely, would be products of pure reason. Such are the *moral* laws, and these alone, therefore, belong to the sphere of the practical use of reason, and admit of a canon.

All the preparations of reason, therefore, in what may be called pure philosophy, are in reality directed to those three problems only. These themselves, however, have a still further object, namely, to know *what ought to be done,* if the will is free, if there is a God, and if there is a future world. As this concerns our actions with reference to the highest aim of life, we see that the last intention of nature in her wise provision was really, in the constitution of our reason, directed to moral interests only.

We must be careful, however, lest, as we are now considering a subject which is foreign to transcendental philosophy,* we should lose ourselves in episodes, and injure the unity of the system, while on the other side, if we say too little of this new matter, there might be a lack of clearness and persuasion. I hope to avoid both dangers by keeping as close as possible to what is transcendental, and by leaving entirely aside what may be psychological, that is, empirical in it.

I have, therefore, first to remark that for the present I shall use the concept of freedom in its practical meaning only, taking no account of the other concept of freedom in its transcendental meaning, which cannot be presupposed empirically as an explanation of phenomena, but is itself a problem of rea-

---

* All practical concepts relate to objects of pleasure or displeasure, that is, of joy or pain, and, therefore, at least indirectly, to objects of our feelings. But, as feeling is not a faculty of representing things, but lies outside the whole field of our powers of cognition, the elements of our judgments, so far as they relate to pleasure or pain, that is, the elements of practical judgments, do not belong to transcendental philosophy, which is concerned exclusively with pure cognitions *a priori.*

son and has been disposed of before. A will is purely *animal* (*arbitrium brutum*) when it is determined by nothing but sensuous impulses, that is, *pathologically*. A will, on the contrary, which is independent of sensuous impulses, and can be determined therefore by motives presented by reason alone, is called *Free-will* (*arbitrium liberum*), and everything connected with this, whether as cause or effect, is called *practical*. Practical freedom can be proved by experience. For human will is not determined by that only which excites, that is, immediately affects the senses; but we possess the power to overcome the impressions made on the faculty of our sensuous desires, by representing to ourselves what, in a more distant way, may be useful or hurtful. These considerations of what is desirable with regard to our whole state, that is, of what is good and useful, are based entirely on reason. Reason, therefore, gives laws which are imperatives, that is, objective *laws of freedom,* and tell us what *ought to take place,* though perhaps it never does take place, differing therein from the *laws of nature,* which relate only to *what does take place*. These laws of freedom, therefore, are called practical laws.

Whether reason in prescribing these laws is not itself determined by other influences, and whether what, in relation to sensuous impulses, is called freedom, may not, with regard to higher and more remote causes, be nature again, does not concern us while engaged in these practical questions, and while demanding from reason nothing but the *rule* of our conduct. It is a purely speculative question which, while we are only concerned with what we ought or ought not to do, may well be left aside. We know practical freedom by experience as one of the natural causes, namely, as a causality of reason in determining the will, while transcendental freedom demands the independence of reason itself (with reference to its causality in beginning a series of phenomena) from all determining causes in the world of sense, thus running counter, as it would seem, to the law of nature and therefore to all possible experience, and remaining a problem. Reason, however, in its practical employment has nothing to do with this problem, so that there remain but two questions in a canon of pure reason which concern the practical interest of pure reason, and with regard to which a canon of their employment must be possible, namely: Is there a God? Is there a future life? The question of transcendental freedom refers to speculative knowledge only, and may be safely left aside as quite indif-

ferent when we are concerned with practical interests. A sufficient discussion of it may be found in the antinomy of pure
reason.

THE CANON OF PURE REASON

SECTION II

*Of the Ideal of the Summum Bonum as determining the
Ultimate Aim of Pure Reason*

Reason, in its speculative employment, conducted us
through the field of experience, and, as it could find no perfect
satisfaction there, from thence to speculative ideas which, however, in the end conducted us back again to experience, and
thus fulfilled their purpose in a manner which, though useful,
was not at all in accordance with our expectation. We may
now have one more trial, namely, to see whether pure reason
may be met with in practical use also, and whether thus it
may lead to ideas which realise the highest aims of pure reason
as we have just stated them, and whether therefore from the
point of view of its practical interest, reason may not be able
to grant us what it entirely refused to do with regard to its
speculative interest.

The whole interest of my reason, whether speculative or
practical, is concentrated in the three following questions:—

    1.   What can I know?
    2.   What should I do?
    3.   What may I hope?

The first question is purely speculative. We have, as I flatter
myself, exhausted all possible answers, and found, at last, that
with which no doubt reason must be satisfied, and, except with
regard to the practical, has just cause to be satisfied. We remained, however, as far removed from the two great ends to
which the whole endeavour of pure reason was really directed
as if we had consulted our ease and declined the whole task
from the very beginning. So far then as knowledge is concerned, so much is certain and clear that, with regard to these
two problems, knowledge can never fall to our lot.

The second question is purely practical. As such it may come
within the cognisance of pure reason, but is, even then, not

transcendental, but moral, and cannot, consequently, occupy our criticism by itself.

The third question, namely, what may I hope for, if I do what I ought to do? is at the same time practical and theoretical, the practical serving as a guidance to the answer to the theoretical and, in its highest form, speculative question; for all *hoping* is directed towards happiness and is, with regard to practical interests and the law of morality, the same as *knowing* and the law of nature, with regard to the theoretical cognition of things. The former arrives at last at a conclusion that *something is* (which determines the last possible aim) because something *ought to take place;* the latter, that *something is* (which operates as the highest cause) because something *does take place.*

Happiness is the satisfaction of all our desires, *extensively,* in regard to their manifoldness, *intensively,* in regard to their degree, and *protensively,* in regard to their duration. The practical law, derived from the motive of *happiness,* I call pragmatical (rule of prudence); but the law, if there is such a law, which has no other motive but to *deserve to be happy,* I call moral (law of morality). The former advises us what we have to do, if we wish to possess happiness; the latter dictates how we ought to conduct ourselves in order to deserve happiness. The former is founded on empirical principles, for I cannot know, except by experience, what desires there are which are to be satisfied, nor what are the natural means of satisfying them. The second takes no account of desires and the natural means of satisfying them, and regards only the freedom of any rational being and the necessary conditions under which alone it can harmonise with the distribution of happiness according to principles. It can therefore be based on mere ideas of pure reason, and known *a priori.* I assume that there really exist pure moral laws which entirely *a priori* (without regard to empirical motives, that is, happiness) determine the use of the freedom of any rational being, both with regard to what has to be done and what has not to be done, and that these laws are imperative *absolutely* (not hypothetically only on the supposition of other empirical ends), and therefore in every respect necessary. I feel justified in assuming this, by appealing, not only to the arguments of the most enlightened moralists, but also to the moral judgment of every man, if he only tries to conceive such a law clearly.

Pure reason, therefore, contains not indeed in its speculative, yet in its practical, or, more accurately, its moral employment, principles of the *possibility of experience,* namely, of such actions as *might* be met with in the *history* of man according to moral precepts. For as reason commands that such actions should take place, they must be possible, and a certain kind of systematical unity also, namely, the moral, must be possible; while it was impossible to prove the systematical unity of nature *according to the speculative principles of reason.* For reason, no doubt, possesses causality with respect to freedom in general, but not with respect to the whole of nature, and moral principles of reason may indeed produce free actions, but not laws of nature. Consequently, the principles of pure reason possess objective reality in their practical and more particularly in their moral employment.

I call the world, in so far as it may be in accordance with all moral laws which, by virtue of the *freedom* of rational beings it may, and according to the necessary laws of *morality* it ought to be, a *moral world*. As here we take no account of all conditions (aims) and even of all impediments to morality (the weakness or depravity of human nature), this world is conceived as an intelligible world only. It is, therefore, so far a mere idea, though a practical idea, which can and ought really to exercise its influence on the sensible world in order to bring it, as far as possible, into conformity with that idea. The idea of a moral world has therefore objective reality, not as referring to an object of intelligible intuition (which we cannot even conceive), but as referring to the sensible world, conceived as an object of pure reason in its practical employment, and as a *corpus mysticum* of rational beings dwelling in it, so far as their free-will, placed under moral laws, possesses a thorough systematical unity both with itself and with the freedom of everybody else.

The answer, therefore, of the first of the two questions of pure reason with reference to practical interests, is this, *'do that which will render thee deserving of happiness.'* The second question asks, how then, if I conduct myself so as to be deserving of happiness, may I hope thereby to obtain happiness? The answer to this question depends on this, whether the principles of pure reason which *a priori* prescribe the law, necessarily also connect this hope with it?

I say, then, that just as the moral principles are necessary according to reason in its *practical* employment, it is equally necessary according to reason in its *theoretic* employment to assume that everybody has reason to hope to obtain happiness in the same measure in which he has rendered himself deserving of it in his conduct; and that, therefore, the system of morality is inseparably, though only in the idea of pure reason, connected with that of happiness.

In an intelligible, that is, in a moral world, in conceiving which we take no account of any of the impediments to morality (desires, etc.), such a system, in which happiness is proportioned to morality, may even be considered as necessary, because freedom, as repelled or restrained by the moral law, is itself the cause of general happiness, and rational beings therefore themselves, under the guidance of such principles, the authors of the permanent well-being of themselves, and at the same time of others. But such a system of self-rewarding morality is an idea only, the realisation of which depends on everybody doing what he ought to do, that is, on all actions of reasonable beings being so performed as if they sprang from one supreme will, comprehending within itself or under itself all private wills. But, as the moral law remains binding upon every one in the use of his freedom, even if others do not conform to that law, it is impossible that either the nature of things in the world, or the causality of the actions themselves, or their relation to morality, should determine in what relation the consequences of such actions should stand to happiness. If, therefore, we take our stand on nature only, the necessary connection of a hope of happiness with the unceasing endeavour of rendering oneself deserving of happiness, cannot be known by reason, but can only be hoped for, if a *highest reason,* which rules according to moral laws, is accepted at the same time as the cause of nature.

I call the idea of such an intelligence in which the most perfect moral will, united with the highest blessedness, is the cause of all happiness in the world, so far as it corresponds exactly with morality, that is, the being worthy of happiness, *the ideal of the supreme good.* It is, therefore, in the ideal only of the supreme *original* good that pure reason can find the ground of the practically necessary connection of both elements of the highest derivative good, namely, of an intelligible, that is, *moral* world. As we are bound by reason to conceive ourselves as belonging necessarily to such a world, though the senses present us with nothing but a world of phenomena, we shall have to accept the other world as the result of our conduct in this world of sense (in which we see no such connection between goodness and happiness), and therefore as to us a future world. Hence it follows that God and a future life are two suppositions which, according to the principles of pure reason, cannot be separated from the obligation which that very reason imposes on us.

Morality, by itself, constitutes a system, but not so happiness, unless it is distributed in exact proportion to morality. This, however, is possible in an intelligible world only under a wise author and ruler. Such a ruler, together with life in such a world, which we must consider as future, reason compels us to admit, unless all moral laws are to be considered as idle dreams, because, without that supposition, the necessary consequences, which the same reason connects with these laws, would be absent. Hence everybody looks upon moral laws as *commands,* which they could not be if they did not connect *a priori* adequate consequences with their rules, and carried with them both *promises* and *threats.* Nor could they do this unless they rested on a necessary Being, as the supreme good, which alone can render the unity of such a design possible.

Leibniz called the world, if we have regard only to the rational beings in it, and their mutual relations according to moral laws and under the government of the supreme good, the *kingdom of grace,* distinguishing it from the *kingdom of nature,* in which these beings, though standing under moral laws, expect no other consequences from their conduct but such as follow according to the course of nature of our sensible world. To view ourselves as belonging to the kingdom of grace, in which all happiness awaits us, except in so far as we have diminished our share in it through our unworthiness of being happy, is a practically necessary idea of reason.

Practical laws, in so far as they become at the same time subjective grounds of actions, that is, subjective principles, are called *maxims.* The *criticism* of morality, with regard to its purity and its results, takes place according to *ideas,* the practical *observance* of its laws, according to *maxims.*

It is necessary that the whole course of our life should be subject to moral maxims; but this is impossible, unless reason connects with the moral law, which is a mere idea, an efficient cause, which assigns to all conduct, in accordance with the moral law, an issue accurately corresponding to our highest aims, whether in this or in another life. Thus without a God and without a world, not visible to us now, but hoped for, the glorious ideas of morality are indeed objects of applause and admiration, but not springs of purpose and action, because they fail to fulfil all the aims which are natural to every rational being, and which are determined *a priori* by the same pure reason, and therefore necessary.

Our reason does by no means consider happiness alone as the perfect good. It does not approve of it (however much inclination may desire it), except as united with desert, that is, with perfect moral conduct. Nor is morality alone, and with it mere *desert* of being happy, the perfect good. To make it perfect, he who has conducted himself as not unworthy of happiness, must be able to hope to participate in it. Even if freed from all private views and interests, reason, were it to put itself in the place of a being that had to distribute all happiness to others, could not judge otherwise; because in the practical idea both elements are essentially connected, though in such a way that our participation in happiness should be rendered possible by the moral character as a condition, and not conversely the moral character by the prospect of happiness. For, in the latter case, the character would not be moral, nor worthy therefore of complete happiness; a happiness which, in the eyes of reason, admits of no limitation but such as arises from our own immoral conduct.

Happiness, therefore, in exact proportion with the morality of rational beings who are made worthy of happiness by it, constitutes alone the supreme good of a world into which we must necessarily place ourselves according to the commands of pure but practical reason. But this is an intelligible world only, and a sensible world never promises us such a systematical unity of ends as arising from the nature of things. Nor is the reality of this unity founded on anything but the admission of a supreme original good, so that independent reason, equipped with all the requirements of a supreme cause, founds, maintains, and completes, according to the most perfect design, the universal order of things which, in the world of sense, is almost completely hidden from our sight.

This moral theology has this peculiar advantage over speculative theology, that it leads inevitably to the concept of a *sole, most perfect,* and *rational* first Being, to which speculative theology does not even *lead us on,* on objective grounds, much less give us a *conviction* of it. For neither in transcendental nor in natural theology, however far reason may carry us on, do we find any real ground for admitting even one sole being which we should be warranted in placing before all natural causes and on which we might make them in all respects to depend. On the other hand, if, from the point of view of moral unity as a necessary law of the universe, we consider what cause alone could give to it its adequate effect, and therefore its binding force with regard to ourselves, we find that it must be one sole supreme will which comprehends all these laws within itself. For how with different wills should we find complete unity of ends? That will must be omnipotent, in order that the whole of nature and its relation to morality and the world may be subject to it; omniscient, that it may know the most secret springs of our sentiments and their moral worth; omnipresent, that it may be near for supplying immediately all that is required by the highest interests of the world; eternal, that this harmony of nature and freedom may never fail, and so on.

But this systematical unity of ends in this world of intelligences which, if looked upon as mere nature, may be called a sensible world only, but which, if considered as a system of freedom, may be called an intelligible, that is, a moral world (*regnum gratiae*), leads inevitably also to the admission of a unity of design in all things which constitute this great universe according to general natural laws, just as the former (unity) was according to general and necessary laws of morality. In this way practical and speculative reason become united. The world must be represented as having originated from an idea, if it is to harmonise with that employment of reason without which we should consider ourselves unworthy of reason, namely, with its moral employment, which is founded entirely on the idea of the supreme good. In this way the study of nature tends to assume the form of a teleological system, and becomes in its widest extension physico-theology. And this, as it starts from the moral order as a unity founded on the essence of freedom, and not accidentally brought about by external commands, traces the design of nature to grounds which must be inseparably connected *a priori* with the internal possibility of things, and leads thus to a *transcendental theology,* which takes the ideal of the highest ontological perfection as the principle of systematical unity which connects all things according to general and necessary laws of nature, because they all have their origin in the absolute necessity of the one original Being.

What *use* can we make of our understanding, even in respect to experience, if we have not aims before us? The highest aims, however, are those of morality, and these we can only know by means of pure reason. Even with their help and guidance, however, we could make no proper use of the knowledge of nature, unless nature itself had established a unity of design: for without this we should ourselves have no reason, because there would be no school for it, nor any culture de-

rived from objects which supply the material for such concepts. This unity of design is necessary and founded on the
essence of free-will, which must, therefore, as containing the
condition of its application *in concreto,* be so likewise; so that,
in reality, the transcendental development of the knowledge
obtained by our reason would be, not the cause, but only the
effect of that practical order and design which pure reason
imposes upon us.

We find therefore in the history of human reason also that,
before the moral concepts were sufficiently purified and re-
fined, and before the systematical unity of the ends was clearly
understood, according to such concepts and in accordance with
necessary principles, the then existing knowledge of nature
and even a considerable amount of the culture of reason in
many other branches of science could only produce crude
and vague conceptions of the Deity, or allow of an astonish-
ing indifference with regard to that question. A greater cultivation of moral ideas, which became necessary through the
extremely pure moral law of our religion, directed our reason
to that object through the interest which it forced us to take
in it, and without the help either of a more extended knowledge of nature, or of more correct and trustworthy transcendental views (which have been wanting in all ages). A concept
of the Divine Being was elaborated which we now hold to be
correct, not because speculative reason has convinced us of
its correctness, but because it fully agrees with the moral principles of reason. And thus, after all, it is pure reason only, but
pure reason in its practical employment, which may claim the
merit of connecting with our highest interest that knowledge
which pure speculation could only guess at without being able
to establish its validity, and of having made it, not indeed a
demonstrated dogma, but a supposition absolutely necessary to
the most essential ends of reason.

But after practical reason has reached this high point,
namely, the concept of a sole original Being as the supreme
good, it must not imagine that it has raised itself above all
empirical traditions of its application and soared up to an immediate knowledge of new objects, and thus venture to start
from that concept and to deduce from it the moral laws themselves. For it was these very laws the internal practical necessity of which led us to the admission of an independent cause,
or of a wise ruler of the world that should give effect to them.
We ought not, therefore, to consider them afterwards again
as accidental and derived from the mere will of the ruler, par-

ticularly as we could have no concept of such a will, if we had not formed it in accordance with those laws. So far as practical reason is entitled to lead us we shall not look upon actions as obligatory because they are the commands of God, but look upon them as divine commands because we feel an inner obligation to follow them. We shall study freedom according to the unity of design determined by the principles of reason, and we shall believe ourselves to be acting in accordance with the Divine will in so far only as we hold sacred the moral law which reason teaches us from the nature of actions themselves. We shall believe ourselves to be serving Him only by promoting everything that is best in the world, both in ourselves and in others. Moral theology is, therefore, of immanent use only, teaching us to fulfil our destiny here in the world by adapting ourselves to the general system of ends, without either fanatically or even criminally abandoning the guidance of reason and her moral laws for our proper conduct in life, in order to connect it directly with the idea of the Supreme Being. This would be a transcendent use of moral theology which, like a transcendent use of mere speculation, must inevitably pervert and frustrate the ultimate aims of reason.

THE CANON OF PURE REASON

Section III

Of Trowing, Knowing, and Believing

The holding a thing to be true is an event in our understanding which, though it may rest on objective grounds, requires also subjective causes in the mind of the person who is to judge. If the judgment is valid for everybody, if only he is possessed of reason, then the ground of it is objectively sufficient, and the holding it to be true is called *conviction*. If, on the contrary, it has its ground in the peculiar character of the subject only, it is called *persuasion*.

Persuasion is a mere illusion, the ground of the judgment, though it lies solely in the subject, being regarded as objective. Such a judgment has, therefore, private validity only, and the holding it to be true cannot be communicated to others. Truth, however, depends on agreement with the object, and, with regard to it, the judgments of every understanding must agree with each other (*consentientia uni tertio consentiunt inter se, etc.*). An external criterion, therefore, as to whether our holding a thing to be true be conviction or only persuasion, consists in the possibility of communicating it, and finding its truth to be valid for the reason of every man. For, in that case, there is at least a presumption that the ground of the agreement of all judgments, in spite of the diversity of the subjects, rests upon the common ground, namely, on the object with which they all agree, and thus prove the truth of the judgment.

Persuasion, therefore, cannot be distinguished from conviction, subjectively, so long as the subject views its judgment as a phenomenon of his own mind only; the experiment, however, which we make with the grounds that seem valid to us, by trying to find out whether they will produce the same effect on the reason of others, is a means, though only a subjective means, not indeed of producing conviction, but of detecting the merely private validity of the judgment, that is, of discovering in it what is merely persuasion.

If we are able besides to analyse the subjective *causes* of our judgment, which we have taken for its objective *grounds,* and thus explain the deceptive judgment as a phenomenon in our mind, without having recourse to the object itself, we expose the illusion and are no longer deceived by it, although we may continue to be tempted by it, in a certain degree, if, namely, the subjective cause of the illusion is inherent in our nature.

I cannot *maintain* anything, that is, affirm it as a judgment necessarily valid for everybody, except it work conviction. Persuasion I may keep for myself, if it is agreeable to me, but I cannot, and ought not to attempt to make it binding on any but myself.

The holding anything to be true, or the subjective validity of a judgment admits, with reference to the conviction which is at the same time valid objectively, of the three following degrees, *trowing, believing, knowing. Trowing* is to hold true, with the consciousness that it is insufficient *both* subjectively and objectively. If the holding true is sufficient subjectively, but is held to be insufficient objectively, it is called *believing;* while, if it is sufficient both subjectively and objectively, it is called *knowing.* Subjective sufficiency is called *conviction* (for myself), objective sufficiency is called *certainty* (for everybody). I shall not dwell any longer on the explanation of such easy concepts.

I must never venture to *trow,* or to be of opinion, without *knowing* at least something by means of which a judgment, problematical by itself, is connected with truth, which connection, though it involves not a complete truth, is yet attended with more than arbitrary fiction. Moreover, the law of such a connection must be certain. For if, even with regard to this law, I should have nothing but an opinion, all would become a mere play of the imagination, without the least relation to truth.

In the judgments of pure reason *opinion* is not permitted. For, as they are not based on empirical grounds, but everything has to be known *a priori,* and everything therefore must be necessary, the principle of connection in them requires universality and necessity, and consequently perfect certainty, without which there would be nothing to lead us on to truth. Hence it is absurd to have an opinion in pure mathematics; here one must either know, or abstain from pronouncing any judgment. The same applies to the principles of morality, because one must not hazard an action on the mere opinion that it is allowed, but must know it to be so.

In the transcendental employment of reason, on the contrary, mere opinion, no doubt, would be too little, but knowledge too much. Speculatively, therefore, we cannot here form any judgment at all, because the subjective grounds on which we hold a thing to be true, as for instance those which may very well produce belief, are not approved of in speculative questions, as they cannot be held without empirical support, nor, if communicated to others, can produce the same effect on them.

Nor can the theoretically insufficient acceptance of truth be called belief, except from a *practical point of view.* And this practical view refers either to *skill* or to *morality,* the former being concerned with any contingent and casual ends and objects whatsoever, the latter with absolutely necessary ends only.

If we have once proposed an object or end to ourselves, the conditions of attaining it are hypothetically necessary. This necessity is subjective, and yet but relatively sufficient, if I know of no other conditions under which the end can be attained: it is sufficient absolutely and for every one, if I am convinced that no one can know of other conditions, leading to the attainment of our end. In the former case my assuming and holding certain conditions as true is merely an accidental belief, while in the latter case it is a necessary belief. Thus a physician, for instance, may feel that he must do something for a patient, who is in danger. But as he does not know the nature of the illness, he observes the symptoms, and arrives at the conclusion, as he knows nothing else, that it is phthisis. His belief, according to his own judgment, is contingent only, and he knows that another might form a better judgment. It is this kind of contingent belief which, nevertheless, supplies a ground for the actual employment of means to certain actions, which I call *pragmatic belief*.

The usual test, whether something that is maintained by merely persuasion, or a subjective conviction at least, that is, firm belief, is *betting*. People often pronounce their views with such bold and uncompromising assurance that they seem to have abandoned all fear of error. A bet startles them. Sometimes it turns out that a man has persuasion sufficient to be valued at one ducat, but not at ten; he is ready to venture the first ducat, but with ten, he becomes aware for the first time that, after all, it might be possible that he should be mistaken. If we imagine that we have to stake the happiness of our whole life, the triumphant air of our judgment drops considerably; we become extremely shy, and suddenly discover that our belief does not reach so far. Thus pragmatic belief admits of degrees which, according to the difference of the interests at stake, may be large or small.

Now it is true, no doubt, that, though with reference to an object of our belief, we can do nothing, and our opinion is, therefore, purely theoretical, yet in many cases we can represent and imagine to ourselves an undertaking for which we might think that we had sufficient inducements, if any means existed of ascertaining the truth of the matter. Thus, even in purely theoretical judgments, there is an *analogon* of *practical* judgments to which the word *belief* may be applied, and which we shall therefore call *doctrinal belief*. If it were possible to apply any test of experience, I should be ready to stake the whole of my earthly goods on my belief that at least one of the planets which we see is inhabited. Hence I say that it is not only an opinion, but a strong belief, on the truth of which I should risk even many advantages of life, that there are inhabitants in other worlds.

Now we must admit that the doctrine of the existence of God belongs to doctrinal belief. For although, with reference to my theoretical knowledge of the world, I can *produce* nothing which would make this thought a necessary supposition as a condition of my being able to explain the phenomena of the world, but on the contrary am bound to use my reason as if everything were mere nature, nevertheless, the unity of design is so important a condition of the application of reason to nature that I cannot ignore it, especially as experience supplies so many examples of it. Of that unity of design, however, I know no other condition, which would make it a guidance in my study of nature, but the supposition that a supreme intelligence has ordered all things according to the wisest ends. As a condition, therefore, of, it may be, a contingent, but not unimportant end, namely, in order to have a guidance in the investigation of nature, it is necessary to admit a wise author of the world. The result of my experiment confirms the usefulness of this supposition so many times, while nothing decisive can be adduced against it, that I am really saying far too little, if I call my acceptation of it a mere opinion, and it may be said, even with regard to these theoretical matters, that I firmly believe in God. Still, if we use our words strictly, this belief must always be called doctrinal, and not practical, such as the *theology* of nature (physical theology) must always and necessarily produce. In the same wisdom, and in the prominent endowments of human nature, combined with the inadequate shortness of life, another sufficient ground may be found for the doctrinal belief in the future life of the human soul.

The expression of belief is in such cases an expression of modesty from the *objective* point of view, and yet, at the same time, a firm confidence from a *subjective*. If even I were to call this purely theoretical acceptance an hypothesis only, which I am entitled to assume, I should profess to be in possession of a more complete concept of the nature of a cause of the world, and of another world, than I really can produce. If I accept anything, even as an hypothesis only, I must know it at least so much according to its properties, that I need *not* imagine *its concepts,* but *its existence* only. But the word *belief* refers only to the guidance which an idea gives me, and to its subjective influence on the conduct of my reason, which makes me hold it fast, though I may not be able to give an account of it from a speculative point of view.

Purely doctrinal belief, however, has always a somewhat unstable character. Speculative difficulties often make us lose hold of it, though in the end we always return to it.

It is quite different with *moral belief*. For here action is absolutely necessary, that is, I must obey the moral law on all points. The end is here firmly established, and, according to all we know, one only condition is possible under which that end could agree with all other ends, and thus acquire practical validity, namely, the existence of a God and of a future world. I also know it for certain that no one is cognisant of other conditions which could lead to the same unity of ends under the moral law. As, then, the moral precept is at the same time my maxim, reason commanding that it should be so, I shall inevitably believe in the existence of God, and in a future life, and I feel certain that nothing can shake this belief, because all my moral principles would be overthrown at the same time, and I cannot surrender them without becoming hateful in my own eyes.

We see, therefore, that, even after the failure of all the ambitious schemes of reason to pass beyond the limits of all experience, enough remains to make us satisfied for practical purposes. No one, no doubt, will be able to boast again that he *knows* that there is a God and a future life. For a man who knows that, is the very man whom I have been so long in search of. As all knowledge, if it refers to an object of pure reason, can be communicated, I might hope that, through his teaching, my own knowledge would be increased in the most wonderful way. No, that conviction is not a *logical,* but a *moral* certainty; and, as it rests on subjective grounds (of the moral sentiment), I must not even say that *it is* morally certain that there is a God, etc., but that *I* am morally certain, etc. What I really mean is, that the belief in a God and in another world is so interwoven with my moral sentiment, that as there is little danger of my losing the latter, there is quite as little fear lest I should ever be deprived of the former.

The only point that may rouse misgivings is that this rational belief is based on the supposition of moral sentiments. If we surrender this, and take a man who is entirely indifferent with regard to moral laws, the question proposed by reason becomes merely a problem for speculation, and may in that case be still supported with strong grounds from analogy, but not such to which the most obstinate scepticism has to submit.*

No man, however, is with regard to these questions free from all interest. For although in the absence of good senti-

---

* The interest which the human mind takes in morality (an interest which, as I believe, is necessary to every rational being) is natural, though it is not undivided, and always practically preponderant. If you strengthen and increase that interest, you will find reason very docile, and even more enlightened, so as to be able to join the speculative with the practical interests. If you do not take care that you first make men at least moderately good, you will never make them honest believers.

ments he may be rid of all moral interest, enough remains even thus to make him *fear* the existence of God and a future life. For nothing is required for this but his inability to plead *certainty* with regard to the *non-existence* of such a being and of a future life. As this would have to be proved by mere reason, and therefore apodictically, he would have to establish the impossibility of both, which I feel certain no rational being would venture to do. This would be a *negative* belief which, though it could not produce morality and good sentiments, would still produce something analogous, namely, a check on the outbreak of evil.

But, it will be said, is this really all that pure reason can achieve in opening prospects beyond the limits of experience? Nothing more than two articles of faith? Surely even the ordinary understanding could have achieved as much without taking counsel of philosophers!

I shall not here dwell on the benefits which, by the laborious efforts of its criticism, philosophy has conferred on human reason, granting even that in the end they should turn out to be merely negative. On this point something will have to be said in the next section. But I ask, do you really require that knowledge, which concerns all men, should go beyond the common understanding, and should be revealed to you by philosophers only? The very thing which you find fault with, is the best confirmation of the correctness of our previous assertions, since it reveals to us what we could not have grasped before, namely, that in matters which concern all men without distinction, nature cannot be accused of any partial distribution of her gifts; and that with regard to the essential interests of human nature, the highest philosophy can achieve no more than that guidance which nature has vouchsafed even to the meanest understanding.

METHOD OF TRANSCENDENTALISM

CHAPTER III

THE ARCHITECTONIC OF PURE REASON

By architectonic I understand the art of constructing systems. As systematical unity is that which raises common knowledge to the dignity of a science, that is, changes a mere aggregate of knowledge into a system, it is easy to see that architectonic is the doctrine of what is really scientific in our knowledge, and forms therefore a necessary part of the doctrine of method.

Under the sway of reason our knowledge must not remain a rhapsody, but must become a system, because thus alone can the essential objects of reason be supported and advanced. By system I mean the unity of various kinds of knowledge under one idea. This is the concept given by reason of the form of the whole, in which concept both the extent of its manifold contents and the place belonging to each part are determined *a priori*. This scientific concept of reason contains, therefore, the end and also the form of the whole which is congruent with it. The unity of the end to which all parts relate and through the idea of which they are related to each other, enables us to miss any part, if we possess a knowledge of the rest, and prevents any arbitrary addition or vagueness of perfection of which the limits could not be determined *a priori*. Thus the whole is articulated (*articulatio*), not aggregated (*coacervatio*). It may grow internally (*per intussusceptionem*), but not externally (*per appositionem*), like an animal body, the growth of which does not add any new member, but, without changing their proportion, renders each stronger and more efficient for its purposes.

The idea requires for its realisation a *schema,* that is an essential variety, and an order of its parts, which are determined *a priori,* according to the principles inherent in its aim. A schema, which is not designed according to an idea, that is, according to the principal aim of reason, but empirically only, in accordance with accidental aims (the number of which cannot be determined beforehand) gives *technical* unity; but the schema which originates from an idea only (where reason dictates the aims *a priori* and does not wait for them in experience) supplies *architectonical* unity. Now what we call a science, the schema of which must have its outline (*monogramma*) and the division of the whole into parts devised according to the idea, that is, *a priori,* and keep it perfectly distinct from everything else according to principles, cannot be produced technically according to the similarity of its various parts or the accidental use of knowledge *in concreto* for this or that external purpose, but architectonically only, as based on the affinity of its parts and their dependence on one supreme and internal aim through which alone the whole becomes possible.

No one attempts to construct a science unless he can base it on some idea; but in the elaboration of it the schema, nay, even the definition, which he gives in the beginning of his science, corresponds very seldom to his idea which, like a germ, lies hidden in reason, and all the parts of which are still enveloped and hardly distinguishable even under microscopical observation. It is necessary, therefore, to explain and determine all sciences, considering that they are contrived from the point of view of a certain general interest, not according to the description given by their author, but according to the idea which, from the natural unity of its constituent parts, we may discover as founded in reason itself. We shall often find that the originator of a science, and even his latest successors are moving vaguely round an idea which they have not been able to perceive clearly, failing in consequence to determine rightly the proper contents, the articulation (systematical unity), and the limits of their science.

It is a misfortune that only after having collected for a long time at haphazard, under the influence of an idea that lies hidden in us, materials belonging to a science, nay, after having for a long time fitted them together technically, a time arrives when we are able to see its idea in a clearer light, and to devise architectonically a whole system according to the aims of reason. Systems seem to develope like worms through a kind of *generatio aequivoca,* by the mere aggregation of numerous concepts, at first imperfect, and gradually attaining to perfection, though in reality they all had their schema, as their original germ, in reason which was itself being developed. Hence, not only is each of them articulated according to an idea, but all may be properly combined with each other in a system of human knowledge, as members of one whole, admitting of an architectonic of all human knowledge which in our time, when so much material has been collected or may be taken over from the ruins of old systems, is not only possible, but not even very difficult. We shall confine ourselves here to the completion of our proper business, namely, to sketch the *architectonic* of all knowledge arising from *pure reason,* beginning only at the point where the common root of our knowledge divides into two stems, one of which is *reason.* By reason, however, I understand here the whole higher faculty of knowledge, and I distinguish therein rational from empirical knowledge.

If I take no account of the contents of knowledge, objectively considered, all knowledge is, from a subjective point of view, either historical or rational. Historical knowledge is *cognitio ex datis,* rational knowledge *cognitio ex principiis.* Whatever may be the first origin of some branch of knowledge, it is always historical, if he who possesses it knows only so much of it as has been given to him from outside, whether through immediate experience, or through narration, or by instruction also (in general knowledge). Hence a person who, in the usual sense, has *learnt* a system of philosophy, for instance the *Wolfian,* though he may carry in his head all the principles, definitions, and proofs, as well as the division of the whole system, and have it all at his fingers' ends, possesses yet none but a complete *historical* knowledge of the *Wolfian* philosophy. His knowledge and judgments are no more than what has been given him. If you dispute any definition, he does not know whence to take another, because he formed his own on the reason of another. But the imitative is not the productive faculty, that is, knowledge in his case did not come from reason, and though objectively it is rational knowledge, subjectively it is historical only. He has taken and kept, that is, he has well learned and has become a plaster cast of a living man. Knowledge, which is rational objectively (that is, which can arise originally from a man's own reason only), can then only be so called subjectively also, when they have been drawn from the general resources of reason, that is, from principles from which also criticism, nay, even the rejection of what has been learnt, may arise.

All knowledge of reason is again either based on concepts or on the construction of concepts; the former being called philosophical, the latter mathematical. Of their essential difference I have treated in the first chapter. Knowledge, as we saw,

may be objectively philosophical, and yet subjectively historical, as is the case with most apprentices, and with all who
never look beyond their school and remain in a state of pupil-
age all their life. But it is strange that mathematical knowledge, as soon as it has been acquired, may be considered,
subjectively also, as knowledge of reason, there being no such
distinction here as in the case of philosophical knowledge. The
reason is that the sources from which alone the mathematical
teacher can take his knowledge lie nowhere but in the essential
and genuine principles of reason, and cannot be taken by the
pupil from anywhere else, nor ever be disputed, for the simple ground that the employment of reason takes place here
in concreto only, although *a priori,* namely, in the pure and
therefore faultless intuition, thus excluding all illusion and
error. Of all the sciences of reason (*a priori*), therefore,
mathematics alone can be learnt, but philosophy (unless it be
historically) never; with regard to reason we can at most learn
to *philosophise.*

The system of all philosophical knowledge is called *philosophy.* It must be taken objectively, if we understand by it the
type of criticising all philosophical attempts, which is to serve
for the criticism of every subjective philosophy, however various and changeable the systems may be. In this manner philosophy is a mere idea of a possible science which exists nowhere
in concreto, but which we may try to approach on different
paths, until in the end the only true path, though overgrown
and hidden by sensibility, has been discovered, and the image,
which has so often proved a failure, has become as like the
original type as human power can ever make it. Till then we
cannot learn philosophy; for where is it, who possesses it, and
how shall we know it? We can only learn to philosophise, that
is, to exercise the talent of reason, according to its general
principles, on certain given attempts always, however, with the
reservation of the right of reason of investigating the sources
of these principles themselves, and of either accepting or rejecting them.

So far the concept of philosophy is only *scholastic,* as of a
system of knowledge which is sought and valued as a science,
without aiming at more than a systematical unity of that
knowledge, and therefore the *logical* perfection of it. But
there is also a *universal,* or, if we may say so, a cosmical
concept (*conceptus cosmicus*) of philosophy, which always
formed the real foundation of that name, particularly when it
had, as it were, to be personified and represented in the ideal

of the *philosopher,* as the original type. In this sense philosophy is the science of the relation of all knowledge to the essential aims of human reason (*teleologia rationis humanae*), and the philosopher stands before us, not as an artist, but as the lawgiver of human reason. In that sense it would be very boastful to call oneself a philosopher, and to pretend to have equalled the type which exists in the idea only.

The mathematician, the student of nature, and the logician, however far the two former may have advanced in rational, and the last, particularly, in philosophical knowledge, are merely artists of reason. There is besides, an ideal teacher, who controls them all, and uses them as instruments for the advancement of the essential aims of human reason. Him alone we ought to call philosopher: but as he exists nowhere, while the idea of his legislation exists everywhere in the reason of every human being, we shall keep entirely to that idea, and determine more accurately what kind of systematical unity philosophy, in this cosmical concept,* demands from the standpoint of its aims.

Essential ends are not as yet the highest ends; in fact, there can be but one highest end, if the perfect systematical unity of reason has been reached. We must distinguish, therefore, between the ultimate end and subordinate ends, which necessarily belong, as means, to the former. The former is nothing but the whole destination of man, and the philosophy which relates to it is called moral philosophy. On account of this excellence which distinguishes moral philosophy from all other operations of reason, the ancients always understood under the name of philosopher the moralist principally: and even at present the external appearance of self-control by means of reason leads us, through a certain analogy, to call a man a philosopher, however limited his knowledge may be. The legislation of human reason (philosophy) has two objects only, nature and freedom, and contains therefore both the law of nature and the law of morals, at first in two separate systems, but combined, at last, in one great system of philosophy. The philosophy of nature relates to all that is; that of morals to that only that *ought to be.*

All philosophy is either knowledge derived from pure rea-

---

* Cosmical concept is meant here for a concept relating to what must be of interest to everybody: while I determine the character of a science, according to *scholastic concepts,* if I look upon it only as one of many crafts intended for certain objects.

son, or knowledge of reason derived from empirical principles. The former is called pure, the latter empirical philosophy.

The philosophy of pure reason is either *propaedeutic* (preparation), enquiring into the faculties of reason, with regard to all pure knowledge *a priori,* and called *critic,* or, secondly, the system of pure reason (science), comprehending in systematical connection the whole (both true and illusory) of philosophical knowledge, derived from pure reason, and called *metaphysic,*—although this name of metaphysic may be given also to the whole of pure philosophy, inclusive of the critic, in order thus to comprehend both the investigation of all that can ever be known *a priori* and the representation of all that constitutes a system of pure philosophical knowledge of that kind, excluding all that belongs to the empirical and the mathematical employment of reason.

Metaphysic is divided into that of the *speculative* and that of the *practical* use of pure reason, and is, therefore, either *metaphysic of nature* or *metaphysic of morals*. The former contains all the pure principles of reason, derived from concepts only (excluding therefore mathematics), of the *theoretical* knowledge of all things, the latter, the principles which determine *a priori* and necessitate all *doing* and *not doing.* Morality is the only legality of actions that can be derived from principles entirely *a priori.* Hence the metaphysic of morals is really pure moral philosophy, in which no account is taken of anthropology or any empirical conditions. Metaphysic of speculative reason has commonly been called *metaphysic,* in the more limited sense; as however pure moral philosophy belongs likewise to this branch of human and philosophical knowledge, derived from pure reason, we shall allow it to retain that name, although we leave it aside for the present as not belonging to our immediate object.

It is of the highest importance to *isolate* various sorts of knowledge, which in kind and origin are different from others, and to take great care lest they be mixed up with those others with which, for practical purposes, they are generally united. What is done by the chemist in the analysis of substances, and by the mathematician in pure mathematics, is far more incumbent on the philosopher, in order to enable him to define clearly the part which, in the promiscuous employment of the understanding, belongs to a special kind of knowledge, as well as its peculiar value and influence. Human reason, therefore, since it first began to think, or rather to reflect, has never been able to do without a metaphysic, but it has never kept it sufficiently free from all foreign admixture. The idea of a science of this kind is as old as speculation itself, and what human reason does not speculate, whether in a scholastic or a popular manner? It must be admitted, however, that even thinkers by profession did not clearly distinguish between the two elements of our knowledge, the one being in our possession completely *a priori,* the other deducible *a posteriori* only from experience, and did not succeed therefore in fixing the limits of a special kind of knowledge, nor in realising the true idea of a science which had so long and so deeply engaged the interest of human reason. When it was said that metaphysic is the science of the first principles of human knowledge, this did not mark out any special kind of knowledge, but only a certain rank or degree, with regard to its character of generality, which was not sufficient to distinguish it clearly from empirical knowledge. For among empirical principles also, some are more general, and therefore higher than others; and in such a series of subordinated principles (where that which is entirely *a priori* is not distinguished from that which is known *a posteriori* only), where should one draw the line to separate the first part from the last, and the higher members from the lower? What should we say if chronology should distinguish the epochs of history no better than by dividing it into the first centuries and the subsequent centuries? We should ask, no doubt, whether the fifth or the tenth belongs to the first centuries? and I ask in the same way whether the concept of what is extended belongs to metaphysic? If you say, yes! I ask, what about the concept of a body? and of a liquid body? You then hesitate, for you begin to see, that if I continue in this strain, everything would belong to metaphysic. It thus becomes clear that the mere degree of subordination of the special under the general cannot determine the limits of a science; but, in our case, only the complete difference in kind and origin. The fundamental idea of metaphysic was obscured on another side because, as knowledge *a priori,* it showed a certain similarity in kind with mathematics. The two are, no doubt, related with regard to their origin *a priori,* but, if we consider how, in metaphysic, knowledge is derived from concepts, while in mathematics we can only form judgments through the construction of concepts *a priori,* we discover, in comparing philosophical with mathematical knowledge, the most decided difference in kind, which was no doubt always felt, but never determined by clear criteria. Thus it has happened that, as philosophers themselves blundered in developing the idea of their science, its elaboration could have no definite aim, and no certain guidance; and we may well understand how metaphysical science was brought into contempt in the outside world, and at last among philosophers themselves, considering how arbitrarily it had been designed, and how constantly those very philosophers, ignorant as to the path which they ought to take, were disputing among themselves about the discoveries which each asserted he had made on his own peculiar path.

All pure knowledge *a priori* constitutes, therefore, according to the special faculty of knowledge in which alone it can originate, a definite unity; and metaphysic is that philosophy which is meant to represent that knowledge in its systematical unity. Its speculative part, which has especially appropriated that name, namely, what we call *metaphysic of nature,* in which everything is considered from concepts *a priori,* so far as it is (not so far as it ought to be), will have to be divided in the following manner.

Metaphysic, in the more limited sense of the word, consists of *transcendental philosophy* and the *physiology* of pure reason. The former treats only of understanding and reason themselves, in a system of all concepts and principles which have reference to objects in general, without taking account of objects *that may be given* (*ontologia*): the latter treats of *nature,* that is, the sum of given objects (whether given to the senses, or, if you like, to some other kind of intuition) and is therefore *physiology,* although *rationalis* only. The employment of reason in this rational study of nature is either physical or hyperphysical, or, more accurately speaking, *immanent* or *transcendent.* The former refers to nature, in so far as its knowledge can take place in experience (*in concreto*); the latter to that connection of objects of experience which transcends all experience. This *transcendent* physiology has for its object either an *internal* or an *external* connection, both transcending every possible experience; the former is the physiology of nature as a whole, or *transcendental knowledge of the world,* the latter refers to the connection of the whole of nature with a Being above nature, and is therefore transcendental *knowledge of God.*

Immanent physiology, on the contrary, considers nature as the sum total of all objects of the senses, such, therefore, as it is given *us,* but only according to conditions *a priori,* under which alone it can be given us. It has two kinds of objects only; first, those of the external senses, which constitute together *corporeal nature;* secondly, the object of the internal sense, the soul, *and* what, according to its fundamental principles in general, may be called *thinking nature*. The metaphysic of corporeal nature is called *physic*, or, because it must contain the principles of an *a priori* knowledge of nature only, *rational physic*. Metaphysic of the thinking nature is called *psychology*, and for the same reason, is here to be understood as the *rational knowledge* only of that nature.

Thus the whole system of metaphysic consists of four principal parts. 1. *Ontology*, 2. *Rational Physiology*, 3. *Rational Cosmology*, 4. *Rational Theology*. The *second* part, the physiology of pure reason, contains two divisions, namely, *physica rationalis,** and *phychologia rationalis*.

The fundamental idea of a philosophy of pure reason prescribes itself this division. It is therefore *architectonical*, adequate to its essential aims, and not *technical* only, contrived according to any observed similarities, and, as it were, at haphazard. For that very reason such a division is unchangeable and of legislative authority. There are, however, a few points which might cause misgivings, and weaken our conviction of its legitimate character.

First of all, how can I expect knowledge *a priori*, that is metaphysic, of objects so far as they are given to our senses, that is *a posteriori?* and how is it possible to know the nature of things according to principles *a priori*, and thus to arrive at a *rational* physiology? Our answer is, that we take nothing from experience beyond what is necessary to give us an object, either of the external or of the internal sense. The former is done by the mere concept of matter (impermeable, lifeless extension), the latter through the concept of a thinking being (in the empirical internal representation, *I think*). For the rest, we ought in the whole metaphysical treatment of these objects to abstain from all empirical principles, which to the

---

* It must not be supposed that I mean by this what is commonly called *physica generalis*, and which is rather mathematics, than a philosophy of nature. For the metaphysic of nature is entirely separate from mathematics, and does not enlarge our knowledge as much as mathematics; but it is, nevertheless, very important, as supplying a criticism of the pure knowledge of the understanding that should be applied to nature. For want of its guidance, even mathematicians, given to certain common concepts which in reality are metaphysical, have unconsciously encumbered physical science with hypotheses which vanish under a criticism of those principles, without however causing the least detriment to the necessary employment of mathematics in this field.

concept of matter might add any kind of experience for the purpose of forming any judgments on these objects.

Secondly. What becomes of *empirical psychology,* which has always maintained its place in metaphysic and from which, in our time, such great things were expected for throwing light on metaphysic, after all hope had been surrendered of achieving anything useful *a priori?* I answer, it has its place where the proper (empirical) study of nature must be placed, namely, by the side of *applied* philosophy, to which pure philosophy supplies the principles *a priori;* thus being connected, but not to be confounded with it. Empirical psychology, therefore, must be entirely banished from metaphysic, and is excluded from it by its very idea. According to the tradition of the schools, however, we shall probably have to allow to it (though as an episode only) a small corner in metaphysic, and this from economical motives, because, as yet, it is not so rich as to constitute a study by itself, and yet too important to be banished entirely and to be settled in a place where it would find still less affinity than in metaphysic. It is, therefore, a stranger only, who has been received for a long time and whom one allows to stay a little longer, until he can take up his own abode in a complete system of anthropology, the pendant to the empirical doctrine of nature.

This then is the general idea of metaphysic which, as in the beginning more was expected of it than could justly be demanded, fell into general disrepute after these pleasant expectations had proved fallacious. The whole course of our critique must have convinced us sufficiently that, although metaphysic cannot supply the foundation of religion, it must always remain its bulwark, and that human reason, being dialectical by its very nature, cannot do without a science which curbs it and, by means of a scientific and perfectly clear self-knowledge, prevents the ravages which otherwise this lawless speculative reason would certainly commit both in morals and religion. We may be sure, therefore, that, in spite of the coy or contemptuous airs assumed by those who judge a science, not according to its nature, but according to its accidental effects, we shall always return to it as to a beloved one with whom we have quarrelled, because reason, as essential interests are here at stake, cannot rest till it has either established correct views or destroyed those which already exist.

Metaphysic, therefore, that of nature as well as that of morals, and particularly the criticism of our adventurous reason, which forms the introduction and preparation of it, constitute together what may be termed philosophy in the true sense of the word. Its only goal is wisdom, and the path to it science, the only path which, if once opened, is never grown over again, and can never mislead. Mathematics, natural science, even the empirical knowledge of men, have, no doubt, a high value, as means for the most part to accidental, but yet in the end necessary and essential aims of mankind. But they have that value only by means of that knowledge of reason based on pure concepts which, call it as you may, is in reality nothing but metaphysic.

For the same reason metaphysic is also the completion of the whole *culture* of human reason, which is indispensable, although one may discard its influence as a science with regard to certain objects. For it enquires into reason according to its elements and highest maxims, which must form the very foundation of the *possibility* of some sciences, and of the *use* of all. That, as mere speculation, it serves rather to keep off error than to extend knowledge does not detract from its value, but, on the contrary, confers upon it dignity and authority by that censorship which secures general order and harmony, ay, the well-being of the scientific commonwealth, and prevents its persevering and successful labourers from losing sight of the highest aim, the general happiness of all mankind.

METHOD OF TRANSCENDENTALISM

CHAPTER IV

THE HISTORY OF PURE REASON

This title stands here only in order to indicate the place in the system which remains empty for the present and has to be filled hereafter. I content myself with casting a cursory glance, from a purely transcendental point of view, namely, that of the nature of pure reason, on the labours of former philosophers, which presents to my eyes many structures, but in ruins only.

It is very remarkable, though naturally it could not well have been otherwise, that in the very infancy of philosophy men began where we should like to end, namely, with studying the knowledge of God and the hope or even the nature of a future world. However crude the religious concepts might be which owed their origin to the old customs, as remnants of the savage state of humanity, this did not prevent the more enlightened classes from devoting themselves to free investigations of these matters, and they soon perceived that there could be no better and surer way of pleasing that invisible power which governs the world, in order to be happy at least in another world, than good conduct. Thus theology and morals became the two springs, or rather the points of attraction for all abstract enquiries of reason in later times, though it was chiefly the former which gradually drew speculative reason into those labours which afterwards became so celebrated under the name of metaphysic.

I shall not attempt at present to distinguish the periods of history in which this or that change of metaphysic took place, but only draw a rapid sketch of the difference of the ideas which caused the principal revolutions in metaphysic. And here I find three aims with which the most important changes on this arena were brought about.

1. With *reference to the object* of all knowledge of our reason, some philosophers were mere *sensualists*, others mere *intellectualists*. *Epicurus* may be regarded as the first among

the former, *Plato* as the first among the latter. The distinction of these two schools, subtle as it is, dates from the earliest days, and has long been maintained. Those who belong to the former school maintained that reality exists in the objects of the senses alone, everything else being imagination; those of the second school, on the contrary, maintained, that in the senses there is nothing but illusion, and that the true is known by the understanding only. The former did not, therefore, deny all reality to the concepts of the understanding, but that reality was with them *logical* only, with the others it was *mystical*. The former admitted *intellectual* concepts, but accepted sensible *objects* only. The latter required that true objects should be *intelligible* only, and maintained an *intuition* peculiar to the understanding, separated from the senses which, in their opinion, could only confuse it.

2. With *reference to the origin* of the pure concepts of reason, and whether they are derived from experience, or have their origin independent of experience, in reason. *Aristotle* may be considered as the head of the *empiricists, Plato* as that of the *noologists*. *Locke*, who in modern times followed *Aristotle*, and *Leibniz*, who followed *Plato* (though at a sufficient distance from his mystical system), have not been able to bring this dispute to any conclusion. *Epicurus* at least was far more consistent in his sensual system (for he never allowed his syllogism to go beyond the limits of experience) than *Aristotle* and *Locke*, more particularly the latter, who, after having derived all concepts and principles from experience, goes so far in their application as to maintain that the existence of God and the immortality of the soul (though both lie entirely outside the limits of all possible experience) could be proved with the same evidence as any mathematical proposition.

3. With *reference to method*. If anything is to be called method, it must be a procedure *according to principles*. The method at present prevailing in this field of enquiry may be divided into the *naturalistic* and the *scientific*. The naturalist of pure reason lays it down as his principle that, with reference to the highest questions which form the problems of metaphysic, more can be achieved by means of common reason without science (which he calls sound reason), than through speculation. This is the same as if we should maintain that the magnitude and distance of the moon can be better determined by the naked eye than by roundabout mathematical calculations. This is pure misology reduced to principles, and, what

is the most absurd, the neglect of all artificial means is recommended as the best way of enlarging our knowledge. As
regards those who are naturalists because they *know no better,* they are really not to be blamed. They simply follow
ordinary reason, but they do not boast of their ignorance, as
the method which contains the secret how we are to fetch the
truth from the bottom of the well of Democritus. '*Quod sapio
satis est mihi, non ego curo, esse quod Arcesilas aerumnosique
Solones*' (Pers.), is the motto with which they may lead a
happy and honoured life, without meddling with science or
muddling it.

As regards those who follow a *scientific* method, they have
the choice to proceed either *dogmatically* or *sceptically,* but at
all events, *systematically.* When I have mentioned in relation
to the former the celebrated *Wolf,* and in relation to the other
David Hume, I may for my present purpose leave all the rest
unnamed.

The only path that is still open is the *critical.* If the reader
has been kind and patient enough to follow me to the end
along this path, he may judge for himself whether, if he will
help, as far as in him lies, towards making this footpath a
highroad, it may not be possible to achieve, even before the
close of the present century, what so many centuries have
not been able to achieve, namely, to give complete satisfaction
to human reason with regard to those questions which have
in all ages exercised its desire for knowledge, though hitherto
in vain.

ANCHOR BOOKS

PHILOSOPHY

AFRICAN RELIGIONS AND PHILOSOPHY—John S. Mbiti, A754

THE ALIENATION OF REASON: A History of Positivist Thought—Leszek Kolakowski; Norbert Guterman, A661

THE AMERICAN TRANSCENDENTALISTS—Perry Miller, ed., A119

AQUINAS: A Collection of Critical Essays—Anthony Kenny, ed., AP8

BASIC WRITINGS ON POLITICS AND PHILOSOPHY—Karl Marx and Friedrich Engels; Lewis S. Feuer, eds., A185

THE BIRTH OF TRAGEDY and THE GENEALOGY OF MORALS—Friedrich Nietzsche; Francis Golffing, trans., A81

BODY AND MIND—Keith Campbell, PP2

THE BROKEN IMAGE: Man, Science and Society—Floyd Matson, A506

COMEDY, "Laughter"—Henri Bergson—"Essay on Comedy" by George Meredith; intro. and supplementary essay by Wylie Sypher, A87

THE COSMOLOGICAL ARGUMENTS: A Spectrum of Opinion—Donald R. Burrill, ed., A586

CRITICAL EXISTENTIALISM—Nicola Abbagnano; Nino Langiulli, trans. and ed., A642

CRITIQUE OF PURE REASON—Immanuel Kant: F. Max Muller, trans., A551

CRITIQUE OF RELIGION AND PHILOSOPHY—Walter Kaufmann, A252

CUSTOM, LAW, AND MORALITY: Conflict and Continuity in Social Behavior—Burton M. Leiser, A669

DESCARTES: A Collection of Critical Essays—Willis Doney, ed., AP5

EITHER/OR, Volume I—Søren Kierkegaard; David F. Swenson and Lillian Marven Swenson, trans., revised with a Foreward by Howard A. Johnson, A181a

EITHER/OR, Volume II—Søren Kierkegaard; Walter Lowrie, trans., revised with a Foreword by Howard A. Johnson, A181b

ESSAYS IN PHILOSOPHICAL PSYCHOLOGY—Donald F. Gustafson, ed., A417

ETHICAL IMPERATIVE—Richard Means, A735

ETHICS AND SOCIETY—Richard T. de George, ed., A512

EVANGELICAL THEOLOGY—Karl Barth, A408

EVOLUTION AND CHRISTIAN HOPE—Ernst Benz, A607

THE FAITH OF A HERETIC—Walter Kaufmann, A336

FIVE STAGES OF GREEK RELIGION—Gilbert Murray, A51

FOUR EXISTENTIALIST THEOLOGIANS: A Reader from the Work of Jacques Maritain, Nicholas Berdyaev, Martin Buber, and Paul Tillich—Will Herberg, ed., A141

FREUD: The Mind of the Moralist—Philip Rieff, A278

FROM HEGEL TO NIETZSCHE: The Revolution in Nineteenth Century Thought—Karl Lowith; David E. Green, trans., A553

FROM SHAKESPEARE TO EXISTENTIALISM—Walter Kaufmann, A213

PHILOSOPHY *(cont'd)*

ANCHOR BOOKS

ANCHOR BOOKS

RELIGION

15Ab

ANCHOR BOOKS

LITERARY ESSAYS AND CRITICISM

LITERARY ESSAYS AND CRITICISM (cont'd)